Lucius D. Clay

Also by Jean Edward Smith

The Defense of Berlin
Der Weg ins Dilemma
Germany Beyond the Wall
The Papers of General Lucius D. Clay: Germany, 1945–1949
Civil Liberties and Civil Rights Debated (with Herbert Levine)
The Constitution and American Foreign Policy
The Conduct of American Foreign Policy Debated
(with Herbert Levine)

First Lieutenant Clay as an instructor,
West Point, 1925.

Lucius D. Clay

· An American Life ·

JEAN EDWARD SMITH

HENRY HOLT AND COMPANY
NEW YORK

Published by Henry Holt and Company, Inc.,
115 West 18th Street, New York, New York 10011.
Published in Canada by Fitzhenry & Whiteside Limited,
195 Allstate Parkway, Markham, Ontario L3R 4T8.

Library of Congress Cataloging-in-Publication Data
Smith, Jean Edward.
Lucius D. Clay : an American life / by Jean Edward Smith.
—1st ed.
p. cm.
Includes bibliographical references.
1. Clay, Lucius D. (Lucius Dubignon), 1897–1978. 2. Generals—
United States—Biography. 3. United States. Army—Biography.
4. World War, 1939–1945—United States.
5. Germany—History—Allied
Occupation, 1945– I. Title.
E745.C47S65 1990
355'.0092—dc20 89-24720
[B] CIP
ISBN 0-8050-0999-X
ISBN 0-8050-1787-9 (An Owl Book: pbk.)

First published in hardcover by
Henry Holt and Company, Inc., in 1990.
First Owl Book Edition—1992

Designed by Marysarah Quinn
Printed in the United States of America
Recognizing the importance of preserving the written word,
Henry Holt and Company, Inc., by policy,
prints all of its first editions on acid-free paper. ∞
3 5 7 9 10 8 6 4 2
1 3 5 7 9 10 8 6 4 2
pbk.

CONTENTS

Book Three

GERMANY

Book Four

THE MILITARY INDUSTRIAL COMPLEX

FOR MY PARENTS

PREFACE

Lucius D. Clay headed the American occupation of Germany from 1945 to 1949, first as deputy to General Dwight D. Eisenhower, eventually as U.S. supreme commander in his own right. Under Clay's stern tutelage, western Germany emerged from the shadow of Nazi tyranny. Under his leadership, a devastated country was rebuilt, an economy restored, and the foundations laid for a prosperous, stable, and democratic government. As Clay's successor, John J. McCloy, once remarked, "the Federal Republic is largely the story of the courage and persistence of this remarkable man."

For many, Clay is best remembered as the father of the Berlin airlift—that dramatic response to the Russian blockade in 1948. But the airlift distorts Clay's role in Germany. He was not a militant cold warrior, and the attention devoted to the blockade obscures the more fundamental and enduring accomplishments of the Occupation, accomplishments due directly to Clay's farsighted and fair-minded governance.

Clay's four years in Germany may have been the most demanding period in his career, yet they are but a small part of the sixty years he devoted to public service. Indeed, his full life reached and touched many of this century's most momentous and threatening events, and he himself was shaped by the tasks entrusted to him. He honed his impressive political skills in New Deal Washington; he developed his planning and engineering abilities while building dams and airports in Depression-wracked America; he established his reputation as a chaos-into-order man of global standing when he headed American military procurement during World War II. And through all of this, including the four years in Germany as America's proconsul—with all the power and the privilege consequent upon that position—there was never a breath of scandal or a hint of impropriety. Sixty years dedicated to the public well-being without a dent on a reputation for probity and rectitude: Clay represents a particular type of American, one that, sadly, seems less in evidence as the century winds down.

Clay retired from the Army in 1949 and went on to make a successful career in business, though he consistently refused to work for defense contractors or to conduct any business with the Pentagon. He participated actively in politics, playing a pivotal role in Eisenhower's 1952 campaign, and then helping Ike to select his first Cabinet. But Clay's politics were essentially nonpartisan. He pioneered the interstate highway program for a Republican president, but returned to Berlin in 1961 as the special envoy of a Democratic president. He helped rebuild the Republican Party financially after the Goldwater defeat, but also provided the money for President Kennedy to ransom the prisoners of the Bay of Pigs. Throughout his long years of service, Clay remained faithful to an American tradition of honesty, independence, and straight-dealing. He was tough and decisive, and he never trimmed his sails to suit a prevailing wind. His integrity was as enduring as his resolve.

General Clay died in 1978, six days shy of his eightieth birthday. Some years before his death, he agreed to a series of interviews with me. In the end, the interviews extended over six years and some twenty-five hundred pages of transcript. He patiently answered every question—always candid, always precise. His extraordinary memory could recall cables twenty-five years old, almost verbatim. No detail was too small to be filed away in his recollection.

General Clay also made his personal papers available to me. The truth is, this was not as helpful as it might sound, because, unlike so many government officials, Clay took no records with him when he left public service. He deposited his official papers in the National Archives, where he believed they belonged. When I sought to use those papers, the Department of Defense resisted, claiming many were still classified. Clay could not understand how documents thirty years old could have any possible bearing on national security, and he intervened directly with the Secretary of Defense to force their declassification.

General Clay's papers as Military Governor were edited by me and published by Indiana University Press. My interviews with him are on file and available to scholars at the Oral History Research Office at Columbia University and at the Eisenhower Library. The biography that follows is drawn insofar as possible from the words and opinions expressed by General Clay. In order to capture the essence of Clay's thoughts as well as his style and manner, I have frequently quoted his answers to my questions directly. By so doing, the portrait that emerges is, I believe, both more accurate and more candid.

General Clay read the first twenty-five chapters of the manuscript in draft form. As was his way, he offered no suggestions or criticisms, except to query jokingly whether I really had to specify his exact birthday. (Clay had lied about his age to gain early admission to West Point.) It is a measure of the man, I believe, that throughout our relationship he encouraged me to probe deeply and write fairly, regardless of the consequences.

Jean Edward Smith
Berlin, 1989

Introduction

> Lucius Clay represents the fiery type of fellow that you see in old-fashioned movies like *Gone with the Wind.* He's the kind of military leader the Confederate Army produced in goodly numbers. They were proud people. They weren't wild entirely, but they weren't afraid of anything.
>
> *Robert A. Lovett*

THE AMERICAN MILITARY TRADITION CLAIMS A VARIety of heroes. First, the demigods of martial spirit: Lee, Pershing, and MacArthur. Then the citizen-commanders, Grant and Eisenhower—men whose military judgment transcended narrow professionalism. Fighting generals like Patton and Stilwell, or Stonewall Jackson and William Tecumseh Sherman, compete for place with generations of military administrators: George C. Marshall, Peyton March in World War I, or Henry W. Halleck during the Civil War.

Lucius Clay fits none of those categories. His austere Roman bearing during the Berlin blockade may have resembled the aplomb of Lee outside Richmond, or the remoteness of MacArthur, yet he lacked the theatrical impulse that drove both to center stage. His executive ability rivaled that of General Marshall, but he lacked Marshall's single-minded military presence. Perhaps he most resembled Grant and Eisenhower, yet Clay never held a wartime command. Both Grant and Eisenhower were rewarded for their victories with the highest office the nation could bestow. Clay, who was relatively unknown outside Washington when World War II ended, was thrust into the desolation of a defeated Germany, and from the ashes fashioned the first stable democracy in German history.

Clay's career is inextricably tied to postwar Germany: the occupation of a defeated nation, its rebirth and reshaping. And were this the sum total of his achievements, it would rank among the major accomplishments of the Second World War. Yet Clay was more than a military proconsul. He was, as John Kenneth Galbraith observed, "one of the most skillful politicians ever to wear the uniform of the United States Army." In a military tradition little noted for its political insight, Lucius Clay stands as a unique figure. His selection to head Germany's occupation reflected a working relationship with the Roosevelt administration that was both close and of long standing.

Clay's political acumen was born and bred in Georgia politics. According to Army records, he was born April 23, 1897.* His father, Alexander Stephens Clay, was a three-term U.S. Senator—a representative of the poor, white yeomanry of Georgia's red clay hills, and Lucius spent several formative years shuttling with his father between Marietta and Washington.

Senator Clay died in 1910, and Lucius, the youngest of six children, was soon packed off to West Point. Like Grant and Eisenhower before him, Clay suffered the Academy with a large dose of skepticism. He graduated first in his class in English and history, but ranked at the bottom in conduct and discipline. As French Marshal Henri Philippe Pétain, the hero of World War I, noted following a visit to the Academy in the 1920s, strong, independent personalities were likely to rebel at the tiresome makework that formed a large part of West Point's

* Clay was actually born on April 23, 1898.

curriculum. In fact, had Clay's class not graduated one year early because of World War I, it is doubtful he would have finished.

Brevetted to the Corps of Engineers in 1918, Clay rose methodically through the ranks of the peacetime Army. But he was as much of a maverick in his way as George Patton would be in his. Clay was an original thinker. He read widely and rapidly—usually about nonmilitary subjects—and quickly formed his own opinions. "He was quite sure that his judgment was correct after he reached it, and rather insisted on it," Defense Secretary Robert Lovett would say in later years, "sometimes to the embarrassment of the people around him."

The trouble was, Clay did not suffer fools gladly—regardless of rank—and quickly tired of garrison routine. His early efficiency reports were peppered with below-average ratings in tact, judgment, and common sense. One commander went so far as to label him a "bolshevik." And in the small peacetime Army, Clay quickly acquired a reputation as a military iconoclast. It was not until the 1930s, when he was given assignments that allowed greater scope for his initiative and independence, that Clay began to flourish.

Then too, Clay moved in unusual circles for an Army officer, most of whom spent the interwar years doing squads left and squads right at small posts scattered across America. As an Army Engineer, Clay experienced a wide range of civilian activity: public works, disaster relief, and local politics from county courthouse to New Deal Washington. Called to the Chief of Engineers' office in Washington when the New Deal came to power, Clay worked closely with Harry Hopkins to establish the WPA (Works Progress Administration). For four crucial years under FDR, he was the Corps of Engineers' principal spokesman on Capitol Hill. When Hopkins and Interior Secretary Harold Ickes feuded over the purposes of New Deal relief activity, it was Clay who levered the Corps onto Hopkins's side. That, and the Civilian Conservation Corps, brought Hopkins into contact with the younger, progressive officers in the Army, and it was from these that America's home-front leadership was chosen once war began.

On Capitol Hill, Clay became close friends with Sam Rayburn, a senior member of the Texas delegation, who would be elected House Majority Leader in 1937 and Speaker three years later. Following a brief year as Chief Engineer at MacArthur's Philippine headquarters, Clay returned to the United States in 1938 to build the Denison Dam on the Red River in Mr. Sam's congressional district. The largest earth-filled dam in the United States, it was the principal project undertaken by the Corps of Engineers that year.

In 1940, Clay was recalled to Washington to head the emergency airport construction program then being established under Commerce Secretary Jesse Jones. Between September 1940 and Pearl Harbor, Clay selected the sites and supervised the construction of some 450 airports in the United States, creating the nucleus of America's commercial air network.

When the Japanese struck Pearl Harbor, Clay requested immediate troop duty. Instead, he was sent to Brazil to negotiate for additional air bases, and then selected by General Stilwell to go to China as Stilwell's chief engineer. But before Clay could leave, Dwight Eisenhower, then head of the Army's War Plans Division, intervened to hold him in Washington. General Marshall announced a sweeping reorganization of the War Department immediately thereafter, and at the age of forty-three, Clay emerged as the youngest brigadier general in the U.S. Army and the head of all wartime military procurement—a very disappointing assignment, as Clay saw it.

From March 1942 until April 1945, Clay was America's soldier in charge of defense production. As the War Department's Director of Materiel, he supervised the vast procurement activities of the Army, set production schedules, doled out military aid to the Allies, and provided the weapons with which the war was won. As the Army's member of the joint U.S.-British Munitions Assignment Board, he was again thrown into close contact with Harry Hopkins, who chaired it. Averell Harriman, who headed the Lend-Lease program in London, and who worked closely with the board, recalled that "Lucius always kept his eye on the ball. He wasn't interested in bureaucratic pettiness. Whenever I had procurement problems during the war, I went to Clay. He immediately saw what the problem was, and could usually figure a way around it."

Clay's role in wartime Washington also brought him in close contact with Secretary of the Treasury Henry Morgenthau. In the summer of 1944, Clay joined the American delegation at the Bretton Woods Monetary and Financial Conference, where he and Morgenthau cooperated to thwart Chinese nationalist leader Chiang Kai-shek's continued raids on the U.S. Treasury.

In the autumn of 1944, Clay was invited by Eisenhower to come to Europe to replace the Allies' supply chief, General John C. H. Lee. But by the time Clay arrived, Ike had had second thoughts about relieving Lee and sent Clay instead to Cherbourg to unsnarl a port tie-up of monumental proportions. Clay then returned to Washington, where he became Deputy Director of War Mobilization and Reconversion—second to former Supreme Court Justice James F. Byrnes in running the American economy.

In light of Clay's extensive political experience in Washington—and his close and easy working relationship with Harry Hopkins, Jesse Jones, James Byrnes, Sam Rayburn, and Henry Morgenthau—it is not surprising that he was quickly tapped to head Germany's occupation. President Roosevelt originally had wanted a civilian for the task, a man like John J. McCloy, the Assistant Secretary of War, or Under Secretary Robert Patterson. But Secretary of War Stimson insisted that in the initial stages the Occupation ought to be headed by a military man. Morgenthau also objected strenuously to McCloy because of his extensive ties to the business world. In that stalemate, Clay emerged immediately as the consensus choice: an Army general who understood Washington's political climate and who could be trusted to carry out Administration policy with the necessary vigor. In fact, Clay's first order of business in Germany in 1945 was to wrest military government from the Army General Staff and place it directly under War Department civilian control.

Despite muted State Department misgivings (Clay had no experience in German matters), Clay's appointment was widely applauded in Washington. Byrnes told FDR that if Clay was given six months, "he could run General Motors or U.S. Steel." And Secretary Morgenthau, who was scarcely a friend of German recovery (or, for that matter, of General Motors or U.S. Steel), agreed with Byrnes's assessment. "The most able fellow around this town is General Clay," said Morgenthau.

In retrospect, it seems striking that Washington's top civilian leadership—Hopkins, Stimson, Byrnes, and Morgenthau—could agree so quickly that Clay was the right man for Germany, while disagreeing so fundamentally on what American policy there should be. But Clay had been completely insulated from discussions about postwar Germany. He was not given a copy of the U.S. directive to govern the Occupation (JCS 1067) until he boarded his plane for Europe; he did not think it necessary to consult the State Department before leaving; and he did not read the Morgenthau Plan for eliminating Germany's industry and creating a "pastoral" society until he reached Eisenhower's headquarters in France.

Clay was no friend of the Germans in 1945. It was widely agreed in Washington that his tough-minded, disciplined direction of America's wartime economy fitted him uniquely for the German task. On April 8, when his appointment was announced, *The New York Times* called him the Pentagon's "stormy petrel" who would put the Germans in their place. The Baltimore *Sun* clucked that it "served the Germans right for losing the war." And *The Washington Post* agreed: "General Clay's exceedingly high abilities are better suited to the German situation than our own. That task calls for authoritarianism." Or, as a senior American industrialist told *Look* magazine, "They've found the right place for him. Ruling over enemies."

In Germany, Clay saw at first hand the devastation caused by the war and was genuinely appalled. The suffering in Berlin moved him deeply. "It was like a city of the dead," wrote Clay, "and I must confess that my exultation in victory was diminished as I witnessed this degradation of man. I decided then and there never to forget that we were responsible for the government of human beings."

As a Southerner who had grown up with first-hand tales of Reconstruction, Clay might have had an extra measure of sympathy with the plight of those being occupied. "I don't know whether it affected me," he said, "but the Civil War was always with us when I was growing up." Whatever the reason, no defeated nation in modern history has fared better as a result of its occupation. And no occupation was more difficult. In Japan, MacArthur ruled and the Emperor reigned. But in Germany, the United States was merely one of four occupying powers, each of which had a veto, and there was no symbolic state on which to build. In addition, the physical destruction that greeted the Allies in 1945 was far more extensive than in Japan. Much of the Third Reich was a rubble-strewn wasteland in which the living often envied the dead. The tasks of political re-education, the eradication of the remnants of Nazism, and the punishment of those guilty of war crimes—crimes that exceeded human imagination in their enormity—were infinitely greater in Germany than in Japan. Finally, the justified hostility of a generation was directed at Germany. And that hostility often did not distinguish between those responsible for the blight of Nazism and the many Germans who suffered under its policies.

Clay's messages from Berlin illustrate the profound changes that took place from 1945 to 1949. As Military Governor, Clay saw his primary task as establishing the foundation for a lasting democratic society. And for Clay, the two most important ingredients in teaching democracy were full bellies and strict impartiality. "We have insisted on democratic processes in the U.S. zone and have maintained a strict neutrality between political parties," Clay told Washington in the bleak winter of 1946. "As a result the Communist Party has made little inroad. However, there is no choice between becoming a Communist on 1500 calories and a believer in democracy on 1000 calories."

If compassion for the plight of the average German played a role in determining Clay's policies, so too did his concern for America's self-interest: if the United States was to be freed from supporting postwar Europe indefinitely, Germany had to be revived. The question of erecting a counterpoise to the Soviet Union did not enter Clay's thinking until late 1947, and until then his relations with the Russians were warm and cordial. Indeed, the record of American military government illustrates the insistence of both Clay and Eisenhower that the United States honor its obligations to the Soviet Union in terms of reparations, German assets abroad, and German patents and scientific data. Many will be surprised that Clay's cutoff of reparations deliveries from the U.S. zone in May 1946 was aimed primarily at the French, not the Russians, and that Clay, who since the Berlin blockade has symbolized American resistance to Communism, deplored the establishment of Radio Liberty in Munich (broadcasting anti-Communist messages in Russian to the Soviet Union) as inimical to the purposes of four-power government. The fact is, Clay believed cooperation with the Soviet Union was essential in Germany, and he blamed Washington for allowing France to scuttle German unity. Later, in 1947, Clay refused to provide American aid to non-Communist political parties in Berlin. "After all," he archly cabled Washington, the tactics used by the Communists were "not much different from election measures sometimes pursued in large cities in democratic countries." When the Truman administration eventually moved to divide Germany, Clay was the last holdout. In his view, German unity and free elections under effective four-power control would extend Western influence into the Soviet zone and assist democratic forces in Poland and Czechoslovakia, but no one in Washington in 1947 was prepared to take that chance.

Clay's experience in government instilled in him a profound respect for constitutional processes. He firmly believed in the beneficial force of public opinion, and was the first Military Governor in history to hold regular, open, no-holds-barred press conferences with reporters from the local press—a lesson both for the press, which Clay believed too timid, and for a new generation of German politicians.

Later, when he became concerned that his orders to military sub-governors in hundreds of villages and hamlets throughout the American zone might go unheeded—or, worse, might be reinterpreted by overzealous commanders—Clay began issuing orders to subordinate commands over the ordinary AM radio so that the Germans might listen and be informed about U.S. policy.

In 1946, Clay successfully initiated free elections in Germany, contrary to the advice of his political advisers, both U.S. and German, and thus took Germany a massive step forward in postwar rehabilitation. In 1948, he overruled another set of advisers to free the German currency from price and wage controls, thereby initiating the astounding economic recovery Germany went on to enjoy.

It may seem curious in retrospect that Clay spoke no German. Furthermore, he deliberately avoided personal contact with Germans at all levels for fear that those whom he approached would be tagged collaborators. Despite this distancing, the Germans soon developed respect bordering on admiration for *der Sieger* (the victor). Reinhold Maier, later Minister-President of Württemberg-Baden, remembered Clay as personifying the best of the German General Staff: "cultivated, taciturn, polished, and clear; an intellectual type with brown, melancholy eyes." Clay was firm and correct—as those who appointed him expected him to be. But he used every trip to Washington from 1945 to 1947 to get the Germans more food.

Clay's readiness to take personal responsibility was the hallmark of his career. A contemporary audience will appreciate Clay's innate political shrewdness in insisting that all U.S. agencies in Germany report to Washington through him exclusively. This was not done for personal aggrandizement but to ensure that American policy was coordinated. To achieve such coordination was a difficult and continuing problem, but Clay succeeded. In the end, even the long arm of U.S. intelligence reported to Washington through Clay's headquarters.

As Military Governor, Clay insisted on doing things his way. If his superiors in Washington objected, they could relieve him, but Clay would not back down. When given orders he didn't believe in, he automatically submitted his resignation. "Of course I will carry out the instructions given me in this teleconference," Clay told Army Secretary Royall during crucial negotiations with Britain and France over creation of the West German government, concluding: "then I will cable requesting my immediate retirement." Clay resigned at least eleven times while serving as Military Governor, but none of his resignations was accepted.

It was Clay's determination to do things his way that saved him from interminable second-guessing in Washington. It also gave American policy a coherent focus. Above all, it provided the firm leadership that occupied Germany required. "Clay was a pleasure to work for," said Donald McLean, a member of Clay's staff and later director of Boston's Leahy Clinic. "I never saw a case in which he said, 'I think we'd better discuss this with Washington.' He made the decision right there." Clay's British counterpart in Germany, General Sir Brian Robertson, phrased it somewhat more colorfully when he noted that Clay not only looked like a Roman emperor—a reference to Clay's unarguably imperious nose—but sometimes acted like one.

Clay's principal achievement was the creation of a prosperous, stable, and democratic Germany. For it was he who presided at the birth of the West German Basic Law (constitution)—goading both German politicians and Allied capitals to timely compromise. And when the Basic Law was approved, Clay retired from the Army. He rented a house on Cape Cod and wrote an account of his role in Germany (*Decision in Germany*). It was typical of Clay that he ignored Army regulations and did not submit his manuscript for military approval before publishing it. "I sent a book to the adjutant general," said Clay. "If he didn't like it, he could have said so."

Clay was a man of quiet dignity: a liberal of the old school who resisted the notion of omnipotent government. Privacy was a right to be jealously guarded, his own as well as others. As Military Governor, Clay halted the military police practice of investigating the personal lives of his officers. "The Army makes enough demands on one's time," Clay once said. "An officer's personal life is nobody's business but his own. Period."

Clay's concern for privacy has obvious drawbacks for a biographer. Unlike Patton, whose personal memorabilia crammed fifty file cabinets, Clay saved virtually nothing. "A man has to have a rather exalted opinion of himself to hang on to everything he ever wrote," Clay said.

Clay's response represented a consistent, pragmatic theme that characterized his life and his achievements: an orientation toward the future, not the past, and an urgent desire to press on with the job at hand. In Clay's case, a neglected childhood and ten years of barracks boredom in the peacetime Army were powerful formative influences. The youngest of six children, so much younger that his parents often overlooked him, Clay subscribed to a strenuous Puritan ethic: nothing could be achieved without hard work. In fact, one cannot understand Clay without appreciating the extraordinary competitiveness that drove him.

Clay was fifty-one years old when he retired from the Army. Too proud to seek out a new position, he waited for industry to come calling. And, as he said, "It was not a very pleasant interlude." In a refreshing expression of old-time civic virtue, Clay refused to work for a defense contractor or any company that did a substantial business with the Pentagon. As the wartime director of all military procurement, Clay believed such employment would be "unseemly" and he declined to use his Defense Department connections for personal profit. Eventual succor came in an offer from Continental Can Company, which signed Clay on as chief executive officer.

When Clay retired from Continental Can in 1962, having driven it from a weak second to a strong first in the packaging field, an ailing Robert Lehman asked him to assume the direction of Lehman Brothers, then one of Wall Street's most powerful and prestigious investment houses. Once again, Clay made the transition smoothly.

For years, Clay played a pivotal role in cementing the ties between big government and big business in the United States. His career is a unique blend of the military, political, and business spheres of American life, yet he was scarcely "the enemy within" that his close friend Dwight Eisenhower warned about. In business, as in the Army, Clay remained a paradox. On the one hand, he was a highly skillful and subtle manipulator of vast financial power; on the other, he remained a throwback to America's past. *Honor, Duty, Country,* remained cardinal principles for Clay, and the thought of using personal influence for private gain was alien to his creed. (When he retired from the Army, having been Military Governor of Germany and, before that, head of all wartime military procurement, Clay's total personal assets amounted to $3,000 in a family savings account.)

Clay's strict sense of propriety imposed rigid limits on how he used his influence. When President Eisenhower flashed signals of not fully comprehending the dangerous import of the 1953 Bricker Amendment to the Constitution, Clay immediately intervened on a personal basis to set him straight. But when Ike's Justice Department indicted Continental Can for antitrust violations, Clay refused to raise the matter.

His personal behavior reflected a similar dichotomy. Among an intimate circle of close friends he was warm and jovial, but his business associates were held at arm's length. "Lucius was an autocrat by nature," said Harold Boeschenstein, chairman of Owens-Corning Fiberglas. "If we lived in an earlier age, he would have been a baron or a duke. He would be a benevolent one, but he'd be an autocrat nonetheless."

Ellison Hazard, who followed Clay as president of Continental Can, remarked: "You never conducted a conversation with General Clay. . . . Either you're telling him something he wants to know, or he's telling you something. But there is no free and easy intercourse."

One of the reasons was that Clay's life was rigidly compartmentalized. "Clay had tremendous self-discipline," said James Boyd, who worked as Clay's wartime executive officer (and later became president of the Colorado School of Mines, and then of Copper Range). "I'd walk in and bring something to his attention—like copper or steel—and often I'd stop in the middle of a sentence. He might not have said anything, yet I would know if he agreed, or was satisfied, and I didn't have to waste his time anymore."

Until the age of seventy-five, Clay continued to arrive at his Wall Street desk at 8:00 A.M. and work a full day. His patrician sense of duty—a combination of Victorian virtue and political cunning—made him available for any government request. President Truman recalled him to Washington in 1950 to help organize the home front during the Korean War. President Eisenhower delegated the initial selection of his Cabinet to Clay, and used him frequently as a personal troubleshooter. As chairman of the President's Committee on Highways, Clay organized the interstate highway program and steered it successfully through Congress. John F. Kennedy sent him to Berlin in 1961, and then asked him to resolve the muddle of America's foreign aid program. When the Kennedys needed funds instantly on Christmas Eve in 1962 to ransom the prisoners of the Bay of Pigs, it was perhaps natural that they should turn to Clay—by then a prominent Republican, but a man who made no political distinctions when the President of the United States was involved.

The book that follows deals with the life of General Clay. It deals with the man—his career, his place in American life, and, above all, his contribution to the development of the first enduring democracy in German history.

World War II and its aftermath were not a simpler time, nor one when the mettle of American leadership was less challenged than today. If anything, the struggle to achieve military victory and the subsequent reconstruction of Europe and Asia posed even greater challenges. Yet America rose to the occasion.

One of the reasons, it appears in retrospect, was the exceptional reservoir of accomplished, dedicated, and incorruptible leaders then in the armed forces. Eisenhower, Marshall, MacArthur, and Clay symbolized American virtue. All had endured the seeming stagnation of the peacetime Army, the endless wait for promotion, the pitiful lack of equipment and manpower. Yet when emergency came, they were ready. Thrust into unprecedented command positions, they excelled. And the political leadership they provided for the postwar world has been unrivaled in its accomplishment.

Strange as it may seem, the leaders of World War II rose to positions of authority through a military promotion system based strictly on seniority (at least through the rank of colonel). They chafed under it and cursed it, but its hidden virtue was that seniority permitted a certain independence of thought and action. A junior officer was not required to flatter his commanding officer's whims to get that outstanding efficiency report upon which rapid promotions now hinge. There were no rapid promotions. Everyone stood in line. And while on the one hand that meant inordinate delays for men like Eisenhower and Marshall to get to the top, it also ensured that when they got there their independence of judgment was still intact.

The postwar establishment of democratic prosperity in Germany and Japan traces to two great military proconsuls: Clay and MacArthur. Were they fitted by their military experience for those responsibilities? It is difficult to say. But what one can say with assurance is that each enjoyed supreme confidence in his own judgment and was prepared to accept the full responsibility for his decisions.

Such a style has its limits. MacArthur's errors and foibles have been widely documented. Clay's are less well known, but equally present. As Paul Cabot, managing director of the First Boston Corporation, once reported, "Lucius was the most arrogant, stubborn, opinionated man I ever met. I remember sitting with him and Sidney Weinberg at Sea Island, Georgia, just after Ike was elected in 1952, discussing possible Cabinet appointees. Lucius had a definite opinion about everyone. Good or bad. Yes or no. Finally, I said, 'Jesus Christ, Lucius, there's a word 'maybe' in the English language. Don't you ever use it?' "

Clay seldom did. At times his decisiveness betrayed a rare snap judgment. At other times his determination became pure stubbornness. Or, perhaps more accurately, he was most stubborn about his own snap judgments, his self-doubt filtered out by fifty years of command.

Clay was at his best in times of adversity. His decisiveness was legendary. The Berlin airlift was but one example: begun on his own initiative, without clearance from the Pentagon, without permission from the President. It was typical Clay, and it saved Berlin.

I once asked General Clay why Continental Can or Lehman Brothers were interested in a retired general. "Well," said Clay, "I don't know of anyone who probably had as much experience with the full range of the nation's economy as I did while Deputy Director of War Mobilization in World War II. And I don't know of anyone else on Wall Street who ever conducted a major currency reform. Or for that matter, who established a government."

· Book One ·

THE EARLY YEARS

· 1 ·

The Clays of Georgia

> Senator Clay is a magnificent specimen of the possibilities of American institutions, a splendid instance of a poor farm boy, who without other advantages than those he made for himself, has risen to eminence in his chosen profession.
>
> Atlanta *Constitution,*
> November 17, 1896

ON NOVEMBER 16, 1896, SEVENTEEN MONTHS BEFORE Lucius Clay was born, his father, Alexander Stephens Clay, was elected to the United States Senate. Clay's father was forty-three: the lawyer son of an impoverished farmer from northern Georgia's red-clay hills. Alexander Stephens Clay symbolized Georgia's New Democracy. As chairman of the state Democratic Party, he led the fight against the Populists in 1894 in the struggle to keep the working man Democratic. Following a decisive victory, he was elected president of the state senate (and lieutenant governor) in 1895. The following year, when General John B. Gordon, last of Georgia's Bourbon triumvirate,* declined another term in Washington, Clay was chosen as his successor.

Senator Clay's humble origin notwithstanding, the Clays of Georgia trace their ancestry to Sir John Claye, knighted by King Edward IV at the Battle of Tewkesbury in 1471. The first American descendant, grenadier Captain John Thomas Clay, landed at Jamestown in 1613. Captain Clay's son, Charles Clay (1638–86), a well-to-do planter, joined with Bacon in the abortive Virginia Rebellion of 1676, and is the common ancestor of the Clays of Kentucky and those of Georgia. But it was Lucius's great-great-grandfather Pearce Clay, a brother of Henry Clay, who first moved to Georgia, shortly after the American Revolution. He established a large plantation at Buffalo Creek, near Milledgeville—three thousand acres of prime Georgia cropland.

In the early 1850s, Lucius's grandfather, William James Clay, severed his family ties, claimed a small inheritance, and moved to Cobb County in northern Georgia, where he bought a rugged hill-country farm of 250 acres. In 1852, he married Edna Ann Peek, daughter of a nearby Baptist parson, and their first son, Alexander Stephens Clay, was born the following year. The name was not chosen randomly. Congressman Alexander Stephens was Georgia's most distinguished spokesman for the cause of the Union in 1852 (though he later became the very reluctant vice president of the Confederacy), and for Will and Edna Clay to name their first son after him was a clear statement of political belief. In fact, the cause of the Union was far more popular in Cobb County than in the plantation country of south Georgia, from which Clay had come.

"It was a moot question why my grandfather moved," said General Clay, "except that he was one of the younger sons of a large family. There wasn't much opportunity where he was, so he acted like they all did in those days: he went out looking for a new and better world. My grandfather was no world-beater, but his wife was an imaginative and

* General John B. Gordon, Joseph E. Brown, and Alfred H. Colquitt have been categorized by historians as a Bourbon triumvirate. During the eighteen years after Reconstruction, either Gordon or Brown occupied one of Georgia's U.S. Senate seats and, after 1883, Colquitt the other. For the major part of the same period, either Colquitt or Gordon was governor. All were identified with the very conservative, planter and capitalist wing of Georgia's Democratic Party. Like the Bourbons of France, they supposedly had "learned nothing and forgotten nothing" when they returned to power after the Civil War and Reconstruction.

wonderful person. Her father had been a minister, and she had a little bit better education. She was always pushing for her children to get better educations, but my father was the only one who responded."

Q: Cobb County is in northwestern Georgia?

CLAY: Yes. Cobb County was the most progressive of the counties in that region. The others were mountain counties, and mountain counties in those days took their politics and everything else very seriously. They were rough people. They were fine people, but they were rough people.

Q: Then it was not a rich agricultural area?

CLAY: North Georgia was a land of small farmers. It was settled relatively late by people who were fighting the Creeks and the Cherokees, and it was never a land of great plantations. Also, north Georgia never had an old, established aristocracy. North Georgia was settled by people who wanted to get away from that. The great houses and plantations are in south Georgia. North Georgia started with small, independent white men who wanted to go away and be independent—where they wouldn't feel the class distinction they felt when they had to live in an area where the white people were rich and the Negroes were poor.

Will Clay, Lucius's grandfather, was not a slaveholder and had little sympathy for Georgia's planter aristocracy. When the Civil War came, he did not serve—except briefly, in the home guard, when Sherman marched through Marietta. He is described by his descendants as a man of fierce independence and striking figure: tall, ramrod-straight, white goatee, with a gracious and courtly manner somewhat out of keeping with his hard-scrabble existence.

The Clay farm in Cobb County was dirt-poor, and Lucius's father worked on it daily until he was seventeen: plowing, hoeing, picking cotton, tending the animals—the never-ending chores of the cracker up-country. Whatever education the young senator received was given to him by his mother "at the fireside." His first experience in a classroom came in 1870, when he went to high school in nearby Palmetto. After two years at Palmetto, he entered Hiwasee College, where he worked his way by raising cotton and teaching during the summer. "Among his students," General Clay recalled, "were my mother and a

D. W. Blair, who later became his law partner. He then read law, which is what you did in those days, was admitted to the bar, and became a very successful lawyer, in the sense of a successful lawyer of the times. He practiced law actively until he went to the United States Senate."

Q: Why did your father enter politics?
CLAY: Lawyers and politics sort of went together in the South. My father had gone to the state legislature and been elected speaker. Then to the state senate, where he had been elected president. He became chairman of the Democratic Party and led it in the fight which prevented the Populists from taking over in Georgia. The result was that when General John B. Gordon's seat became vacant, he was elected to fill the vacancy. In those days senators were elected by the state legislature. Of course, no two men could have been more different than my father and General John B. Gordon. General Gordon waved the banner of the Confederacy 'til his dying day. My father never mentioned it.
Q: Your father's first campaign for the Senate was very close: thirty-one ballots. The second and third times he ran, he was elected without opposition. How do you account for that?
CLAY: This is sort of a habit in Georgia. The first battle is the tough one, then we keep re-electing them. We learned long ago that they get better with age.

The electoral campaigns of the 1890s, pitting the militant Populists against a proud Democratic tradition, were among the most hotly contested in Georgia's political history. But Clay's father emerged relatively unscathed from personal attack. The Atlanta *Constitution,* whose editor, E. P. Howell, was Clay's senatorial opponent, reported that "the nomination of Mr. Clay ends what will go down in Georgia's history as one of the most remarkable campaigns ever known. It has been wonderfully free from bitterness. Mr. Clay's personal relations with all of the candidates were of the very best. He counted on every one of them as his personal friends."

In later years, Senator Clay and Tom Watson, the fiery leader of American Populism, became friends. The fact was that the elder Clay did not oppose the Populist program—free coinage of silver, regulation of trusts and railroads, economic justice for the small farmer and small businessman. But he thought those goals could best be achieved within the Democratic Party.

In the U.S. Senate, Clay aligned himself with the liberal, Democratic minority. From the date of his entry until his death he formed a standing pair with Henry Cabot Lodge of Massachusetts: an arrangement whereby two senators of opposite persuasion "paired" themselves on all issues. If one was absent from the chamber when a vote was taken, the other would rise, announce his pair, and refrain from voting.

Of course, it was only thirty-one years after the Civil War when Clay was first elected to the Senate, and the bitterness still ran deep in Georgia. But, like his famous namesake, Clay was devoted to the idea of Union—and to the *United States.* He rejected the politics of Southern sectionalism, and as chairman of the state Democratic Party (he remained so until his death) worked hard to bring Georgia back into the national consensus. In a front-page interview in 1902, *The New York Times* cited Senator Clay as the leader of liberal Southerners seeking to modernize the party and increase its appeal in the industrialized states of the North. "We should be broad and liberal in our policy, tolerant in our spirit, and cordially invite all Democrats to unite," he was quoted as saying. Clay's progressive views reflected both his upbringing and the principal source of his electoral support: the poor white working class and the dirt farmers of northern Georgia.

Clay was one of the first Senate sponsors of an income tax, a vigorous opponent of monopolies and special privilege, and first chairman of the Senate's Select Committee on Woman Suffrage. His maiden speech in 1898 was a denunciation of U.S. imperialist claims in the Pacific. He opposed the annexation of the Philippines, and led the successful opposition to the Republican "big navy" appropriation bill in 1902 and the exorbitant sugar schedules of the Payne-Aldridge tariff of 1909. He also took up the cudgels on behalf of prohibition, leading an unsuccessful attempt in 1908 to allow the individual states to restrict the importation of liquor.

"Clay was diligent," Senator Lodge said, "and thorough, and especially industrious in that unadvertised but essential task, the work of committees, where law and policies are shaped and where the glaring and deceptive headline rarely penetrates. He was equally diligent and painstaking on the floor. Better than anyone else, perhaps, can I bear witness to his faithful attendance, to his rare absence from a vote. He came well prepared to debate and knew and understood the subjects he discussed, but although he took a due share in all discussions, he wasted no time and never sought to utter words merely for the pleasure of utterance."

Q: When you were a boy, did you go with your father to Washington?

CLAY: When my father went to the Senate, Congress didn't meet year-round as it does now. It usually had a long session one year, and a relatively short session the following year. My mother would always go to Washington with him during the long session. She would not go during the short session. Usually some of the children would go with my mother. I made the trip three times, and, of course, while there I was in school in Washington. In the interim, my mother's mother, my grandmother, lived with us and ran the house in Marietta for those children who stayed home.

Q: Did your early stay in Washington whet your appetite for a political career?

CLAY: No, I don't think it did. I do think it gave me a pretty basic knowledge of how government functions. In those days, government was simple enough so you could see it function. Cabinet members really were the people who ran government, and their staffs were relatively small. You could walk around sightseeing and walk in and see a Cabinet member.

In Washington, Senator Clay and Theodore Roosevelt became close friends. Although they disagreed over America's role in world affairs (Clay opposed foreign involvement), they were in complete accord on progressive domestic policy. "My father once took me to the White House to meet President Roosevelt," said Clay, "my sister and me. I remember Mr. Roosevelt took a rose from his lapel and gave it to my sister—he had quite a way with children. My father invited Mr. Roosevelt down to Marietta once—and Mr. Roosevelt came. His mother [Martha Bullock] was from Cobb County."

Q: According to *The Washington Post,* your father was frequently called upon by the Roosevelt administration to sponsor its legislation.

CLAY: That's right. And because of this he was able to get more patronage and consideration for his appointments and things of that sort than would otherwise have been the case. But my father had a tremendous respect for government, for the apparatus of government, and for the President. He had a tremendous respect for his fellow senators.

Q: Did your father spend much time with you in Washington?

CLAY: Obviously, when we were in Washington he was very busy. But he would often take me down to the office. Then, after dinner, we'd sit around in the living room, in the apartment, unless something was doing. . . . However, I was a little too young to really have very worthwhile talks or discussions with him. I can't say that I really knew my father. I knew the image perhaps better than I did the man.

Q: What impressed you about Washington?

CLAY: I think the thing that impressed me more than anything else was the Library of Congress, where, as a member of a senator's family, I could get all of the books I wanted to read and take them home—which I used to do once a week at least. In fact, I read so much in Washington that I developed a twitch in my right eye. But if I hadn't started to read, I don't think I would have been so happy in Washington. At one time I must have been reading six or eight books a week.

Q: History and biography?

CLAY: Mostly fiction and literature. One book I remember was by a man named Stanley J. Weyman, called *A Gentleman from France.* I don't know what happened to that, but it was a magnificent book in my young days. It was a chivalrous adventure story, like the works of Sir Walter Scott, and it made a tremendous impression on me.

Senator Clay was elected to a third term in 1908. But for several years his health had been failing. In February 1908, he had collapsed on the Senate floor while speaking against the Aldrich currency bill. Clay nevertheless rejected friends' advice that he take a brief rest from Senate chores. "When I become so ill that I cannot attend to the duties for which the people of Georgia have sent me here," he said, "I shall resign and give way to someone who can."

In 1910, with three of his Senate colleagues dead that session, Senator Clay found himself the only Democrat remaining on the Appropriations Committee. When Congress adjourned, his health was spent. He returned to Marietta, rallied briefly, but could not recover. He died on November 13, 1910, at the age of fifty-seven. Lucius was twelve years old.

Senator Clay's funeral in Marietta was attended by five thousand mourners. As the Atlanta *Constitution* records, "not a wheel moved in any industrial plant throughout the day, as the laboring element of the city turned out in force to honor their friend and defender." Two years later, a bronze statue of the Senator, raised by popular subscription, was dedicated on Marietta's courthouse square. According to the custom in Georgia, Clay's likeness was mounted with his back to the north, though no Southern senator at that time was less parochial.

· 2 ·

Marietta Boyhood (1898-1914)

AT THE TURN OF THE CENTURY, MARIETTA BASKED IN McKinley prosperity. The Civil War's wounds had slowly healed; cotton was selling at 15 cents a pound; new peach orchards dotted the countryside; and, in nearby Atlanta, light processing industries were beginning to weaken Georgia's agricultural dependency. Marietta thrived in Atlanta's shadow, its hilly environs recognized as a temperate summer resort for affluent Georgians eager to escape the malaria and typhoid of coastal Savannah. Among its five thousand residents were two former governors, one future governor, a U.S. Senator, and the heads of both the Populist and Democratic parties.

According to official Army records, Clay was born in Marietta on April 23, 1897. The fact is, he was born on April 23, one year later, and lied about his age in order to enter West Point—a not uncommon occurrence, especially in the South, where counties traditionally kept no birth records.

"I hate to put anything like that on the record," General Clay confessed, "because it is so tied up with my whole legal existence—retirement, Social Security, the whole works. We knew you had to be a certain age to enter West Point, but the question was whether you had to be that age by March 17, when you accepted your appointment, or whether you had to be that age by the time of entry [in June]. And it was the time of entry. So there really was no need for anything to have been done in my case. But we didn't know that. So for me it was much easier to change a year than it was to change my birthday. Everybody knows your birthday—family and whatnot. So it was much easier to change the year."

By 1898, the Clays were well established in Marietta. Lucius' father had gone to the Senate two years before. Control of Georgia's Democratic Party rested firmly in his hands, and the legal firm of Clay & Blair prospered. The Clay home reflected the Senator's prominence: a large white-frame Victorian with a veranda overlooking rolling lawns and, across the street, the Confederate cemetery—final resting place for those who died at Kennesaw Mountain.

Lucius was the youngest of the six Clay children. "So much younger," he recalls, "that I knew my brothers much better after I graduated from West Point than I did as a youngster. They were away at college most of the time. Then I was away. I really got to know them much better after I graduated from college." General Clay's Roman first name reflects a tradition of obscure origin but extensive observance among the several branches of the Clay family, which have named others among their offspring Brutus Junius and Cassius Marcellus. His second name, Dubignon, was for Charles Dubignon, Senator Clay's campaign manager in 1896.

Lucius's oldest brother, Herbert, was born in 1881. When Lucius was born, Herbert was already at the University of Georgia, well on his way to a promising political career: mayor of Marietta at twenty-seven, solicitor general of Georgia's Blue Ridge Circuit, president of the state senate and lieutenant governor (1922–23). Herbert's early success was his undoing. Utterly charming but completely self-indulgent, he died mysteriously in a run-down Atlanta hotel the night of June 22, 1923.

Herbert was lieutenant governor at the time, and had just returned from a trip to Washington. "We never knew how my father died," said his son, Herbert Clay, Jr. "Some say he was murdered. But I don't know. He was not an alcoholic, but he drank too much and he enjoyed life too much. He was completely self-centered and totally neglected his duties as head of the family after my grandfather's death.

"He would have been in the U.S. Senate long before that if it had not been for his drinking and womanizing. [Herbert Clay had been prominently mentioned as a candidate against Tom Watson and Walter George in 1920, but abruptly withdrew.] My mother said that he worked hard but had no sense of self-control, and thought he could get away with anything."

Out of deference to the family, Herbert Clay's death was handled gingerly by the Atlanta press, and no taint of scandal was printed. The coroner's jury ascribed death to a "fatty degeneration of the heart tissues," and the appropriate eulogies were sung.

Self-indulgence and a lack of self-control were traits shared by all of Clay's brothers as well as by his only sister, Evelyn. Accustomed to the luxury and easy living of a senator's household, they made few concessions to the prevailing mores of Southern gentility, confident that their father's position would secure them. They were headstrong, hard-drinking, and hard-living—and they burned out quickly.

Senator Clay's second son, Lex (Alexander Stephens Clay, Jr.), twelve years older than Lucius, was dapper, handsome, and generally considered the brightest and wittiest of all the Clays. He was also the most dissolute. A star athlete in high school, he was an alcoholic by the time he left college. Afterward he lived at his parents' home and never held a regular job.

Frank Butner Clay was the third of Lucius's older brothers, born in 1888 and, like Herbert and Lex, high-spirited and undisciplined. Senator Clay often told the story that the University of Georgia had ruined his first two sons, so he "sent Frank to ruin the university."

Denied admission to law school after two years as a hell-raising undergraduate, Frank went to West Point, was given a general court martial for disciplinary reasons, put back a year, and graduated with the class of 1911. He developed aphasia in the Philippines in 1914, was hospitalized off and on, and died in Walter Reed Army Hospital, August 22, 1920.

Ryburn Clay, the fourth Clay brother, was seven years older than Lucius, and for his education insisted on going to Princeton. Unwilling to bear the expense of an Ivy League diploma, Senator Clay told Ryburn he could go either to the University of Georgia or to West Point, but nowhere else. Ryburn's response was typical Clay: if he could not go to Princeton, he wouldn't go anywhere. Instead, he began work at a nearby bank, and by his mid-thirties was president of Atlanta's Fulton

National Bank, a member of the Federal Reserve Board, financial kingpin of Georgia's Democratic Party, and one of the most successful bankers in the South. By his mid-forties—after the death of his first wife—he too succumbed to the vices of his elder brothers and lost out at the bank, though, as Georgia politico Jim Carmichael reported, "Drunk or sober, Ryburn was always the smartest banker in the state."

General Clay's only sister was a similar tragic case. Plump, homely, unable to compete with her handsome and successful brothers, Evelyn Clay flitted about on the fringes of the Democratic Party, living in the reflected glory of her father's reputation: the spoiled, only daughter of a too-indulgent family. She could not stay married, could not hold a job, and shared the family's addiction to strong drink.

When Lucius was born, his mother was thirty-eight. His older brothers, and Evelyn especially, occupied whatever limited time his parents' busy schedule allowed. As a result, Lucius was left to his own devices. Herbert Clay, Jr., who was a number of years younger, recalls that "As a boy, Lucius used to stay with my mother a great deal, because she wouldn't stay in the house alone. And she considered him a nice boy, yet wild and undisciplined. I don't think that meant anything except that his mother didn't pay a hell of a lot of attention to him.

"As it is, Lucius won't show any emotion. Everything is held right smack inside at any price. It all comes from neglect, and the determination to get by in spite of it. His brothers all had the world at their feet, and they went haywire. He saw that, plus unbelievable fits of emotion. Temper tantrums. There used to be a special flowerpot on the front porch in Marietta for people to kick over when they got mad. It was a situation of extreme self-indulgence with a lot of brilliant people going to pot.

"Of course, as far as he was concerned, he was just leading a normal life of a boy in Marietta. I don't think he felt particularly neglected—although he may have later on, especially with the drop in finances at the Senator's death. He occasionally talks as though the family didn't have a cent at that time. That's absolutely not true. It was just that his mother was pouring out every cent she had on her daughter: for clothes, for parties, for schools—anything that Evelyn wanted.

"Like Ryburn, Lucius was told that the only way he could go to college was to go to West Point. And it became a very bitter part of his career. No one ever went up to see him. No one ever commented on his grades. In fact, no one ever wrote to him about anything. He never received one letter whatever while he was at West Point. To stick it out under those circumstances is almost beyond comprehension. You can't help develop a certain fortitude, a certain stoicism."

General Clay's childhood recollections differ, but not markedly. His brothers were "too successful too early," a fact Clay never forgot. "They didn't have to work for what they achieved, and therefore attached too little value to it." For Lucius, life was different: not only as a neglected, perhaps unexpected and unwanted sixth child, but as a junior officer in America's stagnant peacetime Army. Eleven years as a first lieutenant—few challenges, little responsibility, no opportunities to excel. A long, tedious climb that grinds most men down from boredom and inactivity. Clay's childhood necessity for self-motivation, for self-discipline, to succeed in spite of parental neglect where his pampered brothers and sister had failed, gave him an inner confidence that obviously kept him alert during the dreary military routine of the twenties and thirties. Like his siblings, Clay resisted conformity; unlike his siblings, he had a fierce competitiveness that always bridled the family capacity to self-destruct.

As a boy, Clay "never really knew" his father. His brothers were much closer in later life than he remembers during childhood, and his mother was fully occupied in Marietta's civic affairs as the wife of a United States Senator. Ryburn Clay's daughter Zaida remembers that "Momma Clay was old-fashioned, not only in her living, but in her dress. She always wore skirts to the floor. I think she fancied herself as something special. But she was not about to come out for anything. It all revolved around her."

"Momma" Clay—Sarah Frances White—had been born in nearby Lithia Springs in 1860. Unlike her husband, she was a rabid Southerner and an unreconstructed rebel. Her father, Andrew Jackson White, had been a prosperous farmer who joined Lee's Army of Northern Virginia when the Civil War began, was captured at Chancellorsville, imprisoned at Fort Morton, Indiana, and presumably died there.

"She was very bitter about the North, and didn't like Yankees," reports one grandson. "This always made it very difficult when they were in Washington." In Marietta, she founded the local chapter of the United Daughters of the Confederacy and the Confederate Memorial

Association. The Stars and Bars still fly over the Confederate cemetery in Marietta, largely as a result of her efforts.

"I don't know what effect the Civil War had on me," said General Clay. "Of course, we were living very close to it in Marietta, and I was raised in an atmosphere of Civil War veterans, who were all around the town in my younger days. I think I had to go to school in the North to learn that the North had won the war. Because I really was taught two different wars: the War Between the States in Marietta and the Civil War in Washington, D.C. —and you wouldn't have known they were the same war. Confederate Memorial Day, April 26, was quite a day. Schoolchildren were marched to the cemetery, and each child carried a 'flower of love.' They were deposited on the graves, and then there was a band concert and always an oration of the day."

Q: Did the Civil War influence you to go to the Military Academy?
CLAY: Perhaps, but not consciously.
Q: What made you decide?
CLAY: To tell the truth, I hadn't thought very much about it. I knew I wanted an education and I knew this was the way to get an education. I don't think I thought much beyond that, really.

"You must remember, this was the horse-and-buggy age as I grew up. Our transportation was horse-drawn. We used to go to church in a surrey on Sunday. When you see Marietta today, you'll see an industrial town, because the big Bell airplane plant, now Lockheed, was built right next to town, and it changed [Marietta] overnight. In my day nobody had any money, but nobody was really poor. Everybody had plenty to eat. I never thought about money, really, because I don't think anybody had any—in terms of cash. Farmers lived on credit during the winter and paid off when the crops were brought in and sold. The houses were set back from the street with shade trees, most of the roads were unpaved and dusty, but nevertheless it was a very, very nice little town."

Q: What is your strongest recollection of your life in Marietta?
CLAY: Oh, there are a lot of things that stay with me, of course. One is that it was a relatively easy life we led. I could bring anyone home I wanted at any time, and most of the boys I went with could do the same. But in a small town like ours, you didn't worry about where boys were because there wasn't anyplace for them to go. My parents never cared. So long as I got home for dinner, they didn't care where I went

after school. Nor did anybody else's. Because they knew you had to be at somebody else's home.

Dinner at the Clay home was an elaborate affair, always prepared by Gussie, the family cook, and brimming with the staples of a well-set Southern table. "In those days we never knew how many were going to be sitting down to our table in Marietta," Clay recalls, "because every one of us was entitled to bring anyone he wanted. So you never knew how many were going to be there: friends of my father, friends of any of the children. And then there were always visiting political figures."

Q: In other words, it was a very political household?
CLAY: Ours was a political household in every sense of the word. Whoever was there, politics was always the conversation of the day. No question about that. These were the days when you regularly invited the minister for dinner on Sunday. And when the bishop would come to town, you invited the bishop for dinner. As a matter of fact, the important people in town were the ministers, the superintendent of schools, the high-school teachers, and the judge. These were the prominent people in town—people who were held in very great respect.

As a youth, Clay was headstrong and undisciplined, much like his elder brothers. At fourteen, he was expelled from high school for pushing a young chemistry teacher through a first-floor window. "It wasn't serious, really," said Clay. "This young teacher—he wasn't more than a few years older than we were—looked as though he was going to strap a couple of us, and we decided we weren't going to let him."

At fifteen, Clay tried to enroll in Georgia Tech. But because he was underage, he did not qualify for reduced state tuition. Clay returned to Marietta, was elected president of his nine-member high school graduating class, and during the commencement exercises (May 22, 1914) debated affirmatively that "It would be advisable for the U.S. government to grant absolute independence to the Philippine Islands." Immediately upon graduation, he was appointed to West Point by Senator W. S. West of Georgia, who had succeeded to the Senate several months before, upon the death of Augustus O. Bacon, Senator Clay's old colleague.

Although Clay fibbed about his age, he was still too young to enter

West Point in 1914, and that autumn enrolled at Millard's Army-Navy Preparatory School in Washington. "I didn't know whether they would accept my credentials from Marietta High School, so I went to prep school to study for the examination. But they accepted my credentials and I never had to take an examination."

Clay's childhood set him apart from his military contemporaries. As the son of a United States Senator, he was exposed not only to Washington, but to the personal side of political life. That heritage gave him an important entrée when he later represented the Corps of Engineers on Capitol Hill, since many senior congressmen and senators remembered or had served with his father. Clay's habit of voracious reading—formed during his early visits to Washington—stayed with him throughout his career, a habit that allowed him to digest vast quantities of information quickly and coherently. From Georgia and the social position of his family he acquired a remarkable patrician dignity and self-confidence. His later stubbornness may well have reflected his early childhood neglect and the youthful example of his brothers' self-destruction: a determination born of necessity that permitted little leeway for self-indulgence. Throughout it all, Clay remained robustly independent. He retained a supreme confidence in his own judgment. If not placed in a position of responsibility, Clay usually challenged the rules and requirements of prescribed behavior. Unlike the vast majority of his military contemporaries, he took special pleasure in resisting pompous authority. A student who pushes his chemistry teacher through a first-floor window is an unlikely candidate for the Army's comfortable conformity.

· 3 ·

West Point (1915-1918)

In no section of America does West Point enjoy the reputation it holds in the deep South. Its graduates stand pre-eminent in the Valhalla of Southern heroes: Lee, Jackson, J. E. B. Stuart, Jefferson Davis. The élan and glamour of military life excite romantic memories of cavalier first families. And, perhaps most important, at a time when higher education was open only to the South's well-to-do, when commerce and industry were as yet undeveloped, West Point and Annapolis provided free technical educations and a guaranteed title of gentleman—a means of social and economic mobility not otherwise available. Clay's decision to attend the Military Academy reflected those concerns: a combination of tradition, romance, and necessity.

When Clay applied to West Point in 1914, there were no competitive examinations and few merit appointments. Selection was largely by congressional designation, and most legislators looked on their appointments as patronage rewards for the sons of deserving supporters. If the boy had a decent high school record and passed the physical examination—usually more grueling than whatever mental hurdle the Academy might present—he was accepted. Since Clay's father had been a United States Senator, he had little difficulty securing an appointment.

Clay was seventeen when he entered West Point—eighteen according to official records—and his class, like all West Point classes at that time, was a cross-section of white, middle-class America. "There weren't many boys from poverty classes," said Clay, "and the richer boys went to prep schools that sent them to Harvard or Yale." Clay's closest friend was Carroll Tye from Atlanta, whose father was one of Georgia's prominent lawyers. His roommate, perhaps at the other end of the social scale, was Pat Casey (Major General Hugh J. Casey), son of an Irish immigrant family fighting their way up from the streets of New York.

Because Clay had attended Millard's Army-Navy Preparatory School, he knew what to expect from West Point. But, as roommate Casey recalls, "Even then Lucius was a nonconformist. He didn't cater to rank or go out of his way to be deferential—which some people did. He'd be very definite, very opinionated. He was very strong-willed. When he made up his mind, that was it. You couldn't change it. Also, Lucius was not one to talk about his family—which I thought was a bit surprising since his father had been a United States Senator. Here I was his roommate and I have no recollection of his ever talking about his family or reciting any specific instances that I can recall."

When Clay entered West Point, its reputation was in serious decline. Once a leader in some fields, especially engineering and the natural sciences, West Point had gradually secluded itself from the changing currents of higher education. Rote memorization substituted for creative ideas. Instructors routinely graded cadets' performance, but rarely lectured or explained the material, and there were few opportunities for critical discussion. Clay, who was poor in drawing, reports that no one ever demonstrated the proper method to him. "If they had, I'm sure I could have learned it."

If anything, the Plain was saturated with self-satisfaction. With but four or five exceptions, the curriculum was virtually the same as that established by Sylvanus Thayer over a century before. "West Point is not a subject for reform," wrote Superintendent Hugh Scott. "It goes forward on its majestic course from year to year toward the fulfilment of its destiny, moving serenely under its traditions of 'honor, duty, country' . . . without need of radical alteration."

Even the outbreak of World War I made scarcely a ripple on the placid Hudson at West Point. While the armies of Europe bled to death in front of Passchendaele and Verdun, the department of military art continued to concentrate on the battles of Gettysburg and the Shenandoah Valley. Instructors emphasized massed cavalry tactics at the expense of the grim reality of trench warfare. "The Military Academy is forty years behind the times," Army Chief of Staff Peyton March complained bitterly, but not even America's entry into the war could change that—except that the cadets of Clay's class, owing to early graduation, skipped the course in the art of war completely.

Like Grant and Eisenhower, Clay had little patience for cadet life. "I found the studies on the whole relatively easy. I didn't have to study hard or work hard, and I did an awful lot of reading on the side—which I could have done anywhere: Balzac, Dickens, Thackeray, Zola, Dumas, and so forth. I spent so much time walking off demerits that I missed a good deal of the social side of the Academy, but I did like the companionship and I made a great many friends."

Q: Presumably the reputations made there would go with one into the service?

CLAY: Well, many people have maintained that this was one of the great advantages of West Point—that it enabled the officers who served together in war to know more about each other, have more confidence in each other, or less, as the case might be. Personally, I rather doubt that. Of course, you know whether you like them or not. But the later development of some of the members of my class that I knew so well did not indicate that my judgment was any too accurate. Some of those that I thought would go the farthest didn't. And some of those who I'm sure I didn't think would go very far turned out to be outstanding officers. So I just don't think that you have enough maturity of judgment for that to have as much value as it's given.

"Frankly, I don't know how to say it, but I'm sure that the West Point of today offers a lot more challenge academically than the West Point of my day. You didn't have to study to do quite well if you had any reasonable background. Of course, you came out a damned good mathematician. Now whether that was the right type of training for

military service is another question. In those days, it was not considered that officers were very apt to get into running governments or doing the many things that have resulted from modern war.

"I studied my first year. Not midnight oil, but during the hours for study I studied. I'm afraid my last two years there I really didn't. I don't think I opened a textbook after my first year. My roommate used to study the prescribed time—no more. It used to irritate the devil out of me, because he did study the prescribed time. I didn't have to, to do all right, and I wasn't very much concerned about where I stood in class."

Q: Was that important for later promotions?

CLAY: Not in the least bit. It was important for your branch assignment, because you had to be pretty well up in your class to get the Engineers. Many people wanted the Engineers, because in the static service of those days the Engineers offered a much more varied career. I didn't want the Engineers. So I never put in for them. We were one of the few classes where our choices were entirely disregarded, and we were assigned, the first thirty-seven or thirty-eight men, to the Engineers.

Q: General Marshall lamented that he was never taught to write at VMI [Virginia Military Institute]. Did you feel the same way about West Point?

CLAY: We had a pretty good course in English at the Military Academy—amongst other things because it required a considerable amount of writing. You had to write themes and essays on almost everything you read and saw and did. I think, as a matter of fact, they taught a much better course in that respect than they do today.

Q: Because you were required to write?

CLAY: Yes. And you had another factor in those days, and that was your daily recitation. You had to stand on your feet and present your mathematical problem, or whatever it was that you had solved. The result was that the cadets who graduated in my day had time and time again to stand up before their contemporaries and make oral presentations. I think this was an important part of the educational system, and it contributed to the military establishment a group of men who were able to present their views logically and systematically.

Q: Looking back on it, was the preparation you received at West Point adequate?

CLAY: It's very difficult to say, because right after graduation, and after serving only a few months, we went to the Engineer School, where we went through a year and a half of intense engineering training. Perhaps not under the greatest faculty in the world, but done with great thoroughness and great detail. Certainly the combination of the two gave me an adequate preparation for anything I was ever called on to do. I don't know where to separate them, though, really.

Because of the war, Clay's class graduated in June 1918, one year early. Clay stood twenty-seventh in a class of 137: first in English, first in history, and 128th in conduct—a buck private in the Corps of Cadets. His final efficiency report listed Clay's habits as "excellent," his general bearing and military appearance as "very good," although his attitude toward discipline rated merely "good." He was "active but not athletic," a good horseman, a fair swordsman, but "unqualified" with pistol or rifle.

The Class of June 1918 produced few combat commanders in World War II, probably because the first quarter of the class was assigned at graduation to the Corps of Engineers. Another quarter resigned during the twenties and thirties. Only one member of the class died in action: Second Lieutenant Albert Francis Ward, who was killed during the U.S. intervention in Siberia, June 22, 1919. Samuel D. Sturgis, a close friend of Clay's, later became Chief of Engineers. Pat Casey, Clay's roommate, was MacArthur's chief engineer in the Pacific and later chairman of the New York City Transit Authority.

The commandant of cadets when Clay graduated was Colonel Guy V. Henry, later chief of cavalry. Among the senior instructors were Major Geoffrey Keyes, later U.S. Military Governor of Austria, and Major James B. Ord, who served with Clay on MacArthur's staff in the Philippines. Captain Francis A. Harrington, a mathematics instructor, succeeded Harry Hopkins as administrator of the WPA. Captain Adna R. Chaffee, Jr., a pioneer in the development of U.S. armored forces, was an instructor in tactics. Lieutenant Jacob L. Devers, who commanded the Sixth Army Group during World War II, also taught mathematics.

During his three years at the Military Academy, Clay remained aloof from the formal rigmarole of West Point. With the exception of helping to prepare his senior yearbook, the *Howitzer,* he took no part in extracurricular activities. His closest friends at the Academy lived at the fringe of cadet life. None aspired to high rank in the Corps of Cadets, none took his studies seriously, and each sought whatever limited opportunity for good times the Military Academy afforded. Clay smoked heavily ("a source of infinite demerits"), drank whisky whenever he got the chance, and enjoyed especially the company of pretty girls. "Lucius is a true southern gentleman, prolific in southern gallantry and extracts of every poet or novelist known," roommate Pat Casey wrote wistfully in the 1919 *Howitzer.* "With a personality that will make friends anywhere, with a quick temper that is as quickly and readily overcome, and then cements more firmly the bonds of former friendship; with a jovial and generous nature; with an ability to do things quickly and correctly when time is pressing; and with just enough indifference, Lucius will make an efficient, well-liked officer in the service."

Clay's social bent found an outlet in the "Dirty Dozen"—a group of twelve cadet rebels and miscreants that Clay helped organize. Flaunting their independence of Academy regulations, the Dirty Dozen established a clubhouse in an unused room in the cadet canteen. There, behind closed doors, they would drink beer and smoke cigarettes and dance with their girlfriends after football games to records played on a wind-up phonograph.

"It's a funny thing," recalls roommate Casey. "Here is someone who ends up as one of the Army's top commanders, and seven weeks before graduation he had only four demerits to go before he would be kicked out."

One of Clay's most serious problems—and one that would bedevil him throughout his military career—was his unwillingness to accept rank as authority. When his company tactical officer, a senior first lieutenant in the Regular Army, invited an attractive date to West Point for a weekend dance, Clay couldn't resist stealing her away. The result was a personal vendetta that netted Clay more than sixty demerits before he was transferred to another company. "The funny part about it," said Clay, "was that she was really quite a casual acquaintance of mine."

It was at West Point that Clay met Marjorie McKeown, the willowy, blond daughter of another Irish immigrant and successful businessman, John McKeown, president of the New England Button Company. The future Mrs. Clay came to West Point as the weekend date of Clay's Georgia classmate, Carroll Tye. Marjorie was then a student at Barnard, full of life and exceptionally attractive. Tye was ill in the infirmary when Marjorie arrived, and Clay became her escort. From then on, they saw each other regularly.

"Lucius used to get a lot of demerits for silly things," Marjorie Clay remembers. "Once I went up and missed the train to return to New York. In those days, we could only go up with chaperones, and of course, we had to return with them. By that time, I was quite in love with Lucius, and I went back and found him still in sally port. I said, 'Lucius, I missed the train and I'm going to catch hell when I get back —and I'm starving to death.' So he went to the mess hall and stole a piece of cake and gave it to me and that was my supper. When I got back to Barnard, I was campused for six months, and Lucius got three demerits for taking food out of the mess hall."

Clay's stay at West Point was marked by increasing dissatisfaction. His initial decision to attend the Academy was doubtless too lightly taken, an error he could scarcely reverse. If the course had been the usual four years instead of three, it is unlikely he would have graduated. The curriculum offered little stimulation, and the rigid discipline seemed comically out of date. The separation between officers and cadets impressed Clay as painfully unnecessary. "MacArthur changed a good deal of that when he became Superintendent," said Clay. "And while I'm not the most rabid worshipper of MacArthur that there is in this world, I do give him a tremendous amount of credit for recognizing the need for change at the Military Academy to meet the change in the whole national outlook and environment. He knew it had to be changed, and he changed it—against a good deal of opposition from members of his own faculty."

Despite his criticism of cadet life, West Point had a profound effect on Clay. It instilled a sense of discipline and a respect for the values of military service that stayed with him throughout his life. "I think I was out of West Point maybe two or three years before I began to realize how much it meant to me," said Clay. "I think when I went back there as an instructor [in 1924], more mature, having seen at least a part of the world, I really began to understand and appreciate the character formation that takes place at West Point. It left its mark on all of us, no question about that. But I didn't realize how much of a mark until some years later."

The one inspiration Clay found at the Academy was Lieutenant Colonel Lucius Holt, head of the department of English and history, and one of the few Ph.D.s on West Point's faculty. Almost alone until MacArthur's arrival, Holt—who had come to West Point from Yale—tried to inject a tone of modernity into the Academy's curriculum. "Lucius Holt had a very great influence on me," said Clay. "He was an outstanding teacher, and one of the few men at the Academy you could respect on purely intellectual grounds." Clay did his best work for Holt, and led his class in both English and history, two of the subjects he genuinely enjoyed.

Clay's critical, biting intellect resented the tiresome make-work that posed as academic effort in too many subjects. Worse still, he resented the leisurely pace West Point pursued after America entered World War I. For Clay, staying at the Military Academy seemed "an utterly useless waste of time. I wanted to get into the war. A number of our classmates who had been dismissed [from the Academy] were already captains and lieutenants, while we were still at West Point doing nothing."

Q: And the discipline at West Point?

CLAY: The discipline at West Point was mainly petty. I did resist petty discipline. I still do. I didn't like it in the Army. I thought it was foolish. I never used it when I was in command. I thought it was an irritation to harass the troops with petty discipline—which was what they did at West Point. To let you buy tobacco in the cadet store where the only tobacco they sold was Bull Durham, which could only be used in cigarettes, and then to say it was all right to smoke a pipe in your room but not a cigarette, that's what I call ridiculous discipline. And that's the kind of discipline I did resist.

Q: In other words, there was a great deal of Mickey Mouse?

CLAY: A great deal. And I never really believed in it. That was one of my troubles. The discipline at West Point in my day was the type and kind of discipline that you couldn't possibly use on enlisted men. I can remember, at officers' training camp later, where some of my classmates were trying to teach new officers by applying the "stand up and brace" theory of discipline used at West Point, and it just didn't work worth a damn. You were dealing with mature men, and they just weren't going to stand for that type of treatment. I did not try it. I didn't like it even then. I don't mean to say you don't have to have some of it. You do. But it was overdone at the Military Academy, and the rigidity between officer and cadet was terribly overdone.

Clay's disciplinary difficulties were typical of many cadets over the years, whose strength of character simply would not put up with the cant and excessive attention to detail required at West Point. President Charles Eliot of Harvard, then a member of the Academy's board of visitors, lamented in *The New York Times* about the "acquired habit of passing the buck" and "red tape methods" that West Point instilled.

The reaction was best summed up by Marshal Pétain, who was shocked when he visited West Point after the war. "I do not think that young men who are being prepared for the duties of an officer should be required to repeat the same gestures every day during four years," said Pétain. "That seems to me too long and I fear that this monotony must result in fixing the graduate's mind into a groove so rigid that elasticity becomes impaired.

"He comes out a well-instructed and obedient subaltern and a first rate drill-master; but outside of a small category that have exceptional force of character, he has got to pass considerable time before he can break the rigid forms into which his nature has become crystallized and regain his mental vigor."

Clay was one of that small minority who successfully resisted West Point's enervating effect. He graduated from the Academy wearing second lieutenant's bars and the crossed cannons of the field artillery. "I liked horses, I liked riding, and I liked the field artillery," said Clay. "I thought the greatest thrill I could imagine was taking a horse-drawn battery and putting it into action. It had glamour and excitement. I thought that the artillery officers I had known at the Academy were much more glamorous than the very serious-minded Engineers, and so I wasn't the least bit interested in the Corps of Engineers."

Because of the war, Clay's class got only three weeks' graduation leave instead of the usual two months. But after one week, his Marietta sojourn was abruptly ended by a cable from the adjutant general addressed to him as "Lieutenant Lucius D. Clay, Corps of Engineers," and ordering him to report immediately to Camp Humphreys, Virginia.

"I wired the adjutant general that he had made a mistake, that I was in the field artillery. He wired back that he knew what he was doing and that I should follow my orders—or words to that effect. That was when I learned I was in the Corps of Engineers. But, hell, I didn't want the Corps of Engineers. If I had, I would have worked harder and been higher up in my class."

· 4 ·

The Training of a Bolshevik (1918-1933)

> Have known him as a student officer 1 1/2 yrs. Quick mentality but inaccurate. Snap judgment. Inclined to be bolshevistic.
>
> Major Earl North
> [Clay's efficiency report, June 16, 1920]

CLAY'S ASSIGNMENT TO THE CORPS OF ENGINEERS came as an unwelcome surprise, for the field artillery had offered a chance of combat. An assignment to the Engineers in the summer of 1918 made it unlikely he would see action in France. Clay's career was already cast: in thirty-one years of service and two world wars, he would never fight a military engagement. In 1918, fate rested on class standing—a competition for grades that Clay lackadaisically had ignored. In World War II, events were less capricious, though no less galling. For by 1942, Clay was the Army's foremost industrial organizer: a military professional with profound understanding of the civilian economy and what made it tick.

Clay's peacetime career thrust him into the

mainstream of American life. While his colleagues in the combat arms tramped on countless maneuvers at Benning and Sill and Riley, effectively insulated from civilian concerns, Clay built airports and dams and bridges, and spent four important years representing the Corps of Engineers on Capitol Hill: the rivers and harbors assignment so close to the pulse of congressional power. When war came, he knew his way around Washington as well as anyone in the Army.

Camp Humphreys, Virginia—Clay's first post—had been named for Major General A. A. Humphreys, Grant's chief engineer during the siege of Richmond—a gaffe similar to naming a military post outside Atlanta for General Sherman. It was a typical World War I training center: hot and dusty in the summer, muddy when it rained, and surprisingly cold and damp in the northern-Virginia winter. Its major attraction was its location twenty miles south of Washington.

Before the war, Camp Humphreys had been a summer training area for the Engineer School, then located at Washington Barracks. Before that, it had been the decaying, overgrown Belvoir estate of Lord Fairfax, which George Washington once managed. But with the first rumblings of mobilization in 1917, Humphreys was activated as the Engineer training camp: fifty thousand officers and men shunted into the Potomac countryside.

Clay reported to Camp Humphreys at the end of June 1918, and was assigned to a basic training regiment. "My first task was to meet a group of inductees at the rail head and take them back into camp, sort them out, and organize them into companies," said Clay. "I remember it very well because I was the only officer who had drawn mess-hall equipment and rations for the first night. In fact, as it turned out, we were damned near feeding the whole camp.

"But, in any event, that lasted only four or five days. Then they got the idea that they would take our class and a similar number of selected graduates from officers' training camps and put us in a high-speed training group for six weeks so that we could take the new Engineer doctrine out into the service. This was at Camp Lee, Virginia. That again was one of those rigid-discipline things—double time, thump, thump, thump.

"When we graduated, we were all promoted to first lieutenants, and I was reassigned to Camp Humphreys as an instructor. In September, my classmates and I, all of us in the Corps of Engineers, were promoted to captain—promotions were quite rapid in those days—and within a very short time I was commanding a company in the officers' training camp. That's where I was when the war ended.

"After the armistice, I was involved for a month or so liquidating the training camp. And then, with the new graduates from West Point —the class after ours, which was also on an accelerated program— we were put into the regular Engineer School course at Camp Humphreys. It was not a bad course, really. It was called the Engineer School of Application, and we were the last class to go through it."

Clay's courtship of Marjorie McKeown had ripened during the summer of 1918, and on the Labor Day weekend he visited Marjorie's family in East Orange, New Jersey. "I can still remember it," said Clay, "because the temperature must have been close to a hundred, and I had to stand all the way on the train from Washington to New York.

"I don't think I had gone up with marriage in mind—at least, to ask Marjorie at that time. But I did, and then I went in and talked to her father, and I got along very well with him." Clay's Labor Day proposal was accepted and the wedding was set for September 21, a bare two weeks later. There was no ceremony to speak of. Because Clay wasn't Catholic, the wedding could not be held in Marjorie's church. But the vows were exchanged in the rectory of the McKeown family church: East Orange's Our Lady Help of Christians. Clay's West Point roommate Pat Casey was best man, Marjorie's sister was maid of honor, and, except for Marjorie's parents, no one else attended.

No one from Clay's Marietta family came, just as no one had come to his West Point graduation. After Senator Clay's death, each member of the family went his or her own way. Mrs. Clay became postmistress of Marietta—a traditional patronage reward for widows of U.S. Senators; Herbert pursued the pleasures of life, wrecking his promising political career in the process; Lex was drinking himself into an early grave; Frank was in a military hospital; Ryburn worked busily at the bank; while Evelyn led the life of a young lady of leisure in Washington and Atlanta. If Clay resented the neglect he suffered, he never mentioned it. In later years, when his brothers and Evelyn fell on hard times, Clay helped support them as best he could. And during the twenties and thirties, when his own sons were growing up, he sent them regularly to spend each summer in Marietta.

Because of the war, Clay had only five days' leave, and immediately after the wedding lunch (at New York's Hotel Astor), he and Marjorie left for a brief honeymoon at the Delaware Water Gap, then returned to Camp Humphreys and what Clay remembers as two of the most miserable years of his life. "The Engineers tried to treat an officer who had been out of the Academy for six or eight months and was married as though he was still at West Point. And you just couldn't do it at that stage of the game. The fact that we were married made no difference whatever. We had to live in barracks, whereas our wives had to live in town—and we couldn't see them except on weekends. Every Saturday I would go to headquarters and get a weekend pass. One Saturday they told me not to come back again. I said, 'I'll be back next weekend.' And I was. This was an absolutely ridiculous performance [by the Army] and completely unnecessary. And it resulted in several good men in my class quitting."

Marjorie provided Clay with the love and affection he so badly needed. Far more than a surrogate for the family he had missed as a youth—General MacArthur teased her as the prettiest woman in the Corps of Engineers—Marjorie became the one person Clay turned to for advice. Often brusque in official matters, Clay was, as a family man, warm and considerate. In fact, his outward severity was often Clay's method of shielding his personal life from public encroachment. In 1946, he brought American dependents to Germany (against much high-level Washington advice) because, as he frankly said, "I missed my wife, just as I'm sure a lot of other people missed theirs—and I thought the presence of dependents would raise the moral tone of the Occupation."

For the first year, Marjorie lived in a furnished room in an Alexandria boarding house. Then, in the summer of 1919, with Marjorie expecting, Clay's class went to Europe to tour the battlefields. Technically, the war was still going on, "and when I look back on it," said Clay, "we actually had more troops in Europe in 1919 than we did eight months after the Second World War."

While Clay was in Germany—his first of two visits before 1945—Marjorie gave birth to a son: Lucius D. Clay, Jr. The baby was two months premature and weighed only four pounds, and Clay was granted emergency leave to return home. "But I almost didn't make it. When I came through Brest—which was our embarkation port—a

Regular Army captain of Engineers with stateside orders, someone plucked me out to be post engineer."

Four days later, Clay sailed for the United States on the *President Grant,* only to find when he reached Camp Humphreys that the Army expected him to continue to live on post, away from Marjorie and their new son. After moving Marjorie and the baby into a tiny apartment at 106 North Alfred Street in Alexandria, Clay scoured Camp Humphreys for suitable quarters.

"Then one day I found an empty building that had been an infirmary when the camp was larger. It was just an old wooden barracks, but it was divided into a number of small rooms: doctors' offices, an operating room, and so forth. Two of my classmates who were also married went with me to get permission to use it. We had a hell of a time, and I finally had to threaten to resign [Clay's first of many resignations] before we got to use it. We painted all of the rooms, divided it into three apartments, and set up housekeeping. The building had an immense furnace in the basement, and we would stoke the damned thing with wood every morning to keep a fire going for the girls all day—two of them had small babies—and then when we got back at night we would stoke it again. They were miserable quarters. The only thing you could say for them was that they were nearby."

Clay remained at the Engineer School through June 1920. As at West Point, students were assigned to sections based on performance: the best students in the first platoon, the worst in the fourth. Leslie R. Groves, later head of the Manhattan Project, which developed the atomic bomb, and Pat Casey, both dedicated Engineers, stood at the top of the first platoon; Clay in the last section of the fourth—a reflection of his indifference more than his inability. In preparing Clay's final efficiency report, Assistant Commandant Earl North, whom Clay had challenged over the infirmary, rated him below average in attention to duty, as well as in tact, judgment, and common sense.

Such an efficiency report might have marked the end of Clay's career—it probably would in the Army of the 1990s—except that the Corps of Engineers was a tightly knit, elite organization where everyone knew everyone else and junior officers were not expected to amount to much until eight or ten years of service. Efficiency reports had not been inflated to the point where a single derogatory comment could prove fatal, and even promotions, which were based strictly on seniority, were not affected unless an officer was manifestly unfit.

Clay's difficulties with Major North soon became common knowledge in the Corps, for North had originally accused Clay not only of inattention in class but of "bolshevism" as well. When shown the draft report, as regulations required, Clay demanded a court martial. He was testing the system.

"If I am inattentive in class," Clay wrote North, "it is because of the low caliber of instruction. But if I am a bolshevik, that implies disloyalty." Under those circumstances, he said, only a court martial could clear the record. Throughout his career, Clay never hesitated to challenge entrenched authority. In 1948, when most of those in power in Washington wanted to cut their losses in Berlin and evacuate the city, it was exactly such steely determination that steadied the Allied course. For Clay, a matter of principle, particularly if it involved his broad Southern conception of personal honor, was worth fighting for.

Confronted with Clay's intransigence, North backed down. The reference to Clay's inattention in class was deleted, and Clay's "bolshevism" was rephrased to make it clear that it applied to his behavior, not to his beliefs.

From Engineer School, Clay was assigned to ROTC duty at Auburn, then a sleepy land-grant college in southeastern Alabama. There Clay's second son, Frank, was born, also prematurely, delivered by a neighboring professor's wife whom Clay called at the last minute. ROTC provided a pleasant interlude. There was time for football games and leisurely drives in a new Dodge that Clay had bought in Washington. Auburn's students, mostly poor farm boys from rural Alabama, impressed Clay as extraordinarily dedicated, and the engineering curriculum was "on a par with West Point or Georgia Tech." Clay organized the Engineer branch of ROTC, and when given his own responsibility did an outstanding job. When the program was inspected in the spring of 1921, Clay's students performed so well that he was ordered back to the faculty at Camp Humphreys.

Captain Isaac Spalding, Auburn's professor of military science and tactics (and later commanding general of the 77th Division Artillery in the Pacific), wrote on Clay's efficiency report: "For a man of his youth [Clay was twenty-three] I think he is an exceptionally fine officer. He has that excellence of common sense that is so seldom found in Engineers."

Clay enjoyed the tour at Auburn, but was delighted to leave. "If I had had to stay at Auburn for two more years, I would have been bored to death." In addition to the professional problems raised by an extended tour on civilian component duty, Clay and Marjorie missed the social whirl of a large military post: they enjoyed parties, entertained frequently, and were usually in the center of whatever activity was being organized—a different, younger side of Clay from the austere commander who ran America's wartime production or presided over Germany.

While at Auburn, Clay published an article on the ROTC in *The Military Engineer,* the Corps's professional journal. ROTC was then in its first year, and Clay addressed himself to its flaws, some of which later proved fatal on many campuses when the program came under attack during the Vietnam War. He beseeched his collcagucs to improve the caliber of instruction, and "avoid the deadly routine of close order drill. It is in the classroom that the success and efficiency of the program will be determined. The Professor of Civil Engineering does not give dances to attract students to his classes; he does not organize clubs to attract students to his subject. Neither does the Professor of History do these things. Their work speaks for itself. And to make the military cause hold its place, it too must be made to speak for itself."

Back at Camp Humphreys, Clay undertook the usual apprentice jobs of a junior officer: post engineer, assistant quartermaster, instructor in civil engineering. He inventoried the vast mountain of engineer equipment remaining from the war, and was fortunate this time to serve under two distinguished commanders: Mason Patrick, first chief of the Army Air Corps, then commanding Camp Humphreys, and Colonel James A. Woodruff, a level-headed soldier who started his workday at 6:00 A.M. with a canter around the post. Woodruff had a substantial influence on Clay: "He knew how to administer justice without being overly severe, plus the fact that when he went to his office at eight o'clock, he knew more about his command than anyone else."

Clay found his assignment to the Engineer School attractive, and, as at Auburn—as whenever his interest was aroused—he did well. Major Philip B. Fleming, Clay's immediate superior (later director of the Public Works Administration), wrote that he was "An especially intelligent, vigorous and efficient officer. He completed thoroughly and expediently every job assigned to him and asks no questions. He gives promise of a brilliant future." Fleming gave Clay an overall rating of "Superior," the Army's highest category.

Camp Humphreys became Fort Humphreys in 1923—the Army's way of designating permanent installations—and in the timeless routine of peacetime service, Clay found himself writing Engineer training regulations: portable footbridges, explosives and demolitions, principles of field fortifications. Maxwell Taylor, then on his first year's service, met Clay for the first time at lunch one day at Fort Humphreys. "I was terribly impressed," said Taylor. "Here was this young officer, not too much older than I was, slamming his hand down on the table saying he had just found nine mistakes in an Engineer training manual. Well, I'd just come from West Point, and I thought an Engineer training manual was something handed down on tablets from Mount Sinai. But Clay, you see, was an iconoclast even then."

While Clay was at Humphreys, the Army underwent its first major postwar retrenchment. The ranks of the officer corps, swollen by wartime appointments, were reduced sharply to comply with the Defense Act of 1920, authorizing a regular force of 288,000 men. Even that modest figure soon was pared by a parsimonious Congress, so that by the mid-twenties the Army was reduced to fewer than 119,000 actives. Clay and his Engineer classmates, all of whom had been captains since 1918, were reduced to first lieutenants at the end of 1922 and were destined to remain in that grade for another eleven years—though they retained the pay and allowances of a captain. Many of Clay's classmates resigned.

Clay, who took the Army casually at that point, recalls his reduction to first lieutenant with equanimity: "There was no reason to get excited. It happened to everyone. My classmates in the combat branches were still first lieutenants anyway, so I never thought very much about it. A few years later I had second thoughts, but in 1922 I was relatively content."

Q: Five of your first six years of service were at Fort Humphreys. Was that unusual?

CLAY: Probably. It was very lucky for me, because during that period I met so many of the Engineer officers who passed through that I had probably a better-than-average acquaintanceship with most of the officers in the Corps of Engineers.

Q: Was there an "inner club" in the Corps of Engineers, as, for example, in the infantry at Fort Benning under Marshall?

CLAY: No. In the Corps of Engineers, the Corps was the club. It was a very proud group of people. And it was relatively small. There were only a couple of hundred of us. Everybody knew everybody, and it was quite an elite organization. Everyone had his idiosyncrasies, but beneath those idiosyncrasies was a sharp, intelligent mind. And you couldn't help but learn working in that atmosphere.

In January 1924, Clay was placed on detached service with the Marines in the Caribbean, and subsequently was given a letter of commendation by Marine Corps Commandant Dion Williams for his technical assistance during a landing on Culebra Island. "In thosc days," said Clay, "letters of commendation were frowned on. The only reason you got a letter of commendation was because you were on temporary assignment with someone who wasn't making out your efficiency report. Since the war, everybody writes letters of commendation. There are even commendation medals, which was unheard of in my day."

Clay's extended sojourn at Humphreys ended in the summer of 1924, when he was recalled to West Point as an instructor in civil engineering—a choice assignment for a junior officer, although Clay, who had mixed feelings about the Academy, was apprehensive about what he might find. "But MacArthur had done an excellent job of bringing the Military Academy into contact with the world. The disciplinary system was much less rigid; the academic program had been improved considerably; the time devoted to social studies and the humanities was increased, and standards were tightened all along the line."

Q: When you were a cadet, you thought the distinction between officers and cadets was too rigid. How did you react as an instructor?

CLAY: I tried to conduct my classes on a less rigid basis than they had been conducted in my day. But I wasn't trying to beat the system. That would have been impossible. I did try to encourage questions and discussions. In my day, this had been the most difficult part, because if you differed from an instructor you could almost be charged with insubordination. I didn't think that was good then, and I don't think it is good now. I must admit, it may have depended somewhat on how you did it, but it was very difficult in my day to have free discussion between the instructor and the cadet.

Q: Your efficiency reports at West Point are good, but one contained a curious comment: "A good officer, with average tact, ability above average, *who has a rather gloomy outlook on life.*" That was in 1927. [Italics added.]

CLAY: I think it was about that time that I was given the job of taking our entire engineering library at West Point and recording each book on Library of Congress index cards. I resented it then, AND I STILL RESENT IT. It was what I call a minor clerical job, and it made me madder than hell.

Clay's four years at West Point were years of indecision. By 1924, the glorious indolence of the peacetime Army began to pale, and for the first time he seriously considered resigning. "We'd change our minds almost from week to week," recalls Marjorie.

Clay's unhappiness was that of a junior officer with too little to do. "Here you had a man who had spent eight or nine years in the Army, was still a lieutenant, had a great deal of experience, and liked a lot of things that were going on. Other things he was not very happy about. Then too, for young officers particularly, it was very difficult to establish your relative position, because the assignment of responsibilities was so very simple. We didn't know if we were getting anywhere or not. I can remember, somewhat later, when the Engineers were examining the efficiency reports, they found that 71 percent were above average. Of course, this immediately proved their reporting system wasn't worth much."

Clay's search for employment outside the service resembled his aimless decision to attend West Point: if something turned up, he would consider it. One opportunity he examined was with the insurance house of Joseph Choate and Sons, following an advertisement in *The New York Times* to which he had responded. Clay eventually declined the offer—"I don't know why, really"—and turned down a salary more than twice his Army income.

Another opportunity Clay turned down was with the New England Button Company, which Marjorie's father wanted Lucius to take over. John McKeown's health was failing rapidly, and in the summer of 1927 he visited West Point and took the Clays to Europe: first to the family home in Galway, then to England and France. That autumn he died, providing Marjorie with a sizable income. It was a substantial addition to the Clay finances—well above Lucius's 1927 salary, and it enabled them to live considerably more comfortably than many of their contemporaries.

Clay left West Point in 1928 with a final rating of "Superior." Colonel Mitchell, the Academy's permanent professor of civil engineering, said Clay was *"a very capable man, more suited to war than to peace. In peace I would be satisfied with him under me in any grade; in war I would especially desire to have him because of his superior qualities in certain respects."* What this implied, in the cryptic language of Army efficiency reports, was that Clay was quickly bored with peacetime routine. He would excel in assignments that interested him; otherwise, he could be difficult.

From West Point, Clay returned to Fort Humphreys to attend a nine-month course for company-grade Engineer officers, another disheartening episode for Clay, who resented the course and everything associated with it. "This was one of those foolish things they do in the Army. A couple of my classmates and I were sent back because we hadn't been through the course, although we had lectured at it, taught at it, and whatnot. We had to take the course with thirty or forty much [more] junior officers—many of whom I had taught at West Point."

Clay's unhappiness can be judged by his final efficiency report, as prepared by Major H. A. Finch, the assistant commandant: "Intelligent, forceful, ruthless in type; not lacking in ability but lacking in sense of proportion. Needs strong hand for guidance. His judgment does not measure up to his intelligence."

After completing the course at Humphreys, Clay was assigned to the 11th Engineers in Panama. He was plainly dissatisfied with the service, but had found nothing to take its place. Clay, Marjorie, and the two boys left for Panama on an Army transport in early July 1929. The heat in midsummer was overpowering, and as a first lieutenant, Clay was assigned an inside cabin below decks, next to the boiler room. "Talk about the 'Black Hole of Calcutta,' that was the worst trip I ever made in my life," said Clay.

The trip to Panama convinced Clay he wanted a change. He had had enough of peacetime Engineer routine. As soon as he arrived in the Canal Zone, Clay dispatched an urgent letter to the adjutant general requesting transfer to law school. "I believe I could be successful in the legal department of the Army," wrote Clay, "and in the event of securing this detail, I would be glad of an opportunity to serve in the Judge Advocate General's department."

Clay's letter to the adjutant general came at the nadir of his military career. Disgruntled, unhappy, he thrashed around for any way out —short of leaving the service, and even that was not ruled out. Many years later, Clay was surprised and a little embarrassed to learn that the letter he had written in 1929 had been retained in his Army personnel (201) file. After forty years and four stars, it is perhaps understandable that he did not remember the extent of his earlier unhappiness. "I had completely forgotten about that letter," said Clay, "but I think I felt that if I could get a law degree, and get over to the judge advocate's side, I would at least have something I could fall back on if I found there was just no future in the Army. I had just finished four years of instructing at West Point, and I was still a lieutenant after ten years' service. It looked pretty hopeless. I hated the trip. I didn't like any part of Panama at that moment. I don't know what prompted the letter except I simply wasn't happy. Then I took over B Company of the 11th Engineers, and I think within six months we knew we had the best company in the United States Army.

"I really found myself in Panama. It was the first opportunity I ever had to work with the American soldier, the American enlisted man. And while we had very limited money, Panama was an important assignment and you worked at being a soldier. And then we got a general down there by the name of Preston Brown, who had commanded the Third Division during the war, and who was hated in Panama because he was a real disciplinarian. But he had the idea that we were down there to defend the Panama Canal. And while he was rather limited in the facilities at his disposal, he did more to make a military force out of the troops under his command than anyone I'd seen up to that time. I, for one, responded to it, because it all began to seem worthwhile."

The 11th Engineers were the elite of the peacetime Army. Known as the Jungle Cats because of their service in Panama (the regiment wears a black panther on its crest), the 11th had been the first American unit to see action in World War I. Shipped to the Canal Zone in

1920, the regiment undertook a topographic survey of Panama—an enterprise that was still under way when Clay arrived.

"We mapped for more than six months in the roughest kind of jungle," said Clay. "They were rain forests, really. The men would come out after two or three weeks as white as sheets. All of our packing out was done by mules, and pack mules were notorious in the Army for their meanness. We didn't have much trouble, although I learned that a man could outwalk a mule—and carry a bigger load. This was especially true if it involved traversing a greater distance.

"We also went on two maneuvers where we were building roads. Roads had a way of disappearing in Panama, what with landslides and the tropical vegetation. And although a great many companies in Panama were finished at one or two o'clock in the afternoon, and the officers would go to beer call or whatever, in my company we were busy all of the time. Thank God, because that's what made us a good company."

Clay was fortunate in Panama to serve under a series of gifted commanders. In addition to Preston Brown, Clay's regimental commander was "Goff" Caples, a military intellectual whose mind ranged far beyond service routine. "He was a little bit fat and a little bit slovenly, and he was not considered a very snappy soldier," said Clay. "But he had tremendous intellectual capacity and curiosity. He was truly an independent thinker. He read, and he understood ethnic and political movements, and I learned a lot from him—almost as if he were a special tutor. It was really quite inspiring to know him."

It was in Panama that Clay had his first (and only) taste of military action. It was January 2, 1931. As was their custom on Saturday nights, the Clays were in Panama City at the Union Club, a home away from home for Americans in Panama, situated spectacularly on the waterfront and, being Panamanian, one of the few places for an American to get a drink legally during Prohibition.

"Along about twelve-thirty, Colonel Lippincott, the chief of staff of the Panama Department, came around and said, 'You all better go home now. There is going to be trouble tonight.'

"We really didn't take him very seriously as to the trouble, but we took him very seriously on going home. So we went home, and we hadn't been there very long when we began to hear the rally calls being sounded. My first-sergeant was soon knocking at my door to tell me the company was ready.

"I rushed out, the company was formed, and off we marched to our position—the position we were supposed to take inside Panama in case of a revolution. And, sure enough, it was a real revolution. They attacked the President's [Florencio Arosemena] Palace and eventually deposed him. The only person who was killed was an American newspaperman [H. F. Ayres] who got caught in the cross-fire between the two lines."

Clay served in Panama from July 1929 to July 1931. His efficiency reports during that period reflect his change in attitude. At first "above average," he soon settled into a groove of "superior" ratings. Colonel Caples, to whom Clay acknowledges his debt, said that he was "Able, agreeable, loyal, absolutely trustworthy. A born commander. Of some three hundred or more company commanders I have known, I know none his superior. . . . I have never seen his better."

From Panama, Clay returned to the United States and was assigned to the Corps of Engineers district office in Pittsburgh—another routine change of station for a junior officer. Clay was thirty-three years old and, after thirteen years' commissioned service, still a first lieutenant. But rivers and harbors work was a desirable billet, and the Pittsburgh district was one of the most active, handling more annual tonnage than the Panama Canal.

The rivers and harbors work of the Corps of Engineers far overshadows its military responsibilities—except in time of war—and it is the one branch of the United States Army continuously involved in domestic politics. Since 1824, when Congress authorized the President "to cause the necessary surveys, plans, and estimates to be made of the routes of such roads and canals as he may deem of national importance," America's westward expansion hinged on the Corps' activities: the Cumberland Road; the Chesapeake and Ohio Canal; navigation of the Ohio, Mississippi, and Missouri rivers. In the West, the Corps guided the way for settlers across the Great Plains. Congress eventually placed all rivers and harbors work under the Corps, and when Clay reported for duty in Pittsburgh in 1931, the Engineers were at work like beavers improving 192 of America's harbors, 294 rivers, and 83 canals. Annual civil expenditures by the Corps in 1932 totaled $152 million. By contrast, the U.S. Army's total military budget for that year was but $343 million—a figure that the outgoing Hoover administration soon cut in half.

Clay recalls that when he arrived in Pittsburgh in the summer of 1931, "We hadn't quite hit the bottom of the Depression. My work carried me all over the Pittsburgh area, and particularly along the Monongahela River—which was the region that supplied Pittsburgh with its coal. And it was a scene of shocking desolation. The mines were closed. People were out of work. And they were out of money. There was a shantytown in Pittsburgh where thousands of miners came looking for jobs. And there were no jobs. It was a very sad picture."

Q: And in the Army?

CLAY: We were very fortunate to be in the Army with a fixed salary. We were able to live in a community like Pittsburgh much better than we could have under normal conditions. I remember that we rented a house and it was a little more than we could really afford to pay. But the rent was cut twice in the next six months without our even asking.

Q: Did the Army play a role in relief activities?

CLAY: At this time, the rivers and harbors program was going along on a normal basis. It provided jobs, a lot of jobs, but not nearly as many as we were to do later, under the New Deal, when the public works program got under way. Mr. Hoover plunged $300 million into public works while he was still President. Then Mr. Roosevelt came along with $3 billion.

Clay's boss in Pittsburgh was Major Wilhelm D. Styer, three years ahead of Clay at West Point and a former third captain of the Corps of Cadets. Tall, heavy-set, Styer had served with General Pershing on the Battle Monuments Commission, and subsequently became chief of staff of Army Service Forces during World War II. Styer was extraordinarily capable and believed in giving junior officers their head, an attitude that Clay appreciated.

After he had been in Pittsburgh for a year, Clay was assigned as resident engineer in charge of the construction of lock and dam No. 2 on the Allegheny River. "This was a new lock we were building right in Pittsburgh," said Clay, "just before the Allegheny and Monongahela join to form the Ohio. My job was really as chief inspector. The construction contract was won by the Vang Construction Company."

Q: You were still in Pittsburgh in 1932 when Mr. Roosevelt was elected President. Did you follow the campaign?

CLAY: I followed the election very closely, and I can remember sitting up election night listening to the returns. At the time, I was a nonvoting Democrat, and I was thrilled at the election results. It was typical, I think, for the Army to be very interested—but it was what you might call a disinterested interest, since no one in the Army was voting. But we could generate as much nonvoting excitement as anyone else.

Q: Why didn't anyone in the Army vote at that time?

CLAY: For one thing, absentee voting between World War I and World War II was not made easy. Secondly, most of us in the Army had lost home identity, had never registered, and seldom stayed long enough anywhere to register. Thirdly, we seldom had the interest in local affairs which encourages registration. I think these were the reasons, rather than any principle.

Clay's Democratic inclinations reflected more than his Georgia heritage. He was deeply moved by the Depression conditions he encountered in Pittsburgh, and, better perhaps than most military men—isolated in forts and camps across America—understood the great deprivation stalking the nation. Less than five months after FDR took office, Clay was called to Washington to become the number-two man in charge of rivers and harbors, a post vacated by West Point roommate Pat Casey, who had recommended Clay as his successor.

When Clay left Pittsburgh, Major Styer rated him "superior" in all categories. "I consider this officer one of the best in his grade with whom I am acquainted [Styer had known Clay from the time he was a plebe at West Point]. He [is] of excellent character and habits, loyal, able, conscientious, industrious; has initiative to a high degree; willing to assume responsibility; exercises good judgment; capable by reason of his training, experience and natural ability to execute duties and assume responsibilities much beyond those of the average officer of his rank and age; qualified to handle important executive and administrative assignments and to take charge of large construction and other engineering projects in the field."

Clay's assignment to Washington in the spring of 1933 marked the decisive shift in his military career. Until that time, his service had been routine and uneventful: the typical postings of a junior officer who had begun to display a significant ability to lead men and accomplish complicated tasks of engineering detail, but all within the narrow frame of professional service. Except for his exposure to the grim realities of Depression life in Pittsburgh, broader political issues had not intruded. In Washington, Clay was thrust immediately into the excitement of New Deal politics: the organization of vast relief activities, and the disbursement of unprecedented federal funds for projects throughout the country. Clay quickly became an important arbiter of Corps largesse. The political attachments and friendships that he formed at that time endured for the next thirty years. Clay had done well in his junior postings; he would soon prove to be one of the Army's most gifted political tacticians.

· 5 ·

Muddy Waters (1934-1937)

> An officer of outstanding ability, force and character—a tireless worker—tactful and having a highly agreeable personality. He has executed with distinction duties appropriate for an officer with the rank of a Colonel. I know of no officer of more value to the service.
>
> *Brigadier General G. B. Pillsbury*
> [Clay's efficiency report, June 30, 1937]

CLAY REPORTED FOR DUTY IN WASHINGTON ON JUNE 1, 1933. Two weeks later, his name finally at the top of the Army's seniority roster, he was promoted to captain—after eleven years as a first lieutenant. In spite of his promotion, Clay found himself junior man in the Engineers' Washington office. Proud of its heritage, select, independent, the Corps of Engineers stood pre-eminent among the branches of the peacetime Army, its chief ranking second only to the Chief of Staff in power and prestige. In 1933, that post was held by Major General Lytle Brown: a cold, aloof West Point graduate of 1898, the epitome of military conservatism. Reflecting the Corps's dual responsibilities, Brown had two deputies, one for military matters (a colonel), and one for civil functions: Brigadier General George Pillsbury—a New England Yankee with a bent for mathematical problems and a reputation as a stickler for detail. Pillsbury directed the Corps's section on rivers and harbors, center of Washington's public works activities for over a hundred years and the Army's broad back door to Congress. For when it comes to rivers and harbors, or flood control, the Corps of Engineers is a creature of Congress; it does not report to the Army's Chief of Staff or to the President.

Only one President in American history, Chester A. Arthur, ever vetoed a Corps of Engineers appropriations bill, and Arthur's 1882 veto was quickly overridden. Then, as now, the Corps's appropriations package usually included something for everyone: projects, or the promises of projects, in every state and nearly every congressional district. "Thus," as President Arthur observed, "as the bill becomes more objectionable, it secures more support."

In 1933, the rivers and harbors section was headed by Lieutenant Colonel Glen Edgerton, a West Pointer who had led his class in 1908. Clay, eleven years junior to Edgerton, was the only other military person in the office: the Army's entire civil works program (with a 1933 budget virtually equivalent to the Army's total military budget) was handled by Pillsbury, Edgerton, and Clay.

"Clay was terribly industrious," Edgerton recalls. "When I first came to the Chief of Engineers' office, he was new to me. I had met him before, but I didn't know him very well, and I found him already installed as my assistant. I came down to the office the first day at quarter to eight, and about five minutes later Clay came in. The next morning, I came down about twenty minutes to eight, and Clay was there and had been there for half an hour. And never again did I beat him down. As soon as he saw that I was coming early, he was coming earlier.

"Clay, of course, was an original thinker—and that's very rare in the Army: a man who listens to something that's said and makes up his own mind without regard to rank or anything else. And he had terrific initiative. He had a reputation as a young man of being a little radical —in the sense that he didn't conform easily. But I think it was his superior qualities of energy and intelligence that made him a little difficult."

Like most old-line government agencies, the Corps of Engineers awoke to the frantic pace of the New Deal's first hundred days with anguished disbelief. Accustomed to the careful, leisurely consideration of congressional projects, often years in maturing, to time-honored cost-benefit ratios, and to the Army's ancient red-tape bureaucracy, the Corps soon found itself seriously out of step with the new administration. While FDR sought immediate remedies for the nation's jobless, Generals Brown and Pillsbury remained wedded to the rigid patterns of their predecessors: no make-work, no emergency undertakings, no federal involvement, such as the Tennessee Valley Authority, in areas previously reserved for the private sector. Before Roosevelt's first hundred days were out, the Corps saw Interior Secretary Harold Ickes emerge as champion of the very projects they had eschewed—and a serious competitor for congressional favor. It was at this point, shortly after Clay reported to Washington, that General Lytle Brown retired, to be succeeded by Major General "Joe" Markham—a chief after Clay's heart. "General Brown was a very fine, a very able, but not a very flexible man," said Clay. "He did not hit it off with President Roosevelt, and I would hate to say it, but under General Brown we could never have done the work for PWA [Public Works Administration] and WPA [Works Progress Administration] that we did later.

"On the other hand, General Markham got along with the President very well. General Markham was completely unexplainable. Short, heavy-set. When he went down to testify before congressional committees, he never completed a sentence: he never had a subject and a predicate in the same sentence. And yet they understood him. But I'd have to go through all that damned testimony and correct it. And it was frightful. He never studied his lesson, so to speak, and yet he absorbed a tremendous amount. And he was intuitively a good Chief of Engineers. He made all the right decisions, but he made them by intuition. Maybe that's why he got along so well with President Roosevelt, I don't know.

"When he took over from Brown, I think General Markham had his doubts about me. He had been commandant at Fort Humphreys when I was in the company officers' course, and I didn't like it one bit. I thought it was ridiculous. But in spite of that, Markham and I soon became very close."

Q: What was the Army's attitude toward the New Deal in 1933?
CLAY: When the New Deal began, I don't think the Army had any real interest [in it] one way or the other. But it soon became very clear, when the government went into a large public works program, that the Corps of Engineers was going to have to expand and take on a great deal of this work, because we were the only ones, except for the reclamation service, that had programs and projects on the drawing board. And so we were immediately put under pressure to increase the pace of our public works program.

"But that wasn't enough, because public works require a great deal of lead time to get under way. In addition, they do not provide immediately a great deal of large-scale employment. So we embarked on the WPA program. This was set up under Harry Hopkins. And he was having a great deal of difficulty getting under way. And I went over with General Markham to see Mr. Hopkins, and said, 'We would like to lend to you, in each of your regions, a capable, competent Engineer officer who would bring with him a capable and competent chief clerk who knows how to disperse and set up public funds, just to get you going.'

"Mr. Hopkins was very suspicious that we were trying to take over the WPA program, and we assured him that this was not the case, that these people would be reporting directly to him. They would be his people.

"He accepted that, and we sent over a number of officers to become his representatives in various regions all around the country. Sometimes to be in charge, sometimes to be deputies to whomever he picked to be in charge. We selected some of our very best officers to work with Mr. Hopkins, men with outstanding reputations. He picked one of our fine officers, Colonel Harrington, to be his own deputy. And we had General Somervell, then Colonel Somervell, in New York in charge of WPA; and Colonel Connolly in Los Angeles. Harrington, Somervell, and Connolly would have been in the top 5 percent of all the officers in the Army. All around the country, we provided the basic, experienced staff in knowing how to put government money to work under the proper controls, to let Mr. Hopkins get under way."

Q: Was this on the initiative of General Markham?
CLAY: Yes, but it was on my suggestion. General Markham grasped the idea very quickly. You've got to remember that you're always fighting

for position. Somebody wants to take over the rivers and harbors work from the Engineers, although they've had it for years. And so you try to establish yourself. It seemed to me that the best way we could establish ourselves was to make ourselves helpful—without any promise of return. Just to make ourselves helpful in this tremendous, great new effort.

"Frankly, I would have to admit that if we hadn't felt that Mr. Ickes was trying to give us trouble, we might not have thought of going to Mr. Hopkins. It was our theory that Mr. Ickes wanted to turn the Department of Interior into the Department of Public Works, and obviously we didn't want him to. This was one of the reasons why we offered our assistance to Mr. Hopkins. And, of course, Mr. Hopkins and Mr. Ickes didn't see eye to eye. Mr. Hopkins wanted to provide employment, while Mr. Ickes wanted to provide magnificent works that would endure. Both ideas had merit, but the money was being appropriated to provide employment.

"I had great sympathy for Mr. Hopkins. We knew what his task was. We felt that a public works program was not going to provide the necessary employment in itself, but, on the other hand, Mr. Ickes did have a going organization and Mr. Hopkins did not. So we provided the basic elements of an organization for him, and a great many of the men we assigned to him became his lifelong friends. In our subsequent conflicts with Mr. Ickes over flood control, Mr. Hopkins was definitely on our side. But by that time I don't think Mr. Ickes had quite the prestige he had earlier."

Q: What was your impression of Harry Hopkins?

CLAY: I got to know Mr. Hopkins very well. First through our meetings in WPA days, then, during the war, on the Munitions Assignment Board, which handled Lend-Lease and which Mr. Hopkins chaired. I liked Mr. Hopkins. I thought he was a man of great ability and dedication—and in his own way a very effective worker.

Q: And the WPA?

CLAY: I think the WPA did a very fine job. We did many projects for them in the Corps of Engineers. We made work. We did the regular job, but to get the proper work percentage in it we really had to go out and make work. For example, if we were building a dam that was to be faced with stone, which we would have ordinarily placed with a crane, we'd place the stone by hand. This way we would quadruple or quintuple the amount of labor required. Under normal conditions we could not have afforded it, but this was a combination of trying to provide employment and at the same time trying to make the work of that employment useful.

"General Pillsbury, of course, bent over backwards to try to stop such projects unless the ratios of return were extremely good. But this didn't fit the times. Here were projects that had great value, maybe not in accordance with the standards applied by the Corps in the past, but, nevertheless, should you turn them down at that critical stage in American history? In other words, it was my view, and it still is, that we had to take cognizance of the fact that the government wanted to spend money on construction to provide jobs. I don't think we would have ever had a flood control program if it hadn't been for that fact. The United States was not ready to move into a comprehensive, national flood control program at that time. But the need for projects to provide employment was such that I felt it ought to be expedited. Looking back, I think we were right."

Under Markham's skillful direction, the Corps quickly regained its lost prestige. Pillsbury continued to concentrate on cost-benefit ratios, striving to maintain standards, but he no longer rejected the Corps's responsibility to provide emergency employment. Colonel Edgerton became the War Department's representative on the National Resources Board, attempting to reconcile the Administration's water development policies. Clay remained a jack-of-all-trades: on Capitol Hill, at the White House, focus of the Corps's communications with the field, as well as liaison to the National Emergency Council, which was the New Deal's coordinating body for domestic policy, whose representatives included Donald Richberg, Harry Hopkins, Chester Davis, General Hugh Johnson, Harold Ickes, and Frances Perkins.

"Those were exciting years," said Clay. "I can remember the first time I ever met President Roosevelt. This was at the time of the great floods in Connecticut and Vermont in the spring of 1936. President Roosevelt wanted to take a train and tour the flood areas. I was sent over to the White House to work it out with Marvin McIntyre. And we did, and I went on the train with them. It was a tremendous experience for me to see the President at first hand: up the Connecticut Valley, over to Burlington, back to Hyde Park.

"The first evening on the train, we went into the President's car and he mixed the cocktails for us. I was very impressed with that. And it was on the train that I became conscious for the first time of the tremendous physical effort he was making all of the time—just to get around. If possible, it increased my respect for him even more. He was an able, brilliant man, and a very great President. He did the things that needed to be done and got us back on a road that we could travel without breakdown or revolution—which I think could easily have occurred.

"I met Mr. Roosevelt once again in the summer of 1936. I made a trip up to Campobello with a message on the flood control bill for him to sign. I went over to the island—you had to go over by boat—and I got over there about ten-thirty or eleven o'clock in the morning. I went to the house, and they told me: 'Nobody is going to do any work right now. We've got a softball game scheduled, with a picnic luncheon.'

"So they had a softball game. The President looked on for a while, and Mrs. Roosevelt was there too. They served hot dogs, and it was about three-thirty or four before they went back to the house. They said the President had gone to his rooms and that I would have to wait. I waited until about five-thirty; then someone came out and said, 'The President is ready to see you.'

"I went into the living room, and the whole family was there. Mr. Roosevelt was mixing some martinis, and they were having their cocktail hour before dinner. I was introduced around, and then went up to the President.

"He said, 'Now tell me what it is you want.'

"So I went through this whole thing with him while everybody else went along with their cocktails. Finally, he pulled out his pen and signed, and I went back to Washington.

"The only other time I talked to him before I went to Germany was at the international Boy Scout Jamboree in Washington in 1937. Because of the flood control work up in the Connecticut Valley, I had formed a very satisfactory relationship with Marvin McIntyre at the White House. So when he began to get questions about projects, he used to call me for the answers—which was a very helpful thing for the Corps.

"Then, one day in the Spring of 1937, Mr. McIntyre called me over to the White House and told me that they wanted me to set up a Boy Scout Jamboree that summer. Actually, [D.C. Commissioner] George Allen was supposed to be in charge of the thing, but McIntyre said

Allen wanted me to organize it, provide the tenting and camping equipment, and so on."

Washington's 1937 Boy Scout Jamboree, celebrating the twenty-seventh anniversary of American scouting, was conceived as democracy's answer to the mass fascist rallies sweeping continental Europe: twenty-five thousand Boy Scouts from twenty-seven countries camping together on the Washington Monument's grounds—a demonstration of peaceful solidarity. In 1937, over one million Americans had passed through the scouting movement begun by Lord Baden-Powell, including eight of football's 1936 All-Americans, and 65 percent of U.S. Rhodes Scholars that year.

Clay's efforts to organize the scout encampment contrast starkly with the martial enthusiasm displayed by Albert Speer in preparing for Hitler's Nuremberg rallies. For Speer, the problem was to evoke the imagery of might and power, of discipline and obedience to the Führer. For Clay, it was to get the Boy Scouts in and out of Washington with as little confusion as possible.

"Amongst other things," said Clay, "they wanted to have a parade down Constitution Avenue, with President Roosevelt taking the review. And I was supposed to set that up. I got to thinking about it, and I figured that you could never get twenty-five thousand Boy Scouts assembled at a starting point, down a parade route, and pass in review before the President of the United States—and even if you did, he would be there for eight or nine hours until the last units straggled past.

"I suggested that instead they line up all the scouts on Constitution Avenue, and then we'd have the President and his Cabinet and distinguished senators and congressmen drive past in automobiles and review them. And they accepted this.

"So I had all this organized, and the cars assigned: President Roosevelt was to ride in the first car with the professional national scout executive, a man by the name of [James E.] West, who, as it happened, was a prominent and very conservative Republican. And the President turned to me and said, 'I won't ride with that S.O.B. I don't like him, and I won't ride with him.'

"So I had to switch the whole outfit and put the President up front with Vice President Garner. Then I got Mrs. Roosevelt to ride with Mr. West in the second car. I went back to tell Mr. West that we decided the original plan should be changed because this was such a unique opportunity for these boys to see the President and the Vice President together in the first car.

"Mr. West said, 'I understand. He won't ride with me, will he?' "

As for the tents and equipment, Clay once again ran afoul of Army routine. Marvin McIntyre had asked for Clay because he knew Clay would cut through the Army's red tape to do what had to be done for the scouts. But Colonel George R. Spalding, the Army's supply officer, took a different view. "Colonel Spalding was very precise about my responsibility for seeing these things were returned in good shape," said Clay. "We went through with the Boy Scout encampment, the scouts went on their way, and then we were threatened with another veterans' march on Washington.

"McIntyre called me up and he said, 'I don't want those tents taken down. You've got to keep them there, and you can't tell anyone about this.'

"After about four or five days, Colonel Spalding sent for me, and he really raised the roof. Putting up tents for twenty-five thousand people was quite a big deal then. 'You've raised hell around here,' he said. 'The scouts are gone, the tents are still there, the whole organization has gone, and we don't have any money to go and get that equipment. What the hell have you done?'

"I said, 'I assure you that you will eventually get your tents back, but I can't tell you any more than that.' And he really got quite upset with me.

"I reported the conversation back to Marvin McIntyre, and he called up General [Malin] Craig, the Chief of Staff, and there was no longer a problem."

Q: Did you work with Congress during this period?

CLAY: A great deal. General Pillsbury tried to avoid meeting the Congress if he possibly could, and Colonel Edgerton was kept busy with the National Resources Board, which more or less left me to represent the Corps on the Hill. I was the fellow who was always there, and so I began to get the calls from Capitol Hill too about various projects. In those days, I had a very good memory. We had about five hundred projects, and I could recite the details of each from A to Z.

"So I was in touch with various congressmen all the time. In the first place, any congressman, if he knew how to do it, could get a resolution which would authorize a preliminary survey of a waterway improvement. But very few congressmen knew how to do it. They would call me up and say, 'Look, we want to get such-and-such river made navigable up to six feet,' or 'How can we get someone to look at this flood that happened down our way last year?' And I would tell them that the thing for them to do was to go to the clerk of the Rivers and Harbors Committee and present him with a resolution authorizing a preliminary survey. Ninety percent of these things were wiped out with a preliminary survey. Nevertheless, the congressman had gotten some satisfaction by getting this preliminary survey, and at least it involved a hearing where the people in his district had a chance to make their case.

"So, through these preliminary surveys, I became acquainted with a great many congressmen. Then, as we went into active projects, I was the one whom the clerk of the committee (who was always a very powerful person) called to find out what was the status of this or that project. And in that way I was in very close contact with the Senate Commerce Committee, and particularly with Senator Copeland [D., New York]. Actually, he appointed one of my sons to West Point. In the House we had devoted friends in Judge Mansfield [D., Texas], who headed the Committee on Rivers and Harbors, and Judge Whittington [D., Mississippi], who was then chairman of the Flood Control Committee.

"The Corps therefore was in very close contact with these committees. Why shouldn't we have been? This was our livelihood. There was nothing clandestine about it. By contrast, the Public Lands Committee was Secretary Ickes's committee."

Q: You mentioned earlier that the Corps was concerned that Secretary Ickes wanted to play a larger role in public works activities.

CLAY: Yes. The question of flood control was very important in those days. When Mr. Ickes was appointed Secretary of Interior, the federal government was involved in two kinds of water projects: irrigation—which was in the hands of Interior but was restricted to a few states in the Far West—and flood control—which was restricted to the Mississippi River but was done by the Corps of Engineers.

"But shortly after I went to Washington in 1933, we had a series of very disastrous floods. One was out on the Ohio River in Kentucky, and I can remember sending a boat into Paducah to rescue Senator [Alben] Barkley's mother, who was then a very old woman. Shortly after that, we had some very large floods up in Connecticut and Vermont, which were very damaging.

"The Congress was therefore ready for a flood control bill. This was expedited by the fact that they had passed a bill authorizing a survey of every major stream in the United States, the survey to be undertaken by the Corps of Engineers. From these surveys it was possible to draw up the beginnings of a national flood control plan. Fundamentally, it was this flood control plan that the Department of Agriculture and the Department of Interior wanted [to direct], and so did the Corps of Engineers. And so it was inevitable that there would be a struggle to see who would get this bill. It was as simple as that. It was one of those jurisdictional battles in which we at least were in possession. We had been doing this work for a hundred years. The Department of Agriculture's argument was that all the work should be done upstream, with small reservoirs and reforestation and whatnot—all of which had merit, but it would not stop a major flood. And then Mr. Ickes wanted to come in on the basis that this belonged to the Department of the Interior. Actually, he had less logic behind his claim than the Department of Agriculture. So it really got down to where the Commerce Committee was fighting the Land Committee in the Senate, and the Rivers and Harbors Committee fighting the Reclamation Committee in the House. This was where the real battle was fought, because, whichever committee got jurisdiction, it represented a real loss of power to the other committee and for the executive department downtown it worked with."

Q: Did you lobby a great deal for the Corps's version of the bill?

CLAY: I worked on the flood control bill a great deal, particularly with the individual projects that went into the bill. And particularly with Mr. [Sam] Rayburn [House Majority Leader] and Senator Copeland. I don't think anyone in Washington was as close to Mr. Rayburn as I was at the time.

Q: How did you get to know Mr. Rayburn?

CLAY: I first got to know Mr. Rayburn on the Red River project—a program for flood control on the Red River in Texas and Oklahoma in which he was vitally interested—although, curiously enough, Mr. Rayburn had gone to Congress the year after my father died, and a great many of his friends had known my father, and through them he at least knew of me. So I had an initial entrée to him. And he was a very wonderful person. I used to regularly go down and "strike a blow for liberty" with him. He had a special room off the House Chamber where you could go after the House adjourned, and almost everyone would come trailing in for a drink of bourbon and branch water. And this was where I met so many congressmen, particularly the Democrats —in those days, I was far closer to the Democrats than I was to the Republicans.

Q: Was it normal for someone in the Corps to be there?

CLAY: Oh no. I was usually the only outsider. The other people were either congressmen or people like Lew Deschler, the parliamentarian.

When the 1936 Flood Control Bill emerged from Congress, Clay's lobbying activities were amply rewarded. Ickes's longed-for role in flood control was rejected, and the Corps's alliance with Congress remained as formidable as ever. When Ickes attempted to secure FDR's veto of the bill, he ran into a congressional buzz saw: a delicate balance of local needs and public funds—the political pork barrel so important to legislative favor.

Like General Markham, Clay proved exceptionally able at the black art of winning legislative approval; his political antennae were sharply tuned to the nuances of congressional power. "To get along, you have to go along," in Sam Rayburn's classic phrase, and Clay fully understood the rewards the Corps could bestow. "By and large, I think we ran a very careful engineering show," said Clay. "But when you got to the final approval or disapproval of a project . . . I think at that stage of the game a very important congressman or senator, a committee chairman, someone who supported you, got the breaks. But I think that's always true."

Clay's political realism, his experience in a family of politicians, fitted him uniquely to represent the Corps on Capitol Hill. He understood politicians and how to deal with them: an intuitive calculus of mutual reward. "Actually," said Clay, "our problems with Secretary Ickes were more or less the normal ones you encounter in government. The problem of coordination within the federal government is an eternal one, and my answer has always been very simple. The principles require approval from someone. There is no doubt that we need coordination. But I don't think that the tremendous construction activities of the government—reclamation, rivers and harbors, flood control, airports, highways—should all be under one roof. These activities are too many and too varied to be placed in any central agency. It would be too big to be controlled. By breaking it down and decentralizing it, you inevitably get some duplication, but you also get an organization that people can control."

The Corps's role in flood control notwithstanding, it, like most of government, failed to recognize the need to protect America's natural environment.

"Obviously, you can draw quite a case against the Corps on ecological grounds," said Clay, "because the Engineers were never charged with any responsibility concerning ecology. Nor was anyone else. On the other hand, I think many of the Corps's projects have benefited the ecology more than they have done damage. Don't forget it was the Corps of Engineers that staked out and preserved the areas that are now Yellowstone, Yosemite, and Sequoia national parks. The only place where they have done real harm is in granting permits for the discharge of waste products into navigable streams. But the sole legal basis we had for withholding such permits [under the Rivers and Harbors Act of 1899] was whether the waste material would interfere with navigation.

"No matter how some people may feel about them, it is my personal conviction that most of the dams and reservoirs built by the Corps have been a tremendous improvement to the ecology. And they have provided us with several things that are very important: in many instances, with an additional water supply—which is not only important for agricultural purposes but is highly important to navigation in times when there is not enough water flow. Secondly, in flood control, which not only prevents the flooding of cities but prevents a tremendous amount of erosion and other wastes. If you had ever seen the Red River in Texas and Oklahoma before the Denison Dam was put in, and you saw the Denison Dam down there now, providing recreational facilities for a million people, leaving out its flood control and power development, it still would be a great boon to that part of the world.

"Don't forget, it was a necessity to improve our rivers and harbors. If you go to Europe, you will appreciate how inevitable it is for us to increase the use of our waterways. We have some very busy ones now.

But the fact remains that we practically do not have a natural harbor or waterway in this country that would serve our needs without improvement."

Clay's first opportunity to study Europe's highly developed waterways came in 1934, when he attended the Brussels conference of the International Congress of Navigation. For Clay, the trip was especially important because it was his first and only exposure to Hitler's Germany—to which all of the delegates were invited after the conference ended.

"This was just after Hitler came to power," Clay recalls, "and my engineering colleagues were rather pleased with what they saw. The Hitler regime had re-established law and order, and the public works program was very impressive. At that stage of the game, no one had developed an understanding of Hitler, or what was to come later. This was before the persecution of the Jewish people.

"I do remember, however, that as we drove through one little town, I saw the schoolchildren out there goose-stepping. I can remember saying to Marjorie, 'We've got another war coming.' I don't think that I would have had any impression of Germany if I hadn't seen these nine- and ten-year-olds being drilled in these little towns we drove through. Instead of playing at recess, they would be out there goose-stepping. It was obvious they were giving military training to the very young."

Clay's life in Washington revolved around the Corps of Engineers. But prewar Washington was a pleasant, sometimes exciting place to live. "As a captain, we had bought a house in Chevy Chase for $15,000," said Clay. "It was a corner house. White brick. It had a playroom in the basement and an attached two-car garage. Upstairs we had four bedrooms and two baths. This we bought for $15,000. We had a car, we had a cook, and we belonged to the Army-Navy town club and the Army-Navy country club. My wife says we don't live that well anymore."

Like many families, the Clays were not regular churchgoers. But their eldest son, later to become a four-star general in the Air Force, recalled a household in which right and wrong were sharply differentiated. "We were raised in the structured environment of the prewar Army," said Lucius D. Clay, Jr., "and we never had any doubt that my father was in charge. Of course, much of the time we were living on the civilian economy. In Pittsburgh. In Washington. My parents gave us a good deal of freedom to do what we wanted within a fairly close family setting. When it came time to go to college, my father never said we had to go to West Point. He simply said, 'I can get an appointment for you if you want to go.' But he left the choice entirely up to us.

"That's the way he was. I've never met anyone with a greater awareness of right and wrong. Dedication to principle. Some of the things he does amaze me—some of the things he turns down, things we accept as commonplace in business, in the Pentagon today. He was always like that.

"I remember in 1945 I was newly assigned to fly B-26s. I reported to my unit in Germany, and just as I did, a B-26 came in and crashed trying to land. I called my father and said, 'Gee, Dad, I'd really like to fly B-17s instead of B-26s.'

"He said, 'What do your orders say?'

"I said, 'They assigned me to fly B-26s.'

"He said, 'I think you'd better do what your orders say.'

"That was the first and last time I ever asked him to do anything for me in the service."

By the summer of 1937, Clay was due for reassignment. He had been in Washington four important years. He was well known on Capitol Hill, appreciated at the White House, and respected in the Corps of Engineers. "Clay already had developed quite a reputation," said General Edgerton. "He handled this very important work very ably, and everybody knew him. Whenever anyone from the field would call Washington, Clay would be the one they talked to. And the more people called him and got favorable action, the more they were inclined to call him again. If a man gets something done when you call, you're going to continue to call him."

When it became known that Clay was due for reassignment, numerous requests came forward for his services. A congressional delegation from the Mississippi Valley called on General Markham to request that Clay be assigned there. Division Engineers across the country requested that Clay be sent to their division. And from the Philippines, former Chief of Staff Douglas MacArthur put in his plea.

On Capitol Hill, Clay's past services were publicly recognized. Said Congressman J. Buell Snyder, chairman of the Appropriations Subcommittee on the War Department, at the conclusion of hearings on the budget for fiscal year 1938:

> *Mr. Snyder [D., Pennsylvania]:* I am advised that Captain Clay is scheduled for detachment from your office, and I should like you to know that we have learned that with a great deal of regret. When I say "we" . . . I am sure I speak the sentiments of every Member of Congress who at one time or another had occasion to deal with him. His expert knowledge, his fine mind, his personality, and his splendid soldierly qualities need no commendation from me. They speak for themselves. Captain, you have our sincere best wishes wherever duty may call.
>
> *Captain Clay:* I thank you, Mr. Chairman.
>
> *General Markham:* That is very generous of you, Mr. Chairman, but every word of it is deserved by Captain Clay. In the Office of the Chief of Engineers, we have nothing but tears at the leaving of Captain Clay.
>
> *Mr. Starnes [D., Alabama]:* I think he exemplifies the best traditions of the service.
>
> *General Markham:* He certainly does.

Thirty-four years later, on April 30, 1971, General Clay was honored for meritorious achievement at the annual dinner of the Corps of Engineers. In accepting the award, Clay evoked the image of what it had meant to be an Army Engineer in the twenties and thirties. "The Corps," he said, "was formed by the character of the men that made it. Their principal trait was integrity. If you didn't imbibe integrity, you didn't belong in the Corps of Engineers."

Integrity. Another of the watchwords, along with honor, duty, and country, that stand for the military profession, the creed, the oracles of belief for those who wear the uniform. For the officers of Clay's generation particularly, they were articles of faith not lightly disregarded. And so it was—within the military itself. But when dealing with civilians, when confronted by outside values and beliefs, the Corps of Engineers had little difficulty shifting gears to accommodate.

"They always talked integrity," said Brigadier General Richard H. Groves (son of Lieutenant General Leslie R. Groves), who in 1971 held Clay's old post in the office of the Chief of Engineers. "It was the code they lived by. But when it came to wheeling and dealing in Washington, they could be the most devious bastards who ever came down the pike."

Integrity, like all concepts in Washington, was flexible; it was to be interpreted sensibly. According to Groves, "a person who has been through the civil works activities of the Corps of Engineers, who deals intimately and continuously with politics and Congress, comes to realize that truth is not always as simple as it seemed at West Point. At this point, a double standard appears. When a congressman tells you something, you certainly accept it as what he tells you. But you don't necessarily accept it as being the truth. This is not new. The officers of my father's time or Clay's time had no illusions as to what the score was.

"The result was that the people who came up through this system were subtle, and they were cynical. An officer who goes through this is a different breed of cat than the officer who goes through the Infantry School and who commands a rifle company, and who goes to Leavenworth and commands a rifle battalion, and then goes to the War College and commands a regiment.

"An Engineer officer gets involved in the justification of projects which are extremely political in nature. After all, if you look at what we do in the simplest terms, we redistribute wealth. And it becomes very complicated. Whenever you give somebody something, it's from somebody else. And we try to tread our way through that maze. And it's very educational. It makes for quite a different fellow than if you'd just been out doing squads left and squads right—particularly in the period between World War I and World War II, when the average infantry officer did nothing but that. Clay spent twenty years as a junior officer in a very diversified experience. And yet running through it all is this almost puritanical thread of 'integrity.' It almost takes on religious overtones. It is very strange. Almost a devout belief in the Corps: that the Corps of Engineers is good, and that what comes out of the Corps is good."

· 6 ·

Ike and Mac and Mr. Sam (1938-1939)

> A superior officer in all respects. Quick of mind, energetic, loyal and of sound common sense. Willingly assumes responsibility. Exceptionally well informed on general subjects and highly qualified in those applying to his own area. Of unlimited capacity for advancement.
>
> *Dwight D. Eisenhower, Lieutenant Colonel*
> [Clay's efficiency report, June 26, 1938]

EARLY IN 1937, GENERAL DOUGLAS MACARTHUR, who since his retirement as U.S. Army Chief of Staff had been commanding the Philippine Army, returned to Washington with President Manuel Quezon to plead for additional military supplies and equipment. In addition to the standard requests for torpedo boats, machine guns, and airplanes, MacArthur called on General Markham and requested two Engineer officers to make a hydroelectric survey of the Philippines. The two officers chosen would be on MacArthur's staff but would work directly for the Philippine government, from whom they would draw an additional $10,000 over and above their salary from the U.S. Army: a standard arrangement for the few—such as Lieutenant Colonel Dwight Eisenhower—who served with MacArthur.

"General Markham immediately asked me if I wanted the job," said Clay. "I was due to leave Washington, I had just spent four years there, and I was also due for foreign service. So this looked like an ideal opportunity. I was asked to take one officer with me, and so I called Pat Casey, then Captain Casey, who was in Vicksburg, and he said yes."

Clay and Marjorie left Washington in mid-August. As soon as they arrived in the Philippines, they took an apartment in the posh Manila Hotel, where MacArthur and Eisenhower also lived. Clay was still a captain, but his additional salary from the Philippine government, plus Marjorie's income, made a little extravagance possible. Modest to the point of self-effacement in public matters, Clay, like George Patton, always enjoyed a personal style of living better than that of his Army contemporaries—faster cars, larger houses, finer furnishings, cooks, gardeners, polo and country clubs—and in the thirties, Clay's extra income was spent, not saved. In Manila, as in Washington, he and Marjorie quickly became the center of military society. (Later, in Germany, when he could have lived like a Roman conqueror, Clay chose a modest Berlin bungalow and eschewed the trappings of power that beguiled so many Americans abroad.)

Clay and Casey had their office at MacArthur's headquarters in the fortress wall of the old city at 1 Calle Victoria—a relic of the Spanish conquest whose thick stone balustrades and high ceilings naturally insulated them from the tropical heat.

Q: What was MacArthur's headquarters like in 1937?

CLAY: MacArthur was then Field Marshal of the Philippine army, although for all practical purposes the command was exercised by Filipino officers. We didn't attempt to command them from our office. And actually, MacArthur's headquarters was very small. His own office; an aide—Lieutenant [Sidney L.] Huff [USN]; then Colonel Eisenhower, who was chief of staff; Colonel [James B.] Ord, who died in Manila and whose place was taken by Colonel [Richard K.] Sutherland; a sergeant-major; a couple of clerks; and that was about it. Then there was a larger room where Casey and I had our office.

Q: Then MacArthur did not command the U.S. Army in the Philippines?

CLAY: No. The American Army was commanded by [Major] General [John H.] Hughes. But because MacArthur had been Chief of Staff, he was treated with great respect by the American Army. But there was not very much mixing. His headquarters was distinct and separate, and concerned itself primarily with Philippine problems. Socially, the rest of us mixed, but General MacArthur didn't mix with anyone.

Q: What was it like to work for MacArthur?

CLAY: MacArthur was a magnetic personality. When we first went to Manila, he gave Casey and me an hour talk on the Philippines: on its economy, its politics, its relations with America—one of the most inspired talks I've ever heard. But he wasn't a detail man, and actually, I saw more of him socially than I did officially. And that wasn't too much.

"General MacArthur never came to the office but about an hour a day. He would come down about one o'clock and stay until about two. The rest of the time he wasn't in the office at all. I don't mean that he wasn't thinking, planning, or whatnot over in his hotel suite—and at that time he was really studying the Orient, which later stood the U.S. in good stead. The fact was that he did most of his work at home. Every once in a while, he'd call me up and we would go to a prize fight. He loved prize fights. Except for that, we didn't see very much of him. No one did. He simply didn't socialize at that point in his career.

"Actually, I worked much more closely with General [Lieutenant Colonel] Eisenhower. After we were there for a while, Eisenhower asked me to take on an additional job which was not in our contract. MacArthur didn't have an engineer on his staff, and he wanted me to supervise the training and formation of the Philippine engineer corps. Eisenhower asked me if I would take it on.

"He said, 'I know this isn't what you came over here to do, and you don't have to if you don't want to. But I'd appreciate it very much if you would. Particularly, if you would look at their building plans for their cantonments and their training plans.'

"I agreed. And I enjoyed it. I enjoyed working with the Philippine engineer soldiers, who wanted to be good engineer soldiers but had very little experience and very little equipment."

Q: You knew Colonel Eisenhower from Washington?

CLAY: I had known Eisenhower socially in Washington. But it was not until the Philippines that I came in close contact with him. And I became very close to General Eisenhower and remained so until his death. My relation with General Eisenhower was as a friend, but not as a playmate. I was never a bridge partner, and only very seldom did I join their golfing group. Shortly after I got there, in fact, Ike developed a very bad bursitis, and he had to stop playing golf. He didn't play for a number of years. Finally, it disappeared and he started playing again. I did not play bridge, because they normally played in the afternoon. I don't mean it was a three-or-four-hour-a-day job. They went to work very early. And about three in the afternoon he would start his bridge game. Casey and I, on the other hand, were working all afternoon.

"Besides, they were expert bridge players. If you didn't play expert bridge, you were really in the way. And I didn't feel like taking it up again. I didn't have the time. It sounds silly for an officer in the peacetime Army to say that, but I really didn't. Not in Panama, not in Pittsburgh, and certainly not in Washington. Nor in the Philippines, for that matter, where I was now wearing two hats. And we were really busy in the Philippines. We tramped through jungles like nobody had tramped through them for many, many years."

In their search for potential hydroelectric sites, Clay and Casey surveyed the virgin wilderness of the Agno River, northwest of Manila. "We decided to hike up to the source overland and come down by raft," said Clay. "It was quite a hike. I remember walking all day in the rain, and when we finally halted and took off our clothes, we were covered with dozens of leeches. Of course, you couldn't pull them off, because the heads would stay under the skin and get infected. So we had to burn them off each other with cigarettes.

"When we got to the headwaters we built a bamboo raft, put all our belongings on it, and sailed merrily along until we hit the first rapids. Our raft went to pieces, we lost all of our equipment, and I guess we almost drowned. So we had to walk out.

"We also made a survey of the Agus River, which was capable of substantial development—but not in the places where power was needed. The only location of immediate moment we found was a site on the Pasig River just below Manila. By this time, however, I had become very skeptical of what we were doing. From what I had seen, the Filipinos needed other things far more than another hydroelectric plant. They needed education; they needed hospitals; they needed better roads and communication facilities. Plus the fact we were going to be in an inevitable conflict with the Manila Power Company if we tried to build the dam. I knew that if I stayed in the Philippines, I would have to build the dam, and my heart just wasn't in it. So when the opportunity came to return to the States to a very important assignment, I was happy to take it.

"It was June 1938. A cable came in for me Friday afternoon. It was from Major Snow, my successor in the office of the Chief of Engineers. The Denison Dam on the Red River, he said, had just been approved by Congress, and he wanted to know if I wanted to build it. I leapt at the opportunity."

Q: Had this been arranged before you left Washington?

CLAY: I had sort of figured that when the Denison Dam came along, I would be given a chance to build it. I was due for a district, and I had worked very closely on the project with Mr. Rayburn in Congress. The dam was to be in his district. Major Snow told me before I left that he would watch the Denison Dam for me, because he thought I ought to have a crack at building it.

Q: What was Mrs. Clay's reaction?

CLAY: Marjorie wanted to go back too. She missed the boys tremendously, and Frank had just finished prep school and would be entering West Point in the fall. And then I also knew that Pat Casey wanted to stay in the Philippines and build the dam. It was actually he who developed the plans and constructed it. It was finished just about the time the Japanese came in, in 1941, and he had to blow it up.

Q: Was Colonel Eisenhower still in the Philippines when you left?

CLAY: Eisenhower left shortly after I did. The fact that he did indicates that there had been almost a complete break on MacArthur's part against him. I was familiar with the details. It was completely due to a misunderstanding by General MacArthur. A group in the Philippine legislature decided that General [Lieutenant Colonel] Eisenhower was doing all the work and that he was being paid only $10,000 a year, whereas MacArthur was being given a beautiful penthouse apartment in the Manila Hotel and being paid a much more substantial sum. This little group of Filipino congressmen prepared to introduce a bill that would abolish the top job—MacArthur's job—and leave Eisenhower in charge.

"When Eisenhower heard about it, he went to them and told them that if they ever introduced that bill he would immediately ask to be returned to the United States. That under no circumstances would he be a party to it.

"But General MacArthur found out about it. And he simply couldn't believe that anybody in the Philippines would do that to him unless it were planned and manipulated. From that moment he had no more use for Eisenhower. And it was absolutely unfounded, although I'm sure that there were people who deliberately tried to convince MacArthur that Eisenhower was trying to knife him in the back. But I know this was not true. MacArthur's dislike for Eisenhower was based on the fact that he was either given completely false information, or that he misinterpreted it himself. I suspect it was a little bit of both."

MacArthur's prewar career in the Philippines was marred by continual bickering: first with U.S. Governor General Frank Murphy and Interior Secretary Ickes (who presumably forced MacArthur's resignation from the Regular Army in 1938), subsequently with a substantial faction of the Philippine legislature who resented the high cost of military expenditures, especially MacArthur's princely allowance of $35,000—a salary five times that of the Philippine Chief of Staff. MacArthur's friendship with President Quezon also soured. By 1939, Quezon was insisting that MacArthur deal with him only through presidential secretary Jorge Vargas. MacArthur's headquarters was forbidden to order munitions, enroll trainees, or negotiate contracts without Quezon's explicit approval. When former Assistant Secretary of State Francis B. Sayre arrived in October 1939, to become U.S. high commissioner, Quezon talked to him about relieving MacArthur.

Given such a deterioration of his position, it is not surprising that MacArthur thought Eisenhower was conniving to replace him, particularly since Eisenhower's relations with Quezon remained warm and cordial. Rather than a casual alliance of Philippine legislators supporting Eisenhower, the fact was that Quezon had sought a change of military advisers, perhaps with Washington's support. Among other things, it was this Byzantine atmosphere of Manila that made

Clay more than ready to leave as soon as the Denison Dam was approved.

When Clay left Manila, General MacArthur came to the dock and handed him a long, personal letter of appreciation.

> The results you have obtained in your professional endeavors on behalf of the Commonwealth [wrote MacArthur] have been noteworthy indeed and deserving of special praise. . . . I desire to take advantage of this opportunity to add my personal . . . appreciation for the efficient assistance you have rendered in the development of the Engineer Corps of the Philippine Army. Your contribution . . . will long be remembered with pride by your Comrades-at-Arms. My very best wishes will go with you throughout your military career, and I shall follow with personal interest and pride the brilliant record you will undoubtedly achieve in the engineering activities of the American Army.
>
> DOUGLAS MACARTHUR, GENERAL, U.S. ARMY, RETIRED

Denison, Texas, in the summer of 1938 was a hot, dry frontier town of the Old West. One-time trading post, headquarters of Quantrill's Raiders, way station on the Chisholm Trail, and birthplace of Dwight D. Eisenhower, the town itself had been founded for spite by the directors of the Kansas & Texas (Katy) Railroad when neighboring Sherman, Texas, refused a subsidy to the line.

Located near the south rim of the Red River at a passable ford, the Denison area had been an important transportation hub since the first settlers moved to Texas. But by the mid-1930s, like so many towns on the Texas-Oklahoma border, it was in serious decline, its population down to fifteen thousand. Stores and shops were vacant; there were no jobs, little hope, and a large number of people living on relief: planting their few seeds, raising a hog or two, subsisting below the poverty level on land already worn out by one-crop cotton farming.

Denison was fortunate in one respect: it was represented in Congress by twenty-five-year veteran Sam Rayburn, then House Majority Leader and soon to be Speaker—a power in Washington's political constellation determined that Texas's Fourth Congressional District not be overlooked in New Deal largesse.

Since the early twenties, Rayburn had sought federal assistance to harness the capricious Red River—at times no more than a trickle; at others, a raging torrent sweeping everything before it. In 1935, Clay had worked with Rayburn to obtain a preliminary flood control survey of the Red River, with Clay prodding the Corps of Engineers to prompt activity and Rayburn whisking the authorizing legislation through Congress. Money for the survey was ultimately provided by President Roosevelt—overruling a reluctant Harold Ickes and the National Resources Board—and in 1936 the Corps recommended construction of a dam at Denison as a national flood control measure.

As approved by Congress, the dam and reservoir were smaller than the Corps's original recommendations, though not significantly. The Denison Dam remains one of the largest earth-filled dams in the United States: it is four miles long, 1,150 feet wide at the base, impounding a reservoir (Lake Texoma) with a surface area of 145,000 acres and a shoreline of 1,250 miles. It was to build this dam, one of the major projects of the Corps of Engineers in 1938, that Clay returned from the Philippines.

Q: What sort of organization was there in Denison when you arrived?

CLAY: Nothing. No office, no personnel. Nothing. I was it. All we had was the authorization from Congress and the initial appropriation.

Q: In other words, you were just sent out and told to build the Denison Dam?

CLAY: That's right. I had the initial survey, of course, but that was about all. So the first thing I went after was a chief clerk. Then I began to build on him. We went out and rented some office space, such as there was in Denison, and began to assemble a staff: finance people, disbursing people, personnel people on the one hand, land appraisers and land buyers on the other—people who could qualify in court as land appraisers. And then the actual engineering design staff.

Despite the depressed times, not all the citizens of Texas's Fourth Congressional District—or those across the Red River in Oklahoma—shared Sam Rayburn's enthusiasm for the Denison Dam. This was especially true among the few farmers owning large orchards and pecan plantations in the rich bottomland along the banks of the Red and

Washita rivers, lands that would be flooded by the dam. One of Clay's first problems was to assemble the land necessary for the reservoir. "We appraised the land at what we thought was fair value and made an offer. If they didn't accept the offer, we instituted condemnation proceedings and went to court. The court decided almost all the early cases in our favor, and after that we ceased to have many court cases. Because we were being very fair. Of course, everybody has an outrageous idea of the value of their land when the government starts to buy it."

Q: Were you directly involved in the land appraisals?
CLAY: Well, I was, really, yes, because it affects your good will. If you get everybody in the area down on you, if you try to take their land without being fair, they turn very much against you. As a matter of fact, I got a local lawyer, Judge Leslie, and put him in as our trial lawyer on the land cases, because he knew the area and the people, he had a reputation for fairness, and he knew land. So Judge Leslie—he'd been a county judge—was our attorney representing us in the land cases.
Q: How did you set about to establish good will? Did you go on the banquet circuit?
CLAY: A good deal. I went out and paid my respects to all the mayors of the surrounding towns. I held hearings in all of the towns that would be affected by the dam. I called on all the judges, not because I thought I could influence them, but I wanted to pay my respects and meet them and let them know we were there. I called on all of the newspaper people—and I kept an open door for people in the area. By and large, you try to create as little disorder and discontent in the area as you can —without paying too much for it.

Clay's good-will activities were needed to halt a rising tide of local discontent. Fanned by well-placed rumors that the government was offering less than half what the land was worth, opposition to the dam quickly materialized, headed by incoming Oklahoma Governor Leon Phillips—a raucous populist plainsman elected on a cloud of dust-bowl poverty.

Phillips's opposition to the Denison Dam—the governor-elect devoted seven thousand words of his ten-thousand-word inaugural to condemning the project—rested on traditional Oklahoma issues: state sovereignty, diminished tax revenues, lost oil properties within the flooded reservoir, and the accusation that the dam was meant to divert Oklahoma's water into Texas for irrigation purposes. His claims enjoyed substantial credibility, but each was subsequently addressed. The Red River was technically an Oklahoma river (*Oklahoma* v. *Texas,* 260 U.S. 606 [1923]), but the Oklahoma legislature previously had granted the federal government unlimited right to acquire state lands for national projects. The loss of tax revenues was illusory—the lost property taxes were more than offset by increased tourist revenue—and later, when oil was in fact found below the reservoir, provision was made for its extraction.

To head off Phillips's opposition, Clay visited the governor in Oklahoma City. His confidential memorandum to the Chief of Engineers described Phillips's implacable hostility. "The Governor," Clay wrote, "was indignant at work having been placed under way without his consent and threatened both Court action and the use of the National Guard. He appeared bitter at the proponents of the project, which he describes as 'Sam Rayburn's Pet.' While he professed no bitterness toward the Engineer Department and its representatives, he was apparently incensed at the District Engineer [Clay] having talked about the proposed Denison Dam at various meetings held by Chambers of Commerce of neighboring towns."

Phillips had ended the conference with a promise to arrest Clay if he continued with the project. But the governor had misjudged his adversary. As the world discovered ten years later in Berlin, Clay could not be bluffed and was incredibly stubborn. He ignored Phillips's threat and pressed ahead with construction. An infuriated Oklahoma governor thereupon fired off a hot protest to Secretary of War Woodring, requested the U.S. Supreme Court to take immediate jurisdiction, threatened once again to call out the National Guard, and sought an injunction to halt construction. It was a near-run thing, with the outcome frequently in doubt, but Phillips eventually failed. In replying to the governor, Woodring cited the applicable federal and state statutes; an evenly divided Supreme Court declined to take original jurisdiction; and Phillips's request for an injunction was denied. The hoped-for political issue failed to materialize, and the governor eventually backed away from his threat to call out the National Guard.

When Henry Stimson succeeded Woodring as Secretary of War in the summer of 1940, Phillips renewed his attack, again threatening legal action. Clay was concerned about the legal basis of the federal government's position, but pressed ahead with construction nevertheless. "If a suit is brought [by Governor Phillips]," he wrote Rayburn, "there can be no question but that the legal position of the Government would be greatly strengthened if the dam is definitely tied in with navigation and the interstate commerce clause of the Constitution." And Clay advised Rayburn to keep close watch over a bill then pending in the Senate (HR 9972) which declared that it was "the intent of Congress that the construction of the Denison Dam was for the benefit of navigation"—a provision Clay himself had had inserted in special legislation concerning rivers and harbors essential to national defense.

Phillips's suit against construction *(Oklahoma* v. *Atkinson, et al.)* was filed in U.S. District Court for the Eastern District of Oklahoma on September 9, 1940, and was dismissed by a three-judge panel four months later. Curiously, Phillips was an ardent supporter of Franklin Roosevelt. His opposition to the dam had been rooted in a strain of prairie populism that decried government expenditures on public works of any kind. Small government was good government, in Phillips's view, and the Denison Dam was to him a glaring example of what government should not do. But by 1941, with economic recovery visibly under way, the popular appeal of Phillips's position had all but vanished.

Q: What effect did construction of the dam have on the town of Denison?

CLAY: Well, it materially improved the economy during the period of construction. I don't know that it improved too much the lot of individual people living there, because the contractors brought in people from other places to get the skills they wanted. But these people had considerable purchasing power, and obviously the payroll was very substantial.

Q: And Denison? How did you enjoy living there?

CLAY: I suspect that I enjoyed it more than my wife. Of course, it was a small town. There was not much in the way of recreational facilities available. There was a small country club with a nine-hole golf course, which all of our people were invited to join. And I think, all in all, we had a very decent social life: nothing to be excited about, but we had dances at the country club, dinners in various homes, and that sort of thing.

In 1940, with the Army beginning to mobilize, Clay was promoted to major—a routine advancement for an officer with twenty-two years' service. That autumn, with construction activity in full swing, he was abruptly ordered to Washington to head FDR's newly established emergency airport construction program.

Q: How did it feel to leave Denison before the dam was completed?

CLAY: These are the kinds of things you get used to in the service. You very seldom get to finish anything, so in a way you get used to it. Organizing the work, getting the designs out, getting the initial contracts out are perhaps the most thrilling aspects. Perhaps after the last contract is let there would have been somewhat of a letdown because the design work was through. I think it is a hard question to answer, but I don't think that to stay there until the final days would have been very thrilling.

"On the other hand, I think that there is no greater satisfaction in the world than being a construction engineer, than to see a complicated structure materialize. When you get all through, it's there, finished, ready for operation. I don't know very many things you can do in life where you can enjoy seeing the pieces put together. Obviously, architecture is one. And I presume, in a way, this is the same sort of satisfaction a painter gets out of a painting."

Clay's Denison sojourn provided a brief interlude from top-level politics. In Washington during the early thirties, he had played a vital role in integrating the professional Army with the New Deal—a far more important role than his junior rank might have warranted. In the Philippines, he had served for a year in close, intimate contact with Eisenhower and MacArthur—both destined to become the dominant military figures of World War II. But in Denison, Clay had the opportunity to operate on his own: to fashion a major engineering structure and initiate its construction. The Denison Dam was a massive undertaking, and Clay enjoyed the challenge. It provided an enormous opportunity to prove himself as a practicing engineer.

· 7 ·

B-17s on the Runway (1940-1941)

A good organizer. Full of energy. Brilliant and original in thought. Practical. Conscientious. Able to get a mission accomplished in spite of difficulties and without arousing unnecessary opposition. A strong character who can be politely firm without being hard boiled.

Brigadier General Donald H. Connolly
[Clay's efficiency report, October 29, 1941]

SEPTEMBER 26, 1940. THE EARLY AUTUMN SUN BEAT down heavily on the tin roof of Clay's Denison field office as he gave a last-minute check to the day's construction schedule. Over the shack's portable radio blared the day's news: FDR barnstorming across the Midwest in pursuit of a precedent-shattering third term; Willkie in California; and over Britain, the air war approaching a climax as Goering turned the Luftwaffe's attention to London while Hitler massed an invasion armada at the Channel ports.

The harsh reality of the world situation was

jarred by the ring of Clay's telephone. "Lucius, this is Don Connolly in Washington. We need you here to head the airport construction program the President wants rushed through. Five hundred airports in two years. Six hundred million dollars. It's part of the emergency defense program. Can you drop Denison and come to Washington?"

"It'll take me a day or two to close out here," Clay remembers replying, "but I'll come to Washington next week."

Civil Aeronautics Administrator Donald Connolly was one of the New Deal's most effective executives. An outstanding Army Engineer, he had been among those selected by General Markham to help Harry Hopkins organize the WPA, and was assigned to run its sprawling Los Angeles district. Connolly's work in Los Angeles so impressed Hopkins that, when Hopkins became Secretary of Commerce, Connolly was brought back to Washington to head the Civil Aeronautics Administration (CAA). A tall, jovial Irishman, Connolly got along famously with politicians of every stripe, his unfailing fund of stories always on tap. When war came, Connolly was given the Persian Gulf Command, where he opened up the supply route from Abadan to Tehran and then into Russia. It was a tribute to Connolly's rare ability that he became the only U.S. general ever given a full tour of the Red Army front, and was able to work with the Russians without friction. (In 1945, when it appeared that Justice Byrnes might not release Clay to go to Germany, Connolly was Secretary Stimson's second choice to head the Occupation.)

FDR's defense airport program was the type of boom-time construction America does best. It repeated the emergency experiences of the WPA on a national scale, with the emphasis once again on speed. In 1940, the United States had only thirty-six airports equipped for all-weather flying. Under Clay's direction, 457 new airports were under construction by mid-1941—the nucleus of America's postwar air transportation net.

Clay knew nothing about building airports in 1940, though, like Eisenhower, he had taken advantage of his stay in the Philippines to learn to fly. But Connolly and Clay were old, dear friends and enjoyed "something of a mutual admiration society." Connolly knew the job he was asking Clay to do was going to involve great pressure. "So he called me and asked if I would take it. It was that simple," said Clay.

Q: Was the airport program approved at that time?

CLAY: I thought it was. But actually it turned out to be not clear. After I got to Washington, we had to go to hearings and do quite a bit of work on it. The whole matter had been rather badly handled, it seems.

Q: What was the difficulty?

CLAY: In the first place, the Civil Aeronautics Administration was a comparatively new agency working with a comparatively new committee of Congress. You didn't have long-established rules and precedents to govern your relations. And the committee had not yet attained the power of the Military Affairs Committee or the Commerce Committee. Plus the fact that in 1940 almost no one in Congress was prepared to go out on a limb for what might be a military program. They were too clever for that. You've got to remember that Mr. Roosevelt got his draft bill through [the House of Representatives] by only one vote. That's how divided sentiment was in the country when we were only a few months from war.

"So the CAA had this bill before Congress for civilian airports, and in the bill they were called 'civil airports for defense,' because basically we didn't want to recognize the possibilities of war to create an airport network. On the other hand, the Air Force was expanding very rapidly, and for training particularly they needed a large number of airports across the country. But there was also a real growth taking place in commercial aviation, which Congress recognized; hence we got a bill out aiding that. And since the WPA was still in existence, we were able to augment those funds with WPA money."

Q: But you say this was not clear when you arrived in Washington?

CLAY: That's right. I didn't realize it at the time, but my experience in Washington during the first four years of the New Deal was invaluable: I was working in an historic era, although I didn't realize it at the time. Working between Mr. Hopkins and Mr. Ickes more than qualified you to deal with a Donald Nelson [chairman of the War Production Board] or a Paul McNutt [chairman of the War Manpower Commission]. I had learned the highways and byways of government —how you have to proceed to get things done, what you do, what the steps are. And so, when I went back to Washington, this gave me a tremendous advantage that many of my associates didn't have. It enabled me to do things faster and quicker than they could, because they didn't have that type and kind of background.

"You learned, for instance, that you had to have an authorizations bill passed before you could have an appropriations bill passed. You learned that the best way to get something done is to talk to the committee clerk—to find out from the committee clerk what the procedures are, and then go to the congressman to ask if he'll do this, that, or the other to help you.

"You also learn who the executive assistants are downtown [in the Executive branch]. And they are the people that by calling on the telephone you can get answers and decisions from. You don't get them from a Cabinet member. As a matter of fact, you probably couldn't reach him. And you wouldn't get an answer from him if you did. But three times out of four, you can get an answer from his executive assistant.

"So, to get this airport program moving, I went up to the Hill and called on the clerks and the chairmen and the congressmen. I explained very frankly what we were trying to do. And I did it on an individual basis. That way they didn't have to ask embarrassing questions in public hearings. That had been one of our problems."

Q: Was there much political pressure? Pressure to have airports located in particular places, and so forth?

CLAY: In any program like that, when you're spending that much money, there are always political pressures, pressures from congressmen and the like. The best way of handling the problem, it seemed to me, was to make it clear on an informal basis that this was an important military program which also had important civilian aspects. I made it clear that the airports were going to be designed to be useful to both commercial and defense aviation. We didn't want any white elephants. And with that in mind, after I took the job I made direct contact with Colonel [Robert] Olds of the Army Air Forces, who was one of our great bombing experts, and I worked out with him the location of the airports we put into the program. National Airport in Washington, Newark, O'Hare, L.A. were obvious choices. Some became very important in the war, because we put a few in Alaska [Ladd, Kodiak, Nome] and on several islands in the Pacific: Midway, Palmyra, Johnston, and Christmas islands.

Officially, Clay became secretary of the Airport Approval Board and assistant to the Administrator of Civil Aeronautics. The board had three members: Secretary of Commerce Jesse Jones, Secretary of War

Stimson, and Secretary of the Navy Frank Knox. But the board never met, and for practical purposes Clay ran the program.

"Actually, my boss was Jesse Jones," Clay recalled. "Mr. Jones was a canny old fellow, and when I first went there and we were putting in our recommendations for these various and sundry airports—maybe for a couple of months—I had to go up to see him with a detailed list of every one of them. Then all of a sudden one morning he said, 'O.K. Go ahead. It's your show.' And I never had to see him again."

Q: Was there any reason he signed off?
CLAY: That was the way he worked. He was rating me to find out what he thought of me, and he finally decided that I was all right and could go ahead. He didn't give you freedom of action until he decided whether he wanted to or not. From then on, we were very fine friends. I remember later, when he was on the War Production Board, he threw his support very heavily to us. But the Airport Approval Board never functioned. I functioned.
Q: Did you consult with the other two secretaries?
CLAY: The Navy wasn't really interested. I consulted with Colonel Olds. When we agreed, that was it. When we disagreed, we might have gone to one of the secretaries, but we made it a point to resolve our differences ourselves. Our job was to determine the sites, determine the degree of local cooperation that was required, work out with WPA how much support we could get, approve the plans and specifications, and then be sure they got the work under way.

Clay's responsibility for selecting the sites of the new airports once again placed him in a position of important political leverage. For the most part, the proposals he received from state agencies represented careful compromises of local and national interests. But occasionally he intervened to bestow favors where discretion permitted. Clay's decision to reward his hometown of Marietta with a new airport—a fact of lasting military and economic import—is one such example. "Sure, I put an airport at Marietta," said Clay. "The military wanted an airport in the Atlanta area, and I thought that this was the best location. As a matter of fact, I thought then, and I still do, that this really was the correct location for Atlanta's principal airport. It is so much nearer to town than the one they have now."

Occasionally, Clay's selection of the sites riled local politicians, as, for example, when he chose to install an airport in Westchester County, New York. According to Clay, "Mayor La Guardia made up his mind that this was designed to take traffic away from La Guardia [Airport], and he wasn't going to stand for it. That was all right. He had his right to do whatever he wanted. But I felt it was absolutely essential for the New York metropolitan area to have another airport, and I wasn't about to give in to him. In any event, he came to Washington and invited me and the Assistant Secretary of Commerce, Mr. [Robert] Hickley, and Mr. [Robert] Lovett [Assistant Secretary of War for Air] to have breakfast with him in his suite at the Mayflower. Which we did. And La Guardia started off with a violent attack on the Corps of Engineers. Not on me specifically, but on the Corps of Engineers. 'Untrustworthy, political, unreliable,' and so on. After this had gone on for two or three minutes, I just got up and said, 'I'm sorry, Mr. Mayor, I simply do not have to take that kind of thing and I'm not going to. Good morning.' And I walked out. He went down and complained to the War Department, but apparently didn't get anywhere." As La Guardia discovered, and as the Russians were ultimately to find in Berlin, Clay would not be bullied, even by the most popular mayor in the United States at that time. In fact, Robert Lovett said afterwards that he had never seen a political figure as dumbstruck as La Guardia when Clay walked out.

In 1940, Washington was a bustling boom town of commercial and government activity. When the New Deal had come to power in 1933, the size of government expanded five-fold. In 1940 and 1941, as the nation prepared for war, another five-fold expansion took place. From all over the United States, businesspeople, laborers, clerks, and civil servants flocked to Washington. The city's tight housing market became even tighter, hotels and restaurants were perpetually jammed, schools and amusement parks hopelessly overcrowded. "There was a real 'Let's get going' atmosphere," Clay recalls, "because we had started to substantially increase the size of our defense forces. General Marshall had recently taken over from General Malin Craig as Chief of Staff, and the excitement of these changes acted as a real stimulant. There was a general feeling that we might soon be at war whether we wanted to or not, and that we'd better by a damn sight get ready."

Q: Were you concerned at that point that you had never attended the Command and General Staff School at Fort Leavenworth, or the War College? Wasn't that the avenue to higher command?
CLAY: I never worried about it at all. For this reason: Until 1941, promotion was strictly by seniority. Under the ordinary course of events, I could not even be sure that I would reach the grade of colonel. Until I did reach that grade, it was all by seniority. So my life at that time was engineering, construction, building—and obviously the defense airport program was an engineering program.
Q: In retrospect, what do you think about a promotion system based on seniority?
CLAY: Seniority? It was the only system by which you could have kept the Army alive in the days when appropriations were very limited, when the opportunities for competition were on the whole limited. You didn't have enough ways to measure people to go by any system other than seniority. In wartime, I think we had a much better system. But it wouldn't have worked in the days between World War I and World War II.

"If you were in the [West Point] Class of 1916 or before, you had an opportunity to become colonel at an age young enough that you might be selected for general officer. We were in what was known as the 'hump' in our class. We wouldn't have had that opportunity if the Army hadn't expanded."
Q: But didn't the seniority system tend to reduce efficiency?
CLAY: When the war came in 1941, there were many officers who became ambitious and worked hard who, without that type of incentive, didn't put out during their earlier periods. It was a little bit easier, perhaps, not to work too hard before the war than it was to work hard. If you worked hard, you got a district maybe two or three years before the other fellow. But he'd get one too—unless he was manifestly unfit. So your only real return from what you did was your own self-satisfaction.

"Since World War II, the military service has had assignments around the world of great importance. We've had to get along with people of other nations, train people of other nations, as well as train ourselves. The Army has had money for new and exciting equipment. It's been an entirely different world. My sons don't know the world that I knew: the world of an Army that sometimes didn't even have ammunition to shoot. But I can remember when we didn't have our target practice for the entire year simply because we didn't have ammunition."

Q: What type of Army did this create?

CLAY: An Army kept alive by its schools—and the challenges of such things as the engineering work which the Engineers had. Leavenworth, the War College—these were the places that kept the Army alive in those days.

Q: And the insularity? The isolation from civilian life?

CLAY: Well, I don't know that I could talk about that so much, because I spent so much of my time in rivers and harbors work that I was meeting with civilians more than I was with Army personnel, so I'd be a poor judge of that.

"There are a lot of strange ideas about the peacetime, prewar Army. But the peacetime Army was poor. My family lived in converted barracks at Fort Humphreys for four years. When I was instructing at West Point, I had to live in a house at Highland Falls I'm damned sure you wouldn't live in. I lived in Newburgh for a year and commuted at six o'clock every morning to get to a class at seven-thirty. It was a poor Army. It had no vehicles, no equipment. It had only a certain sincerity, particularly among the younger officers, who had been the junior officers of World War I and who knew how badly we did during World War I and who dedicated themselves to building a better Army. And the only way they could do it was through the school system: Fort Benning for the infantry, Fort Sill for the artillery, and, of course, the Command and General Staff School at Fort Leavenworth. And the school system, although I didn't participate in it, was highly competitive.

"But it was these younger officers of World War I who carried the torch, so to speak. Styer, Connolly, Somervell in the Engineers; Patton and Chaffee in the cavalry; Marshall, Bradley, and Eisenhower in the infantry. They had seen how poorly prepared we were in World War I and were determined to do better. And I think they did. This was one of the reasons why the [West Point] Class of 1915 achieved such an outstanding World War II record. They were the ones who came back from World War I thoroughly convinced that we had to be more professional, and they really introduced a spirit of professionalism into the armed services. We were amateurs in World War I. We were professionals in World War II."

Q: But aren't careers in business or law more demanding than a career in the military?

CLAY: Well, I've been in the business world for twenty-five years, and the biggest jobs that I've ever seen done were done by Army officers—bigger than any jobs I've ever seen done by anybody in the business world. And they were well done. Marshall and General Eisenhower, for example. I've never known anybody in the business world who had handled as big a job as they did.

Q: To return to 1941, General, do you recall where you were on December 7, when the Japanese attacked Pearl Harbor?

CLAY: Yes. I recall that very well. I was with Jesse Jones. I was his guest that Sunday at Griffith Stadium, watching a football game between the Washington Redskins and the Philadelphia Eagles. [Redskins 20, Eagles 14.]

"During the half-time, they began to call out all of the admirals: 'Is Admiral so-and-so here, and if he is will he report immediately . . .' After they'd done this half a dozen times, everybody got to wondering what this was all about, and Shirley Povich, who was a sports writer for *The Washington Post,* came up to see Mr. Jones and said that the rumor they had in the press box was that there had been an attack on Pearl Harbor.

"I immediately proved my great military expertise, because when Mr. Jones turned around and asked me, I said, 'The Japs would attack Guam or the Philippines, but Pearl Harbor is impregnable. I just can't believe they would attack Pearl Harbor.' Well, within a very few minutes we knew they had attacked Pearl Harbor.

"That night, I went to a hastily assembled meeting in General [commanding general, Army Air Corps] Arnold's office in which the Air Forces asked that we get out orders stopping all civilian airplanes from flying at all airports in the country as of the next day. That we close all civilian airports. And I wouldn't do it. I said, 'This is the surest way in the world to create panic. It doesn't make sense. You're not going to have Japanese planes coming in and taking off for sabotage. I just don't think you have that kind of danger.'

"Well, after a while they cooled off a bit and we didn't do it. But we did get out orders about checking each pilot before he was allowed to take off. That's how disconcerted the people in the War Department had gotten by that night. Because we were told that night what we had lost, and it was unbelievable."

Q: Your concern at that point was to get back into the military? Into a military position?

CLAY: Very much so. Of course, the announcements on the radio called for all of us to report to work next day in uniform. And it was quite a job. We'd been wearing civilian clothes until then to de-emphasize the military nature of the airport program, and I hadn't had a uniform on in several years. Getting it out and getting the right insignia on and so forth—I must have been the sorriest-looking soldier you ever saw the next day. I'm not even sure that I had my colonel's insignia. I think I had to borrow it from somebody.

"On Monday, I reported to the Chief of Engineers and said I was available at the CAA and expected to be recalled for military duty immediately. In a day or two, I got a call from Colonel Mark Clark at the War Department, and they wanted me and an Army Air Forces officer [Colonel Robert C. Candee] to go down to Brazil in civilian clothes and determine where we should have airports in Brazil —and whether the Brazilians would let us build them. At that point, the Brazilians had not made up their minds to go to war. So we went down semi-incognito. We were in civilian clothes and we didn't call ourselves colonels, we called ourselves misters. On the other hand, quite a few of the Brazilian army officers knew who we were.

"We went up to Belém and Natal, where we were already building airfields under contract with Pan American. Ostensibly, Pan American was building them. The question was whether the Brazilians would let us use them.

"While I was in Belém, a B-17 and a B-24 came through to try to make it to the Philippines—believe it or not—with no maps and no charts. They went by Dakar, and then over. But the Brazilians wouldn't allow Pan American to refuel them with their trucks. So they had to refuel these big bombers with five-gallon cans."

Q: Was the Brazilian army cooperative?

CLAY: The ones I went with were. Most of the Brazilian air force was on our side, but the Chief of Staff [Air Force General Eduardo Gomez] had been educated and trained in Germany. Fortunately for us, while we were there German submarines sank a Brazilian ship off Pôrto Alegre with substantial loss of life. They immediately threw in with us, and it was no longer a problem. By that time, we had picked out the sites and had roughly laid out the airfields—the completion of Belém and Natal, also at Pôrto Alegre and Recife, which were added to the Pan American contract. And they went ahead with the whole series—which became very important in 1943, when we were ferrying aircraft across the Atlantic.

Q: And then you returned to Washington?

CLAY: I returned to Washington and reported to General Eisenhower, who had just taken over the War Plans Division. He was fresh from the Louisiana maneuvers, and it was the first time I'd seen him since the Philippines.

" 'That's fine,' Eisenhower said when I made my report, 'I think you ought to give this to General Marshall, and I will arrange it.' Which he did. And after I made my report to General Marshall, Ike said, 'Now, before we determine your next assignment, you can sit down here [in War Plans] and take one of these desks and help us out right here.'

"I said, 'I don't think that's my talent.'

"He said, 'Well, in any event, you take a desk here for the time being until we see what's happening.' Which I did.

"Well, that afternoon, [Lieutenant General Joseph W.] Stilwell walked in. I knew him. Not intimately, but I knew him. And he looked over and saw me sitting there and said, 'How would you like to go with me?'

"I said, 'I'd like to go with you anywhere.' I knew wherever Stilwell was being sent he was being sent as a fighting general, because that was his reputation.

"And he said, 'All right. You come with me as my engineer. We'll be going in a day or two. All I can tell you is to take summer clothes.'

"I went home and started getting ready with summer clothes. Next day, down at the office, I ran into [Major General] Bill Somervell. He asked me what I was doing, and I said I was getting ready to go somewhere with Stilwell.

"Somervell didn't say anything. The following day, General Eisenhower said, 'I'm sorry, but you're not going with Stilwell. You'll just have to stick around here. I'm sorry, I can't tell you any more than that, but you're not going with Stilwell.'

"I sat around there, doing whatever odd jobs they gave me to do, and about two or three days later General Eisenhower announced a big conference to be addressed by General Marshall. I was told to attend.

"Well, the purpose of the conference, it turned out, was to announce the reorganization of the War Department and the creation of the Services of Supply, which was to be in charge of all of the Army's service and supply functions. General Marshall said the commanding general of the Services of Supply would be Lieutenant General Brehon B. Somervell—he was a major general at the time, so obviously this was his promotion. Then Somervell got up and announced that he was going to start out with Major General Wilhelm D. Styer as his chief of staff, Brigadier General Lucius Clay as his chief of materiel (whatever that was), Brigadier General LeRoy Lutes as his chief of distribution, and a couple of others.

"And so it was announced that I was promoted and whatnot, and to me it looked like a very disappointing assignment. It probably worked out all right. But I had never been in supply work. I didn't want to be in supply work. It wasn't what I wanted to do by any manner of means. Of course, if I had gone with Stilwell, it would really have been a dead end. But no one knew that in those days, and we all wanted to be where the action was."

Q: In retrospect, did you find your experience with Civil Aeronautics useful once war began?

CLAY: I guess every bit of experience helps you. I suppose you could say it made me somewhat air-conscious, Air Force–conscious. As a matter of fact, I was invited by General Arnold once to take over the command of the Air Transport Service during the war.

Q: Why did you decline?

CLAY: I didn't. General Somervell declined for me. I wasn't asked to express an opinion on it. And, in a way, I'm glad that I wasn't, because at that stage of the game you've got to rely on others as to where you can make your best contribution. Actually, I think I made a better contribution to the war effort in Services of Supply. There were plenty of top-flight people like C[yrus] R[owlett] Smith, president of American Airlines, with the experience to handle air transport, whereas in the job I was doing I was exploring new territory, almost without precedent. The other was a job where an old airline expert like C. R. Smith certainly should have been able to do much better than I could.

Clay's dedication to the Army was complete, his youthful indecision now far behind him. For the past ten years, he had been given assignments that increasingly tested him, and he had fulfilled each in an outstanding manner. When war began, Clay was one of the most junior colonels on active duty. But his efficiency ratings for the past seven years put him at the head of the class. In a marking scheme that ran from one to seven, seven being the highest, Clay had received perfect "sevens" since 1933. No other colonel could claim such an achievement.

· Book Two ·

WARTIME WASHINGTON

· 8 ·

Director of Materiel

> Hopkins told me a long time later that during the months in the hospital he thought endlessly about how the various . . . bottlenecks had been broken and the desperate shortages of strategic materials converted into surpluses, and it all seemed in retrospect as if it had been easy. . . . But, he said, there was one miracle that he could not explain: how did it happen that the United States, an unwarlike and unprepared country if there ever was one, was suddenly able to produce so large and so brilliant a group of military leaders, competent to deal with situations that had never before existed in the history of the world? Where did they come from? And what had they been doing during all those twenty years when our Navy had been used purely to pose for newsreels and our Army had been kicked around like "a mangy old dog"?
>
> Robert Sherwood,
> *Roosevelt and Hopkins: An Intimate History*

When America confronted the possibility of war in 1940, her defenses suffered from years of neglect. Appropriations were niggardly, equipment outdated, and the profession of arms lay in ill-repute. Congressional insistence on using up whatever remained from World War I kept procurement funds low and equipment dangerously obsolete. In point of fact, the United States was a third-rate military power: the U.S. Army ranked seventeenth among the armies of the world; the Army Air Corps possessed only forty-nine modern bombers, while the Navy habitually purchased sufficient ammunition only for target practice.

Even worse, the Army high command had little appreciation of industrial mobilization and the inescapable time lag between placing an order and receiving a finished weapon. The War Department's elaborate budgeting procedures caused further delay. General J. O. Mauborgne, the Army's chief signal officer, complained in 1940 that it took twenty-seven months just to complete the paperwork for a new item of equipment—and six years to get it into production.

Military purchasing officers, weaned on years of adversity, were temperamentally incapable of moving with the speed that total war required. Peacetime purchasing was routine: small in magnitude, leisurely conducted, and relatively unencumbered by issues calling for on-the-spot judgment and strong initiative. Thus, when Henry Stimson became Secretary of War in the summer of 1940, he found that the Quartermaster Corps had handled the negotiations for the construction of new barracks "without a taint of scandal," but that, come winter, half the American army would be without housing.

Research and development were equally retarded. The German Mark IV heavy tank had crashed through the Ardennes in 1940 and outflanked the Maginot Line, but the United States did not have a heavy tank, and when one finally did go into mass production, it was a model designed immediately after the British offensive on the Somme in 1916 that fired in one direction only. The M-1 Garand rifle, developed as a replacement for the 1903 bolt-action Springfield, came from the factories so slowly in 1941 that training plans had to be adjusted to its delivery, while the 105mm howitzer, already the standard field piece of all European armies, was still undergoing tests at the Aberdeen Proving Grounds.

Between the wars, American public opinion dwelt in splendid isolation. A riptide of pacifism led to the Neutrality Act of 1935, punishing equally the aggressor and his victim by denying American aid to both. The ill-conceived Ludlow Amendment, which would have required a national plebiscite before the United States might declare war, came dangerously close to passing the House of Representatives in 1938. An opinion poll conducted by the American Institute of Public Opinion at that time found nine of ten Americans indifferent to Japanese encroachment in China, while FDR's famous October 1937 speech recommending that aggressors be quarantined fell on deaf, if not hostile, ears. The small military appropriations of 1938 and 1939 passed the Congress, but never in the amounts Roosevelt requested and never without overcoming substantial isolationist opposition. Even the Administration's request to amend the Neutrality Act following Hitler's occupation of Prague was defeated by a defiant Congress determined to keep America out of war.

The sentiments of isolationist America found responsive echo in both the War Department and the State Department. Secretary of War Harry Woodring, a brittle Kansas Democrat wedded to the pacifist fundamentals of the rural Midwest, and Army Chief of Staff Malin Craig were determined to stay out of Europe's quarrels; they made little effort to remedy the nation's unpreparedness. A 1938 Army staff study recommending a modest fleet of long-range B-17 bombers was rejected summarily by Deputy Chief of Staff Stanley Embick with the biting reminder that "Our national policy contemplates preparation for defense, not aggression."

From 1936 to 1939, the War Department's high command systematically reduced the Army's meager research funds, preferring "proven" World War I models to "needless expenditures for unessential research." Attempts of leading scientists such as Vannevar Bush to enlist the National Research Council and the National Academy of Sciences in the defense effort languished without response from the Army's leadership.

A determination to resist war with Nazi Germany resonated even more strongly among the old-school diplomats of America's foreign service. Starchy and class-conscious as they were, a war for democracy did not stir them deeply or elicit their prompt support. George Kennan, then a mid-level diplomat posted in Prague and Berlin, and more sensitive than most, wrote darkly about the political pressure from "vocal minorities" in the United States that was leading America into war. "I could not get excited," he wrote later, "about this fancied issue . . . of dictatorship vs. democracy."

Like the War Department, the State Department remained anchored to the humdrum days of the past, when the life of an American diplomat was consumed by the genteel passions of an international elite, laced with occasional obligations to negotiate, represent, and report. To a degree much greater than in the Army or the Navy, where West Point and Annapolis provided entry-level opportunities for at least a cross-section of middle-class America, the foreign service was an upper-class avocation, the province of high-caste Eastern Protestants with a taste for European society and the leisure to indulge it. Of those recruited by the State Department between 1914 and 1922, three-quarters had attended prep school, often St. Paul's or Groton. Virtually without exception, all were well-to-do. Not only were they strongly Republican (the more ardent New Dealers often considered them crypto-fascists), they were incredible dandies as well. King George VI, for example, had actually complained to Roosevelt that he hoped in the future the United States would send real Americans to London, not imitation Englishmen. Roosevelt himself was only too well aware of the problem. Drafting a 1940 fireside chat, the President wrote that some American citizens in high places were aiding and abetting the Nazis. When the manuscript came back from the State Department with the words "in high places" circled in red, FDR agreed to change it. He said it should read, "There are also American citizens, many in high places, *especially in the State Department* . . ."

To circumvent military and diplomatic obstructionism, Roosevelt devised a series of stratagems. The defense airport program that Clay headed was one of these. Another was FDR's plan to divert Allied weapons orders through Treasury Secretary Henry Morgenthau, Jr., who in turn placed them directly with American industry, in effect bypassing both the State Department and the War Department. Then, in the summer of 1940, with France defeated and his third-term candidacy looming, Roosevelt replaced Woodring with seventy-two-year-old Henry L. Stimson, former Secretary of War (under Taft), former Secretary of State (under Hoover)—a fighting Republican whose hostility to the Axis rivaled that of the most rabid New Dealer. The President was less successful at State, where the aging Cordell Hull of Tennessee clung to office until 1944, forcing FDR to maneuver around the reluctant diplomats for most of the war.

To complement Stimson at the War Department, FDR provided three younger men: Judge Robert Patterson of the U.S. Court of Appeals as Under Secretary of War; investment banker Robert A. Lovett, of Brown Brothers, Harriman, as Assistant Secretary for Air; and John

J. McCloy, of the prestigious Wall Street law firm of Cravath, deGersdorff, Swaine, and Wood, as the Assistant Secretary of War—all destined to play a decisive role in the next two decades of American policy. Stimson's new team revitalized the War Department: a building Lovett characterized as "so full of dead wood that it was an absolute firetrap."

Nevertheless, when war came in December 1941, the United States was still remarkably unprepared. Draftees trained with broomsticks instead of rifles. Scarcely any 105mm howitzers or 81mm mortars were in the hands of troops. Vehicles were in chronic short supply, stovepipes substituted for antitank weapons, and gas masks and medical supplies were virtually nonexistent. Three weeks after Pearl Harbor, the United States had a grand total of one infantry division, two bomber squadrons, and three pursuit groups ready for combat.

Even worse, the War Department still had little idea of America's military needs or of how to convert the nation's economic potential to war. In the first place, Lend-Lease to the Allies competed directly with U.S. rearmament efforts, while problems involving the allocation of scarce resources, manpower, and civilian supply were just beginning to be grappled with.

Much of the Army's unpreparedness stemmed from the antediluvian organization of the War Department itself, a problem that Stimson's new team had not yet solved. Under the National Defense Act of 1920, military procurement was the responsibility of the Under Secretary of War, not the Army's General Staff. This was a negative reaction to World War I and represented an attempt by Congress to curtail the peacetime activities of the military. By separating purchasing and procurement from ongoing military activities, civilian control supposedly was enhanced. And preventing the military from dealing directly with industry snuffed out the potential dangers of a "military-industrial complex." The unfortunate result, however, was that plans for industrial mobilization were formulated in isolation from the rest of the War Department. With too few officers and too little coordination, the Under Secretary procured for the Army at arm's length: military plans were prepared by the General Staff, procurement plans by the Office of the Under Secretary. Coordination between the two was virtually nonexistent. During the critical years 1940–41, the two sections were not even located in the same building. The Army General Staff remained in Washington's old Munitions Building on Constitution Avenue, while the Under Secretary and his staff resided two blocks north in the building that now houses the Department of the Interior. Coordination supposedly was to be achieved at the topmost civilian level, but Secretary Woodring and Under Secretary Louis Johnson rarely spoke to each other, and when they did it was usually acrimonious. As a result, Army mobilization plans had serious defects, and FDR quickly discarded them. Clay, who was later charged with all of the Army's procurement efforts, never recalled referring to them, nor was he familiar with them.

To replace the procurement sideshow run by the Under Secretary, General Marshall, with Stimson's approval, reorganized the War Department and combined the Army's supply and service branches under General Somervell, whom he appointed commanding general of the Services of Supply. Somervell became the Army's administrative head: an appointment uniformly resented by the previously independent branch chiefs, such as the adjutant general and the chief of ordnance, who now found themselves shut out from the War Department high command.

Marshall's reorganization represented far more than a routine reshuffling of housekeeping responsibilities. Since 1933, Roosevelt had wrestled to gain control of the military, just as he had sought to place his stamp on the State Department. But it had been a painful, step-by-step process. General Douglas MacArthur, who had little sympathy for the New Deal, was not eased out as Chief of Staff until 1935. He was replaced by the impeccably correct but slow-moving Malin Craig, who was scarcely the general FDR needed to defend democracy in a global war. When Craig retired in 1939, Roosevelt passed over General Hugh Drum, the candidate of the conservative military establishment ("I'm tired of hearing Drum beat the drum for Drum," FDR told Hopkins), and selected George C. Marshall, an officer who had worked closely with Hopkins and the Civilian Conservation Corps and who was far more sympathetic to the New Deal than most of the Army's West Point–trained senior officers.

Nine months after Marshall's appointment, Roosevelt had replaced Woodring with Henry Stimson. The top echelon of the War Department was thus consolidated. But the problem of effective political control involved control within the military itself. Independent branch chiefs such as the Chief of Engineers, or independent commanders

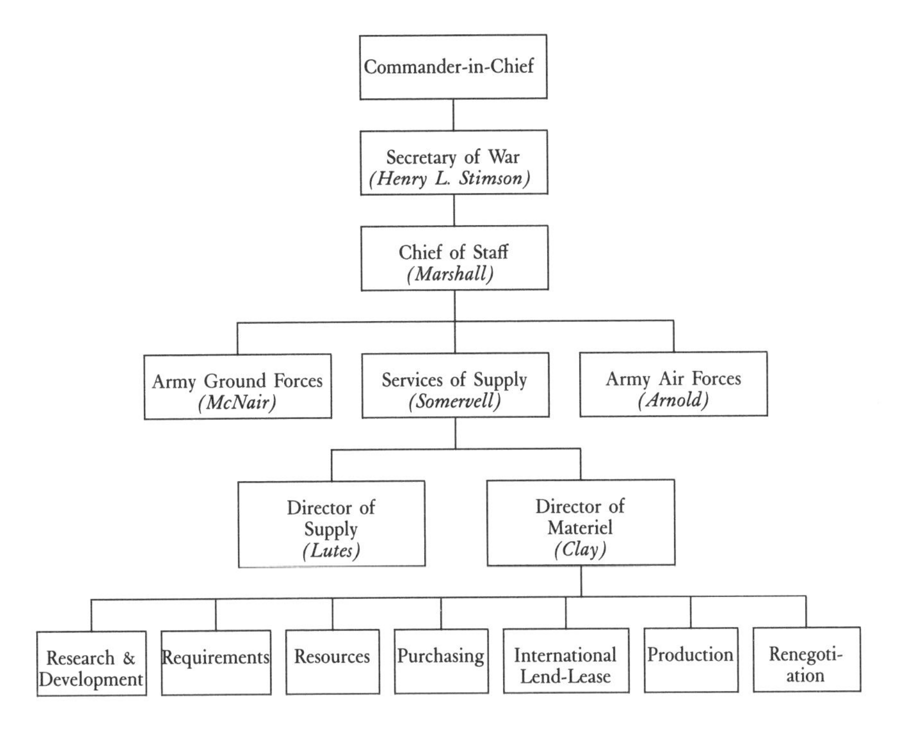

War Department Reorganization, 1942 (Extract)

such as John J. Pershing in World War I, habitually played one set of superiors against another to gain additional leverage for themselves. And many were not in the least bit of sympathy with the New Deal, or with Roosevelt's foreign policy.

Marshall's 1942 reorganization of the War Department met that problem head-on. For the first time in American history, the Chief of Staff assumed indisputable control over all elements of the Army, reporting directly to the Secretary of War. Marshall chose as his immediate lieutenants men who were equally adept at working with the Roosevelt administration. Generals "Hap" Arnold and Leslie McNair, designated to command the Army Air Forces and the Army Ground Forces respectively, already had demonstrated their ability to work smoothly in wartime Washington, and Somervell, whose Services of Supply was destined to become the most powerful military organization on the home front, was an old hand at political infighting and had proved himself to be a loyal friend of the New Deal during his years as head of the WPA in New York City. Indeed, with the military now completely realigned, it should not have been surprising that the War Department, not the State Department, became the vehicle of FDR's wartime diplomacy.

Within the War Department itself, Somervell quickly took control of everything other than the fighting forces. "Somervell shook the cobwebs out of their pants," Marshall said later. "If I went into control in another war, I would start out looking for another General Somervell the first thing I did, and so would anybody else who went through that struggle on our side."

Q: Prior to the 1942 reorganization, a number of staff sections, such as the adjutant general, reported directly to Mr. Stimson. Afterwards they reported through General Somervell and General Marshall. Did this make any difference?

CLAY: This relieved the Secretary from a lot of detail that was relatively unimportant and let him concentrate on the real job of winning the war. Today, Defense Secretaries are ruined by the detail they go into. You have to remember that in 1941 we were very fortunate in having men who had gone through a war before. Mr. Stimson had been Secretary before. And he'd known and worked with Army officers for many, many years. Judge Patterson had been a very gallant soldier in World War I and had great respect for the military service. We could not have been more fortunate in having two men who knew how to work with the military without giving up any of their own decision-making and policy-making responsibilities. They were two very exceptional men.

Q: Some might argue that they had been captured or bamboozled by the military.

CLAY: I think it was just the opposite. If Mr. Stimson and Mr. Patterson had felt for one minute that the military were getting out of hand, they would have been over there on the other side just as fast as they could be. Knowing these two gentlemen, I don't see how anyone could think otherwise. They were tremendously strong-willed men.

Q: How did Patterson react to the creation of the Services of Supply?

CLAY: Patterson and Somervell had offices adjoining each other. Patterson didn't try to command anything. But he was always ready to support you or carry the battle for you. When we ran into obstacles which required help from above, we went to Mr. Patterson. We used to say jokingly about Judge Patterson to be damned sure, if you got him carrying a fight for you, that you wanted it carried at all, because once he got into it you could never stop him. There were times when I thought that we might have compromised on issues, but there was no compromising with Judge Patterson.

Q: Could you describe Judge Patterson?

CLAY: A very intense kind of person. Rather indifferent as to dress. He used to wear old GI shoes. But he was highly motivated, highly dedicated, and completely sincere. The rumor was that the belt he wore had been taken from a German soldier whom he had killed in World War I, but I have no first-hand knowledge of that.

Q: And Somervell?

CLAY: I had no difficulties with Somervell. Probably less than anybody. He didn't bother me. That's not the right way to express it. He delegated authority to me and let it rest. I had much more freedom of operation under General Somervell than most people had. The first year of the war almost drove him crazy, because there was nothing you could put your finger on. I think that's why we had the Alcan [Alaska-Canada] Highway and a number of other projects: he just had to do something. I have great respect for General Somervell. We had many differences before the war. But I don't think he brought me up there because he liked me personally, or that I went there because I liked him personally.

Brehon B. Somervell was the handsome only son of a happy-go-lucky doctor father and a doting but determined mother who founded the Belcourt Seminary for Girls in Washington, D.C. Somervell grew up in Washington and, like Clay, stumbled through West Point without much effort. Later, he served on the Mexican border with Pershing, earned a Distinguished Service Cross for gallantry in France, and spent the twenties and early thirties conducting a series of economic surveys, first on the Rhine, then in Turkey for Kemal Atatürk. After a brief stint in the office of the Chief of Engineers in 1935—where he and Clay clashed frequently—Somervell took charge of New York City's massive WPA program and ran it successfully for four years, earning the lifelong confidence of Harry Hopkins.

In November 1940, when too many senior officers in the Army found too many reasons for doing nothing, Marshall recalled

Somervell (at Hopkins's suggestion) to head the Army's lagging construction program. Trading money for time—Somervell later admitted that the rush cost taxpayers an additional $100 million—he built enough barracks to house the Army before the worst of winter. Marshall rewarded Somervell by promoting him to major general and made him the Army's assistant chief of staff for logistics (G-4), where Somervell's ruthless energy catapulted him ahead of many more senior officers and made him a logical choice to head the Services of Supply.

Somervell's selection was greeted with mixed emotions by many, including Senator Harry S Truman. "I will say this for General Somervell," Truman allowed. "He will get the stuff, but it is going to be hell on the taxpayer. He has a WPA attitude on the expenditure of money."

A rigid disciplinarian gnawed by unlimited personal ambition, Somervell boasted that he never had a subordinate who made the same mistake twice. Yet the top leadership of the Services of Supply—Styer, Lutes, and Clay—remained at their posts throughout the war, an unusual continuity in wartime Washington. Of the four, only LeRoy Lutes had previous experience in supply, having served as supply chief for General Krueger's Third Army (for which Eisenhower was chief of staff) during the famous 1941 Louisiana maneuvers. Somervell, Styer, and Clay, on the other hand, were all Engineers—veterans of the highly politicized Civil Works Division of the Corps of Engineers.

Somervell's chief of staff, Major General Wilhelm D. Styer, was an old and trusted friend for whom Clay had worked in Pittsburgh in 1933, and who, in fact, first recommended Clay to Somervell. But where Somervell was brusque, curt, and abrasive, Styer was calm, affable, and judicious. "Styer complemented Somervell perfectly," remembers Lutes. "He was completely different: big, comfortable looking. Quiet. Very impressive. He wasn't going to get into a fight with anyone unless he had to. But he was no pushover. He could be tough. But in an atmosphere that was already supercharged, he served as a damper, as a lightning rod, so to speak. He was always a counterbalance for Somervell."

Clay and Somervell shared mutual respect but little affection. They were too much alike to cherish each other, and in the small peacetime Army they had been less than friends. When Somervell had been assigned to the office of the Chief of Engineers in 1935, following his return from Turkey, he had sought to take over the work Clay was doing on Capitol Hill, although Clay, who could be just as rigid, obstinately refused. "Somervell complained very bitterly that I wouldn't turn over the work for which I was responsible," said Clay. "I don't blame him. Here was this very successful young officer who was all of a sudden without a job. He was just assigned to our office as a stopgap, pending assignment elsewhere. And with his usual drive and energy, he wanted to take it over. Well, I wasn't about to let him do that, and neither was Colonel Edgerton."

Somervell forgave Clay, but he never forgave Edgerton. In 1943, when General Edgerton returned to Washington—by this time, he was the senior officer in the Corps of Engineers, having just completed a tour as governor general of the Canal Zone—Somervell assigned him to work *under* Clay as chief of military Lend-Lease. The assignment was demeaning, but Clay and Edgerton made the best of it. ("I never sent for General Edgerton," said Clay. "Whenever I needed to talk to him, I went down to his office. That was the least I could do.")

Such vindictive moves were typical of Somervell—"he was a man without a drop of human kindness," according to one three-star general who worked for him—but Somervell also could recognize talent and exploit it. First he interceded with Eisenhower to snatch Clay from Joe Stilwell. Then he convinced General Marshall that Clay could handle the Army's procurement efforts. Marshall initially thought Clay too young for the assignment: he was officially forty-four. But, to Marshall's surprise, Clay had the highest efficiency report of any colonel on active duty—a perfect score of 7.0 for the past eight years. "I'll promote him, if you want him," Marshall told Somervell. "But he's still too damn young."

Q: Do you recall your immediate actions after General Marshall made his announcement?

CLAY: I went up to see General Somervell, asked him what my job was, and told him how unhappy I was to get it.

Q: How did he explain it?

CLAY: He didn't. Somervell never explained anything. "That's too goddamn bad," he said. Then he told me, "Your job is to find out what the Army needs and get it." As a matter of fact, those are the only instructions I ever had from him. Much later we had organizational charts and job descriptions, but that was much, much later, and I don't recall that I ever paid much attention to them, truly.

Q: In retrospect, was your lack of experience in Army procurement an advantage or a disadvantage?

CLAY: Well, to tell the truth, in the magnitude we were dealing with, nobody else had any experience either. It certainly wasn't any disadvantage.

Somervell's crisp imperative, *find out what the Army needs and get it,* was the only instruction Clay was ever given. From March 1942 until he went to Germany in 1945, Clay headed the War Department's vast procurement effort: compiled the requirements for an eight-million-man Army; let the contracts; wrangled priorities; supervised production; rode herd on research and development; coordinated military Lend-Lease; renegotiated costs; disposed of scrap and surplus property—all without a breath of scandal. In three and a half years, the United States produced 88,000 tanks, 178,000 artillery pieces, 2.3 million trucks, and billions of rounds of ammunition. To clothe the Army alone required 50 million field jackets and 229 million pairs of pants. Given the magnitude of America's wartime effort, it was an unprecedented assignment, combining under the Director of Materiel all of the functions performed by the office of the Under Secretary before Marshall's reorganization.

"We were building an Army in which we in supply found ourselves having to determine its size and how it was to be constituted," said Clay. "We were flying blind. It wasn't until late 1943 that the General Staff came up with plans for the number of armored divisions that would be required, the number of paratroop divisions, and so forth. My God, if we had waited for them, we would never have supplied the Army."

Q: In World War I, General [George W.] Goethals [head of military procurement] had great difficulty with Congress, and so did the Navy in World War II. Why didn't the Army?

CLAY: Perhaps it turns on the fact that most of us had a good bit of experience in working with the Hill and knew a great many of the congressmen and senators—which is always helpful. Another factor was success. I think the speed with which we equipped our troops, while at the same time giving huge amounts of equipment to our

Allies, combined with our rapidity in sending fighting men into action, kept the Congress so enthused that we escaped the investigations and criticisms that were so prevalent in World War I. General Styer had a lot of experience working with Congress; I had a lot of experience working with Congress. And all through the establishment that was true. We had worked with civilians, and we also knew Washington. When you bring people to Washington, particularly in wartime, it takes them quite a little time to learn how government works.

Q: Were you called to the Hill frequently?

CLAY: I went to the Hill many times during the war, but I think I was there because I had a great deal of experience with Congress, rather than because it pertained to my job particularly. I was up there an awful lot on things I had no business being up there on. For example, Secretary Patterson told me to go up and defend the Alcan Highway, and I was probably the only man in the War Department who wrote a memorandum against it. I thought it was utter foolishness at the time —a waste of resources—and I wrote a memorandum to that effect. But they went ahead and did it anyway. Yet I had to go up and defend it before the Truman Committee.

Clay's explanation of the relatively smooth sailing enjoyed by the Services of Supply neglects one crucial factor. It is true that Somervell, Styer, and Clay had long experience working with Congress. It is also true that the American supply effort performed miraculously. But, perhaps equally important, by mid-1942 the Army leadership was completely in step with the Roosevelt administration. From General Marshall down, the Army's high command had worked with the New Deal, trusted it—and in turn were trusted by it. Hopkins recommended Marshall to FDR, just as he recommended Somervell to Marshall, and he had known Clay since the very beginning of the WPA. All three were as much a part of Roosevelt's political team as Morgenthau and Hopkins. In the later squabbles the Army had with Donald Nelson and the War Production Board, the simple military-civilian dichotomy does not fit. For the fact was that Marshall, Somervell, and Clay were usually closer to the White House, and certainly closer to Hopkins and Morgenthau, than Nelson and the WPB.

Q: General, in retrospect, what were the major mistakes on the home front in World War II?

CLAY: Unquestionably, we made many mistakes. I think that fundamentally, if you went down through all the lists of inventory and so forth, you would find that we built an awful lot of equipment that became obsolete before it was ever used. This was inevitable in a country that had not really prepared for war and from its existing designs could only build relatively obsolete equipment. When new designs were available, this became waste. And there was an awful lot of that. But I don't know what else we could have done. You couldn't wait for new tank designs before you went into production, because you didn't know when you were going to need those tanks. In 1942, we didn't know if we were going to be on the defensive—either here in America, or in Great Britain, or elsewhere. And so we had to have something. I think perhaps this was our greatest mistake: that we did not have modern, up-to-date designs ready to go and that we had to use our first production for things that turned out to be relatively obsolete.

"Our tank was always a problem. As a matter of fact, we never did really develop a top tank during the war. We did all right because we made enough of them, and that offset some of their weaknesses. But we never had a tank that equaled the Russian or the German tank."

Q: President Roosevelt pushed the tank program. Did every program have its own sponsor?

CLAY: In many ways, yes. Somervell, for example, had to push the landing-craft program. We had found by bitter experience that we could make successful landings if we had the appropriate landing craft to go in. It was almost mathematical. But the Navy didn't believe in it, although it was really a Navy program. So Somervell became the prime pusher. It was his drive and insistence that was behind the program. He even wanted to man them with SOS [Services of Supply] troops, which of course the Navy would never permit. But it was his impetuosity and initiative that forced the program to be put under way. And if he hadn't, I don't know whether we would have ever landed on a beach or not.

Q: And you?

CLAY: I became the sponsor of the pipeline that the British rolled across the Channel on D-Day. And I didn't believe in it a damned bit. But General Marshall asked me to push it. So I did. And it worked. A tiny, flexible pipeline for pumping gasoline. The British unrolled it and sank it on the bottom of the Channel to carry gas. I thought it was absolutely crazy. But they went to General Marshall on a personal appeal, and he told me to please go ahead with it. And so I pushed it. And, much to my surprise, it was a success.

"But these were exceptional, unforeseen items. Ninety percent of everything else went through on a routine basis. But if you had an emergency, if you had to get something out of the ordinary—landing craft, heavy ammunition when it was in short supply, something like this pipeline, tires, high-octane gasoline—all of these things had to have special treatment. And, in a sense, the only way you could give it this special treatment was to put it under a very strong man and have him fight it through. When these crises developed, you had to be able to go over to the War Production Board and say, 'Look, we want to take this material away from here and put it there.' Anytime you picked out a special program—or someone else did—you either were supporting it or fighting it. It couldn't succeed otherwise."

· 9 ·

America's Victory Program

CLAY'S FIRST TASK AS DIRECTOR OF MATERIEL WAS TO devise a coordinated program of military procurement. In March 1942, the War Department still had no firm idea of what it would take to defeat the Axis, much less a production schedule. There was no strategic plan upon which military needs could be computed, no determination of ultimate manpower requirements, and no resolution of the competing demands of Lend-Lease, the Army (which then included the Air Force), the Navy, and the home front. The only guidelines the military had were the dramatic production goals announced by President Roosevelt in his State of the Union message to Congress, January 6, 1942: sixty thousand airplanes, forty-five thousand tanks, and eight million deadweight tons of merchant shipping.

"Mr. Roosevelt had spoken up very forthrightly and said our program was sixty thousand airplanes a year and forty-five thousand tanks," said Clay. "And this was the Bible. Everybody was out to build sixty thousand planes and forty-five thousand tanks. But nobody at that stage of the game had considered, if you were going to have forty-five thousand tanks, how many people it would take to operate them, how many guns and how much ammunition you would need, what you would have to have in the way of gasoline to run the tanks—and, most important, whether the United States could really produce that in 1942."

Roosevelt's production targets provided the inspiration the United States badly needed in the dark days of 1942. But FDR had drawn his figures more or less out of a hat, believing that it was better to aim too high than too low. "Oh—the production people can do it if they really try," he told an incredulous Hopkins the night before delivering his address.

Rather than the careful product of systematic, well-reasoned, staff studies, Roosevelt had relied primarily on the judgment of Lord Beaverbrook, who visited Washington with Churchill in late December 1941, and who had cautioned the President against underestimating the capacity of American industry. Taking planned Canadian production for 1942 as a base, Beaverbrook estimated that the excess of U.S. over Canadian resources should permit the United States to produce fifteen times as much. According to Beaverbrook's rough figures, this would mean forty-five thousand tanks and sixty thousand planes—figures that Roosevelt relied on in drafting his speech.

Both the War Department and the newly created War Production Board took Roosevelt's goals at face value. At its first meeting, the WPB considered FDR's production aims and pronounced them "reasonably certain of attainment."

In the Army, General Somervell informed Marshall that "the items in the President's directive are indices of balanced production [already] contemplated." What Somervell meant was that Army planners already had been thinking of figures similar to the President's and that a new procurement plan would be drawn on the basis of FDR's goal of forty-five thousand tanks.

Using FDR's forty-five thousand tanks as their planning datum, the Army General Staff completed a new War Munitions Program on February 11, 1942. But whereas prewar Army planners had been too cautious, the military now assumed the sky was the limit: the War Munitions Program carried a price tag of $63 billion for the Army alone in 1942—almost twice what the War Production Board (in its most optimistic mood) considered American industry capable of producing.

For officials of the War Production Board, the Army's $63 billion program came as a shock. The President's goal for airplanes and tanks could be achieved, they maintained, but not in conjunction with the multitude of ancillary items that the Army needed to procure on a similar scale. At the heart of the matter was the question of a balanced program, for "balance" meant something different to everyone involved.

General Marshall's reorganization of the War Department coincided with these difficulties. "When the Services of Supply was established," said Clay, "the various branches had each built up their own procurement programs and were letting contracts and moving ahead more or less on their own. But the necessary coordination and the setting up of a true requirements program—and a production schedule based on that program—just had not evolved.

"The fact was that nobody had really established any requirements. To build up the requirements for an army, the first thing you have to start out with is a troop basis. And we had no troop basis. We didn't have any figures from the General Staff as to how many infantry divisions we would have, how many armored divisions, how much artillery—all of the things that go together to form an army."

Q: In other words, the War Munitions Plan you inherited simply arrived at its figures by computing what the Army would need to go along with the forty-five thousand tanks President Roosevelt requested?

CLAY: That's right. Ordinarily, the nation's strategic goals would determine how many armored units you would need, how many infantry divisions, how many artillery units, what caliber artillery, and so forth. But these goals had not yet been formulated.

"So this was the first thing I did: to establish what we thought was the troop basis of the Army. And this should not have been our job: this should have been given to us by the General Staff. But it was months before they ever determined the ultimate size of the Army, let alone its composition.

"Sometime in late 1943 the General Staff sent a memorandum over to us wanting to know by what authority we in the Services of Supply had determined what the troop composition of the Army would be. I wrote back and said, 'We haven't. But this is what we procured for, and if we hadn't done it you wouldn't have had any procurement.' "

Q: And you were given no guidance by the General Staff?

CLAY: I don't want to say we were given no guidance. We were given no *official* guidance. I knew the Operations people—Eisenhower and [Brigadier General Robert W.] Crawford—and I talked about it with them and told them what we were doing. Of course, the people in Operations changed all during the war, so you were really working with different people all the time. For line officers, the [War Department] Operations Division was just a stepping-stone to a combat command.

Clay raised the matter initially with Eisenhower, then assistant chief of staff (war plans), who then flashed the first distress signals about the War Munitions Program on February 20. "Careful analysis by those charged with running the economy," he wrote General Marshall, "determined that the total program could not be accomplished by 1943." Accordingly, Eisenhower recommended that the War Munitions Program be revised, and that a properly balanced program be developed "in accord with the strategic concept and the capacity of industry."

Admiral Ernest J. King, the crusty Chief of Naval Operations, agreed with Eisenhower. "It is of little use to go all out on tanks unless there are ships to ferry them, trained and equipped troops to man them, anti-aircraft guns and field artillery to protect them," he told Secretary Knox.

On March 4, Clay and Somervell, along with Donald Nelson, chairman of the War Production Board, attended a showdown meeting in the office of the Chief of Ordnance. Speaking for those charged with running American industry, Nelson pointed out to Somervell that the Army's $63 billion program simply could not be met. Instead, he recommended adjusting the President's objectives for 1942, "with a view to securing a better balance in the program as a whole."

Somervell, who had been chosen to head the Services of Supply because of his ability to accomplish what others thought impossible, was not convinced. On March 8, he asked Clay for a detailed list of President Roosevelt's production objectives. "The success or failure of the new Services of Supply," said Somervell, "will be judged, to a considerable extent, by the success or failure in meeting the objectives laid down by the President. You will remember that at our meeting with the Ordnance Department [March 4, 1942] it was stated that the objectives would not be reached in certain items. We cannot afford to make any such reply, or to take any such attitude towards the instructions of The Commander in Chief."

The difficulty, of course, came in recognizing what truly were the outside limits of U.S. production and what were simply outdated estimates. And Clay frankly had no idea. But four days of discussions with the Army's branch chiefs and officials at the War Production Board convinced Clay that Roosevelt's goals were unattainable and had to be modified. On March 12, Clay sent Somervell two memoranda, one setting forth possible reductions in presidential objectives, the other indicating the measures necessary if the targets established by Roosevelt were to be met. "These memoranda are submitted to you in separate form," wrote Clay, "in order that you may have a complete statement . . . of the effect on the program . . . under either . . . course of action."

In each memo, Clay made the same point: the Army's War Munitions Program could not be achieved, and President Roosevelt's production goals should be reduced to obtain a balanced fighting force. FDR's forty-five thousand tanks, said Clay, were 50 percent more than the Army required in 1942, whereas the President's target for antitank guns amounted to only 30 percent of the Army's anticipated need. That, and similar imbalances, made prompt revision essential. Equally important, the tank designs then in production were far from satisfactory. To devote excessive materiel to their production seemed an unnecessary waste.

Somervell, whose first impulse when told that something could not be done was to suspect someone of malingering, was shaken by Clay's report, but still not convinced. On his own initiative, Clay took the issue to the Army-Navy Munitions Board, where he sat as the War Department's representative. Ferdinand Eberstadt, the Wall Street banker who presided over the Munitions Board, accepted Clay's point immediately and gave board approval for a modified set of production goals on March 25.

The joint U.S.-British tank committee, which was also meeting in

Washington, weighed in strongly on Clay's side when it reported in mid-March that total Allied tank requirements for 1942 (including eight thousand earmarked for the Soviet Union) would equal only 21,415. That was less than half of what FDR had asked for.

The combination of Clay's own strong feelings, plus the messages from Eberstadt and the joint tank committee, finally convinced Somervell that FDR's production goals would have to be modified. On March 26, he authorized Clay to prepare a memorandum to that effect for Under Secretary Patterson. Clay carefully pointed out to Patterson that "the proposed shift [in presidential objectives] would not represent a decrease in production but, on the contrary, would probably increase production and certainly would increase the fire power that could be brought to bear on the enemy."

Patterson accepted Clay's argument, and a memorandum of agreement between the Under Secretary and the WPB's Donald Nelson was drafted by Clay, preparatory to carrying the case to the White House. Clay suggested a joint approach. Nelson would advise FDR of the economic infeasibility of the goals contained in his State of the Union message, while General Marshall, for the War Department, would explain the military items the Army wanted to substitute.

Nelson agreed, and on March 30 drafted a letter to the White House for Somervell's approval. Unfortunately, Nelson, who was reluctant to be the bearer of bad tidings to the President, waffled to such an extent that the military began to doubt his candor. Rather than ask Roosevelt to revise his original goals, Nelson indirectly blamed the military for demanding a balanced program. "If it is your instruction that the specific objectives which you set are to be adhered to," he wrote the President, "I shall request the Services to submit new requirement schedules . . . in general correspondence with our agreement as to what constitutes a maximum production effort."

Somervell, whose patience was already sorely tried by six years of all-out effort (to control his temper, Somervell would go into an adjoining office and walk violently up and down), penciled his dissatisfaction on the margin of Nelson's letter and returned it to him. Wrote Somervell:

> We are asking for a revision [of presidential objectives] on the basis of our knowledge backed up by what you advised. This does not state the

> question. What we want is to tell the President the military situation and have your backing on the economic side. [Your] letter is not in conformity with our understanding of agreements reached . . . and not at all conducive to the cooperation we must have.

Pulled up short by Somervell, Nelson advised Roosevelt that, "in my judgment, it will not be possible to provide all of the items set forth in your list of objectives, and at the same time produce everything else now called for. . . . Under these circumstances, I feel that I must come to you for instructions upon what is clearly a matter of major policy."

On April 1, the War Department's position was made known to the White House in a letter that Clay had written for General Marshall's signature. Marshall told the President that the Army's "serious deficiency in armored cars, artillery and antitank weapons" could only be remedied by reducing his goals for tanks and anti-aircraft guns. It was a bitter pill for FDR, who saw his production targets as the one bright spot in the dismal days of 1942. For Roosevelt's benefit, Marshall again pointed out that "the proposed modification does not represent a decrease in production. . . . It would meet all requests . . . now foreseen for tanks and, at the same time, would provide equipment for a balanced military force. It would strengthen our offensive power as it would increase the fire power which could be developed on the battlefront."

To ensure that FDR got the point of their plea, Clay prepared a large chart showing what the Army would have if the President's goals were achieved—and what it would lack, especially artillery and antitank guns. Then, to be doubly sure Roosevelt understood the problem, Clay entrusted both the letter and the chart to Harry Hopkins, who quickly saw the point of the changes the War Department was asking for.

"Mr. Hopkins got the President's personal OK," said Clay, "although he never gave it a public OK." The fact was that Roosevelt did not want to make public that he was retreating from his announced goals of forty-five thousand tanks—a point the War Department readily appreciated.

When Hopkins informed Clay in mid-April that FDR had agreed to the modifications the Army wanted, Clay drafted the President's

RECOMMENDED ADJUSTMENTS IN PRESIDENTIAL OBJECTIVES

Item	Estimated Production to Meet Presidential Objectives and Additional Estimated Production for Other Major Items of Program — Quantities Required for a Balanced Program, Calendar Year 1942 (1)	Production in Excess of Balanced Program Requirements, Calendar Year 1942 (2)	Conversion of Excess Production to Provide a Balanced Program, Calendar Year 1942 (3)	Estimated Cumulative Production to Provide Balanced Requirements by Dec 31, 1943, Calendar Years 1942 & 1943 (4)	Recommended Presidential Objectives Required to Achieve the Balanced Programs Shown in Columns 3 & 4 — 1942 (5)	1943 (6)	Remarks (7)
Light Tanks 19,500	10,588	8,912	10,588	28,532	10,588	17,944	
Medium Tanks 25,000	14,000	11,000	14,000	49,178	14,000	35,178	
Heavy Tanks 500	115	385	115	115	115	115	
90mm. AA 5,400	2,800	2,600	2,800	8,600	2,800	5,800	
37 & 40mm. AA 14,600	9,800	4,800	9,800 (a)	38,400 (b)	9,800	28,600	(a) Includes 3,100 S.P. Mounts for 40mm. Guns AA. (b) Includes 15,100 S.P. Mounts for 40mm. Guns AA.
37mm. AT 17,000	17,000		17,000 (c)	47,000 (d)	17,000	30,000	(c) Includes 2539 S.P. Mounts (d) Includes 10,788 S.P. Mounts
3" or 57mm. AT 12,000	3700	8,300	8,300 (e) 3,700	26,900 (f)	8,300	18,600	(e) Includes 7,241 S.P. Mounts (f) Includes 15,250 S.P. Mounts.
Cal. .30 MG. 275,000	275,000		275,000	605,000	275,000	330,000	
Cal. .50 MG. 125,000	125,000		125,000	295,000	125,000	170,000	
75mm. How. SP 1,839	312	1,527	1,839	5,723	Estimated Production in Other Major Items: 3,050	5,886	
75mm How. FLD. 0	0		0	310			
75mm. PK 1213	258	955	1,213	2,903			
105mm. How. Wheeled 3035	3035		3,035	7,299	5,817	14,558	

Excess Converted to Shortage To get

Clay's Recommended Adjustments in Presidential Objectives

official reply. In place of the original forty-five thousand tanks, Roosevelt now asked for 46,523 tracked vehicles (tanks, armored cars, and self-propelled artillery), "of which 24,700 shall be tanks." On May 1, President Roosevelt dispatched Clay's letter to Donald Nelson. "The accomplishment of the above objectives," FDR instructed Nelson, "must include the complementary weapons . . . required . . . for offensive action. . . . However, a balance in these latter items must not be attained at the expense of the specific items which I have enumerated herein."

Roosevelt's modification of his State of the Union goals gave those charged with arming America targets they could reasonably achieve. Not only was the number of tanks reduced, but FDR's call for sixty thousand airplanes was cut by 25 percent, and a balanced procurement program (known officially as the Army's Supply Program) was set in motion.

Clay's success in altering FDR's production targets saved America valuable time and raw materials. It avoided the worst of a production situation in which scarce machine tools and facilities were devoted to items not really needed by the services—a contrast, again, to the production pattern followed in Nazi Germany under Hitler's absolute direction—and allowed the services to procure for a "balanced" fighting force commensurate with American industry's capacity to produce. In a curious way, the Army's prewar, tradition-bound seniority system had permitted Clay the necessary confidence in his own judgment to confront Somervell (and the President), for it had afforded him the luxury of his own opinions. As Secretary Stimson remarked repeatedly in his diary, the United States was extremely well served during World War II by its professional soldiers. "They are in many respects the best educated men in the country in regard to the basic principles of our Constitution," wrote Stimson.

One of Clay's hallmarks, both as Director of Materiel and later in Germany, was his ability to recruit and retain a professional staff of the highest caliber. Clay eschewed yes-men and sycophants. He sought expertise and independence. The qualities Clay saw in himself, he looked for in his staff. And, like Somervell, he was ruthlessly demanding.

"When I first took over the job," said Clay, "there was already some staff there, and then, as we began to build up, I went out to get people, either using some of the people we had or going to people that I had known before. For example, I wanted to get a production expert, so I tried to get O. I. Hunt of General Motors. Well, he didn't want the job, but he recommended Chuck Skinner of Oldsmobile.

"We had Bill Marbury of Baltimore as our legal counsel, and through Bill we got a group of brilliant young lawyers. Not entirely through him either, because Judge Patterson was a great help too. Now, this is the way these things operate. For example, General [Albert J.] Browning [president of United Wall Paper Factories of Chicago], whom I brought over to head up my purchasing section, had come to Washington when it first looked like we were going to war. And Brigadier General Bill Draper, who had been in the same Wall Street firm as Forrestal, was over in Hawaii as an assistant division commander, and I pulled him back."

Q: Had you known him before?

CLAY: Only by reputation. Then there was Bill Harrison [vice president of AT&T] and Doug MacKeachie [purchasing director of the Great Atlantic and Pacific Tea Company] over at the War Production Board. They came over because they were unhappy in the War Production Board, and most of them were people who had become friends of mine in the course of our operations.

Q: Why did they want to leave the WPB?

CLAY: Both of these men were doers, and I think they felt they could do more with the Services of Supply than they could with the War Production Board. And both of them wanted the satisfaction of being in uniform during the war. I think that had something to do with it too.

Q: In choosing your staff, why did you stick so much to big business and Wall Street and the big law firms?

CLAY: Well, I don't think we really did. Most of these people became associated with big business and Wall Street after they left us, and not before. Many of them were young lawyers, like Bob Bowie of Harvard and Don McLean, who runs the Leahy Clinic up in Boston. These were the type of brilliant young men that we had.

"When it came to production, obviously we went to the people that had experience in these things. I had to put into production schedule the largest procurement program the world had ever seen. Where would I find somebody to do that? I went to General Motors. I think this was logical. If you'd gone to our shipping division, you'd find that they had people from the shipping industry in it, or that the personnel division—which, among other things, was concerned with enforcing the standards of the Wagner Labor-Relations Act—had labor people in it. And so on. Our job was production. And where do you find people who are knowledgeable about it except from the big companies? But by and large the businessmen who came with us became top industrialists later in their career. I think for a man to have had a position of responsibility in the greatest undertaking that the United States has ever had was certainly a help to him. For the benefit of our country, it would have been far more sinister for him not to have been there."

Q: President Eisenhower, when he left office, warned of the dangers of a military-industrial complex. To what extent were you concerned about that in 1942?

CLAY: I don't know that General Eisenhower ever meant that as strongly as it was taken. I don't know otherwise either. There can be no question but that the manufacturer of a B-52 and the general commanding the Strategic Air Command have a common objective to get more B-52s. But the problems of the military-industrial complex are a recent phenomenon. We don't have the time to produce military weapons that we had in World War I. We couldn't have had so much time in World War II, were it not for our fine Allies.

Q: Do you think there are any aspects of that that might have been handled differently?

CLAY: No, I think you've got a different situation today. You must remember this. We had the same kind of a buildup in World War I. The minute World War I was over, we demobilized. We didn't build anything of a military nature. And the relationship between the military and industry just disappeared, because we were practically doing no procurement. World War II, when it ended, we did about the same thing, and for a couple of years we let our defense establishment go very much downhill. We took a look at ourselves in 1947—two years after the war—and we had only a handful of B-29s, which was the new plane of the period, and we weren't ordering any more. And all along the line we were running into shortages of equipment and manpower. And we began a buildup.

"Then came Korea, and we went into a bigger buildup. And then, of course, came Vietnam. This is the first time in history that we've had years and years of major military procurement. There's no precedent with which to compare it. The relationships formed during World War II would have all disappeared in two or three years if we hadn't embarked on a national defense program of tremendous magnitude.

"Traditionally, we always thought that defense production would not be predominant in the thinking and action of American industry. But the airplane has complicated the picture. Until the airplane came along, you were using U.S. Steel and the automobile companies, the Remingtons and the Olins and so on, to take on defense contracts without it ever becoming the predominant part of their business, so that they were never really a defense industry.

"But then the aircraft industry came along, and with military demands so great, our airplane companies became defense companies. Then you have the shipbuilders and submarine-makers. This is highly specialized work. It's so enormous that an existing company can no longer take it on as a part of their business. Thus you saw the growth of these predominantly defense industries.

"This was further enhanced by the space program. It's paid for by the government, and it's being built and used by the same people, so that when both defense and space spending fall off, you have the same group of people that are being hurt. And they are going to exert pressure. Not only as manufacturers—and don't make any mistake about it, it's not the manufacturer who exerts pressure in Congress. It's that workman who is laid off. And the community. If the payroll is gone, what happens to the grocery stores, and what happens to the butcher? This is something we have not solved. What do we do with the defense industry in the period when it is not building defense? And it's a very important problem. It no longer can be solved by assuming that it is a relatively small part of the defense effort and ignoring it."

Q: And the pernicious aspects?

CLAY: What do you do? This is the old theme that munitions-makers cause war. I don't see what in God's world they do to create war that we wouldn't know about and quickly take in hand. On the other side of the picture, their ability to influence legislation—authorizing more airplanes and the appropriations to provide these airplanes—is certainly used all the time. But if you examine our defense industries in World War II, particularly in view of contract renegotiation, nobody has yet been able to find a case of excess profit.

Clay's concern for the military-industrial complex stayed with him. Throughout his life, he refused to work for defense contractors, or any company that did a substantial business with the Pentagon. Clay believed it was "unseemly"—a favorite word of his—and he could not understand how a retired military officer could do it. Clay's attitudes were formed in an era of American idealism. He genuinely believed that the United States was unique, and in his view one of the things that set America apart from other countries was its high standard of public integrity. Government service was a trust, and a military officer had a special responsibility to serve his country proudly. It was old-fashioned and slightly sentimental, but Clay believed it deeply.

· 10 ·

Lend-Lease

> We have to deal with big leaguers here who know the game from A to Z, and they are quick to seize upon any weak spot in the statement of our requirements.
>
> *Cable, Lieutenant General Maurice Pope* to Ottawa, November 14, 1943

FROM THE BEGINNING OF THE AMERICAN REARMAMENT program in 1939, competition for equipment between the U.S. Army and America's Allies was intense. During the height of the Battle of Britain, for example, General Marshall resisted delivery of much-needed planes to England, fearful of denuding America's all-but-defenseless shores. The passage of the Lend-Lease Act in March 1941 intensified the Allies' demands. In fact, of the armaments included in the War Department's pre–Pearl Harbor procurement program, over 80 percent were earmarked for America's allies.

With Pearl Harbor, the needs of the American Army became paramount, and in January 1942, at the ARCADIA Conference in Washington, Roosevelt and Churchill established the Combined Munitions Assignment Board (with Harry Hopkins as chairman) to allocate military supplies between Britain and the United States. At General Marshall's firm insistence, the board was made responsible to the Combined Chiefs of Staff, for, as Marshall forthrightly told Roosevelt, he "could not continue to assume the responsibility of Chief of Staff" if the assignment of munitions was not under his control. Churchill, who had wanted to exercise direct supervision, reluctantly accepted the arrangement "for a month," but was never happy with it and repeatedly tried to circumvent the control that the Combined Chiefs enjoyed.

Nevertheless, at least with regard to allocating supplies between the United States and Great Britain, the Munitions Assignment Board worked smoothly and efficiently. The principal difficulty arose within the U.S. Army itself, for there were two parallel bodies in the War Department determining military requirements: the Division of Requirements and Resources, which reported to Clay, and the Division of Foreign Aid, under Brigadier General Henry Aurand, which handled Lend-Lease. Both were coordinate and coequal. With responsibility divided, friction was inevitable. The Division of Foreign Aid believed that Clay and Somervell were unresponsive to the needs of America's Allies; the leaders of the Services of Supply believed that those charged with foreign aid were pressing Allied claims at the expense of the American Army.

"The whole trouble with Foreign Aid," Somervell wrote Clay, "is that it is an entirely separate and uncoordinated outfit without any knowledge of, or interest in, the supply problem as a whole."

Worse still, Somervell and General Aurand shared an abiding dislike for each other. Aurand had been head of Foreign Aid since its inception and before that a senior member of the War Department's G-4 (supply) division. Accustomed to dealing at the highest policy-making level (he was a 1915 classmate of Eisenhower and Bradley), Aurand played little role in the creation of the Services of Supply and resented the subordination of his division to it.

Aurand was a strikingly handsome West Point ordnance officer with a natural flair for political maneuvering. But to Somervell, Aurand was a prima donna: an unreliable subordinate who sought personal aggrandizement through his role as chief of Foreign Aid. The issue came to a head in June 1942, when Aurand incautiously accepted appointment as executive director of the Combined Production and Resources Board—a body set up at British suggestion under the War Production Board's Donald Nelson to allocate strategic materials between the United States and Great Britain. The British, who were still smoldering over the decision of the ARCADIA Conference to place the Munitions Assignment Board under the Combined Chiefs, and who were continually seeking ways around it, saw the new board as a means of removing strategic materials from the control of General Marshall and the War Department.

It was one of those jurisdictional battles for control, to which Washington was so prone in 1942. Donald Nelson, who was having his own difficulties with the military, also welcomed the new board, since it raised his status to a par with the Combined Chiefs of Staff. But the division of responsibility between the Munitions Assignment Board, chaired by Hopkins, and the Combined Production and Resources Board, chaired by Nelson, was never clear, and a showdown battle for jurisdiction was inevitable.

The Combined Production and Resources Board convened for the first time on June 20, 1942, with Nelson presiding. The War Department was represented by Aurand, who, as executive director, presented a British request that ten thousand tons of armor-piercing steel shot be transferred from the September quota of the American Army to the British. Aurand recommended approval, and Nelson readily agreed—promising to forward the decision to the War Production Board's Requirements Committee, the body that had final control over such requests (and on which Clay sat as the Army's Director of Materiel).

When the Requirements Committee convened for its regular meeting that afternoon, Clay was informed of the Combined Board's action, and objected heatedly. Such matters, he maintained, were to be decided in the Munitions Assignment Board, under Hopkins, not in the new CPRB. At Clay's insistence, the Requirements Committee deferred action on Nelson's request, and Clay returned to the Pentagon, where he protested vigorously what had transpired. There could not be two bodies with equal jurisdiction making contradictory decisions, he said.

Somervell solved the problem immediately by promoting Aurand to major general and sending him to Chicago to command the Sixth Service Area. The Foreign Aid Division (renamed the International

Division) was placed under Clay—where it remained for the duration of the war—and the Combined Production and Resources Board was relegated to a purely advisory role under Hopkins and the MAB.

"Aurand was a damn fine, capable officer," said Clay. "He was moved because he couldn't get along with his superior officer, and that's a damn good reason for moving anybody. Foreign Aid had always been quite a problem. It had been in operation for some time, and it looked like it was doing better in terms of supplies than the American Army. General Somervell decided that this wasn't a job for competition."

Q: So, in effect, Somervell was moving the Foreign Aid Division one echelon lower?
CLAY: Well, I guess you could call it that. He moved it from reporting directly to him to report through me, just as he did procurement. I'm not sure whether he moved them down one or me up one.

Clay's control of the International Division ensured that Lend-Lease would not take precedence over the needs of the U.S. Army. The Munitions Assignment Board under Hopkins, on which Clay sat as Somervell's representative, determined final Lend-Lease policy, and Clay implemented it for the Services of Supply. The long-range requirements of the U.S. Army and America's Allies were consolidated in the Army Supply Program (which was administered by Clay) and, curiously, because of Clay's long and friendly association with Harry Hopkins, the net effect was to improve Lend-Lease deliveries rather than curtail them. The incessant back-biting within the Services of Supply, which had embittered the atmosphere, ended abruptly, and military aid became fully integrated within the Army's supply system.

Averell Harriman, then in charge of Lend-Lease in London, reports that once Clay took charge of military Lend-Lease things moved with gusto. "Lucius was always so goddamned direct that it was easy to do business with him," said Harriman. "He was above the petty jealousies of Washington. He dealt with issues—not on a department-versus-department basis. Whenever I had problems in Lend-Lease and I went to Clay, I always got a fair shake. He was terrifically informed, very determined, very sound. I had a tremendous respect for him. And so did Hopkins. I know, because on Lend-Lease I reported through Hopkins."

Q: And the actual supply allocations for Lend-Lease were made by the Munitions Assignment Board?

CLAY: Yes and no. The general allocations were made by the individual services, meeting with British representatives in Washington. When we differed and were not in agreement, then we went to the Munitions Assignment Board for the final allocation. Theoretically, the British had equal representation with us on the board, with the exception that Mr. Hopkins presided. But we never went to the board where there was agreement. Only where there was disagreement. And we agreed about 95 percent of the time.

Q: And Mr. Hopkins?

CLAY: Mr. Hopkins was the chairman of the board. Actually, our problems weren't with the British so much as among the Americans. We had a representative of the General Staff always present—a [Brigadier] General [Patrick H.] Tansey, a mad Irishman who was a classmate of mine—and he would get up in a meeting, with all the British there, and charge me with being pro-British. Then we had an American admiral by the name of [Joseph M.] Reeves, who hated the British with a passionate hate, and he would chime in.

"The trouble was that at this time the British were the only ones fighting. Our armies were still getting ready. And I recognized that we would never fight if they didn't get the supplies. But I also recognized that Mr. Roosevelt and Mr. Churchill were always going to compromise issues and that we were not making life any easier for them if we couldn't find reconciliation and ways to do it down below.

"So, by and large, I had agreed with my British opposite before the meetings as to what we were willing to do and what we were not willing to do on military items. We were working every day with [Lieutenant] General [George N.] Macready [chief of the British Joint Staff Mission]—my staff and his staff—and I never made any bones with him as to what our production figures would likely be and what we thought we could let them have. The only time anything would come up as an argument before the Munitions Assignment Board was when he was trying to get more than I was willing to give him, and actually that didn't happen very often, because I tried to give them a fair break and I think they appreciated that. As a matter of fact, Macready and Sir Walter Vinning and Robb Sinclair remained good friends of mine after the war. Vinning was the ablest of the lot. Macready was not very popular in Washington, whereas Vinning was—which always has a lot to do with how successful you are."

Q: You said General Tansey was a classmate of yours.

CLAY: As a matter of fact, he is the godfather of my eldest son. But at this time, I was thoroughly disgusted with his position—as I'm sure he was with mine. Of course, his position would not have been supported by the people whom he worked for if I had gone to them. Because Tansey was a classmate, I never carried the issue to [Major General Thomas T.] Handy [Army G-3] or General Marshall. But Hopkins would have ripped them apart if that had been accepted as the official Army position. He didn't pay any attention to it. He accepted what I said as the official Army position, and that made Tansey even madder.

"Don't forget, we were working for some pretty hard-driving people who wouldn't take no for an answer when it came to supplying our own troops. Whenever I'd agree to give anything to the British or the other Allies, I'd have to go back up and convince General Marshall that we hadn't sold our own troops down the river. If General Tansey had had his way, we wouldn't have given a rifle to the British."

Q: And Russian Lend-Lease?

CLAY: This was handled in the Soviet Protocol Committee, which Bill Batt chaired, although under Mr. Hopkins's general direction. This was an entirely different picture. With the Soviets, we concluded a series of bilateral protocols spelling out in detail the items they would receive. It was not a continuing arrangement like the Munitions Assignment Board.

"The trouble was that as early as 1943, when we were negotiating the third Russian [Lend-Lease] Protocol, the Russians were no longer interested in military equipment. They still wanted trucks, but their real demand was for railroad signal equipment, locomotive engines, machine tools, all sorts of devices to help restore their economy but which could not possibly contribute to this particular war.

"This is where I ran into my first argument with Lend-Lease. Bill Batt was determined that the Russians were going to be helped, so we used to have battles royal in that committee. As a matter of fact, we fought the third Russian Protocol down every alley we could (without breaking up the meeting), on the basis that it was building them up for after the war, not during the war. By contrast, we knew the military equipment that we wanted and were ordering, and that the British wanted and were ordering, was going to be given to troops and used to fight a war. And you couldn't figure out how railroad electrical equipment or signal equipment, sent over to electrify the Russian railroads, could possibly be shipped and installed in less than two or three years, and you had to think of an awfully long-drawn-out war for that to be of any value."

Q: In other words, you were looking to the postwar period?

CLAY: No. Not to the postwar period then. But if you sent railway electrical equipment, you knew that even if they got it, it would be two or three years before they could electrify the signal systems on their railroads. You were tying up shipping, you were tying up copper and other materials that were in short supply—all to give something to a country that might very well need it to sustain a war effort two or three years down the road, but at the expense of your own immediate war effort. It didn't make sense. Later, when the Russians came in with their last request, it was my contention that they were asking us for rehabilitation of their country after the war, and that this wasn't within our province as a military aid committee.

"Mr. Hopkins was the compromiser on it. We fought Bill Batt to the point where the Russians were being ugly about it, and at that stage of the game Mr. Hopkins stepped in and said 'Let's go.' When we finished, and the agreement went over to Mr. Stimson to sign, he flew into a rage. He thought I'd given the Russians too much. He sent for me, and he was very harsh in his criticism of what I had accepted. Very harsh. About two or three hours later, he called me back up to his office.

"He said, 'I've signed the agreement.' And he said, 'Do you know what happened? Harry Hopkins called me up and told me what a son of a bitch you had been all during this thing, and that they had cut this thing down to get you as the Army representative to go along. And Hopkins thinks it has been cut back too far.' At which stage Mr. Stimson began to see the problem and, as he always did with his insight, he called me back immediately. And for him it was an apology. Mr. Stimson didn't apologize to anybody. But for him it was an apology. He knew damn well after Hopkins called that he was going to sign it, and if he was going to sign it, I think he began to realize the pressures under which we had been operating."

Clay's insistence that the Russians justify the nonmilitary items requested in the third Protocol should not be misinterpreted. It reveals no deep-seated suspicion of the Soviet Union. "If you think that behind all of this," said Clay, "was a fear that we were helping build them up so they could fight us, it was a very, very remote consideration." Clay's opposition was simply an attempt to maximize the production potential of the United States for the war then under way. In fact, once the Protocol was approved, the British—who were indeed suspicious of Russian motives at that point—requested that the military items be reviewed once again by the Munitions Assignment Board, on which they were represented. Clay replied forthrightly to Hopkins that "such a procedure is unnecessary and would unduly delay the accomplishment of the Protocol."

In fact, Clay's files are replete with messages to subordinates to expedite the shipment to Russia of precisely the type of equipment he had opposed before the Protocol was approved. When Lieutenant General L. G. Rudenko, chief of the Russian mission in Washington, requested a variety of steam shovels and cranes "for the rehabilitation of the liberated areas of our country," Clay quickly agreed.

"Let's try to do this," Clay penciled in the margin of Rudenko's letter as he sent it to General Edgerton for action. When Edgerton replied that the shipments of cranes to the USSR "have already exceeded the offering for the first half of [the] Protocol period," Clay chided him for being "too legalistic."

"After all," wrote Clay, "we want to help USSR with what it needs to support the war and it would seem fair to recognize the importance of cranes and shovels." Clay instructed Edgerton to round up whatever used cranes were available— "by phone or by having them condemned —while we are thrashing out protocol technicalities."

Clay was equally ready to help America's other Allies with special requests. Lieutenant General Maurice Pope, chairman of the Canadian Joint Staff Mission to Washington, reports that Clay made extraordinary efforts to obtain scarce ball bearings for Canada (which, it turned out, Canada didn't need). "If I am put in the clink because of this," Clay told Pope, "I hope you will rescue me with a Canadian guard."

Lend-Lease was but one of many pressing problems during the bleak spring of 1942. "Very early in the game," said Clay, "I was caught with the problem that we were running out of rubber. And I called the heads of all of our rubber companies and most of our large oil companies and brought them to Washington for a conference. It was quite obvious that there was no possibility of getting enough natural rubber for our needs, and the problem was how fast could we get into the production of artificial rubber. This required cooperation from the oil companies, because it took certain byproducts of the refining process to make the chemicals that went into the making of the artificial rubber.

"After the meeting, when we found out their problems and really were determined to set up a priority program which would enable them to go ahead, I discovered that they were completely bogged down by their inability to get materials. At the time, I thought this was the greatest bottleneck that we had. Anyway, I decided this was the type of problem where Bernard Baruch's past experience from World War I would be very helpful, and I got into an airplane and flew to New York to see him."

Q: Was this the first time you had met Mr. Baruch?

CLAY: That was the first time I talked to him about the war. After that, the President moved in and asked Mr. Baruch to develop a plan for the production of rubber. Mr. Baruch came down to Washington with John Hancock [of Lehman Brothers], made his report, and developed a program. And under this program, Mr. [William M.] Jeffers of Union Pacific was brought in to be the "Rubber Czar," with authority just below that of the chairman of the War Production Board. He could establish special priorities and do whatever was necessary to get rubber going. And he did.

"After that I came to know Mr. Baruch very, very well. Whenever any major problem would come up that went back to a similar problem in World War I, I would often go up to see him. There was still an awful lot of wisdom in that experienced old head—if you could separate the wisdom from the vanity. And that's what you had to do.

"As for rubber, Jeffers came in and did a great job. He got us rubber. But after he had done that job (and in the process we found that we had gained more access to raw rubber than we thought we could), we were running short of high-octane gas. And to make high-octane gasoline required the same type of fittings and special components as synthetic rubber. But Mr. Jeffers wouldn't give way. So here we were—the ones who had started the fight for rubber—we had to go in and have a battle with Mr. Jeffers to divert some of the equipment and materials that was going into rubber to get high-octane gasoline."

Q: Did Jeffers back down?

CLAY: Hell, no. He fought it to the bitter end. He was finally overruled. And I'm not trying to be critical of him. He did a hell of a job. He got us rubber. But when we tried to call him off, he was still going to provide us with rubber. And if we were going to be short of rubber, it was not going to be because he backed down.

In spite of his responsible position, Clay continued to be disappointed with his Washington assignment. On September 28, 1942, he commiserated with his West Point classmate Sam Sturgis, then on Mississippi River duty, later to become Chief of Engineers. "As a matter of fact," wrote Clay, "if I could find an Engineer Combat Regiment with a sick Colonel and the Engineers would have me, I would very gladly change the [brigadier general's] insignia on my shoulder and start out. . . ."

Two months later, Clay wrote classmate Pat Casey, who was with MacArthur in Australia, that he was "doomed to stay in Washington a long time unless I get fired, and I don't even see any prospects of that at the moment. It would be worth deliberately doing," Clay added, "if it were not for the fact that no one of us can let down that way. Washington is filled with families with husbands at various fronts, and I am beginning to feel like a draft dodger every time I walk down the street."

Overall, however, Clay thought the war effort was going well. He concluded his letter to Casey on an optimistic note:

> While, to the ordinary observer, Washington appears somewhat in a state of confusion, I really think that orderly procedure is developing here and there and that by and large the situation is greatly improving. Production is good although not as large in volume as we expect to reach. Civilian restrictions are increasing, however somewhat slowly, and that is an encouraging sign.

The production and procurement organization that Clay created literally converted America into the arsenal of democracy that Roosevelt had proclaimed. And it was America's productive capacity, harnessed for war, that so decisively helped turn the tide of battle. But

Clay's staff was small by wartime standards, and those in responsible positions exercised direct hands-on control. The vast procurement infrastructure that drains defense dollars in the 1990s simply had not evolved. The result was that Clay was able to retain personal control of virtually all aspects of the procurement picture, and when things went wrong, he could take immediate action to correct them.

The idea of direct personal control came naturally to Clay. In his view, a commander must know more about the status of his organization than anyone else in it. Old Colonel Woodruff had taught Clay that at Camp Humphreys. As a result, throughout his career Clay was a firm believer in undiluted military responsibility. He had little patience in 1942 for schemes then being hatched to employ what we now call "defense consultants," and he mocked the idea of turning the control of military operations into a "group responsibility." As he wrote to Deputy Chief of Staff Joseph McNarney in September 1942 about one such proposal:

> [The proposal] defines the primary duty of these civilian analysis groups to be the analysis of battle experience to "indicate the real merits of various tactics, items of equipment, scientific procedures and methods of training." The civilian analyst is to become "the auxiliary brain of the commander." . . . The head of the group must be of "such age, experience, and high standing that he can deal with his commander on a basis of substantial equality." The group itself must be composed of "brilliant, energetic young men with specialized training in science, mathematics, or other specialties."

"Apparently," Clay continued, "the head of this group will be a super–Chief of Staff, and the group itself will cut across all other staff groups in its access to the commander to whom it is attached." This proposal, said Clay, "must be based on a belief . . . that our Army is officered by inferior personnel lacking in the intellectual capacity requisite for the prosecution of the war. . . ."

> It is difficult to understand why operations analysis can be conducted more advantageously by men without uniforms. Perhaps the intellectual capacities of our commanders need to be watched by civilian analysts, even as the Red Army at one time placed commissars in its organization to determine the political loyalties of its officer personnel. If we have reached that point, we have lost the war before we have started to fight it.

> My own experience with the statisticians, analysts, economists, and the many other "ists" with new formulae each day to solve the problems of war economy even in the field of military decisions, convinces me that our present need is to adhere ever more closely to the well-established channels of military command and to avoid the pitfalls of a new order.

Clay's skepticism was well placed. A postwar generation of defense consultants has removed most strategic thinking from the military services, spawning a growth industry of alarming proportions and imparting an abstract artificiality to America's military planning. The officers of Clay's generation retained responsibility for military strategy; authority was not diluted, and, in a curious way, the ultimate political control of the President and the Secretary of War was enhanced. They could decide major policy questions, and military execution was automatic. Unhindered by a legion of civilian analysts, the military moved confidently to accomplish the tasks it was given.

· 11 ·

The Battle of Washington

> No appointment was more strategic or more fortunate. An officer of unlimited courage and crystalline resolution, Clay happened also to be a virtuoso at the art of General Staff planning of material flow and logistical support. His was the responsibility for budgeting enough of everything in the right place at the right time for each fighting unit; and his was the responsibility for transforming paper budgets into fire power.
>
> Eliot Janeway,
> *The Struggle for Survival*

BY LATE 1942, THE COORDINATION OF MILITARY PROCUREMENT, Lend-Lease, and the various production goals set by President Roosevelt was well under way. But the more prickly problem of balancing military needs with those of the home front remained largely unresolved, an unfortunate side-effect of Roosevelt's understandable desire to keep the reins of domestic politics in his own hands.

Before Pearl Harbor, FDR steadfastly resisted a

rising tide of high-level advice that he turn economic responsibilities over to one man. "Who is this 'Czar' or 'Poobah' or 'Alkoond of Swat'?" he petulantly asked. "The final responsibility is mine, and I can't delegate it."

The result was a succession of temporary agencies, each independent of the permanent government structure, their duties ill-defined—free to make the best of it in the everyday whirl of Washington politics. Finally, in January 1942, under the impact of total war, FDR yielded and established the War Production Board, with Donald Nelson as chairman. Nelson was delegated full power to direct America's wartime economy, although, as Justice Felix Frankfurter prophetically wrote Roosevelt, "It took Lincoln three years to discover Grant, and you may not have hit on your production Grant first crack out of the box."

Nelson was not a felicitous choice. As Frankfurter was well aware, he was a man whose reputation had outrun his ability. A former vice president for sales of Sears-Roebuck, Nelson had been sent to Washington in 1940 by the president of Sears (General) Robert Wood to assist Treasury Secretary Morgenthau in handling British and French defense purchases. Morgenthau had originally requested Sears' vice president for plants and factories, E. Penn Brooks, but General Wood declined to let Brooks go and sent Nelson instead, apparently without bothering to consult Nelson beforehand.

After coming to Washington, Nelson moved adroitly up the preparedness pecking order, a businessman with a faint New Dealish flavor. As more experienced industrialists, such as General Motors' William ("Big Bill") Knudsen, and seasoned labor leaders like Sidney Hillman were consumed by the Roosevelt administration's political infighting in 1941, Nelson emerged after Pearl Harbor as the least objectionable candidate to become czar of the home front: the lowest common denominator among Washington's mobilization policy-makers. Nelson's appointment reflected the hale and hearty manner of a successful salesman. But that bonhomie concealed a disturbing inability to act decisively, to rule in favor of one claimant against another, or to provide the moral leadership for a home front asked to make continuing sacrifices.

"Donald Nelson was a compromiser and something of a trimmer," said his one-time deputy, WPB vice chairman Harold Boeschenstein.

"He had an awfully hard time making up his mind. He had a quick mind, but he couldn't make hard decisions. And you couldn't be sure he was going to stay put after you thought he had made it up. You couldn't get him nailed down. You never knew just where he stood, and too often you couldn't get a decision when you needed one."

No sooner was Nelson installed as chairman of the War Production Board than he began to dissipate the authority FDR had given him. In January 1942, the authority to ration civilian consumer goods was transferred to the newly created Office of Price Administration (OPA). In April, manpower policies were stripped out of the War Production Board and placed under another new "czar," Paul V. McNutt, and the War Manpower Commission. Interior Secretary Harold Ickes, who doubled as fuel coordinator, made it clear from the beginning that he considered his office independent of Nelson, while Rubber Director William Jeffers became a "czar" within Nelson's own organization. The result was that the War Production Board, instead of making top policy, became one of many competing agencies vying for control.

Even worse, Nelson's reputation suffered a series of near-scandals which cast serious doubt on his personal dedication. Understandably perhaps, given his background as a successful sales executive, Nelson enjoyed night life, alcohol, and the company of attractive women, and wartime Washington provided abundant opportunity to pursue all three. "Stimson, Patterson, Somervell, were all interested in ending the war just as soon as possible," said Clay. "But no one could ever figure out what Nelson's purpose was. And so, where you were willing to take a lot from someone like Patterson, because you knew what his aim was, you weren't willing to take it from a Donald Nelson."

The basic task of the War Production Board was to maintain the balance between military and civilian supply, while the Army and Navy retained statutory authority for military procurement. But the division of responsibility was sometimes murky, and by mid-1942 military production was falling behind schedule. Artillery pieces were being turned out in Army arsenals without breach blocks; tanks were being made in sufficient quantity but then sat for weeks in supply depots waiting for radios and armament. The production of rifles and machine guns was on target but ammunition was in short supply. The steel tubing used for 60mm mortars was needed by the Air Force for airplane construction. And so it went. Overall production was generally on schedule, but individual shortages threatened to throw the entire munitions program seriously out of balance.

The issue hinged on competing military and civilian requirements. Nelson thought military requirements were being set too high, whereas the War Department resented the business-as-usual attitude taken by the WPB toward civilian luxuries. Nelson believed the matter would be solved if the War Production Board could take over from the Army the responsibility for establishing military requirements and the actual scheduling of production; Clay and Somervell contended that the matter would be solved if Nelson would face up to the task of restricting civilian supply. It was a battle for prime Washington turf: who would control defense production?

This dispute, known as the "scheduling controversy," was one of the home front's most bitter struggles in 1942. But the controversy was not a matter of the civilians in Washington lining up against the Pentagon. It was not an issue of civilian control so much as a personal power struggle waged by Nelson and his staff at the WPB on the one hand, and the War Department from Mr. Stimson down on the other. In the final denouement, Washington's political leadership, from FDR to Hopkins to Morgenthau (not to mention all of the vice chairmen of the WPB), supported Clay and Somervell, not Nelson. None wished to remove from the Army the control of military production.

The scheduling controversy arose in the summer of 1942, when Nelson's office issued a feasibility study prepared by Johns Hopkins economics professor (later Nobel Laureate) Simon Kuznets, arguing that U.S. munitions goals would absorb three-quarters of the nation's GNP if not curtailed. To remedy the problem, Kuznets recommended the creation of a "Supreme War Production Council" under Nelson's control. Such a council would supersede all other domestic agencies (the Joint Chiefs of Staff would be members), and responsibility for production scheduling would shift from the Pentagon to the planning staff of the War Production Board, which, of course, would also be the planning staff of the SWPC. In effect, the WPB would supplant the Army as America's prime defense contractor.

Kuznets's report hit Somervell's desk late on a hot Saturday afternoon in September. Overworked and out of sorts, Somervell glanced hastily through it, and then penned a caustic note to WPB economist Robert Nathan (who had sent the report to Somervell). The proposed

Supreme War Production Council, said Somervell, "is an inchoate mass of words"—a flippant rejection of what Somervell recognized as a Nelson power play. Rather than taking Kuznets's memorandum seriously, Somervell's instinct—which often betrayed him on such occasions—led him to mock both the idea and the author. "I am not impressed with either the character or basis of the judgments expressed in the reports," he told Nathan, "and recommend they be carefully hidden from the eyes of thoughtful men."

Somervell's gruff, off-the-cuff comments did little to appease those at the War Production Board, such as Kuznets and Nathan, who were honestly concerned whether America's economy could withstand the demands being placed upon it, and played directly into the hands of those, like Nelson, who wanted the WPB to assume direct procurement control. "I hesitate to take your judgment seriously," replied Nathan. "There is no reason for now adopting an ostrich-like attitude, [and your conclusion] that these judgments 'be carefully hidden from the eyes of thoughtful men' is a nonsequitur."

Nathan's impertinent reply jolted Somervell, who had thought the matter was settled. The following day he sent Kuznets's report to Clay for a more serious appraisal. Clay shot back a blistering reply. According to Clay, the WPB study

> was purposefully designed to lead to the conclusion that the requirements established [by the armed services] have not resulted from a careful analysis of strategic considerations and a careful computation of the munitions . . . necessary to support our main effort. In other words, all data . . . have been formulated to arrive at a general conclusion that there must be a Supreme War Production Council composed of strategists working hand in hand with economists and statisticians.
>
> Certainly the War Production Board and its Chairman should have the advice of economists and statisticians. The major decisions of the Board must be based on an intimate knowledge of production and the capacity of industry of the United States; and by trial and error that portion of our output necessary to support the war economy must be determined *so that the remaining supply* may be made available for the military effort. . . . [But] we need no more super-boards and super-committees to guide a war effort which is already hampered by the constant committee sessions absorbing the time and talents of men whose full daily effort is needed to direct various phases of the war effort.

Q: Then you were more concerned about the proposed Supreme War Production Council than about whether production goals could be met—the so-called "feasibility" aspect of the report?

CLAY: Absolutely. It was another effort to remove the control of the war to a committee. But all of this was tied up with personalities. Somervell didn't like Bob Nathan. He knew Nathan was behind it, and that may have had something to do with it. Also, if you gave in, there was always the feeling that you'd immediately get a demand to give in further. We revised our figures downward, but I don't think it meant much, because we hadn't reached those figures. We simply couldn't raise the troops and put them into action as fast as we thought we could.

"Nevertheless, at this time there was an effort for the War Production Board to take over the procurement of supplies from the armed services, somewhat following a pattern which existed in Great Britain —a system which failed. But hell, I was opposed to the centralization of procurement in the Army itself—much less in the WPB—for the simple reason that we were talking about something that was much too big for us to even attempt to centralize at that stage of the game. Production scheduling was done in the branches [e.g., Quartermaster, Ordnance, Signal, Engineers], surely under our supervision, but it had to be done in the branches. They were the only ones equipped by virtue of experience to do that type of thing."

Q: But Nelson apparently wanted to?

CLAY: This is where all of the fighting took place. It had very little to do with the actual division of materials. Nelson and his planning staff wanted to take over the scheduling of military production. This represented a centralization that I thought would be completely damaging to the war effort. In my opinion, it would have been a complete disaster. Even if we'd tried to take it over in our office, it would have been a disaster. There were just too many items.

"So much of the fighting was personalities, unfortunately. And it was almost entirely with Mr. Nelson and his personal staff, his statistical group, and his planning group. I got along with Tom Blaisdell and Robert Nathan [two of Nelson's most prominent staff members]. We disagreed vigorously, but we didn't try to slug each other. I think one of the troubles was that everyone felt he had to take sides for or against Mr. Nelson. In fact, if Nelson had visualized his job as one of establishing policy, rather than attempting to assume operational control, there would not have been all the trouble that developed later. He just didn't see it that way.

"But Nelson was a weak man. He was being pushed by his economics staff to take over the scheduling of military production, which really meant control of production. He moved right up to the brink of doing it, then found he didn't have the power. [Military procurement was vested in the Army and Navy by statute.] But he was always maneuvering at the brink."

Q: You mentioned that Nelson was being pushed by his staff. Was this Robert Nathan?

CLAY: Bob Nathan was a statistician who, because of real ability, exercised a great deal more influence around Washington than was justified by his job. But I always got along with Bob, and he was a damn able statistician. We simply were able to produce more than Nathan thought we could. He may have been right if we were talking about fighting a six-, seven-, eight-year war. But in the type and kind of war that we were fighting, we were perfectly capable of going twice as far as we did in restricting the civilian economy without suffering unduly.

"I lived on the civilian economy during the war, and I never felt very restricted. I had an apartment in Washington. I bought everything on rations, I did everything on the civilian economy. And then I'd go in there and hear these civilian supply people talk about how terrible it was. But I never felt very restricted, really."

Q: Did you have a car?

CLAY: I had a car—a second-hand Cadillac—but because of the gasoline situation we pooled our use of it. Four of us [Lieutenant General Styer, Major General Walter Woods, Harold Bruce, and Clay] used to go to the Pentagon and come back in the car of one of the four. In those days, the government didn't give cars to generals.

Q: In your view, then, the organization of the home front in World War II was satisfactory?

CLAY: I think the organization of the home front was very good. Obviously, there were conflicts. In the first place, I don't see how you can make a war effort without having conflicts. I think they were necessary. People who were fighting for materials for the civilian economy were naturally going to be in conflict with those who were fighting for materials for the Allies and the armed forces. Someone had to resolve this: I think to have it resolved in the War Production Board, after give and take and battling for what you needed, was the only sound way in which it could be done. I personally think the War Production Board, set up with the actual procurement authority vested in the armed services, on the whole worked better than the procurement of military supplies anywhere else in the world. We had, I think, much greater success in the speed with which we converted to a wartime industrial setup than did England. That doesn't mean that we necessarily had the right people in the right places all the time.

"As a matter of fact, we could have doubled our military production for two years. Then the economy would have been in a hell of a shape. But for two years, we could have doubled our production.

"This is one thing we learned about Germany. With all our bombing and whatnot, we didn't make very serious inroads on their military production. And when the damned war ended and they surrendered, their military production—in spite of the bombing and everything else—had been very little reduced."

Q: How would you compare your job to that of Hitler's production chief, Albert Speer?

CLAY: Speer had a completely different kind of job. He had a job where he had complete authority to issue orders and to roll heads if they weren't carried out. On the other hand, he had the same problem of maybe arriving at work tomorrow morning and finding his own head cut off—which is not conducive to a man's best effort. But on the production front, the Germans didn't make anywhere near the all-out effort we made until the last year of the war. And then it was too late.

Joseph Weiner, who was the deputy chairman of the War Production Board in charge of civilian supply, agreed with Clay that the American system worked as well as it possibly could have. There were inevitable mistakes and always a little friction, but Weiner said that his division "had nothing but the closest working relations with the military. This was based on the principle that we were just as anxious as they were to see that the military got everything they needed—and maybe a little more. After all, it wouldn't have been natural for them to have come before an allocation authority and ask for exactly what they needed and take the chance of getting less. We recognized that, and there were never any serious problems. Certainly none of a policy nature. In fact, Lucius became one of my close friends in Washington. The disputes we had were the type that occur every day in any organization where you are dividing resources that are in short supply. We recognized that these disputes were inevitable, and operated on that basis. From time to time, the Joint Chiefs needed their knuckles rapped, but the issues weren't fundamental or particularly earth-shaking."

Under continued prodding by the services, Nelson finally brought Charles E. Wilson, president of General Electric, to Washington to serve as the WPB's deputy chairman to coordinate military and civilian production. A huge, strapping man (he had been a prize fighter in his youth), Wilson was a recognized production expert and one of the most respected leaders of American industry. According to Stimson, Wilson had been "loath to come" to Washington because he feared he would be "crucified" by "the petty gang that Nelson had allowed to accumulate around him." But at Secretary Stimson's urging, Wilson finally agreed, and he arrived in Washington in early November 1942. Under Wilson's direction, a new committee, the Production Executive Committee—composed of the heads of the procurement services—was established by the War Production Board to coordinate military production.

Q: Did the Army object to the Production Executive Committee chaired by Mr. Wilson?
CLAY: Hell no. We were in favor of the committee. As a matter of fact, we were the ones that urged that the committee be formed. We thought that if we could get the discussion out of the hands of the planners [at the WPB] into a group of managers and responsible executives, we could resolve all the problems without rancor and bitterness. And I think we were right. The Production Executive Committee really did the work. We met a couple of times a week and we solved, reconciled, all the differences that we were having.

At first, the Production Executive Committee encountered heavy going. Despite Wilson's presence, Nelson's office continued to press for full scheduling authority in the WPB. When Nelson drafted a proposed Executive Order for FDR's signature that would have granted Mr. Wilson complete authority for scheduling "the entire war production program," Clay appealed directly to Stimson and Hopkins. For Clay, it was another of Washington's jurisdictional battles. In four separate memoranda—each a condensed version of the memo that had preceded it—Clay detailed the Army's case. In particular, Clay objected to the overcentralized control that Nelson's plan required, although "the administrative unsoundness of the proposal is of minor import in comparison with its basic concept which would place the responsibility for the production of military weapons in an outside agency."

> Modern warfare is largely a war of logistics and control of military procurement and production is essentially a part of the strategy governing the . . . use of our armed forces [wrote Clay]. It must be the basic responsibility of civilian agencies to direct our national economy into the war effort, and, clearly, it must be the basic mission of the Services under the supervision of the President as Commander-in-Chief to organize, equip, dispose and direct our Armed Forces in conjunction with those of our Allies to defeat the armed forces of the enemy completely and without delay.

Clay insisted that the present system was working. "Thirty-nine percent of our output is devoted to the war effort, equal to England's effort after three years." If there were shortcomings in particular items, said Clay, these were traceable to the failure of the WPB "to increase the supply of raw materials and finished products—a responsibility which has been fixed in the War Production Board since it was first established."

> Why should it be assumed that an agency which has been incapable to date of exercising its responsibility for increasing the supply of raw materials and for converting the available supply into balanced semi-finished products, both relatively simple to achieve, has demonstrated its ability to take over the enormous and complicated task involved in centralized scheduling of end products?

Stimson took the Army's case to the White House, and FDR, who was always reluctant to jettison an ineffectual subordinate, finally decided Nelson had outlived his usefulness. Roosevelt convinced South Carolina's James F. Byrnes to step down from the Supreme Court and assume the total direction of the home front. The move epitomized Roosevelt's style. Rather than replace Nelson, the President simply inserted Byrnes above him, although, as Stimson accurately observed, FDR had brought the troubles on himself "by faulty organization which places on him the decision for too many things." As Bruce Catton (then Nelson's press officer) reported, the news of Byrnes's appointment—which Nelson learned from the news ticker— "landed on [him] with the impact of half a ton of bricks falling from a high building."

On November 25, 1942, Roosevelt summoned the demoted Nelson, along with Stimson and Navy Secretary Frank Knox, to the White House, and instructed them "to compose [your] former differences"—a clear victory for the services, since Nelson's proposed Executive Order was immediately shelved. The following morning, Nelson called on Stimson at the War Department, and presented him with a conciliatory letter disclaiming any intent to take over scheduling responsibilities from the military services. For all practical purposes, the scheduling controversy was at an end. Nelson had lost his attempt to centralize military purchasing in the War Production Board, and Clay quickly formed a close working partnership with Charles Wilson on the Production Executive Committee.

The following day, Clay was awarded his second star. "Congratulations on your promotion," wrote Navy Under Secretary James Forrestal. "There is no one in the Army that the entire Navy thinks deserves it more than you do."

New Year's Day, 1943, marked the turn of the tide in Europe. During January, the siege of Leningrad ended, Berlin underwent its first daylight bombing, and, in Casablanca, Roosevelt and Churchill agreed on the doctrine of "unconditional surrender." In February, Field Marshal von Paulus surrendered the German Sixth Army Group at Stalingrad. May saw the link-up of American and British forces in North Africa. During the summer, the U-boat menace in the Atlantic was brought under control, Sicily occupied, and Mussolini overthrown. Before the year ended, the turn toward victory was unmistakable. Italy surrendered and declared war on Germany; round-the-clock bombing of German industry began; and late in December, General Eisenhower was named supreme commander of the cross-Channel attack.

On the production front, 1943 saw military production hit its peak. Defense spending rose to $106 billion, of which $83 billion was earmarked for military procurement (a figure equal to four-fifths of total

U.S. production in 1940). By mid-1943, America's production emphasis had shifted from the capital equipment necessary to outfit the Army initially to replacement parts and ammunition. Combat losses had to be made good, battle experience had to be incorporated in new designs, and the tremendous daily expenditure of materiel had to be maintained.

Though still denied a combat command, Clay could point with pride to the production achievements of 1943: FDR's "balanced" program was 94 percent complete; the U.S. economy had absorbed military production in stride. In stark contrast to the Pentagon of the 1980s, no scandals or congressional exposés marred the procurement effort, and unit costs of most items were dropping rapidly as the mass-production techniques of American industry took hold. The M-1 Garand rifle, which had come from factories so slowly in 1941, was being produced in half the man-hours at half the cost. Hand grenades, which had cost $1.32 to fabricate in December 1940, cost 54 cents in June 1943. More important, the delicate art of translating automatically, back and forth, between fighting-front requirements and home-front commitments, seemed to be in hand.

In January, the Clays had been confronted with the unhappy problem of finding an apartment in wartime Washington. Until then they had been living comfortably at Tilden Gardens on upper Connecticut Avenue (where the Harry Trumans also lived). But Tilden Gardens had become a cooperative, and Clay and Marjorie doubted they would be in Washington "long enough to make it worthwhile." With housing scarce, they took an apartment next door to Mamie Eisenhower's in the baronial Wardman Park Hotel, and then, in the summer, moved to quarters 12A at Fort Myer, the sanctum sanctorum of the Army's high command.

The Clay children, "June" (Lucius Junior) and Frank, had graduated from West Point as classmates in June 1942 (June, who later became a four-star general in the Air Force, busted math at the Academy and was put back a year), and were both at war: Frank in North Africa with the 1st Armored Division; June in England with the 395th Bomber Squadron.

Clay's Washington life remained remarkably regular. At his Pentagon desk by seven-thirty in the morning, he rarely left before ten or eleven in the evening. James Boyd, who was Clay's executive officer, reports that it was not unusual for Clay to work seventy-two hours at a stretch, pausing only for a quick trip home to shower and shave. Clay's staff tried to maintain the pace, then gave up, working in shifts to accommodate his hours.

The WPB's Production Executive Committee meanwhile had shaken down into an effective instrument for controlling production. Charles Wilson had won the respect of the services, and under his leadership the PEC resolved the complex problem of dividing scarcities. In the process, Wilson and Clay became close friends—a friendship that continued until Wilson's death in 1964.

Clay's role as head of military procurement made him a figure of considerable power in Washington. Clay did not bestow contracts directly, but as the Army's Director of Materiel he exercised substantial influence in such matters. Thus it seemed natural that when new defense plants were established, his hometown of Marietta should be among the areas considered. In fact, the airport he had already put there (subsequently dubbed Rickenbacker Field) made Marietta an ideal site for a new bomber plant the air force needed.

"The air force had to have a new plant—and a big plant," said Clay. "And they came to me to ask for a list of possible places where there was both a labor supply available and an existing airport. And I happened to remember Marietta, so I gave it to them as one of the names. It had a tremendous labor potential—both from Atlanta and from the surrounding mountain area.

"Larry Bell [of Bell Aircraft] went down there. He liked the area, and so they built a plant there, the Bell bomber plant. And I think Larry Bell was always very happy with it. I don't know about Lockheed since. [Bell Aircraft merged with Lockheed in 1955.] But they brought labor out of those hills that had never had an opportunity to work before, and they did remarkably well."

Q: And you helped put the plant there?

CLAY: I helped them every way I could. It was my hometown. I had no financial interest of any shape, form, or fashion [in Marietta], and none of my relatives did either. But I did have an interest in the town. I thought it was a worthy town and that it would live up to whatever commitments it made. And I think it did.

One of the valid complaints against military procurement in World War II was that the Army seriously overbuilt munitions facilities, some of which never became operative, and others of which were closed down without ever reaching maximum production. Clay's response was to admit that mistakes were made, although, like Roosevelt, he believed it was better to err on the side of too much, rather than too little. It is also important to consider the context. When America entered the war, her Pacific battle fleet rusted at the bottom of Pearl Harbor, and an attack on the continental United States was considered imminent. No one could be sure what the future held, much less whether beleaguered Britain (or the Soviet Union) could withstand Hitler's onslaught. The threat of sabotage loomed ominously over the entire production picture, with ammunition plants particularly susceptible. As Clay advised the Truman Committee in April 1943:

> An excess capacity for ammunition . . . does not indicate lack of sound planning. . . . Ammunition and explosives are the life blood of the war machine. We may fight with comparative efficiency without certain caliber of weapons, without certain types of armored cars, and without other special equipment . . . [but] we cannot fight without ammunition. The making of explosives and the loading of ammunition are both hazardous, and plants devoted to the purpose are susceptible to fire, sabotage and bombing. While the latter threat may be regarded as somewhat remote at this time, it was not considered remote when the [ammunition] capacity was planned and placed under construction.

If the construction of excess ammunition capacity was a dark spot, the military's control of costs, and the refusal of the Army under Clay's stern leadership to permit manufacturers to reap exorbitant profits, were truly heroic achievements. There were no scandals involving massive cost overruns in World War II, no $800 toilet seats, and no reported instances of the Army's paying significantly more for a contracted item than that same item sold for on the open market. In this respect, one of the most important means Clay developed to control costs was to compel industry to renegotiate contracts that had already been awarded when the Army found it no longer needed the item contracted for, or when it became clear that the contractor was making an excess profit out of the deal. Mandatory contract renegotiation and the recapture of excess profits faced repeated court challenges, but in the end the Supreme Court upheld the Army's authority. In the view of the Court, the mobilization of the nation's industry in a time of total war was no different than the conscription of manpower in that same war, and it was a legitimate expression of the war powers to allow the government to set a reasonable price for what it obtained.

But it was Clay, with important support from Judge Patterson, who was the Army's prime mover on contract renegotiation. "This had been one of the great aftermath problems of World War I," said Clay, "and I was very conscious of that: the Nye Committee looking into the munitions industry and all of the other investigations. On the other hand, I was also conscious of the fact that we weren't going to get a good job unless manufacturers and industries felt that we would be fair and rapid in our decisions. I think that fundamentally it was with this in mind that I sent for [Brigadier] General [William] Draper. Then we got Joe Dodge [president of the Detroit National Bank] in on the contract side, and a very fine lawyer from Houston by the name of [Maurice] Hirsch, who came in as his assistant and later took over from him."

Q: But the initial move was yours?

CLAY: The problem fell into my lap after I took over the Procurement Division. The idea of contract renegotiation was already there as a result of World War I. But the rules and regulations and procedures under which it would be conducted had not been established.

Q: And, on balance, this effort was successful?

CLAY: I think it was the greatest job we did during the whole war. As a matter of fact, you haven't heard any criticism of excess profits or anything else from World War II, and no one else has. Our job really was twofold: on one side to convince industry that we were going to be fair, and on the other side to win the confidence of Congress and the public that you weren't going to overpay. We weren't afraid to pay a profit, but we were damn sure we weren't going to pay an excess profit.

Q: And surplus property?

CLAY: That was a very definite concern of mine. I wanted people to dispose of what we didn't need rather than building up huge surpluses. Of course we'd make a mistake, order too much of something, and then we'd put it on the market and try to sell it. The newspapers would use it as a terrible example of Army miscalculations and Army errors and Army mistakes. None of that bothered me. I wanted to get the material back into circulation.

Paul Cabot, the hard-bitten chairman of First Boston Corporation, who directed the WPB's salvage operations, reports that Clay was "forceful, persuasive, and bright as hell. He was a pleasure to do business with in the froth of wartime Washington. I went down there and was told I was to head the scrap drive. I didn't know a goddamned thing about scrap, but we needed twenty-two million tons of iron and steel, and I had no idea how to find it. I went out and looked at the scrap industry, and it was 99.4 percent Jewish. The remaining six-tenths of one percent who were Gentiles were the crookedest bunch of bastards you ever saw. So I got myself a Jewish deputy—Jake Wolff from Cincinnati—and we decided that one of the best places to collect scrap was from the military: the most wasteful goddamned people you ever saw.

"We were also hard-pressed for nonferrous metals, and yet the Navy was still ordering thousands of brass cuspidors. I went over to the Navy Department to see if we could substitute galvanized steel, and I got the damnedest runaround. One admiral told me that they couldn't use steel because if it were hit by a shell it would splinter, whereas a brass cuspidor would just collapse.

" 'Christ', I said, 'if that's the problem we'll give you cuspidors made of papier-mâché.' Then I found out the real story. The Navy felt it had to have brass because they had to have something for the sailors to do when they were at sea. And the only thing they could think of was keeping the damned things polished.

"Well, we thought we'd get the same runaround from the Army, but Wolff and I went over to see Clay, who was in charge of that sort of thing, and it was a completely different story. Lucius understood our problem immediately and gave us first-rate cooperation."

One of Clay's continuing problems was to combine all-out military production with the eventual reconversion of industry to civilian production. The War Production Board bore the primary responsibility for balancing requirements, but Clay was in the uncomfortable position of extracting the maximum possible military output from an American industrial structure designed primarily for peacetime production. As the war dragged on, industry looked increasingly to the postwar period. No company wanted to be placed at a competitive disadvantage, or to lose market share once civilian production resumed.

Q: Could you describe the pressure for reconversion in 1943?
CLAY: I don't think there was any pressure for reconversion in the sense of providing employment, or even from the industrial managers themselves, because they were all far too busy producing for the war. But the economists and planners were terribly concerned that all of a sudden the war orders would be cancelled, there wouldn't be any orders for nonwar material, there would be a necessity to reconvert machines, and that out of this we would have a terrific amount of unemployment.
Q: The planners in the War Production Board?
CLAY: Some of my own planners were concerned about it. I was never concerned about it, for two reasons. It seemed very clear to me that the fact that you still had a major war to fight [against Japan] after the Germans surrendered gave you a period to let down, which would avoid the worst of this. And, second, I had confidence that American industry really wanted to go out and build automobiles and refrigerators and this, that, and the other thing, and that if given the chance, they would really go to town. Which they did. The planners just didn't give enough credit to the ingenuity and speed with which American manufacturers could be ready to go back to work. And remember, most of those special tools for their particular industry had just been stored. They hadn't been thrown away. So all you had to do was bring them out of storage and put them into action.
Q: And the dangers of premature reconversion?
CLAY: The dangers of premature reconversion were that it was very difficult at that time to know what you wanted to cut back. We were still fighting a very furious war with Germany, and we hadn't begun to fight Japan. Remember, we were all thinking then of having to make amphibious landings in Japan and fight on the ground. This not only made the problem of selective reconversion very difficult, it also meant that you had to build up great stores on the opposite sides of the world. Whether you could get them from Europe, and how fast you could get them, was a question too, because we weren't too sure what kind of Europe we were going to have.
Q: Do you think it would have helped if the War Department had

had more sophisticated accounting devices—computers and so forth—to keep track of inventory and supplies?

CLAY: Well, if we'd had a better computer system, or had *any* computer system, we might have been able to have done some sort of an inventory control. Theoretically, we tried to establish one on IBM systems during the war, but I don't think it was worth a damn after the supplies once left the United States. It was a hopeless thing. Hopeless. How could you work out an inventory when a hundred shiploads of equipment were off-loaded and stored on the mud fields of Normandy, where you couldn't get to them?

Q: And this was a major difficulty?

CLAY: I think it was our principal difficulty. That, plus the fact that even if you had an inventory, the supplies weren't where you needed them. For example, a great deal of the equipment that we off-loaded over the beaches at Omaha and Utah was demobilized for three, four, or five months because you couldn't get through the mud to move it out. Even if it was included in an inventory it didn't do you any good, because you couldn't get it to the troops who were in the front lines of fighting. So an inventory has to mean more than just the number of items. I suspect that there were a great many items that were abandoned on islands in the Pacific because no one thought it was worth the transportation to move them.

In the spring of 1943, Clay again tried to shed his desk job in the Pentagon and go overseas, this time as deputy to his old friend Major General Donald H. Connolly, head of the Persian Gulf Command. But Clay's request was denied. On June 20, 1943, he wrote Connolly dejectedly that he would not be coming. "I had hoped that by now my job would be in such shape and would have developed so many enemies that it would be most obvious to everyone that my departure from Washington would be helpful in procurement of military supplies. It just hasn't worked out that way yet," said Clay.

By 1943, Clay had formed strong opinions about the appropriate management style and the virtues of individual initiative. Or, to be more accurate, his wartime experience confirmed his long-held predilections. Within the War Department, he continued to preach the virtues of decentralization. In a memo to General Styer on August 6, he bitterly attacked a proposal then current to combine the procurement staffs of the Army and Navy. "We have progressed too far [wrote Clay] to accomplish any further centralization of procurement between the several Departments. In fact, this office is of the view that further centralization would not result in increased efficiency."

But the battle against overcentralization and bloated procurement staffs was a continuing one. No sooner was one proposal defeated than another would arise: a hydra-headed, bureaucratic reflex. Such, at least, was Clay's reaction to the scheme hatched by General Somervell in the autumn of 1943 to abolish the Army's supply branches (Ordnance, Quartermaster, the Corps of Engineers, etc.) and incorporate them into a unitary Services of Supply. To Clay, Somervell's plan was similar to Donald Nelson's Supreme War Production Council, but this time centered in the War Department.

"I was not in on this scheme," said Clay, "because Somervell knew I was bitterly opposed to it. I was bitterly opposed to it because our work was of such volume and magnitude it had to be decentralized."

Q: And the reaction of the branches?

CLAY: They were all very much opposed to it. General Somervell envisaged a setup under which [Major] General [Levin H.] Campbell would be his chief of production. Campbell was Chief of Ordnance and he wouldn't buy it. He wasn't going to sell his Ordnance Department down the river, so to speak.

Somervell presented his reorganization plan to General Marshall and Secretary Stimson in late August 1943, just before embarking on a two-month worldwide inspection trip, accompanied by Clay. Stimson and General Marshall apparently looked kindly on Somervell's plan, although both later pulled back when Judge Patterson and John McCloy expressed doubts similar to Clay's. "Whatever critics may say," Stimson confided in his diary, "we have done an almost miraculous job and I therefore am *prima facie* against stirring up a hornets' nest right in the middle of a war when things are going well."

Somervell's reorganization proposal coincided with well-placed rumors that he would replace General Marshall as Chief of Staff when Marshall went to Europe to command the invasion of France—an arrangement similar to that of Pershing and Peyton March in World War I. Whether Somervell had the inside track to succeed Marshall remains open to conjecture, but the fact is that at the Quebec Conference in August, Roosevelt and Churchill agreed that Marshall would command the cross-Channel attack—a decision with which both Stimson and Hopkins readily agreed.

Marshall evidenced little enthusiasm for leaving Washington, although he and Mrs. Marshall surreptitiously began moving their belongings out of the Chief of Staff's quarters at Fort Myer to their Leesburg estate. But the remaining members of the Joint Chiefs of Staff—Leahy, Arnold, and King—lobbied openly against Marshall's transfer, and old General Pershing (who usually took his cue in such matters from Marshall) wrote Roosevelt from his Walter Reed Hospital bed to caution against the move.

By late September, with Clay and Somervell already on their world tour, the issue of Marshall's transfer leaked to the press when the quasi-official *Army and Navy Journal* reported that "powerful influences would like to eliminate Marshall as Chief of Staff." The equally authoritative *Army and Navy Register* claimed that "the European Command would not be a promotion" for Marshall but a means of removing him from Washington. "It is understood," said the *Register,* "that Harry Hopkins prefers Lt. General Brehon B. Somervell" as Chief of Staff.

The charge that Somervell would succeed Marshall was quickly picked up by America's right-wing press. "GLOBAL W.P.A. SEEN AIM IN MARSHALL PLOT," announced Sissy Patterson's Washington *Times-Herald.* And in Congress, Representative Paul Shafer (R., Michigan) charged that the New Deal palace guard—Frankfurter, Hopkins, Judge Samuel Rosenman, and David Niles—sought to build Somervell up as an Army running mate for FDR on a fourth-term ticket, should Douglas MacArthur be nominated by the Republicans.

Q: Did Hopkins support Somervell for Chief of Staff?

CLAY: Everybody thought Mr. Hopkins was supporting Somervell because Somervell had worked for Hopkins in the WPA. They were on a first-name basis, and in our various difficulties in Washington Somervell got a great deal of support from Mr. Hopkins. Judging from Somervell's actions on our trip, I'm sure he had some reason to think it was going to happen. General Marshall may have too, for he got very cold to Somervell. On the other hand, I can't believe that either President Roosevelt or Mr. Hopkins ever for one minute thought of moving Somervell up to be Chief of Staff.

Q: But during the trip?

CLAY: Yes. In Chungking, for example, a situation arose concerning Stilwell. Chiang Kai-shek wanted Stilwell relieved, and Somervell stepped in and tried to mediate. But it was none of his business. He should have stayed completely clear of it. That was one of Somervell's troubles: he got involved in everything. General Marshall finally sent him a cable that, if Stilwell was relieved, Somervell would take his place. That stopped him right there. That was one job I know damn well he didn't want.

Q: Were you involved?

CLAY: Not at all. I was kept busy with the Kungs and the Soongs. I was supposed to negotiate a settlement for the cost of the airports we were building in China at the time. I figured out that on the most generous of terms—namely, what those airports would have cost us to build in this country—they would be worth $200 million. Which I was willing to pay. The Chinese wanted $2 billion. So we didn't reach an agreement.

From China, Clay and Somervell flew to India, and then on to the Persian Gulf, where they once again met General Connolly. In his efficient way, Connolly was on top of the situation—organizing the shipment of supplies through Iran to Russia. "Connolly had three separate assembly lines putting trucks together," said Clay. "He had found out that if you put Jews, Christians, and Moslems on the same line they spent most of their time fighting with each other. So he had one line manned by Moslems, one by Christians, and one by Jews. And the competition was terrific. Of course, that's something you can't talk about today."

After a brief inspection tour with Connolly, Clay flew to North Africa, where he tried to find his son Frank ("one of the two times I cheated and pulled rank during the war"), then a lieutenant with the 1st Armored Division. "I knew that if I went through that area and didn't see him, I wouldn't have a very good welcome when I got home. So I wired [Major General] Tom Larkin, who was the Services of Supply general in North Africa, and asked him if it would be possible for me to see my son for a few minutes. And I received a wire back from him saying, 'Don't worry about it. When you land in Cairo he'll be at the airport.'

"Well, we landed in Cairo and he wasn't at the airport. But Larkin was, and he said, 'We just haven't been able to find him, but when you get to Algiers tomorrow, he'll be in Algiers.' Well, he wasn't in Algiers either, but there they said, 'The 1st Armored Division has now moved up into Italy, and he'll meet you in Naples.'

"So I landed in Naples and he still wasn't there. I went up to the front where [Major] General [John] Lucas was fighting a battle, and I came on back that evening, and we were sitting down to dinner, and I commented that I had not been able to find my son.

"Colonel Case said, 'Oh my God. The 13th Armored Regiment of the 1st Armored Division, why that's Colonel Howze's regiment. I saw him just before we got into Cassino. I passed him in the road and waved at him. That must be where they are.'

"We were leaving the next morning for Dakar, from where we were going to fly back to the United States. I said to General Somervell, 'I'll meet you in Dakar,' and I got hold of [Major] General Eddie House of the air forces and asked if he would set up a plane to take me to Dakar. He said he would, and so I got into a jeep with a driver and I started out on this damned road at about four o'clock in the morning. And it was pitch-black. I've never been so damned scared in my life—not of German bullets or artillery—but have you ever traveled during a blackout on a dark night with military trucks moving bumper to bumper and you're traveling in a jeep in the opposite direction with no lights on? God! It looked like we were going to get run over on every damned turn we made.

"In any event, just as day was breaking—and if it had been any earlier, we would have missed it—but just as day was breaking, I looked over and saw a sign by the side of the road and it said, 'Headquarters, 1st Armored Division.' I got out of the jeep and walked maybe twenty or thirty yards into an olive grove, and there was a sergeant there. And I said, 'Sergeant, I'm looking for the 13th Armored Regiment.'

"He said, 'It's right here.'

"I said, 'Well, I'm looking for a Lieutenant Clay in the 13th Armored.'

"And he said, 'Well, hell, there he is.'

"And there he was. And they had just gotten in that night. Howze had been in the advance, and they were scheduled to make an attack the next day. So I had about twenty minutes with my son. I remember it so distinctly, because he said, 'Gee, Dad, have you had breakfast?'

"I said, 'No, I haven't.'

"And he said, 'Well, why not have it with me?'

"I said, 'Fine.'

"And he said, 'Oh, I forgot, we're not having breakfast this morning. Our rations haven't reached us yet.' "

Clay returned to Washington in mid-November to find the reconversion kettle boiling furiously. Within the Services of Supply, James Mitchell, director of industrial personnel and, later, Secretary of Labor under Eisenhower, advocated a committee to study pockets of unemployment as contracts were canceled. But Clay, who was always distrustful of committees, rejected the idea. "I do not believe that the problem is one which can be well solved by committee action," Clay wrote Styer on November 16.

With the war in full swing (and the landing in France still six months away), Clay found the increased demand for civilian production disheartening. As he often did when the going got rough, he sought out Sam Rayburn for advice and counsel. "It looked to me that we were running into a period of unhappiness with the war," Clay said, "and I remember going up to see Mr. Rayburn. And afterwards he went down into the well of the House to make a speech—which the Speaker does very seldom. He told everyone we were still fighting a war and let's remember that. It was a wonderful thing."

That night, Clay wrote to Rayburn expressing his appreciation. "I am grateful that I had the opportunity to hear your speech to the House today," he said. "It was inspiring and cannot help but bring about a better understanding."

To head off possible conflicts over reconversion, Clay issued a memorandum in early December establishing War Department policy on civilian production. Above all, Clay warned his staff to ensure that the relative position of manufacturers in competitive fields not be jeopardized. In particular, Clay sought to avoid difficulties with the War Production Board. "It is now essential," he told his staff, "that a close and friendly relationship be reestablished at all levels of contact with the civilian agencies so that mutual problems can be understood and worked out with a minimum of friction. It should not be the attitude of the Army representative that the War Department is fighting the civilian agencies in reaching an equitable adjustment in the very difficult problems which will arise when reconversion faces us. It should be clearly understood by every officer concerned with the problem that unless the representatives of the civilian agencies clearly understand the War Department's problems, the day-to-day action they take can do more overall damage to the munitions programs than any generalized policy decisions. Consequently, if opposition is expressed by a War Department representative to any action, . . . it should be accompanied by a careful explanation of the reasons for such opposition. There is no War Department policy which requires general opposition to any claimant agency's program in whole or in detail."

Clay coupled his memo with a proposal that the Production Executive Committee of the WPB be designated to handle all matters relating to reconversion. Clay felt that Charles Wilson was a man of sound judgment with whom the services could get along. Also, since Wilson's first job was to assure fulfillment of military production schedules, it would be unlikely that the jurisdictional fights that had characterized so much of the WPB's past activity would recur.

Clay's request that reconversion be handled by the WPB's Production Executive Committee outflanked Nelson before the battle was joined. By proposing that reconversion planning be placed under Wilson, the War Department made it virtually impossible for Nelson to intervene. Nelson temporized for several months, never really recognized the extent to which his position had been undercut, and eventually was ordered by Byrnes to put Clay's plan into effect.

Robert Nathan, Clay's frequent antagonist at the War Production Board, respected Clay's concern to handle reconversion in an orderly manner—though he often disagreed on specific proposals. "If Lucius Clay had been in charge of the Services of Supply," said Nathan, "I don't think there would have been as much conflict, or the conflicts would have been more readily reconciled. In my judgment, Clay was as tough as Somervell ever was—I mean tough in the tough-minded manner, having a conception of where he wanted to go and being firm in what he wanted to achieve. But he was also very direct. Somervell, on the other hand, had a streak of deviousness in him. Clay didn't. I had a tremendous respect for Clay, because I think he had an amazingly clear conception. He fought like a tiger, but he did it in a gentlemanly manner and very forthrightly. And in this respect I think that the conflicts that did occur would have been less bitter and left less scars. But there's no use kidding ourselves. These conflicts were very fundamental and inevitable."

At the end of December, with production rising again, Clay once more sought to go overseas—with a reduction from major general to the rank of colonel, if necessary. Clay wrote Somervell requesting that he be relieved as Director of Materiel. "The undersigned has served under your Command with staff responsibility for production and procurement since the formation of Army Service Forces," Clay said. "During this period, the military programs have been balanced within the national economy, scheduled, and controlled through the allocation of materials. The peak production necessary to equip our army and our allies has been reached and production rates are beginning to decline." Clay told Somervell that he thought "a fresh mind would be of more use now in meeting the transition problems ahead. It is realized that the rank which I now hold results from the staff responsibility with which I am vested and that a field assignment in this rank is unlikely," said Clay. "However, I believe that I am qualified to command an Engineer regiment in the field and such assignment in the grade of Colonel would be welcomed."

Somervell replied the following day. "I know of no officer in this organization to whom I feel more indebted for a high character of service which has been rendered to the A.S.F. than yourself," he wrote. "Though I would very much like to gratify your ambition to see service overseas, the needs here in Washington are too pressing to permit favorable consideration of your request."

Q: Was your letter motivated by any particular difficulties you were having at that time?

CLAY: No, I never had any difficulties—other than the constant ones. I simply wanted to get into the war. I'd been through World War I without seeing combat, and to go through the second one as a professional soldier without seeing combat was about as humiliating as anything I could think of. And I'm still ashamed of it.

· 12 ·

Saving the Taxpayer from Chiang Kai-shek

AS 1943 DREW TO A CLOSE, FDR ENDED THE SPECULATION as to who would head the invasion of Europe with the selection of General Eisenhower. Marshall would remain in Washington, and Somervell would continue to head the Services of Supply.

In the United States, the focus of the production battle shifted again, as manpower and reconversion became Clay's principal concerns. In 1942, the problem had been plant and material shortages. In 1943, it was production scheduling—the shift from capital equipment to replacement parts and expendables. But in 1944, as the Army and Navy grew to exceed twelve million men and women, serious labor shortages, exacerbated by the growing clamor to resume civilian production, threatened to disrupt the flow of critical items to the front.

In Washington, the sniping over reconversion continued intermittently throughout the spring of 1944. Former U.S. Supreme Court Justice James Byrnes, who had supplanted Donald Nelson as overall coordinator of the home front, directed the War Production Board and the military services to prepare a reconversion program to take effect on Germany's surrender, and Clay pressed once again to have the matter assigned to the Production Executive Committee, headed by Charles Wilson. But Nelson temporized and, in the absence of agreement, the reconversion problem continued to drift.

The ongoing difficulties with Nelson caused Clay to yearn for combat more than ever. General Eisenhower's selection as supreme commander provided a brief glimmer of hope when Ike offered Clay the job of chief engineer for the cross-Channel attack, but once again the request was rejected by Somervell and Patterson. As Clay wrote to his old engineering friend Jack Sverdrup, then on MacArthur's staff, "Just last week, I had another opportunity for overseas service in what appeared to be a most promising assignment. However, the net result was another emphatic 'no.' I am afraid that my almost thirty years of military service is going to wind up with me still behind a desk filled with papers, while you and others are doing the things that are really worthwhile. I really feel quite hopeless and blue about it, but suppose there is nothing to do but to continue to try to do the best one can on whatever his assignment might be."

In the summer of 1944, with Allied forces now fighting in France, the reconversion battle approached a climax. The War Department urged Byrnes to restore a "sense of urgency" to the lagging war production program, while Nelson sought Byrnes's help to tone down the Army's claims of front-line shortages. On July 21, Clay summarized the issue for Secretary Stimson. According to Clay, "the Army is experiencing its greatest difficulty since the beginning of the war in meeting production schedules. . . . This difficulty . . . is accentuated by the 'peace jitters' now sweeping the country. The Chairman of the War Production Board, although presumably responsible for meeting the needs of the armed services, has been a major factor in developing 'peace jitters' by his relaxation of major controls over civilian production in spite of the shortages in war output."

Finally, on August 4, Byrnes acted by transferring Nelson's authority over reconversion to Paul McNutt's War Manpower Commission, a move that Clay strongly supported. Said Byrnes:

> There is a public psychology in the country that the end of the war is near at hand. No man knows when the war will end. We must produce

> until the last shot is fired. People want to leave their jobs in war plants in order to get back to civilian business. If the exodus from war plants continues, it is going to interfere seriously with the possibility of an early end to the war.

Immediately after Byrnes's announcement, Clay and Nelson were called to testify in closed session before the Truman Committee on Capitol Hill. Once again, Clay argued that the dispute was a matter of timing, not substance.

> The War Department is certainly not opposed to reconversion. Neither is reconversion primarily or basically our responsibility, and we appreciate that. [But] we are vitally concerned with war production and with a failure to meet war schedules. We insist and urge in every way that we can that the responsible authorities meet our war schedules before doing anything that might interfere with [those] schedules, and that is the extent of our objection, if it could be called an objection, to reconversion.

Public opinion in the United States strongly supported the War Department's position. The war was still too hot, and too many men were still actively engaged in combat to condone a full resumption of civilian production. According to *The Washington Post,* "General Clay's report of shortages in specific items needed at the fighting fronts gives us detailed information supporting a frequently told story. . . . There is only one way to change that dismal outlook on the home front during this hour of exhilaration and triumph in the military phase of the war. That is for every community to put forth an extraordinary effort to meet its wartime obligation."

Two days after Clay's testimony, Donald Nelson was relieved as chairman of the War Production Board. The White House announced that he was going to China as the President's confidential representative. Nelson's departure caused little regret. "From my own observation," Secretary Stimson wrote in his diary, "Nelson is a weak, dishonest, and inefficient man who has done little good in Washington."

Treasury Secretary Morgenthau shared Stimson's view. "You get three years in Washington to find out whether or not you are a schlemiel," Morgenthau told Assistant Secretary Henry Dexter White.

"And if you are, you get promoted," said White, referring to Nelson's impending trip to China.

General Marshall was also delighted that Nelson was leaving, but worried about his impact in China. He agreed that Nelson could go, providing he didn't "meddle with policy or strategy but confined himself to selling razor blades."

The day after Nelson's relief, Clay requested overseas assignment. With Nelson gone, Clay believed the principal impediment to increased production had been removed. In Clay's name, General LeRoy Lutes, who had a parallel post to Clay in the Services of Supply as chief of distribution (Clay procured the equipment; Lutes saw to it that it was distributed to the right place at the right time), cabled Somervell, who was then on an inspection trip in Europe:

> DONALD NELSON LEAVING FOR CHINA IN NEXT FEW DAYS FOR WHAT IS REPORTED AS SHORT STAY. [CHARLES E.] WILSON WILL STAY IN CHARGE. PRODUCTION DIFFICULTIES LESSENING. CLAY SAYS NOW MAY HE PLEASE GO TO WAR.

Once again, Clay's request was denied. In Somervell's view, strongly seconded by Judge Patterson and Mr. Stimson, Clay had become the linchpin of America's military production. He was too important a fixture, and the outcome was still too iffy, to allow the War Department to gratify his personal desire for combat. Equally important, Clay served as a valuable lightning rod on Capitol Hill. For almost nine years, including his work with the Chief of Engineers and the Civil Aviation Administration, Clay had been in continual touch with the leadership of the House and Senate. He had built the Denison Dam in Speaker Sam Rayburn's district, and during the great floods of 1936, he had sent a Corps of Engineers boat into Paducah, Kentucky, to rescue the mother of Senator Alben Barkley, who was now the Senate's Majority Leader. Clay counted Rayburn and Barkley among his closest friends. In fact, as a result of his flood control activities for the Corps, and his later work building airports across America, Clay knew most of the senior members of Congress personally and enjoyed enormous credibility on the Hill. He could be relied on by the War Department to protect that important flank, while Stimson and Marshall got on with fighting the war. The Truman Committee, in particular, was one of Clay's responsibilities.

Q: What was your opinion of the Truman Committee?
CLAY: The Truman Committee was an investigating committee. And the whole point of the counsel of the Truman Committee [Hugh Fulton] was to prove you were wrong. You were always on the defensive; you wouldn't have been there otherwise.
Q: Did the Truman Committee help the war effort?
CLAY: If you asked me that at the time, I would have given you a definite answer, "no." They took the time of people who didn't really have the time to give, and by and large the things they investigated were things that had already happened. And while those things were mistakes, they were mistakes that had gone by the boards. Nobody could do anything about them. However, I think it is wise to have congressional investigations, and I think that the investigation of some of those mistakes at that time resolved issues that might have been far more worrisome if we'd tried to investigate them in the aftermath of the war.

As Director of Materiel, Clay was often called on to handle the unexpected. One such crisis involved Montgomery-Ward, the large mail-order distributor, which was shut down by one of the few full-scale labor strikes in 1944. In addition to its catalogue business, Montgomery-Ward was engaged in producing and procuring numerous items for the Army's quartermaster, and the strike threatened to disrupt military delivery schedules. The government, acting under its wartime authority, seized temporary control of the company and ordered the strikers back to work. But Sewell Avery, Ward's president, refused to surrender control to the government, or to vacate his office. "This didn't really come under my jurisdiction," said Clay. "General Aurand, who was the area commander in Chicago, called General Somervell for instructions, but Somervell was away and they put him on to me. Mr. Avery wouldn't leave his office, and they wanted to know what to do. So I said, 'Pick him up and carry him out,' which is what they did. Whether it was right or wrong, whether it had to be done or not, is another matter. I think it did have to be done, because he was defying authority and we didn't have time to follow ordinary procedures."

No sooner was the reconversion controversy resolved than Clay was summoned to Bretton Woods, New Hampshire, by Treasury Secretary Henry Morgenthau to take part in negotiations with China concerning the airfields the United States was building there. Clay had had his first exposure to the sinkhole China situation in October 1943, when he and Somervell visited Chungking on their round-the-world tour. At that time, Stilwell complained bitterly that Chiang Kai-shek was stalling on building the fields, intent on extracting the maximum possible "take" from the United States.

The problem was that the official exchange rate for U.S. dollars was pegged at 20:1, while the true market value of the Chinese yuan was 120:1 and falling weekly. To Stilwell, and especially to Clay, who had to defend the Army's expenditures before Congress, China's failure to establish an equitable exchange rate was a clear case of Chiang's duplicity—a case compounded by the rampant corruption of the Kuomintang. (The Treasury had discovered $867,000 of U.S. aid funds stashed away in the private accounts of members of Madame Chiang's entourage.)

Somervell, with his usual brusqueness, told Stilwell to go ahead and build the airfields, while Clay spent his days in Chungking trying to negotiate a more favorable exchange rate with China's finance minister, Dr. H. H. Kung, the Oberlin-educated brother-in-law of Madame Chiang. To save Chinese face, Clay proposed that the official exchange rate of 20:1 be continued, but that for every dollar exchanged at that rate, the Chinese furnish the United States an additional 80 yuan, either as reverse Lend-Lease, or as China's contribution "to our joint war effort." Clay reported to Washington that Kung "appeared to view these proposals as feasible and promised to place them before the Generalissimo for approval."

But before action could be taken on Clay's proposal, Chiang Kai-shek was invited to Cairo to meet with President Roosevelt and Churchill before the two Western leaders met Stalin at Tehran. Uncertain of America's island-hopping advance across the Pacific, Roosevelt was determined to keep China in the war. "With all of their shortcomings," he confided to his son Elliot, "we've got to depend on the Chiangs." The chronic American fear of China's collapse (Admiral Leahy, in particular, fretted lest "Chiang drop out of the war") failed to consider that Chinese self-interest would keep her in under any circumstances.

The question of support for Chiang Kai-shek split the Roosevelt administration along ideological as well as departmental lines. Leahy and the State Department (with the notable exception of old China hands like John Stewart Service) wanted to buy Chiang's favor, while Clay and the Treasury wanted to take a firm line. In later years, Clay had no sympathy with the debate about "Who lost China?" From his experience dealing with the Kuomintang, the clear answer was Chiang Kai-shek.

In Cairo, Chiang beseeched Roosevelt for a $1 billion loan to ease China's financial plight, a demand FDR declined, although he did agree that the United States would "bear the cost of its military effort in China." The conference's final communiqué pledged that "Manchuria, Formosa, and the Pescadores, shall be restored to the Republic of China."

To appease Chiang further, Roosevelt and Churchill agreed to a major military operation to recover Burma in 1944, a promise quickly retracted at Tehran. As Churchill later wrote, "the talks . . . were sadly distracted by the Chinese story, which was lengthy, complicated and minor."

Informed upon his return to Chungking that the Burma operation was off, Chiang assuaged his pride with a renewed request for the $1 billion loan, pleading that his task had now been made "infinitely more difficult" and that China's military and economic weakness made it "impossible" to hold out for six months. China's collapse, said Chiang ominously, would have "grave consequences on the global war."

Roosevelt passed Chiang's request on to Morgenthau, who wrote a scathing memorandum cataloguing China's economic problems. A billion dollars was the last thing the United States should be giving Chiang, Morgenthau concluded. "This looks good," said Roosevelt, who then, to the anguish of Secretary of State Cordell Hull, dispatched Morgenthau's memo virtually verbatim to Chiang Kai-shek.

While Chiang smarted over his second rebuff from Washington, costs skyrocketed on the Chengtu airfields the Army was building. On January 2, 1944, Clay told Morgenthau that "our principal concern is the exchange situation in China," and he suggested that the Treasury redouble its efforts to achieve a better rate. Then, to Stilwell, Clay cabled renewed authority "to expend, regardless of exchange rates, such funds as may be necessary to prosecute work vigorously" on the airfields.

Stilwell replied through Ambassador Clarence Gauss that "Progress is being made . . . on only four of the seven bases which China promised to construct." Work on the other three, "which are much more urgently needed," said Stilwell, had not been started, because "the United States Government has not committed itself to pay for these latter bases at the official exchange rate and China is, therefore, holding up work for them."

Clay and Morgenthau were appalled. After telling Clay that the important thing was to get the bases built, Morgenthau cabled Chungking on January 15 that "Nothing could be more conducive to lowering the prestige of China in the United States . . . than the knowledge China was not cooperating fully in the building of these airbases." At the same time, Clay asked Stilwell to remind the Generalissimo of "the adverse effect on Congressional and American public opinion if there is any delay in the military construction program or if it has to be completed at unreasonable cost. We should take as firm a position as necessary to develop a speedy decision."

Exactly how firm the United States intended to be was immediately put to the test, for Chiang's reaction to his billion-dollar turndown was to give the American government a new ultimatum. If the Treasury would not grant the loan, said Chiang, the United States would have to pay its expenses in China at the official rate. If the United States were not prepared to do so, then China "could not make any further material or financial contribution," and the "American forces must look out after themselves."

Morgenthau's response to Chiang's threat was immediate. "Tell them to go jump in the Yangtze River," he said to Assistant Secretary Harry Dexter White. If the U.S. needed yuan to build the airfields, then Morgenthau suggested selling gold on China's black market. "I am not going up on the Hill," he told White, "and ask the bastards for anything. They [the Chinese] are just a bunch of crooks, and I won't go up and ask for one nickel."

Chiang's alternative—that the United States build the Chengtu fields at the official rate of 20:1—was equally repulsive, for the cost was estimated at $800 million, and rapidly rising. "I am mad as hell," Morgenthau told Somervell. "Now he is holding a pistol at our head. Is this something that I have got to stomach and vomit and take it, or have you got some way to wiggle out and do something else?"

Somervell told Morgenthau that the Army was "very dissatisfied" and "willing to go to the limit if necessary." The military were "prepared to stop building airports in China and . . . approach Japan from another direction" if a suitable exchange rate could not be worked out, said Somervell. But it was Clay who had the immediate staff responsibility for the Chengtu airfields. At a meeting between the War Department and the Treasury, he suggested that they send no more Lend-Lease to China, or divert it to Chiang's rivals, "or, if necessary, even pull out of China, or just do nothing and continue doing it at a slow pace."

Since the United States had already furnished over $340 million worth of Lend-Lease to China, Chiang's stubbornness quickly eroded whatever sympathy the Kuomintang once enjoyed in the War Department. Clay had already complained bitterly that under the official exchange rate the cost of the airports would be astronomical, while Mr. Stimson, once China's most ardent partisan, agreed that the time had come for firm measures. "I do not fear that the Chinese are going to drop out of the war now that we are so close," he noted in his diary.

The State Department, which was always nervous whenever it came to a showdown with Chiang, struck a more conciliatory pose. Wouldn't it, asked Alger Hiss of the Office of Far Eastern Affairs, at a meeting with Clay and Harry Dexter White, be "almost as cheap" to grant the loan? (In 1944, Hiss was a solid defender of Chiang's.) But Clay bristled at the prospect. If Chiang got the loan, he said, "it wouldn't be long before he would be asking for another one." When Dean Acheson, the assistant secretary of state for economic affairs, also spoke in favor of the loan, Treasury Under Secretary Daniel Bell said "it was just throwing money down a rat hole."

The day after the meeting at Treasury, Clay met once more with Bell, Harry Dexter White, and Alger Hiss to draft a reply for the President to Chiang's demand. Above all, Clay was determined that the loan not be granted, a position endorsed by Bell and White. A conciliatory State Department draft was reworked by the three; no loan was offered, and Chiang was told to work out a new exchange rate with Stilwell.

Despite the yuan's continued decline on China's black market, Chiang refused to consider devaluation. "Mere phrase 'exchange rate' sends GM [Generalissimo] into tailspin," Stilwell cabled. As a result, U.S. purchasing officers found themselves paying exorbitant prices for basic necessities. At Chengtu, a simple wooden chair that might have cost $7 in the United States now cost the Army $95, reported Major General Thomas G. Hearn, Stilwell's chief of staff. Chiang's only concession was to offer an additional 10 yuan for each dollar, an unofficial 30:1—which Hearn characterized as "ridiculous."

Confronted with Chiang's obstinacy, Clay met again with Bell, White, and Hiss to answer Stilwell's cable. Hiss again favored a conciliatory tone, although Daniel Bell and White maintained that military considerations were primary and agreed with Clay that a firm stand was essential.

Clay returned from the Treasury meeting and asked General Marshall for a policy decision. According to Clay's recommendation, Chiang Kai-shek should be told that unless a satisfactory exchange rate was established, "the United States must reduce the scope of its planned military operations" in China. For Marshall's benefit, Clay included a draft cable to that effect for the President's signature.

Marshall initially accepted Clay's recommendations. According to Clay's figures, it would cost "more than $1 billion" to build the airports at the official rate of 20:1, which Chiang insisted upon. But General H. H. Arnold, the chief of the Army air forces, wanted the airports finished nevertheless, and Marshall reluctantly agreed. Clay thereupon suggested a compromise, giving the Chinese $25 million monthly if they would make 2.5 billion yuan available to Stilwell—in effect establishing an exchange rate of 100:1. State and Treasury agreed immediately, and Clay cabled the proposal to Stilwell on February 20. This was a quick fix. It would provide Stilwell with the yuan he needed, and the rate would be tolerable.

Kung responded by agreeing to provide the United States with the currency it needed while leaving the exchange value to be established in future negotiations. This suited Clay perfectly, since he was confident the Treasury could negotiate a better rate in Washington than Stilwell could in Chungking. Meanwhile, Clay prepared a chart for Secretary Stimson illustrating the high price of Chinese cooperation. According to Clay's figures, the United States was paying a $1.2 billion premium to Chiang if business was transacted at the official exchange rate.

The root of the problem was China's spiraling inflation, which the Chiang government was either unwilling or unable to control. As U.S.

Ambassador Gauss cabled from Chungking, unless something was done, the China theater "ultimately will become the most expensive theater of the war." Thus, when Kung suggested that he be provided with $20 million in American currency to buy yuan in the black market (ostensibly to improve their value), Clay reluctantly agreed to provide $5 million, although, as he cabled Hearn in Chungking, "we are unable to see any advantage to the U.S." Simultaneously, Clay asked Harry Dexter White for a list of economic sanctions the United States might apply against Chiang if push came to shove.

When the Chinese black-market rate for U.S. dollars continued to rise, Madame Chiang reopened the question of a loan with President Roosevelt. Clay countered by suggesting that Morgenthau himself go to Chungking to settle the matter. Recognizing the ultimate futility of such a mission, Morgenthau declined. "I have had a rule that when it comes to doing business I never want to get more than a hundred yards away from the White House," said Morgenthau.

Vice President Henry Wallace, who lacked Morgenthau's instinct for survival, quickly jumped at the chance to go to China, and Morgenthau insisted that Clay brief him before he left. "Just as long as the Army and the Treasury stick together, I'm not going to worry," said Morgenthau. Wallace's mission brought no breakthrough on the financial front (as usual, Morgenthau was correct in his assessment of Chiang's perfidy), and though China continued to advance yuan for U.S. expenses, the Bretton Woods international monetary conference opened in July with Dr. Kung still insisting on an exchange rate of 20:1.

The Bretton Woods conference was called to lay the groundwork for postwar financial cooperation: the International Monetary Fund and the World Bank. But insofar as the United States was concerned, it also brought together America's principal Allies for some hard bargaining; an opportunity to settle wartime accounts and negotiate postwar assistance. In the case of China, the bill for the Chengtu airfields required immediate attention, and Morgenthau asked Clay to lead the discussion, for as Morgenthau told Harry Dexter White, "the most able fellow around this town is General Clay."

Like Morgenthau, Clay was determined to save the American taxpayer any unnecessary expense in buying Chiang Kai-shek's favor, especially in the face of China's rapidly disintegrating economic situation. Clay particularly resented that Chiang kept his "biggest and best equipped army" standing guard against the Communists rather than fighting the Japanese. "The Japs move forward in the summer and early spring and they move back when they destroy the harvests, and the Chinese have won a great victory when the Japs move back," Clay told Morgenthau at Bretton Woods.

In the negotiations with Kung, Clay offered to settle the Chinese account for $100 million—which, in effect, amounted to an exchange rate of 120:1. Kung replied in what Clay described to Somervell and Stimson as "a magnificent piece of acting which covered the entire range of human emotion." Blaming the United States for China's inflation, Kung protested the high costs of feeding the American Army. "We in China are vegetable eaters, but your boys must have roast beef and must have eggs for breakfast—six eggs a day." To Clay and Morgenthau, it was obvious that Kung was going to hold out "for the maximum possible 'take.' "

In the interest of quick and prompt settlement, Clay raised his offer to $125 million. Kung was still dissatisfied, arguing that at Cairo President Roosevelt had promised to pay the total costs of American involvement—an amount to which Clay and Morgenthau could see no limit. Morgenthau replied that he had "no record" of FDR's promise, and after lunch, Clay raised the American offer to $150 million—the final figure as far as he was concerned.

Again Kung balked, at which point Morgenthau terminated the discussions. "That is the best we can do," he said reluctantly.

The Chinese account was eventually settled in November 1944, at a cost of $185 million, but since it covered an additional three months' work on the airfields, both Clay and Morgenthau were satisfied. In reviewing the episode with Solomon Adler, the Treasury Department's representative in China, Morgenthau confided that "the man who helped the most was General Clay."

But if Clay was in good odor with Morgenthau and the Treasury, his opposition to providing unlimited funding for Chiang Kai-shek had made him the *bête noire* of the numerous China-firsters in the American diplomatic community. In Chungking, pro-Chiang intelligence officers vented their outrage by adopting "Lucius" as the code name for a then little-known Vietnamese leader who was fast becoming a thorn in the flesh of colonial rule: the redoubtable Ho Chi Minh.

Clay himself was not aware of that, and certainly it would not have pleased him. But in the context of his struggles with Chiang, the appellation makes a point. For Clay could not tolerate the corruption he encountered.

Q: What did you think of Mr. Morgenthau?
CLAY: Well, on the few occasions I did work with him, I had nothing but pleasant relations with him. There was no strain at all. He was a very effective Secretary of the Treasury. I did not discuss Germany with him. That was not my job at the time. But on Chiang, we were in complete agreement.

It was in the late fall of 1944 that Clay was finally granted his wish for combat duty overseas. The Allied offensive in Europe had ground to a halt. Field Marshal Montgomery's advance into Holland and Belgium was stymied by the bitter resistance the Germans were putting up before Antwerp, while General Bradley's 12th Army Group confronted the Germans in their dug-in positions along the Siegfried Line. In the face of these determined German efforts, Eisenhower found himself to be desperately short of supplies and reinforcements. Artillery ammunition—particularly the heavy ammunition required to dislodge the enemy from concrete fortifications—was in especially short supply. The urgent need for heavy artillery ammunition "can not be minimized," cabled Eisenhower in early October. "I urge that every possible expedient be applied now to step up production."

Eisenhower's plight caused immediate dismay in Washington, where one year earlier it had been assumed that, if anything, the United States had too much artillery ammunition on hand. To check the situation first-hand, Under Secretary Patterson flew to Europe, where he discovered not only that Ike was short of heavy ammunition, but that supplies of every kind were becoming a problem. One difficulty, of course, was Montgomery's failure to capture Antwerp, for without that key Belgian port, Eisenhower's supply line was thrown back on the inadequate port facilities of Normandy—now far to the rear of the fighting front and poorly linked by rail and highway.

A more serious difficulty, in Patterson's view, was Eisenhower's supply setup, which limped along from crisis to crisis, rent by dissension and jealousy, split down the middle between competing Allied and American jurisdictions. Supply chief for SHAEF (Supreme Headquarters, Allied Expeditionary Forces) was Lieutenant General John C. H. Lee, an Engineer officer of exceptional ability who, like Somervell and Connolly, had done yeoman service for Harry Hopkins and the WPA. Six years Eisenhower's senior in the Regular Army, Lee's demonstrated organizing ability recommended him to Marshall (and Somervell), who were desperately eager to avoid the logistical snafus of North Africa and Italy during the all-important cross-Channel attack. Marshall's judgment was amply rewarded. Lee's preparations for D-Day left little to be desired, and the Allies crossed the Channel in fine shape—an accomplishment of enormous magnitude. But over the long haul, Lee wore badly. A slightly pompous officer with the religious ardor of a Chautauqua evangelist—his initials, JCH, caused him to be dubbed "Jesus Christ Himself"—Lee doled out supplies with a supply sergeant's eye for rewarding past favors and punishing grievances. Lee's crowning fiasco, however, was to divert scarce transportation and gasoline in early September 1944 in order to move his bloated Com Z headquarters of eight thousand officers and twenty-one thousand enlisted men to Paris without Eisenhower's knowledge. (The French subsequently complained to Eisenhower that U.S. Army demands in Paris were greater than those made by the Germans.)

When informed of Lee's action, Ike flew into a rage. Bradley and Patton, who badly needed the gasoline and trucks Lee had pre-empted, clamored for his scalp, and Lieutenant General Walter Bedell Smith, Eisenhower's chief of staff, who usually ran over anyone in his way, simply threw up his hands and began dealing directly with Lee's subordinates.

Judge Patterson, who arrived in Europe shortly afterward, recognized that nothing could be done to hasten Montgomery's plodding advance on Antwerp, but they could remove Lee, and in his private discussions with Eisenhower, Patterson recommended Clay, LeRoy Lutes, and Henry Aurand as possible replacements. Whether they could be spared, Patterson realized, was another question, but Eisenhower, who was still smoldering over Lee's move to Paris, said he would be delighted with any of the three. Ike knew Aurand slightly from the prewar Army, but Lutes had been his supply chief on the make-or-break 1941 Louisiana maneuvers, and Clay was an old, dear friend whose ability he prized highly.

Immediately upon Patterson's return to Washington, Marshall cabled Eisenhower that he had gained the "definite impression" that the "assignment of Lutes, Clay and Aurand" would greatly improve SHAEF's chaotic supply setup. "Investigation here discloses that I can assign Aurand to you at once, that Clay can be loaned for a 2 or 3 month period beginning next week and that Lutes can be sent for a period of about 1 month."

Eisenhower replied he was "sure" the "three men mentioned" would help a great deal. "I sincerely trust that General Clay particularly can start to this theater without delay."

Clay was thrilled at the opportunity of joining the campaign in Europe. The battle with Donald Nelson over reconversion had been won, the Chinese problem was still smoldering, but Treasury and the War Department were in agreement that Chiang would not play one against the other, and, to Clay, it looked like another long winter in Washington dealing with the same manpower and production problems with which he had been wrestling for the past three years.

"I am taking off," he rejoiced to his old friend Tom Farrell, who was serving with Stilwell in China. "While I am going in the opposite direction from where you are, I am at least having the opportunity which I have wanted since the war began, to do some service other than in Washington."

But when Clay arrived at Eisenhower's Versailles headquarters, Ike had experienced a change of heart about relieving Lee. After all was said and done, Lee did have unquestioned organizing talents, and, most important, he had gotten the Allies across the Channel—for which Eisenhower was profoundly grateful. He was sorry, Ike told Clay, but since victory was in sight, he had decided to go the rest of the way with Lee. The supply system might not work perfectly, but at least it worked, and he didn't want to swap horses in the middle of the stream. "I'm glad you are here, all the same," Eisenhower told Clay, "and if you'd be willing to take it on—although I know it's not what you came over here to do—after it's cleared up, I'll give you a division. What I'm asking you to do is to go down and take over the Normandy Base Section and try to clean up that shipping mess at Cherbourg."

To Clay, any assignment out of Washington was a gift horse into whose mouth he dare not look, and Ike's promise of a combat division more than consoled him. Besides, it was never clear what blooper Lee might pull, and if he could stay in Europe, Clay was certain things would work out all right. "Nevertheless," said Clay in retrospect, "I was really quite surprised when I was told to go down to Normandy.

"When I got down to Normandy I saw what the problem was. Patton and Bradley were being held up because they couldn't get supplies, yet there were a hundred ships tied up in Cherbourg and off Omaha and Utah beaches. It was a bottleneck that was slowing down the attack, and it resulted primarily from the fact that we had had to use the port facilities in Normandy far more than we had thought, because Montgomery was way behind in taking Antwerp, and nobody could persuade him to make a frontal assault.

"Because of the delay in taking Antwerp, we were having to put pressure on these areas, which were not really designed for this type and kind of traffic. We also found a great deal more destruction at Le Havre than we had anticipated, and we were having difficulty restoring it. Brest we didn't capture until much later. So the only ports we had to support the entire front were Cherbourg, and Omaha and Utah beaches—and the British with their 'Mulberry,' a floating dock that was assembled in Britain and floated across the Channel, and wasn't really designed for that much usage.

"This tie-up also contributed to our shipping crisis. Obviously, if we could unload the ships sitting off Cherbourg and not use them as floating warehouses, we'd have nothing like the shortage of ships that people in Washington were complaining about. This was one of our troubles. We had literally a hundred ships lying offshore and we were unloading maybe two or three a day."

Clay's Washington reputation preceded him to Cherbourg, where the bickering and petty jealousies that had snarled the port quickly dissipated. Two days after he arrived, Eisenhower wrote Somervell that Clay "has already taken charge at Cherbourg. I know he will do a bang-up job."

The real problem at Cherbourg, Clay discovered, was too many bosses. "We had a very experienced port commander who for years was director of the Port of Philadelphia. The only trouble was that he was being so hounded by higher staffs checking up on what he was doing that the poor fellow was spending all of his time explaining why he wasn't doing the job that he was perfectly capable of doing.

" 'Can you run this port?' I asked him.

" 'Yes,' he said, 'if you can take all of these other things off my shoulders—and if you can give me control of the port railroad.'

" 'Fine,' I said. 'You've got seventy-two hours to do it. No staff representative from General Lee's headquarters or anywhere else is going to bother you during that period. And the railroads will be yours as of tomorrow morning. If anybody gets in your way, call me. Is that satisfactory? Are you willing to accept it on that basis?'

" 'You give me seventy-two hours and I'll show you,' he replied.

"I said, 'Fine. You've got them.' And at the end of seventy-two hours, he showed me. He had corrected the problem.

"The more serious problem was that they were unloading at Omaha and Utah beaches and putting the supplies into mud fields at a rate three and a half times greater than we could move it out. We knew where everything was, but it didn't make a goddamned bit of difference, because we couldn't get to it. Obviously, with the front moving forward, our input into those beaches should have been less than our output. But it was just the reverse. All we were doing was transferring the ship bottleneck into a worse bottleneck on the ground. And so I stopped unloading over the beaches. There wasn't a damn bit of sense in unloading ships at Omaha and Utah beaches if you couldn't move those supplies forward."

Q: Because of the mud?

CLAY: We had just been piling up the material—in a very orderly fashion, it's true—in the pastures and fields of Normandy. But the rains came, and then the frost came, and I'm sure that fifteen or twenty thousand years from now, when they dig down in the fields of Normandy, they'll find supplies that we put there in 1944.

Q: And the railroad?

CLAY: There was a port railroad at Cherbourg that served all the docks. In our takeover of the French railroads, our transportation division had taken over control of that railroad too. So it was being operated from General Lee's headquarters, not from Cherbourg. This meant that the port superintendent had to call somewhere else to get railroad cars when he needed them. And this turned out to be a real bottleneck because, if you have a dock that is sagging with equipment, and if you haven't got any railroad cars to take it off, there is not a damn thing you can do about it.

Q: And you changed this?

CLAY: I just turned the railroad over to the port commander.

Q: But was the railroad under you?

CLAY: It should have been under me. It wasn't, but it should have been. I called up General [Frank S.] Ross, who was Lee's chief of transportation, and told him what I had done. If he'd wanted to have a fight with me, I might have lost, but he didn't. The port railroad belonged to the port, and it should have been controlled from there.

Q: General, E. J. Kahn, in his *New Yorker* "Profile" of you, refers to some six cases of Scotch whisky that you expedited for an unnamed U.S. general in Paris.

CLAY: General [John M.] Franklin was in Paris. He'd been the head of U.S. [Steamship] Lines, and took a leave to become the deputy of General Gross [Army chief of transportation] for ocean transportation, and was sent over to Paris from Washington to investigate the shipping problem. While I was in Cherbourg, he called me from Paris and told me that he was awfully tired of drinking champagne and cognac, the only things you could get in Paris, and that U.S. Lines had a warehouse of Scotch liquor, and he could arrange for six cases to be put on the *Ferry Queen,* one of the big ferryboats we had running across the Channel, but he couldn't get them off the boat and couldn't get them to Paris. Would I take care of them for him?

"And I said, 'You know you're not talking to your friend Lucius Clay, you're talking to the commanding general of Normandy Base Section, and I'm certainly not going to take off six cases of Scotch and send you six cases.' I think he almost fell off of his chair at the other end. I said, 'However, I will see that you get three of them. The other three, I'm keeping.' And I did."

Two weeks after Clay arrived, the difficulties at Normandy Base Section had been ironed out, and Ike summoned Clay back to Paris.

"Clay has already proved most helpful," the chastened Lee wrote Somervell. "He has more than deserved the Bronze Star which we have dignified by awarding one to him—along with Hodges and Huebner for their cracking the Siegfried Line. Clay's cracking open the Cherbourg and beach situation is no less important."

Eisenhower's reason for pulling Clay out of Cherbourg was the even more desperate shortage of artillery ammunition SHAEF faced.

Already Patton's drive against Metz had been called off because of the lack of ammunition—Third Army artillery could fire but one round per gun per day—and the situation was little better in Bradley's Twelfth Army Group, now up against the heavily fortified positions of Germany's West Wall. Lee's difficulties in Com Z and the port problems in Normandy only partially accounted for the shortage, for the United States just wasn't producing ammunition in the quantities Eisenhower needed.

"General Eisenhower wanted me to find out how serious the ammunition shortage was at first hand," said Clay, "and then return to the United States and get it. Eisenhower said he just simply hadn't been able to convince Washington of his need.

"The difficulty was that about six or eight months before, Donald Nelson had protested that we were stockpiling too many items, and artillery ammunition was one of these. So in response to Nelson's protests, the War Department convened a board of retired officers—the McCoy Board—to look into the matter. I argued our requirements at the time before the board, but nevertheless they found that we were piling up artillery ammunition beyond our needs and ordered us to cut back. So here I was again, a little while later, arguing the same case for General Eisenhower, who now was caught short of ammunition."

Q: It was a question of not knowing how much was enough?

CLAY: This was one of the troubles that dogged us constantly. For a long period of the war, we were not doing the type of fighting that required heavy artillery ammunition. And suddenly you run into the Germans in a well-prepared defensive position—as we did. We knew with almost mathematical certainty that the use of maximum firepower saved lives. And the heavier the artillery, and the more you had of it, the more lives you saved. But we hadn't used much of it up to that point, so the need for it had been denied.

Q: This was the McCoy Board?

CLAY: Yes. We were firing ammunition at a rate far in excess of any rate in any other war. This was made possible by trucks, self-propelled artillery, and transportation of a type and kind that we had never had before. And it was very difficult for the older military men on the McCoy Board to visualize the rates of fire we were predicting. You couldn't have used those rates in World War I. Horse-drawn caissons, slow-moving trucks, poor roads, mud—all would have prevented you from firing that rapidly. And so at the McCoy Board's recommendation, production was cut back.

In an effort to look into the situation at first hand, Clay visited Bradley, Devers, and Patton and then flew immediately to Washington with Lieutenant General "Pinky" Bull, Ike's operations officer (G-3). Eisenhower pinned high hopes on Clay's mission. To Marshall he cabled, "General Clay has been especially selected to present the ammunition problem principally because of his general knowledge of the subject and the fact that he has come here recently and his views are therefore relatively objective." Ike asked that Marshall receive Clay and Bull as soon as they arrived, "so that they may return at the earliest possible date."

To emphasize his plight, the supreme commander passed on to Marshall a message from Bradley, who complained that his reserve stocks would soon be exhausted. Without more ammunition, said Bradley, "the crossing of the Rhine is out of the question unless enemy resistance collapses."

Clay made his report, "and it was a very upsetting report, unquestionably, to General Marshall. I asked for a little time, and went into consultation with Ordnance, with the manufacturers, checked on warehouses and whatnot. And I found that, by what we called 'compressing the supply line,' we could get about sixty to ninety days' additional ammunition to General Eisenhower. It worked out very well, because the war in Europe ended just as we reached the bottom of the larder, and we never had to use any heavy ammunition on Japan. And, actually, we in the Services of Supply had done a much better job of forecasting requirements than anybody had thought during the period when we weren't using heavy ammunition."

· 13 ·

Deputy Director of War Mobilization

General Clay gets his results by direct action. Conferences are brief, brusque and to the point. He scorns the usual Washington practice of carrying reams of documents in bulging brief cases, a trait he shares with Mr. Byrnes. A small scratchpad with a few notes jotted upon it are enough for the General. Figures, he carries in his head. The result is that he gets quickly and clearly to the point. Time is saved, and, with General Clay, time is precious.

United States News [*& World Report*],
December 20, 1944

After Clay and General Bull reported Eisenhower's precarious ammunition situation, Clay set to work to "compress the pipeline." In the meantime, General Marshall, whose usual unflappability was set on edge by Clay's disturbing survey, appealed to Justice Byrnes to "use all the resources of your office" as Director of War Mobilization "to get heavy ammunition going again."

Like Clay, Byrnes had just returned from Europe, and was more than sympathetic to Ike's predicament. But Byrnes already had a full plate. Not only was he FDR's "assistant president" for the home front, but Congress had just given the Office of War Mobilization statutory authority to plan for reconversion as well—a grant of power that represented the broadest delegation of legislative authority ever bestowed by Congress on an executive agency.

Just as Clay and Marshall made their pleas for more ammunition, Field Marshal von Rundstedt launched his devastating counterattack in the Ardennes. The Battle of the Bulge left no doubt that victory was far from won. As Clay told *Newsweek*, "Our need for military supplies will be at [its] peak on the date the Germans quit. Those who think that date is predictable and would taper off military production accordingly risk prolonging the war."

Byrnes responded to the Army's request with a proposal of his own. "All right. That's fine. I'll do what I can," he told Marshall. "But send General Clay over to be my deputy."

Although Eisenhower had requested that Clay be returned to Europe immediately, Marshall readily agreed to Byrnes's suggestion, and Byrnes telephoned Clay the unwelcome news. "I'm sure you are mistaken," said Clay. "I have a letter here from General Eisenhower asking that I be returned immediately."

"I think you are coming with me," Byrnes cryptically replied.

Clay immediately went to see Somervell, who was sympathetic but said Clay would have to see General Marshall.

Q: And General Marshall?
CLAY: General Marshall said I was going to work for Justice Byrnes. Period.

Somervell broke the unwelcome news to Eisenhower in a long, rambling letter stressing the "immense help" that Byrnes had been to the armed services. "[Byrnes] asked for General Clay . . . and General Marshall thought it was the appropriate move to make. I know that you will miss him and I want you to be sure that I have not double-crossed you on his assignment. The initiative was with Byrnes and not in this office and I believe, however, that Clay will do you more good there . . . though he personally was greatly disappointed in not being able to go back."

Once Clay was installed in the Office of War Mobilization, Byrnes delegated to him complete responsibility for war production. Clay was authorized to act in Byrnes's name whenever the situation required. Clay's ability to act quickly and decisively—the combination of ruthlessness and finesse that had untangled the mess at Cherbourg in three days—made him invaluable in restoring a sense of urgency to the war effort. "More and more decisions were gravitating to Byrnes," said WPB deputy director Harold Boeschenstein, "and someone had to be deputized who could handle them. Clay was a very logical choice, because he could make decisions rapidly and be arbitrary about them."

Clay's appointment caused an immediate outcry against creeping "militarism" in Washington, although, as Byrnes later told Roosevelt, "I . . . obtained his assignment to my office, because, after dealing with officials of all the departments, I found no man more capable than Clay and no army officer who had as clear an understanding of the point of view of the civilian."

Q: When did you meet Mr. Byrnes?

CLAY: Well, I don't know that I can answer that. Certainly I met him when I was working on rivers and harbors and he was Senate majority leader—but not in any real sense. Then, during the war, when he left the Supreme Court and went into this particular job, I was sent over representing the War Department on a number of issues that came before him for settlement. Out of it, he asked me to come over and be his deputy. He didn't ask me—he told me I was coming. In that particular period I became very close to him. Then he became Secretary of State while I was in Germany, and we kept up really a very close relationship.

Q: And you thought highly of Mr. Byrnes?

CLAY: He was one of the outstanding men of his generation. He'd held practically every position that his state could give; he'd served both in the House and the Senate, and I think he was generally conceded to be one of the great legislative experts of the period. He'd then gone to the Supreme Court, and when the President asked him, he stepped down from the Court to run war mobilization. He believed that politics was the art of compromise: that you didn't put any venture on a do-or-die basis. If you got halfway to your goal on your first try, you'd had a great success—and you kept chipping away until you reached your goal. Which was probably why he was such a great legislator.

Q: Did he regret leaving the Court during the war?

CLAY: I don't think that he ever regretted leaving the Court, no. He left the bench to become head of war mobilization, then he became Secretary of State, after which he practiced law for a while and made a little money, which he had very little of, and then went back and became governor [of South Carolina]. I think these active jobs were more appealing to him than the judicial job.

Q: What was your job under Mr. Byrnes?

CLAY: I was his deputy. There was no specific assignment. I just had the general responsibility—the same as he did. I ran the office, made up the reports, wrote the letters, kept track of our responsibilities, that sort of thing.

"On the other hand, Mr. Byrnes exercised a great deal of person-to-person leadership, particularly with his old friends like Marvin Jones, who was agricultural stabilizer, and Fred Vinson, who was price administrator. Obviously, he was over consulting with the President fairly often. One of my real difficulties in being the Justice's deputy was to find out what he had said at these meetings, because he didn't keep a record except for his own shorthand notes. So every time he had a visitor, I had to go in afterwards and find out what they had discussed."

Q: But you and he were very close?

CLAY: Very close. We never had any problems, then or later. Every evening, after the office closed, we would sit down together and discuss the problems over bourbon and branch water. That way each knew what the other was thinking. If I had any problems, I told him then.

Q: And your offices were in the White House?

CLAY: When I joined Mr. Byrnes, we were in the East Wing of the White House. By that time, however, the office had been set up as a statutory agency by Congress, which required that we keep certain records and make certain reports that we hadn't done when it was simply a staff office of the President. I got the office set up for that type of work. But our rooms in the White House were so small that when I built up a reasonable staff I got offices for them over on the top floor of the Reconstruction Finance Corporation. All of the routine work I took over there, so that Mr. Byrnes didn't have to be bothered with it. This was a very informal office. There were never more than seven or eight of us. That assured that only policy problems got our attention. We didn't try to run anything. I don't think Justice Byrnes could have been anywhere near as effective if he'd really expanded his office and brought a lot of people in. His effectiveness was due to the fact that he listened personally to the people who had problems. In other words, you only went to Mr. Byrnes if you were a Cabinet officer or the head of the War Production Board or the price administrator and so forth. He was really dealing with people who ordinarily would have been dealing with the President.

Q: Presumably this is the way the President conceived it?

CLAY: Mr. Roosevelt wanted this type of decision-making taken out of his office. He was sick and tired of all of these clashes coming to him for decisions. He didn't want his time taken up by having to resolve all of these jurisdictional battles and disputes. He wanted to be relieved of it so he could give his main time to running the war and foreign policy. So he got Mr. Byrnes in there and made him his deputy for that particular purpose. The President gave him the authority and Mr. Byrnes took it, and by and large took that load off the President's shoulders.

Q: Then the descriptions of Mr. Byrnes as "assistant president" are accurate?

CLAY: No question about it. He was the assistant president so far as the domestic scene was concerned. Not so far as the conduct of the war or foreign policy was concerned. He was not involved with that until he went to Yalta. And he didn't go to Yalta as an official member of the delegation. He went because the President asked him to go as a friend. But when he got there, Mr. Hopkins was sick, the President was sick, and General Watson [FDR's military aide] was sick. And so Mr. Byrnes found himself practically running the delegation.

Q: Was there any conflict of interest in your being Director of Materiel for the Army and deputy director of war mobilization for Mr. Byrnes?

CLAY: I think it worried a few people in the War Production Board. I don't think they had any cause to worry, but I'm rather inclined to believe they did, from what some of them have said in memoirs and otherwise. The last place that I wanted to end the war was in Mr. Byrnes's office. I'd practically given up then on getting back to Europe, but I still hoped to get into the war on the Pacific side.

"The fact is, however, that my relationship with this whole thing depended entirely on the confidence Mr. Byrnes had in me. Period. If there were conflicts of interest, I didn't let them develop. I ceased acting as Director of Materiel when I worked for Mr. Byrnes."

Although Byrnes and Clay became very close, it would be incorrect to describe Clay as Byrnes's protégé. As Robert Lovett recalled, "Lucius was too goddamned independent to be anyone's protégé." Nevertheless, the mutual esteem and respect between Clay and Byrnes became crucial for American foreign policy when Byrnes was Secretary of State and Clay was Military Governor. Both were southern New Dealers, from the piedmont of South Carolina and Georgia (Byrnes's hometown of Spartanburg and Marietta are barely one hundred miles apart). They spoke the same soft cadences of the Appalachian plateau and understood each other instinctively. Both were skilled manipulators of broad governmental coalitions, and devotees of pragmatic compromise. Above all, both were firm believers in the direction FDR had charted for the United States, and both tried loyally to carry it into effect.

"Obviously," said Clay, "my job was to take the necessary action to get the war program moving again, particularly the heavy ammunition program. But we had a great many problems. One of the most important at that time was the legislation before Congress for drafting manpower—not just for military service, but for industry. I had a conflict there, a very serious one, because Mr. Byrnes had gone to Yalta and left me in charge."

Q: Didn't Mr. Byrnes have an advisory council?

CLAY: We had one, but Mr. Byrnes never embraced it. It was composed of a number of distinguished Americans plus several labor leaders. It was a difficult council because it was so diverse in its opinions. Each member represented a special interest. Every time you had a meeting, it ended up in a shouting match across the table. There was never any unanimity of thinking or opinion, and I think he just naturally began to hold the sessions of the council further and further apart.

Q: Weren't Phil Murray of the CIO [Congress of Industrial Organizations] and Bill Green of the AFL [American Federation of Labor] members of the council?

CLAY: And one or two others. It was nothing personal. Phil Murray and I got along very well together. Bill Green too. And especially Walter Reuther. But they were very much opposed to the manpower bill—

which our office was for. If we hadn't had the manpower problem in the closing year of the war, I don't think we would have had any difficulty whatever. I am sure that many members of the council felt that I had pushed Mr. Byrnes into the manpower problem, which is absolutely not so. Mr. Stimson got him into the manpower problem, not I. Then, when Mr. Byrnes was at Yalta and I presided over the council, they liked it even less. But that didn't bother me. I didn't expect them to like it. For them it was a symbolic question, and they didn't want an Army officer telling them what the policy would be.

America's manpower shortage in late 1944 was not in the military services but on the home front. With twelve million men and women serving the colors, labor scarcity in key defense industries had become a chronic problem. Mr. Stimson and the War Department sought to relieve the difficulty through congressional legislation that would have empowered the Selective Service System to draft workers for essential defense work, only to run into a hotbed of opposition from organized labor. Byrnes, whose skill at achieving a compromise on such issues was unparalleled, devised a scheme whereby the Army and Navy would draft men with essential skills directly into the services and then "furlough" them to man critical positions in industry. Selective Service would reciprocate by inducting men in higher age groups to replace those released, while the Army, on its part, would not be too sticky about physical standards for the older replacements. The result would be essentially what all desired: critical jobs would be filled; pressure would be exerted indirectly on the labor force to take jobs with defense industries; and the principle of drafting men only for military service would be preserved.

The compromise was embodied in a press release issued by the Office of War Mobilization and Reconversion in mid-December. But the War Department was never happy over its lack of statutory authority to force workers into essential jobs and, despite Byrnes's order, continued to press for national manpower legislation in Congress. Judge Patterson, in particular, insisted that vital defense production "should not depend on coaxing people to take war jobs." At Patterson's urging, Mr. Stimson, who had long advocated national service legislation, prevailed upon Navy Secretary Forrestal to make a joint appeal to President Roosevelt.

But FDR needed no convincing. As early as New Year's Day, 1944, the President had come out for national service legislation. He again endorsed the measure in his State of the Union message in 1945. "The Lord hates a quitter," Roosevelt said, and the nation would have "to pay for slackers with the life blood of its sons."

President Roosevelt's message notwithstanding, there was faint hope for the passage of any form of national service legislation in 1945. The war clearly was won—it was only a matter of time—and organized labor strongly resented the idea of drafting men into the labor force. "It's like using a shillelagh to pick your teeth," said the AFL's Bill Green.

"Quack medicine," sniffed Philip Murray.

Byrnes and Clay, both of whom were in close touch with congressional leaders, were prepared to support the War Department insofar as the compromise formula of Justice Byrnes might be enacted, but no further. Unlike Judge Patterson and Mr. Stimson, Byrnes and Clay recognized that the country was not ready for broad national service legislation, but would support some type of stopgap to ensure that vital defense jobs were filled. Indeed, Byrnes's position became the basis for identical bills introduced in the House of Representatives by Andrew J. May (D., Kentucky) and in the Senate by Josiah Bailey (D., Connecticut), chairmen of the respective committees on military affairs. Byrnes was able to enlist limited labor support for the compromise measure—"I'm all for the labor draft," said Harry Bridges of the longshoremen's union—and it seemed just possible that passage might be secured.

On January 10, 1945, Judge Patterson presented the War Department's case to the House Committee on Military Affairs. And though he had agreed beforehand to Byrnes's compromise strategy, Patterson abruptly switched signals, condemned the idea, and demanded passage of far-reaching national service legislation for all men between eighteen and forty-five.

Before Patterson could be called off, Byrnes departed abruptly for Yalta and left Clay in charge. "In my absence from the City," Byrnes wrote Clay, "I request and authorize you to serve as Acting Director of War Mobilization and Reconversion." With both Byrnes and FDR out of the country, Clay suddenly found himself in nominal control of the home front.

But Clay faced a dilemma. On the one hand, he was firmly committed to enforcing the compromise measure Byrnes had worked out. On the other, he was confronted with the War Department's demand for the full national service package. Clay knew that even if the War Department's bill passed the House it would fail in the Senate, and so he intervened directly with the congressional leadership to preserve Byrnes's formula. When news of Clay's action got back to the Pentagon, Stimson and Patterson were furious.

Stimson called Clay immediately. "I got on the phone," Clay said, "and then Mr. Stimson came on. 'Stimson speaking,' he said. Then he said, 'I understand that you are trying to obstruct the War Department's manpower proposal.'

"I said, 'Mr. Stimson, I'm not trying to obstruct the War Department's manpower proposal.'

"He said, 'I don't want to hear any of that. General—you are a general, aren't you?'

"I said, 'Ycs sir.'

"He said, 'Well, you may not be one.'

"I said, 'Yes sir,' and about an hour later I got another telephone call. We were going to have a conference in Mr. Stimson's office. I went over. Patterson was there, and Mr. Stimson started off by lighting into me. Whereupon Judge Patterson spoke up.

" 'Colonel,' he said—he always called Mr. Stimson 'Colonel'—'I'm the one that's completely wrong in this. I entered into the agreement which General Clay is trying to carry out in Byrnes's absence. I went up to the Hill and violated that agreement. I had no business to do it. I accept full responsibility for what has happened and I again want to tell you I shouldn't have done it.'

"That ended the conference," Clay remembers. "I don't know what would have happened if Judge Patterson hadn't spoken up. I'd probably have been a colonel of Engineers in a few hours. But Mr. Stimson never held it against me. When I returned from Germany in 1949 and made a talk at the Council on Foreign Relations, he came in his wheelchair. He was a giant. He was in the mold that we don't see many of."

Q: But Mr. Stimson was in his late seventies in 1945. Was he still alert and active?

CLAY: Mr. Stimson did not work many hours a day. But in the five or six hours that he was in his office, he was completely alert and active. He gave General Marshall the kind of support without which General Marshall could not have accomplished what he did. And respect. The respect and esteem in which he was held by the President and the Congress was almost unbelievable. He went down there and got the appropriation for the Manhattan Project without any explanation of it except that it was necessary.

Byrnes's judgment about the infeasibility of national service legislation proved correct. The House passed (246–165) the War Department version Patterson had advocated, only to have it killed in the Senate. Clay's role, far from being that of an advocate of the military's plan, was to encourage a compromise that labor could support. "Rightly or wrongly," said Clay, "the Army took the position that if you could draft men to go to war and possibly be killed, then it was not restrictive of the liberty of those that stayed home to be drafted and told where to work. This is where organized labor resisted very, very bitterly. We didn't need to draft labor to put it to work, but we did need to move it from one part of the country to another in some instances, and Mr. Byrnes's compromise achieved that."

Q: In terms of American national security today, how do you feel about an all-volunteer Army?

CLAY: I have spent most of my service in an all-volunteer Army. But I honestly don't see how in a volunteer Army, if you offer it as a career, you can avoid it becoming too old. I think such an Army would be far less effective for that reason. Secondly, I think that we're letting an unpopular war in Vietnam distort our vision. It seems to me that to retain the responsibility of a citizen to defend his country in the form of the draft is a very important thing, whether you exercise it or not. In the period prior to Vietnam, I don't believe that the number of draft calls was sufficient to bother anybody. But the fact that there was a draft led a good many young men to enlist who might not have otherwise. The present dislike of the draft is tied up with a dislike of the war in Vietnam rather than whether the draft is good or bad for our country. I think we have passed the stage where we can depend on a mercenary Army.

Q: Are the problems of political control exacerbated in a mercenary Army?

CLAY: I don't think so. We had a mercenary Army throughout most of our history, and we had no problems. And I don't think we ever will. But it becomes a question of physical stamina. Younger men are better able to adjust to severe conditions than are older men. I don't think motivation *per se* is a problem, because professional soldiers have always given a good account of themselves—not only in our Army but in all armies. They are given a much higher standard of discipline than a draft army. But I don't think we have anything to fear in terms of [loss of] civilian control.

Clay's battle with the War Department over manpower was a prelude to his fight with the Navy over the massive naval construction program undertaken in 1945. Early in January, Fleet Admiral Ernest J. King, the Chief of Naval Operations, who usually dealt directly with the President in such matters, requested White House approval for eighty-four new combat ships, including eight battleships. FDR approved King's request immediately. "The President did not have time to study your recommendation," the White House naval aide wrote Forrestal, "but said that you could inform the Budget that he favored the construction."

Budget Director Harold Smith, who had not been informed of the Navy's request—a not unusual situation in FDR's freewheeling White House—issued an immediate reclama. But Roosevelt, who relished his role as commander in chief and was always partial to the Navy, replied in no uncertain terms: "I am inclined to support the proposal of the Secretary of the Navy," said FDR. At that point, Smith hesitated to make another appeal to the President and took his case to Byrnes.

"The President was a great Navy man," said Clay, "but no one in our office thought the war could possibly last long enough for those battleships to be built. Fred Searles, who was on our staff and who was always a stormy petrel, wrote a blistering memo against the program. But since the President had approved it, Mr. Byrnes was reluctant to take it up. Finally, he did. Or at least got the President to allow him to look into the matter. Then we stirred up things so much with memos back and forth that the Navy decided, as a discretionary matter, not to push it anymore. And the ships were not built."

Q: In the spring of 1945, the Joint Chiefs wanted to build forty additional tankers.

CLAY: These are the types of problems that were coming up all the time. And we opposed that on the same grounds: the time that it took to build them meant they would not be available for use in that war.

Q: And the Air Force?

CLAY: We had trouble with them too. They were building too many different types of airplanes. No one wanted them to cut back on B-29s, but they were still building B-17s. We couldn't see the need for both.

Q: And the military services accepted Mr. Byrnes's decisions?

CLAY: The services were perfectly prepared to accept Mr. Byrnes's decisions—in contrast to those of the War Production Board—because they felt he was impartial and above the fight. On many occasions, he helped the services. So there was a feeling of even-handedness. I never heard his decisions questioned, really. You've got to remember that Mr. Byrnes was really operating for the President. And everybody knew it. If they went to see the President, he'd say, "Go see Jimmy." He didn't have to do that many times until, as far as people in government were concerned, Mr. Byrnes was the authority. Don't forget, the conflicts weren't just between the Army and the War Production Board. There were conflicts within each service. Constant conflict. The only way you could possibly solve many of these problems was by conflicting demands. This way it got resolved in the best fashion. Each side had to yield. If ammunition at that moment was more important than soldiers, then soldiers had to yield.

Q: This was generally done with good spirits?

CLAY: By and large, I think it was. When you have this kind of battle going on between the various interests—let's say the railroads and somebody else—somebody's going to get mad, but by and large I think it was done in a spirit of understanding and highly competitive demand.

"We did two or three things which seemed childish, and nevertheless seemed awfully important then. And I think they were. One was to close the racetracks. Gasoline and tires were scarce—people were complaining about not having enough gasoline to go to work—yet here were the races going on, and you always saw a great number of cars parked at the racetracks in spite of rationing. Then there were all of the people who worked there. We needed them in war work too."

Q: By what authority did you close the tracks?

CLAY: We just issued a statement urging the operators not to open. That was all that was needed.

Q: And no one questioned it?

CLAY: Not then. Later, when we asked the nightclubs and cabarets to close at midnight, [Mayor] La Guardia questioned it. He refused to order the clubs in New York to close. So we sent MPs and the Navy's Shore Patrol into all of the clubs at midnight to tell the soldiers and sailors to go home, and, believe it or not, practically everybody else got up and went out with them.

Q: Was that your idea?

CLAY: I can't be sure, but it probably was.

Q: When you were with Justice Byrnes, did you meet with the press?

CLAY: No. I held no press conferences at all. I saw members of the press who were interested in specific issues, but I was working in the White House. I deliberately avoided the press. The press could see Mr. Byrnes and the President. Not me.

Clay's service as deputy director of war mobilization proved invaluable when he went to Germany, for his experience in the full range of the American economy was unparalleled—a vital consideration in a devastated country that had to be put back together. Equally important, Clay was on intimate terms not only with Justice Byrnes (who quickly emerged as Truman's Secretary of State) but with Washington's entire civilian leadership. He enjoyed the respect of Harry Hopkins and Henry Morgenthau no less than that of Colonel Stimson and Judge Patterson. And on Capitol Hill, he was a familiar figure. Sam Rayburn was as close to Clay as Justice Byrnes was, and from both Clay learned the art of Washington politics. Years later, reflecting on his work under Byrnes, Clay called it a "postgraduate course in government."

· 14 ·

Selection of a Proconsul

> Being Military Governor was a pretty heady job. It was the nearest thing to a Roman proconsulship the modern world afforded. You could turn to your secretary and say, "Take a law." The law was there, and you could see its effect in two or three weeks. It was a challenging job to an ambitious man. Benevolent despotism.
>
> *John J. McCloy*

AMERICAN PLANNING FOR THE OCCUPATION OF GERmany divided the wartime Roosevelt administration as did few other issues. Secretary Morgenthau and the Treasury Department, often joined by Cordell Hull and Harry Hopkins, favored the harshest possible treatment for Germany. Secretary Stimson and the War Department, frequently joined by the career foreign service, favored a firm occupation and a swift rehabilitation. And as was often the case, President Roosevelt stood in the no-man's-land between—at times agreeing with Morgenthau, as at Quebec, when he and Churchill initialed the "Morgenthau

Plan" for Germany's pastoralization; at times agreeing with Stimson, as when FDR reminisced with his Secretary of War about the Germany of Goethe, Schiller, and William I.

For the most part, the battle over postwar Germany focused on the policy to govern the occupation. Throughout late 1944 and early 1945, representatives of State, War, and Treasury worked diligently to fashion a directive that would accommodate the divergent views of Morgenthau and Stimson, and in the end produced a document (JCS 1067) that largely succeeded. The need for tough treatment was recognized, yet the occupying authorities were given sufficient discretion to avoid "disease and unrest"—a pragmatic formula that reflected the drafting skill of John J. McCloy, who put the directive in final form.

What is curious, in retrospect, is that Washington's top political leadership, in spite of fundamental differences over what American policy should be, could agree so quickly in the spring of 1945 that Clay was the man best qualified to head the occupation. By then Clay was a recognized fixture in Washington. His efficient, scandal-free conduct of military procurement had earned him the lasting respect of the War Department's civilian leadership: Stimson, Patterson, and McCloy. Harry Hopkins valued Clay's work with Lend-Lease, Byrnes had asked personally for him to be deputy "czar" of the home front, and Morgenthau considered Clay one of the ablest men in government. In sum, Clay was a politically sensitive general on intimate terms with the Roosevelt administration— "one of the most skillful politicians ever to wear the uniform of the United States Army," in the words of John Kenneth Galbraith. His selection to head Germany's military government reflected the unanimous choice of the key figures of the Roosevelt administration. He was chosen, not simply because of his demonstrated organizing ability, but because he was in tune with the goals and aspirations of wartime Washington. That he knew nothing about Germany, or about the discussions that had taken place concerning its future, appeared of little importance to men like Hopkins and Byrnes, who had known Clay since the earliest days of the New Deal.

The news that he was going to Germany came as an unwelcome surprise to Clay. Washington's initial discussions on who would head Germany's occupation had focused on naming a top-ranking civilian. On September 4, 1944, the Cabinet committee on Germany (Hull, Morgenthau, Stimson, and Hopkins) recommended to FDR that an

American High Commissioner be appointed immediately. No names were suggested, although Harry Hopkins (who may have wanted the post himself—at least, Hull thought so) put forward Averell Harriman, then Ambassador to Moscow, and Mr. Stimson recommended the Assistant Secretary of War, John J. McCloy. But Morgenthau objected to both. After all, he told Hopkins, McCloy's "clients are people like General Electric, Westinghouse, General Motors" and "the same thing would apply" to Harriman.

The following morning, in Hull's outer office, Hopkins buttonholed Morgenthau with the name of Under Secretary of War Robert Patterson. Morgenthau was delighted. "If you have that kind of directive [JCS 1067] and put it into the hands of someone like Patterson, I wouldn't worry," he said. Morgenthau and Hopkins agreed that whoever was appointed "should start now under Eisenhower"—Morgenthau, in part, because of his distrust of Robert Murphy, then Ike's political adviser.

But when Morgenthau, together with Hull, Stimson, and Hopkins, discussed the matter with Roosevelt, it appeared that FDR had other plans. As Morgenthau told Harry Dexter White afterward, "they got off on the question of the high commissioner and the President didn't see why there should be one now. Then he told me, 'Well, if there is one it should be Jimmy Byrnes.' " FDR's suggestion of Byrnes was disheartening to Morgenthau, but as he later admitted, "I was told that Jimmy Byrnes is quitting [as director of war mobilization] in a couple of weeks and they have to find a spot for him."

According to Morgenthau, after Roosevelt mentioned Byrnes, Hull suggested Hopkins.

"Well, I don't want to see Harry go into a German hospital right away," the President said. "Harry needs a lot more pipes in his insides and I don't know whether we can get any pipes over there."

"In fencing, that's known as touché," said Morgenthau.

Roosevelt, who continued to believe it was premature to name anyone to the German post (Eisenhower's armies had not yet set foot on German soil), allowed the matter to drift—although Morgenthau pressed Patterson's candidacy aggressively. The day after the White House meeting, Morgenthau consulted with John McCloy. (Despite Morgenthau's distrust of McCloy's big-business connections, the two worked together closely in wartime Washington.) McCloy, who handled German matters for the War Department, had already heard of the meeting with Roosevelt from Harry Hopkins.

"So far as Patterson is concerned," said McCloy, "he certainly will go right down the line . . . whatever it is. He is quite a different breed of cat than your friend [Robert] Murphy on that."

"Oh well," replied Morgenthau, as if to dismiss Murphy. "There couldn't be a higher type person than Bob Patterson for this job or any other. I would be delighted if the President would give it to Bob Patterson. One hundred percent."

On September 8, Morgenthau called on Hull, the aging Secretary of State increasingly enfeebled after eleven years in office and, as Morgenthau reported, "looking very tired and very badly." Morgenthau sought Hull's assistance in persuading Roosevelt to issue the directive (what later became known as JCS 1067) on Germany immediately.

"The President," said Hull, "should have someone like Jimmy Byrnes who could advise him to go ahead on this matter. But I don't think Byrnes is going to take it." Hull told Morgenthau that it would be a "nice gesture" to give it to Hopkins, and, when pressed by Morgenthau, revealed that Hopkins had indicated he was interested in the job.

At Hull's direction, a representative of the State Department called on Byrnes but, instead of offering him the post of high commissioner, proposed that Byrnes take a secondary job on the Economic Control Commission for Germany. "Oh God, it was terrible," Hopkins told Morgenthau. "They didn't even talk to him about the high commissioner." When Hopkins asked Hull why, Hull matter-of-factly replied, "I have been assuming all along that you were going to have that job" —meaning the high commissionership.

Byrnes abruptly declined State's offer, and when Hopkins later asked him about the high commissioner's post, Byrnes said he wasn't interested in that either. "It wouldn't make any difference because it would be in effect the same kind of job," Byrnes said.

Byrnes's resolve not to be sucked into the German problem was final, as Hopkins immediately informed Morgenthau. Hopkins "wanted me to know that the position of high commissioner was wide open," Morgenthau confided to his diary. "Of course, it is perfectly obvious that he wants it for himself."

The following week, Morgenthau accompanied FDR to the Quebec Conference and another meeting with the British, where, among other things, Roosevelt and Churchill gave their approval to Morgenthau's plan for a Carthaginian peace—a plan Churchill dictated into final form. But little, if anything, was said at Quebec as to who should lead the American occupation, and on September 26, Hopkins again met with Morgenthau and Harry Dexter White at Treasury to discuss the matter further. "If we don't do something," said Hopkins, "Murphy will be running this show and he shouldn't. The thing [will] go by the board and we [will] wake up and find some Army officer like [Brigadier] Gen. Julius Holmes [deputy G-5, SHAEF] or somebody running the show." Hopkins believed that "some topflight civilian should be put in uniform and given the job" now. When the war was over, he could revert to civilian status.

"I know Hopkins so well," Morgenthau later told White. "He always has so many things you never know really what he is aiming at. . . . [W]hether [his] real reason for coming over here was trying to interest me in his candidacy for this job of being high commissioner—first the lieutenant general and then the high commissioner—I don't know, but he certainly got no encouragement." Nevertheless, Morgenthau and White agreed that it was "time to stick somebody in there," and Morgenthau again mentioned Patterson—a choice with which White concurred.

The next day, Morgenthau invited Patterson to lunch at Treasury to discuss the matter first-hand.

"Bob," he said, "I want to talk to you about a matter which I am doing wholly on my own initiative and I am not being sent by anybody to sound you out. So let's understand each other.

"If you were asked would you go now as an assistant to Eisenhower to do the civil affairs thing in Germany and even have to put on a uniform and subsequently become high commissioner, would you be interested?"

"The thought of putting on a uniform wouldn't bother me a bit," replied Patterson, "and I would be interested. I owe it to my wife and children to go on and earn a living, but I will be interested."

"Can I, without committing you," asked Morgenthau, "back your candidacy to the President?"

"Yes," Patterson replied. "Understand, I haven't made any commitments, but if it is offered to me I will give it serious consideration."

Morgenthau was delighted. "I am going to walk across the street [to the White House] in a few minutes to see [Fleet Admiral William D.] Leahy [chief of staff to the President]," Morgenthau noted in his diary, "and when I am over there I will drop in and see Grace Tully [FDR's secretary] and give her this little suggestion about Bob Patterson"—a revealing insight into the decision-making hierarchy of the Roosevelt White House.

Patterson, on his part, immediately reported the conversation to Secretary Stimson, then weekending at his New York estate, Highhold. Stimson, whose judgment was colored by his own experience as Taft's Secretary of War during the Philippine occupation, strongly advised Patterson against taking the job. The more Stimson had thought about the matter, he said, the more he had come to believe that the occupation should be headed by a "military man": it simply wouldn't do to put a civilian in uniform and call him a soldier.

On Monday, Hopkins suggested Patterson to FDR, and, as Hopkins later told Morgenthau, "the President . . . seemed to like the idea." Two weeks later, Roosevelt raised the matter with Stimson after a Cabinet meeting, and Stimson—perhaps not ready to press his case for a military man with the President—allowed that the initiative should come from Eisenhower, a judgment with which Navy Secretary Forrestal concurred.

Stimson's views weighed heavily on Patterson, for the following day he told Stimson "he thought a regular officer could be found who could do a better job than he could, and he mentioned particularly [Lieutenant General] Johnny [John C. H.] Lee." Stimson thought the suggestion of Lee, then Ike's supply chief, was a good one, "as well as a generous one" on Patterson's part—a reference to Patterson's earlier desire to have Lee replaced at SHAEF. Nevertheless, Stimson thought Patterson still "was a little tempted to try it."

Whatever doubts Stimson had were removed October 17, when Patterson sent him a four-page memo summarizing their discussion. In brief, Patterson argued that the initial occupation should come under Eisenhower's direct control, and that it should be staffed with soldiers, not civilians. In addition to very compelling reasons involving unity of command, Patterson maintained that "civilians would by no means command the respect of the Germans that military men would command." They would also be "controversial figures and would not receive the united support of our people when the going gets rough.

"There is no need to run these risks," Patterson continued. "The Army has plenty of officers . . . who are thoroughly qualified to deal with the difficulties to be encountered," and Patterson thereupon suggested four names: Omar Bradley, Lee, Clay, and Brigadier General Kenneth Royall, later Secretary of the Army under Truman. "The time may come when it will be necessary to have a [civilian] high commissioner," Patterson concluded. "But the appointment should be made when the need arises, not at the present time."

Patterson's memorandum effectively established the War Department's position. Two days later, on October 19, Stimson lunched with Hopkins, "whom I understand from McCloy has been very active in this matter." Stimson read Patterson's memo to Hopkins and, as Mr. Stimson later noted, "Hopkins agreed that Eisenhower should do the choosing."

With Stimson's intervention, the initiative shifted from Treasury to the War Department. Morgenthau resigned himself to Patterson's apparent unavailability and, perhaps content that he had headed off more objectionable choices, seemed satisfied to allow the Army to staff the Occupation with soldiers of the caliber Patterson and Stimson had suggested. "I would put myself in the hands of the generals," he later told Treasury's Frank Coe, "and there would be a Russian general there, and an American general, and a French general."

On October 25, 1944, McCloy wrote Eisenhower to acquaint him with what had transpired. "In the War Department we have all taken the view that the first phase of the administration [of Germany] must be on a military basis," McCloy said. "We have been quite clear that the Commanding General [Eisenhower] should not be surrounded by a group of separate 'advisers' who owed allegiance and reported back to others than the commanding general himself.

"Although there were some indications originally that the President might be of a different mind in this regard, I now believe that both the President and Mr. Hopkins are impressed with the wisdom of this course."

McCloy told Eisenhower that Judge Patterson had been mentioned for the post, but had turned it down unless Ike "desired him to undertake it," in which case "he would not refuse."

Eisenhower replied on November 1. "I now understand recent events much more clearly," he told McCloy, "and I want you to know how much I appreciate your efforts . . . to protect us from a complex system of advisers which would only add to the difficulties of a straight forward problem of military government." Ike told McCloy he was surprised by the suggestion of Judge Patterson, "not because there is any question . . . as to his complete acceptability, . . . but because I always had you yourself in mind for this particular assignment." In any event, Eisenhower concluded, "I would be delighted to take either Judge Patterson or a senior Army officer whom the Secretary and General Marshall consider to possess the necessary qualifications."

The following week, Lieutenant General Walter Bedell Smith, Ike's chief of staff at SHAEF, wrote Major General John Hilldring, then chief of the War Department's Civil Affairs Division, that McCloy's letter had come as a shock since "we have actually hoped to get McCloy for this job. I assume there is little likelihood that he will be made available," said Smith, "so I think the best thing is either to make a major general of Judge Patterson and send him along or send the best soldier you can find. . . . This decision should be made as quickly as possible." Smith's reference to a temporary rank of major general reflected Smith's own view that whoever headed the Occupation would report to Ike through him as chief of staff.

In spite of general agreement in Washington and at SHAEF that the Occupation post should be filled as soon as possible, the issue remained unresolved until the early spring of 1945. One of the reasons was that State, War, and Treasury concentrated on drafting the policy directive for Germany, not on the man to administer it. But, perhaps more important, Field Marshal von Rundstedt's sudden offensive in the Ardennes in December 1944 not only made planning for Germany's occupation premature, but totally occupied both SHAEF and the War Department for almost two months.

By early February, when it was clear that the Germans had gambled and lost in the Bulge, the search for an American occupation head resumed, with public speculation again focusing on Judge Patterson. But Patterson had by this time become even more firmly convinced of the unwisdom of sending a civilian to Germany, at least for the initial phase of the Occupation. When both *The Washington Post* and *The New York Times* mentioned him as the leading candidate, Patterson drafted a telegram to the President (then at Yalta) for Stimson's signature, strongly recommending that Patterson not be named.

After reflecting upon the matter, Stimson decided it was unlikely that FDR would make a decision until he was back in the White

House. *"Hold until President's return,"* Stimson wrote in longhand across the top of Patterson's draft, and four days later he discussed the matter at length with McCloy. "As far as we got," Stimson confided to his diary, "Justice [Owen] Roberts seemed to be the best man."

Stimson's reference to Supreme Court Justice Roberts suggests that he was still not certain Roosevelt would agree to the selection of a military man to head Germany's occupation. The day after his talk with McCloy, Stimson dictated a memorandum for his files. Again Stimson stressed the need for Patterson to remain in Washington. Military production was threatened by the pressure for reconversion, said Stimson, and "I cannot exaggerate the difficulties that he [Patterson] will face or the unique confidence I have in him for that purpose." Stimson summarized his discussion with McCloy under two headings: soldiers and civilians. Among the soldiers who might be selected to assist Eisenhower, he listed Generals Joseph McNarney (deputy supreme commander, Mediterranean), Clay, Charles H. Bonesteel (SHAEF inspector general), and Henry Aurand (commanding general, Sixth Service Command). If it had to be a civilian, Stimson listed but one choice: Supreme Court Justice Owen Roberts.

On March 3, Stimson approached Roosevelt for a decision. Once again the President exhibited that streak of procrastination that so often infuriated Stimson. FDR agreed that Patterson "couldn't possibly go" at the present time, although Roosevelt said he admired Patterson's "judicial qualities and his ability to put punch behind the judgement." On the other hand, Roosevelt said he recognized that the single-minded Patterson lacked "the political and worldly wisdom" that such a job entailed and that he might not be such a good choice after all. Somewhat encouraged by Roosevelt's attitude, Stimson made his case for sending a soldier, at least to handle the early days of the Occupation. "I told [the President] that the situation there now was chaotic and nothing effective was being done. . . . [The man selected] must begin at once and he must be a most effective organizer. I told him he should be a man like General Clay with his ability."

Roosevelt told Stimson he knew Clay and said, laughing, "You will break Jimmy Byrnes' heart, he is so dependent on him." FDR then allowed that he might like to try the job himself, reflecting on the old, uncorrupted Germany he knew as a schoolboy.

"This reassured me," wrote Stimson immediately afterward, "that at bottom he did not differ from McCloy and myself in respect to the basic organization to be aimed at in Germany . . . and although no further progress was made towards the selection of personnel, he approved of the types I have mentioned—Clay for the soldier, and somebody like Roberts for the civilian."

The following week, McCloy advised the working-level interdepartmental committee on Germany that Patterson would not be going to Europe and that the War Department preferred to assign a soldier instead. McCloy's announcement apparently met with general approval (no names were suggested), for it was conceded that "a soldier could better assure liaison with SHAEF and General Eisenhower."

Eisenhower, who had his own sources of information in Washington, may have learned that Clay was being considered by Stimson and McCloy, for on March 14 he wrote to Somervell indicating that he had heard via the grapevine "that Lucius Clay may become available for assignment to a theatre." In December, Ike had been distressed when Byrnes intervened to keep Clay in Washington, and with victory now in the offing, he wrote Somervell that he again needed Clay for "a job of the greatest responsibility." "My idea," Eisenhower said, "is that he would be the Herbert Hoover [the reference is to former President Herbert Hoover, who headed American relief activities in Europe after World War I] of this war and would have the job of handling civil affairs in Germany."

At the moment Ike was writing to Somervell, Secretary Stimson met with his top civilian advisers (Patterson, McCloy, Harvey Bundy, Goldwaithe Dorr, Julius Amberg, and John Martyn) to resolve the issue. It may seem strange that Stimson did not consult the military side of the War Department in making his choice, but the fact was that Stimson knew Marshall supported his old Fort Benning associate Bedell Smith, and Stimson wanted no part of Smith. "Smith has indicated that he thinks he could run it [Germany's occupation] in addition to his other duties. That is silly and I won't stand for it," Stimson noted in his diary entry that day. The issue hinged on whether Eisenhower's deputy for military government would report directly to Ike or through Smith as Chief of Staff. And Stimson was adamant that if military government were to succeed, it must be independent, with direct access to Eisenhower on a parallel basis with U.S. combat forces, and not through the Chief of Staff.

Stimson's colleagues agreed that Clay was the general officer best qualified to head a military government, but no one felt that Byrnes would release him. Their second choice was Lieutenant General Donald H. Connolly, Clay's old boss in the CAA, now heading the Persian Gulf Command, who had demonstrated a remarkable ability to get on with the Russians and British in Iran. LeRoy Lutes and Lieutenant General Wilhelm Styer, both in Army Service Forces, were considered next best qualified.

On March 16, Stimson approached Byrnes after a Cabinet meeting to see if Clay could be released. "Byrnes was very nice about it, and said that Clay, he thought, was the most able man he had ever worked with and he didn't know how he could get along without him." Stimson was unaware that Byrnes himself was leaving office at the end of the month, and was therefore surprised when Byrnes agreed that Clay could be made available. "I came back from the Cabinet meeting feeling that I had scored a good day's work . . . securing . . . Clay for this vital position," Stimson recorded in his diary. "I called McCloy and he was tickled to death. . . . He may go over himself for a few days to make things ready for Clay when he comes."

But FDR remained uncommitted. When John McCloy called on the President several days later, Roosevelt greeted him with a Hitler salute. *"Heil McCloy,"* said Roosevelt, *"Hochkommisar für Deutschland."*

Roosevelt's greeting took McCloy by surprise, but FDR's failing health startled him even more. "I was impressed that the President was not his vigorous self," McCloy recalled. "His whole manner had been somewhat changed from that which I had been used to."

"I've made up my mind," said Roosevelt. "McCloy, you're going to be the first high commissioner for Germany."

McCloy remembers that Roosevelt was "pretty unequivocal" about it. "I said, 'Mr. President, we haven't won the war yet. Furthermore'— I was just sort of gasping for air—I said, 'Furthermore, I think you could probably be making a mistake to put a civilian in there right away. The great heroes, the military heroes, will be marching and countermarching around. It will be primarily a military problem at first. And the person who goes there is going to find himself in a situation like a Mississippi River disaster. Where are the rations going to come from? How are the people to be fed? Basic logistics. And with all of the armies there, with the military conquest so recent, I think a civilian might be submerged.' "

"McCloy," Roosevelt replied, "I'm too tired to argue with you. I think you're wrong, but you tell me. Amongst the soldiers, who could do this job?"

"I said, 'Lucius Clay. You must have heard of him. He's Jimmy Byrnes' right-hand man. He's an Army Engineer. He has dealt with disasters of this kind. Furthermore, he is the son of old Senator Clay, and he used to be a page boy in the House of Representatives.' And that interested Mr. Roosevelt," McCloy remembered.

"Well," Roosevelt answered, "as I said before, I'm too tired to argue with you, McCloy. I haven't changed my mind, but I'll think it over."

When McCloy left the President's office, he stopped in to see Jimmy Byrnes, to tell him what Roosevelt had said. "I'll take care of the boss," Byrnes told McCloy. "You go back to the Pentagon and get Clay promoted."

Two days later, McCloy confirmed to Morgenthau that the Army was sending Clay to Germany to head the Occupation. Morgenthau entered the conversation in his diary without comment, apparently in full agreement.

On March 24, Byrnes had a long talk with Roosevelt. Byrnes was resigning that day as director of war mobilization, and his discussion with FDR rambled over many problems, including Germany's occupation. Roosevelt indicated once again that McCloy was going to Germany, but when Byrnes told him the War Department had decided to send Clay instead, the President accepted that decision. Roosevelt then told Byrnes that he had not met Clay, and that Byrnes should bring him in.

Everyone in Washington connected with postwar Germany was now aware that Clay was to head the Occupation. But Clay had not yet been informed; nor, for that matter, had Eisenhower. Indeed, neither had been consulted. (Eisenhower's letter to Somervell, which envisaged Clay as G-5 and thus under General Staff control—not the independent deputy Stimson had in mind—languished unanswered in the headquarters of Army Service Forces.) It was Robert Murphy, then in Washington for a series of conferences, who first informed Clay of the decision. Clay was manifestly surprised, and as Murphy reports, somewhat cold and hostile. "I guess I was," said Clay. "I didn't know anything about it. I wasn't interested in the job, and it was the last thing I wanted."

Shortly after Murphy left Clay's office, Byrnes informed Clay that the appointment was official. Clay drove immediately to the Pentagon, hoping to decline the post. As he explains in *Decision in Germany,* "I did so because it looked then as if the Japanese war would last for some time and I hoped for a tour of duty in the Pacific which would carry with it some combat experience. I had been a soldier in two wars, and like any other professional soldier, I believed that my career would be a failure without combat experience. My plea," Clay noted, "was ineffective."

Clay's concern was but partially related to his desire for combat. As he remembers, "The minute I was told that I had this job I visualized trouble. I knew that the military people at SHAEF would want to keep it under General Staff control. I was convinced that it could not be under General Staff control. Even as far back as Cuba [in the Spanish-American War] we learned that. And so we had set up a special branch of the War Department to handle the government of Cuba and the Philippines.

"I also visualized that whoever was chief of staff at SHAEF [Walter Bedell Smith] would try to see that this was a job that came under his bailiwick. I did not believe it could succeed that way. Furthermore, I believed it was in the best interest of the Army to do everything that we could to show that we were not trying to hold the job [of Occupation government]; that we wanted somebody else to have it. And therefore we had to set it up as an independent organization that could be severed from the Army at a moment's notice. And we had to proceed to make it civilian in character as fast as we could.

"I mentioned these problems to Mr. Byrnes. That's when he intervened to make sure that I was designated as General Eisenhower's *deputy* for military government. That meant that I reported directly to Eisenhower, not through the General Staff. And the appointment was announced from the White House. That made it official.

"As I was saying my goodbyes—I don't remember if I was in General Marshall's office or Mr. Stimson's—but I asked, more or less in an offhanded manner, what General Eisenhower thought of my coming. To my great surprise, and I guess to everyone else's, they suddenly realized that no one had consulted Ike. Here I had been appointed by the President, and no one had asked General Eisenhower what he thought about it—which was certainly not very polite, to say the least. Well, McCloy was dispatched post haste to tell General Eisenhower what had happened and that I was coming.

"And I'm sure General Eisenhower was none too pleased. Not that I was coming, but that he had not been consulted. General Eisenhower's reaction to me was always as a friend. That doesn't mean just because he's a friend you like to have someone sent to you without being asked. But actually, I experienced no difficulty from General Eisenhower."

Q: In *Decision in Germany,* you state that Mr. Byrnes "insisted" that your appointment be announced from the White House.
CLAY: If Mr. Byrnes insisted on it, it was because I asked him to.
Q: Before you left for Germany, did anyone suggest to you that four-power government might not work?
CLAY: Nobody professed any philosophy of that kind and type to me at all. Neither General Marshall, nor Judge Patterson, nor Mr. McCloy. And I saw them all before I left. Also, I saw Secretary Stimson before I left.

McCloy left Washington for Eisenhower's headquarters in Reims on March 31 and, like Stimson, he anticipated heavy going. As Stimson noted in his diary that day: "We have had so much vacillation and trouble about getting this matter of the rule of Germany arranged that the people in Eisenhower's staff are all mixed up over it and we are afraid that Clay would have a hard time unless his place was explained to Eisenhower by McCloy in whom Eisenhower has great confidence. Bedell Smith, the chief of staff at SHAEF, is said to want to have the position himself and thinks he can carry it on with his other duties. This is sheer nonsense and McCloy is to tell Eisenhower so. Bedell Smith has gotten a little bit of a big head and he has also unfortunately let this be appreciated by people as high up as the President who has told me several times he has lost confidence in Smith. Consequently we have got to have the right man there and Clay is the right man in the opinion of all of us. Bedell Smith has quite enough to do to take care of his own matters as chief of staff without trying to include in them such entirely different matters as the civilian affairs of Germany."

Stimson's and McCloy's opposition to Smith deserves further explanation. It was based on two points: first, a belief that military government, because of its distinctly political character, should be set up on an independent basis, parallel to the combat forces at SHAEF, and reporting directly to Eisenhower, not through the military Chief of Staff; second, a considerable distrust of Bedell Smith's political sensitivity. It does not detract from General Smith's justly deserved reputation for staff efficiency to note that, like many Army officers, he had a limited understanding of civilian values. For example, Smith could not understand why Robert Murphy was so horrified at Smith's suggestion that part of the captured German gold horde be distributed among the American generals chiefly responsible for defeating Germany. "Can't some of us quietly arrange some of our own bonuses?" he had asked.

McCloy arrived at Eisenhower's headquarters on April 5 and, as he anticipated, "ran into a little roughneck on the part of Bedell. But Eisenhower had the highest regard for Clay, and I didn't sense any opposition at all on the part of General Eisenhower."

Eisenhower was understandably disturbed that he had not been notified before Clay's appointment was announced, but the fact was that he had previously written to Somervell asking for Clay, and he was delighted with the appointment. And although it had not been Ike's original plan, he quickly grasped McCloy's point that military government was too important to be treated as a General Staff function.

Meanwhile, in Washington, Clay conducted a last-minute round of interviews to familiarize himself with Administration policy on Germany. On March 31, Byrnes took Clay to see the President.

"Remembering the number of times that I'd seen President Roosevelt," Clay said, "I guess I didn't make much of an impression on him. But I think it was pretty hard for him to think of Major General Clay as the Captain Clay who a few years before had been in his office on several occasions.

"In any event, we walked over there. On the way, Mr. Byrnes said, 'He's going to ask you some trick question like, "What would you do if in Heidelberg during the night Germans rose up and attacked and killed a few soldiers?" '

"Well, we went over to see Mr. Roosevelt, and he got to talking about his childhood, when his father would take him every year to one or another of the German spas where his father apparently went for the cure. And he got to talking about what he considered the real problem in Europe, which was energy. That a giant TVA [Tennessee Valley Authority] for Germany—indeed for all Europe—was something that would have great meaning and great significance.

"Two or three times Steve Early [Roosevelt's press secretary] tried to break it up, but without success. Finally we left, and when we got out, Mr. Byrnes sort of teasingly said, 'You didn't answer any questions, Lucius. You didn't say very much.'

"I said, 'No, I didn't. The President didn't ask me any questions, but I'm glad that he didn't. Because I was so shocked watching him that I don't think I could have made a sensible reply. We've been talking to a dying man.'

" 'Oh,' Byrnes said, 'you're crazy. I've seen him. He's been like this for a long time.'

"I didn't say anything more. As a matter of fact, I think ours was the last official appointment Mr. Roosevelt had in the White House. He left that afternoon and went to Hyde Park, and from Hyde Park to Warm Springs."

The White House announcement of Clay's appointment was greeted enthusiastically. *The New York Times* called him the Pentagon's "stormy petrel," who would put the Germans in their place. *The Washington Post,* whose editorial writers had criticized Clay frequently for his insistence that civilian consumption be curtailed, observed that "General Clay's exceedingly high abilities are better suited to the German situation than our own. That task calls for authoritarianism." The New York *Herald Tribune* stated that "life will be hard for the German citizen" as a result of Clay's appointment, "but things may be a little easier for the American." *United States News* presciently observed that "the German civilian can expect a minimum of the things that make life more comfortable. But he can expect that as quickly as possible the debris of war will be cleared away and civil affairs set to moving on the basis of a solid organization." Even the British seemed pleased. "For over three years Clay was Director of Materiel in the War Department where he did a remarkably fine job," the British Staff Mission told London. "He is a very able and forceful character who can be expected to be tough."

Before leaving, Clay consulted with Secretary Stimson, John McCloy, and General Hilldring of the War Department's Civil Affairs Division. He telephoned Morgenthau to ask for help in staffing the economic side of military government. (Specifically, Clay requested that Treasury Under Secretary Daniel Bell be made available for six months to organize the American economic element—a request Morgenthau declined.) But, as Clay acknowledges, he did not consult the State Department.

"It never occurred to me that they had anything to do with it. And this was a different type of occupation from Cuba or the Philippines. This one was based on diplomatic agreements among the Allies, in which the State Department was closely involved. But no one advised me of the role of the State Department in Occupation matters, and I'm inclined to believe that no one had thought it out."

Clay's failure to consult the State Department has sometimes been cited as an example of the military's determination to run its own show in Germany. But in fact, Clay was appointed precisely to ensure that political policy not be short-circuited by the military. That he did not consult the State Department probably says more about the position of the State Department in the closing days of the Roosevelt administration than it does about Clay.

Unlike his success with the War Department, FDR never succeeded in bringing the State Department into the New Deal corral. Cordell Hull, Roosevelt's first Secretary of State, a banner conservative from Tennessee, proved infinitely more durable than Harry Woodring, and ultimately would serve in that post for a record twelve years—providing the President no opportunity to replace him with someone more congenial. Hull rejected the liberal thrust of the New Deal, but provided Roosevelt with indispensable insurance among the southern Democrats on Capitol Hill. (Hull had served in Congress for twenty-four years.) As Secretary, aside from sporadic forays into negotiating reciprocal trade agreements, he restricted himself to protecting "his boys"—the equally conservative, class-conscious diplomats of the foreign service—from FDR's efforts to replace, retire, or transfer the most reactionary of them to less sensitive positions.

Accordingly, when World War II came, Roosevelt relegated the State Department to the role of a bystander. This was partially by mutual consent, since the old-school diplomats were ill-suited by training and mental outlook to ally themselves with Communist Russia, which they despised, or to fight against Nazi Germany and Fascist Italy, which some of them rather admired. In fact, in a relaxed moment shortly after Pearl Harbor, the President confided to a friend that thus far the State Department had been neutral in the war, and he hoped that it would at least remain that way.

Instead of entrusting major wartime responsibilities to State, FDR organized foreign policy around it. Lend-Lease and military aid to the Allies were initially handled by Morgenthau and the Treasury, later by Hopkins. Economic matters pertaining to the conflict were entrusted to a newly created Office of Economic Warfare under Leo Crowley, while information and propaganda became the responsibility of Elmer Davis and the new Office of War Information. Perhaps most important, foreign intelligence activity was delegated to a specially created Office of Strategic Services headed by William "Wild Bill" Donovan—all of which effectively pushed the State Department to the sidelines.

To the extent that State was consulted, and that was not very much, Roosevelt invariably dealt with Under Secretary Sumner Welles, bypassing Hull completely. Welles was another Harvard-Groton product, but he was an old companion of the President and had served as an usher at Franklin's marriage to Eleanor. And he tolerated the New Deal with a modicum of grace and wit. But Welles was forced from office by Hull in 1943 in an unfortunate personal episode, and as a result Roosevelt cast the State Department into the Washington equivalent of outer darkness. With the exception of Charles Bohlen, who served as an interpreter, no one from State accompanied Roosevelt to the Big Three meeting at Tehran; FDR's correspondence with Churchill and Stalin bypassed State completely; and the Army's General Staff declined to discuss occupation boundaries in Germany with the State Department, insisting that it was a military responsibility. George Elsey, then a Navy commander manning the White House map room, reports that he was explicitly forbidden to pass incoming cable traffic to the State Department, lest it be misused.

Clay, who was unusually punctilious in such matters, certainly understood the Washington power structure under President Roosevelt, and was undoubtedly aware of the irrelevance into which the State Department had fallen. As a close associate of Harry Hopkins, he was also very likely aware of the ideological differences that separated the European Affairs Division at State from the White House. But whether this motivated his decision not to consult the State Department is unclear.

Q: General, in retrospect, wasn't your selection to head the Occupation a bit of an unusual choice?

CLAY: Well, I can't answer as to why the choice was made. But I can say that in my dealing with the War Department and working as I did with the War Production Board and with Mr. Byrnes's office, it had given me about as much familiarity with an entire economy of a nation as one could have. There weren't very many people that had had much experience in that field. I think I'd probably had as much as most of them.

Q: When you were leaving for Germany, did you consider your lack of familiarity with the German problem a handicap?

CLAY: You don't think about handicaps when you're given a job in the Army. You go do it. Period. I don't think I was ever asked in the Army, did I want to do something.

Q: What was Mrs. Clay's reaction?

CLAY: I don't know that she or I could answer that. We were at war and the kids were at war. We came and went with such speed that I don't think we thought too much about it. I don't think she was too happy about it. In the first place, she had to find a place to live. Because I got kicked out of Fort Myer immediately. It's a lovely way the Army has. When your difficulties start, they make it more difficult.

Q: When you left the U.S., what did you think you would find in Germany?

CLAY: I knew pretty much the type and kind of physical destruction we were going to find. But I don't think I appreciated that there would be a complete breakdown of government (and all other services, really), largely through unconditional surrender.

Q: Were you in favor of unconditional surrender?

CLAY: I don't know what else we could have done. But it certainly made our job—at least in the short run—a bit more difficult. In the long run, I don't think we had any alternative, unless we wanted to negotiate with Hitler. And I don't think we should have done that.

Q: How did you think Germany should be treated?

CLAY: At the time I left I certainly was not averse to a tough peace. Remember, we were still fighting; we were still seeing our people killed.

Q: But you were not familiar with U.S. Occupation plans at that time?

CLAY: I think I was given a draft of JCS 1067 to read when I got on the plane. But I didn't know anything about the agreement in the European Advisory Commission [on zonal boundaries], or the Morgenthau Plan. I was at Quebec. I knew that Mr. Morgenthau had gotten a document signed and that Mr. McCloy was very unhappy about it and had enlisted Mr. Stimson's aid in getting it changed. But I never read it. I truly wasn't the least bit interested at that time. I didn't care what they did to Germany. I hadn't thought about it. It wasn't going to be my responsibility, and I was still hoping that one of these days I'd be back in the combat Army.

· Book Three ·

GERMANY

· 15 ·

Ike's Deputy

> Nobody was more devoted to the Army than Clay, but he deliberately organized a predominantly civilian administration in Germany. Of all the Army officers I have worked with, none has matched Clay's respect for the civilian viewpoint, none has revealed more talent for true statesmanship.
>
> Robert D. Murphy,
> *Diplomat Among Warriors*

CLAY ARRIVED IN PARIS ON APRIL 7, 1945, AND THE following day he reported to SHAEF headquarters at Reims. As Eisenhower's deputy for military government, Clay was walking into an entirely new position and, for the Army General Staff at least, a new concept of military government. Rather than a simple staff function (G-5) under the normal military command structure (at top, page 225), Clay's task was to fashion a parallel organization for military government that, while reporting to the supreme commander, was as much civilian in character as it was military. This was resented by many in the

Army, and as Clay had anticipated, his reception at SHAEF was none too cordial.

The traditional organization of the U.S. Army provided for a small General Staff section (known as "G-5") at each headquarters to handle matters of military government. In combat situations, these G-5 staff sections furnished a few officers and enlisted men capable of dealing with the population in the immediate area of military operations, a useful function. But as far as the tactical commanders were concerned, G-5 activity was ancillary to the main combat function, and it tended to attract less gifted personnel. In addition, the G-5 staffs were governed by military necessity. Their task was to assist the combat mission of their unit, not to oversee a lengthy political occupation. But this distinction was not clear to many of those at SHAEF in the spring of 1945, and it quickly became the basis for a serious confrontation between Clay and some of Eisenhower's staff, particularly General Walter Bedell Smith.

Clay insisted that the long-term occupation of Germany was a political issue, not a military problem. He believed that the traditional "G-5" structure was unsuited to the task of a major occupation; if the United States was to be successful in Germany, the responsibility for the Occupation had to be removed from the Army's General Staff and placed in an entirely separate political structure, reporting directly to General Eisenhower, as supreme commander, and to the Secretary of War. In Clay's view, Eisenhower should have two deputies: General Smith as Chief of Staff for U.S. military forces, and Clay as deputy military governor to handle Occupation matters. Eisenhower quickly saw the merits of Clay's plan and endorsed it wholeheartedly. But the U.S. military below Ike were never happy with it and continued to resist it until Clay became overall U.S. military commander in Europe in 1947.

Clay's insistence that military government be removed from the General Staff was not a minor matter of military protocol. It was a fundamental necessity if the occupation of Germany was to be responsive to political control. And Clay, in his brusque, arbitrary manner, insisted upon it. The ultimate success of the American occupation of Germany from 1945 to 1949 traces in the first instance to that decision —and to Clay's ability to develop a structure independent from General Staff control.

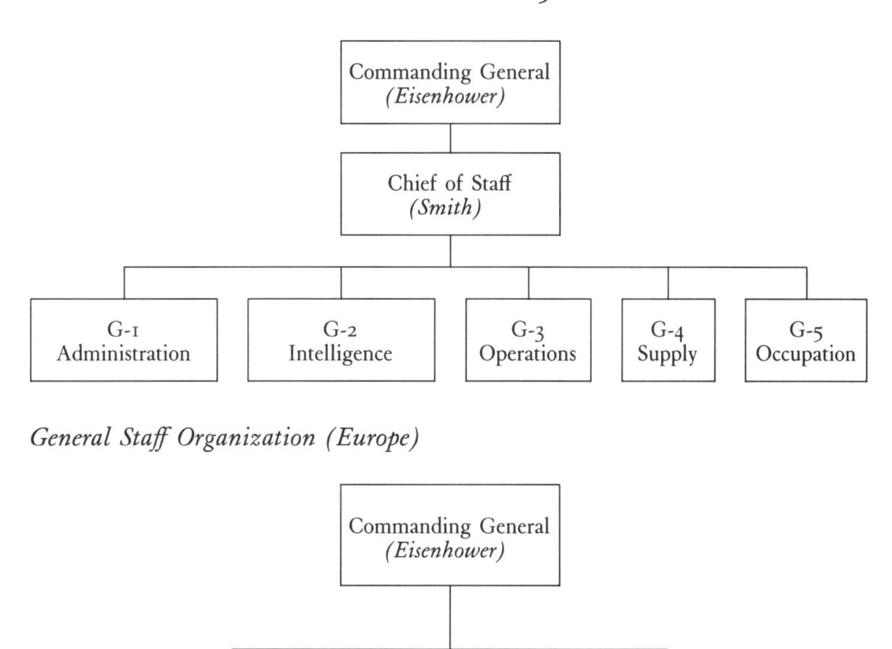

General Staff Organization (Europe)

Clay's Alternative Organization (Accepted by Eisenhower)

Q: As deputy military governor, you reported directly to General Eisenhower?

CLAY: I reported directly to him, with no intermediaries. Beetle [Bedell Smith] always wanted me to report through him as Chief of Staff. But I resisted that. Military government would have fallen apart if it was responsible to the tactical military command structure. I could never have gotten the type and kind of civilians I had if we had been down there reporting to the General Staff. And more important, I wanted to get military government out of the hands of the Army and into the hands of the State Department as quickly as we possibly could. It was my view, and it still is, that military government had to be independent; that it had to be set up in such a way that it could be severed from the Army on a moment's notice. And we had to make it civilian in character as fast as we could get the money and the people.

Q: Had you discussed this with General Marshall?

CLAY: I don't think I discussed it with anybody in the War Department. I did discuss it with General Eisenhower immediately after I got there, and I found very quickly that it was my concept he liked and approved of.

Q: How did you proceed after that?

CLAY: Well, after General Eisenhower approved my concept, the major problem was setting up an organization which could take over from the tactical troops, because, when we moved into Germany, each little area was being administered by the tactical troops with their separate military government detachments. This meant there was very little coordination. And the tactical commanders were not really very interested in military government.

Q: What sort of military government organization did you find when you arrived in Europe?

CLAY: When I got there, the military government headquarters group, which was called the U.S. Group, Control Council, was quartered in Paris, where British and French teams also had been set up. And these people were organized by government ministries, all on the theory that they were going to go in and take over an existing German ministry from the top and administer it. Well, within a week it was clear to me that this was just a lot of damn foolishness. That there weren't going to be any German ministries in existence, and if there were, under our instructions [JCS 1067]* they would never be allowed to serve, and that we were going to have a far more chaotic condition than was visualized by this rather academic organization. So I began immediately to lay much more stress on the tactical units and how to get them into an organization reporting to military government.

Q: This meant that the tactical Army commanders would become Military Governors?

CLAY: Yes, temporarily. General Patton at that time was commanding the Third Army, and he became Military Governor of Bavaria. He helped us. But when he made his famous statement about Nazis' being no different from Republicans and Democrats, we relieved him as Military Governor, and we never restored that post to the [Third] Army commander. Instead, we got [Brigadier] General [Walter] Muller

* For the text of JCS 1067, see Appendix.

made our deputy for military government in Bavaria, and this hastened our getting these posts into a separate channel outside the tactical command structure.

Q: Were you consulted on General Patton's relief?

CLAY: Yes. [Major] General [Clarence] Adcock made the recommendation in his capacity as my deputy. He called me up and told me what had happened and that he was going to recommend that we replace General Patton as Military Governor, and I gave him my blessing and approved it. Let me put it this way: It wasn't just [Patton's statement] that made me do it. It was my firm belief that military government should not be under the Army commander. So I was relieving General Patton not just because of that statement, but because I would have liked to have gotten all of the Army commanders out of the picture—and did. They did not belong in it. In the first place, they were not going to be there very long. It was obvious that we were not going to keep our armies in Germany. In the second place, I did not want military government handled as a General Staff matter. I wanted it distinct and separate and reporting to General Eisenhower in a parallel structure with the military. And General Eisenhower quickly accepted this concept.

Q: But General Smith resisted it?

CLAY: Well, General Smith was never in favor of it. I won't say he resisted it, because after General Eisenhower had made it so very manifest that he was going to back me on it, General Smith didn't officially resist it any longer. He didn't like it, though, and he made it plain that he didn't like it. Nor did the rest of the Army.

Q: Even in Washington?

CLAY: The whole time I was there, the Army wanted to control us. But I refused. I never reported through the tactical military command structure. I reported directly to General Eisenhower and to the Secretary of War. This meant that military government in Germany was separate and distinct from the Army field forces. And it had to be, because the issues with which we were dealing were not military issues. They were political.

Q: This continued after General Eisenhower was replaced by General McNarney?

CLAY: It continued. Again, his chief of staff tried to take over.

Q: Who was that?

CLAY: General [Harold R. "Pinky"] Bull, a good friend of mine. I could understand why they wanted to do it. As a matter of fact, I think that's the way General MacArthur started running it in Japan. He had his problems too, and he didn't get out of his economic problems until Joe Dodge and Bill Draper, who had done such a terrific job to get us out of ours, went over there to help him. I personally think MacArthur made a great mistake staying in Japan. We were very lucky, General MacArthur and certainly myself, that we came out of an occupation as well as we did.

Q: After General Eisenhower left, did you have difficulties with General McNarney?

CLAY: I had no difficulties with General McNarney. I got along with him very well, and I never had any difficulties with him personally. He was not as interested as General Eisenhower, put it that way, and he was also having some problems with discipline on the military side. But I had great trouble with his staff. I had continuing difficulties with the [U.S.] military—until I took over [as U.S. commander in Europe]. The demands they made on the German economy, for example; their unwillingness to submit a budget for us to include in the overall budget of the German economy—all of these were really insurmountable problems. We were the German government, but we had a military that did not want to be held accountable.

Q: And since you were responsible for the German economy, you wanted to hold down the Army's demands?

CLAY: Yes, and I insisted that the Army had to submit its budget to us and that we have a chance to resist its budget.

Q: For Occupation costs and so forth?

CLAY: Yes. I insisted that my finance department prepare the budgets. The problem was that we'd get a budget from the Army in the form of an order: *This is what the Occupation forces will require.* And it was always more than I thought the German economy could afford, and, in the long run, all the Army was doing was increasing the cost to the United States. And then, when we combined with the British zone, we had the problem of making both armies come to us.

Q: Could you describe your relations with General Smith?

CLAY: General Smith and I were always very good friends. Later, when he was Ambassador in Moscow, he and his wife always stayed with us [in Berlin] on their trips to and fro. We visited him in Washington, and vice versa. It was certainly a mutual respect, because he was a very able and competent officer. However, Bedell did want to be at that time a full general and he also wanted to be Military Governor of Germany. And he was very close to General Marshall, much closer than I.

Q: Smith was close to General Marshall?

CLAY: They were close personal friends. I'm sure closer in the sense of friendship than General Eisenhower was to General Marshall. They'd hunted together at Fort Benning, and so forth. So they had a very, very special relationship. On the other hand, I have no reason to say that General Smith wasn't completely loyal to Eisenhower, and I never heard General Eisenhower complain about his lack of loyalty. I just don't think they were ever close and intimate friends.

Q: Whereas you and General Eisenhower were close?

CLAY: We had been [close] in the Philippines, and we became so again. I think General Eisenhower regarded me, and I certainly regarded him, as one of my closest friends. But we were not playmates. I mean by that, General [Alfred] Gruenther was also one of his great friends; General Gruenther was also one of his bridge companions, who played bridge with him constantly and frequently. There were also friends who played golf with him constantly and frequently. I didn't do either of these. So I had put my friendship on a different basis. I was not one of his golf or bridge companions. I was often invited—I could have been invited more often—but I wasn't that good of a bridge player and I didn't care that much about it. And when bridge was over, you got down and played golf. This was a great relaxation for General Eisenhower. But it wasn't for me, so I didn't do it. General Smith was not a bridge player and he didn't give much attention to golf either. And he and General Eisenhower were not socially close at all. Yet they had a mutual respect, which I think is more important.

Q: And professionally?

CLAY: We were a pretty good team. General Eisenhower gave me a complete delegation of responsibility as long as I would keep him informed and we were seeing eye to eye on policy. He wasn't always the easiest man in the world to work for, but he was for me.

Q: General Eisenhower is often pictured as benign.

CLAY: Better talk to some of the generals who worked for him. He was a tough taskmaster. As long as you were doing all right, he'd hand more work to you. And if you weren't doing all right, you wouldn't last very long. Eisenhower had a terrible temper. I'm probably one of the few people that never did experience it. And he was a very intelligent man. You didn't have to go down and explain things in detail a second or third time.

"I think he was the only President in my lifetime that had a philosophy of administration in the White House. He believed that his Secretaries were responsible for their departments, and they had to make the decisions. And he wouldn't let them run to him for decisions. The result was, he kept his mind and his desk pretty free from clutter. I think his regime looks pretty good as you look back on it."

Q: And Sherman Adams [Eisenhower's Chief of Staff in the White House]?

CLAY: I think that's the biggest bunk in the world. It's just like saying Bedell Smith ran the war. He didn't do any damn such thing. General Eisenhower ran the war, and Sherman Adams didn't run the White House. I'm sure General Smith and Sherman Adams didn't think they were running it. Let me say this: when Bedell Smith was after my job, as soon as I had General Eisenhower's support I never worried about Bedell Smith. I got along with him. I didn't get mad because he wanted my job. Maybe if I'd been in his place I would have too. Because instead of being Chief of Staff of a huge Allied effort, he was becoming Chief of Staff of a relatively small military force, with most of the responsibility for whatever work was done in Germany over on the military government side, not on the military side. So you can't blame him for being unhappy and wanting something else.

Q: How long did you assume you were going to stay in Germany?

CLAY: I really had no idea. After I saw the chaotic conditions, I knew I was there for a longer spell than I thought in the first place. It was very difficult for me to see how anyone but the Army had an organization to cope with it in the initial phase. Among other things, there was the tremendous problem of displaced persons: feeding them, clothing them, housing them. We also had to import food to keep the Germans alive until their agriculture could be put back on its feet. All of these things required an organization, and the Army had an organization. No one else did. There was no German government. We were it. Absolute and sovereign.

Q: How did you recruit your staff for military government?

CLAY: Well, I recruited a few people before I left Washington, people that agreed to come over later. And I set up an office for recruitment back in the Pentagon, where I would write and let them know what type and kind of people I wanted, and they could go out and get them for me.

"And then I took some people with me who had been working for me: General Draper; Joe Dodge; Judge [Charles M.] Fahy. And I also took two bright young men with me on my personal staff, Bob Bowie of Harvard and Don McLean, who's now the administrator of the Leahy Clinic up in Boston. They were a tremendous help, getting out the instructions as to how we would operate and writing some of the early proclamations."

Q: Did the fact you could only offer one-year contracts pose a problem?

CLAY: Not really. The type and kind of people we wanted were not people who were looking for a job. They were people who wanted experience. They were taking these jobs [in military government] because it was challenging and because they thought it was an important and worthwhile undertaking. Professor [James K.] Pollock [Clay's adviser on German government and politics] wasn't looking for a job. He was on leave from the University of Michigan. And this was true of Joe Dodge, who was on leave from his bank, and General Draper, who was on leave from Dillon, Reed.

Q: How was Professor Pollock recruited?

CLAY: I think he'd been a consultant to the School for Military Government in Charlottesville, and in that way had become well known to and highly regarded by our Civil Affairs Division, and they recommended him to me. I did not know him before.

Q: And Professor [Herman] Wells [Clay's adviser on education matters]?

CLAY: He was recruited by my office in Washington. Obviously, one of the first places I went to in looking for various members of our staff was the universities. And we obtained some outstanding individuals. Professor Pollock was president of the American Political Science Association. Professor Wells was president of Indiana University and remained so for many years. Professor [Edward] Litchfield [Clay's adviser for administration] later became president of [the University of] Pittsburgh. Professor Carl Friedrich of Harvard became my adviser on constitutional matters, and Professor [Walter] Dorn of Columbia was my adviser on de-Nazification. My science adviser, Roger Adams, was one of the leading scientists in the country. I believe he was a professor of chemistry at Illinois.

Q: Would he have been involved in recruiting Wehrner von Braun [the German rocket scientist]?

CLAY: No. He was involved, however, in what we did to save what we could from the Kaiser Wilhelm Institute. The movement of von Braun and the other scientists in that particular field was handled by the Army, not military government.

Q: How did you get Lewis Douglas and General Draper?

CLAY: General Draper had been working for me [in Army Service Forces] before I went over. I learned to have very great respect for his energy. Draper was a hard worker, and I wanted to have him with me. As for Douglas, when I got this job, the first thing I could foresee was the financial problems that were going to result. So I went after a man who had a great deal of financial experience—Lew Douglas—and he agreed to go with me. Unfortunately, although he never gave his exact reasons, but I think when he saw the extent of the economic problem in Germany and the instructions that we were to do nothing about it [JCS 1067], he said to me, *"I've got to go back home and see if we can get these changed."* He went back. He couldn't get them changed. He never came back [to Germany]. Before Douglas, I'd tried to get Daniel Bell, the Under Secretary of the Treasury—whom I knew—but Mr. Morgenthau wouldn't let him go. Then, when Douglas didn't come back, I got Joe Dodge. And he was a tower of strength. Later, when MacArthur was having problems with the Japanese economy, I sent Dodge and Draper over to him. And they did a bang-up job.

Q: Unlike Douglas, General Draper stayed?

CLAY: He didn't have much choice. He was in the Army.

"Of course, the staff situation in Germany was very different from the one I had in Washington during the war. In Washington, I could choose from almost anyone in the country, and I had a staff that you couldn't possibly duplicate no matter how much money you had. In Germany, it was an entirely different situation. You couldn't pick the staff that you would have liked to have picked. I don't mean by that that I didn't develop and have a good staff, but nevertheless you just couldn't pick off the tree anybody you wanted, once the war was over.

"Second, you had a tremendous amount of understandable bitterness and hatred that failed to, or wouldn't, recognize that you couldn't have an empty void in the center of Europe, and any efforts that you made to fill that void you knew were going to be met with tremendous criticism and resentment. Even Washington didn't really know what it wanted.

"So I don't think you can compare the two. Our effort in building up and rearming our forces in World War II was almost a miracle. But it was done because everybody was for it and behind it. You had no such thing as real opposition. The German cause was a bitter one, a difficult one."

Q: What about your basic directive to govern the Occupation, JCS 1067?

CLAY: It was on the whole too vindictive a directive to have long suited the American people, because we are not a vindictive people.

Q: Was the Potsdam Agreement [signed by Truman, Attlee, and Stalin in July 1945] an improvement?

CLAY: Not much. Potsdam was just about the same thing.

Q: Did you try to get your directive changed?

CLAY: Well, I tried to get it changed through Mr. Douglas in the spring of 1945, and we got nowhere. I must admit, I didn't think it would work—my instructions, that is—and I said, "The surest way in the world to get this changed is to try and make it work." And I think that's what happened. If we hadn't had 1067, I am sure that our original approach would have been quite different.

Q: What would that have been?

CLAY: I think we would have been instructed from the very beginning to assist in getting the Germans back on their feet. Not because they were Germans, but because it was essential if we were going to have any chance to make them citizens of the world again, and if we were to get Europe back on its feet again. This was already a very evident factor for me. And I would like to have started out on a less restricted and more cooperative basis. I think we would have been better off in the long run, because the change, when we made it, was a very costly one.

Q: And the British and French?

CLAY: Well, the British, with all of their experience, wanted no part of it [JCS 1067]. The French ran their zone like a prized possession. They didn't give a damn about 1067. They didn't give a damn about fraternization. They lived in pomp and luxury and they took the maximum out of Germany that could be taken. Period.

Q: Did the economic recovery of the French zone lag behind?

CLAY: In many ways it did. On the other hand, it was a very rich part of Germany.

Q: JCS 1067 required the breakup of large German agricultural estates?

CLAY: Under our instructions, we went to work to break up the big estates in Bavaria and put our law on land reform into effect. I think it was utterly ridiculous in a way, because compared to the land holdings in this country, the biggest holdings [in the American zone] involved only a few hundred acres. There weren't any huge real estate holdings, at least not in one spot. The Prussian royal family might have a dozen residences with a few hectares around each, but they didn't have any real land holdings. So the question of land reform was not really applicable to western Germany. It may have been more applicable to eastern Germany, East Prussia, Silesia. There may have been large land holdings in that area. There were very few in western Germany.

Q: Your heart wasn't really in this?

CLAY: Well, we did it. I don't know whether it lasted or not. I doubt it.

Q: Did Secretary Stimson consult with you at the Potsdam Conference about Occupation policy?

CLAY: Mr. Stimson was not a member of the Potsdam delegation, but he came to Germany at that time, and I happen to know that he was rather hurt at not being a part of the conference. But he had lunch with General Eisenhower in Frankfurt, and General Eisenhower invited me to attend. Just the three of us. We had a very long luncheon, with an hour or two afterwards.

"Mr. Stimson, in his very calm way, was really talking primarily to me, because I think he knew this was not a job at which General Eisenhower would stay any great time. And he said, 'No matter how vindictive the American people may feel now, no matter how stringent your orders may be, just remember that in the long run, unless you restore an economic life to these people under which they have some hope, you will be repudiated by the very people who have given you these instructions.' "

Q: Then Mr. Stimson was not in favor of a punitive Occupation?

CLAY: Well, I think he and McCloy had tried to get JCS 1067 changed, but they didn't have much success. And so I think it was in light of this that he was trying to give me this philosophy. "Sure, you've got to live with 1067," he said, "but don't live with it to the extent that you let this country starve to death or break down with the lack of opportunity for economic life. In the long run, the American people will never tolerate an area under American control in which there is chaos and hunger." And I think he was probably right.

Q: And you had this much flexibility under JCS 1067?

CLAY: In many ways, I had too much flexibility. There were many times that I would have loved to have had instructions. But where did I go to get them? I never knew. I don't think I ever got any instructions. At least, I don't remember any, except in the very early stages. I'd get suggestions, and these suggestions might come in a hundred different ways. They might come in a telegram from the State Department to [Robert] Murphy, who'd advise me of the suggestions. Sometimes they'd come by visits—Forrestal, representatives of the State Department.

Q: Most of the interpretations of the Occupation argue that you thrived on the lack of instructions.

CLAY: What the hell do you do when you don't get any? When I tried to get our government to explain what it meant by the "federalization" of Germany and similar details, I never got answers.

Q: Decentralization?

CLAY: That too. Maybe I was happier that way, I don't know. All I'm saying is that I had no choice. After Mr. McCloy left the War Department, I don't think there was anybody in Washington that paid much attention to the Occupation. Except how much money it was costing us.

"The State Department wasn't interested either. They were interested in Germany's relations with other countries, not in Germany itself. I went back to Washington in November [1945] to discuss 1067. I don't remember too much about it, except we weren't too successful. But my primary purpose was to talk to the War Department about our need for food, our need for funds, and our need to get the German economy moving. In the back of my mind was to tell the War Department that 1067 was unworkable, and I left Washington fairly confident —in my own mind, at least—that I wasn't to interpret it rigidly or narrowly. But I didn't get it changed. And then, when we finally got to the point, in 1948, where we recognized and accepted that there had to be a rebuilding of Germany, then they all wanted to move in."

Q: What was General Eisenhower's headquarters like in the spring of 1945?

CLAY: Well, our headquarters [in Reims] were in what had been a schoolhouse. It was not a very impressive headquarters—simple furniture and equipment. We were billeted in various homes around the city, which had been requisitioned for the purpose. I lived in a villa with [Major] General [Robert W.] Crawford [SHAEF G-4] and a couple of his aides, which was the Krug family home—the champagne family. That made it very pleasant, but we didn't see very much of it, because we went to work early and came home rather late. In addition to that, I was commuting back and forth between Reims and Paris.

"There wasn't much social life in the ordinary sense. You always had a full crew of visitors whom you knew, whom you'd take home to dinner, and they'd bring you up to date on what was happening in other parts of the war. Every once in a while we would break the monotony by playing bridge, or, in my particular case, by joining a poker game. But that wasn't very often—once or twice a month. We had one the night of the surrender. The only reason we had it was that we couldn't accept the German surrender until they [the German officers] had authority from [Grand Admiral Karl] Doenitz [Hitler's successor].

"I happened to have been in Paris the day the Germans surrendered. And General Smith called me up about three or four o'clock in the afternoon—he was in Reims—and said, 'Lucius, come up to Reims.'

"I said, 'I can't do it, Bedell, I've got appointments tomorrow.'

"He said, 'Well, I can't say anything more over the telephone, but you'll be very disappointed if you don't come up here.' So I got into a liaison airplane and flew up to Reims and got in there at 6:00 P.M. And of course, when I got there, the other officers in Reims were in the schoolhouse, and as I opened the door to my office there was a German general sitting behind my desk. Actually, I thought it was a joke of some kind or other, but it turned out to be General [Alfred] Jodl. So we were there all that night. We sat in [General Carl] Tooey Spaatz's house playing poker until two or three in the morning, because he was waiting for the call to sign the surrender agreement."

Q: Did you talk with General Jodl?

CLAY: No. In the first place, I had thought this was an intelligence agent, our intelligence people putting up something, and I wasn't going to be caught with that. So, perhaps instinctively, I backed out and went around to see Carter Burgess, who was secretary of the General Staff, and then I found out from him what it was all about. I happened to have had the only vacant office, because I was in Paris, so they put Jodl in there.

"The next day, the Germans had surrendered, and General Eisenhower invited us all over for lunch at his billet. There were twenty-five or thirty of us, British and Americans, many of whom had been serving together for a good many months. In any event, it started off as a great victory celebration. By the time the lunch was over and everybody began to tell everybody else goodbye, all of a sudden this group of generals recognized that they no longer had a job. The companionship of months and days was gone. And it was almost like having attended your own funeral, really. By the time we left, everybody was sad, and General Eisenhower was saying goodbye with tears in his eyes. It was a very sad occasion—which I think you have to translate into terms of what happens to you when you've achieved the greatest objective that you ever had in your life and all of a sudden that objective is achieved; you have initially a great feeling of satisfaction, and then you no longer have the objective. So you have a terrible letdown."

Q: After the surrender, you moved immediately into Germany. What were your first impressions of Germany in 1945?

CLAY: I think my first impression was that the destruction was unbelievably massive and distributed throughout Germany as a whole. We were already faced with the problem of getting food to many of the cities and getting transportation going, so I think I was probably too busy to form any impressions.

Q: What was your first personal contact with German officials?

CLAY: I suspect my first direct contact was probably with either the post office or the railroad officials. Both of these were civil service organizations, and I met with them to be sure that they had an organization which, if given authority, could function, and that rail and other facilities could get back into operation.

"But I never had any general relations with Germans, for several reasons. I avoided social relations. I thought that I had to deal at arm's length, and I did deal at arm's length. That didn't mean that I didn't form a very real respect for a great many people who worked for us, but I also felt that any social efforts would in the long run be very harmful to them. So I lived at arm's length with the Germans the whole time I was in Germany.

"The tactical Army commanders didn't have that problem. They found Germans they liked. And a lot of the German intellectuals, a lot of German society, they found attractive. And after the nonfraternization rule was lifted, they met with them and dined with them and so on. I did not."

Q: Were you involved in the nonfraternization law?

CLAY: No, that came from Washington. I was certainly involved in having it lifted, because we were removing an absolutely ineffective law. It had absolutely no effect as far as the individual soldier was concerned—who was the one you were mostly concerned with. The only thing it stopped was decent fraternization.

Q: After you had been in Germany two or three weeks, you wrote Mr. McCloy: "I hope you won't think . . . that I am getting soft. I realize the necessity for stern and spartan treatment. However, retribution now is far greater than realized at home and our planes and artillery have really carried war direct to the homes of the German people." Was the destruction greater than you had anticipated?

CLAY: Well, not only was it greater, but we also very quickly began to realize that there was a real shortage of manpower. Much of the manpower that had constituted the work force was now in internment camps—another great responsibility for us—and our big job was to get work, agriculture, going, to keep this country alive. We couldn't let starvation and mass deaths take place, and we were responsible. I also realized that the cost to the United States was going to be terrific unless we could get this thing moving again—which we were not permitted to do if we literally followed our instructions [JCS 1067].

"Technically, our instructions prevented us from doing anything to help the Germans financially or economically. Well, this had been based on the theory that there was going to be a German government there that could function. But there wasn't any government. So I began to think about this thing in terms of reconstruction, in a period when even to talk about reconstructing Germany would have been enough to get you hung on the Ellipse in Washington."

Q: How did General Eisenhower feel about reconstruction?

CLAY: General Eisenhower was completely in sympathy, and saw this picture just as I did. Now whether his military commanders understood this is open to conjecture.

Q: Did General Eisenhower intend to remain in Germany?

CLAY: I don't think he had thought it out. The surrender came so very suddenly, and here was General MacArthur firmly in command in Japan, and General Marshall firmly installed as Chief of Staff. There wasn't anything else for him to do. I think he'd made up his mind that to stay in Europe in command of a constantly decreasing American Army was not what he wanted to do. But obviously, until General Marshall decided to retire, there wasn't any place for him to go.

Q: Did you and he discuss this?

CLAY: Well, I discussed it with him in terms of getting him out of there as quickly as possible. Frankly, yes, we discussed it, because I couldn't see that he could get any additional appreciation of his work by remaining in this disaster-stricken and chaotic country. If he tried to help them bring it back, he was going to be damned for too much sympathy for an enemy, and if he didn't and it did become, as I thought it might, the vacuum that would help to destroy all of Europe, then he would be equally damned. I didn't see where he could win on this. I don't think he could have, unless he had stayed there for the full duration. Nobody recognizes it now, but for the first year and a half, nobody ever said a kind word about the military government. You had to have a pretty damned thick skin, and be pretty confident, not to let it get you down. It was a pretty hard road.

Q: Did the fact that you were a Southerner and familiar with Reconstruction influence you?

CLAY: I don't know how to answer that. I think that newspapermen used to make a lot out of it, because at one of our meetings I said I was going to be damn sure that there weren't any carpetbaggers in the military government: that no one, if I could help it, was going to make an exorbitant profit out of Germany's defeat. Well, a lot of them didn't know what a carpetbagger was. But they went out and looked it up, so they immediately determined that I'd been influenced by my background. Maybe I had. I don't know. I don't think I had any predetermined views. Certainly, I was not at all sympathetic to the Germans when I went there, and I had no desire to do things because it was for their good.

Q: But how did you get the Occupation off the ground, so to speak?

CLAY: We began by establishing local government, and finding and putting into office Germans, and getting the courts going. Getting the police working. Getting the tax collectors out. All of this required the selection of Germans who were willing to do this, who at least were not obviously members of the Nazi Party, and who did have the experience and background to do the job. And it was very difficult, because we had to throw out such a large percentage of the people who had worked for government as having been involved in the Nazi Party one way or another.

Q: Was the prohibition against former members of the Nazi Party successful?

CLAY: I think we carried it too far.

Q: The British and French?

CLAY: The British and French didn't have the same feeling toward the Nazis that we did. Neither one had a huge Jewish population that had developed a hatred you can well understand. I am not critical of it at all, because I can understand how it developed. Nevertheless, this was a pressure that did not exist in Britain and France.

Q: How successful was the *Fragebogen,* the questionnaire about their past activities that all Germans were required to complete?

CLAY: Well, it wasn't a very successful thing. But I don't know what else you could have done.

"You've got to remember that we were being constantly attacked by our press, which had the unerring ability to find some Nazi that we had put in military government. And the bitterness and feeling [in the United States] were so strong that we had to have some way to let our people know that we were investigating and trying to find out who these people were and do something about it. So we instituted the *Fragebogen.* As I said, we were the only ones doing this. The British and French zones weren't doing it. So this put us in a somewhat different position. But I still think it was the right answer. We may have gone too far, we may have carried the definition of who was to be tried and who wasn't to be tried too far.

"Certainly it penalized those who worked for the government most: schoolteachers, postmen, and so forth. But, then again, under our directives, we couldn't let them teach until they were tried and cleared. At least after they had been tried and given a punishment, they were rehabilitated and could go back and do their jobs. Until that time, we had a blanket order under JCS 1067 that barred them from public positions. That was one of the purposes of this thing: to get some of these people cleared if they had committed no crimes, so they could get back into the stream of political and economic life."

Q: To return to the question of local government, did you select the Germans who worked in the Occupation?

CLAY: No. No, outside of [appointing] the Minister-Presidents [of the German provinces], at that time I made no selections. Later on, when we formed a more or less centralized government, I selected certain ministers to have various responsibilities—agriculture, economics, and so on. But I didn't try to play any part in the selection of the Minister-Presidents' staffs or of the people who worked for them in running the state governments.

"Of course, we had the initial problem of re-establishing state governments. Bavaria had been a state. But Hesse-Darmstadt and Hesse-Nassau had been two separate states—or, rather, a state and a Prussian subdivision—so when we combined them, that state had no experience in state government. We were in the unfortunate position of occupying half of Württemberg and half of Baden, with the French in the other half. We didn't think either one of those was enough for a government of its own, so we put the two of them together for a new state. Getting these states set up, and getting the Minister-Presidents, getting our governors down there to help in the selection of the Minister-Presidents and get them going, was my basic first job. And these things moved with great rapidity. I can't tell you, really, just how the priorities went, but they moved with great rapidity."

Q: In selecting the Minister-Presidents, what criteria did you use?

CLAY: Find the best man you can who has some background and experience, who has not been a member of the Nazi Party. That's just about it. I went mainly to the universities for political scientists, for professors, because they were on the whole more free from the Nazi taint than any other group.

Q: Could you describe the Minister-Presidents?

CLAY: They were all very different in type. Dr. Reinhold Maier [of Württemberg-Baden] was a big, heavy-set German with considerable political experience. He had been married to a Jewish woman and had gone through the process of divorcing her so she could get out of

Germany and be free of danger. The minute the war was over, he brought her back immediately. Very anti-Hitler. Conservative. At that time, his life was made more difficult by having to rule over a divided Württemberg and a divided Baden—although, interestingly enough, when the time came [in 1949], both Württembergers and Badeners decided to stay together in a single state. I'd been told that this would never happen, but this is what did happen.

"Our first Minister-President from Hesse, Dr. Karl Geiler, was a distinguished professor at Heidelberg, and later rector of the university. Definitely an intellectual. Extremely intelligent and attractive. He was followed by a Social Democrat [Christian Stock], who was much more a man of the people. Our first Minister-President in Bavaria, Dr. [Wilhelm] Hoegner, was a Social Democrat, had been a member of the resistance, and was a very able and practical type of a person. His successor, [Dr. Hans] Erhard, had been a successful jurist in Bavaria. He also was an intellectual—quiet and very able. He became the first head of the Bundesrat after the West German government was formed. Then we had [Dr. Wilhelm] Kaisen from Bremen, who was the typical go-getter city manager. Hustling, energetic. Would have loved to go to Rotary meetings, if they had Rotary. But a very alert, very capable fellow. And very closely identified with Bremen. A Socialist, but not very doctrinaire."

Q: Did you find it easy to work with the Minister-Presidents?

CLAY: Well, they had to work with me. Actually, I got along with them very well. But I never saw anything of them in a social way. I never met them with my family. After the *Länderrat* meetings, they would join me for coffee and we would talk informally. And I got to know quite a lot that way. It wasn't because I didn't want to know them socially. But I didn't think it was the right thing to do. In the first place, I felt if they became too friendly with us, it would ruin them politically. I was wrong on that, but I had great concern that the Germans who worked with us and got too close to us would be ruined in Germany. This was one of the reasons I operated at arm's length with them—which I'm sure they didn't understand.

"Altogether, I think they were a very exceptional group of people. We were very fortunate to have been able to find men of this caliber to take on such a hopeless job, given the odds against them. The British had pretty good Minister-Presidents too. Also very capable men.

"The first problem I assigned them was that of dealing with all of the [German] displaced persons. It was a tough one too. Here they were, running states that had a tremendous shortage of houses for everyone, and also tremendously short on food, clothing, and all of the essentials of life, and they were being asked to make an equitable distribution to these hundreds of thousands of people: people who had been bombed out, people who had fled west, Sudeten people from Czechoslovakia, and the Swabians from Hungary, who were moved out just after the war. Inexcusable, in my book. The Swabians had been in Hungary for over a hundred years.

"I gave the problem to the Minister-Presidents for several reasons. In the first place, they could do a better job of it than we could. They would have a greater interest than we would. They would certainly work to see that it was done fairly insofar as their own people were concerned. Second, it was going to be a damned unpopular job, so I thought they might just as well suffer the unpopularity as us. Third, it was a real test of whether they could establish a government that could function."

Q: But basically you wanted to return the responsibility for local government to the Germans?

CLAY: I was determined to return local government to the Germans as soon as possible. For several reasons. In the first place, I didn't know how long the United States was going to be willing to support an occupation, and therefore, if I was going to establish law and order, I felt the best way of doing it was by the utilization of Germans. Second, I felt that the more we could reduce American personnel in military government, the more apt we were to obtain the proper support at home. Third, I thought the Germans could do it better than we could.

Q: How did you know you could trust them?

CLAY: The only way you can find out is by giving people the responsibility and seeing how they react. You cannot find out by not doing it.

"This was a question that was always raised—even by the Germans. But I think it gave us the best local government in Germany. Better than the British or the French. For example, I think it was in December of 1945, we set up a transport directorate under the *Länderrat* to handle rail traffic. Our military chief of transportation predicted a railroad collapse as soon as the Army gave up control. I did not believe this, because I was certain that German railway technicians were more competent to direct their own rail operations than we were. In the first month after the transfer, the Germans removed several thousand Nazi employees whom the Army had found indispensable to adequate service. And the Germans actually increased passenger traffic and freight tonnage.

"One of the real problems in running an occupation is your own people. They want to be czars. They resent very bitterly when they suggest to the Germans that certain things be done and the Germans don't do them. This is one of the hardest things you have to face in an occupation situation: your own staff are zealots, and they're often zealots for reforms that go far beyond anything that's ever been done in your own country."

Q: Was this part of the problem in decentralization?

CLAY: Part of the problem with decentralization, part of the problem in civil service reform, part of the problem in education reform. The people we had in all of these branches were leading exponents of reform in these fields in the United States. And I'm not passing [judgment] on the merits of what they wanted to do in the United States. But I held very much to the principle that we had no right to make the Germans accept reforms that we had not been willing to get authorities in the United States to accept.

Q: Is that why you pushed authority and responsibility onto the Germans?

CLAY: Yes, but there were other reasons. One, over the long run, they were obliged to have a greater degree of competence than we could demonstrate: we had some fine people, but running Germany was not their life's work. Number two, if we were building for the future, we had to leave in Germany people that were able to prove what we had done wasn't wrong.

Q: Some German critics of the Occupation have suggested that it really took the Cold War to modify the harsh policies of American military government.

CLAY: Well, I think you could also say that it probably took the Cold War and fear of the Russians to make the Germans accept the Occupation so well. But there's certainly some truth in the charge. We began to look like angels, not because we were angels, but we looked [like] that in comparison to what was going on in Eastern Europe.

Q: What about teaching democracy? Free speech and a free press? For example, when did you begin holding press conferences in Germany?

CLAY: Almost from the beginning.

Q: And with German reporters?

CLAY: That was after I became Military Governor in 1947. I invited the Germans to attend. And I had a lot of opposition from the American press at first. So I had a special meeting with them. I remember that very well. I said, "Look, if you people believe in what you say you believe in, that the press conference is an important part of democracy, what can be better for the German reporters than to come in here and watch the way you ask questions and the way they're answered? Maybe we can make them do what you do." They had a meeting on it and agreed it was OK. You know, it's a funny thing, press conferences are an important part of political life in Germany today. They never held them before. But now the press demands it.

Q: E. J. Kahn in his *New Yorker* "Profile" reports that you refused to revoke the license of a German newspaper that was critical of you.

CLAY: That's right. My information bureau sent out an order curtailing the issue of this newspaper because it had an article quite critical of me, and I remember it very well, because I said, "I think this is wonderful." It was. So I revoked the order, and I think it helped the Germans understand what a free press meant.

Q: In 1945, what did you see as the principal bottlenecks to German economic recovery?

CLAY: Well, number one, Germany could not raise enough food to be self-supporting. Therefore it had to import food. The only place it could get food was from the United States. Number two, it was difficult for Germany to export without having its revenue from these exports confiscated by the country buying those products, since all of them held unpaid German securities. Number three, in view of the fact that you were paying people to work in a currency that was depreciating all the time, there was very little incentive for people to work. Finally, many of the things that were needed in Germany—raw materials, for example—required importation . . . and this required money. So the only way in which you could get a true economic recovery in Germany was to provide sound money internally, to find some credits on the outside, and to get agreements on the outside that money paid in exchange for exports would not be confiscated. "Confiscated" is not the right word. Enjoined.

Q: So money was the crucial problem?

CLAY: Yes. For example, we had to get a standby agreement from the major banks in the United States against a $100 million German government bond issue that was in default. We had to get an agreement from the banks that they would not try to seize the money that we developed in the U.S. from German exports, being assured that in the final rendition of accounts for Germany, we would recognize that this money was owed.

Q: Would it be fair to say that as a result of the defeat, everyone in postwar Germany started out at the same level?

CLAY: No, not at all. There are two or three reasons for that. One was that our currency reform program did not have a capital tax on land. Actually, I had proposed one, and it was concurred in by the British and French. But our government turned it down. They didn't want any part of a tax on capital, a capital levy, which, in effect, a land tax would have been. Thus the landowner escaped relatively unscathed from currency reform. In addition, and I think this is an important thing to remember, there was no way to devalue equity, and the equity owners had just as much equity after reform as they did before. For those who could afford to hold it, this represented a possible return to affluence. And it was not only possible; it actually materialized. We did close down the [stock] exchanges, and we tried to make the exchange of equity stock very difficult, because we recognized the consequences. You also had another wise group—which is always true in Europe—which escaped the general devaluation. And that was those who owned jewelry, antiques, and valuable paintings. And many of the very wealthy families in Germany held these in large measure. Take the trial that we had [over the ownership] of the jewels taken by the military people from the home of the Prince of Prussia. Those jewels were appraised at $3.5–4 million in 1945. The Hohenzollern jewels—or, rather, the Kaiser's jewels that were in our possession for a few weeks—which had been spirited out of East Germany—were also appraised at $3–3.5 million. And of course some of the art collections were of immeasurable value. So I suppose you would have to accept that in any currency devaluation, the poorer you are, the more you are affected.

Q: And people with liquid assets?

CLAY: People also who were on pensions and people who held bonds. The exchange for them was one to six, so obviously they were badly hurt. Actually, I don't really think they were hurt, because the new currency bought more for them than they'd been getting. Currency reform always hits the pensioner and the people who are living on fixed incomes, because they have no other way to recoup.

· 16 ·

Withdrawal from the Russian Zone

THE DIVISION OF GERMANY INTO EAST AND WEST was a direct result of the location of the military zones of occupation in 1945. It was surely one of the ironies of World War II, for no one anticipated or intended that the zonal boundaries in Germany would become permanent: they were merely lines on a map indicating where each victorious army would be deployed once Germany was defeated. The general assumption was that all of Germany would be under joint four-power control; that common policies would be set by the four military governors meeting together; that those policies would be uniform throughout Germany; and that the Occupation would be brief.

But almost from the beginning the zonal boundaries took on a transcendental importance. Each nation focused on the territory that had been designated for its army to occupy, and, pending the development of agreed quadripartite policies—a lengthy process under the best of circumstances—each nation was forced by sheer necessity to promulgate unilateral directives affecting only its zone. In this context, one of the most important issues that initially confronted the four victorious powers was the withdrawal of each army to its designated area. In particular, the evacuation of that vast territory in central Germany overrun by American and British forces, but designated to be part of the Russian zone of occupation, posed one of the earliest tests of Allied unity. Clay and Eisenhower vigorously insisted that the withdrawal take place as soon as possible. Churchill and the British government sought to delay: to use the captured territory as bargaining leverage with the Soviet Union concerning matters elsewhere.

The actual boundaries for the occupation of Germany had been drafted by the European Advisory Commission (EAC) meeting in London in 1944. These boundaries (which reflected a proposal prepared initially by the British Cabinet) provided for three separate zones of occupation, with Berlin—which was located 110 miles within what was to be the Soviet zone—jointly occupied by all three powers.*

The British zone, located in northwestern Germany, included the industrial heart of Germany and the port city of Hamburg. The American zone, in southwestern Germany, included the provinces of Bavaria, Hesse, Baden, and Württemberg, as well as the port cities of Bremen and Bremerhaven. The Russian zone extended more or less from the Oder and Neisse rivers in the east to the Elbe in the west, plus the ancient kingdoms of Saxony and Thuringia.

When hostilities ended in 1945, the U.S. and British armies held territory far into the area that had been designated as the Russian zone. Eisenhower and Clay recognized that the quadripartite occupation of Germany could not begin until each army was installed in its designated area, and they urged Washington to move quickly to authorize them to coordinate such a withdrawal with the Russians, lest the atmosphere of wartime cooperation be impaired.

As early as April 5, 1945, with Allied troops advancing into Germany, Eisenhower had sought permission to allow his Army Group commanders (Bradley, Devers, and Montgomery) to arrange mutually with their Russian opposites for a withdrawal behind the agreed zonal boundaries once contact had been established. But the British objected

* France was subsequently added as an Occupation power, its zone composed of territory previously designated for Britain and the United States.

COPENHAGEN
SWEDEN
DENMARK
NORTH
SEA
Flensburg
SCHLESWIG-
HOLSTEIN
JOINT
AMERICAN-BRITISH
Stralsund
Rostock
Lübeck
Schwerin
Wesermünde
HAMBURG
MECKLENBURG
Oldenburg
OLDENBURG
BREMEN
HANNOVER
NETHERLANDS
BRITISH
Neuruppin
JOINT
AMERICAN-SOVIET-BRITISH
BERLIN
Brandenburg
Potsdam
Hannover
Braunschweig
MAGDEBURG
Hildesheim
BRAUNSCHWEIG
Magdeburg
Münster
LIPPE
Detmold
MARK BRANDE
SOVIET
WESTPHALIA
ANHALT
Dessau
ESSEN
DORTMUND
Cottbus
Krefeld
HALLE-MERSEBURG
Halle
Torgau
DÜSSELDORF
Kassel
LEIPZIG
COLOGNE
KURHESSEN
DRESDEN
Aachen
Bonn
Weimar
Erfurt
THÜRINGEN
SAXONY
RHINE
BELGIUM
Giessen
NASSAU
Koblenz
PROVINCE
Plauen
Wiesbaden
FRANKFURT
LUXEMBOURG
Main R.
Trier
Bamberg
Worms
Kaiserlautern
SAARLAND
Saarbrücken
BAVARIA
Mannheim
Nürnberg
AMERICAN
FRANCE
Karlsruhe
Regensburg
BAVARIA
Stuttgart
Baden-Baden
WÜRTTEMBERG
Neckar R.
Reutlingen
Ulm
Augsburg
Freiburg
MUNICH
AUST
Kempten
Rosenheim
L. Constance
SWITZERLAND
R. Clinton

Zones of Occupation and Location of Western Forces

strongly. Both the Foreign Office and Prime Minister Churchill believed it preferable for the Allies to stand fast. They maintained that if the Western powers should come into possession of large parts of the Soviet zone, such territory would provide "a powerful lever to obtain concessions" from the Russians.

Eisenhower and Clay had little sympathy for the British position. Eisenhower, especially, was concerned to avoid a possible military clash with the Russians and, in the absence of instructions, authorized his field commanders on April 10 to negotiate "directly" with their Soviet counterparts to work out Allied withdrawals if necessary.

"Let's put it this way," Bradley told General Simpson (Commanding General, Ninth Army) immediately afterward. "We would prefer to hold our present line until we can arrange for an orderly changeover. But if the Russian insists on going forward to his line of occupation, we're not going to start any trouble. Work it out as best you can and allow him to." According to Bradley, the U.S. military was "not going to risk an explosion that might bring a sequel to the war and bring World War III."

On April 15, Eisenhower once more pressed Washington for instructions. He told General Marshall that he could find no justification for refusing to vacate territories allocated to the Soviets by the EAC, except on pain of "grave misunderstandings if not actual clashes."

Acting again on his own initiative, Eisenhower then cabled Major General John R. Deane, head of the American military mission in Moscow, to arrange the details for linking up with the Red Army. Eisenhower told Deane to propose to General Antonov, chief of the Soviet General Staff, the "simplest possible" coordinating procedures when the Allied and Russian armies made contact. He also told Deane to assure the Soviets that the Allies had no thought of altering the EAC zones of occupation.

Still with no reply from Washington, Eisenhower once more cabled Marshall that he deplored the "monkey wrench" the British had thrown into the negotiations. "Frankly," said Eisenhower, "if I should have forces in the Russian occupation zone and be faced with an order or 'request' to retire so that they may advance to the points they choose, I see no recourse except to comply. To do otherwise would probably provoke an incident with the logic of the situation all on the side of the Soviets."

But the Combined Chiefs of Staff (CCS) meeting in Washington saw the issue differently.* On April 20, 1945, they instructed Eisenhower that he should order his forces to hold their positions, and that he should seek CCS approval for any major adjustments. The issue of withdrawal from the Soviet zone was thus removed from SHAEF's control and placed at the governmental level.

This did not sit well with Eisenhower and Clay. Like Eisenhower, Clay fervently believed that the wartime example of military cooperation with the Soviet Union would have "a happy and definite effect upon the whole question of whether communism and democracy could find a way to get along together in the same world." Clay strongly resented the impediments the British were placing in the way of establishing the Occupation.

Indicative of Clay's views at the time were his comments at a press conference at the Hôtel Scribe in Paris on May 16, 1945. When questioned about the possibilities of four-power cooperation, Clay emphatically replied, "It's got to work."

> If the four of us cannot get together now in running Germany, how are we going to get together in an international organization to secure the peace of the world? We are going to have to give and take and do a lot of things which the American public will not believe in, but we cannot go in there with four nations without being prepared to give and take, and if the people at home will recognize that the experiment of four nations means much to the future of the world, then we have hope for the future of the job.

The views of Clay and Eisenhower reflected not only those of the wartime Roosevelt administration, but their own deeply held convictions about the necessity to cooperate with the Russians. Even the State Department at that time shared SHAEF's view that the withdrawal of Allied forces into their designated occupation zones was not a bargaining chip. According to officials in the Division of European Affairs, "For governments to direct [this] movement of troops definitely indicated *political* actions." *"Such movements,"* these officials advised the

* In World War II military terminology, the Combined Chiefs of Staff refers to the U.S. and British Chiefs of Staff acting in their combined capacity. It stood at the apex of the Allied command structure, and determined Anglo-American military policy.

Joint Chiefs of Staff, *"should remain a military consideration."* Under Marshall's direction, the U.S. Joint Chiefs of Staff thereupon prepared a letter for President Truman to send Churchill that incorporated Eisenhower and Clay's position. The letter also contained a draft message to Stalin that would have permitted SHAEF to begin the withdrawal in coordination with the Russian military. That same day, Eisenhower himself cabled Truman recommending that the withdrawal be handled as a routine military matter:

> I do not understand [said Eisenhower] why the Prime Minister has been so determined to intermingle political and military considerations in attempting to establish a procedure for the conduct of our own and Russian troops when a meeting ultimately takes place. My original recommendation submitted to the CC/S [Combined Chiefs of Staff] was a simple one and I thought provided a very sensible arrangement.

But Churchill remained adamant. After the German surrender on May 8, the British pressed their point that Allied forces not retire from the Soviet zone until the whole question of future relations between East and West had been resolved. Eisenhower and Clay just as persistently insisted that the withdrawal take place as soon as possible.

When Churchill proposed to meet with Truman to discuss the general issue of Soviet relations, the President declined. Instead, he dispatched Harry Hopkins to Moscow to arrange a Big Three meeting with Stalin and informed Churchill it was his intention "to adhere to our interpretation of the Yalta agreements"—which meant that the United States would withdraw to its zonal area prior to the Big Three meeting. The President was not prepared to support Churchill at that time, and certainly did not wish to disrupt U.S. relations with the Soviet Union.

When Eisenhower visited Churchill in London on May 16, he found the Prime Minister still determined to prevent a withdrawal from the Soviet zone. Eisenhower emphasized to Churchill that the four-power occupation of Germany could not begin until each power was in control of its own zone and the Allied Control Council, the quadripartite body that was to govern Germany, had been established. Until that occurred, said Eisenhower, the legal basis of the Occupation was shaky. But Churchill remained unconvinced. As

Eisenhower advised Washington afterward, the Prime Minister "did not appear to be in any real hurry" to have four-power occupation begin.

For Eisenhower and Clay, the problem of administering Germany in the absence of four-power government was fast becoming critical. The Allied armies were still holding their battle positions, and Eisenhower technically was still in supreme command. The complicated tasks of dealing with occupied Germany simply were not being addressed. On May 23, Eisenhower advised Washington that he "could not carry out his mission much longer" in the absence of four-power government. He suggested that SHAEF be abolished and that the withdrawal from the Russian zone begin immediately.

The British continued to oppose withdrawal, but suggested a compromise: the four military Commanders-in-Chief (Eisenhower, Montgomery, de Lattre de Tassigny, and Marshal Zhukov) should meet in Berlin the following week to establish the Allied Control Council for Germany (ACC). The ACC, said the British, would be empowered to discuss the withdrawal from the Soviet zone, but until all outstanding issues with the USSR were resolved, the Allied forces should stand fast.

After a week of protracted negotiations between Washington, London, and Moscow, it was agreed that the military commanders would meet in Berlin on June 5, 1945, where they would sign the formal Declaration Regarding the Defeat of Germany and the Assumption of Supreme Authority—the legal basis for the Occupation—and then promulgate the EAC Protocols on zonal boundaries and the Allied Control Council.

But differences between the United States and Great Britain persisted. Whereas Eisenhower was authorized by Washington to work out the withdrawal from the Soviet zone with Zhukov, Montgomery's instructions from the Foreign Office specified "that the de facto occupation" by the British and American armies of large parts of the Soviet zone was an "important bargaining counter for obtaining satisfaction from the Soviet government on a number of outstanding questions."

On June 2, Clay cabled Washington for instructions. In particular, Clay and Eisenhower were concerned that they be authorized to begin the withdrawal from the Russian zone as soon as possible. Said Clay:

> It is anticipated that one of the questions which will be raised at Berlin meeting . . . will be date on which our forces will begin their withdrawal from Russian zone. It is possible that Russians may establish such withdrawal as a corollary to the establishment of the Control Council on a functioning basis in Berlin and to turning over the several zones [sectors] in Berlin. . . . Any cause for delay in the establishment of Control Council due to delay in withdrawal would be attributed to us and might well develop strong public reaction.

Clay noted that SHAEF as yet had "no instructions covering such withdrawal," and suggested that separate instructions be sent to Eisenhower and Montgomery by their respective governments as to how they should handle the issue.

Thc following day, the Joint Chiefs of Staff, with President Truman's approval, replied that "the question of withdrawal to our zones should not be a condition precedent to establishing the Control Council. . . . If the Russians raise the point, you should state in substance that the matter of withdrawal of forces to their own zones is one of the items to be worked out in the Control Council. As to the actual movement of U.S. Forces, you should state that this . . . is primarily a military matter; its timing will be in accordance with U.S. ability to withdraw their forces . . . and Russian ability to take over."

On June 4—the day before the meeting in Berlin—Churchill repeated his "profound misgivings" to President Truman over "the retreat of the American Army to our line of occupation in the Central Sector [i.e., Germany], thus bringing Soviet power into the heart of Western Europe and the descent of an iron curtain between us and everything to the eastward. I hoped that this retreat, if it has to be made, would be accompanied by the settlement of many great things which would be the true foundation of world peace. Nothing really important has been settled yet, and you and I will have to bear great responsibility for the future."

Churchill's reclama failed to move Washington. On June 5, the four military Commanders-in-Chief, with their deputies for military government, met in Berlin as scheduled. But as Clay noted afterward:

"This was not a very satisfactory meeting. The Russians kept us waiting—General Eisenhower, Montgomery, and the French general [de Lattre de Tassigny]—for five or six hours because of some wording in the document that could have implied they were at war with Japan. It didn't specify Japan, but it could have been interpreted that way. But it took them six hours even to tell us what the problem was. When they finally told us, it wasn't any problem to us. I thought we had sufficient authority to make clear that the document didn't apply to Japan, so I just added a note to that effect in the document. The British and French agreed, and that was it. But it had taken six hours. And General Eisenhower and Montgomery were furious, as was the French general."

Q: Did the Russians explain the delay?
CLAY: Not for six hours. We didn't have any fear that we were being held prisoner or anything, but it was so discourteous and so obviously unexplained that we were awfully damned mad at being treated that way.
Q: And the Russians sensed this?
CLAY: Well, I can't answer that. They finally came around, and afterwards they wanted to have a big banquet, and General Eisenhower said, "I'm leaving at six o'clock." And he did. And so did the British and French.

With the texts reconciled, the ceremony in Berlin began. In the glare of arc lamps, each of the four military Commanders-in-Chief signed the Declaration assuming total power over Germany. Afterward they met briefly. Eisenhower proposed that Clay and the other deputies for military government (Lieutenant General Sir Ronald Weeks, Lieutenant General Louis Marie Koeltz, and General Vassily Sokolovsky) meet immediately to organize the Control Council machinery. But as Eisenhower and Clay had anticipated, Zhukov made it clear that any steps to set up the control machinery would have to await the Allied withdrawal from the Soviet zone. Zhukov said pointedly that he would be willing to join in establishing the control machinery *as soon as the withdrawal began.* When Eisenhower and Montgomery suggested that the withdrawal could be discussed by the Control Council after it was established, Zhukov replied that he could not consider the Control Council issue until a date was set for the withdrawal.

Upon their return to Frankfurt, Clay composed a cable to the Joint Chiefs of Staff for Eisenhower's signature. In it, he made clear once again that, in his opinion, "the question of withdrawal must be . . . resolved by the U.S. and U.K. governments before any further discussion of control machinery with Zhukov will serve any useful purpose."

Clay told the JCS that Eisenhower had suggested that there were many problems the Control Council could deal with before the withdrawal, and that the two problems were not necessarily related. "However," wrote Clay, "there is some justification for Zhukov's position that he is unable to discuss administrative problems in Germany when he is not in control and hence not familiar with the problems of the zone for which he will eventually be responsible."

Eisenhower added his personal observation that, as a result of his conversation with Zhukov, he was "optimistic that the Russians will join in some form of control machinery when withdrawal is accomplished and will agree to our force entering Berlin concurrently with our withdrawal from their zone."

Clay concluded the cable on a somber note. He warned Washington to consider alternatives to four-power government, should agreement with the Russians not be possible. "As I see it," he said, "if quadripartite government does not treat Germany as a whole, we must either establish tripartite control of Western Germany to permit its treatment as an economic unit, with full realization of all the implications involved, or else be prepared to govern our zone on practically an independent basis. I realize the undesirability of either alternative and hope that the necessity for adoption of either will not materialize."

Robert Murphy, who attended the Berlin meeting with Eisenhower and Clay, dispatched a similar note to Washington from Paris, using the State Department's separate communications facilities. "For the Department's secret information," said Murphy, "I believe that General Eisenhower does not consider that the retention of our forces in the Russian zone is wise or that it will be productive of advantages."

Two days later, Harry Hopkins passed through Frankfurt on his return journey from Moscow to Washington. Hopkins had achieved mixed results in Moscow. He had no success with Stalin over the fate of Poland—one of the principal outstanding issues between the United States and the Soviet Union—but he had arranged for a Big Three meeting to be held at Potsdam on July 15 and had also settled the voting procedure in the United Nations General Assembly pursuant to American wishes, thereby salvaging the upcoming San Francisco Conference that would establish the U.N.

Hopkins and Eisenhower knew each other slightly and shared a common Midwestern heritage. But Clay and Hopkins were warm friends whose association traced back to the early days of the New Deal, and Hopkins had strongly supported Clay's appointment to be Eisenhower's deputy for military government. In a series of conversations lasting over the next twenty-four hours, Hopkins summarized his talks with Stalin for Eisenhower and Clay and listened at length to the problems confronting the Occupation. All three agreed that the withdrawal of Allied forces from the Soviet zone as soon as possible was essential if there was to be any hope of achieving postwar cooperation with the Russians. The following cable to President Truman, which Clay drafted for Hopkins's signature, reflected their consensus:

> . . . I am convinced [said the message] that the present indeterminate status of date for withdrawal of Allied troops from area assigned to the Russians is certain to be misunderstood by Russia as well as at home.
>
> It is manifest that Allied control machinery cannot be started until Allied troops have withdrawn from territory included in the Russian area of occupation. Any delay in the establishment of control machinery interferes seriously with the development of governmental administrative machinery for Germany and the application of Allied policy in Germany.

At Clay's suggestion, Hopkins told Truman that a delay of a week or so "would not be disastrous," but that the question should be resolved before the July 15 meeting with Stalin at Potsdam.

Clay's draft also contained the note that "As a concurrent condition to our withdrawal we should specify a simultaneous movement of our troops to Berlin under an agreement . . . which would provide us with unrestricted access to our Berlin area from Bremen and Frankfurt by air, rail, and highway on agreed routes."

Hopkins indicated that, despite the predictable British response, a cable should still be sent by the President to Stalin indicating that the withdrawal would commence June 21, in accordance with plans to be worked out by the respective military commanders. "As matters now stand," said Hopkins, "Eisenhower is in [the] embarrassing position of not being able to discuss a specific date for withdrawal with the Russians." Accepting Clay's language verbatim, Hopkins noted that he considered the decision on the date of withdrawal "of major import to our further relations with Russia," and urged that prompt action be taken. To add urgency to the request, Hopkins, whose health was failing badly, volunteered to remain in Europe if President Truman thought it would be helpful.

Hopkins's message had the desired effect. Whereas Eisenhower and Clay had not been able to overcome British resistance on the Combined Chiefs of Staff, Hopkins was able to drive home to the President the urgency of withdrawing Allied forces. On June 11, Truman pointedly informed Churchill that he was "unable to delay the withdrawal of American troops from the Soviet zone in order to use pressure in the settlement of other problems," since "advice of the highest reliability [indicates] that the Allied Control Council cannot begin to function until Allied troops withdraw from the Russian zone." The President said that SHAEF's overall responsibility for the Occupation should be terminated immediately and that separate U.S. and British zones under Eisenhower and Montgomery should begin to function forthwith. Truman added that "it would be highly disadvantageous to our relations with the Soviets to postpone action . . . until our meeting in July."

To the surprise of almost everyone in Washington (and at SHAEF), Churchill promptly conformed to Truman's decision. "I sincerely hope," he said, "that your action will in the long run make for a lasting peace in Europe."

As soon as Churchill's agreement had been obtained, Truman cabled Stalin that he was prepared to order the withdrawal of U.S. forces from the Soviet zone on June 21, "in accordance with arrangements between the respective commanders, including in these arrangements simultaneous movement into Greater Berlin and provision for free access by air, road and rail from Frankfurt and Bremen to Berlin for U.S. forces." Churchill sent a similar cable to Stalin on June 15. The following day, Marshal Stalin replied that Zhukov would be in Moscow for a victory celebration on June 24 and requested that the date for the changeover be delayed until July 1. The President agreed, and on June 19 General Marshall informed SHAEF of the arrangements.

Q: Could you review your meeting in Frankfurt with Mr. Hopkins?

CLAY: Mr. Hopkins was very ill at that time, but President Truman had gotten him to fly to Moscow to see Stalin to arrange the Potsdam

Conference. General Eisenhower and I saw Mr. Hopkins, and we stayed up very late that night talking to him. And there was no question but that he thought we [the Soviet Union and the United States] were going to get along. I also think that the Russians wanted to get along at that time.

Q: Then the atmosphere was relatively good?

CLAY: At that time, the Russians were so impressed with our strength and power, they would not have attempted anything. Knowing that the Russians all through the years have had the desire to create a huge buffer area between themselves and the rest of Europe, a policy they had devoted their lives to, and then to see this great and powerful United States—and powerful England, for that matter—demobilize as fast as they could, move out, reduce their strength, I think that if I had been in their place, I would have assumed that the Americans didn't give a damn for Europe. They didn't after World War I, and they didn't after World War II. I think the Russians felt we were very foolish to demobilize as fast as we did. I don't think we would have had a Cold War if we'd kept a strong army in Europe in 1945.

Q: The Russians would have respected that?

CLAY: They would have known we were going to be there, and they respected us. And we would have accomplished more. But I'm not sure we could ever have made four-power government work over a long period of time. The differences between our systems were just too great. But I thought then, *and I still do,* that we had an obligation to try and make it work—that if it failed, it wasn't going to be our fault.

Q: Was there any talk of dismembering Germany at that time?

CLAY: Cutting it up permanently? Not at that time. The question of whether the Ruhr should be separated from Germany was not raised until 1947. And that was a battle royal. (Of course, the French always wanted to detach the Ruhr.)

Q: At this particular time in 1945, did the Russians and Americans get along better than, say, the Russians and British, or the Russians and French?

CLAY: At that particular time, yes. No doubt about it. General Eisenhower and Zhukov became quite friendly. I was very friendly with Zhukov, and especially friendly with Sokolovsky [Clay's opposite number, who was highly regarded in military circles for his brilliant strategic victory in the battle for Smolensk]. This is one of the reasons I think we could have avoided the worst of what followed. Because it looked in the beginning as though we were going to get along. That is why I think that the Soviet behavior grew out of events rather than having been predetermined. For the first five or six months after the war, we didn't do anything of consequence. But, then, neither did we battle. Then, Zhukov left and Sokolovsky took over, and we began to find that we just couldn't deal with them.

Q: Could you describe your contacts with Zhukov and Sokolovsky?

CLAY: In the first place, every time the Control Council met, whoever was chairman gave a reception after the meetings right in the Control Council building. Not a very elaborate party, just tea and coffee and sandwiches, a little wine or champagne. No hard liquor. No, I take that back: when the Russians were hosts, they had vodka.

"Then, of course, we had a regular exchange of dinners. Eisenhower would give a dinner for Zhukov. I would give one for Sokolovsky. And vice versa. They were relatively informal dinners. They were done in considerable style, but nevertheless they were relatively informal and friendly. And after dinner we'd have a nightcap together and chat and talk. Sometimes until very late.

"Eisenhower and Zhukov would always reminisce. Both of them had fabulous memories, and they were always telling what happened here, there, and everywhere. Each country also celebrated their holidays: Red Army Day, Bastille Day, the King's birthday, and so on. I used to bring up half a dozen generals from the [American] zone for Red Army Day. It usually turned into a drunken affair—not for the top people, but the Russians really did it up.

"Then, after Zhukov left, Marshal Sokolovsky's wife came. She used to come over with him and have dinner with us every once in a while, look at a movie. We went over and had dinner with them a couple of times. In other words, it was really very friendly until '47."

Q: And Sokolovsky?

CLAY: I liked Sokolovsky, I really did. He could quote the Bible more frequently and more accurately than anybody I'd known. He was very intelligent. Very interesting. Loved to read English novels, especially Jane Austen.

Q: Had he studied for the priesthood?

CLAY: I don't know. I don't think so. But he had been a schoolteacher before he went into the Army.

Q: So the difficulties during the first year and a half . . .

CLAY: There were no real difficulties during the first year, except that we couldn't get anything moving. But there were no personal difficulties. We got along with each other.

Q: And in Berlin?

CLAY: It was the same thing. We had a Victory Day Parade, which was quite a show. That was the 82nd Airborne, and that was very well done. They were spit-and-polish soldiers. I had General Patton come up to take the review, and Zhukov was there with all of his medals on. Patton later gave me hell for not telling him that Zhukov would be wearing his dress uniform. I think he felt upstaged. So, up until the departure of the 82nd Airborne, we certainly were putting up a very military appearance. But it sure went to pot after that. By early 1946, we were down to three battalions. But that was sufficient for Berlin. What we lacked was any back-up in the [American] zone.

Q: You visited Moscow with General Eisenhower in August? Was there any special reason for you to go?

CLAY: I suppose it was because I knew Zhukov better than anyone else. Zhukov was our host. Interestingly enough, when we first arrived, Zhukov met us at the airport and came with us to the American Embassy. [Ambassador Averell] Harriman asked him in to have a drink, and, much to Harriman's surprise, Zhukov and his staff came in and had a drink. It was almost unheard of, any of them visiting the embassy except on very formal occasions. All during our visit, they were very, very friendly. They really were. They had a dinner party for General Eisenhower. Then they had a massive review for him. He was invited out to the huge Moscow stadium with Stalin. We went there, went to a soccer match, with eighty thousand, maybe a hundred thousand people there. And when they were introduced, the Russians gave Eisenhower and Zhukov a tremendous ovation. We went to Leningrad and had a delightful reception. Nothing could have been any more friendly. There was no tension whatever. Of course, this was a matter of a victorious army. The war had just ended, and we still had all of this big military strength in Europe.

Q: Did you question the pace of American demobilization?

CLAY: General Eisenhower did. He was the military commander, and he very definitely queried the number of troops to be left in Germany. He wanted ten divisions. That was not my job. I was not the troop commander at that time.

Q: Did the protests against demobilization continue?

CLAY: I would have to say that certainly General Eisenhower contemplated ten divisions and requested them. I'm sure General McNarney [Eisenhower's successor as military commander] made presentations for more than he had. In addition to that, General Marshall and General Arnold, and later General Eisenhower when he became Chief of Staff, made very great protestations to Congress that we were cutting back too fast. But that was not the mood of the country. The country just wanted to "bring the boys home."

Q: But as Military Governor, this was not your primary concern. It was General Eisenhower's?

CLAY: That's right. My concern was to run military government. Obviously, the only concern I had was that we have sufficient military strength to do the job. But we didn't really need a lot of military strength for that.

· 17 ·

Access to Berlin

NO CITY IS MORE CLOSELY LINKED TO THE COLD WAR than Berlin. Even today the former German capital still symbolizes the division between East and West: the division of Europe, the division of Germany, and the division of the city itself. East Berlin, the Soviet sector, was the capital of Communist East Germany, the German Democratic Republic, and for twenty-eight years (from 1961 to 1989) was separated from the rest of the city by the infamous Berlin Wall. West Berlin, composed of the American, British, and French sectors, was linked economically and politically with prosperous West Germany, the Federal Republic of Germany—located some 110 miles to the west. In a technical sense, the entire city of Berlin remains under four-power occupation—the last relic of World War II. And its precarious location inside East Germany gave rise to two major international crises: the Berlin blockade of 1948–49, and the building of the Berlin Wall in 1961.

The Berlin blockade represented an imperialist thrust by Communism ascendant: a blatant attempt to force the Western powers from Berlin and incorporate the city into the Soviet occupation zone. The Wall, some thirteen years later, reflected Communism in decline: a desperate attempt to shore up the sagging East German regime by closing its open border to the West. Both crises, and the curious isolation that engulfed Berlin, were a direct legacy of the wartime agreements concerning Germany's occupation and of the failure of East and West to make quadripartite government a success. In particular, these problems traced to the glow of wartime amity and the desire of victorious statesmen to make Berlin a symbol of Allied unity after Hitler's defeat. In that heady atmosphere, the fact of its location well inside the Soviet occupation zone was deemed irrelevant.

Berlin was to be the seat of the Allied Control Council, the meeting place where quadripartite policy for all of Germany was to be fashioned. Impressive military contingents from each of the four powers would occupy separate sectors of the city, and the four Military Governors, who would be based in Berlin, would provide the leadership for creating a peaceful and democratic Germany. It is not surprising that in the context of victory, detailed arrangements for Western access to Berlin were overlooked.

Following the agreement by Truman, Churchill, and Stalin to begin the withdrawal of Western forces from the Soviet zone, a military conference of Allied commanders was arranged at Zhukov's headquarters for June 29. The purpose of the conference was to coordinate the movement of the U.S., British, and Russian armies into their particular occupation zones and the simultaneous transit of the American and British garrisons into Berlin—which was then occupied solely by the Russians. Because General Eisenhower and Field Marshal Montgomery were both on home leave, the United States was represented at the conference by Clay, and Great Britain by Lieutenant General Sir Ronald Weeks—the respective deputies to Eisenhower and Montgomery for military government. Clay was accompanied by the State Department's Robert Murphy; Weeks by Sir William Strang of the Foreign Office, who had been Britain's representative on the European Advisory Commission (EAC).

General Marshall already had impressed upon Clay the importance of securing access arrangements to Berlin. On June 25, he cabled:

> It will be noted that the proposed directive [drafted by the EAC] contains no action to obtain transit rights to Berlin and Vienna [both of which were located within Soviet-occupied territory and both of which were to be under four-power occupation].
>
> In accordance with the President's message [of June 14] to Stalin, these should be arranged with Russian commanders concerned simultaneously with arrangements for other adjustments.

"I don't remember ever seeing that cable," said Clay many years later. "I must have seen it, but I don't remember it. I suspect what happened was that we had urged the government (through Mr. Hopkins) to take up the question and they were putting it back into our hands."

Marshall had cabled a similar message to Major General John R. Deane, chief of the U.S. military mission in Moscow, and asked him to confirm the arrangements with the Soviet General Staff. Deane immediately responded that "I have requested General Antonov [Chief of the Soviet General Staff] by letter to confirm fact that Soviet commanders have been authorized to agree with American commanders on freedom of access by road, rail, and air to Berlin. . . . Will meet with Antonov or his representative today and hope to get an answer at that time."

The following day, Andrey Vishinsky, then deputy foreign minister, told Ambassador Harriman in Moscow that Marshal Zhukov had been authorized to discuss the access arrangements to Berlin. On June 27, Deane radioed SHAEF that Zhukov was asking urgently for the details of the matters the Western commanders wished to discuss. "It is my opinion," said Deane, "that when our representatives meet with Zhukov there will be little difficulty in arranging for free access for our troops to Berlin."

Upon receipt of Deane's message, Clay provided the U.S. military mission in Berlin with a summary of Allied wishes, along with instructions that they be passed on to Zhukov immediately. The main features of this summary were that Western forces should enjoy the unrestricted right to use two autobahns (preferably Berlin-Magdeburg-Hannover and Berlin-Halle-Frankfurt) and three rail lines, as well as the right of unrestricted air travel, including the right of fighter escort between Bremen and Frankfurt in the Western zones and Staaken, Gatow, and

Tempelhof airfields in Berlin. Clay also sought agreement that all Western traffic would be free from border search or control by customs or Soviet military authorities. These proposals appear to have been drawn up originally by the American delegation to the EAC but were never presented. They were given to SHAEF by Robert Murphy in mid-May 1945.

Q: The agreement on zonal boundaries was drafted by the European Advisory Commission in London. Do you recall your reaction when you first saw it?
CLAY: I saw it for the first time when I got to Reims. I've always been told that the Army took the matter of access [to Berlin] up with Mr. Winant. But that Ambassador Winant [the American representative on the EAC] said, "Look, these protocols have been agreed to by everybody. If we tried to get them changed now, after all this work and effort, we can forget about it. There wouldn't be any point in trying to get them modified." Whether that is true or not, I don't know.

The EAC had briefly considered the matter of access to Berlin but, as Clay observed, had taken no action. In September 1944, when Murphy raised the matter with Winant, Winant "vehemently" objected to introducing the issue into negotiations at that late date. The right of access, Winant claimed, was implicit in the right of occupation. Sir William Strang—Winant's opposite number from Great Britain—apparently shared that view.

Paradoxically, when the United States had agreed to occupy the southwestern zone of Germany just two weeks earlier, at the Quebec Conference between Roosevelt and Churchill, the Joint Chiefs of Staff had insisted not only on explicit American access rights through the British zone in northwestern Germany, but full control of the ports of Bremen and Bremerhaven as well. These demands were incorporated in a November 14 amendment to the Protocol on Zones of Occupation. Yet, although Fedor Gousev, the Soviet representative to the EAC, advised the American delegation at that time that "similar transit arrangements would be made, providing Western forces . . . 'full access to the Berlin zone across Soviet-occupied territory,' " the matter was not pursued by either Winant or Strang in the EAC.

Clay, who was not consulted on the zonal boundaries, and who in fact was scarcely aware of them at the time of his appointment, nevertheless shared the view of the American military. "If we were going to have those boundaries," said Clay, "we wanted the northwest portion of Germany, so that we weren't cut off from our lines of communication. It was much more logical from a military viewpoint for us to have that part of Germany that was on the coast. That was our direct route from the United States. England's direct route was across the Channel."

Q: Did you agree with the zonal concept?
CLAY: That is a very difficult question to answer because at that time I believed we would be able to establish a central German government at the national level operating under the Allied Control Council, as was contemplated in the [Occupation] Protocols. And in that context, the zones would have had little significance.
Q: Did the question of access to Berlin concern you?
CLAY: Well, the question of access did not really concern me because I thought then, *as I do now,* that to agree on a route of access, when you have already agreed on a central government being established under four-power control in Berlin, would have been accepting the fact that the whole thing wasn't going to work.
Q: You met with Marshal Zhukov to arrange for the occupation of Berlin on June 29, 1945. Do you recall the details of that meeting?
CLAY: We met at Zhukov's headquarters. I can't tell you the place; I think at that time they were still in battle positions. But our relations, and the meeting, were very friendly, very cordial. There were no problems whatever, other than the fact that we didn't agree.

"Zhukov was below medium height, heavy-set, but powerful rather than fat, and his bearing indicated that he had become accustomed to power and authority. It was largely the bearing of a professional soldier who had exercised high command with perhaps a little more consciousness of position than would be normal with us. He was polite, with a sense of humor and with the obvious desire to seem friendly. I liked [Zhukov] instinctively and never had any reason to feel otherwise."

Marshal Zhukov opened the meeting by saying the principal problems to be settled were the takeover of their sectors in Berlin by the

Western powers and the Soviet occupation of its zone to the west of Berlin. When Zhukov asked Clay what the United States would bring to Berlin, Clay replied that the 2nd Armored Division with its tanks would be part of the original Occupation force, but would soon be replaced by the 82nd Airborne Division. All told, he said, the Americans would have thirty thousand troops in Berlin. The British planned to bring twenty-five thousand, and the Russians said they would have about twenty-five thousand in the city itself (the French sector had not yet been agreed upon).

Zhukov asked when the occupation of the Soviet zone could take place. Clay replied that because the amount of territory occupied by the United States was so great, the withdrawal would take about nine days. Zhukov thought that was too long: "The quicker the move, the quicker the entry into Berlin." Years later, Clay said he thought that Zhukov was correct, that nine days was too long. Clay was convinced that the highly motorized U.S. Army could move far more quickly than the Russians, and he was eager to complete the move into Berlin and get four-power government established. The British had less territory to evacuate, and thought four days would be sufficient. It was thereupon agreed that the Western movement into Berlin, and the corresponding Soviet movement into their zone, would commence July 1 and be completed by July 4.

The meeting then turned to the question of transit to Berlin. Zhukov said that he thought Clay's request for two highways and three rail lines would create difficult administrative problems, since those facilities were also needed by Soviet forces. The problem of protecting the communication routes, he said, was considerable. Zhukov suggested that one autobahn and one rail line—preferably the one through Magdeburg—should be sufficient to supply a garrison of fifty thousand troops. Clay replied that because the U.S. and British main forces would be stationed in different parts of Germany, and because the U.S. port of entry was in Bremen while the U.S. zone was in southwestern Germany, one highway would not be sufficient. The United States was not asking for the exclusive use of the roads, he said, "but must have the right to use them as we need."

Zhukov replied that he was not turning down the American request and that if they didn't like the Magdeburg autobahn, it could be changed later. He chose that route, he said, because it was central for both U.S. and British forces and would be the most economical. Clay and Weeks thereupon accepted Zhukov's offer of the Hannover-Magdeburg-Berlin autobahn, while reserving the right "to reopen the question at the Control Council in the event the one road is not satisfactory."

Clay and Weeks also accepted the Berlin-Magdeburg rail line, on the understanding that the gauge would not be changed (to the Russian narrow gauge) without prior notice. It was agreed that the railroad bridge over the Elbe, near Magdeburg, would be repaired by Russian engineers using American materials. Zhukov concluded the meeting by stating that all of the items discussed could be changed later.

Q: You didn't press the access problem?

CLAY: Yes, I pressed the access problem. But Zhukov offered a logical explanation. He said they were moving back and demobilizing their armies and that they would have the highways and railroads filled, and it might create problems [if we were using the same routes]. They'd rather assign us a highway and a railroad which they would stay off of. And then, later on, when they'd finished their demobilization, everything would be OK, and all the roads would be open. I think he meant it. I know that he would have been very happy to have written me a letter, or to have put it in a signed agreement, but I wouldn't take it, because I thought that would be a limitation on the overall [Occupation] agreement.

Q: Was there any record of the meeting?

CLAY: When I went back to headquarters, I dictated a memorandum on the meeting.

Q: That was the closest thing to an official record?

CLAY: That was the only record.

Q: Was Mr. Murphy there?

CLAY: Yes. And he wasn't concerned about the problem of access either.

Q: And General Weeks?

CLAY: General Weeks was there and concurred. I don't think he was interested in the access problem. It was not really a problem at that time. He was really much more concerned about whether or not we should bring food in [to Berlin]. He was very much opposed to it. He felt that Berlin was in the only part of Germany that had the ability to support itself agriculturally and that there was no reason or need for us to send food unless the Russians were taking food out.

Q: Could you describe General Weeks?

CLAY: Weeks was an industrialist. He had gone into the Army in 1940 from Vickers, where he had been chief executive, and had become Deputy Chief of [the Imperial General] Staff. I think he had been basically responsible for the logistics and supply. I'd met him in Washington when we were negotiating Lend-Lease. He was a very fine-looking British officer. He'd been in World War I. He was strong-looking; a very keen man. A little on the pompous side, but that may be an overstatement.

"I remember one time during the war, flying over to Europe with him and General Franklin. We were going from a military depot on Long Island. In any event, after we got ready to take off, word came back that the only plane available was a cargo plane with medical supplies and bucket seats. I said, 'That's fine with me.' But he was horrified at the idea of riding in this bucket-seat job. He did, though."

Q: And Sir William Strang, Murphy's opposite number?

CLAY: Yes, Strang was there. He was a completely professional diplomat of outstanding abilities. Small and wiry. Quiet in his operations but never missing a trick. I thought he was a very, very good man. He'd been the British representative on the European Advisory Commission, and came to Germany as Montgomery's political adviser. He later left to go back and be Permanent Under Secretary of State for Foreign Affairs, and I think they eventually made him a baron. A very able professional.

Q: Presumably, since he'd been through all of the negotiations on zonal boundaries in the EAC, if this arrangement on access hadn't looked right he would have said so?

CLAY: Well, I have a feeling he didn't want to raise it either—that he'd rather assume that the fact we had a general agreement setting up Berlin as the capital of a quadripartite government was so strong in its implication of free and general access that to ask explicitly for it was to weaken the agreement.

Q: That is what all of you thought at that time?

CLAY: If anybody had asked me then, that's certainly what I thought. Nobody challenged it when I went back to Frankfurt. I don't think it would have made a damn bit of difference now. I don't think it would have changed a thing.

Q: Even though . . .

CLAY: No, I don't think a written document on access would have changed anything. A written document on sector boundaries, on keeping our sectors open in Berlin, didn't change anything in 1961 [when the Berlin Wall was built]. That was a written document.

Q: But wasn't the question of access to Berlin an issue in 1945?

CLAY: Not at all. It was part of the general Occupation agreement. I never visualized for one minute that we would have trouble with this road, this highway. And with all the troops we had behind us at our disposal, I didn't give a damn. I could go to Berlin anytime—then. I didn't sit there thinking that we'd be in Germany six months later with only a division and a half of green troops.

Q: And this vacuum had much to do with the problem?

CLAY: I'm certain it did. I'm just absolutely convinced of it, because as we began to get weaker and weaker, the Russians began to get more and more aggressive. I don't think we would have had a Cold War if we'd kept a strong Army there in 1945.

Q: Your hopes were to make four-power government a success?

CLAY: Well, if we hadn't hoped that and believed in it, we would have kept our position in the Soviet zone, which was a very substantial part of eastern Germany. We would have established our capital there and gone ahead. Because the territory that the Russians controlled at that time was a very small part of Germany. This is what Mr. Churchill wanted to do.

Q: Did you consider this a useful negotiating . . .

CLAY: I didn't consider it negotiable. I thought it was a solemn agreement of our government. Never for one minute did I consider it negotiable. And I think this is the way our government looked at it. We don't have enough experience in this business to consider an agreement as simply a basis from which to negotiate a new agreement. Thank God.

In 1949, after returning to the United States following the Berlin blockade, Clay wrote that he thought he "was mistaken in not . . . making free access to Berlin a condition of our withdrawal into our zone of occupation. The import of the issue was recognized but I did not want an agreement in writing which established anything less than the right of unrestricted access. We were sincere in our desire to move into Berlin for the purpose of establishing quadripartite government, which we hoped would develop better understanding and solve many problems. Also, we had a large and combat-experienced army in Germany which at that moment prevented us from having any worries over the possibility of being blockaded there. However, I doubt very much if anything in writing would have done any more to prevent the events which took place than the verbal agreement which we made. . . . In any event General Eisenhower had delegated full authority to me to conduct the negotiations and the responsibility for the decision was mine."

Despite the subsequent difficulties about access to Berlin, President Truman admired Clay's forthright acceptance of responsibility. Clay "is honest about it," Truman wrote in his memoirs. "He admits this was a mistake. He doesn't blame the civilian side of government."

Q: Did the upcoming Potsdam Conference weaken your negotiating position?

CLAY: Well, I suppose it did. But you'd have to say that it weakened the Russians' too, because they also wanted the conference to take place.

Q: So it was a two-way street?

CLAY: I think so. I don't think it weakened us any more than it weakened them.

Q: Ambassador Murphy argues that you were under great pressure to conclude an agreement on access with Zhukov because of the conference.

CLAY: I was. But so were they. I never visualized for one minute that we'd have difficulty with this highway.

Q: You had a full division in Berlin?

CLAY: A whole tank division of combat-ready troops. The 2nd Armored.

Q: When were they taken out?

CLAY: Well, we didn't really need the tanks in Berlin, and I got them replaced by the 82nd Airborne Division under [Major] General [James] Gavin. That was another crackerjack outfit. But we started to demobilize almost immediately, and I think they were taken out in November [1945].

Q: Between June and November, you had exclusive use of the autobahn and rail line?

CLAY: I won't say we had the exclusive right of way, but I don't think the Russians were using them. But local people, local German people, were using them.

Q: As 1945 went on, didn't the limited-access arrangements seem awkward?

CLAY: We had no trouble whatever with the access arrangements really until '47. On several occasions I tried to get some more roads and railroads released to us, particularly in the direction of Bremen [the U.S. port of entry], but we never got anywhere, and I didn't take it too seriously. After that, in late 1946 and '47, our relations were becoming more and more strained. Not just in Germany, but between the two countries.

Q: In that sense, was the situation in Germany more of a reflection of strains elsewhere, or did strains elsewhere develop as a result of tensions in Germany?

CLAY: We hurried into making peace settlements with all the satellite countries. Out of them, we formed coalition governments that were supposed to have free elections. Obviously, as we began to pull out, reduce our forces, the Russians remained with the threat of military force. They didn't have to use it, but the threat was there. And the Communist parties in each of these countries began to take the lead, with the coalition governments falling and the Communists taking over. It was about this time that we recognized that our own four-power government in Germany was not going to work. But I don't think you can say which came first.

Q: And your experience negotiating with the Russians?

CLAY: I had reservations, of course. I had dealt with them on Lend-Lease, and I had enough experience to know how tough and difficult they were and how inflexible they could be. So I don't think I felt it was going to be easy, but I certainly felt we had to give it a go. That if it failed, it had to fail not from lack of effort but from complete lack of ability to agree.

"If we had withdrawn and not gone to Berlin, would we have had a better world? I don't know. I only know that we had an agreement and were going to try to make it work. As far as I'm concerned, I never thought for a minute of America not trying to carry out that agreement. And I didn't really go beyond that, or behind it, to question whether it was right or wrong.

"I certainly had my views about what we might have done later on, but they were not the views that governed me at the time. Perhaps they were self-serving views."

Q: Were you satisfied with the agreement on access?

CLAY: No, I wasn't satisfied with it. But I wasn't as unhappy about it as I would have been if we hadn't had all those divisions there. I was confident that if we were cut off, they'd know how to get there.

Q: Is there any reason why the headquarters of the Allied Control Council was established in the American sector of Berlin? Why not the British? Or the French?

CLAY: I suspect it is a little like the president of General Motors wanting to do business with the president of General Electric, not with the president of Sun Electric Company. I think it was a matter of pride with the Russians. We were three to one, and I think they felt that it had better be in our sector. They'd rather have it in our sector than in the British or the French.

Q: In 1945 and 1946, could you go freely into the Russian zone?

CLAY: You could drive over to East Berlin whenever you wanted to. But whenever I drove into the Russian zone, I always got General Sokolovsky to give me a permit. And he did likewise coming into the American zone.

Q: Before the United States withdrew its troops, did the Russians give any indication that they wanted to control all of Germany?

CLAY: They had not given any indication at that stage of the game, other than what they had done in the rest of Europe. I think that later, along in 1947, with the Communist Party so strong in France and Italy, they felt that if we withdrew, the Communists could literally take over in Germany.

Q: Did the actions of the Red Army in 1945 hurt the Communist Party in Germany?

CLAY: No question about it. That, and this failure to return German prisoners of war. It destroyed the Communist Party in the Western zones. Remember, the Russians didn't return their prisoners for several years, and then only a very small percentage of those that had surrendered.

· 18 ·

General Clay and the Russians

THE ORIGINS OF THE COLD WAR ARE COMPLEX AND controversial. The traditional Western interpretation places the blame exclusively on the Soviet Union. Revisionist scholars cite American economic imperialism as the root cause. Both approaches overlook the crucial role played by Stalin and Truman themselves, along with their immediate advisers, in creating the atmosphere of recrimination and hostility that developed following President Roosevelt's death.

The division of Germany is a good example. Although this is often cited as the principal cause of the Cold War, the fact is that throughout 1945 and 1946, while relations between Washington and Moscow progressively deteriorated, cooperation between the U.S. military government in Germany and its Russian counterpart remained remarkably cordial. When ties between the occupiers weakened in 1947, it was not because Clay and Sokolovsky were unable to work together, but because the growing tension between the Soviet Union and the United States demanded it.

Clay and Eisenhower saw the quadripartite government of Germany as a model of postwar amity. Both were dedicated to FDR's goal of meaningful cooperation with the Soviet Union, and both rejected bellicose advice from American diplomats that confrontation was inevitable. Based on the enormous military strength that the United States deployed in Europe in 1945, both were confident that a lasting accommodation with the Russians could be attained. As Eisenhower wrote afterward, "We in Berlin saw no reason why the Russian system of government, and democracy as practiced by the Western allies, could not live side by side in the world, provided each respected the rights, the territory and convictions of the other, and each system avoided overt or covert action against the integrity of the other."

Clay not only shared Eisenhower's view, but may have been even more determined to get along with the Russians. As an unabashed admirer of the wartime leadership of Franklin Roosevelt and an intimate of Harry Hopkins, Clay had worked effectively during the war to facilitate military Lend-Lease to Russia—overcoming substantial bureaucratic resistance in the process. He knew the Russians at first hand. He knew how difficult they could be, but he genuinely respected what they had achieved against the full weight of Hitler's undefeated military juggernaut. In the last television interview Clay granted before his death, he recalled World War II and reminded his audience that while "we try to make Stalin out as a murderer and all of the things he was, [we overlook the fact that] he saved his country." Those views were even more pronounced in 1945. Clay saw the Russians as political and military allies in the common struggle against Nazism. He discounted their revolutionary ideology, and he was profoundly committed to making four-power government a success. As he wrote to John McCloy one month after Germany's surrender:

> I am somewhat optimistic that we will be able to forge a national administration [for Germany] with the Russians as well as with the British and the French. We will not develop such arrangements overnight and we must be prepared to expect much criticism from home for the slowness with which we will be able to restore administrative machinery to carry out agreed policies. . . . [But] anything we accomplish in Europe effecting agreement of four nations will mean more for history than individual policies which could be applied immediately in the respective zones.

The views of Eisenhower and Clay were reciprocated by Zhukov and Sokolovsky. In fact, personal relations between Eisenhower and Clay on the one hand, and Zhukov and Sokolovsky on the other, were warm and friendly, far warmer than American relations with the prickly Montgomery or the obstinate French.

At the official level, Clay was cautiously optimistic. "It is difficult to predict the attitude of the Russians," he informed the War Department in late June 1945. "However, I still feel that with patience and understanding we will be able to work out central controls [for Germany] over a long period of time." Clay warned that he was "just as apprehensive over possible impatience and lack of understanding at home of our failure to obtain rapid progress, as I am of our ability in the long run to work out many problems of the Allied Control Council."

In mid-July, when the Army's Berlin newspaper published an uncomplimentary article about the capabilities of the average Russian soldier, Eisenhower and Clay took immediate action to counter the adverse publicity with a feature article on Soviet forces in Berlin. Said Eisenhower to Clay, "A prompt initiation of indoctrination would seem to be indicated."

After the first meeting of the Allied Control Council on July 30, 1945, Eisenhower cabled General Marshall that he found Zhukov "most friendly and [I] feel rather hopeful that he will cooperate in making the Berlin organization an effective machine." Clay reported in a similar vein to McCloy one month later, saying that the Control Council already was functioning smoothly. "The Soviet and other representatives have cooperated cordially in getting things going," he reported. In fact, Clay said that Marshal Zhukov had "highly praised" Eisenhower's work as chairman "and that of the entire American delegation as well. While recognizing that the really difficult matters are yet to be faced, I am much encouraged by the general attitude of cooperation and the apparent desire, *especially on the part of the Russians,* to work with us in solving the various problems." Clay said he and Eisenhower "were making real headway in breaking down [the Russians'] feelings of suspicion and distrust. I am hoping that by the time conflicting views develop on the major issues, we will understand and trust one another sufficiently to deal with the problems objectively and work out sensible compromises of our views."

In November, Eisenhower returned to the United States to succeed

General Marshall as Chief of Staff. Before leaving Germany, he joined Zhukov at a formal State dinner celebrating the twenty-eighth anniversary of the Bolshevik Revolution. Afterward the two adjourned for a long private discussion concerning the many problems confronting the Occupation. Eisenhower summarized his discussion with Zhukov in an extensive memorandum to Clay. "The whole purpose of my long talk," Eisenhower wrote, "was to renew and strengthen the spirit of understanding that he has seemed to show toward you and me so cordially and to get certain concrete concessions that I thought would do much to prove the sincerity of both sides." Eisenhower told Clay that he hoped Clay would "follow these things up with General Sokolovsky and move instantly to meet them always at least half way."

Clay replied to Eisenhower shortly afterward that "Marshal Zhukov was particularly affected by your departure and said . . . [he] wanted to carry out everything you requested." Clay went on to note that "military government continues to make real, if slow progress; except of course in the field of [establishing] central administrative machinery. There is no improvement or change in the French attitude in this respect." Clay's reference to difficulties with the French would have come as no surprise to Eisenhower, for both he and Clay believed it was the French (and, to a lesser degree, the British) who were blocking four-power agreement in the Allied Control Council. In fact, Clay believed that Washington was being duped by the British and French into taking unwarranted anti-Soviet positions.

Clay's wartime experience confirmed that view. He was well aware of the proclivity of old State Department hands to take pro-British, pro-French, anti-Soviet stands. Clay had seen this through his work with Hopkins on the Munitions Assignment Board, as well as with Lend-Lease. In fact, the Lend-Lease program, set up under Hopkins, had been a deliberate end-run around exactly the type of anti-Russian sentiment Clay feared was now emerging in American policy.

By contrast, what Clay saw in Berlin reinforced his belief that cooperation with Russia was possible. "Ike and Zhukov became close personal friends," said Clay many years later. "I think Eisenhower felt very strongly about his friendship with Zhukov. Let me put it another way: if Zhukov had been able to survive, four-power government might have worked. I really believe Zhukov wanted to be friends."

Eisenhower shared that assessment. As he reported in his memoirs,

"While Clay and I had always fought for the rehabilitation of the Ruhr and the development of an economy in western Germany sufficient to support the population, we likewise insisted that every firm commitment of our government should be properly and promptly executed. We felt that for us to be guilty of bad faith in any detail of omission or execution would defeat whatever hope we had of assisting in the development of a basis of intimate cooperation."

The truth is that official Washington was divided at that time as to the appropriate treatment of the Soviet Union. Secretary of State Byrnes and many of the liberal holdovers from the New Deal, as well as Eisenhower and Clay, favored developing the full potential for cooperation with Russia. They genuinely believed a lasting accommodation could be achieved. President Truman appeared skeptical but undecided. However, many around the President, particularly Fleet Admiral William D. Leahy, who was the President's Chief of Staff, Navy Secretary James Forrestal, the career diplomats at the State Department, and many in Congress, were not only staunchly anti-Communist, but believed that a serious confrontation with Russia was inevitable. Some believed that a war could not be ruled out. One of the leading advocates of this hard line toward the Soviet Union was George Kennan, then chargé d'affaires at the American Embassy in Moscow. Kennan and many of his foreign service colleagues, men like his fellow Princetonian H. Freeman Matthews ('21), head of the State Department's Division of European Affairs; Matthews's assistant, John Hickerson; Elbridge Dubrow, head of Eastern European Affairs; and Loy Henderson, director of Near Eastern Affairs, deeply distrusted the Soviets. Matthews, Hickerson, Dubrow, and Henderson were the principal cogs in the State Department's diplomatic machinery, and all four were charter members of the old guard: the high priests of the anti-Communist dogma that had frustrated the Roosevelt administration since 1933. During the war, for example, Henderson, as head of State's Russian desk, had doggedly fought sending supplies to the Soviet Union, and at FDR's firm insistence had been transferred to Iran in 1943. By 1945, he was back in Washington, now in a more senior position, helping to shape American policy under Truman. Like Kennan, all four claimed to be experienced in the ways of Communism, and had watched it through the prism of Russian émigré politics in Warsaw, Bucharest, or the Baltic States during the 1920s and early '30s.

All subscribed to the doctrine that the only language the Soviets could understand was superior force, that negotiations were futile, and that confrontation was inevitable. Men of narrow political outlook, they fretted that Secretary Byrnes, as well as Eisenhower and Clay, were insufficiently aware of the menace of Communism, and they sought as best they could to reorient American policy in a more militant direction.

While Roosevelt was President, the impact of the diplomats on American policy had been slight. FDR had handled most major foreign policy issues, particularly those concerning the Soviet Union, directly from the Oval Office, and staffers like Matthews, Dubrow, and Henderson were largely ignored. But with the President's death, the situation changed abruptly. Unlike Roosevelt, Truman and his personal staff were unfamiliar with European politics and needed the expertise the foreign service could provide. In addition, and again contrary to Roosevelt, Truman believed strongly in working through established channels. In his view, the State Department was America's foreign policy arm, and he turned to it increasingly for advice and direction. Where FDR had relied on a wide array of informal, *ad hoc* consultants and intermediaries, Truman, in effect, made the foreign service his foreign policy staff: Roosevelt's command post in the White House map room was disbanded, direct contact with the leaders of foreign governments diminished, and the control of cable traffic was returned to the State Department. The result was that the conservative values and strong anti-Communist predilections of the professional diplomats moved from the sidelines of American policy to assume a central place in its direction. After thirteen years in the diplomatic wilderness, the old foreign service clique stood poised to resume control.

Initially, insofar as Matthews, Hickerson, and the Division of European Affairs was concerned, this involved siding with the needs of France, and against the effective quadripartite occupation of Germany. That attitude paralleled a similar position assumed by the British Foreign Office. Both in Washington and London, the career diplomats despaired of continued collaboration with Russia and rekindled the doctrine of militant anti-Communism. In particular, the insistence of Clay and Eisenhower on restoring essential German services on a unified basis in all four zones was looked at skeptically by the career diplomats at the State Department. As Matthews wrote to an incredulous John McCloy on June 15, 1945, "the most persistent effort must be made in all quarters to offset the human tendency of all our high-powered people in Germany [Eisenhower and Clay] to use the German economy to make that country run and to disregard completely the vital needs of the liberated areas of northwest Europe."

Clay confronted this pro-French, anti-Soviet mood for the first time when he returned to Washington for policy talks at the War Department and the State Department in November 1945. When Clay told the assembled mandarins at the State Department that it was the French, not the Russians, who were blocking four-power government in Germany, it was like talking to a stone wall. When Clay pressed Matthews in particular as to whether the United States was prepared to bring pressure on France to cooperate, Matthews demurred. When Clay (according to the minutes of the meeting) "took sharp issue with the point of view that it was the USSR which was failing to carry out the Berlin [Potsdam] Protocol," his arguments were dismissed by the diplomats as naïve.

But Clay held his ground. He rejected the State Department's suggestion that reparations be used as a lever against the Soviets. Clay pointed out that the Russians favored the creation of central administrative machinery for Germany, but that the French had continued to veto such arrangements. In fact, Clay said there was some merit to the Soviet position that barriers to creating a single economic structure in Germany could only be removed after the establishment of central administrative machinery.

Clay also argued that the Russians "had gone further than the French in the introduction of the democratic procedures in their zone" —an observation that apparently fell on deaf ears in Washington. When his listeners pointed to the land reform in the Soviet zone (in which the large estates of Prussian landowners had been broken up) as a blatant example of Communist behavior, Clay reminded them that the Russians were "acting unilaterally in the absence of quadripartite agreement." But, then, he said, "so was the Commanding General, U.S. Forces, European Theater." According to Clay: "The entire record of the Control Council showed that the USSR was willing to cooperate with the other powers in operating Germany as a single political and economic unit. The USSR had blocked no more than one or two papers in the Control Council, which is more than can be said for the other members."

Despite Clay's urgent pleadings, the anti-Communist obsession of the foreign service officers prevented military government's case from getting a fair hearing. For Matthews and Hickerson especially, the idea of dividing Germany along East-West lines had already taken hold. The possibilities for cooperation with the Soviet Union had been written off. And in that scenario, French intransigence in the Allied Control Council was an essential ingredient. As Charles Bohlen told Clay afterward, the French were saving the United States with their continued vetoes. In effect, the sharp disagreements that would bedevil American Occupation policy were now apparent. Clay and the War Department favored German unity and effective quadripartite government; the diplomats at the State Department favored a divided Germany, with the Soviets excluded from the Western portion.

That Clay was not alone in 1945 when he argued that it was France, not the Russians, who were blocking quadripartite government was quickly demonstrated. The War Department, which, unlike the State Department, continued to subscribe to FDR's global ideals, fought a determined battle in behalf of German unity. Judge Patterson, who had succeeded Mr. Stimson as Secretary of War in August 1945, picked up the argument where Clay left off. On November 21, he wrote to Secretary Byrnes that "there is a great danger of a breakdown in the provisions of the Berlin [Potsdam] Protocol with respect to the treatment of Germany as an economic unit. Should *the French* continue to impede development of central German agencies . . . the very basis of quadripartite administration in Germany might be jeopardized."

One month later, in December 1945, Patterson repeated the message to Dean Acheson, who had been appointed Under Secretary of State by President Truman in September. Patterson told Acheson that the War Department was "gravely disturbed by the continued French refusal to treat Germany as an economic unit."

John J. McCloy shared that assessment. Following an inspection trip to Europe in January 1946, he told the American Academy of Political Science that, "contrary to the general conception, the difficulty we are now encountering in our attempt to achieve a central machinery [in Germany] does not emanate from the Soviet Union but from France." McCloy said that "the French have been reluctant to permit any form of central administration."

Similarly, on April 5, 1946, Major General Oliver P. Echols, Clay's former chief of staff in Berlin, who had succeeded Hilldring as head of the War Department's Civil Affairs Division, told the Senate's Kilgore Committee (named for Senator Harley Kilgore of West Virginia, who chaired it) that France, not Russia, was the principal impediment to four-power government in Germany.

Even as late as June 1946, Howard Petersen, a distinguished Philadelphia banker who had replaced McCloy as Assistant Secretary of War, repeated the message to the Chamber of Commerce in Columbus, Ohio. "The four powers have not been able to agree [in Germany] because of French, and to a lesser extent, Russian objections to the formation of the central administrative agencies contemplated at Potsdam."

The point is that the evidence from Germany in 1945 and early 1946 unmistakably suggests that those in command of the American occupation believed that France, not Russia, was the nation obstructing quadripartite government. This pitted the War Department against the State Department in a bitter struggle for the control of American Occupation policy. On issues such as the vesting and marshaling of German external assets, the restitution of looted property, and reparations claims against Germany, Clay accepted the merit of Soviet arguments while the State Department already was fashioning an Anglo-American common front that at the very least worked at cross purposes to quadripartite government.

A pertinent illustration involves the use of German patents and scientific data. On May 27, 1946, Clay protested a planned meeting of Western countries in London (organized by the State Department) to discuss German patents. The Soviet Union was to be excluded. But as Clay saw it, "If we are to adhere to the principles of quadripartite government of Germany, advance agreements among the western powers add to our difficulties. . . . Patents belong to Germany as a whole. It would not appear that they could be made available under the Potsdam Protocol except under such conditions as would be agreed by quadripartite machinery."

Similarly, when the State Department sought to establish Radio Liberty in Munich in August 1946 (broadcasting in Russian to the Soviet Union), Clay protested vigorously. "I cannot agree," he told Washington, "that the establishment of a broadcasting station in Germany to broadcast to the Soviet Union in the Russian language is in the spirit of quadripartite government."

But if Clay, Patterson, McCloy, and the War Department pointed to France as the principal impediment to cooperation in Germany, the State Department, particularly at the working level of Matthews and Kennan, insisted on blaming the Russians for the deteriorating situation. France's role was deliberately obscured. In fact, there is substantial evidence to suggest that French obstructionism in Germany was to some degree encouraged by those at State (including U.S. Ambassador to France Jefferson Caffery) who sought to force a showdown with the Soviet Union.

George Kennan's celebrated cable from Moscow on February 22, 1946, pertaining to the sources of Soviet conduct, is a useful case in point. Kennan's message was not so much a fresh analysis of postwar Communist behavior as a restatement of the ingrained distrust of the Soviet Union shared by America's diplomatic establishment. The cable was not volunteered by Kennan, but was sent in direct response to a request from Matthews, who had concluded that the policy of accommodation with Russia advocated by Clay and the War Department, as well as by Secretary Byrnes, was not only dangerous but potentially catastrophic. Kennan, of course, shared that assessment. In fact, at one point in late 1945, he had been on the verge of resigning from the State Department in protest. Accordingly, when given the official opportunity by Matthews to suggest an alternative policy, Kennan eagerly complied.

Kennan's message stressed the implacable fear and hostility of the Soviet leadership toward the West. It suggested that Communist imperialism was the inevitable result of the Soviet system, and that the West was in mortal danger of being engulfed. The Cold War doctrine of "containment" is traced by many scholars to Kennan's cable.

When Kennan's telegram was circulated to American military commanders throughout the world, General Clay was appalled. Its negative tone, he said, simply did not conform to his daily experience in working with the Russians. As Ambassador Robert Murphy (Clay's State Department deputy) informed Washington shortly afterward:

> [General Clay] believes . . . that the [Kennan] telegram represents the British line and that it is evident that the British technique of needling our people over a period of months is bearing fruit. As you know, General Clay has regarded the responsibility entrusted to him to succeed in [the] quadripartite government of Germany most seriously and conscien-

> tiously. An inventory of what has been accomplished in Germany he finds not too discouraging. He points out with a certain justice that while some Americans are prone and eager to blame the Soviet representatives for everything that is unhappy in the situation, an important portion of whatever blame there is clearly attaches to the French Government which thus far has done everything it could to sabotage [the Potsdam] agreements. Clay points out, and rightly so, that apart from an active interest in reparations, restitution and intelligence matters, the French have thus far not contributed one single solitary constructive idea or effort in the entire quadripartite management of Germany.

Murphy reminded Washington how the British had long predicted that quadripartite government would fail, and that "the only solution lay in dividing Germany, probably at the Elbe." He even went so far as to suggest that the Soviet representatives in Germany could not be accused of violating the Potsdam Agreement.

> Whatever secret cynicisms they may maintain, it has not been manifest in their negotiations or official action. On the contrary, they have been meticulous in their observance of the several principles of the Potsdam Agreement. . . . That their attitude toward the British and the French is permeated with distrust and suspicion, is, of course, obvious. It is also obvious that they know of British and French lack of faith in the four power cooperative management of Germany. The fact of the matter is that there is foundation for the Soviet suspicion and distrust in this particular instance.

In contrast, Murphy said that the Soviet representatives "have gone out of their way repeatedly and throughout the months to be friendly with the Americans." In the eyes of many in U.S. military government, said Murphy, this reflected "a sincere [Russian] desire to be friendly with us and also a certain respect for the U.S. . . . The Soviet representatives are not obtuse. They know that the American effort has made the Allied wheel go round here, and that it would have stopped moving were it not for the American contribution."

Murphy also took issue with Kennan's disparagement of the importance of personal relations between U.S. and Soviet leaders. He said that the mutual respect between Eisenhower and Zhukov had made a definite impact in Berlin. "Zhukov, Sokolovsky and [Arkady Alexandrovich] Sobolev [Chief, Political Section, Soviet Military Administration in Germany] have told me in different times and in different ways that they sincerely want the friendship of Americans, that there will never be a war between the two countries, that they are grateful for what the United States has done for the Soviet Union, but that they simply do not trust the U.K."

Murphy concluded by noting that, while the increasing appearance of tension between the United States and the Soviet Union might aid the passage of the Administration's universal military training (UMT) bill, "I would like to make it quite clear that in our local innocence [in Berlin] we have never and still do not believe for a minute in imminent Soviet aggression." Murphy's reference to the UMT draft legislation illustrates one of the techniques used increasingly by the Truman administration to secure congressional support for Administration policy. By emphasizing problems with the Soviet Union, the Administration effectively undermined congressional opposition to preparedness measures.

In retrospect, it may appear odd that Murphy's letter is not reprinted in the American government's official collection of diplomatic papers, *Foreign Relations of the United States.* Those papers were assembled and printed by the State Department in 1969, and presumably Murphy's message did not conform to the image of Soviet hostility that Washington sought to convey. There is no explanation as to the cable's omission. Nevertheless, Murphy's message once again makes it abundantly clear that those closest to the Russian presence in Germany did not despair of Soviet cooperation. General Clay, in particular, saw no reason for alarm. Throughout 1946, he continued to stress the importance of Great Power harmony. In fact, Clay, who met regularly with the Russians on the Allied Control Council, had not presented a single complaint to Washington concerning Soviet belligerence or lack of cooperation.

When Kennan's cable arrived in Washington in February 1946, the direction of American policy was not yet established. In fact, it was still very much in flux—which is why Matthews had asked Kennan to provide his assessment. But if Kennan's "long telegram" represented a consensus of Cold War professionals, it scarcely reflected the informed judgment of many who understood the Soviet Union at least as well as Kennan. Knowledgeable observers both in and out of government decried the pessimistic tone of historic inevitability that pervaded Kennan's message. Walter Lippmann, for example, attacked Kennan's analysis in a series of columns, pointing out that the Soviet Union was far more concerned with Russian security than Communist ideology, and suggesting that Washington's hard-line policy, particularly in Europe, was intensifying those concerns. Like Clay, Lippmann argued that the Russians were scarcely the devils incarnate that Kennan believed them to be.

More important, perhaps, Kennan's message was directly contrary to an almost simultaneous report produced in the State Department's own Research and Analysis Branch, formerly a part of William Donovan's Office of Strategic Services. The OSS had been established by Roosevelt in 1942 to provide the Administration with independent intelligence estimates, and it is not surprising that R and A's report differed so fundamentally from Kennan's pessimistic analysis. Unlike the foreign service, the academic analysts who staffed R and A believed that cooperation with the Soviet Union was both feasible and desirable.

In a lengthy memo that corresponded to Kennan's long telegram, the chief of R and A's Russian division, Geroid T. Robinson, noted that the Soviet Union was so devastated and war-weary that the political initiative in Europe rested with America. If the United States sought compromise and accommodation, R and A suggested that the Russians would probably respond in kind. On the other hand, if the United States exerted significant pressure, the Soviet Union would be encouraged to adopt a counterpolicy of revolutionary expansion. Most significantly, the R and A report rejected the fundamental premise of Kennan's analysis:

> It is by no means certain [said R and A] that Soviet intentions are set irrevocably in the pattern of expansion facilitated by revolution. . . . Marxist ideology does not by any means prescribe overt conflict at all times and all places. Furthermore, it is by no means to be expected that in the future the foreign policy of the Soviet leaders will be determined entirely by Marxist theory.

The contrast between Kennan and the professional diplomats at the State Department on the one hand, and the OSS remnants of the Roosevelt administration on the other, reveals the tug-of-war then going on for control of American policy in Europe. George Kennan's cable reflected the cherished beliefs of the foreign service. It was promptly distributed throughout the government and became the rallying cry for the anti-Soviet policy the Truman administration was inching toward. The Research and Analysis Branch's report was perused by Charles Bohlen and relegated to the State Department archives, where it gathered dust for the next forty years.

The differences among American policy-makers in 1946 can scarcely be overstated. Clay, for example, firmly believed that Kennan's influence on American foreign policy was pernicious. In fact, when Kennan unexpectedly appeared in Berlin en route from Moscow to Washington in the spring of 1946, Clay took the opportunity to object to what he saw as a dangerous shift in U.S. policy. At a dinner party at Robert Murphy's, Clay told Kennan of his own friendly relations with Sokolovsky, suggesting that he might trust the Russians more than he did the British. As Kennan recalled the dinner years later:

> I was being upbraided by the general over what he considered to be our anti-Soviet prejudices. I remember him somewhat suspicious of the Moscow embassy because he lived in the atmosphere that radiated at that time, not only from General Eisenhower but from other high military figures. . . . These men were strongly influenced toward the end of the war by the feeling that they could get along with their Soviet military opposite numbers much better than any of us had been able to get along with the Soviet government. I'm sure that Zhukov's personality played a considerable part in this. I think it is quite true that a number of the Soviet military, senior military figures, like their American counterparts, were influenced by the fact that they had a certain comradeship of arms with their American opposite numbers during the war, and would have liked to continue to have close and good relations with them. I'm sure this was as true of Zhukov as it was with Eisenhower. However, I think this atmosphere and these mutual feelings were somewhat misleading, because the military did not play so great a part in the Soviet Union as our people thought. In fact, Stalin kept things under very close control and rather eliminated them from influence as soon as the war was over.

According to Kennan, "Clay took seriously the line of policy that had been developed in the wartime conferences and in the Potsdam

Conference, whereas I was skeptical about all this. I had the impression of a very strong man who looked in one direction with great physical and nervous intensity. I don't believe he thought much of me."

Kennan's recollection rings true. "Kennan is all theory," Clay told Marjorie immediately after their meeting. One of the problems was that Kennan and Clay differed on far more than the Soviet Union. Clay was a command personality: a tough administrator who dealt daily with the practical problems of administering an occupied country; Kennan was a reflective theorist, "an impressionist, a poet, not an earthling," in Eugene Rostow's trenchant characterization. Clay, the West Pointer, believed deeply in democracy, and the good sense of the electorate. Like his father and grandfather before him, he embraced the cause of the common man whether he was working in America to establish the WPA with Harry Hopkins, or in Germany to implant the roots of responsible government. By contrast, Kennan, the Princeton diplomat, was an elitist to the core. He deplored popular government and brooded darkly about the negative influence of democratic institutions on the conduct of foreign policy. Whereas Kennan had written scathingly about the role of blacks, women, and Jews—all of whom he considered inferior—in the politics of the United States, Clay (whose father had chaired the original Senate committee on women's suffrage) was moving unilaterally in Germany to integrate the combat units under his command and was in the forefront, along with Eleanor Roosevelt, of those fighting for increased American immigration quotas for European Jews brutalized by the Nazis. Clay, the democrat, favored free elections and German unity. Kennan, the philosopher-king, preferred not to take that risk.

Another Berlin visitor at that time in 1946 was John Kenneth Galbraith, then in charge of economic security policy at the State Department. Unlike Kennan, Galbraith saw eye to eye on policy with Clay, and Galbraith enjoyed breaking out of the bureaucratic confines of Foggy Bottom to take his ideas directly to Clay in Berlin. "Clay did not welcome interference from Washington intruders," wrote Galbraith, "but neither could he resist any idea that seemed worthwhile." Galbraith was distressed at the time by the fear of Communism that pervaded American policy. He reports that "Clay and such of his staff as the highly intelligent William H. Draper, Jr., were contemptuous of such fears. That Russia, recovering from by far the worst devastation of

World War II, was physically or even emotionally in a position to begin a new war was dismissed by Clay as fantasy." Against Clay's views, said Galbraith, was arrayed "the professedly deeper insight of the old priesthood" of the foreign service. Galbraith was as dubious of that revealed dogma as Clay was.

It is not surprising, therefore, that in July 1946, when General Eisenhower, then Army Chief of Staff, queried all military commanders "on the manner in which agreements have been carried out by the Soviets," Clay replied:

> It is difficult to find major instances of Soviet failure to carry out agreements reached in quadripartite government of Germany. Our difficulties in this field arise not so much from failure to carry out agreements but rather from failure to agree on interpretations. . . . In most such instances, French unwillingness to enter into agreements relative to governing Germany as a whole makes it difficult to place blame on Soviets.

Eisenhower's inquiry had been prompted by President Truman's request to White House staffers Clark Clifford and George Elsey to prepare a speech for him detailing Soviet failure to live up to their international commitments. Clifford and Elsey, assisted by Kennan, would later expand that speechwriting assignment into the preparation of a full-dress policy report that emphasized the inevitability of military confrontation with Russia. That report, coming in late 1946, helped to channel Washington policy away from the wartime goal of peaceful accommodation and into a more militant direction. As written by Clifford and Elsey, "The language of military power is the only language" that the Soviet leadership understands. As a result, the document concluded, the United States must be prepared "to wage atomic and biological warfare" if necessary, and establish a global doctrine designed to "support and assist all democratic countries which are in any way menaced or endangered by the U.S.S.R."

In the case of the Clifford-Elsey report, as with many others in 1946 and 1947, the wish of Washington's Cold War policy-makers was apparently father to the thought. Theories of Soviet belligerence prevailed over the fact of Russian cooperation in Germany. Clay's reports to the contrary were either ignored or dismissed.

But Clay was as determined in his way as those who sought confrontation were in theirs. He repeated his message two weeks later to Assistant Secretary of War for Air Stuart Symington, then on a global inspection of U.S. forces. As Symington later reported to President Truman: "It was from General Clay in Berlin [that we heard] the first counter-thinking to the heavy anti-Russian sentiment characteristic [of Administration policy]." According to Symington:

> Clay felt that the Russian story was not being reported accurately. He said there were incidents of arrests and detentions [in the Soviet zone], but that there were comparable incidents of Americans picking up Russians and holding them over a period; that it was to be regretted the [news] stories were on a purely unilateral basis; that in the American zone we had arrested, imprisoned and killed far more Russians than they had Americans.

Symington went on to say that "Clay felt the Russians antagonized the old school diplomats, because they were rude and did not have social graces. 'For example, if you ask them a question on the phone which is embarrassing, they click off. But it is only their way,' said Clay, 'and they are improving.' " Secretary Symington reported that Clay also worried that the American, British, and French interpreters in Berlin were hostile to the Russians. " 'They come in [to quadripartite] conferences prejudiced, and may well reflect such prejudice in their interpreting.' "

Symington told Truman that Clay felt "it was a mistake not to have carried out the policies of General Eisenhower; *i.e.,* to have our zone open to the Russians." (At Washington's explicit direction, the American zone was closed to Soviet entry in December 1945.) In Clay's view, closing the zone "irritated [the Russians] because of their knowledge of the change in policy, but, and more important, when it went into effect, it stiffened the attitude of all American personnel against the Russians."

Clay had told Symington he thought that "the situation was far from hopeless and could be worked out." When Symington had queried Clay as to how he "correlated this thinking with Mr. [John Foster] Dulles' statement that the Russians felt their ideology could not live in a world which contained capitalist countries," Clay had replied forthrightly: "If things go on this way, a scrap with Russia is inevitable. I am one who believes we can get to know them, and they can get to know us. I believe we can, over a period, work out the prevention of that war which so many people think inevitable."

Clay steadfastly backed the policies of FDR. He told Symington that, until recently, "thanks to the diplomatic genius of Mr. Roosevelt, the United States had been between Russia and Britain as mediator, and that the British were very satisfied to be back in the accustomed place in the middle again, as mediators."

By the summer of 1946, Clay was growing increasingly alarmed at the anti-Soviet line emanating from Washington. On July 25, he wrote to his former finance adviser, Joseph Dodge, then with MacArthur in Japan: "While I appreciate the great difficulties involved in working with the Russians, I still refuse to be a pessimist and I am apprehensive that the old 'red scare' is receiving too much emphasis at home these days."

The reason Clay was alarmed was that the militant tone of anti-Communism emanating from Washington was so at odds with his own experience. Clay's view amply demonstrates that, as far as Germany was concerned, the Cold War was neither inevitable nor inherent in U.S.-Soviet relations. Certainly, it was not sought by those in command of the U.S. military government. Indeed, an interesting gauge of the standards of political propriety that motivated America's overseas command is illustrated by General Clay's response to advice from Washington in the summer of 1946 that he intervene in forthcoming Berlin elections on behalf of non-Communist parties. To Clay, such intervention was unthinkable. "If we did this," he said, "military government would have clearly violated its announced principles of political neutrality and such action . . . would prove a step backward in teaching democracy."

In a refreshing glimpse of an older and perhaps wiser America, Clay advised the War Department that: "We have created a reasonably healthy political atmosphere in our zone in which there is little evidence of Communist gains. It is my view that the direct support of political parties by military government would harm our political gains and would do little to retard the development of the Socialist Unity [Communist] Party and its efforts in Berlin."

Clay, whose practical political experience exceeded that of most in Washington, then put the matter into context. After all, he said, the measures about which some persons in the State Department "have become most excited are not too different from election measures sometimes pursued in large cities in democratic countries." By that, Clay meant that the Communists did not have a monopoly on rigging elections.

While James Byrnes was Secretary of State, Clay's position in Germany was secure. Like Clay, Byrnes, whose attitude in dealing with the Russians was one of pragmatic compromise, genuinely believed that cooperation with the Soviet Union was possible. As a result, 1945 and 1946 were years of flux in Germany. American policy was torn between the desire to cooperate with the Soviets—the policy of Byrnes, Clay, and Eisenhower—and the need to construct a Western bulwark against Communist encroachment—the policy espoused by Kennan, Matthews, Leahy, and the career officers of the foreign service.

· 19 ·

War Crimes Trials

THE TRIALS OF GERMAN WAR CRIMINALS TOOK PLACE at three levels. At the highest level, an International Military Tribunal at Nuremberg tried twenty-two Nazi leaders on a four-count indictment for conspiracy to commit war crimes, war crimes, crimes against peace, and crimes against humanity.* When the four-power International Tribunal completed its work in October 1946, the United States undertook a dozen additional trials against subordinate German leaders. These cases included the industrial combines

* Of the twenty-two defendants, thirteen were sentenced to death by hanging: Hermann Goering (who committed suicide before the punishment could be carried out); Martin Bormann (who was tried in absentia); Joachim von Ribbentrop; Arthur Seyss-Inquart; Alfred Rosenberg; Field Marshal Wilhelm Keitel; Ernst Kaltenbrunner; Walther Funk; Wilhelm Frick; Julius Streicher (who committed suicide during the trial); Hans Frank; Fritz Sauckel; and General Alfred Jodl. Six were sentenced to prison and subsequently incarcerated at Spandau: Rudolf Hess and Admiral Erich Raeder for life; Albert Speer and Baldur von Schirach for twenty years; Konstantin von Neurath for fifteen years; and Admiral Karl Doenitz for ten years. Three were acquitted: Franz von Papen, Hjalmar Schacht, and Hans Fritzsche.

of Flick, Krupp, and I. G. Farben; the physicians and surgeons who had used prisoners for experimental purposes; the Nazi SS leadership; the Gestapo and concentration camp hierarchy; the military leaders who exploited occupied territories; the Justice Ministry and judicial leadership that had condoned mass exterminations; and those Foreign Ministry officials who had plotted aggressive war. These dozen trials were also conducted at Nuremberg under American legal experts headed by Brigadier General Telford Taylor, who had been the assistant U.S. chief prosecutor at the International Tribunal.

Finally, and concurrently with these major trials, the United States Army conducted a series of trials of individual offenders at Dachau. These were lesser Nazis—concentration camp guards, policemen, minor officers and soldiers—charged with such specific crimes as the torture or murder of captured Allied soldiers and airmen. These trials, conducted by military courts martial according to military trial procedure, pronounced numerous death sentences. Altogether, the Dachau trials convicted 1,416 persons and acquitted 256. Four hundred and twenty-six of the convictions carried the death sentence. Clay, as Military Governor, reviewed all of these sentences. He set aside 69 convictions, commuted 119 death sentences, and reduced 138 other sentences. The remainder of the sentences were carried out.

Q: What was your opinion of the Nuremberg trials of the major war criminals?

CLAY: I was convinced they were a very good thing, and that without them you would have a very different Germany today. Because it would have been impossible, without these trials, to have convinced the German people how terrible their government really was.

"I saw to it that the record [of the trials] was widely printed in the German press. And a substantial proportion of the German legal profession—those who were lawyers for the accused—examined the evidence in great detail. They knew that the charges with respect to mass murders and what went on were backed by solid evidence. So, on balance, I think the trials served a useful purpose, and I say that because the Germans are still bringing to trial themselves those people who have been found who participated in those events.

"Now, when you get to the separate trials—not the Nuremberg International Tribunal but the war [crimes] trials we ourselves conducted—you get into a more difficult area. Krupp was sentenced by one of our courts, not by the international court. He was released by my successor [John J. McCloy]. The perpetrators of the Malmédy Massacre [of captured U.S. troops during the Battle of the Bulge] were tried by our courts. Because of certain methods used to secure evidence, I commuted the death sentences. But they were also pardoned by my successors. I would suggest that these pardons indicate that we were not too happy in the United States that we had conducted these separate trials.

"Part of that may well come from the fact that, with a few notorious characters excepted, neither the British nor the French pursued a similar policy. The Russians didn't either. If they wanted to remove somebody, they just sent him to Siberia. Period. So we were alone in what we were trying to do."

Q: Did you visit the concentration camps?

CLAY: I visited *all* of the concentration camps, at one time or another. And, believe me, it was a dreadful sight.

Q: And Krupp?

CLAY: I have no doubt that Krupp should have been found guilty. Not for using slave labor. He couldn't avoid that—nor would we, if our economy had been in the same straits. But because he permitted it to be abused. Now a good many of the industrialists who used slave labor also fought, resisted the abuse of that labor. But Mr. Krupp didn't do that. So for that reason it was not hard for me to approve his sentence. But I don't think these other trials added much, if anything, to what the German people already knew from the Nuremberg trials. On balance, I think our unilateral pursuit of this was wrong.

Q: What about the military defendants at Nuremberg?

CLAY: Well, there were great differences among the military men tried at Nuremberg. Examining the record as I did, I had no doubt whatever but that [Field Marshal Wilhelm] Keitel had been closely associated with many of the atrocities which were developed at Nuremberg. But I was never too sure that [General Alfred] Jodl was. I'm not too sure that Jodl—maybe it was ill-conceived, but nevertheless, given his conception of his duties [as director of operations for the German high command]—didn't do what almost any other military man would have done in the circumstances.

"This makes it harder to analyze. Where do you go, where do you stop? Take Karl Doenitz, the admiral who commanded the German

U-boat fleet. He had been a top member of government and was primarily involved in illegal use of submarines. I'm not too sure that, when we talk about that type and kind of use of submarines, and at the same time we lay down nuclear bombs on Nagasaki and Hiroshima, that you aren't making a distinction that won't stand up in the light of history—or that will stand up in the light of history. The point is, don't lose the war. That's all.

"You've always had, since the beginning of time, penalties to be paid by those who were defeated, sometimes in the form of humiliations, sometimes in the form of reparations and damages, frequently in the form of punishments for those who took part. I don't think it was too many hundreds of years ago—in the border wars in England—they'd take a raider who came across the border and just hang him in a cage outside the castle window. This was a punishment for losing.

"I've spent most of my life as a soldier, and I could not honestly tell you today, in my own mind, when I could make a distinction between refusing to obey an order because I decided it was not a legal order, or obeying it because I was a soldier."

Q: But you could distinguish the activities of General Keitel from General Jodl?

CLAY: I can, because many of General Keitel's actions were not those of a soldier carrying out orders. He was a participant in the development of the programs in France. He was a co-conspirator. When he did that, he ceased to act as a soldier; he acted as a member of government. Between that and a soldier who is given orders to do something and then is charged with a crime because he's carrying out the orders he's given—this is the place where it's so difficult for my conscience to tell me when it's wrong and when it's right. I just don't know.

Q: Both Keitel and Jodl were in Berlin. Can you distinguish between their activities and someone like Field Marshal von Rundstedt, who was in command on the Western front?

CLAY: Well, I don't think von Rundstedt ever had anything to do with decisions such as how you would run a prisoner-of-war camp, or how you would make labor available for factories and plants. I don't think generals in the field had anything to do with that sort of thing. Perhaps if you were a gauleiter, in France or Holland, you would get orders as to how many laborers you had to produce. However, very few of those people were in the [military] chain of command.

Q: But some of the German generals were tried by the United States.

CLAY: I don't remember any that we tried except those charged with specific war crimes, like the Malmédy Massacre. We didn't try any just because they were soldiers fighting a war. We kept the generals in prison—not exactly in prison—we kept them in a camp in Bavaria for a good many months. But the purpose of that was to get them to write the histories of the war, from their viewpoint, which we thought was a great project, and I think it was. And then also to determine what we were going to do with them. I'm not too sure in that respect that—aside from the fact that they were restrained—they weren't in much better shape living there in that camp than they would have been trying to live in the rather rough way of life that was available to Germans elsewhere. They had heat and food.

Q: Did you supervise the camps in which the Germans were being held?

CLAY: I went down a couple of times just to satisfy myself that it was decently done and decently run. I did insist that the German generals and German prisoners of war be given proper treatment.

Q: Was there much vindictiveness on the part of American personnel?

CLAY: Actually, not very much. We had the usual problem of combat soldiers going home and young recruits taking their place. That created a substantial lessening in discipline. This did result perhaps in some mistreatment or maltreatment of civilians, but I don't think it ever reached the proportions that were alarming or even aroused any great German resentment. It was more than offset by the kindness of Americans who gave out food and CARE packages and candy and what not to literally thousands of Germans. There was not very much vindictiveness. We are not a vindictive people.

"When you get to the question of the trials we conducted, I think you have to accept that prosecuting attorneys want convictions. They probably wouldn't be good prosecuting attorneys if they didn't. So if you ask me about the conduct of our war [crimes] trials, I would say they were conducted by prosecuting attorneys who were determined to win their cases. We did have what we thought were adequate courts set up and established. I personally reviewed every sentence that involved either the death sentence or life imprisonment. I did that after they had been gone over by my legal staff, and I went through the whole transcript very carefully.

"That was one of the reasons I revoked the death sentence of Ilse Koch. There was absolutely no evidence in the trial transcript, other than she was a rather loathsome creature, that would support the death sentence. I suppose I received more abuse for that than for anything else I did in Germany. Some reporter had called her the 'Bitch of Buchenwald,' had written that she had lampshades made out of human skin in her house. And that was introduced in court, where it was absolutely proven that the lampshades were made out of goatskin. In addition to that, her crimes were primarily against the German people; they were not war crimes against American or Allied prisoners. As a military government, our mandate was to try those who had committed crimes against the United States, or our Allies, not against the German people. So I revoked that sentence. Later she [Ilse Koch] was tried by a German court for her crimes and sentenced to life imprisonment. But they had clear jurisdiction. We did not.

"The only military men that were tried, that I can remember, were tried for specific offenses against Allied troops. Those tried for the Malmédy Massacre, for example. That was the cold-blooded murder of captured troops. There was no question of the guilt of those convicted. And they were sentenced to death. I rejected the death sentence, not because I wasn't convinced of their guilt but because, to break them in the first instance, we'd brought in American troops who had witnessed the results and recovered the bodies after Malmédy as their jailers. And these troops used very rough methods to get the first breaks. After you got the first breaks, we got plenty of breaks, so that we did not have to use this first evidence for the conviction. But whether you could ever have gotten the conviction without that first break so bothered me that I cut the death sentences to life imprisonment."

Nevertheless, Clay rejected a blanket appeal from the Vatican in 1948 for mercy for all Nazi war criminals who had been condemned to death. "These trials . . . were for specific offenses, many of which included brutal murder in cold blood," Clay told Washington in response to the Vatican's request. "Each case has been examined painstakingly to determine that [the] evidence is irrefutable, and death sentences are approved only when the offense was clearly committed in cold blood and without mitigating circumstances." Subsequently, when Washington ordered a stay of execution for those sentenced at Nuremberg and Dachau, Clay sought to have it lifted before he retired as Military Governor. "This request must make me seem ghoulish," he cabled Army Assistant Secretary Tracy Voorhees, "but I would again urge that present stay[s] of execution . . . be lifted. I would not like to have a mass execution, and yet I do want to free my successor from this thankless task. . . . It is one of my inheritances I do not want to pass on."

Q: After the trial of the major war criminals, wasn't there a danger of making martyrs of some as the process continued?
CLAY: One of the reasons I wanted to get the de-Nazification process out of American hands and into German hands was just for that reason. This was conceived in my office, written up by Bob Bowie and Don McLean, and the primary purpose was to get us out of the business of punishing Nazis. . . . We couldn't have tried [all of] them in a hundred thousand years. So we either had to have mass punishment or we had to get somebody else to try them. So we got the Germans to do it. The British and French never did anything about it, and I don't think that they gave a damn, really.
Q: When the de-Nazification process was turned over to the Germans, was there a great deal of controversy?
CLAY: Not at first. Let me put it this way: I really believe the Germans preferred to do it themselves than to have us do it. Afterward, when they began to get a tremendous amount of criticism, I'm not too sure that they were as happy about it as they had been in the beginning.
Q: Was there a problem with the statute of limitations?
CLAY: Well, that had not run out by the time I left. That became a problem later. But the separate trials we conducted were a problem. Unlike the Nuremberg trials, they didn't develop a tremendous amount of data to prove to the Germans and everyone else what really happened under Hitler. I have no doubt the trials were conducted fairly. The cases were reviewed with great care, and if our assumptions were correct and we had the right to try these people for their criminal acts against the United States, against our Allies, then the record is clear that it was done under the rules of justice. This was important to me—so important that I conceived the idea very quickly of getting men

who'd had judicial experience in the United States to come over and conduct the trials.

"Judge [Charles] Fahy, the former Solicitor General of the United States, was on my staff as head of the legal department. I wish I could have kept him. He was a great tower of strength. But it was through him that I got many of the experienced judges to preside over these courts, to be sure that we were following the rules of law.

"In addition to that, when we got to the problem of restitution of Jewish property [property seized by the Nazis], I insisted on establishing a court of law to hear those claims. And originally, when I instituted the court, there was tremendous opposition from the Jewish people to having to go through a court. I met with some of the Jewish leaders, and I said, 'I just can't understand this. Of all the people I know of, you should especially want a rule of law.' And, as a matter of fact, they accepted that immediately, and I think the restitution court did a good job. I've certainly never heard any complaints."

Q: In the period immediately after Germany surrendered, was military discipline a problem?

CLAY: Looting was never serious. I think it has been overplayed. It was more serious in Berlin. It wasn't really looting, it was buying and selling on the black market. As a matter of fact, you'd be surprised what some [Americans] did at the Potsdam Conference: sold watches and other things in the black market for huge amounts of military currency, which they could exchange for dollars.

Q: You stopped the exchange?

CLAY: I stopped the exchange in Berlin, but I couldn't stop it in the [American] zone. Of course, it never reached the proportions in the zone that it did in Berlin. Most of the exchange of military currency was with the Russians, who also had [printing] plates. So we were not only underwriting the currency we put out, but we were underwriting the currency the Russians put out from the plates we had given them. That was one of the reasons why we wouldn't give them plates for German currency later on.

Q: Was there any way to tell the difference between Russian and U.S. Occupation currency?

CLAY: Not really. Same plates exactly. I suppose there must have been some difference in paper. Nevertheless, at least at that time, they looked the same.

Q: The people at the Potsdam Conference who exchanged watches—was this prevalent among high-ranking Army officers?

CLAY: No, not among high-ranking officers. But it was damn prevalent among a lot of people. Some of Mr. Truman's personal staff sold wristwatches and whatnot in Berlin, and turned the military Occupation currency in for dollars. I don't want to be critical. I'm just trying to give you the atmosphere, because, really and truly, I don't believe they fully appreciated the fact that the United States government was paying for all that.

"I stopped the conversion. Then the Treasury repudiated the fact that they would take this [Occupation] money. I think I was left with $150–200 million. Something like that. We worked it out by expenditures in Germany. Maybe it was just a bookkeeping payoff, but at least it was a payoff."

Q: The military constabulary was created in 1946. Was that your idea?

CLAY: I really can't tell you whose idea it was. It was not mine. The idea was that if we were going to have trouble in Germany, we needed light, fast, highly mobile troops that could be moved to where they were needed very rapidly. Since this did not fit in with any of our existing organizations, we developed a light armored group that would replace the cavalry of older days. So we established the constabulary. [Major] General [Ernest] Harmon was given the job of setting it up. When I assumed the full military command [in 1947], the first thing I did was to convert it back to regular armored regiments with supporting artillery and infantry. It was obvious to me that we weren't going to fight the Germans. If we were going to do any fighting over there, it was going to be a major enemy, and we weren't going to do it with lightly armored troops.

Q: In November 1946, you criticized the Germans for not moving fast enough on de-Nazification. Was this related to the congressional elections that month?

CLAY: No, I don't think it was. As a matter of fact, by that time, here in the United States, most of the pressure was the other way. But I wanted to proceed with de-Nazification as fast as we could, to get these people back into the normal stream of German life. We captured a large number, and as long as we had the system [JCS 1067], if they had been a member of the party—whether guilty or not guilty of any specific offense—we had to have them cleared before they could go back into the stream of German life. And I think it was sometime around that time that I pardoned all those under a certain age.

Q: General Telford Taylor said that he received great support from you during the war crimes trials. The one instance in which you overruled him—which he said he really couldn't object to—pertained to his request to the British that Field Marshals von Rundstedt, von Manstein, von Brauchitsch, and General Strauss be transferred to the Americans for trial.

CLAY: I was never quite sure of [the legality of] our attempts to try the German military commanders simply because they held high commands. And these were not our prisoners, they were British prisoners. I couldn't see why we should take on the responsibility for making that decision.

Q: General Taylor thought that the trials of individual offenders at Dachau, conducted by the Army's Judge Advocate General, caused more difficulty with procedural due process than the Nuremberg trials.

CLAY: I think they did. In the first place, you were getting down to the nitty-gritty details. We were getting down to trying unimportant people who may have committed or not committed major crimes. This is always more difficult than when you are trying principals. The Nuremberg court procedures were much better established than the other courts we set up. Taylor and Fahy did that. As a result, the verdicts there didn't require the attention and reviews and the care and the worry. The Dachau trials were different. When you have the responsibility of whether someone is going to die, before you sign a paper you worry about it an awful lot. And I never signed any of those papers without going through the trial record from A to Z. And if there was any doubt in my mind, *any doubt,* I commuted the sentence. In terms of procedure, the Nuremberg trials were much easier to follow; it was much easier to determine whether justice had been done. In Dachau, I had some doubt.

"So long as Judge Fahy and Mr. [Herman] Phleger [a prominent San Francisco lawyer who subsequently became legal adviser to the State Department] were there, that also helped a lot. But with their departure, in 1947, the caliber of our legal talent fell sharply. You can't lose two men like Judge Fahy and Mr. Phleger without having lost quality in your legal office."

Q: And the trial of the major war criminals?
CLAY: They were not a function of military government. This was the International Tribunal. The only authority we had as military government was the power of abrogation of any sentence, providing it was done by unanimous consent of all four Military Governors. This gave the military governors an utterly ridiculous responsibility which was without meaning, because the Russians were going to support every sentence and therefore it was impossible to get any sentence changed.
Q: Did you try to change any sentences?
CLAY: We did try to reduce the punishment in a couple of sentences, but we were vetoed by the Russians. Even today I'd rather not say who we tried to save and why, because it was done under the utmost secrecy and confidentiality. I do think I could say with complete justification that we tried to reduce some of the sentences but that it was impossible to get unanimous consent.*

According to General Telford Taylor, chief prosecutor during the American war crimes trials, "General Clay's attitude toward my work was continually a very supportive and helpful one. As far as I was concerned, our relations were good. I can only recall one substantial disagreement on a matter of policy in the three years I was there. I would say that I received full and very helpful support from Clay all the way through.

"The area of our disagreement was a very particular thing. One of the last trials we held, Trial Number 12, the High Command Trial, was one in which we had assembled a great deal of material showing the responsibility of high military commanders of the German Army, and to a lesser extent of the Air Force, for war crimes committed during the course of the war. And it had been my intention—I had worked this out with the British—that they would make available to me four generals for trial who at the time were in British custody. I had made available to them Field Marshal Kesselring, who was an American prisoner but whom they wished to try in Italy. And I'd made available to them an SS general named Karl Wolff. And part of that

* Subsequent discussion with General Clay indicated that, among others, General Jodl's death sentence by hanging was thought by the United States to have been excessive. Clay sought a firing squad for him, but was vetoed by Marshal Sokolovsky.

general arrangement was that I would prepare charges against most of the other high-ranking German military commanders. They would therefore make available to me Rundstedt, Brauchitsch, Manstein, and Strauss. That was the arrangement General Clay vetoed. He said our program of trials in the American zone had been so much more extensive than the British that he was afraid that if these four officers came to be tried by us—and, of course, Brauchitsch and Manstein and Rundstedt were three of the leading German field marshals—that it would give the impression that we were conducting a revenge effort, that we were being much more harsh about this than the British. And he put it very simply. He said the British ought to do this themselves. He had not objected to some of the other transfers, but he thought this was going too far. And therefore those four generals did not get tried at Nuremberg.

"I can't say in retrospect that he was wrong, and we had no unpleasantness over this. But he did overrule this arrangement which I had made. I think if this had happened a few years sooner—actually, this came up in 1948, close to the end of our program—I think he would probably have raised no objection.

"By 1948, the political situation had changed a great deal. The Iron Curtain was a good deal thicker, and the problems of relations to the West Germans were beginning to loom larger than it had before. The West German government was about to be set up in Bonn, and I think these were the considerations that were dominant in his thinking. He didn't object to their being tried. He just thought they ought to be tried by the British and not by us. And, indeed, Manstein was tried by the British. The reason the other three weren't was primarily age and illness. All three died quite shortly afterward."

According to Taylor, Clay was much more dubious about some of the sentences given out at the Dachau trials than he was with the Nuremberg sentences. "The Dachau trials were conducted by military courts martial. They were therefore lay benches with Army judges, whereas in Nuremberg we used professional judges from the United States. Furthermore, there was a period at Dachau when they were turning out a lot of death sentences. We didn't at Nuremberg. There is a lot of confusion about that. We had seven death sentences in the medical trial. They were all carried out; Clay commuted none of those. We had half a dozen death sentences in the concentration camp cases.

We had a lot more in the SS case. As far as I can recall, General Clay commuted from the Nuremberg trials exactly one sentence, and that was with my approval. The trial of the concentration camp leadership involved one death sentence for one man where the evidence to me seemed a bit sketchy. General Clay consulted me about that. I remember talking to him about that on his plane when we flew into Berlin during the airlift. I told him a commutation to life imprisonment would be justified, and that is what he did. But as far as I can recall, that is all he commuted. After [John J.] McCloy came in [as U.S. high commissioner of Germany in 1949], there were only three death sentences carried out.

"Sometime around 1948, there was a general reshuffle in military government, and one of the recommendations made to General Clay was that Nuremberg not be as autonomous as it had been—that it be assimilated into an Army field command. This would have changed the whole command setup, and [General Leroy] Watson [U.S. military commander at Nuremberg] and I both thought that this was a bad idea. I remember flying up to Berlin with Leroy [Watson] and going to see Clay with General [Charles K.] Gailey [Clay's chief of staff] and some of his staff—who had proposed the new scheme. They put their case to Clay, and Watson and I put our case that things should be left as they were, that things were working well. Clay listened at some length without saying a word. Then he turned very sharply to Gailey and this colonel and said, 'You guys never understand me. You're always trying to get me in command of troops. You know that I have other responsibilities and I don't want direct responsibilities for troop command. The way it is is much better. Throw your plan in the wastebasket and let's keep things as they are.' Quite humiliating for Gailey and the other guy, and, needless to say, quite gratifying for Watson and me.

"This was one of a number of meetings in Clay's office that I attended. He would listen and decide quickly and firmly. I liked him. I thought he was a fine commanding officer and I had very high regard for him."

· 20 ·

Saving Germany's Art Treasures

> Perhaps never in the history of the world has a conquering army sought so little for its own and worked so faithfully to preserve the treasures of others.
>
> Lucius D. Clay,
> *Decision in Germany*

When World War II ended, the United States Army became the custodian of what Clay described to Secretary Stimson as "the greatest single art collection in the world." This collection included not only the various masterpieces of Rembrandt, Rubens, Tintoretto, and El Greco (to name but a few) looted from Nazi-occupied Europe, but almost all of the really valuable German artworks that had been removed from their museums during the war and stored for safekeeping in that portion of western Germany liberated by U.S. forces.

Clay took an immediate personal interest in preserving the artworks the Americans captured. He expanded military government's Monuments, Fine

Arts, and Archives branch to include some of America's most celebrated art historians and curators (including James Rorimer, of the Metropolitan Museum of Art), and instructed them "to identify, salvage and restore everything worth saving." And Clay told Stimson he hoped to get immediate approval to return to their original owners the works the Nazis had looted throughout Europe, and to preserve the prewar German art collections in trust for the German people.

Stimson applauded Clay's plan and assured him of his support. To Stimson, the preservation of Europe's cultural treasures and of Germany's own important artworks bespoke the dignity of America's war aims, and he recommended Clay's plan strongly to Secretary of State Byrnes, who was then at Potsdam. Stimson suggested to Clay that he raise the matter immediately with President Truman, and Byrnes concurred.

The art that had been looted by the Nazis posed an immediate problem. The Nazis had been insatiable in their quest for art and plunder, but evidenced little discrimination in terms of quality. Pictures less valuable than their frames were found by U.S. forces side by side with the greatest treasures of painting; statues unworthy of a suburban garden had been stacked against works by Michelangelo; and fake antiques of the shoddiest kind were piled up beside the finest attainments of the French eighteenth century *ébénistes.*

The pattern of Nazi looting also varied. In Western Europe (officially referred to by the Nazis as the "Western Confiscation District"), the Germans had initially taken very little from state or ecclesiastical collections. The Louvre, the Rijks Museum in Amsterdam, the Brussels Museum, and, for the most part, the churches were left intact. The two notable exceptions were the famous altarpiece of the *Adoration of the Lamb* by the van Eycks—the greatest masterpiece of Flemish painting—and the Louvain altarpiece by Dirk Bouts. Both had been reconstituted after World War I with panels taken from German museums, in accordance with the Treaty of Versailles. And in both cases, Hitler ordered the removal to the Reich of the altarpieces in their entirety.

But toward the end of the war, German policy changed, and there was considerable looting of public collections in Antwerp and elsewhere, which resulted in the removal of the Bruges *Madonna* by Michelangelo and other important works. Nevertheless, for the most part, the Nazis had confined their looting in Western Europe to the great private collections (such as the Rothschild collection, the collection of David Weill, the Koenigs' collection) and Jewish-owned property of all descriptions. In the East, far less discrimination was shown. The Nazis simply took what they wanted, regardless of where it was located. All of this was of concern to Clay.

But he was equally concerned to preserve Germany's own public art collections. The most famous and most important German collection was that of the great European masterpieces belonging to the Kaiser Friedrich Museum in Berlin, discovered by General Patton's Third Army in the salt mines of Thuringia, where it had been hidden by the Nazis. The collection included fifteen paintings by Rembrandt, six by Rubens, five by Botticelli (including the famous *Saint Sebastian* and the *Venus),* two by Pieter Brueghel the Elder, two by Vermeer, three by Raphael, five by Titian, three by Watteau, and five by Jan van Eyck, as well as works by Fra Angelico, Bellini, Lucas Cranach the Elder, Dürer, Giorgione, Frans Hals, Hans Holbein the Younger, and Manet—in all, a total of 202 of the greatest art treasures of the world, many painted before Columbus crossed the Atlantic.

The nucleus of the collection had been given to the Kaiser Friedrich Museum in 1821 by the British merchant Edward Solly, then living in Berlin. And when Patton's army found the collection in Thuringia, many still had the Solly mark on the back, including the famed Titian *Self-Portrait.* Clay was particularly concerned about the fate of the collection—for a variety of reasons. First, the Kaiser Friedrich Museum, which owned the paintings, was located in the heart of downtown Berlin. It was now in the Soviet sector and, like most of downtown Berlin, the building had been severely damaged during the war. The massive dome was shattered, most of the roof demolished, the lower floor piled high with rubble, and the museum's stone walls so cracked that the cellars were flooded with several feet of water. It clearly was in no condition to receive the collection back. Clay was afraid that if he were ordered to return the paintings, they would likely be shipped off to the Soviet Union.

Second, Clay worried about the tide of revenge and retribution sweeping Europe. If he retained the collection in the American zone, he feared that the German masterpieces might become trading fodder in a struggle for reparations that could see them shipped off to Allied countries as restitution for paintings looted by the Nazis that had not been recovered. In Clay's view, that would merely sow the seeds of revenge once again, and he believed it contrary to fostering the long-term goal of a peaceful and democratic Germany.

Third, Clay was legitimately concerned about the condition of the paintings, many of which dated from the fourteenth and fifteenth centuries. Although the salt mines had proved less harmful than at first thought (because salt absorbs moisture, the humidity in the mines was not ruinous), some of the collection already had been destroyed in Berlin before it could be evacuated, including such renowned works as the *Pan* by Luca Signorelli, the *Conversion of Paul* by Rubens, and Cosimo Tura's *Madonna Enthroned.* Others were badly damaged in the shipment to Thuringia, having been spirited out of Berlin in March 1945 in small, dilapidated open trucks, sometimes uncrated and always at the mercy of the elements. If the paintings could be removed to the United States, Clay was confident they could be properly cared for. And, more important, by shipping them to the United States, Clay was ensuring the collection could be preserved intact for the German people.

Clay met with President Truman on July 19, in the midst of the Potsdam Conference, and secured the President's oral approval to send the Kaiser Friedrich collection to the United States "as rapidly as arrangements can be effected." Clay suggested that they be placed on exhibit, "but that an announcement be made to the public, *to include the German people,* that these works of art will be held in trusteeship for return to the German nation when it has re-earned the right to be considered as a nation."

Despite the President's approval, Clay's plan ran into immediate difficulty with those American agencies charged with obtaining reparations from Germany. Although they agreed with Clay that the German masterpieces should be taken to the United States, they balked at announcing that the art was being held in trust for the German nation. Instead, Ambassador Edwin W. Pauley, head of the U.S. reparations team, and Assistant Secretary of State William L. Clayton proposed that the eventual disposition of the paintings "be subject to future Allied discussions." Clearly, such an announcement would have left their return to Germany in doubt; beyond that, Clay feared the U.S. reparations team wanted to use the Kaiser Friedrich collection to settle reparations claims in France and Belgium.

Clay protested immediately. On August 7, 1945, he cabled the War Department that he had "presented to the President and secured his informal approval for removal for safekeeping to the United States" of the Kaiser Friedrich collection, "with public announcement that they be held for safekeeping and ultimate return to the German people." Clay said that, since obtaining President Truman's informal approval, he had received a letter from Pauley and Clayton objecting to the issuance of a "public statement of future intent" concerning the collection. This, Clay told the War Department, not only conflicted with Truman's wishes, but would have an unfortunate impact on public opinion throughout the world. "I am apprehensive," said Clay (in an unaccustomed tone of understatement), "that removal of German art without statement of future intent to return [the paintings to Germany] would not be acclaimed by the public at large." Clay said he doubted that Pauley and Clayton had been informed of President Truman's approval of the United States' acting as trustee for the Kaiser Friedrich collection, and he requested further instructions.

Shortly thereafter, Robert Murphy confirmed to Clay that the State Department wanted to use the collection as "replacements in kind" for articles that the Nazis had looted from elsewhere in Europe. Again Clay protested immediately. It was essential, he told the War Department, that a public announcement be made that the paintings were being "removed to the United States for safekeeping and eventual return to the German people."

Clay's sense of military rectitude bristled at the prospect of taking the German collection for others. As a soldier he could not condone it, and as a Southerner raised on recollections of Reconstruction he was appalled. When confronted with Clay's determination, the State Department backed down. On September 17, a joint press release was issued in Washington and Berlin stating somewhat elliptically that important German art treasures "not readily identifiable as looted property" would be sent to the United States for safekeeping on behalf of the German people.

Ironically, Clay's plan to ship the Kaiser Friedrich collection to the United States was criticized by many, including *The New York Times, The Washington Post,* and the Baltimore *Sun.* In the fine arts community, John Nicholas Brown of Rhode Island, a prominent collector who briefly assisted the military government in Germany, protested the removal to the United States, claiming that the works could be taken care of just as well in the American zone. (Brown was unaware of Clay's fear that the paintings might be used for restitution.) On September 20, 1945, John McCloy asked Clay for his assessment of Brown's views.

Clay replied the following day. Although conditions were improving in the U.S. zone, he said, it would require coal to heat the areas where the paintings were stored. And coal, Clay reminded McCloy, "is not even available for [the] heating of homes . . . Moreover it is very difficult for us to see the future as to the American personnel which will be available to safeguard these art collections *which in large part do not belong in the US zone. I doubt the advisability of returning them to other zones if we desire to preserve them for the German people.*" Referring to Brown's criticism, Clay said that "the same people who do not approve of the removal of German art objects to the United States urged immediate and early action on the return of objects to liberated areas on the grounds that our facilities were entirely inadequate to protect these pieces. It was their concern over the art objects belonging to liberated areas that developed my concern for the preservation of German art objects." Clay thought that much of the opposition to shipping the paintings to the United States was motivated by a desire to see the collection broken up and used as reparations. That made him all the more determined to see that it was safeguarded.

Clay also told McCloy that he thought the American public was entitled to see the paintings and that "they will certainly not be available for anyone to see for some time in Germany." Moreover, his recommendation to safeguard the paintings by shipping them to the United States "was based on my best judgement. It will not be helpful to us here if such recommendations are changed because of the views of subordinates who have returned home."

The interest in using the Kaiser Friedrich collection for reparations did not die down quickly. Officials at the State and War departments continued to agitate for use of the German masterpieces as restitution to other countries. On November 12, 1945, the War Department once again asked Clay's opinion. His reply, dated November 14, illustrates, as well as any message could, the basic decency of the American Occupation and the integrity of those who directed it.

> I feel very strongly that we should not accept responsibility for replacing unique cultural works with similar or comparable property as restitution. I do not believe we could ever agree as to what constituted unique cultural objects nor as to what museums and collections in the several [occupation] zones would provide replacement items.
>
> Much of the German art is in the United States zone. I am of the view, in any event, that this should be returned to other zones of occupation where it originally came from before it is used for replacement purposes.
>
> However, I sincerely believe that cultural objects belonging in Germany should be left in Germany if we expect to be successful in implanting democratic processes, and that the United States should not take responsibility of taking these German works of art and other cultural objects to turn over to other nations even as replacements.

Clay's stress on America's ultimate role of teaching democracy in Germany carried the day. On November 15, 1945, the War Department authorized him to proceed as he desired. Immediately thereafter, German cameramen painstakingly photographed the paintings to record their condition. Then, using packaging materials scrounged from Army stockpiles, they were carefully packed and loaded onto two German Red Cross railway coaches for shipment to Le Havre. At the French seaport, the paintings were unloaded under tight security and carried aboard the Army transport *James Parker.* After an uneventful crossing, they arrived in New York on December 6, where they were offloaded onto specially prepared Army trucks, again under the tightest security arrangements, and driven to Washington in a convoy under police motorcycle escort. At the National Gallery, they were unloaded, uncrated, minutely examined, and moved one by one to a barred, air-conditioned storage room, where they were placed under twenty-four-hour guard. Chief Justice Harlan F. Stone, chairman of the board of the National Gallery, accepted responsibility for the paintings on behalf of the United States. But aside from maintaining the paintings at a constant temperature and humidity, no effort was made to restore them, and despite Clay's recommendation, they were not put on public display.

In October of the following year, the War Department asked Clay if he was ready for the paintings' return. By then, U.S.-Soviet relations had become strained, and Clay was reluctant to place further strains on those relations by bringing the works back. The paintings, he said, belonged to the Kaiser Friedrich Museum in East Berlin. If they were returned to the American zone (the War Department had proposed Wiesbaden), it would be a needless affront to the Soviets. Instead, Clay preferred to wait "until we have established some form of central German government. . . . There appears to be no agitation in Germany for their return. It is my view that responsible German leaders would be happier for the pictures to remain in the United States than to be returned to Berlin."

> I repeat again [said Clay] that it is difficult to justify their return to Wiesbaden except as a direct challenge to Soviet good faith. It is my personal view that it would be most desirable to place the pictures on exhibition stating that they are to be kept on exhibition until a responsible German government has been formed to whom the pictures can be returned as national property belonging to all the German people.

Nothing of the sort was done. The paintings remained in storage at the National Gallery, and, for whatever reason, were not put on display. In the beginning of 1948, when it appeared that the State Department was prepared to take control of Germany's occupation, Clay became concerned that his tenure as Military Governor would conclude with the Kaiser Friedrich collection still in the United States and his pledge to return the collection to Germany unfulfilled. On January 31, 1948, he cabled the War Department in a "Personal and Eyes Only" message to Under Secretary Draper. Clay said he would "like very much for the Army to arrange [the] return of German paintings now in National Gallery for safekeeping prior to the Army's transfer of responsibility" in Germany to the State Department. By 1948, relations with the Soviet Union seemed less important to Clay than his personal obligation to return the collection to Germany. He recommended that the paintings be exhibited in Wiesbaden and Munich.

But the War Department had become cautious. Draper replied the following week that the Department had "serious doubts" as to the advisability of returning the paintings, which "have been subject to considerable press comment and have been subject to considerable controversy in the Art World." If they were to be returned to Germany without prior exhibition in Washington, Draper anticipated a renewal of criticism.

For the last year or so, Clay had heard rumors that the National Gallery wanted to retain the paintings in the United States. He replied to Draper that same day, saying that, whereas he had previously recommended against returning the paintings to the American zone because he thought it would offend the Soviets, "we had not reached present position in which far more important actions have been taken against Soviet protest. Hence, to my mind, this represents no longer a valid objection" to the return of the paintings. "For almost three years I have tried to get paintings exhibited at home without success, and it seems very late to do so now."

The museums in Munich and Wiesbaden were now in excellent repair, Clay said, and the return of the paintings "would mean a great deal psychologically to the German people [who are] being propagandized heavily to believe we are exploiting Germany." Clay proposed that if the paintings were to be exhibited in the United States, "it should be done now with an early date for their return announced simultaneously. I assure you that the effect in western Germany would be worth a great deal."

Before action could be taken on Clay's request, Senator J. William Fulbright of Arkansas introduced legislation to "retain and display" the Kaiser Friedrich collection in the United States. The Department of the Army informed Clay that it was supporting his view that the paintings be returned, but that Fulbright had "refused the Army's request that [his] Bill be withdrawn."

Clay was dumbfounded. Not only did he feel personally committed to the return of the collection to Germany, he told Draper that he "could not understand how a United States Senator could have such an elastic conception of America's international obligations." Clay questioned "the legal right" of the United States to keep "German art objects which belong to the German people," and suggested that, if necessary, the Attorney General be asked for an opinion.

Clay also opposed the Army's suggestion that the four Minister-Presidents in the American zone be asked to leave the pictures in the United States. In Clay's view, such a request would be grossly unfair, "since it is quite obvious that these pictures are not their property or responsibility. . . . In point of fact, because there is no German government, the pictures will remain in the custody of military government if, and when, they are returned to Germany, until there is a German national government."

Clay stressed the symbolic importance of the paintings. "There is no one single item which would lend itself more to Soviet propaganda," he said, "than to leave these pictures in the United States as a result of legislative or executive action." Clay said that "it is difficult to believe that the majority of the Members of Congress would desire to retain these pictures, thus seriously damaging our national reputation in Germany and in central Europe. It seems to me that such action could well place us in the same position as the Soviet representatives who allegedly took the Sistine Madonna to Moscow so that it would be in 'safekeeping.'

"In point of fact," said Clay, "the return of these pictures in the light of the well-known works of art taken from Germany to the Hermitage in Moscow [Leningrad], would be better understood as representing America's real stand in the world than thousands of words over the Voice of America and in our overt American publications. It seems to me that we are prepared to spend millions for propaganda and billions for recovery while undertaking actions which destroy the value of our recovery expenditures."

Clay reminded Draper that it was the Department of the Army that was somewhat at fault. "When these pictures were returned to the United States [in 1945]," said Clay, "I urged that they be placed on exhibition immediately so that they could be viewed by millions of Americans. At that time, public opinion was the other way and military government was charged with acting as a vandal in having returned the pictures home. In the face of that public criticism, the Department of the Army and our Government placed the pictures in a dark basement hidden from the light of human eyes for more than two years in the hope that public opinion would subside. Now that public opinion has turned the other way, I hope that the Department will not accept it as it did when public opinion did not desire that the pictures be shown. I know of no action that could be exploited more effectively by Soviet representatives."

In an "Eyes Only" message to Major General David Noce, the new chief of the Army's Civil Affairs Division, Clay stated that "The proper ownership under international law of the German art objects lies directly in the Kaiser Friedrich Museum, which of course was the property of the German nation. Under international law these paintings remain the property of the German nation and are entitled to the protection of the occupying power under whose control they passed by virtue of occupation. This was clearly recognized at the time the art objects were [sent] to the United States, and this matter was felt so important that the President of the United States was requested and did affirm our intent to return the art objects when conditions in Germany provided for their safe protection."

Clay did not mince words. He told Noce:

> From the very beginning I have had serious doubts as to the real desires and intent of the directors of the National Art Gallery. Their representatives on an early visit talked about the possibility of obtaining these pictures either in reparations or in payment of Occupation costs, and I am afraid their desire to increase the prestige of the National Gallery lies behind the Fulbright measure.

Clay concluded that "this type of thinking is difficult to understand, as the effect of such action on American reputation and prestige would be devastating indeed and would place us in the same position as the Red Army and other vandal hordes who have overrun Europe throughout the centuries."

The following week, Draper told Clay that the Army had not been able to convince Fulbright of the unwisdom of retaining the pictures in the United States. Draper then asked whether the Minister-Presidents would be willing to have the paintings shown in the United States "as a tangible German appreciation for American help in feeding Germany."

Two days later, Clay informed Draper that the Minister-Presidents were agreeable to exhibiting the paintings "as long as they do not have responsibility. My views are unchanged as to resulting propaganda." As a compromise, Clay proposed that the paintings "be divided into four representative lots of approximately fifty each. First group to be returned immediately for exhibit in Germany and announcement made that remaining groups will follow: Three remaining groups to be exhibited in United States and returned over next nine months at three months' intervals." Clay ended by saying that this was "a compromise to help you which I believe will be satisfactory although I still prefer return as scheduled."

On April 23, Draper organized a teleconference between Clay in Berlin and three ranking members of the Senate Armed Services Committee: Senator Wayne Morse of Oregon, Senator E. V. Robertson of Wyoming, and Senator Burnette Maybank of South Carolina. Draper told Clay that the Department of the Army was inclined to follow his compromise suggestion. The proceeds of the exhibition would go to a fund for German children, and Congress would pass legislation stating that the paintings belonged to the German people. Draper then asked for Clay's comments.

Clay replied that the return of the paintings had been widely publicized in Germany but that, if it were clear that they would be shipped quickly, he thought there would be no objection to exhibiting them briefly in the United States prior to their return. But he cautioned against passing any legislation. An Act of Congress, he said, would imply a legal right to control the paintings. "If you can by legislation hold [the paintings] for a year, then it would appear that further legislation could continue this right indefinitely." Clay proposed as a compromise that the pictures be exhibited "at the suggestion and with the approval of the [Senate] Armed Services Committee, based on recommendations of the Military Governor after consultation with representative Germans."

Senator Morse replied that the committee basically agreed with Clay, and that he believed exhibiting the paintings in the United States would be of "great public relations value." Morse said he was certain that he and his colleagues did not want to exhibit the paintings unless German public sentiment would support it. "Your suggestion on legislative point appeals to me," said Morse. "I shall be glad to advise Armed Services Committee that I think your suggestion on that point should be followed."

On March 17, 1948, without preview or special fanfare, the entire collection was placed on display in the National Gallery in Washington. To everyone's astonishment, the exhibition was a huge and immediate success. Almost one million people swarmed in to see the collection. On April 11, 1948, an all-time Gallery record was set when 67,490 people filed past the exhibit. President Harry Truman, out for his morning stroll, appeared at the service entrance one Sunday morning well before the Gallery opened. He was shown the collection and enjoyed it so much that he made arrangements to come the following evening with Mrs. Truman and his daughter Margaret. At a press conference later, the President lauded the collection and pronounced his preference for the famous 1532 portrait of the merchant Georg Gisze by Holbein the Younger. Senators, representatives, and Cabinet officers attended special showings. From Washington, all but the most fragile went on tour to thirteen American cities before being returned to Germany. The tour raised over $2 million for German children's relief and marked the beginning of a new era in German-American relations.

On May 17, 1948, again under police and military escort, the first group of paintings were loaded onto the military transport *General Edwin D. Patrick* for the return journey to Bremerhaven. From Bremerhaven they were shipped by special train to Munich, where they were put on exhibition once more, this time in the Haus der Kunst, one of Munich's most famous exhibition halls. All German newspapers carried full accounts of the collection's return, and as the chief German curator remarked in Munich, "The paintings arrived without damage. They are in better condition than when they left Germany [in 1945]. Their convalescence in America has done them good." Since 1950, the paintings have formed the core of the Prussian State Collection in West Berlin.

"The Kaiser Friedrich collection," said Clay in retrospect, "was a magnificent collection of artworks, and they did come back from the United States, and they raised a good deal of money for children's relief. Very interesting thing, though, because at that time, when they were to be brought back [to Germany], one of our Senators [J. William Fulbright] introduced a resolution in the Senate that they be kept in the United States as reparation for the war. I can remember very well getting on the teletype communications with the State Department, telling them that this would absolutely ruin us in Germany. That the paintings had gone to the United States with my own personal assurance as to their return, and for us to keep them would never, never be accepted in the light of history. It's exactly what the Russians were accused of doing with the Sistine Madonna, and I couldn't understand how anybody in the United States Senate could have such a low conception of the responsibilities and duties of the U.S. government. . . .

In any event, they were returned, and I think that it would have been ruinous if they had not been returned.

"On the other hand, we were also very fortunate in recovering as much as we did of the artworks that had been stolen from France and Holland and, above all, from Italy. Italy involved an interesting case at international law, because Goering and Hitler had bought and paid for their Italian artworks. The owners had been well paid. Mussolini had violated or set aside the Italian law that made it illegal for these works of art to be taken out of Italy, but nevertheless they had been bought and paid for. The Italians had provided us with some art experts who were putting this collection together and urging its return. Our government couldn't give me an answer because they said, 'This is a question of international law. The art has been paid for. This has got to be decided at international law.' Or, rather, they didn't say it had to be decided at international law—they said they couldn't decide. So I just adopted the rule that in my opinion these belonged to Italy, and that they didn't belong to anyone else. So I told the Italians that I was willing to send them back, provided I had their assurance and that of the Italian government that the artworks would not be returned to the owners who sold them, but would be placed on permanent public exhibition. They agreed. We sent them back, and I haven't heard any more about them."

Q: What was your attitude toward Americans' buying valuable artworks on the black market for food and cigarettes?

CLAY: It was against the law. I tried in every way possible to stop it. Finally, I developed a legitimate system by establishing a regulated barter market, with official appraisers, where Germans could bring things they wanted to dispose of and Americans could barter for it with coffee, food, and whatnot, but not with cigarettes. Lots of people were very critical of this, perhaps rightly so, but it was very difficult to convince anybody that trading coffee for paintings or a chair or furniture, when the other fellow was a willing part of the transaction, that there was anything wrong with this. It was very difficult. Particularly women. So, since we couldn't stamp it out, I made this so-called outlet by providing a barter market in Berlin. Subsequently, I think there was one in Frankfurt and perhaps a couple of other places. I still think it was a good out. Obviously, the prices were somewhat in favor of Americans, but nevertheless no German had to come.

Q: How would you have felt if Union troops in Marietta had established a barter market?

CLAY: I would have felt a lot better about it than if they were doing it around the corner with uncontrolled and unregulated prices. We certainly tried to set up a system where at least there was some reasonable return to the Germans—far more than they were getting around the corner in off-the-street business, where they were operating between three and four and five go-betweens who were operating illegally. I don't think this was a unique problem, because I had just as much trouble with my people when they would go [on leave] to France and Italy, buying their currency in the black market, where they got four and five times as much for their money as they did at the official rate. And this is really the same thing. How do you prevent that? I don't know. The British and French just didn't pay any attention to it.

Q: How did the black market in the U.S. zone compare to that in the British and French?

CLAY: Hell, ours was the biggest one because our people had more money to spend and could get things like coffee. The British couldn't get coffee, so they couldn't get the things that we could. Our affluence made us the biggest black-market area. The French didn't pay any attention to it; they just took what they wanted anyway.

Q: Mrs. Clay arrived in Berlin with the first dependents in early 1946. What was life in Berlin like before that?

CLAY: When I first went to Berlin [in July 1945], I lived in a house on the Wannsee with two or three of my associates [William Draper and Robert Bowie]. Very quickly I knew that was not for me, for two or three reasons. One was that my hours were very irregular. Number two was that what might be important to them was perhaps the least of importance to me at that particular moment. And, third, I was working very, very hard, and I didn't feel very much like dining and having conversation afterwards. So I finally moved into a smaller house. This is the one Mrs. Clay joined me in. And I guess I lived there alone from September of '45 until April of '46, when she joined me. My aide and my secretary lived in the house next door. By that time, I also began to get visitors from the United States. And that was another one of the reasons I moved into a small house. This gave me the opportunity to put visitors up in the official guest house. I couldn't have taken the hours I was working if I'd had to be sitting up and talking with visitors and whatnot.

Q: You had frequent dinner guests?

CLAY: By and large, there was almost always someone for dinner, either from my staff or, mainly, visitors from the United States—both military and civilian. Usually we'd have a relatively early dinner and then they'd go home to the guest house or wherever they were going, and I'd try to get to bed pretty early.

"Of course, every chance I got, I was visiting our field installations. I had a train and I had an airplane at my disposal all the time. And I suppose that two or three days a week I was visiting places in the zone. I made frequent visits to Stuttgart and the government we were establishing there; frequent visits to Frankfurt, where we had our main administrative branches of military government. Everybody was living the same kind of life. My closest intimates of the period were Bob Murphy, Bill Draper, and Joe Dodge. Down in Frankfurt, it was [Major] General [Clarence] Adcock [Clay's deputy], and [Lieutenant] General [Bedell] Smith—in spite of the fact that we had our differences. Down in Stuttgart, Professor [James K.] Pollock and Colonel [William] Dawson. It was pretty much a round-the-clock job."

Q: When Mrs. Clay came over, you continued to live in the same house?

CLAY: Yes. I don't know how long the United States kept it after I left [in 1949]. But for the very reasons I liked it, it was not suitable for an official residence. It really had only two large bedrooms and a bath. Up on the third floor there were three very small bedrooms and one bath. They were certainly not suitable for a distinguished guest. So after I left, nobody really wanted this house. It was a lovely house, but it was a small house.

Q: When you went back to Berlin in 1961, as President Kennedy's special representative after the Berlin Wall, did you go back to that house?

CLAY: No. It had been given back to the original owners. But as a matter of fact, the people who owned it and were living there offered it back to us in 1961 if we wanted it. I thanked them very much, but I didn't take it.

Q: In 1946, when Mrs. Clay came over, how did it change your life?

CLAY: It changed for the simple reason that you had somebody at the house when you got there, and to get over the feeling of lonesomeness was obviously a very welcome factor. And also we began to have a little more of a social life. Not much, but a little more. You know, when you get to be a commanding officer, life gets pretty lonesome anyway. You put a damper on most parties, whether you mean to or not. Furthermore, particularly from '48 to '49, we were in a rather critical situation. I never knew when I was going to be on the teletype to Washington, what time of night or anything else. So parties were not the answer for me. We led a quiet life and went to bed fairly early. And night after night, I'd have to get up and go back to headquarters to hold a teleconference with Washington.*

Q: When did your day begin?

CLAY: I usually got up about six-thirty, had breakfast, read the *Stars and Stripes,* got to the office about eight. I did not go home for lunch. Too much of the time, really, we'd have someone for dinner, because there was always somebody, a congressman, a senator, visiting general or Cabinet officer, almost always somebody you thought you ought to have for dinner.

Q: Was there opposition to bringing the dependents over in 1946?

CLAY: Some. For different reasons. Some people, particularly in Washington, thought it added to the security problem. Also, some people in Germany, I think, rather liked the life that was going on. And certainly there was a problem in taking further housing from the Germans. But, fundamentally, [bringing the dependents] gave a stability to our Occupation that I don't think we could have gotten any other way. It brought back a much higher moral standard. I think this was necessary and important.

Q: Your primary concern was to raise the moral tone?

CLAY: I don't believe in keeping families separated too long. They'd been separated, many of these people, for quite a long time already. Perhaps I was carried away by my own feelings. I wanted my family with me. I felt I would be more efficient. I think it was timely and logical. That it was really a very wise move. It really gave an entirely different tone to the Occupation.

Q: What was the German reaction?

* In 1948, there were no instantaneous-scrambler telephones linking Washington and Berlin. Communication was by coded teletype messages punched out on what was known as a "teleprinter." Clay would write out his statement in longhand, give it to a code clerk for transmission, and wait for Washington's reply. Such "teleconferences" usually consumed two or three hours, because each exchange had to be separately typed in and transmitted.

CLAY: Locally, where we had to take a few more houses, it probably created some very deep resentments. But I think amongst the top Germans, they appreciated the stability that was implied. And by that time they were very anxious to have us over there. The Russian menace had already loomed up, so I think they felt a little better that our dependents were there.

Q: Wasn't your son, who was stationed in Germany, married about that time?

CLAY: I think it was somewhere about November 1945. His fiancée, General Casey's daughter, was in Berlin. She had come over on a Treasury team, a team that had been recruited by the Treasury, as a junior economist. I had nothing to do with her being there; didn't even know it until after she got there. She'd graduated from William and Mary, and they'd known each other as youngsters. So they got together and wanted to be married. Their mothers both were not very favorable to it. Not that they didn't want them to get married, but they wanted them to wait until they could come back home and have a home wedding. They even thought of having the wedding in London, so the two mothers could come. But I decided that this wasn't the thing to do. They were in Germany and we were in Germany. So my aide and I put on a wedding. Marshal Zhukov and General Sokolovsky were there. General Casey came from Japan, and we put on a very lovely wedding. They weren't the first. I'd given my permission—I had to give my permission for Americans to get married—and I had earlier given permission to two or three reporters to marry women reporters.

Q: I asked Robert Murphy how you relaxed while Military Governor. He said you didn't. But he finally came up with the fact that you once went skiing with him. Had you skied before?

CLAY: No, I hadn't gone skiing before or since in my life. That was my only attempt. We were at his home having a cocktail with some distinguished visitor, I can't remember whom, maybe about six-thirty, something like that. I don't know whether it was Christmas or New Year's, but there was a holiday coming up that weekend. This was a Thursday. And one of the Murphy daughters said, "Oh gee, it would be wonderful if we could go down to Bavaria skiing. It must be wonderful down there."

"All of a sudden, I said, 'Why not? Let's go.' So I got my aide working on it and got hold of the Berchtesgaden hotel and got reservations. The hotel had been taken over by military government, so that wasn't too difficult a job. And we all got in my airplane and flew down there and spent the evening in the hotel, ice-skated the next day, went up the mountain on the chair lift and tried our hand at skiing, and came back to Berlin the next day. And we had a wonderful time."

Q: Your first and only encounter with skis?

CLAY: My first and only encounter. I'm not too sure it wasn't the only weekend I took off while we were in Germany. I can't remember any other.

"The Bavarians put on one of their singing and dancing parties at the hotel. We could hear them yodeling and coming in from miles away, and finally they all got there and put on their dances. It was a cold night. It was a very entertaining evening."

Q: Did they know you were coming?

CLAY: They did by that time. I don't know whether they staged it just for us or whether they'd already planned it, but, knowing the Bavarians, I expect they staged it. They were very nice people that way. I don't think it was trying to bootlick one way or the other. It's just that entertaining people who come to Bavaria is their business in life. This is why they attract tourists. It's become a way of life with them.

Q: You found this unique to Bavaria?

CLAY: Oh yes. Native costumes, native dancers—the Bavarians put on quite a show. I think they enjoy it. Northern Germans are not much more demonstrative than we are.

· 21 ·

Clay Takes Control

> We had much advice from those who professed to know the so-called German mind. If it did exist, I never found it. German minds seemed to be remarkably like those elsewhere. This meant we had to reach them with hard convincing facts.
>
> Lucius D. Clay,
> *Decision in Germany*

When the Allies overran Germany in 1945, the U.S. Army not only captured vast art treasures (as well as the Nazi gold horde), it also fell upon the archives and records of the German Foreign Ministry—which had been evacuated from Berlin during the closing days of the war. These records were assembled by the Army at Kassel, and when the Allied Control Council was established, Clay announced that they were available to each of the four powers for research and review.

The British objected immediately. As Clay would later note, Great Britain's leadership was concerned that wartime cables from the German embassies in Lisbon and Madrid pertaining to the Duke of Windsor's pro-Nazi sympathies might compromise the position of the royal family. Clay's own view, summarized in a cable to Washington on November 21, 1945, was that "all documents in the possession of any occupying power should be equally available to all occupying powers."

Q: The British were concerned?
CLAY: The British are very protective of the royal family. I respect the royal family too, but we were part of a quadripartite arrangement in Germany. I thought the only way we could engender trust among our partners was to be absolutely open and aboveboard. I still feel that way.

When Clay declined to restrict French and Russian access to the documents, Harold Macmillan, on behalf of the British government, appealed directly to General Eisenhower. And Eisenhower—always sympathetic to Anglo-American unity—told Clay to let the British remove the documents they felt might be embarrassing. Clay protested, but acquiesced. As he told Washington, "I know of no reason from American viewpoint here, why Russians and French should not be given full access."

Dealing with an occupied country required a keen sense of history. It demanded an acute awareness of the needs, the aspirations, and the desires of a conquered people. Clay more than provided the political sensitivity FDR and Stimson had been looking for in Germany. He combined it with an obstinacy that was remarkably unaffected by pressure from the State and War departments to take actions he believed would be detrimental to long-term American interests. In that respect, Clay in Germany and MacArthur in Japan were similar. Both had enormous confidence in the correctness of their own on-the-spot judgment and would not tolerate second-guessing by distant headquarters.

Like Clay, MacArthur had been born in patrician comfort. His father, who had been awarded the Congressional Medal of Honor for gallantry at Lookout Mountain during the Civil War, had served as the Army's senior general. Clay's father had been a U.S. senator. Both sons were accustomed to public life from childhood and were intensely aware of the subtleties, the give and take, and the ambiguities of political success. After West Point, both had entered the Army as Engineers, had lived and worked among American civilians, and had spent many years in Washington: MacArthur as Chief of Staff under Hoover and Roosevelt, Clay as the Corps of Engineers' liaison with the New Deal and later as wartime head of all military procurement. Both knew the ins and outs of government far better than most political appointees.

In 1945, MacArthur was at the apex of a brilliant career. As supreme commander of Allied forces in the Pacific, he had avenged the loss of the Philippines and directed the island-hopping ground attack that helped bring Japan to its knees. He had been prominently mentioned as a potential GOP candidate for the presidency and was every inch a national hero. In Japan, he ruled over an exclusively American occupation, and his years in the Orient fitted him uniquely for that task.

Clay was many years MacArthur's junior. The youngest Army general when war began (just as MacArthur had been the youngest U.S. general in World War I), he had received his third star only when he left for Germany in 1945. (MacArthur was a five-star General of the Army.) In Germany, Clay was subordinate to the U.S. theater commander and represented but one of four occupying powers—whose decisions were required to be unanimous. Unlike MacArthur, Clay eschewed personal publicity and lacked a flair for drama. But his crystalline insight into the nature of democracy and his grim determination to instill its roots deeply in German soil fitted him just as uniquely for the task in postwar Europe. A more senior officer, a military icon like Eisenhower or MacArthur, would likely have stumbled in the roughhouse of quadripartite control. Clay's work habits and mastery of detail, his ability to put together patchwork solutions to seemingly intractable problems, an ability honed over many years in Washington, gave him a special advantage in working with the British and Russians in Berlin. Indeed, without Clay, four-power government would undoubtedly have collapsed much earlier than it did.

Clay's major disadvantage was that, unlike MacArthur in 1945, he could not dictate the terms of the Occupation to Washington. He could be just as obstinate, but his stubbornness had to be constantly explained and reinforced in thousands of cables that passed between him and the War Department. In October 1945, for example, General John Hilldring, chief of the War Department's Civil Affairs Division, suggested to Clay that German POWs still held in the United States be trained to work for the military government. As Hilldring saw it, the use of POWs would not only save the United States money, but could provide a valuable political cadre of German supporters.

Clay was skeptical. As a native son of Georgia, he wanted no scallywags or carpetbaggers. He told Hilldring that a POW training school might be a good idea, but that the military government should not hire them. "We believe that if these trained prisoners of war are discharged and returned to their home areas they will quickly find places in the German administrative machine." But Clay said that the military government should not exert any pressure since it might "make these persons [appear to be] collaborators and therefore destroy their future value. While this will not guarantee the fullest immediate use of all repatriates it is our view that, in the long run, it will permit them to contribute more to the re-education of Germany."

Similarly, Clay resisted attempts to use German POWs as indentured labor in liberated countries. Clay acknowledged to the War Department that the Geneva Convention permitted the use of military prisoners to repair war damage, but he said the political fallout in Germany would be disastrous. To send German POWs to liberated countries, Clay told Washington, "savors quite a lot like the labor practices employed by Hitler. The view is widely held among the German people that large numbers of these prisoners were soldiers through compulsion and had much less to do with the causes of war than much larger numbers of the German population remaining in Germany and under no restraints. . . .

"I am very much of the view that the placing of a monetary value as reparations on prisoner of war labor and its allocation as a matter of reparations, will make Germans doubt the sincerity of our efforts to develop liberal and democratic thinking."

In a similar fashion, Clay opposed American exploitation of German scientific achievements. He believed that the United States should pay for any scientific achievements produced by the Germans. In October 1946, he protested American actions to Washington. "We are taking from Germany all information we can obtain relative to trade processes and advanced scientific thought," said Clay. "We took this information first to facilitate our war against Japan and then definitely for commercial purposes. *The taking of this information to my mind without accounting is parallel to Soviet action in taking current pro-*

duction and to French action in removing capital equipment. . . . Finally, we are taking the thought of German scientists and fashioning it to our own purposes." Clay insisted that Washington put an immediate monetary value on the contribution of German scientists to the United States and credit it against American reparations claims.

The War Department was unmoved. Clay was told that it was impractical to put a value on German scientific information because there was no way of knowing how it would be used. Clay persisted—as he usually did when he believed he was correct. On January 22, 1947, he repeated his concern to Major General Daniel Noce, head of the War Department's Civil Affairs Division. When Washington once again declined to act, Clay moved on his own authority. He informed the War Department that he planned to terminate the collection of scientific data in Germany on March 31, 1947. When the Department of Commerce (which supervised the project) protested, Clay remained adamant. He told the War Department that all collection efforts would cease unless he received specific orders to the contrary. When no orders came, Clay halted the project.

Q: General, as a military commander you have appeared to some people as a paradox: a tough disciplinarian who believed deeply in civil liberty.

CLAY: I have been averse all my life to doing anything under what might be considered the slightest duress. When I was in Germany, I supported the American Civil Liberties Union as much as I could. I thought they were serving a very useful purpose. Arthur Garfield Hays [director of the ACLU] used to come over to see me in Germany, and I gave him free access to go anywhere and see anything he wanted. I thought he was very sincere. I thought it was part and parcel of teaching the Germans the meaning of democracy.

Q: Shortly after you left Germany, you spoke at Columbia University. You said: "American business cannot exist except in an atmosphere of free thinking, which is formed in free educational institutions such as Columbia."

CLAY: I still feel that way. I suppose it's my old Democratic background bubbling out. I don't believe in McCarthyism. I don't believe in the use of the power of government to stifle people in expressing themselves freely. However, a civilized society must have a certain discipline. And that discipline must consist of a respect for law and order.

"In the Army that I belonged to it was understood that you spoke your piece freely and forcefully before a decision was made. But once a decision was made, you loyally carried it out. And I don't think you can have any real discipline otherwise. I think I believe in free speech as much as anyone in this country. But I also recognize that when you go into an army, you give up certain of your rights as a free citizen.

"But the Army should not take advantage of that. I'm against spying on someone's private life. When I was in Germany, I had to order my CID [Criminal Investigation Division] to stop spying on officers in my command. I said it was no one's business who visited their quarters or who spent the night with them. I've always believed that the Army made such demands on one's privacy that whatever little there was had to be jealously protected. And I tried to do that."

Q: And the danger of espionage?

CLAY: We supposedly had a security risk in one of our sections, because the fellow had belonged to some book club or other back in Washington during the war. I called the fellow in and told him that our security board had received this word from Washington and that as a result he had to go.

"He said, 'General, what do I have to do to prove myself a good citizen? I went into the Army. I got a battlefield promotion. I was a captain. I took my discharge. I think I performed my duties satisfactorily. Is this going to plague me all of my life?'

"I said, 'You've convinced me. And you're going to stay.' So I wired Washington that I was keeping him. And the cables back and forth got hot and heavy. I practically had to say, 'If he goes, I'm going!' Well, finally they accepted my decision. He went back to work. And that day when I told him it would be all right, he brought his wife and his two young children to see me—charming little children—just to say thank you.

"About six or seven weeks later, I got a telephone call from our ambassador in Czechoslovakia. And he said this man had been in Prague consorting with all the Communist leaders. Did I know anything about it?

"I said, 'Yes, I'm afraid I do.' I immediately checked back with his office and found that he had gone on a weekend leave and had not returned. He was a couple of days overdue.

"That same day, he called a press conference in Prague and announced he was there to seek political asylum and was taking a post in a Communist indoctrination school.

"That was the last I heard from him until about ten days ago [April 10, 1971]. I got a letter from a Midwestern university saying that this American professor who had been teaching at universities in Czechoslovakia for the last several years was applying for a chair at the university and had stated that he had worked for me at one time. They said they would appreciate it if I would tell them what I thought of him.

"I thought about it a lot, and I simply wrote them a letter that he had been with me in military government and had left voluntarily in 1947 to go to Czechoslovakia. And as far as I knew, he had been engaged in teaching in Czechoslovakia in the intervening years.

"I don't know what happened, nor can I possibly imagine the chain of circumstances which led him to seek so earnestly to retain his position in military government and then a few weeks later to change. The only thing I could think of was that the Soviet agents had something on him. It was known that he had met with the Russians a good many times in Berlin, but this in itself meant nothing, because almost everybody was [doing that] at that time. I can't really believe that he was insincere or that he would have brought his family in to say thank you, and then six weeks later do as he did. He certainly put me up against the guillotine.

"But I've always believed in the right of people to express themselves freely. One of the most amazing experiences I ever had came at the Harvard commencement in 1949, when I was to be given an honorary degree. I'd been given one by Yale the preceding day, and there had been a great deal of talk at Yale because they'd awarded the Bollingen Prize for Poetry to Ezra Pound. When I went to Harvard, I listened to some of the graduating class exercises that morning, and one of the student speakers said what a great thing Yale had done to award a prize to a man who was a defector from his country during the war.

"Well, that afternoon I was sitting on the platform at Harvard with the honorary degree recipients, Ambassador Frank [from Great Britain] and Ralph Bunche. We'd been to dinner at Dr. Conant's [president of Harvard] house the night before, and nobody had ever said a word to me about speaking at the commencement. We went up to get our degrees, and Frank was scheduled to make a speech, which he did in short order. Then Dr. Conant said, 'We're very fortunate because we're now going to hear from General Clay,' or words to that effect. I almost jumped out of my skin. I hadn't been paying too much attention by that time, and then, my God, here was my name called to address the Harvard commencement. I drew an absolute blank, and I had to figure out what I was going to say between my seat and the rostrum.

"I can't remember what I said, except for one thing. I said I knew I was back in America, and how wonderful it was, because I had just listened to a student supporting the right of a sister university to give an award to a defecting American citizen. And that perhaps in doing this we were providing our greatest example of what freedom really means. It had certainly impressed me."

Clay's chief of staff in Berlin, Major General William Whipple, said that he saw few military characteristics in Clay's methods. "He could do everything that a military man was supposed to do, of course, but I never saw a marked military orientation in what he did. Perhaps his habits of orderliness and punctuality might be considered military. But when we came to discussing things around a conference table—Clay had a staff conference every week and it lasted about two hours—it was freewheeling. Clay had all of his division chiefs around that table. He had all kinds of people with all kinds of expertise: Bill Draper from Wall Street; Joe Dodge, who'd been president of the American Bankers Association; Ambassador Murphy, a man thoroughly familiar with diplomacy; former Solicitor General Fahy; and so on. And he'd go around the table talking to each one about that person's business. And he never seemed to be at a disadvantage no matter what the subject was. He'd argue legal matters with Fahy, for instance, and Fahy didn't always win the arguments, because Clay would remember some historic point that Fahy hadn't thought of.

"Then he'd talk about German political parties and the relation between the monarchists and the Catholic Right in Bavaria with Professor Friedrich. And he obviously knew more about it than anyone, with the possible exception of Friedrich. The same on the financial or economic side. Clay would go around this table with a bunch of experts, and he knew as much or more than they did.

"And don't forget that Clay had one of the most expert staffs ever created. He didn't build it up out of the military. I happened to be there because I was a Rhodes Scholar, not because I was regular military. The Regular Army personnel were not the key men at Clay's headquarters. He brought in former governors, educators—a really varied and talented group. No one else could have done it, because no one else knew as many people in as many fields as Clay did.

"Of course, although the staff meetings were freewheeling, they were also very tense. Everyone was apprehensive that Clay might ask them something they didn't know, because it wasn't easy to keep ahead of him. He wasn't trying to embarrass anyone, but he frequently did it anyway. I remember things had gotten dull at one meeting and someone mentioned that the sentinel at headquarters had been rude: that some American wife had passed through the gate, the sentinel had asked her to stop but she didn't hear him, and so he whistled at her. And this staff director said that was disrespectful.

"Clay said, 'Whistle at her? You mean like this?' And he suddenly whistled through his teeth in a way that almost took everyone out of their chairs. You suddenly got the picture that when this man was young he must have been a great party boy. And he grinned in such a way to make everyone realize that what this young soldier had done hadn't been so bad.

"Clay directed me to set up a system of communications from Berlin," said Whipple, "and I suggested that we do it by radio, because it took too long to go through all these intermediate headquarters between us and the military government units in the field. [These intermediate headquarters] might change the orders, or add something of their own, just sit on them, or never issue them. So we set up a radio system broadcasting directly from Berlin, and we issued radios to each military government detachment throughout Germany. Each man out there had his little radio. And between six-thirty and seven every evening, we'd make a daily broadcast of information and directives. And these directives would take effect as of the time of the broadcast.

"One of the amusing things was that the Germans started listening to this. We broadcast in the clear. We didn't try to hide anything. Clay had what he called a 'goldfish bowl' policy, and there was remarkably little going on that he wasn't willing to talk about. That was one of the secrets of his success. He was always candid and frank with the Germans—and everyone else.

"But the transmission of our instructions in the open on the radio had a big effect on the Germans. They found out they could listen themselves. And this was *the* official information coming directly from Clay's headquarters in Clay's name. And since the Germans were listening too, there couldn't be any nonsense. You couldn't have some military government man running his own show. And you have to remember that there were a lot of people in Germany with different ideas from Clay as to what should be done. Many of them were there for personal or ideological reasons. Including some people high in military government. They would implement their own policy as far as they could, and we had terrible injustices in a number of cases as a result. So to have our directives out in the open was a big help. The Germans got radios, and they listened. And we wanted them to."

Clay's lengthy experience in Washington made him uniquely sensitive to the media. According to Whipple, "we started with a horrible press. The Army was portrayed as a bunch of idiots. But Clay organized trips for newsmen and publishers to bring them over and show them what we were doing. He'd let them go all over Germany and see everything they wanted to see and talk to everyone they wanted to talk to. When they went home, they were all converted. And Clay used them to get information about what was happening in Germany and a perspective that he couldn't get through official channels.

"He'd talk to the press that were assigned to Germany just as frankly. He'd get them in and tell them exactly what he was planning to do and why. As a result, the press was perfectly delighted and didn't bug him about details. Because he was not only telling them what was going on, but if something was wrong he'd admit that it was wrong and say how he was going to correct it. And he did. They began to get confidence in Clay, and then we began to get a good press.

"About September [1945], General Clay told me he wanted a monthly military government report made up to go back to Washington each month. Well, as always happens, the contributions were very uneven and in most cases very unimaginative, particularly the one from the Economics Division. I worked the original contributions up into a report, then I added an opening statement that I thought reflected General Clay's policies. In it, in this opening paragraph, I said, 'Contrary to the view that Germany should have its economy dismantled, which would prevent a resurgence of its war potential, it was urgently necessary that Germany have its economy brought up to a satisfactory level to maintain its population at a decent standard of living.' That, of course, was a direct challenge to the Morgenthau concept of a pastoralized Germany, and I thought that General Clay probably agreed with that. So I brought the report in to him, not in draft form but in final form, all ready for his signature. He read through it—he reads remarkably rapidly—and he brought it back to me and said, 'This first paragraph on economic policy—where did you get that?'

"I said, 'This is what the staff believes is your policy.'

"He said, 'Have I ever said that?'

"I said, 'No sir.'

"He said, 'Who wrote it?'

"I said, 'I did.'

"He said, 'Suppose I don't like it?'

"I said, 'Well, we'll retype it.'

"He looked down at me and said, 'Well, it's all right.' And he signed his name and off we went. But that was the first statement of his economic policy, of what had to be done. And it had a tremendous effect."

General Whipple minimized Clay's often stated rationale that his primary interest in German recovery was to reduce the drain on the American taxpayer. "That was part of it," said Whipple. "Certainly that was the official justification. But I do not believe that was his primary reason. General Clay, although he is regarded as cold and efficient, is not all that cold. He simply didn't like to see the Germans starving."

But Clay was indeed worried about financial support from Washington. His years of dealing with Congress had taught him to take nothing for granted. "If the Congress failed to appropriate the money, and we had to continue with the Occupation, where would we be?" asked Clay. "I didn't know whether Congress would support the Occupation. And for how long?

"But on the whole we had very good support in Congress. Much better than we had any reason to expect. The War Department made a concerted effort to invite congressmen to visit all of the theaters. The result was that we had a constant flow of visitors—sometimes whole committees, sometimes subcommittees, sometimes individuals. They never came that I didn't meet them and try to answer all of their questions, and to try to give them any and all of the information they wanted. I felt that was the duty of any United States representative abroad. I worked at it, and I worked at it hard. I doubt if the military side of the picture worked as hard as we did in military government. I think it would have been helpful if all members of the Senate and House had visited Germany."

Q: And other visitors? Mrs. Roosevelt? Former President Hoover?
CLAY: Mrs. Roosevelt visited me in Berlin shortly after the war ended. I had great respect for her. She was a great lady.
Q: Did she support your efforts in Germany?
CLAY: I think that as far as her newspaper columns were concerned, they were very much in support of what we were trying to do in Germany. At that time, she was writing her column "My Day," which was carried in many, many newspapers.
Q: You arranged her visit?
CLAY: I think she wrote and asked if she could come over, and she was actually my houseguest in Berlin. But Mrs. Roosevelt was very busy. She was on the go every minute: women's clubs, hospitals, schools, everything. But she was always there in the mornings, so we'd have breakfast together, and then she'd always return for dinner.
Q: And President Hoover?
CLAY: The first time that he came to Europe after the war, I met him in Brussels when he arrived, had dinner with him at his club there, and invited him to visit Germany. That's the trip he made independently. Later he came under a mandate from President Truman. There again I set up a train for him to take him all over Europe, and brought him to Berlin and gave him a house to live in, and arranged for all the people in Germany who were working on the food problem to come up there and report to him.
Q: What made you decide to go to Brussels [to meet former President Hoover]?
CLAY: I heard he was coming. He was a former President of the United States, and I thought it was my duty to go over and pay my respects to him when he landed. I would have done it for any former President.

"Mr. Hoover's support was important for Germany then [in 1945], and it was even more important later, when we had the whole European problem on our hands. And then, when the Republicans won both houses of Congress in 1946, it became even more important. Because Mr. Hoover was still a powerful voice in the Republican Party.

"At that time, everybody needed food. And Mr. Hoover was determined that in that distribution [of food], the needs of Germany would also be given consideration. He was a tower of strength to us in getting food. I frankly doubt we would have gotten it without him.

"On the other hand, we had to convince him. And he was no easy man to convince. I had to bring in our agricultural people—both our own and the Germans'. And they had to come in with the data. We had a very fine German Minister of Agriculture [Dr. Hermann Dietrich], and he made an excellent showing. Because, when it came to dealing with figures and statistics, Mr. Hoover was right in his element."

In addition to the primary problem of feeding Germany, one of the most important issues confronting military government in 1945 was the future capacity of German industry. The issue focused on the level of the German steel industry, which would be used as a benchmark. According to Clay, "The British and French wanted a much higher level of steel production than did our government. Ours was higher than the Russians'. Actually, my instructions for a 'suggested level' for the steel industry was something around 4.5 million tons. This the Russians could have accepted, but the British and French were talking ten million tons.

"So I developed a compromise solution. The fact is that after all is said and done, no steel industry could work at 100 percent capacity. And it was foolish to talk in those terms. So I proposed that we temporarily agree to limit production to 4.5 million tons a year, subject to further agreement. And that we accept the fact that to accomplish that would require 7.5 million tons of capacity. And this was the formula that was finally accepted. That way I was trying to meet the British and French, while I was technically within the limits I had from my government.

"I might say that I was almost alone on this—and rightly so, from an economic standpoint—because all of my staff were very much in favor of the higher limit. I either had to persuade my government that the higher limit was justified, or fight for the lower limit [in the Allied

Control Council]. When I got into that kind of fight, I didn't put the blame on Washington. I took the responsibility for the decision, and I think it probably worked out as well as any other decision."

Q: How closely did Washington watch you on matters like that?
CLAY: Ha! That's a very difficult question to answer. The level of steel production was a hotly debated topic because it was a part of the Morgenthau Plan. And so, on the question of steel, Washington was quite specific.

"Also, this came particularly early in military government, and I'm not too sure that we ourselves had formulated very deep convictions as to what type and kind of Germany we wanted to have. When you have practically no steel capacity—as was the case in late 1945—4.5 million tons looks like a lot. And if you have a capacity of 7.5 million tons, that looks like a great deal too. And you're also measuring this against neighboring countries whose capacity at that time wasn't too high either. I don't think France had more than thirty million tons at the time.

"So when we're talking about levels of industry, or the amount of industry to be reduced or dismantled because of its value for future military purposes, I had very specific instructions. When it was a question of the internal German economy, I had none. And I think the steel industry was being scrutinized [in Washington] by the same people who were concerned with what should be denied to Germany to prevent it from ever again becoming a strong military power."

The compromise on the German steel industry was an exception to the stalemate among the occupying powers on the Allied Control Council—pushed through by Clay's determination to seek a common ground between the Russians and the British. But the more fundamental issues—the treatment of Germany as an economic unit, the free interchange of goods and services among all four occupation zones, and the crucial issue of an all-German administrative apparatus—remained unsolved. And they remained unsolved primarily because of deliberate French obstructionism. In 1945, it was the French, not the Russians, who blocked German unity. France wanted to take no step that might lead to a revived, centralized Germany, and her representatives in the Allied Control Council vetoed all proposals that might lead in that direction. The unhappy and inevitable result was that each zone was thrown increasingly upon its own resources.

French obstructionism should have come as no surprise. De Gaulle had been excluded from the Potsdam Conference, and was properly miffed. Not only did he feel that France was not bound by the accord, but immediately after the conference he informed the United States, Britain, and the Soviet Union that he rejected key portions of the agreement, including the treatment of Germany as an economic unit, central administrative machinery, and the re-establishment of national political parties in Germany.

De Gaulle had been even more specific when he met President Truman in Washington at the end of August 1945. De Gaulle told Truman that France wanted to control the left bank of the Rhine "from one end to the other" to insure against another German invasion. "Separation of the Rhineland from Germany is a necessary geographic guarantee, as well as a psychological necessity for the French people," said de Gaulle. He added that the huge industrial potential of the Ruhr should be placed under international control and warned once more of the dangers stemming from a united Germany.

De Gaulle's views in 1945 were the views of Eternal France. There was no room for compromise. And regardless of the changes in government during the early years of the Fourth Republic, those views dominated French policy.

French obstructionism surfaced for the first time in the Allied Control Council on September 22, 1945, when France vetoed all proposals for central transportation, communications, and postal services throughout Germany. Clay, who had little sympathy for French intransigence, later openly condemned the French action. Privately, he advised the War Department, "the establishment of sufficient central administrative machinery to govern Germany as an economic unit at earliest possible date is essential to execution of our policy in Germany and of the policy agreed to at Potsdam." Clay again told Washington that the "Russians and British are in full agreement" with the need for central administrative machinery but that the French opposed such plans. Unless there was a change in the French attitude, "it would appear essential to suggest to Russians and British that they join us in establishing such machinery for our three zones." Clay requested

Washington's immediate permission to do so. The alternative, he said, was to operate the U.S. zone as a separate unit—an unfortunate alternative that Clay believed would "lead to practical if not actual dismemberment of Germany."

Two weeks later, Clay informed Washington that the situation in the Allied Control Council had reached an impasse. General Pierre Koenig, the French Military Governor, had formally advised the ACC that France could not agree to centralized administrative agencies in Germany until the future of the Rhineland and the Ruhr was settled. This was deliberate obstructionism in Clay's view, because the Potsdam Agreement had made it clear that the Ruhr and the Rhineland would remain German. "Yesterday's meeting," said Clay, "developed almost complete inability to reach unanimous agreement [on] any of fifteen papers under consideration. Eleven were supported by three of four parties but [were] defeated due to necessity for unanimous agreement. *Any real progress appears impossible as long as the French delegation continues to prosecute their recently developed antagonism to the establishment of central German administrative units.*" Unless the situation changed quickly, "it will be manifest to the press and to the public that quadripartite government in Germany has failed. We have done, and continue to do, everything possible to make it succeed."

The following day, Clay wrote a depressing letter to John J. McCloy. "We've made little progress on important matters," said Clay. "So far the French have blocked the creation of any of the central German administrative machinery called for by the Potsdam Agreement. When the concrete proposals to establish central agencies for transport and for communications and posts came before us [the French] refrained from approving them." Clay said the French were intent on detaching the Ruhr from Germany and would not agree to anything in the ACC until that had been achieved.

Clay went on to tell McCloy that he had requested permission to negotiate directly with the British and the Russians to set up central agencies at least in their three zones, but that he had received no reply. "The creation of some central machinery is essential to permit us to administer Germany as an economic unit," said Clay. "Under the circumstances, I can only repeat my request for permission to proceed on a three-way basis, pending agreement by the French."

When Clay returned to Washington in November 1945 for consultations with the State and War Departments, there had been no change in the French attitude. If anything, it had become more rigid. Clay told a specially convened meeting of State Department officials that the French representative on the Allied Control Council (General Koenig) was opposing the establishment of central German administrative machinery until France's claim for the internationalization of the Ruhr and the Rhineland was settled. Clay said that the Russians assumed that France's obstinacy "was receiving tacit support from the British and the United States." Indeed, when Clay asked H. Freeman Matthews, chief of the State Department's European Affairs Division, what the United States was doing diplomatically, Matthews replied that Washington had taken "no steps to bring pressure to bear upon the French to cooperate with other members of the Control Council in carrying out the Berlin [Potsdam] Protocol with respect to the treatment of Germany as an economic unit and was unlikely to do so."

When Clay asked about France's proposal to detach the Ruhr and the Rhineland from Germany, Matthews, who was one of Washington's most dedicated cold warriors, replied elliptically that Secretary Byrnes had invited French Foreign Minister Georges Bidault to Washington to discuss the matter and that it was "unlikely that the Secretary would desire to prejudge the United States position in advance of hearing French arguments." As Clay saw it, to Matthews and his colleagues the danger in Europe was Russia, not France, and they would do nothing to upset the fragile French government. Not for the first time in U.S. foreign policy, the weakness of an ally, not the strength of the United States, determined the direction of American policy.

As Clay flew back to Berlin, he and Murphy analyzed the changed atmosphere in Washington. Murphy mentioned the preoccupation of the State Department with the domestic situation in France. Communist influence was growing, and American diplomats were urging Byrnes not to apply pressure for fear of toppling the weak French government and bringing Maurice Thorez and the Communists to power.

Clay acknowledged but rejected Murphy's analysis. To Clay, letting France scuttle the quadripartite government of Germany was letting the tail wag the dog. The future of Europe hinged on the future of Germany, in Clay's view, and the situation in France was (at best) a disagreeable sideshow. Clay told Murphy that he was determined not to let France destroy Germany and bring all of Europe down with it.

One month later, Clay advised his old friend Donald Russell, who had become Assistant Secretary of State for Administration, that, although some progress was being made in the American zone, restoration of the German economy "depends almost entirely on the establishment of central machinery and the elimination of artificial zone boundaries. *The situation here has not improved as the French have not deviated in the slightest from their position of opposition.*"

When France continued to oppose a quadripartite formula for the restitution of property that had been looted by the Nazis, Clay brusquely told the Allied Control Council that the United States might find it necessary to proceed on a tripartite basis, excluding France. Clay's remark caught the French off guard. Until then their intransigence appeared to be at least passively supported by the State Department. But Clay had become a wild card. His independence was to be a source of continuing puzzlement to the French. When the French government protested Clay's statement to Washington, they received mixed signals. Under Secretary Acheson and Matthews reported that Clay did not speak for the United States. Secretary Byrnes, however, in direct contact with Clay, remained firmly on his side. And Clay was in no mood to back down. He told the War Department bluntly that France was making the four-power government of Germany impossible.

"Quadripartite government must necessarily be a government of compromise," said Clay. "The Russians have gone a long way to meet with French views on restitution and . . . I cannot but feel that the French are being quite stubborn in their unwillingness to compromise. In point of fact, *French position in quadripartite government is not understandable to me. To date, their only contribution has been insistence on adoption of their restitution policy and opposition to central administrative machinery. They have made no constructive contribution to quadripartite government.* . . . It seems to me that we are on a one-way street in which we support France to the full and get absolutely no support from France for the policies which . . . were adopted at Potsdam."

In January 1946, de Gaulle resigned as head of France's provisional government. U.S. Ambassador to France Jefferson Caffery, reporting on the resignation, indicated the strong likelihood that de Gaulle would be succeeded by a coalition government headed by Maurice Thorez and the Communists—already the largest party in France. When a coalition Cabinet under moderate socialist Félix Gouin eventually emerged, Washington was even more anxious not to shake its weak foundations by confronting France over the quadripartite government of Germany.

But Secretary Byrnes continued to support Clay. Byrnes suggested to Caffery that he "might discreetly inject the thought that any steps which the French government may publicly take at this time in the way of cooperating with American aims [in Germany] should help to create a more favorable atmosphere for the impending economic and financial talks [with] Bidault in Washington." When, four weeks later, Caffery replied on his fruitless conversations with Bidault, he assured the Department he would continue his efforts to bring about an evolution in French thinking but cautioned that Bidault's resignation might cause a governmental crisis "on which the Communists would capitalize." As Caffery saw it, "it would be definitely unwise at this juncture to press this matter further." Caffery's message fell on receptive ears in the European Affairs Division of the State Department. He was told that "the French should not be pressed to a point where there is a real danger of Bidault's resignation and of a split in the coalition government which would have wide political ramifications in France."

If Washington was reluctant to pressure the French to cooperate in Germany, Clay had no such qualms. At one point in the bleak winter of 1945–46, he sought to hold up American wheat deliveries to the French zone until France complied with the Potsdam accords. "I am convinced the situation in the French zone from a food viewpoint is quite serious," Clay told Hilldring in Washington. "However, it results in substantial part from failure of the French to look ahead, and particularly to their initial policy of supplying their forces in the occupying territory from indigenous sources." Clay told Hilldring that if France had cooperated in the establishment of central administrative machinery for Germany, it "might well have eased the existing [food] situation." He suggested that "our cooperation in the existing food shortage in the French zone might well be conditioned on a change of attitude by France on quadripartite government."

The change in leadership from de Gaulle to Gouin brought no change in French policy. On February 18, 1946, the new French government officially informed the United States, Britain, and the Soviet Union that it sought permanent control of the Saar—Germany's rich coal-and-steel basin, adjacent to France—and that it opposed the creation of any administrative apparatus for a united Germany until the Ruhr was detached and placed under international control. Once again, Clay protested vigorously. In an "Eyes Only" cable to Hilldring, he warned the War Department of the political consequences in Germany should French policy be accepted. Clay said that while pro-Western German political parties such as the Christian Democratic Union (CDU) and the Social Democrats (SPD) were prohibited by Occupation law from criticizing the French, the Communist Party was exploiting the situation.

"The Communist Party has made a unified Germany a rallying cry," said Clay. "This rallying cry is one of tremendous appeal to all Germans regardless of class, religion or political affiliation. It places the Communist Party in a most favorable light as compared with other parties in Germany." Clay told Hilldring that although this development was "embryonic," it had "more future political significance than any issue to date."

When spring came and there still was no softening in the French position, Clay recommended direct action. On April 11, 1946, in a joint cable to Secretary Byrnes and Secretary of Agriculture Clinton P. Anderson, Clay said that it was of "paramount importance" that the establishment of German central administrative machinery provided by the Potsdam Agreement be undertaken immediately. "Recommend [that] French be informed that unless they prepare to concur immediately in the establishment of such centralized administrative agencies, all shipments of wheat to French zone of Germany will be discontinued." Clay also proposed halting shipments of wheat to France itself.

Not surprisingly, given Washington's increasing fixation on the Communist threat in France, the medicine Clay proposed was too strong. Two weeks later, Acting Secretary of State Dean Acheson informed Judge Patterson that it "would be unwise to exert such direct pressure on France" at this time.

It was at this point that Secretary Byrnes asked Clay directly for his opinion on France's plan to internationalize the Ruhr. Byrnes was now under intense pressure from State Department professionals such as Matthews and Charles Bohlen to accede to French wishes, and he sought Clay's views as a counterweight. Clay replied on April 20 with a thirty-page memorandum stressing the Ruhr's indelible identification with Germany, its crucial role in German recovery, and the massive political implications for the future of Germany should the Western powers permit the Ruhr to be severed. Once again Clay told Washington that "The Communist Party in Germany has adopted as its battle cry, 'A Unified Germany,' " and the popular appeal was enormous.

Clay emphasized the importance of the Ruhr for German recovery. Even before the war, he noted, the industrial economy of Germany was based on the coal and steel produced in the Ruhr. Germany's dependence on the Ruhr was even greater in 1946 than before the war, since its prewar land area had been reduced by 25 percent, and that, combined with the influx of refugees and expellees from the East, meant that a population more or less equal to its prewar size "must live in about three-fourths of the pre-war land area. The density of population in Germany which will result is approximately four times as great as in the rest of Europe. This population must be sustained in an area which has never been self-supporting in food."

But above all, Clay stressed the political implications. "The Potsdam Protocol visualized the democratization of Germany. It encouraged the development of democratic parties and the return of self-government to Germany under democratic procedures. It looked forward to a restoration some day of German government and the return of the German nation to the family of nations." Clay said that it was assumed that the new Germany would some day be admitted to the United Nations, and that the desire to partition Germany "shows a lack of faith in the success of UNO."

> Democratic processes may be expected to grow only in an atmosphere of political and economic stability. The removal of the Ruhr with its thirteen million inhabitants would reduce remaining Germany . . . to almost a pastoral economy. The inevitable low standard of living would create permanent unrest, and the lack of fuel and raw materials would create a condition of permanent unemployment. *Political stability would be impossible.*

"Communism and totalitarianism thrive on political unrest," said Clay. "If the Ruhr were separated from Germany, the remaining part of Germany would dedicate its political life to regaining the Ruhr. Internationalization could succeed only if supported with force. The desire of the people of the Ruhr to return to the Reich would rise again and again. It would have to be suppressed either with force or by rigorous political control. Each of these methods would become repugnant in the years to come to the democratic countries."

Clay concluded that "Any real faith in developing democratic processes in Germany and in bringing a peace-loving Germany back into the family of nations would be rendered much less likely through the severance of the Ruhr." Not only would American Occupation costs be increased, but removal of the Ruhr "would have to be sustained by armed force at variance with democratic principles." And as for military security, Clay suggested that French efforts to detach the Ruhr reflected "a prehistoric concept of warfare which [became] outmoded with the overrunning of the Maginot Line."

Throughout 1946, Clay continued to press Washington for some indication as to when the Army might relinquish its responsibilities in Germany and turn the Occupation over to the State Department. On March 1, 1946, Clay thought things were moving in the right direction when Hilldring called from Washington to say that he would be leaving as head of the War Department's Civil Affairs Division to become Assistant Secretary of State for Occupied Areas. Hilldring said the change should reduce the time required to get answers from Washington. "It's the first step in the right direction," he told Clay. Hilldring said that his place in the War Department would be taken by Major General Oliver Echols, who was Clay's deputy for local government. That would ensure continuity. From Clay's point of view, the return of Echols to Washington meant that the War Department would be even better informed about conditions in Germany, and he applauded the move. But he chided Hilldring for using military government "as a personnel reservoir." First Hilldring, then Echols, then Colonel Mickey Markus (who later headed Israel's defense forces in Jerusalem and was accidentally killed in Palestine in 1948), whom the War Department had snatched from Clay's headquarters, and now, Clay said, the State Department wanted Charles Fahy. "Those are four top people that they've pulled out of us at a very crucial period." Clay told Hilldring that one of the complicating problems in attracting top-quality civilian personnel for military government was the Army's insistence that they wear uniforms. "I've spent fifty percent of my time fighting to protect the civilians on that particular regulation," said Clay. "I don't blame USFET [United States Forces, European Theater] too much. USFET has an entirely different calibre of civilian from the ones that I have. They slop around USFET headquarters in a semi-military uniform and look like hell, and that keeps USFET and its staff terribly disturbed all the time. They can't appreciate that here in Berlin I have an entirely different type of person."

Clay complained to Hilldring that even in Berlin the caliber of persons being assigned from Washington "is going down hill. . . . All of my division directors tell me that the people that we are getting in don't measure up as well lately as they did at first."

Finally, he warned Hilldring that the three *Länder* (provinces) in the American zone were going to promulgate laws punishing former members of the Nazi Party. Clay said they were good laws and he was going to approve them. "You will find that we will get a tremendous amount of abuse on it from those of us that will say that we are turning back responsibilities to the Germans too quickly. Actually, if you gave me 10,000 people over here, I couldn't do that job. With 10,000 people I couldn't do the job of denazification. It's got to be done by the Germans." Clay said that he was going to take responsibility for the law himself, and not send it back to Washington for approval.

No issue has figured more prominently among the so-called origins of the Cold War than Clay's cutoff of reparations deliveries from the American zone in May 1946. Traditional and revisionist historians alike have suggested that Clay's move was designed to force the USSR into concessions. But the fact is, Clay's action was not directed primarily at the Russians; it was designed to put additional pressure on the French to cooperate in the quadripartite government of Germany. When the State Department declined to pressure France, Clay decided to do it with the means at his disposal in Germany. And reparations, which France sought with a rapacious appetite, provided one such opportunity.

By early May of 1946, the Allied Control Council had reached an impasse. The Americans, British, and French agreed to a pooling of German resources based on a common standard of consumption and the use of export proceeds to buy essential imports, while the Soviets maintained that exports should be conducted on a zonal basis. When Clay pointed out to the Russians that their position was contrary to

Potsdam, Sokolovsky asked whether the French were ready to establish central administrative machinery. As Clay advised Washington, "the French answer was their usual statement that they favored treatment of Germany as a single economic entity but still opposed central administrative machinery." That brought the issue to a head.

Clay told his colleagues on the Allied Control Council that the Potsdam Agreement had to be accepted as a whole. He said that the reparations program assumed a common export-import program and without the latter, "the U.S. zone could not provide reparations." Clay emphasized that a common export-import program "definitely required central administrative machinery to be effective."

On his own initiative, and without clearance from either the State Department or the War Department, Clay then announced that he was terminating further reparations deliveries from the American zone. "In the absence of a decision by the Allied Control Council to develop a common import-export program," said Clay, the United States "would have to cease further dismantlement of plants and [reparations] deliveries."

In reporting his action to Washington, Clay said that "this was not a bluff," and that he had already ordered any further dismantling of plants designated for reparations to be discontinued. "While we are prepared to continue the paper allocation of plants for reparations, we do not propose to take any further physical efforts to carry out the reparations program until major overall questions are resolved and we know what area is to compose Germany and whether or not that area will be treated as an economic unit."

Clay repeated his concerns in a lengthy message to General Eisenhower, who was now Army Chief of Staff.

> After one year of occupation, zones represent airtight territories, with almost no free exchange of commodities, persons and ideas. Germany now consists of four small economic units which can deal with each other only through treaties in spite of the fact that no one unit can be regarded as self-supporting. . . . Economic unity can be achieved only through free trade . . . and a common trade policy designed to serve Germany as a whole. A common financial policy is equally essential. Runaway inflation accompanied by economic paralysis may develop at any moment. . . . Common policies and nationwide implementation

> are equally essential for transportation, communications, food and agriculture, industry and foreign trade, if economic recovery is to be made possible.
>
> Central administrative agencies either under a provisional government or to be placed under a provisional government at an early date should be established without delay. As it now stands, economic integration is becoming less each day with the Soviet and French zones requiring approval for practically each item leaving their respective zones, and with the British and U.S. zones in self-defense moving in the same direction.

Clay told Eisenhower that he had halted the dismantlement of plants in the U.S. zone for reparations, but that "if economic unity is obtained, there is no reason why the reparations plan should not be implemented promptly."

Clay was equally eager to revive German political life, telling Eisenhower that he thought it was feasible to establish a provisional government for all of Germany and urging that the United States move without delay. Clay suggested that a Council of Minister-Presidents from the various *Länder* be assembled and "charged with the preliminary draft of a constitution to be placed before an elected constitutional convention, which would prepare for ratification by the people the future constitution for the German state."

Clay thought his views were generally acceptable to the British, and told Eisenhower that, "in theory, since they accord with Potsdam, they should be acceptable to the Russians." But, he noted, they "will be strongly resisted by the French," and if some agreement was not reached, he warned, "we face a deteriorating German economy which will create political unrest favorable to the development of Communism in Germany and a deterrent to its democratization. The next winter will be critical under any circumstances and a failure to obtain economic unity before the next winter sets in will make it almost unbearable. The suffering of the German people will be a serious charge against democracy and will develop a sympathy which may well defeat our other objectives in Germany."

If French and Russian agreement could not be obtained, Clay strongly recommended "that the British be approached to determine their willingness to combine their zone of occupation with ours.

If the British are willing for this merger to be accomplished, the French and Russian representatives should be advised that it is our proposal to effect this merger before winter, even though we would much prefer to obtain Allied unity in the treatment of Germany as a whole."

The following day, Clay met with reporters in Berlin in one of his regular press conferences. He was asked if he could expand on his remarks in the Allied Control Council pertaining to the cutoff of reparations deliveries and whether it was directed at the Russians. "Not to the Russians. It's to everybody. We simply announced, insofar as the U.S. zone is concerned, we are not going to dismantle any further plants except the ones that have already been allocated . . . until the economic unity on which reparations [are] based has been attained." He was then asked on what level that decision had been made:

> Right here. It has been reported, of course, to our government. We've always regarded Potsdam as a whole and not its parts, and . . . until economic unity is agreed . . . we don't feel that we can proceed further to dismantle plants. . . . The fact remains we do not have economic unity or agreement to obtain it. That doesn't mean there is any change whatever in U.S. policy with respect to reparations. There isn't. The U.S. policy with respect to reparations stands just as it was written at Potsdam. We are fully prepared to carry it out as soon as the conditions involved in Potsdam are also carried out.

Clay was pressed by the reporters as to whether the action was aimed at Russia or France. He avoided answering, except to stress the need that Germany be treated as an economic unit. Later he told Arthur L. Mayer of *The New Republic* that his differences with Sokolovsky on the Control Council were not that great, that the problem was France. "The Russians are tough horse-traders," said Clay, "but we are negotiating with them daily on a basis of reasonable give and take and are not faring too badly. The French, with their demand for the Saar and the internationalization of the Ruhr, are far more intransigent." Similarly, Walt Whitman Rostow, who was in Berlin in the spring of 1946 on a special mission for the State Department, confirms that Clay's action was aimed primarily at France. In a cable on June 10, 1946, to Charles Kindleberger in Washington, Rostow stated that "Whether correct or not it is the Berlin view that Clay's hold-up of reparations is designed rather more to get the French obstruction cleared up than to show up Russian intentions.

"As we have already gathered," said Rostow, "the OMGUS [Office of Military Government, United States] attitude towards the Soviets is one of cautious optimism. They feel, out of their experience, that hard-bargaining, straight-forward Americans who know their objectives, and who have reasonable objectives, can do business with the Russians. They emphasize the need for clarity, simplicity, and directness in all relations."

The cordial relations between Clay and Sokolovsky continued despite the reparations cutoff. When the Communist East Berlin press blasted Clay (in violation of Control Council regulations), Clay recalls that Sokolovsky tried to soften the blow. "We have always been good friends and I hope we will remain so despite the political differences between our governments," he told Clay at the next meeting of the Control Council.

Indeed, it was not until the second session of the Paris Council of Foreign Ministers, in July 1946, that the Russians seriously protested the reparations halt. For they realized that Clay's target had been the French, and that his purpose had been to force France to cooperate in quadripartite government.

In reflecting on the episode many years later, Clay said, "I don't think it [the reparations cutoff] really affected our relations with the Russians." But in Washington, Clay's action was immediately seized upon by the State Department and reinterpreted. What had been aimed at the French was deflected against the Soviets, in effect heightening the tension between Washington and Moscow. In what the 1980s would dub "spin control," Dean Acheson told the press that until Russia complied with the Potsdam Agreement (the specifics were left vague), the United States would continue to withhold reparations from the American zone. What had been a tactical maneuver by Clay to bring pressure on France had been converted by Washington into an important benchmark in the Cold War. As Professor John Gimbel, the leading American historian of the Occupation period, has written: "State Department functionaries [he mentions Acheson, Kennan, Cohen, and Matthews] shamelessly misled the American public about the reasons for Clay's reparations suspension and for the failure of the four powers to agree at Berlin." In Gimbel's words, the State Department "refused either to apply sanctions against France or to admit publicly that France was indeed the major problem in Germany. Instead, State Department functionaries expressed suspicions about Russian intentions and long-range objectives in Germany, and they did so despite evidence and arguments by Clay and Robert Murphy . . . that the Russians were cooperating to fulfill the terms of the Potsdam Agreement and that the French were much more recalcitrant."

· 22 ·

Coping with Crises

> No country can regain its self-respect nor progress to maturity in democratic processes in the presence of large occupying forces. No country will recognize its own guilt over a period of years if it lives in economic squalor under the shadow of mighty occupying armies. . . . Allied control over Germany should be exercised through leadership and not through command.
>
> Lucius D. Clay, July 19, 1946

BEFORE WORLD WAR II, GERMANY PRODUCED 83 PERcent of the food it consumed. When the war began, consumer intake was rationed at two thousand calories daily, not including the fresh fruit and vegetables that were frequently available from occupied Europe. And so long as the German army was able to live off the land in occupied countries, that ration was maintained. But by January 1945, Germany's military situation had worsened and consumer rations were cut to sixteen hundred calories, and then, in May 1945, to even less. As Colonel Hugh Hester,

Clay's agricultural adviser, noted, it would have been difficult to feed the Germans from domestic sources even under optimal conditions, but the division of Germany into four separate zones of occupation presented the United States and Britain with an almost impossible task.

To begin with, the vast German agricultural areas east of the Oder and Neisse rivers had been divided between Poland and the Soviet Union. The best cropland remaining in Germany was concentrated in the Soviet zone, but the fighting that had taken place in the spring of 1945 had made most of it temporarily unusable. Crops had not been planted; fuel and fertilizers were unavailable; most farm animals had been slaughtered; and much of the original work force was either in flight or in captivity.

In addition, most of the German regional food and agricultural offices had ceased to exist. National ministries no longer functioned. Nazi officials had gone into hiding, their offices closed and all records removed or destroyed. Warehouses, grain elevators, and food storage places had been heavily damaged. Germany's communications system had broken down completely, and it was virtually impossible to transport even the most essential supplies by truck or rail.

Clay, who was firmly committed to quadripartite control, was especially concerned about the situation in the Soviet zone. In 1945, the average ration in that part of Germany occupied by the Red Army had been reduced to one thousand calories a day, consisting mostly of bread, potatoes, and limited amounts of sugar. As he advised McCloy on October 5, "many will receive much less than this average" because of the almost total breakdown in transportation and distribution. The low food ration was already having its effect, said Clay:

> The death rate in many places has increased several fold, and infant mortality is approaching 65 percent in many places. By the spring of 1946, German observers expect that epidemics and malnutrition will claim 2.5 to 3 million victims between the Oder and the Elbe. Shortages of essential drugs, serums, and medicines further complicate the picture.

Clay was touched deeply by the suffering. He told McCloy that the "tragic situation was made even worse by the large influx of refugees and expellees from east of the Oder-Neisse, and from the Sudetenland —estimated conservatively at 9 to 10 million persons. No coordinated measures have been taken to direct this stream of refugees to specific regions or provide them with food and shelter. They gravitate toward the larger towns and cities which are becoming dangerously overcrowded. . . . During the last three months, they have been passing through Berlin alone at the rate of 500,000 or 600,000 per month. Of these, over 40 percent are children, many of them without parents."

The situation was better in the French zone, but not much. Baden and Württemberg had suffered less initial damage than the Soviet zone, but the French had confiscated all food within reach, and France's Army of Occupation was living rapaciously off the land. At the end of January, Clay received an emergency request from General Koenig for 110,000 tons of wheat "to avoid immediate cut in ration of Germans in French zone from 1380 calories to 1145." While Clay blamed French Occupation policies for most of the shortfall, he acknowledged that the situation was critical.

The following month, General Sir Brian Robertson was forced to cut rations in the British zone to a thousand calories—the lowest level of all four occupation zones, and, as Clay informed Washington, barely enough to sustain life, "and far below any minimum standard for the average consumer to maintain health for even a short period." Clay said that he did "not believe that such a ration could be continued in British zone without repercussions in all other zones, particularly if we continue a ration of 1500 calories," and he urgently requested Washington to seek means of raising the food level throughout Germany to fifteen hundred calories.

By March 1946, the situation had become critical in the American zone as well, owing primarily to the War Department's cancellation of scheduled wheat shipments from the United States. Washington urged Clay to share the dwindling food supply in the U.S. zone with the British and French. Clay balked. On March 6, he notified Hilldring that he was prepared to pool U.S. food resources with the British and French if ordered to do so, but not otherwise. "Such action," said Clay, "prior to treatment of Germany as an economic unit, is establishing in effect a unified policy in the three Western zones, which would adversely affect quadripartite control."

Reminding Hilldring that, based on War Department assurances, Clay had told the German Minister-Presidents that the United States would support a daily ration of 1,550 calories if the Germans supervised food collections from the countryside, where many farmers were hoarding their harvest, he noted: "This they have done. In point of fact, the Germans themselves were unwilling to raise the previous ration level until this commitment was given to them, and since the level was raised a considerable portion of the increased ration has been met from indigenous sources, leaving the Germans less than they formerly had to meet whatever ration is now established." Clay said that, in contrast to the other zones, "The U.S. zone has made every effort to husband indigenous resources and military authorities have contributed substantially from Army stocks to the feeding of displaced persons, relieving in part this drain on German resources."

Clay told Washington that, unlike commanders in other zones, he had not used German resources to meet American Occupation needs. However, "while we were conserving our resources, the French in particular used large quantities of indigenous resources to support their own needs. It would seem unjust to the Germans in the U.S. zone who have met our requirements to make them pay the penalty for such action in other zones." And, he added, "Perhaps I am off-base, but I find it difficult to understand when I see the exploitation which has taken place and is taking place in at least two other zones, why the U.S. should divide its resources without requiring as a condition thereto an agreement for the future treatment of Germany as an economic unit."

By the spring of 1946, it was clear that all Europe was suffering a disastrous food shortage. America's wartime Allies were forced to cut domestic rations; the liberated countries of Western Europe suffered even more, and defeated enemies such as Germany and Austria were relegated to the meager leavings of an already overburdened supply line. The United States had become the breadbasket of the world, and food exports desperately needed to sustain life in the U.S. zone of Germany were diverted elsewhere.

On March 16, 1946, Clay cabled Washington that the failure to receive wheat shipments as scheduled made it impossible to maintain a 1,550-calorie ration in the American zone. He said that unless new shipments were scheduled, the ration would be reduced to twelve hundred calories immediately. "The reduced ration will bring a rapid deterioration in health. It is inadequate to comply with the 'prevention of disease and unrest' formula [in JCS 1067]. . . . The seriousness of the situation cannot be overemphasized."

The following day, Clay prepared an emergency cable for General McNarney, the European Theater commander, to send to General Eisenhower in Washington. After restating the urgent need for the wheat previously promised by the War Department, Clay asked to be relieved of command—his first of many resignations over the next two years, all of which were triggered by his overriding concern that German interests be protected. Clay refused to accept the residual role into which Germany had been cast. He preferred to resign rather than be responsible for a policy he did not believe in. As McNarney advised Washington: "Clay feels strongly in view of his commitments to the German officials made in good faith, that the reduction in ration will destroy his usefulness as Deputy Military Governor. He has asked me for his relief after the reductions have been ordered."

Clay mentioned McNarney's cable in his memoirs, but made no reference to any resignation. He was, it seems, ready to resign if Germany was short-changed, but his rigid code of professional behavior prevented him from mentioning it publicly. Nevertheless, the threat that Clay would leave galvanized Eisenhower to intervene in Washington, as Clay had hoped it would. The following week, the War Department told Clay that an additional 150,000 tons of wheat would be forthcoming.

One of Clay's problems at this time was that officials in Washington, particularly at the Department of Agriculture, were still fighting World War II. And they preferred to calculate German needs using their own figures. Agriculture's statisticians arbitrarily added two hundred calories daily to each German's ration because of presumed black-market purchases—a figure that Clay pointed out was available only to those few Germans with the means to buy on the black market. Clay told Washington the additional grain shipments would help (he had withdrawn his request to be relieved), but that he was reducing the daily ration in the U.S. zone to 1,275 calories, and if additional commitments from the U.S. were not received quickly, a further reduction to a thousand calories was inevitable. Clay compared the deteriorating situation in the American zone with that in the Russian zone, where the Soviets had made a surprising amount of food available from Red Army sources in late 1945, and were now feeding fifteen hundred calories, "and will continue to do so until the next harvest season," when it would presumably increase. For the first time, Clay couched his appeal to Washington in anti-Communist terms. Clay did not yet see the Soviet Union as an adversary. But if it would get more food for the American zone, he was willing to cry wolf. Said Clay:

> We have insisted on democratic processes in the U.S. zone and have maintained a strict neutrality between political parties. As a result the Communist Party has made little inroad. However, there is no choice between becoming a Communist on 1500 calories and a believer in democracy on 1000 calories. It is my sincere belief that our proposed ration allowance in Germany will not only defeat our objective in middle Europe but will pave the road to a Communist Germany.

For a brief period in early 1946, conditions in the Soviet zone compared favorably with those in the West. The Red Army had provided sufficient rations to bring daily food consumption up to a level of fifteen hundred calories, and a major financial restructuring temporarily provided full employment. Inflationary pressures eased; work incentives were quickly re-established; and there was a much smaller black market than in the Western zones. The people simply had less time for it, and the penalties for being caught were severe.

It was at this point that Clay first acknowledged the possibility of potential competition with the Soviet Union over the future of Germany, but he still did not believe that it was inevitable. To the contrary, he thought quadripartite government could succeed. And in the unlikely event of a split, Clay was confident that the West would prevail, unless Washington deliberately kicked away the opportunity. Failure to provide minimum food rations for the German people could do just that. To this end, Clay told the War Department he knew of no additional information he could send that had not already been provided. "As the occupying power in our zone we have assumed some obligations even though the Germans are an enemy people." Clay said he would contact former President Herbert Hoover, who was then in Europe, and seek his assistance in meeting the food crisis.

Clay credits President Hoover with recognizing the calamitous situation facing Germany and bringing the necessary pressure to bear on Washington to increase grain deliveries. Where Clay could not move the government's bureaucracy, Hoover rolled over it. President Truman had rehabilitated Hoover's standing as a former president (Truman believed FDR had treated Hoover shabbily) and frequently used him when bipartisan efforts were required. In the early spring of 1946, he appointed Hoover chairman of the Emergency Famine Commission, seeking to employ his administrative talents in a fashion similar to the great role in European relief Hoover played after World War I. As a result, Hoover's prestige was at its height. But it was several months before Hoover's influence made itself felt.

When April grain shipments once again fell below War Department commitments (there was a thirty-four-thousand-ton deficit), Clay exploded. "The physical condition of the population is deteriorating," he told Washington. "In my view it is imperative that the ration be restored to 1,275 calories, and particularly that the bread ration be raised within the next several weeks. This we cannot do until we know what we are going to get."

Clay said he would "rather be told we are going to get nothing than to be given commitments which we, in turn, pass on to our German officials for planning purposes and then not have these commitments met. Twice now we have been forced to go to our German officials to back down on commitments made by the government of the United States. Nothing could be more damaging to our prestige."

Also in May, a special tripartite team examining the food situation in the three Western zones reported what Clay described as a "nutritional disaster." According to Clay, "rickets is becoming prevalent in children from zero to six years of age. Retarded and arrested growth is evident in those from six to eighteen years of age with the children underweight and continuing to lose weight. Signs of malnutrition are common and anaemia is prevalent. Famine edema, which was evident immediately after the Occupation began but which had disappeared, has reappeared in many urban areas and is becoming more prevalent." The deterioration would accelerate unless more food was provided promptly, Clay said, concluding, "our objectives are facing certain failure unless some relief is forthcoming."

By autumn, with a slightly better-than-average harvest, the situation had improved to the point where Clay could restore the ration in the U.S. zone to 1,550 calories. But the relief proved temporary. The winter of 1946–47 was the most severe in Europe since World War I, and food again was in short supply.

"We have only a three weeks' supply of grain," Clay told Assistant Secretary of War Howard Petersen during a teleconference in May,

1947, "and there is nothing left to collect [in Germany] until the next harvest." Clay then said that unless shipments from America were resumed immediately, the Germans would soon be without bread.

PETERSEN: Recent newspaper stories in *New York Times,* some by-lined by Jack Raymond and Edward Murrow . . . blame crisis on failure to ship food from this country.
CLAY: We do not see why you have to read *New York Times* to know the Germans are starving. Our own cables have again and again pointed out our need for import schedules to be met. You are reading only the results which we tried to point out in January, February, March, and April.

Saying that he did not "censor any newspapermen nor American personnel working for military government," Clay continued: "I do not believe such censorship would work and in fact am sure we get more good than harm for our unrestricted press policy. I think all of us blame crisis on our failure to receive scheduled imports from wherever they were supposed to come."

Once again, President Hoover came to Clay's assistance. With the Republicans now in control of both houses of the 80th Congress, Hoover intervened directly with the Appropriations Committees to insist that food to Germany be given a higher priority. In particular, Congressman John Taber of New York, chairman of the House Appropriations Committee and a tight-fisted fiscal conservative, was a lifelong admirer of Herbert Hoover and had complete confidence in his judgment. At Hoover's request, Taber introduced and steered through Congress a $300-million deficiency appropriation to buy food for Germany in 1947, with an additional $600 million slated for 1948. Also at Hoover's urging, the War Department authorized Clay to use high-nutrition Army field rations to provide a noon meal for the 3.5 million schoolchildren in the American and British zones. And as Clay later acknowledged, "The child feeding program did more to convince the German people of our desire to re-create their nation than any other action on our part."

Q: During the worst of the food crisis, you started to weigh Germans?
CLAY: It was as effective as anything we could think of to get the

money to import food, because we had to make a case before the Bureau of the Budget and Congress, and we needed some objective figures. My surgeon general, Dr. Morrison Stayer, came up with the idea of weighing a representative sample of Germans after I had asked him to develop some means of illustrating what was happening.

The history of the American occupation of Germany, and of western Germany's subsequent democratic development, cannot be understood without an appreciation of the bitter struggle waged by the military government to provide food and the other necessities of life to a defeated enemy. Clay used every weapon in his arsenal of political support to circumvent the *vae victis* mood in Allied capitals, and when one path was blocked, he found another.

Clay was equally concerned that the Germans be provided quickly with the means for limited self-government. He was fearful that the long-term effects of a military occupation would snuff out what he believed was a growing democratic sentiment, and he was alarmed that the Russians were moving much more quickly than the Western powers to re-establish German political life. In September 1945, the Soviets announced the establishment of five *Länder* governments in their zone and the creation of twelve German administrative agencies to conduct essential services. Fearful that the Russians would score an important breakthrough and possibly establish the pattern for a future German government, Clay advised Washington on October 15, 1945, of his intention to move quickly to re-establish political life in the American zone. "As you know," he wrote McCloy, "the Russians have set up a complete German administration for their zone. I have been reluctant to create any such agency for our zone for fear it might impede the treatment of Germany as an economic entity. In view of the delay in establishing the central agencies, however, we have concluded that some German machinery is essential for coordinating the activities of the three *Länder* in our zone."

Clay said that he planned to create a council of the three *Länder* in the U.S. zone (the *Länderrat),* which would enable the Germans to coordinate their activities and "relieve our staff of the direct coordination to some extent," and he told McCloy he did not believe this would "impede the creation of the central agencies" for Germany as a whole, and he hoped that what had been agreed at Potsdam would be realized eventually.

On October 17, 1945, Clay met for the first time with the Minister-Presidents of the American zone in Stuttgart. Responsibility for day-to-day administration, he told them, would be returned quickly to German hands. While economic unification and the creation of all-German administrative machinery remained the goal of U.S. policy, the fact was that neither existed at the present time. Nonetheless, said Clay, "policy coordination will be your job, not ours. I would like to emphasize that within the framework of the policies of the United States, the responsibility will be yours. We shall not dictate so long as you abide by these policies."

Clay's staff believed that he was moving too quickly, and that the Germans were not ready for self-government. For the most part, Washington agreed. Nevertheless, Clay pressed ahead with elections at the local level. In the first place, he believed the Germans could do most jobs in Germany better than the officers and enlisted personnel assigned to military government. But, more important, he saw the elections as an essential first step in restoring democracy. "If the Germans are to learn democratic methods," he wrote McCloy, "I think the best way is to start them off quickly at local levels." As he told James Pollock, his senior civil affairs adviser, "in order to swim, you have to get into the water." Clay later remarked that he "enjoyed teasing" Pollock about "liberal professors of political science trying to restrain hard-bitten soldiers from restoring the ballot to a people who had been deprived of their right to vote."

Giving the newly established *Länderrat* increased responsibility enabled Clay to reduce the size of military government still further. Already down to twelve thousand (from an initial twenty thousand), it would be cut by another four thousand in the next six months.

Despite the fact that he spoke no German, Clay's monthly meetings with the Minister-Presidents in Stuttgart were a source of considerable personal satisfaction. With his patrician Southern manner barely concealing his intensity and drive, Clay was a man of extraordinary personal dignity. His demeanor demanded respect, and he was punctilious in respecting the dignity of others. If he dealt with the German Minister-Presidents at arm's length, it was abundantly clear that he had the highest regard both for the men themselves and for the offices they held. After each official session with the Minister-Presidents, Clay initiated informal conversations over coffee. Similarly, he obviously enjoyed talking to the German press. "The German reporters at first could not believe that they were permitted to question the Military Governor," said Clay. "They watched the give and take with the Allied press for several meetings before they gained enough confidence to ask questions themselves."

Clay's satisfaction with the Stuttgart meetings was reciprocated by the Germans. According to a German observer at the sessions, "the General's speeches were concerned with subjects that were frequently unpleasant but always vital. They were masterpieces of precision. Delivered for the most part without notes in an unobtrusive but soldierly and distinct voice, concise and to the point, occasionally spiced with a sprinkling of humor, Clay minced no words without being offensive. Never repeating or correcting himself, the General spoke in brief sentences which were individually translated. He never failed to impress his audience with his sincerity and determination. It was through Clay's appearances at the *Länderrat* that the American government presented itself at its best to the representatives of the German people."

In late 1945 and early 1946, the Soviets stepped up their efforts to appeal to the Germans politically. The food provided by the Red Army was one example. In addition, a far-reaching land reform broke up the large Prussian agricultural estates and redistributed the land to those who had worked it. The educational system was also turned upside down in the Soviet zone, and a thoroughgoing purge removed all teachers not considered reliable. Although this initially reduced educational standards (and caused many middle-class Germans to flee westward), it provided an essential base for implanting Communist ideas. The most important move undertaken in the Soviet zone was the attempt to broaden Communism's attraction by establishing a common front with the Socialists, in effect uniting German Marxism under a common banner.

Western observers, particularly in the early postwar period, too frequently overlooked the fact that Marxism was not an alien philosophy in Germany. Marx and Engels were nothing if not German, and the entire logical structure of Marxist thought traced directly to eighteenth- and nineteenth-century German philosophy—particularly the works of Hegel and Feuerbach.

Historically, German Marxism was the dominant force in the international Socialist movement. Before World War I, the German Social Democratic Party (SPD) was not only the largest Marxist party in Europe, but the largest party in the German Reichstag as well. It brought together under a common leadership (and rigid party discipline) both the revolutionary left wing of German Marxism and the trade-union right wing.

In August 1914, the SPD had bitterly divided over the military appropriations for World War I. But the appeal of German nationalism, and the electoral force of the trade union movement behind it, led the party caucus to support the appropriations in the Reichstag. And despite the bitter division in the caucus, the SPD vote when it was announced was unanimous. As the war dragged on, however, the divisions within the SPD increased. When a second appropriations measure came before the Reichstag in 1915, the left wing of the party broke ranks, voted against the measure, and formed themselves into the Independent Social Democratic Party of Germany (USPD). That split in the German Marxist movement was traumatic for all involved. It became a permanent fixture on the political landscape. The majority Socialists, the SPD, remained the largest party in Germany until 1932 and continued to draw their principal support from the trade unions. The SPD supported the German war effort in World War I, was instrumental in founding the Weimar Republic, and provided Germany with its first president, Friedrich Ebert. It also was the only party in the Reichstag to vote against Hitler's Enabling Act in 1933.

The revolutionary Socialists, the USPD, went into opposition in 1915 and opposed the war effort; its leaders were quickly imprisoned. Released in 1918, they reorganized into the Spartacus League, took to the streets, and fomented the Spartacus Revolution of 1918–19. That revolt was brutally put down by the German army. Although its leaders, Karl Liebknecht and Rosa Luxemburg, were executed, the membership of the USPD reorganized into the German Communist Party (KPD) in 1920. Throughout the period of the Weimar Republic, the German Marxist movement remained divided between the SPD and the KPD—that is, between the two traditional wings of Marxist thought: one revolutionary, the KPD; the other evolutionary, the SPD. And the rivalry was bitter. In fact, the failure of the two parties to cooperate in 1932–33 was one of the major contributing factors to Hitler's rise to power.

This had several important ramifications for postwar Germany.

First, and most important, Communism enjoyed significant indigenous support; it did not depend solely on the bayonets of the Red Army. Revolutionary Marxism, organized as the Communist Party since 1920, was an important political movement with deep roots in Germany's past. Its heroes and martyrs, particularly Luxemburg and Liebknecht, were authentic German personalities. And though the party's leadership had coexisted under Soviet tutelage since its inception (and many had spent World War II in the Soviet Union), it had always enjoyed the consistent support of 15–20 percent of the German electorate.

Second, the idea of Marxist unity had a transcendental appeal for many Germans. The division of the party in 1915 was viewed with genuine regret. And the failure of the two divergent wings to unite against Hitler in 1932 was clearly recognized as a major error.

The Soviet occupation authorities sought to capitalize on both factors. In June 1945, the KDP was quickly revived in the Soviet zone (Walter Ulbricht and other Communist leaders accompanied the Red Army when it rolled into Germany), and a concerted effort was made to organize a broad coalition of so-called antifascist parties with the KPD in the forefront. These efforts culminated in the Soviet zone in February 1946 with the merger of the KPD and the Social Democratic Party into a new, consolidated Marxist party, the Socialist Unity Party (SED). The Social Democrats in the three Western zones resisted the idea of merging with the Communists, but the SPD in the Soviet zone had little choice. Nevertheless, it must also be recognized that the idea of a single Marxist party had substantial theoretical support in Germany.

The Soviets at that time believed that it was possible to win broad public support under the banner of the Socialist Unity Party (in pre-Hitler elections, the combined vote of the SPD and KPD approached 40 to 50 percent of the electorate), and scheduled parliamentary *(Landtag)* elections in their zone for March 1946—well before any of the three Western powers were prepared to hold similar elections. And, of course, the Soviet authorities openly supported their new party, the SED.

Concerned with the developments in the Soviet zone, many of Clay's political advisers urged him to challenge Soviet actions in the Control Council. He flatly refused. Similarly, when Washington requested that he take steps to aid the democratic parties, Clay disagreed.

"If we did," he cabled the War Department, "Military Government would have clearly violated its announced principles of complete political neutrality. Such action would be misunderstood in Germany and would prove a step backward in teaching democracy."

Clay also refused to license a political press in the American zone. Party newspapers, he thought, were contrary to the open democracy he sought to encourage. In a critical decision that was to set the pattern for postwar Germany, Clay resisted pressure from Washington to restore Germany's prewar tradition of party-owned newspapers. Clay said the British had tried it and now believed that it was a mistake. By contrast, the independent press in the American zone "reflects differences of political thought since its publishers and editors come from several political parties. They are responsible to their readers and are not responsible to the dictates of party leadership. We are confident that we are obtaining a more objective press as a result."

A further example of Clay's attitude toward the press is illustrated by his refusal to intervene in early 1947 when elements of the German press bitterly attacked Dr. Reinhold Maier, the Minister-President of Baden-Württemberg, and one of Clay's most effective German subordinates. The charge against Maier was that, as a prewar member of the old Center Party (Germany's Catholic party), he had voted for Hitler's Enabling Act in 1933. Maier asked Clay to intervene to halt the press attacks and to order Radio Stuttgart to grant Maier airtime to reply. Clay refused. In a personal letter to Dr. Maier, Clay commiserated about the vulnerability of those in public life and advised Maier that "the development of a skin impervious enough to withstand the barbs of one's enemies, and the courage and will to fight in the arena of public opinion" were essential attributes for a politician. In a kind but blunt way, Clay told Maier that his request reflected a "fundamental misconception of the function of the press and radio in a democracy," where radio and press criticism were inevitable.

In a passage that now seems remarkable (how many Army generals have read Milton?), Clay paraphrased the famous statement in the *Areopagitica,* "If truth and falsehood grapple in the open, my philosophy is that one should never be afraid of the result."

> If military government should do as you request and intervene directly to require that Radio Stuttgart be instructed to use its time to broadcast certain specific speeches you desire to be broadcasted, . . . in

> my opinion military government would be doing you, and the newly elected government of Württemberg-Baden, and the cause of democracy a serious disservice.
>
> Government in a democracy cannot control the press and other media without destroying them, as has been so disastrously demonstrated during the Nazi regime. I feel sure that you will recognize this essential principle after a little further consideration.

Throughout his tenure in Germany, Clay refused to imitate Soviet methods of favoring one party over another or one politician over another. Under his tight direction, military government maintained a strictly hands-off attitude. The idea that the United States might promote a future German leader was alien to Clay's democratic creed, but, perhaps more important, he believed it would prove counterproductive.

The results of the first elections in the Soviet zone confirmed the correctness of Clay's policy. The SED, despite significant Soviet support, received 47.5 percent of the vote in the Russian zone—a figure comparable to the support the SPD and KPD had enjoyed before Hitler—but there had been no decisive breakthrough. In Berlin, where elections were also held, the traditional Social Democratic Party, the old majority Socialists, retained control with 48.7 percent. There the SED received only 19.8 percent—which was less than the German Communists had received in any election from 1928 to 1933.

When 1946 had begun, Clay's hopes for Allied unity were high. As he was fond of telling Washington, quadripartite government was a government of compromise, and the agreement he had reached with the Russians, British, and French on the level of German industry had led him to be cautiously optimistic.

Unfortunately, the agreement on German industry fell apart in February, when the French informed the Control Council that they planned to annex the Saar and attach it directly to France. Clay objected vigorously, once more reminding the French that the Potsdam Agreement contemplated treating Germany as a single economic unit—a position with which Robertson and Sokolovsky strongly agreed. Afterward Clay told the War Department that the French had thrown a wrench into the works, and he was convinced that no further progress could be made in Germany until the question of the Saar was resolved "at the governmental level." Clay recognized that the future of quadripartite government was out of his hands. Two weeks later,

Secretary of State Byrnes formally advised Clay that the question of Germany's western frontier was a matter to be solved by the four powers at the Council of Foreign Ministers.

The Council of Foreign Ministers (CFM) was one of the positive byproducts of the Potsdam Conference. Composed of the foreign ministers of Britain, France, the Soviet Union, and the United States, the CFM was mandated to meet quarterly, rotating the site of the meeting among the four powers. The purpose was to continue grappling with the unfinished issues of World War II and such other problems as might arise: drafting the peace treaties, removing troops from various theaters (Iran and Korea, for example), atomic energy, and of course, the central issue of postwar Germany.

The Council convened for the first time in Moscow in the fall of 1945, and then in January 1946 in London. The third session convened in Paris in late April 1946. Altogether, Secretary Byrnes, British Foreign Secretary Ernest Bevin, Bidault, and Molotov would spend almost one hundred days negotiating the fine points of the Italian and satellite peace treaties. But the main issue, the future of Germany, once again proved intractable.

In both plenary sessions and informal conversations, Bidault pressed French claims for a splintered Germany: the Ruhr, Germany's industrial heartland with a population of thirteen million, should be detached and placed under international control; the left bank of the Rhine, including the great cities of Cologne and Mainz, should be garrisoned permanently by Allied troops; and the Saar, Germany's westernmost province, integrated economically with France. Bidault made it clear that until those issues were resolved to France's satisfaction, there would be no progress on German unity.

Byrnes, Bevin, and Molotov deferred action on Bidault's demands. Each insisted on the urgent necessity for treating Germany as an economic unit, but, for different reasons, none of the three wanted to pressure France. Byrnes and Bevin strongly opposed French plans to detach the Ruhr and the Rhineland, but were reluctant to make a public issue of it for fear of embarrassing Bidault and his pro-Western Mouvement Républicain Populaire (MRP) in upcoming French elections. Soviet Foreign Minister Molotov shared Byrnes's and Bevin's distaste for French plans but did not want to compromise the chances of the French Communist Party (PCF) in those same elections.

Secretary Byrnes, hoping as always to fashion a compromise that might bring France along, proposed accepting the French proposal on the Saar, if that might make it possible for France to agree to a central, unified administration for Germany. Clay, who attended the conference at Byrnes's invitation, reluctantly went along with Byrnes's strategy—partly out of personal obligation to the Secretary, partly because the Saar was so small that the overall effect on Germany would be minimal, and partly because, like Byrnes, he hoped that it would be the bait that might entice France into quadripartite cooperation.

Whatever hopes Byrnes and Clay had were soon dashed. The French evidenced no sign of settling for the Saar, and throughout the summer and fall of 1946 they continued to resist all efforts to establish the common administrative agencies upon which German recovery depended. As Clay reported subsequently:

> General Robertson and I were to try many times to obtain agreement to central German administrations only to find that there was no change in the French position. In one of our last meetings in 1946 Robertson made an eloquent plea for progress in this field, pointing out that the gap between us was widening and that it could be closed in no other way. Unless it was closed, he felt, we would inevitably drift so far apart that unification would become impossible.

The question of the Saar proved to be one of the most disagreeable issues Clay confronted during his entire stay in Germany. Sharing a common border with France, and with less than one percent of the German population, it was the smallest of the *Länder,* and had suffered considerable destruction during the war. In 1919, the Versailles Treaty had granted France a mandate over the Saar for fifteen years, to be followed by a plebiscite in 1935. When the Saarlanders, under strong Nazi influence, voted to return to Germany at that time, many in France believed the results were tainted. After Germany's defeat in 1945, successive French governments sought to regain permanent control of the Saar (it contained one-tenth of Germany's coal deposits and 12 percent of its steel capacity), hoping initially to persuade the Saarlanders to request economic fusion with France. But despite the Nazi defeat, those living in the Saar were no more interested in joining France in 1945 than they had been after the First World War. Accordingly, on December 20, 1946, General Koenig informed his colleagues on the Allied Control Council that in the absence of any agreement on

Grandfather William James Clay (1829–1911).

Grandmother Edna Peak Clay (1829–1914).

Frances Sarah Clay (1860–1941).

Senator Clay (left) *and his father.*

Senator Alexander Stephens Clay (1853–1910).

Clay and Lucius D. Clay, Jr., Camp Humphreys, 1919.

Captain Clay, Camp Humphreys, 1919.

Clay on ROTC duty at Auburn, 1921.

To Sail for Philippines

CAPT. AND MRS. LUCIUS D. CLAY,

Who will sail shortly for the Philippines, where Capt. Clay will take over his new post as aide to Gen. Douglas MacArthur, military adviser to the Commonwealth Government of the Philippine Islands. Capt. and Mrs. Clay will spend a few days in Marietta, Ga., before leaving for the West Coast.—Hessler Photo.

Washington Evening Star, *August 4, 1937.*

The Philippines, 1938. Wrote Clay: "Kaliwa River showing communication facilities now available" (above) *and "Lunch on the Kaliwa River"* (below).

Major Clay as District Engineer, Denison, Texas, 1939.

Clay and Marjorie celebrate Christmas in Denison, 1939.

Clay receives the news that he has been ordered to head the Emergency Airport Program.

Joking with Harry Hopkins at a meeting of the Combined Munitions Assignment Board, 1943.

Berlin victory parade, 1945. Left to right: *Sokolovsky, Clay, Patton, Zhukov, Douglas, Robertson.*

Eisenhower and Clay, 1945.

Ike, Clay, Zhukov, and Sokolovsky at the ceremony following the award of the Order of Kutuzov to Clay, 1945.

Clay and Mrs. Roosevelt leaving Clay's quarters in Berlin, 1946.

Among the paintings rescued by Clay: (opposite, clockwise from top left) *Botticelli,* Venus; *ter Borch,* Fatherly Advice; *Holbein the Younger,* George Gisze; *Cranach the Elder,* Fountain of Youth. (This page, clockwise from top left) *Dürer,* Hieronymus Holzschuher; *Rubens,* St. Sebastian; *Canaletto,* St. Mark's Square; *Rembrandt,* Hendrikje Stoffels.

Clay with Secretary of State Byrnes in Stuttgart in September 1946. Economics Minister Ludwig Erhard at right.

Clay as Sokolovsky's guest at a Soviet reception. Political advisers Sobolov and Murphy look on.

American delegation at Moscow Conference of Foreign Ministers, March 1947. Left to right: *Dulles, Mark Clark, Bedell Smith, Marshall, Ben Cohen, Murphy, Clay.*

Clay and Marjorie, Berlin, 1948.

Military Governor opens the baseball season in Berlin.

Military Governor of Germany, 1948.

Clay and Sokolovsky at the Allied Control Council, 1948.

Berlin airlift. WALTER SANDERS, LIFE

Clay, at the Alfred E. Smith Memorial Foundation dinner in New York, November 1, 1948, announcing President Truman's decision to reinforce the Berlin airlift. Left: *Governor Thomas E. Dewey.* Right: *Francis Cardinal Spellman.*

The Military Governor pays an unprecedented call on Mayor Reuter in a gesture of respect, May 1949. ASSOCIATED PRESS

Clay and sons, Major Lucius D. Clay, Jr., and Frank B. Clay, with Frank B. Clay, Jr., in Berlin, 1949.

500,000 Berliners turn out to honor Clay in a special ceremony at the Schöneberg Rathaus. WIDE WORLD PHOTO

Clay addressing the House of Representatives, May 1949. Speaker Rayburn in the chair. UNITED PRESS INTERNATIONAL

New York greets Clay with ticker-tape parade.

Clay displays interstate highway system to Ike.

An emotional Clay addresses Berliners at the Berlin Wall in August 1961. LBJ and Brandt look on.

Clay chins himself up the Berlin Wall for a glimpse of East Berlin.
UNITED PRESS INTERNATIONAL

With JFK during his 1963 visit to Berlin. Adenauer is at left, Brandt at right.

Discussing the 1971 Berlin Accords with Dewey, Nixon, Kissinger, and Acheson (hidden by Kissinger).

Formal portrait for Continental Can, 1960.

Clay's headstone and footstone. RAYMOND AALBONE COPYRIGHT © 1989

the Saar at the Council of Foreign Ministers, France would unilaterally establish a customs barrier the following day between the Saar and the rest of Germany. The effect would be to integrate the Saar economically with France.

Clay responded with a blistering attack on the French and followed up by speaking directly to the Allied press in Berlin—a sharp departure from normal procedure. Clay's instructions from Washington had been to support the economic integration of the Saar with France in quadripartite discussions, but to oppose any unilateral French action. Unfortunately, the State Department had its wires crossed. Secretary Byrnes, in a personal letter to Bidault after the CFM had adjourned, indicated that while the United States could not support unilateral French action to incorporate the Saar, neither would the United States oppose it. For whatever reason, Clay had not been informed of Byrnes's commitment.

In the dust-up that followed, Byrnes told Clay of his letter to Bidault and said that he did not think that the United States could now protest. Embarrassed at being caught off base, Clay pointed out that he had not been informed of the shift in U.S. policy, but in any event he thought that the French action "was another example of French contempt and disregard of Allied Control Authority which defeats the purpose of quadripartite government."

When Clay's opposition to the French move was reported by the press, Under Secretary of State Acheson announced at a Washington press conference that Clay's views did not represent the policy of the United States. In a teleconference with the War Department immediately afterward, Clay asked to be relieved.

> I know I have talked a lot about leaving Germany [Clay told Assistant Secretary of War Howard Petersen]. However, if [Acheson] is quoted correctly I feel my usefulness here is at an end and I would like to be recalled immediately.

Clay said that his "difficulties with the French have been too real over too long a time for me to continue to sit with them in view of State Department repudiation of my actions, which were based on specific State Department instructions. I feel deeply in this matter, completely let down, and I am sure there is no other answer."

Telling Clay that he thought his protest of the French action on the Saar was "wholly warranted" and that he would speak to Acheson at once, Petersen said, "If I cannot get satisfaction from Acheson, will get matter to Byrnes soonest."

The next day, Clay followed up with an "Eyes Only—Top Secret" cable to Petersen in which he again objected to the unilateral nature of the French action. "If we condone such action by France," Clay asked, "how can we ever protest unilateral action by others?"

On December 30, Secretary Byrnes did his best to reassure Clay. Saying that he was "distressed that the misunderstanding as to the Saar should cause you embarrassment," Byrnes took full responsibility for the confusion. "I am disturbed about it," said Byrnes, "chiefly because you are the only person I would not want to embarrass in any way."

That settled it. Clay told Petersen that since Byrnes had taken personal responsibility, the matter was closed. "As far as I am concerned, I cannot feel hurt by anything done personally by Mr. Byrnes due to my high regard for him and to my appreciation for the confidence which he holds for me. I shall try to work myself out of the position which I have been put in here as best I may, but in view of Mr. Byrnes' personal cable, no further action appears necessary."

To Byrnes, Clay cabled a special New Year's greeting. "Regardless of embarrassment in present instance, I would be more embarrassed if I did not accept cheerfully any personal action which you have taken or may take. Marjorie joins me in affection and best wishes for Mrs. Byrnes and yourself for a Happy New Year." Throughout his public career, and later in private life, Clay cherished Byrnes's friendship and counsel. Clay gave the eulogy at Byrnes's funeral in 1962, and later headed a fund drive to establish a scholarship fund in Byrnes's honor at the University of South Carolina.

The French annexation of the Saar in late 1946 reflected France's long-standing concern with the preponderant size of its German neighbor, and was simply one more manifestation of an intense desire to prevent German unity in any form. After World War I, France had followed a similar strategy by actively encouraging separatism among the various German *Länder,* particularly in the Rhineland and Bavaria: an attempt to undo what Bismarck had put together in 1870–71. But after World War II, the appeal of outright separatism had paled in Germany. Only in Bavaria was there any glimmer of incipient independence, and as Clay recalled:

"It was not a *major* problem. But it was always a problem. It was particularly acute at first because of the difficulty in getting the Bavarians—who had a food surplus—to cooperate in making that surplus available for distribution elsewhere. And in fact, they never did. The Bavarian farmer lived very well all during the Occupation.

"But out-and-out separatism existed only on a very minor part. Our Bavarian Minister-Presidents were really not so inclined and they were very able people. And it was completely foreign to my way of thinking. It is alleged that the French may have encouraged it. I personally have no knowledge of that happening, and I doubt if it did."

Q: General, the Free University of Berlin was established at about this time. Were you involved?
CLAY: Very much so. Ken Foss, who was a newspaper reporter in Berlin [for the *Neue Zeitung*]—I think he had been a Rhodes Scholar—came to me and told me that some German students and German professors from the Humboldt University [in the Soviet sector] had approached him to find out what were the chances of moving over to West Berlin. I put Foss on our payroll and gave him the job of working it out. We found that we could vacate a number of our military government buildings, which were part of the old Kaiser Wilhelm Institute, and that we could make them available as well as a substantial grant from the German funds in our budget. This was sufficient to make the professors feel secure that their tenure would continue, and so they moved over.
Q: Did you clear this with Washington?
CLAY: No. This was entirely within my powers as Military Governor. Later, after we got this moving, the Ford Foundation helped tremendously. But that was later, after it had already proven that it was a going university.

Not only did Clay not clear the founding of the Free University with Washington, but he overruled his own education division in the military government to do so. Clay was a shrewd judge of character. He was impressed by Foss and the students he represented, and had no doubt that the university (which is now the largest German-speaking university in the world) would succeed. Instead of taking the advice of the professional educators in military government—who offered some two dozen reasons why a new university could not be created—Clay relied on his own instincts, and the informal advice he received from Herman Wells, Carl Friedrich, and James Pollock. Wells, Friedrich, and Pollock were not in the education division of OMGUS, but Clay more than respected their judgment. And when they confirmed to him that the idea of a new university in West Berlin was feasible, Clay went ahead. According to Wells, who was then president of Indiana University, Clay's boldness "took my breath away." But Clay "brushed aside all doubts, said it could be done, and asked me to put the machinery in motion."

Walter Heller, who was Clay's financial adviser at the time (and later chairman of the Council of Economic Advisers under Presidents Kennedy and Johnson), suggested to Clay that interim funding could be provided from local funds generated by the military government, and Clay, unknown to anyone, authorized Ken Foss to transfer 20 million Reichsmarks from a military-government account to a German trustee on the eve of the West German currency reform. Had the money stayed in the military government account, it would have been liquidated. The move provided the Free University with a 2-million-Deutsche mark nest egg, and the conversion was conducted entirely in secret, at Clay's personal direction.

By the summer of 1946, Clay had become thoroughly dispirited. His problems with the French showed no sign of letting up; he was having great difficulty convincing Washington to provide the necessary food to prevent mass starvation in Germany; quadripartite government had gone off the rails; and, to make matters worse, U.S. military headquarters in Europe (USFET) was seeking once again to subordinate military government to tactical Army control. When the staff at USFET declined to submit its Occupation budget to the military government for approval, Clay requested immediate retirement. In a Top Secret-Eyes Only cable to General Echols in Washington, Clay said that he had "applied for immediate return home and retirement." Clay said Echols would understand. "My stated reasons are I am tired and want a long rest. Hope I am not letting you down, but [I am] convinced action is [in the] best interest of military government."

Not surprisingly, Clay had become the subject of considerable resentment at USFET headquarters in Frankfurt. His determination to keep military government independent of the Army's General Staff annoyed former combat commanders, while his increasing concern for developing democratic procedures in Germany confused the brown-shoe generals of America's peacetime military establishment. Clay's long friendship with Byrnes and Eisenhower may have rankled even more, since Clay was seldom reluctant to call on their support when necessary to carry his point. Even the threat that he might do so was unsettling to many at USFET. But above all, it was Clay's absolute determination to restore German economic and political life, to reduce the Occupation as quickly as possible, and—in the view from USFET—to place long-term German interests before the Occupation perks of a victorious Army that made Clay so objectionable.

Most senior military commanders lacked an understanding of the political and economic problems of a military occupation, and few enjoyed the give and take that teaching democracy required. For far too many, the Germans were merely another conquered people: the maids and servants of a life-style no uniformed officer could afford in the United States. In fact, it was Clay's determination to cut Occupation costs, and curtail the excessive high living by U.S. forces in the zone, that had brought matters to a head. General McNarney, in particular, evidenced little regret that Clay might leave, and was supported in this by his staff at Frankfurt.

For the very reasons that USFET wanted Clay replaced, Robert Murphy had become convinced that Clay's presence in Germany was essential. When Murphy secretly advised Byrnes of Clay's intentions, Byrnes and Secretary of War Patterson brought the Army into line. As Murphy reported with his usual diplomatic tactfulness, "McNarney's combat record was impressive . . . but he lacked the flair for politics which distinguished both Eisenhower and Clay, and he seemed to take little interest in German affairs." Or as Jacob Beam, later U.S. Ambassador to the Soviet Union, said, "McNarney showed little understanding for the problems of the occupation, and even outsiders could not help noticing what little interest he took in his work."

Following a month's recess, the Paris meeting of the Council of Foreign Ministers reconvened in mid-June. The French Communists had retained the support of 25 percent of the French electorate in the June elections but had not improved their standing significantly. Instead, the pro-Western MRP had emerged as France's largest party, and its leader, Georges Bidault, became Premier. This heralded absolutely no change in the French position at the conference, since Bidault was still wedded to Germany's dismemberment. But it did free Molotov from having to aid the French Communists' election bid, and on July 10, 1946, the Soviet Foreign Minister suddenly proclaimed strong Russian support for German unity, economic recovery, and political rehabilitation. If the Communists could not win power in France, Molotov appeared determined to capture popular support in Germany.

The abrupt Soviet shift caught the Western powers by surprise. Until then, the USSR had been the harshest of the occupying powers, and the Soviet Military Administration in Germany was considered the most vindictive. In Paris, Molotov still insisted on the need for reparations, but he now said Russia did not seek vengeance. Instead, he emphasized the importance of a united and prosperous Germany restored to the family of nations and free to develop civilian industries beyond the minimum levels fixed by the Allied Control Council (minimum levels previously insisted upon by the Soviet Union). As a first step toward a future German government, Molotov called for the immediate creation of central German administrative machinery—which the French continued to oppose. In fact, Molotov's speech was carefully crafted to appeal to all Germans regardless of party and to hang the Western powers on French intransigence.

> It has become fashionable [said Molotov] to talk about dismembering Germany into several "autonomous" states, federalizing her and separating the Ruhr from her. All such proposals stem from the same line of destroying and agrarianizing Germany, for without the Ruhr Germany cannot exist as an independent and viable state. But the destruction of Germany should not be our objective.

Molotov's speech was widely publicized in Germany, and it had an electric effect on public opinion. For the first time, one of the occupying powers had broken ranks and was offering the German people the prospect of a swift recovery. More important, Molotov had filled the vacuum created by the Allies' inability to make quadripartite government effective. While Britain and the United States were still clinging to the discriminatory remnants of Potsdam, and France was openly advocating dismemberment, Molotov was providing the Germans with a glimpse of a brighter future.

Clay and Murphy, who were attending the Conference as Byrnes's advisers, recognized immediately that the United States had been thrown on the defensive. That evening, Clay told Byrnes that in light of Molotov's statement, the United States could no longer have its policy in Germany based on the punitive strictures of JCS 1067 and fulfillment of the Potsdam Protocol. With Byrnes's approval, Clay returned to Berlin, where he drafted a revised statement of American aims: one that conformed more closely to Clay's ideas of a just peace, and which offered the Germans some hope of redemption. After obtaining General McNarney's concurrence, he dispatched it to the War Department for approval on July 19.

Clay disguised his handiwork as a routine restatement of American policy. He told Washington that Potsdam and JCS 1067 were "too bulky and too legalistic" for general distribution, and that without a crisp statement of U.S. objections, the Russians, now championing German unity, would continue to gain momentum in the battle for German support.

Clay's draft, entitled "A Summary of United States Policy and Objectives in Germany," represented a sharp break with the Carthaginian tone of JCS 1067. Germany was to be demilitarized, but the main thrust of U.S. policy shifted to recovery, re-education, responsible self-government under democratic procedures, and the eventual acceptance of a united Germany into the United Nations on terms of equality.

Clay called for all-German elections "at the earliest possible date" and the prompt establishment of a provisional government. He said the United States supported a vigorous trade-union program and the removal of all controls from the press and radio. Clay added that existing zonal restrictions should be removed "to permit the free exchange of commodities, persons and ideas throughout Germany. . . . The United States insists that the air-tight territories now created through the establishment of the four zones be eliminated and that zonal boundaries serve only to delineate the areas to be occupied by the armed forces of the occupying powers."

As for Germany's boundaries, Clay acknowledged the transfer of the territories east of the Oder and Neisse rivers to Soviet and Polish control, and he accepted the economic linkage of the Saar with France.

These concessions were important. Subsequent historians, particularly those of a revisionist persuasion, have argued that Clay (and Byrnes) sought to rectify Germany's eastern border at Polish expense. Nothing could be further from the truth. But Clay did reject any *further* reduction of German territory. "The United States believes the Rhineland and the Ruhr to be essential to the German economy. Moreover, it is convinced that the severance of the Rhineland and the Ruhr would make impossible the accomplishment of other objectives in Germany. The people remaining in the Rhineland and Ruhr areas would have as compelling a desire to return to the control of German government as the remainder of the German people would have for their return. As a result, continuing unrest would be certain throughout Germany."

As for Germany's political structure, Clay urged the early establishment of a Council of the Minister-Presidents from all four zones to coordinate the work of central administrative agencies, and to draft a constitution to be submitted to a special convention before ultimate ratification by the German people.

> The United States believes that this constitution must contain the following minimum essentials of democracy:
>
> a. All political power must originate with the people and be subject to their control.
> b. Programs and leadership must be referred frequently to popular elections.
> c. Elections must be held under competitive conditions. . . .
> d. Political parties must be democratic in character. . . .
> e. The basic rights of the individual must be defined in the constitution and preserved by law.
> f. Government must be exercised through the rule of law.
> g. The power of the central government must be limited. . . .

Clay recognized that America was playing for high stakes in Germany. And he knew that Molotov's speech was having a powerful effect. To counter that, Clay relied on the fundamental appeal of freedom and individual liberty. He said that the military occupation should be terminated quickly.

Clay blamed the French, not the Russians, for the plight the West was in. He was convinced that a united Germany could be attained and that liberal, democratic values would ultimately prevail. The result would be to extend Western influence to the Soviet zone and bring Poland and Czechoslovakia into direct contact with democratic ideas. Assistant Secretary of War Howard Petersen strongly agreed with Clay's proposed statement. But most in Washington did not. As was frequently the case, Clay was far in front of official American thinking. Under Secretary of State Acheson, for example, was convinced Clay had gone too far, that a united Germany would complicate U.S. relations with France. Rather than act on Clay's proposal, he created a special study committee "to consider and report on long-range U.S. policy for Germany" and to prepare a policy summary to be used by military government.

In early August, the War Department's Civil Affairs Division informed Clay that his statement did not reflect existing U.S. policy. Clay was nonplussed, especially since he knew what he had written had the full support of Secretary of State Byrnes. He fired back an immediate query. "Since we are and have been operating under my summary of policy [since 1945] we must indeed be drifting." Somewhat disingenuously, Clay said that his proposed statement contained nothing that had not been published before except for "our stand on Ruhr and Rhineland." He reminded Washington that he did not seek a revised policy, but "a statement of the policy under which we are operating now. We are really in a mess if we are unable to give a summary of our policy to our own people or if we are operating at variance with United States policy." Clay then told the War Department that unless instructed otherwise, he proposed to issue the statement to military government personnel in one week. "Otherwise," he said, "I can only tell them that I don't know what our policy is."

As Clay saw it, the State Department and now the War Department were becoming increasingly timid about U.S. policy in Germany. Either they had not been informed of Byrnes's views, or they were pursuing their own policy independent of the Secretary of State. He thought it was probably a combination of the two. Clay was also determined to prevent what he thought was unwarranted second-guessing by Washington. Throughout his military career, Clay had believed that the commander on the spot should be given broad general instructions and left free to determine the means best suited to accomplish them. If the President, or Secretary Byrnes, or Judge Patterson, or Eisenhower instructed him, Clay complied quickly. But staff-initiated cables from Washington that directed Clay to take action contrary to his political instincts were usually appealed, ignored, or rejected outright.

In early August, for example, Clay received fresh instructions from the War Department to halt German de-Nazification trials. A new policy, he was told, was being devised in Washington. This, in Clay's view, was another example of subordinate staff officers initiating policy contrary to the views of those politically responsible.

Clay dispatched a sharp response to his old friend John Hilldring, who was now Assistant Secretary of State for Occupied Areas. Arguing that a quadripartite law pertaining to de-Nazification (largely the work of Clay, former Solicitor General Charles Fahy, and Robert Bowie) was already in effect so that it was far too late to change U.S. policy, Clay said he was committed to "denazification by Germans—unless it fails, which it won't. . . . If policies are going to be changed after the fact, or if we are to be given instructions on procedures, I am through." Clay told Hilldring that he knew Byrnes supported the existing de-Nazification policy and asked pointedly whether the State Department had been consulted. "I cannot tell you how strongly I feel" that this procedure of second-guessing is all wrong, said Clay. "It seems to me that when the going was tough and everyone was critical, you didn't have many people climbing on the bandwagon to crowd you. Now they are all hopping on."

Concluding that he felt hopelessly let down by Washington, Clay said that he planned to return immediately "to determine whether or not our Government desires me to continue on this work. I am not issuing ultimatums, but the present situation is completely intolerable."

Clay's dismay became even greater on August 12, when he was told unequivocally by the War Department not to publish his policy statement on Germany. "We are fearful that issuance now," said Washington, "might commit this government in [a] manner more binding than desirable." In particular, Clay was told, the State Department objected to Clay's statements "relative to the early establishment of a provisional governmental structure in Germany"; to the eventual admission of Germany to the United Nations; and to U.S. acceptance of Germany's eastern frontiers at the Oder-Neisse as provided by Potsdam.

It was now apparent to Clay that his continued tenure in Germany was problematic. The Army General Staff—which continued to smart over Clay's independence—and those members of the State Department who leaned toward France rather than Germany, appeared to be making common cause. Both preferred someone more tractable in Germany than Clay.

An additional source of friction with the State Department was the German food budget voted by Congress. Germany's European neighbors sought to replenish their scant dollar reserves by selling fruits and vegetables to the Germans for U.S. dollars. Clay, on the other hand, insisted that Germany's food-import money be spent exclusively for the high-calorie food the nutritional emergency required. Washington diplomats invariably backed Germany's European neighbors; Clay, who controlled the budget, just as consistently refused to yield.

The conflict heightened on August 14, 1946, when General Thomas T. Handy, the Army's operations chief (G-3), informed McNarney that Clay's de-Nazification policy was contrary to War Department wishes. De-Nazification, said Handy, should not be delegated to the Germans.

That same day, Clay was informed by Hilldring that the State Department proposed to send a top-level committee to Germany, headed by James Riddleberger, chief of the Division of Central European Affairs, to discuss Occupation policy with Clay's staff. Clay, it appeared, was being bypassed.

Clay wrote to Hilldring on August 15, protesting both actions. "I must confess that I am more at sea than ever," said Clay. The War Department, he said, had been informed in February of his plan to turn over to the Germans the responsibility for de-Nazification and it had not objected. "To change our plans now would indicate a lack of confidence in our German administrations and also a lack of confidence in military government." Clay also told Hilldring that Justice Robert H. Jackson, the chief U.S. prosecutor at the Nuremberg war crimes trials, had approved the de-Nazification plan and that he could not understand the War Department's belated objection.

When the USFET intelligence chief (G-2) criticized the German de-Nazification proceedings as a threat to U.S. security, Clay shot back a brisk reply. If there were still dangerous Nazis at large, said Clay, it was because Army intelligence had not arrested them when it had been G-2's responsibility. In a note to McNarney, Clay criticized the Army G-2 for a lack of knowledge of the de-Nazification program. "His criticism is largely destructive . . . and I cannot accept the conclusions of the G-2 report as other than an expression of opinion." Clay summarized his views in a message to Washington on September 6: "If Nazism and militarism are to be permanently suppressed, only the German people themselves will do it, and arbitrary interference by Military Government would completely negate this principle."

But Clay's major concern was the committee of State Department officials Hilldring proposed to send to Germany. "With all due respect," said Clay, the committee "cannot expect me or my staff to enter into such discussions. We shall be very glad to provide factual information," Clay told Hilldring, but any policy recommendation from military government

> will be in writing under my signature. I cannot accept the interpretations which may be given by a committee to views obtained from members of my staff.
>
> The general situation as it exists today appears impossible to me. . . . I realize that many others are available to undertake this task. Nevertheless, it has no glamour and becomes meaningless unless we have the confidence and support which will permit on-the-spot decisions, under broad policy instructions. Believe me, John, retirement and a tour of catfishing look awfully good to me.

The following day, Clay sent a personal letter to Judge Patterson. Clay said that he had thrown his policy statement "in the waste basket." He told Patterson that he thought the memorandum had been misunderstood. "It was not my intent to submit it as a recommended policy for Germany. Rather it was an effort on my part to summarize our policy in Germany as we understood it, based on directives modified by the passage of events.

"I was disappointed to find out how mistaken I was and I must confess [that I am] somewhat at sea to know how to proceed further. I realize that it is not our task to originate or even to recommend policy but it is distressing to find after more than a year that our interpretation of policy must be variant with the facts."

Clay was visibly upset. As yet, there had been no effective Western response to Molotov's overture in Paris, and German sentiment, in Clay's view, was shifting slowly but unmistakably toward the East. There was but one recourse. From military government headquarters in Berlin, he called Secretary Byrnes in Paris. Byrnes sensed that a crisis was at hand and invited Clay to Paris immediately. Clay, accompanied by Murphy and Mrs. Clay, took off from Tempelhof that afternoon. In Byrnes's hotel suite that evening, he catalogued for the Secretary the array of problems suddenly confronting military government: the War Department wanted the quadripartite de-Nazification policy rescinded; the State Department was sending a group of experts to consult with Clay's staff about Occupation matters; and, worst of all, despite the inroads on German public opinion that Molotov had achieved, no one in Washington wanted to approve the policy summary Clay had submitted in July.

Byrnes heard Clay out and then responded as Clay had hoped. On every point mentioned by Clay, the Secretary of State was in full support. His being in Paris so long, said Byrnes, had prevented him from giving personal attention to the State Department. It was possible that they had not been fully aware of his views, or of his complete agreement with Clay as to how Germany should be treated.

After a week of uncertainty, Clay felt he was back on solid ground. With Byrnes's backing, Clay sensed that victory was in the offing. To exploit that possibility to the fullest, Clay invited Byrnes to come to Germany when the foreign ministers' conference ended in September and suggested that the Secretary make a policy statement while there. In Clay's view, Byrnes's physical presence in Germany would not only help counter Molotov's appeal, but would clearly help military government in its struggle with Washington. And if Byrnes would restate in public what he had told Clay in private, Clay was certain that the German cause could be won.

Byrnes needed little convincing. He immediately agreed to go to Germany, and, at Clay's suggestion, John Kenneth Galbraith was set to work in Washington preparing Byrnes's speech. Clay returned to Berlin confident that his position had been sustained.

"Marjorie and I enjoyed our trip to Paris more than I can express," Clay wrote Byrnes on August 19. "How you could take time to raise my spirits in the midst of your worries is almost unbelievable. I am sorry that I bothered you with some of my own problems in Germany which while so important to us are local in character. . . ."

But Byrnes's support for Clay's German policy did not resolve his problem with USFET. Throughout 1946, Clay believed he was fighting a two-front war in Germany. In front of him were the French and

Russians (who were becoming progressively more difficult in the ACC); behind him was the U.S. Army, which wanted to subordinate military government to tactical Army control.

On August 21, Clay met with McNarney and repeated his desire to resign. As Clay saw it, if McNarney would not support him in his jurisdictional struggle with the General Staff, he would step aside and let McNarney find a suitable replacement.

Curiously, it was Bedell Smith who, from the U.S. Embassy in Moscow, intervened in Clay's behalf. Smith had made one of his periodic trips to Berlin to escape the rigors of his Russian assignment and, after trying to dissuade Clay from resigning, sent a long handwritten letter to Eisenhower warning him of Clay's intent. "Clay is still indispensable in Germany," wrote Smith, and he suggested that Ike intervene. Eisenhower wrote Clay immediately. The Chief of Staff said he was coming to Germany in mid-September, and he asked Clay to wait until then. Clay replied on September 8 that he would of course wait for Eisenhower's arrival. "However, I am more convinced than ever that it would be a serious mistake for me to continue here."

In writing his memoirs, Clay made no mention of his bitter struggle with Washington in the summer of 1946. He merely published his policy recommendations and highlighted Byrnes's pivotal speech at Stuttgart—which incorporated Clay's suggestions. To read Clay's 1950 version, it was as if U.S. policy had never wavered, and as if there had been no disagreement in Washington as to how Germany should be treated. Clay also failed to mention that his robust constitution was paying a price for the two-front war of attrition he was waging. With the exception of his one-day ski trip to Berchtesgaden, Clay had not had a vacation since he returned to the United States by ship from the Philippines in 1938. He repeatedly worked around the clock, and, as in Washington, his staff in Berlin staggered their hours to accommodate him. He survived on countless packs of cigarettes and massive infusions of black coffee. His stomach would tolerate little food, he slept fitfully if at all, and his nerves were raw. But he took no medication and refused to see a doctor: the stakes in Germany were too high.

Byrnes's speech at Stuttgart was a ringing endorsement of Clay's policy: the establishment of an elected provisional government, the drafting of a new constitution, and Germany's eventual admission to the United Nations—all of which Clay had proposed but subordinate

State Department officials had rejected—figured prominently in the Secretary's remarks.

In fact, the text of Byrnes's speech, to the obvious dismay of many in Washington, was a virtual paraphrase of Clay's message of July 19—and at times a direct quotation. According to Galbraith, it had been prepared with the help of Charles Kindleberger and taken to Paris, "where it was reviewed by Benjamin Cohen, then counsel to the Department. I then took it on to General Clay in Berlin. He read it with great approval while smoking the usual six cigarettes."

Like Clay's policy statement of July 19, the speech had a remarkably positive tone. It was time for the German people to be given "the primary responsibility for running their own affairs," said Byrnes. "All that the Allied governments should do is to lay down the rules under which the German democracy can govern itself. The Allied occupation forces should be limited to the number sufficient to see that these rules are obeyed."

As for Germany's borders, Byrnes reiterated America's commitment to the Soviet Union and Poland on the Oder-Neisse (the professional cold warriors in the State Department previously had objected to Clay's mention of it) and to the economic integration of the Saar with France. But with regard to the Ruhr and the Rhineland, Byrnes vehemently rejected any plan to detach them from Germany. "So far as the United States is aware," said Byrnes, "the people of the Ruhr and the Rhineland desire to remain united with the rest of Germany. And the United States is not going to oppose their desire [loud and sustained applause]."

Clay could not have been more pleased. Not only had the Secretary of State come to Germany at his request, but he had delivered a major policy address in Stuttgart—the seat of the German government for the U.S. zone—that incorporated all of Clay's policy recommendations, sometimes verbatim.

Q: What lay behind Secretary Byrnes's visit to Germany and his policy speech at Stuttgart in 1946?

CLAY: Mr. Byrnes sensed my distress in Paris, and he asked me what did I think about his coming to Germany? I grabbed at the idea and suggested the place and the type and kind of the meeting. I think that I made much more out of his suggestion than he intended. But I also think that after I did it, he liked the idea. And, of course, he came to

Berlin first. We went over his speech. And I had only one suggestion: that he put in there that, as long as anybody else's troops were in Germany, ours would be there too. He did add it to the speech, and he recognized fully the importance. He tried very, very hard to get Mr. Truman on the telephone to get his approval. He did not get him on the telephone, although he tried very hard, but he went ahead and put it in his speech anyway. And to my way of thinking, it was the most important thing in the speech. To the Germans, there were other things that were very, very important. But to the Europeans, the fact that the United States had committed itself to stay in Germany probably did more to stop Communist political gains in Western Europe than any other one thing that ever happened.

Q: What was Mr. Byrnes's attitude toward Germany?

CLAY: The same as mine. I don't mean that it necessarily reflected my view, but it was the same as mine.

Q: Did you write Mr. Byrnes's speech?

CLAY: Well, you can always say these things. It was very close to the messages that I had sent to Washington. But to say that I wrote the speech would not be correct. To say that Mr. Byrnes listened to and accepted many of my ideas and suggestions would be much closer to the truth.

"Mr. Byrnes was very unhappy with the Paris foreign ministers' conference, and he thought that by visiting Germany and expressing his interest he would be strengthening the hand of American military government. Which it did. Then, when this carried along to his major speech, it was really a European declaration of policy by an American Secretary of State. It set the pattern under which we've been in Europe ever since. And this was something Europe didn't believe: that we were going to stay. This was something neither the Russians nor Western Europe believed. The result was it did do something to discourage Russian aggression, and it did even more to build up the morale of non-Communist political forces in Western Europe—particularly in France and Italy."

Q: Was there any immediate Russian response?

CLAY: There is never an instant Russian response in the field, because when they are caught by an event they didn't know would take place they have no instructions. So they don't react.

"Mr. Byrnes's speech was aimed at the Germans. It was an attempt to give them some hope. It was also aimed at Western Europe, to give them some assurance. And I think it had an immediate and marked effect in both respects. It was a speech which was received with tremendous enthusiasm in Western Europe. It was received and accepted as a far more important and greater speech in Europe than it was in the United States."

Q: What was the German response?

CLAY: The Minister-Presidents were at the meeting [in Stuttgart] and they were tremendously impressed. And I think that view was shared by the Germans at large. We were going to stay there and yet at the same time we were going to give them a chance to work out their own future and their own destiny.

"I had taken the Minister-Presidents down that morning to the Secretary's official train, and they'd had a chance to meet and talk with Justice Byrnes before he made his speech. Our seat of government was in Stuttgart, and that's why I wanted the speech to be in Stuttgart. I wanted it to be a speech to our own headquarters, to our own people. Obviously, Berlin wasn't the place. So the logical place was in the seat of the Germans who were running military government under our jurisdiction."

Q: What sort of reception was Mr. Byrnes given by the Germans?

CLAY: It was very interesting to me, because I had made all sorts of security arrangements for Justice Byrnes's train, but nevertheless the train stopped in an unscheduled station which we didn't have guarded. Everybody on the train, I thought, was taking a nap. I was in my stateroom when the train stopped. I got up to find out what the trouble was, and when I got out there in the rear car, there on the observation platform was Mr. Byrnes, and there must have been five hundred or a thousand Germans gathered around, and he was signing autographs for them all.

"By that time, he had made his speech, it had been in all of the newspapers, and he was greeted with enormous enthusiasm. It was unbelievable to me. Here was an American Secretary of State out there signing autographs for the Germans little over one year after the end of the war."

But Byrnes's speech did not relieve the tension between Clay and USFET. While Clay and his largely civilian staff in military government were encouraging the Germans to take local initiatives and restore political activity, the tactical Army tended to resent any German activity that suggested independent action. On October 8, 1946, for example, just as work was being completed on the draft constitutions for the *Länder* in the American zone, the USFET chief of staff gratuitously informed the War Department that the Germans were showing "increasing disregard for Allied authority. There is no evidence of true growth of democratic spirit."

Clay was appalled. Not only did Clay believe that the charge was factually wrong, but USFET's cable to Washington seemed a deliberate attempt to undermine military government. In a blistering message to Frankfurt, Clay said he had "no evidence which indicates any increase in efforts to circumvent laws or to indicate a rising disregard of Allied authority."

> Obviously the German people are recovering from the chaotic condition which followed surrender and are slowly gaining a renewed hope and confidence. It is very difficult to translate this into disregard of Allied authority. . . . This office also doubts the factual nature of the statement that there is no evidence of true growth of democratic spirit and, in point of fact, the recent work of the three constitutional assemblies in the American zone would indicate just the opposite.

In fact, the constitutional assemblies in each of the *Länder* in the American zone had just completed work on new constitutions that were to be submitted to the German people. Here again Clay had forced the pace. After Clay called the constitutional assemblies in each province into session, Washington became nervous about the outcome. On August 21, the War Department told Clay to furnish draft texts of the proposed constitutions to the State Department before approving them. Once again Clay resisted what he believed was an unwarranted intrusion by the United States into German self-government. Clay said he would furnish the State Department with drafts for their general comments, but any "detailed comment to the constitutional assemblies would be inconsistent" with the ideals of democracy America sought to instill.

> These constitutions [said Clay] are being developed by the Germans in an atmosphere free from military government direction or interference.

> We have told the German authorities of the basic principles which we consider necessary to a democratic constitution and these principles have been furnished to you and the State Department. As long as these principles are safe-guarded in the constitution, we do not propose to comment on the details or on the governmental procedures established in the constitutions.
>
> These constitutions must go to the German people as a free creation of their elected representatives and with the least possible taint of military government dictation. We have every confidence that the constitutions thus prepared will meet the requirements of democracy and will be recognized by the German people as the creation of their own representatives.

Nevertheless, when the constitutional drafts were completed and sent to Washington for comment, State Department officials in the Division of European Affairs sought detailed changes to conform more closely with U.S. political procedures. Clay bluntly told the War Department that the proposed changes could not be obtained except by military government decree, and that if such a decree were issued, it would destroy German political support for the new constitutions, probably defeating ratification.

In a "Personal and Confidential" cable to General Echols dated October 15, 1946, Clay discussed each of the State Department's proposed changes and indicated why they were inappropriate. But above all, Clay maintained that "The constitutional assemblies of the three *Länder* [were] composed of representatives freely elected by the people. They have devoted three months of sincere and conscientious effort to the drafting of these constitutions. They are major advances over the Weimar constitutions. Our own experts [Professors Carl J. Friedrich of Harvard and James K. Pollock of the University of Michigan] have worked with them through this period but by power of suggestion rather than by instruction.

"The assemblies believe and proclaim that the instruments as they now stand truly represent their own work. It is our view that this belief will be shared by the German people . . . and we are confident of ratification by substantial majorities. The enthusiasm in the three *Länder* is high now. The constitutional assemblies will lose this enthusiasm unless they are permitted to take a final vote at an early date." Once again Clay said that Washington's proposed changes could not be made by suggestion but would require an order from him, which would be "disastrous to the work accomplished to date."

Assistant Secretary of War Petersen, who was in Germany at the time, concurred in Clay's analysis. If the State Department insisted on the changes, he told Dean Rusk (then a colonel on active duty with the Army) to "take the matter up with the Secretary of War [Judge Patterson], recommending that he go to the President if necessary."

By December 8, 1946, the three *Länder* constitutions had been ratified overwhelmingly in popular referendums. Two days later, when speaking to a zonal meeting of military government officers in Stuttgart, Clay told the assembled American officers that the new German constitutions "must become the Bible for our actions. You must be as zealous in guarding German rights as if you were a constitutional lawyer in the United States."

Q: As Military Governor, you vetoed provisions in the Hesse constitution that would have provided for public ownership of certain industries, and for co-determination [requiring trade union representation on company boards of directors].

CLAY: I opposed both proposals. For different reasons, but obviously I didn't like either one of them. They were foreign to my way of thinking—and to the American way of thinking. On the other hand, I've always believed in the right of people to determine what they want themselves. My concern was for the future. If we were going to have a German government, and if it was to be a federal government, it couldn't leave to the individual states the right to determine what kind of economic life they wanted. My view—and I expressed it in my veto of the Hesse proposals—was that this was not a matter that should be decided by the individual states. That it had to wait until there was a government for Germany as a whole.

"Now, the fine points of that, which really were very sincere on my part, have always been lost in the charges that I was an ultra-conservative and violently opposed to these ideas. I was opposed to them. But that had nothing to do with my veto. If the Federal Republic of Germany had been in existence at that time, and if I had been high commissioner and had the power of veto and the same questions were presented to me, I would have acquiesced without any question. But at the time, the Federal Republic was not there. And we did not know what a new German constitution might provide. And I didn't want state actions taken that would make it impossible for a new German constitution to provide a free choice."

Q: Did you see the role of U.S. military government as one of promoting free enterprise?

CLAY: I thought it was the job of military government to maintain free enterprise in Germany until the Germans were capable of making that choice for themselves. Yes.

"I did not go back and change state enterprises—try to change railroads, telephones, post offices—to private ownership. Never thought of it. On the other hand, I didn't want the dire straits of the economy to be used as a basis for the state to take over other enterprises. This was a choice for all of Germany—not by each individual state. However, as long as I was there, I was going to try my best to prove that in encouraging free enterprise we were encouraging a more rapid recovery for Germany than would have occurred otherwise. Certainly, I came from a free enterprise country, and I represented to the best of my ability the advantages of free enterprise.

"My opposition to co-determination for labor was similar. I did not oppose it if it could be for Germany as a whole, but I did not think it was wise to require it for industry in one state and not require it of industry in another state. I was determined not to preclude choice for the Germans themselves later on."

Q: And your relations with organized labor?

CLAY: My relations with labor were very good. I had Joe Keenan of the AFL-CIO on my staff and I saw a great deal of him. I respected his views and I think he did mine. The AFL-CIO also had a representative in Germany working directly for them, whom we gave freedom to travel anywhere he wanted to go in the American zone—Irving Brown. He was very helpful, particularly in the elections in which the Communists were voted out of office in the unions.

"I've never heard any accusations that American military government was anti-labor. I had complete rapport—I won't say complete, because you never have that—but I had excellent rapport in Germany with George Meany [of the AFL] and his people. Joe Keenan is one of my very close friends." (In 1974, when Keenan celebrated his sixtieth year in the International Brotherhood of Electrical Workers, Clay—a dying man then—traveled to Chicago to honor his friend as the banquet's principal speaker.)

Q: And the banking system?

CLAY: We tried to create a new German banking system modeled to some degree on our Federal Reserve system. First Joe Dodge, and then Jack Bennett from the Treasury, were in charge of this.

"Then Colonel Wilkinson and his economics staff played a major role in getting Germany into the European economic group to enjoy the benefits of the Marshall Plan. We maneuvered it so that we could take German experts with us to the early meetings, although the neighboring countries were by no manner of means ready to receive Germans as participating members. But by the simple device of taking them there as advisers, we got them accepted as members much, much quicker than we could have any other way."

Throughout 1946, Clay believed that it was possible to achieve a united Germany. In a special memorandum that he hand-carried to Secretary Byrnes at the December meeting of the Council of Foreign Ministers in New York, Clay recommended settling the reparations question with the USSR by raising German production and using the excess to meet Russian claims. Sokolovsky, he said, supported the idea. The historian John Backer has called Clay's proposal one of the most far-reaching to emerge from Germany, but it was never acted upon.

Clay told Byrnes the reparations question appeared to be the basic problem that needed to be resolved with the Soviet Union and that "American objectives in Germany should not preclude serious consideration being given to the utilization of some current production for reparations." Clay resolutely believed that the united Germany that would result from such a deal would be worth the trade-off, a country strongly democratic in character. Said Clay:

> We have much at stake in gaining the opportunity to fight for democratic ideals in Eastern Germany and in Eastern Europe. This opportunity would result from the true unification of Germany under quadripartite control.
>
> Therefore, it does appear worthwhile to investigate fully this possible solution to the internal German problem. How much we are willing to pay to achieve our objectives is unknown, but it is possible that the investigation may indicate that the cost in dollars is not too high, particularly when measured in terms of European stability and the possible contribution of such stability to world peace.

While Clay was tireless and, indeed, uncompromising in his efforts to establish liberal democracy in Germany, he was equally assiduous in not disturbing traditional social and economic values. Clay was not a social engineer. He did not seek a social revolution, nor was he ever instructed to do so. Instead, Clay believed firmly in the basic human dignity of the German people. He believed in leading by example; if he as Military Governor could demonstrate the way democracy worked, the Germans would quickly see its benefits. An American liberal of the old school, Clay exemplified a tradition of public service that cherished openness, integrity, and the absolute observance of legal norms. Procedural correctness was no less important than substantive results.

Not surprisingly, the Germans could relate to that. The ideals of American democracy personified by Clay were quickly embraced. For many Germans, it was a restoration of the Prussian *Rechtsstaat* (the rule of law) with a Georgia accent.

· 23 ·

CINCEUR

> I like to think that during the years our flag was flown in Germany, it stood for something more than military power.
>
> Lucius D. Clay, *Decision in Germany*

WHEN JOSEPH MCNARNEY SUCCEEDED EISENHOWER as European Theater commander in November 1945, he also became Military Governor of Germany and Austria. But in McNarney's case, the title was largely *pro forma*. As deputy military governor, Clay continued to set Occupation policy in Germany, reporting directly to the War Department, while General Mark Clark performed the same function in Austria. McNarney retained the final authority, but devoted himself primarily to military command problems and tactical control of America's rapidly dwindling military establishment.

In fact, by mid-1946 military discipline had become the most serious problem for what remained of the U.S. Army in Europe. When three thousand GIs demonstrated outside American headquarters in

Frankfurt shouting "We wanna go home," McNarney blamed it on Communist agitation and chastised the press for reporting it. McNarney, an Army Air Corps officer who had served as General Marshall's deputy in Washington for most of the war, belatedly ordered a crackdown on discipline, but to little effect. Raymond Daniell of *The New York Times* described the U.S. Army in Europe in 1946 as "an aggregation of homesick Americans shirking their jobs to figure out ways to make money, courting German women, and counting up points [required for discharge]." Shortly afterward another journalist wrote that "The average American soldier learns only two things from his occupation experience. He learns how to drink and how to pick up a Fräulein."

McNarney's problems with military discipline coincided with the difficulties Clay was experiencing with the Army General Staff. The relationship between military government (OMGUS) and U.S. Army headquarters in Frankfurt (USFET) had never been satisfactory. After Eisenhower's departure, the General Staff at USFET sought to reassert military control over OMGUS activities. Clay resisted and refused to accommodate them. By August 1946, the situation had become intractable. When the Army refused to submit its Occupation budget to OMGUS for approval, Clay resigned. That forced the issue. His resignation brought both Secretary of War Patterson and Eisenhower to Berlin, and both had a similar message: Clay's views would be upheld; USFET would be forced to back down.

During his visit in early October, Patterson told Clay that McNarney seemed either unable or unwilling to restore military discipline in Europe. He had handled the press badly after Daniell's report in *The New York Times,* and the War Department had been severely embarrassed. Patterson asked Clay if he would stay in Germany if McNarney was relieved. It was an extraordinary question from the Secretary of War. McNarney, after all, was Clay's superior, and Clay felt the question was improper. He declined to give Patterson an answer. Nevertheless, Patterson left Europe convinced that unless a change was made at USFET, Clay definitely would seek retirement.

Eisenhower arrived in Berlin two weeks later. As Chief of Staff, Ike had borne the brunt of U.S. demobilization, and the troop disturbances in Frankfurt (as well as much more serious demonstrations in the Pacific) had put him in a black mood. A trip to Berlin, he thought, might restore his spirits and give him a chance to review the situation at first hand with Clay. Ike was accompanied by Mrs. Eisenhower, who was a close friend of the Clays'. For a brief period during the war, and then when Clay and Eisenhower were both in Germany in 1945, Mamie Eisenhower and Marjorie Clay had lived in adjoining apartments at the Wardman Park Hotel in Washington, and had spent a great deal of time with each other—just as they had in Manila in 1937. In Berlin, Ike and Mamie stayed with the Clays in their small Dahlem bungalow, the tight quarters a relief from the formality of Washington, and providing the intimacy that both families sought.

Speaking for Secretary of War Patterson, Eisenhower told Clay that "We want you to take over the complete military command in Europe." He said that McNarney would be offered a newly created post as U.S. military adviser to the U.N. Security Council. Eisenhower told Clay that he was going to write McNarney a letter to that effect. "I want you to deliver the letter personally," Ike said.

Clay insisted that he really wanted out; that he genuinely wanted to retire. "It was not a very happy period," Clay recalled many years later. "I wanted to leave Germany. I won't say it was because of the problems of military command, but obviously that had something to do with it. I really didn't see what future there was to it. If I wasn't in a position to make the decisions, and if I was going to do all of the work in Germany, I couldn't see any point to that. I wasn't very happy. Period."

But Eisenhower was not prepared to take no for an answer. His letter to McNarney was a masterpiece of political subtlety, and helps explain Ike's justly acquired reputation for walking through mine fields unscathed. "Dear Joe," he wrote, "Please do not take this letter as anything more than it is intended to be, namely, advance notice of something that *may* happen with respect to your assignment.

"Certain civilian officials of the Government have been urging upon the Secretary of War that you be brought home to be the Air Force representative at the United Nations in New York, coupling this recommendation with a further one, that Clay take over the European job. The recommendation comes from very high sources."

Ike told McNarney that he couldn't predict the outcome, and that although he, Eisenhower, had previously assured McNarney that he could remain in Europe for two more years, he now saw "no ground for interposing opposition" to the move. "I realize that if this proposal should be carried into effect it may involve disappointment for you but the work [at the U.N.] is of the utmost importance," he said. In effect, McNarney, a ranking four-star general, was being deftly transferred into a not yet existing job at the U.N. that would normally have been filled by a much more junior officer, and the responsibility for the change was being placed by Ike on unnamed but "very high sources" —presumably Secretary of State Byrnes. Finally, to add to the impact, Eisenhower was having the letter delivered by Clay himself. That was Ike's way of announcing the change without having to do so directly, and without having to take actual responsibility. Presumably, McNarney would recognize the handwriting on the wall and take the necessary action.

When Clay went to USFET headquarters on November 6, he told McNarney that he should make his decision independently: that he should not be concerned about Clay's own wishes. McNarney, who was undoubtedly stunned by Eisenhower's letter, made no reply at the time. One week later, he called Clay from Frankfurt and asked him directly whether he, Clay, would stay on in Germany if McNarney remained. Clay said that he would not, that he would not remain under present conditions.

When McNarney procrastinated, the War Department told Clay that the shift was definite and that he should inform McNarney immediately. That troubled Clay. As he wrote to Assistant Secretary Howard Petersen, "during my entire service in the Army I have had but one standard, and that was complete loyalty to my immediate superior. I am unwilling to have any suspicion cast on that standard as long as I am in the Army." As a result, Clay told Petersen that he could not deliver the message. In fact, Clay said he had reached the following conclusions about the changeover:

1. While I am not seeking the job in Germany, I would undertake it if the War Department desired me to do so, but only in the event that General McNarney accepted his proposed assignment [freely].
2. If General McNarney is unwilling to accept his proposed assignment in such spirit, I would not care to stay in Germany as his successor. . . .
3. If General McNarney stays in Germany, I will assist [him] in every way possible prior to my departure.

Clay told Petersen that he didn't know what McNarney's decision would be, but that "self-respect is the most precious possession one can have. I could not take over command in Germany and maintain my own self-respect under all the conditions involved, unless it were accepted in good grace and understanding by General McNarney."

On December 16, 1946, McNarney wrote Eisenhower that he had discussed the matter with Clay and "could find no fault with his attitude, which was that the matter was entirely one for my decision. Realizing that Mr. Byrnes reposes complete confidence in Clay and knowing the closeness of the association between them, it is only logical to assume that Mr. Byrnes desires to keep Clay on the job. When one considers the magnitude and complexity of the international problems confronting the Secretary of State it is only right and proper that he should have the major voice in picking the executor of his policies in Germany." McNarney then authorized Eisenhower to announce that he, McNarney, had "requested reassignment."

On March 15, 1947, Lucius Dubignon Clay assumed total command of the European Theater. He was given a fourth star, the first full general in the history of the U.S. Army never to have served in combat. His promotion ended two years of bickering with the Army about the role of military government in Germany. Clay now had the authority to make the changes he believed necessary. Military government was immediately put on a parallel footing with the tactical military forces. The old USFET headquarters—Clay's nemesis—was abolished. Clay became the first U.S. commander-in-chief, Europe (CINCEUR). CINCEUR headquarters was established in Berlin and was little more than a personal headquarters for Clay himself. Like Grant in 1864, the commander-in-chief in Europe traveled light. Unlike most senior generals, Clay never accumulated a personal entourage. His secretary, Captain Margaret Allen, had already been working for the Army in Europe when Clay arrived in 1945. One aide was assigned to him, Captain Edloe Donnan, but Clay did not replace him when Donnan returned to the United States in 1947. Even George, the Scottish terrier who accompanied Clay constantly, had been given to him by a former driver, Sergeant John De Boer, when the sergeant went home.

Reporting to Clay's personal CINCEUR headquarters were the two operational commands. Military government (OMGUS), now headed by Clay's deputy, Major General Frank Keating, and the tactical military command (redesignated EUCOM), now headed by Lieutenant General Clarence Huebner. Huebner was a tough disciplinarian who had come up through the ranks and was a superb troop leader. He had commanded the 1st Division during the war, and Clay had requested his reassignment to Germany to shape up the military command. Clay had visualized this parallel command structure since his arrival in Europe in the spring of 1945. As a result, his assumption of supreme command was handled almost routinely.

By delegating operational control to Keating and Huebner, Clay freed himself to concentrate on Occupation policy. He was acutely aware of how Grant had retained Meade to head the Army of the Potomac when he became commanding general during the Civil War, and he was more immediately conscious of how Justice Byrnes had directed the American home front in 1944–45. Like Byrnes and Grant, Clay wanted to be free of the operational details. He established a command structure that permitted him to do that.

As Secretary Patterson and Eisenhower had recognized, the military command problems in Europe were enormous. The few tactical units that remained in Germany in 1947 were in dreadfully poor shape. Undisciplined, disorganized, engaged in black-market trading, with high AWOL and VD rates, the American Army in Europe was seen by many observers as a blemish on the United States.

Q: When you assumed the full military command in Europe, how did you change things?

CLAY: My first directive to General Huebner was to move immediately to re-establish the 1st Division from the units of the constabulary. It was really a move. The constabulary was not a tactical force; it was a mobile police force. It was obvious to me that we did not need troops organized to fight German resistance: there was no German resistance. If we were going to fight in Europe, it was going to be against a major enemy. And to do that we needed tanks and artillery, not light cavalry. And that change back to a traditional division structure gave evidence of our intention to remain in Europe.

"Secondly, I made General Hall, who was my chief of intelligence [in military government], the chief of intelligence for the whole theater. I wanted this right by me at all times. Quite obviously, if anything was to happen in Germany in which I had to make an instant decision, I wanted the latest intelligence right with me. [Clay relieved the USFET intelligence chief (G-2), who previously had complained about turning de-Nazification over to the Germans.]

"Other than that, I delegated full authority to General Huebner and General [Curtis] LeMay, who commanded the Air Forces. However, I held monthly staff conferences with the military staff at Heidelberg. And I went on immediate and constant inspection trips to all of our military activities. I covered every installation in Germany—barracks, quarters, training facilities, everything—to get a feel of what needed to be done. Actually, as a result of my inspections I probably knew more about what our military establishment in Germany looked like and what needed to be done than anybody else. I think I'm the only person at that time who had visited all of our installations in Europe."

According to Clay's former aide, whenever the general inspected troops, "he would not go to Army or division headquarters. He would go down to the company or platoon. He would go through at kind of a half-run, with a bevy of generals behind him trying to keep up. He would go through the mess halls and through the latrines to check their condition. And he would look into their rooms to see what kind of uniforms, clothing, and laundry service the men had. He would talk directly to the troops and ask questions of the junior officers, the NCOs, and the enlisted men. When he found something he thought was wrong, or that he could not get an answer to, then he would go back up to division headquarters to run down the solution. He would have nothing to do with the protocol around higher headquarters. He would go to the end product."

Q: How many people reported to you directly?

CLAY: General Huebner was in command of all our military activities. General LeMay also reported directly to me. The chief of intelligence, General Hall, reported directly to me. That was it on the military side. On the military government side, General Keating was my deputy in Frankfurt. And then I had the four provincial [*Länder*] military governors reporting to me. Five, if you count Berlin. The German Minister-Presidents reported to me through the provincial military governors.

And [Lieutenant] General [Geoffrey] Keyes in Austria. As Military Governor of Austria, Keyes also reported to the Secretary of War. [Keyes succeeded General Mark Clark in May 1947.]

Q: How did you use your chief of staff?

CLAY: He ran the office. Period. But all of these people had direct access to me.

Q: Not through your chief of staff?

CLAY: No sir. That, I've never believed in. Some commanders do, but I've never worked for anyone who did, and I certainly never used that system.

"Bedell Smith was a very strong chief of staff, but I never felt he could cut me off from General Eisenhower, or that I had to go through him. And I don't think there was ever a day in the world when General Bradley didn't think he could walk into General Eisenhower's office directly. I'm sure Montgomery felt that way too. I know Jakie Devers [CG, Sixth Army Group] did.

"All routine matters were handled by my chief of staff. Anything that was consistent with existing policy, he could approve. He had no authority to disapprove anything in my name. I was not cut off and would not be cut off from the people that were supposed to report directly to me. I wanted to know what they were thinking and I wanted them to know what I was thinking. And I don't think you can do that through an intermediary. And our staff conferences were very important and uninhibited give-and-take sessions for hammering out a common policy."

Q: How does one create good morale in a military unit?

CLAY: You have to make people proud of themselves. One way to make a soldier proud of himself is to have him dress up and go on parade. I established these very early in Berlin. I wanted to show our presence there, and I thought they were good for morale.

"As a soldier, I never went to a parade that I didn't get a thrill out of it—even though I might bitterly resent having to go. When it came time for retreat to be sounded and 'The Star-Spangled Banner' to be played, you couldn't help but feel proud of your profession.

"A soldier fights a war and spends most of it in fatigue clothes, slogging in the mud and dirt. And he gets a little sloppy. The soldier in peacetime who gets himself sloppy is a sorry soldier. You either have to keep him in shape by tough, hard-boiled discipline, or by making him proud of himself. I have always believed the latter was more effective.

"One of the first things I did after I took command in 1947 was to tell my quartermaster in no uncertain terms that I didn't want to see any soldier whose uniform did not match. We had used all kinds of materials during the war, and the quartermaster just handed out the coats here and the pants there. You'd see a man with one shade of OD [olive-drab] trousers and another shade of coat. I stopped all that. And, interestingly enough, you'd be surprised at how much less trouble we had with men being in railroad stations with their blouses unbuttoned and looking sloppy—which is no way to impress an occupied country."

Q: The Army was still segregated at that time?

CLAY: There was no integration of black and white troops at the time. When I took command, our Negro troops were primarily in service units. Their disciplinary record was not good, and the number of incidents involving Germans was excessive. I have always felt that we were making a great mistake—as we had in World War II—in using our Negro troops largely in supply jobs: that if we were going to have the type and kind of black soldiers that we wanted, we had to show that we had confidence and pride in them. So I directed the transfer of Negro soldiers from service units to form three infantry battalions. In Berlin, I created a black honor guard. I never got to full integration (that was contrary to War Department policy), but it was a step in that direction. Actually, I would have been perfectly prepared to try integration. You certainly weren't doing anything for the Negro soldier or anyone else in keeping him in supply services.

"In any event, we set up these Negro combat units and morale really increased. The incident rate, which records the number of disciplinary violations that occur, fell below that of the white incident rate. The esprit was terrific. Before I left Germany, Walter White—who was the president of the NAACP—asked me if he could cite the example of our successful integration of Negro soldiers at the battalion level in a presentation he was making to President Truman. And I agreed. And, as you know, President Truman ordered the complete integration of the Army during the Korean War."

As a Southerner, Clay was keenly aware of racial discrimination and bitterly opposed it. That was unusual for someone of his generation. It was particularly unusual for someone reared in the segregated Regular Army. Later, first as chief executive officer of Continental Can Corporation, and then as managing partner of Lehman Brothers, Clay headed fund-raising efforts for Tuskegee Institute for many years, and was a member of its board of governors.

BIZONIA

The bizonal merger of the American and British zones, which Clay had initially proposed to Secretary Byrnes at the Paris meeting of the Council of Foreign Ministers in July, was accepted by the British on July 30, 1946. Final arrangements for the merger—initially restricted to economic matters—were concluded during the following session of the Council of Foreign Ministers in New York that December. Clay did not conceive "Bizonia" in order to divide Germany. He saw it as a way to bypass French and Russian intransigence: a first attempt to put the splintered pieces of Germany back together.

Q: What led you to think in terms of a zonal merger with the British?

CLAY: Two things. There was simply not enough in the way of resources or industry in the American zone to give it anything but a pastoral economy. And on the other hand, we were supplying the money and the food to keep both our zone and the British zone alive. It was quite evident to me that, with the coal and industry of the Ruhr [located in the British zone] added to our zone, we would have a self-supporting economic area. If we were ever going to be rid of the financial burden of carrying an occupied territory, it was clearly in our economic interest for them to be united.

"It was equally clear that maintaining four small occupation zones made no political sense. If we were going to restore a democratic Germany, we had to create units that at least would be reasonably acceptable to the Germans. So this again made it important to enlarge the sphere we were operating in. And since our thinking was much closer to the British than [to] anyone else, obviously the first merger to be considered was with the British zone."

Q: Had you come to the conclusion that four-power government was not going to work?

CLAY: I think I had advised our government by that time I did not think it was going to work, at least not in its present form. The French were not cooperating in any way whatsoever, and the Russians were becoming far less cooperative than they had been. But I had a feeling that if we combined the British and American zones, and if that yielded evidence of immediate and rapid recovery—as I thought it would—that this might be helpful in making four-power government effective once more. If the Russians and the French saw that we were successful, I thought that they would want to become a part of it.

"My Minister-Presidents knew what I had in mind and they were a little wary of it. Basically, they were afraid that this [zonal merger] would be detrimental to an eventual union of all of Germany. But I saw it just the other way. And you must remember that a merger with the British meant a reduction in their powers to some degree. The Minister-Presidents were the top government in the American zone, and in the bizonal area they wouldn't have nearly that much power."

Q: Did the concept of zonal merger originate with you?

CLAY: I think it did. I don't want to be absolutely positive in that, because this may have occurred to any number of people. But I know I didn't do it because someone recommended it to me.

Q: But the merger was only in economic matters?

CLAY: At first we tried to keep the bizonal merger purely in the economic realm, because of the fact that we had two other partners and we weren't trying to kill quadripartite government—we were trying to find another formula for it. So we tried to avoid this being a political union at that time. It was not until after the 1947 fall meeting of the Council of Foreign Ministers in London that we went full speed ahead with a political merger.

Q: Your British opposite number at the time was General Sir Brian Robertson?

CLAY: Brian Robertson was completely different from his predecessor [Lieutenant General Sir Ronald Weeks]. Brian's father had been Chief of the Imperial General Staff. Brian had gone to the military schools. He'd been a sapper [engineer]. After some years in the Army, Brian got out and went with Dunlop Rubber. When war came, he went right back into the Army and became head of supply for Alexander and

Montgomery. And he was unquestionably Montgomery's choice to be his deputy for military government.

"I don't think Ronnie Weeks was Montgomery's choice. I don't mean by that that Montgomery wasn't satisfied with him. But I think he was picked by the British government for the job, whereas Robertson was Montgomery's choice. Then he stayed as deputy under [Air Marshal Sir Sholto] Douglas [who succeeded Montgomery].

"Neither Montgomery nor Douglas really cared very much about military government. If you read Douglas's book, it's almost amusing, because he says that he always found out what I was going to do, and since he agreed with me, he did the same. That was the way Douglas operated. I liked him.

"Brian Robertson was a man of great intelligence. Some of our Americans didn't like him because he was very, very British. He was immaculate. . . . He looked like a Guards officer, both in uniform and in civilian clothes. Quite serious minded, although he played an outstanding game of bridge. He liked to play polo. He was a man of great intellectual capacity. I had tremendous respect for him. And we didn't have very many differences. When we did, it was usually because we had been launched on separate courses by our governments. We got to the point [in Bizonia] that regardless of which one of us presided over bipartite meetings, we never had to interrupt or change a word. We could feel and sense when we had each other's approval.

"From my point of view, I could not have had a better working partner. In the period when I was Military Governor and Robertson was deputy [on the British side], I still worked with him more than I did with Douglas, although I was very fond of Douglas. He was a fine person, but he didn't really care. And Robertson did. He had both great pride and perhaps some feeling of having to outdo himself because his father had risen from the ranks to become Chief of Staff. The only time it's ever happened in Britain."

Q: And your French opposite, General Koenig?

CLAY: General Koenig was a very bright, able Frenchman. He'd had a very gallant record fighting with the Free French forces up from Bir Hacheim to join Montgomery at El Alamein. Fundamentally, he wasn't interested in military government or the quadripartite control of Germany. He had a little kingdom down there [in the French zone], and he wanted to keep it that way. He was bright enough and understood what was going on. But one of the problems was that he was an absolute out-and-out Gaullist. And de Gaulle was no longer in power. The result was, I always thought he was reporting to and taking his orders from de Gaulle rather than from the French government.

Q: Why didn't the French government replace him?

CLAY: The French government, I think, wanted to move him. But the fact is, the French government changed with such rapidity at that time that it never got around to it.

"I happened to visit Mr. [Maurice] Schuman in Paris just before the NATO founding session, and I gave him a report on what we were doing and trying to do in Germany [concerning the formation of the Federal Republic]. He said, 'That's what I suspected. That isn't what I've been told [by General Koenig]. But this is the way I suspected it was.' And Schuman was Foreign Minister. As a matter of fact, Mr. Schuman originally sent word to me that he was going to try to slip into Germany secretly and wanted to know if I could meet him at Bad Homburg. But I decided to go to Paris instead. Mr. [James] Riddleberger [who had succeeded Murphy as Clay's State Department adviser] went with me. We were joined by Mr. [Jefferson] Caffery [U.S. Ambassador to France], and we went around and had lunch with Mr. Schuman. At this time, the French were blocking all of our efforts in military government to create the Federal Republic. And we talked to Mr. Schuman for about two hours. This is when I told him what our plans were for a federalized Germany and what it was that we wanted to do. But he had not been able to get that information from his subordinates in Germany. And Mr. Schuman agreed with us completely. This broke the logjam. He immediately came over to the United States and signed the agreement [to establish the Federal Republic] with Mr. Bevin."

Q: And Mr. Bevin? He was British Foreign Secretary when Bizonia was created.

CLAY: Ernie was a great man. I enjoyed him. I had the greatest respect for him. He murdered the King's English, but he knew where he was every minute and what he wanted to do. I think he thought Robertson and I were both working for him. He was really bipartite in every respect, and I saw him much more often than I saw members of my own government. As a matter of fact, he was the first government leader of stature to endorse the airlift [in 1948].

"But Mr. Bevin was quite a character. We had been in London for the foreign ministers' conference [in 1947], and the King and Queen gave a reception in Buckingham Palace for the delegates. Out of their usual custom, the King stood in one place in the room, the Queen in another, and the Queen Mother in another. The equerries took you to meet one and then another. Robertson and I were standing together talking, and Ernie came over and grabbed each of us by an arm and took us over to the King. He said, 'King, here are a couple of my boys I want you to meet.' I don't think there was anybody else in the British Isles who would have addressed the King as 'King' or told him that here were a couple of 'my boys' that 'I want you to meet.' But that is exactly the way he put it. And with it all, he was extremely intelligent, knew what he was doing, and I had great respect for him. Certainly a rough character, as you would expect from his background and his appearance, but innately a gentleman and a very fine and highly intelligent man."

Q: And the zonal merger?

CLAY: He accepted the zonal merger fully. As a matter of fact, I don't think that there was ever any problem between the United States and the British in connection with the bizonal merger. We had the right of veto. We never used it. Never.

"Eventually, the French joined us. I had the idea that if we set up something like Bizonia, and if it really worked—and it was working—maybe it would encourage the others to come in. Maybe we could reestablish effective quadripartite government for all of Germany. And the fact that it was working is what brought the French in. But it didn't bring the Russians in."

Q: Why was Frankfurt selected as the seat of Bizonia?

CLAY: It was the largest city, a central city with good communications. I don't think that it was necessary that it be in the American zone. Frankfurt just seemed the logical place. We had the facilities for a bizonal headquarters there. We could give office space in the headquarters building to General Robertson and his staff, and later to General Koenig and his staff. So it worked out very well.

"So far as I know, there was never any discussion of any other place. Frankfurt was so logical—far more logical than Bonn to have become the German capital—except that Mr. Adenauer loved the Rhine. Period."

But establishing Bizonia was far easier than making it work. As Clay advised Under Secretary of War William Draper shortly after its founding, "The basic difficulties in making the bizonal economic agencies effective are more fundamental than appear on the surface. The tendency of the Germans is to an almost complete regimentation of the German economy and they have considerable British sympathy for this purpose."

Clay said that, "having been intimately involved with wartime controls [in Washington], I know that many thousands of people would be required and these people are not available. The present German [economic] agency is much too large for broad policy actions and yet many times too small for detailed control."

Clay believed that the British wanted to nationalize industry in the bizonal area and were encouraging the Germans to push for tighter central controls. In particular, Clay thought General Robertson was under strong pressure from Britain's Labour government to promote socialism in Germany, and he told Washington that the centralized control the British sought "would destroy the political gains we have made in our own zone."

Nevertheless, on the whole Clay believed that important progress was being made in restoring Germany's economic and political life. The bizonal structure still had bugs in it, but Clay saw it as a necessary first step toward eventual German unity. More significantly, his November 1946 agreement with Sokolovsky on the hitherto intractable issue of reparations led him to hope that effective quadripartite government could be resuscitated. If that were so, he was convinced that free elections would restore a democratic government to the Soviet zone. Above all, his personal difficulties with the Army command structure had been resolved. As CINCEUR, Clay restricted the General Staff to purely military matters, and was able to devote most of his own energy to the more politically charged issues of military government.

But Clay's optimism suffered a severe setback on January 20, 1947, when Justice Byrnes abruptly announced his resignation as Secretary of State. Byrnes had just been named by *Time* magazine as its "Man of the Year" for 1946, largely as a result of his successful negotiation of the Italian and satellite peace treaties with the Soviet Union, and his resignation was totally unexpected. In fact, for a brief moment at the end of 1946 and the beginning of 1947, it looked as if the wartime amity between Washington and Moscow might be restored and the momentum of the Cold War reversed. Byrnes himself certainly thought he was on the verge of a decisive breakthrough. In a widely publicized speech on January 11, 1947, Byrnes stated:

> The development of a sympathetic understanding between the United States and the Soviet Union is the paramount task of statesmanship. Today, I am happy to say I am more confident than at any other time since V. J. Day that we can achieve a just peace by cooperative effort if we persist with firmness in the right as God gives us the power to see the right.

Byrnes added that "Nations, like individuals, must respect one another's differences," which was a theme that had characterized his long career. Like British Foreign Secretary Ernest Bevin, Byrnes had had little experience in foreign affairs when he became Secretary of State in 1945. But he shared President Roosevelt's belief that cooperation with the Soviet Union was essential if world peace was to be achieved. Byrnes had accompanied FDR to Yalta and, within the limits of diplomatic possibility, he felt that he had always been able to work with the Soviets. At Potsdam, for example, when Truman and White House Chief of Staff Admiral William Leahy had despaired of the outcome, Byrnes had fashioned a package deal with Molotov temporarily settling the reparations question on largely U.S. terms in exchange for moving the Polish frontier westward to the Oder-Neisse.

At the Moscow Council of Foreign Ministers in December 1945, Byrnes had come close to restoring wartime amity: procedures for drafting the Balkan peace treaties were agreed upon; the Soviet Union endorsed the U.S.-British-Canadian proposal for a United Nations Atomic Energy Commission; an Occupation council for Japan was agreed upon; Stalin consented to the presence of U.S. troops in China; and provision was made for the unification of Korea. The only issue that had not been resolved was the withdrawal of foreign troops from Iran.

Unfortunately, Byrnes's pragmatic attitude appalled many ideologues in Washington. President Truman, his immediate advisers—

particularly Fleet Admiral William Leahy, Judge Samuel Rosenman, and the career foreign service officers of the State Department—believed Byrnes was on the threshold of a policy of dangerous appeasement toward Russia. Senator Arthur Vandenberg of Michigan, the ranking Republican on the Senate Foreign Relations Committee, who accompanied Byrnes to the various foreign ministers' conferences, later wrote that his principal task at that time had been to prevent Byrnes from "loitering around Munich." Like many in Washington, Vandenberg believed that the "policy of tolerance, patience and respect" for the Soviet Union that Byrnes and Clay advocated would lead straight to disaster.

Byrnes also encountered the unremitting hostility of State Department professionals. Part of this was due to Byrnes's preference for handling the important issues of foreign policy personally. In Acheson's words, "As far as Mr. Byrnes was concerned, the State Department consisted of about six people. . . . What the rest of the Department did was no concern of his and he did not want to be bothered about it." But, more important, the key members of the U.S. diplomatic establishment shared an ingrained distrust of the Soviet Union. As Bedell Smith expressed it from Moscow: "The career U.S. Foreign Service Officer felt that the Soviet Union . . . was almost incapable of collaborating with other governments in the manner which Americans have in mind when they speak of collaboration."

In addition, and despite Byrnes's accomplishments, the chemistry between him and President Truman was not good. To some degree, Byrnes may have felt that he, not Truman, should have been FDR's running mate in 1944, and, for his part, Truman was never completely comfortable with his Secretary of State. In fact, Truman went so far as to ask Congress to alter the line of succession to the presidency in 1946 to put the Speaker of the House (Sam Rayburn) and the President *pro tem* of the Senate (Kenneth McKellar) ahead of the Secretary of State. As Clay phrased it, "I think [Byrnes] sort of patronized Mr. Truman when he was Secretary of State, and you can't patronize the President of the United States."

Whether Byrnes's unexpected success with the Russians (and the positive press coverage he received) triggered Truman's move is unclear. Truman always believed Byrnes harbored presidential ambitions, and the President's own popularity was at an all-time low. The Republicans had just captured both houses of Congress, and Truman undoubtedly feared that Byrnes might be planning to supplant him as the Democratic nominee in 1948.

Byrnes's failure to keep him fully informed of the Moscow negotiations heightened Truman's suspicions. The result was that in early January 1947, the President contacted General Marshall in China and asked him to return to Washington as soon as possible. Marshall had been aware of Truman's dissatisfaction with Byrnes for some time, and indicated from China that he would take the job as Secretary of State "if that continues to be [Truman's] desire." When Byrnes learned of the President's message to Marshall, he promptly resigned.

The sudden announcement of Byrnes's departure filled Clay with dismay, and he wrote the Justice on January 27 of the "unbelievable shock" his resignation had caused. "Somehow or other," said Clay, "my own assignment here in Germany does not seem the same." Clay told Byrnes that he would continue in Germany, "although I shall again urge the War Department to look for an ultimate successor."

> All of this is not why I am writing to you. Now that you have left the arena, perhaps I can try to say the things that have been in my heart since I first had the privilege of working for you. That privilege has given me a new faith in America and in democracy. It has proved that an American can spend his life in politics and at the same time keep the faith and maintain the highest levels of service. . . . I can only add that I personally have been a better man because of my association with you.

The departure of Secretary Byrnes removed Clay's most important supporter in Washington. While Eisenhower remained as the Army's Chief of Staff and Judge Patterson stayed on as Secretary of War, the replacement of Byrnes by General Marshall meant that Clay could no longer count on the automatic approval of his German policy by the Secretary of State. To the contrary, General Marshall and Clay were not close, and Marshall had been especially selected by Truman to take a tough line with the Soviet Union: an implicit repudiation of the policy that Byrnes and Clay espoused.

The result was that American policy, both toward the Soviet Union and in Germany, changed abruptly. Unlike Byrnes, Marshall abhorred ambiguity. His experience as Chief of Staff in World War II led him to place exceptional emphasis on orderly process, administrative efficiency, and chain-of-command decisions. He relied exclusively on the State Department professionals Byrnes had avoided, and like them he shared an abiding distrust of the Soviet Union. During Marshall's tenure as Secretary of State, U.S.-Soviet relations slipped to their lowest ebb.

And it is also true that after Byrnes's resignation, Clay felt shut out from the top policy-making level in Washington. He did not wish to attend the upcoming meeting of the Council of Foreign Ministers in Moscow. Above all, he did not want to become window dressing for the hard-line attitude that now dominated U.S. thinking toward the Soviet Union. Clay believed that the Moscow conference would "become the basis for an intensive propaganda campaign" and could trigger "a period of unrest in Germany. If this is correct, obviously my place is in Germany," Clay told the War Department on January 28, 1947.

Clay's fears were confirmed on March 7, when Secretary Marshall's party arrived in Berlin on their way to Moscow. The only friendly face, the only holdover from Byrnes's tenure with whom Clay felt comfortable, was Benjamin Cohen, whom Marshall had retained as State Department Counselor. Instead of the positive aura of pragmatic compromise that Byrnes exuded, Clay found the U.S. delegation mired deeply in the permafrost of the Cold War. The State Department professionals H. Freeman Matthews and Charles Bohlen set the tone for the delegation, and Marshall had added John Foster Dulles to ensure bipartisan support. Dulles's presence disturbed Clay. Widely touted as the next Secretary of State should the GOP win the presidency in 1948, Dulles saw himself as the defender of Western civilization against a rising tide of atheistic Communism. Not only did he reject any accommodation with the Soviet Union, but Dulles was also the leading advocate of detaching the Ruhr from Germany and placing it under international control.

In the delegation's discussions at the Army's Wannsee guest house in Berlin, Clay found himself dangerously isolated. At Marshall's request, he summarized his November memorandum to Byrnes advocating an accommodation with the Soviets on reparations and said that his discussions with Marshal Sokolovsky indicated that a deal could be struck. That, in Clay's view, would restore quadripartite government in Germany and extend Western influence into the Soviet zone. Clay thought German unity could be attained and that democracy along Western lines could be established in all of Germany.

Dulles responded with a paper he had prepared especially for the meeting. The basic premise was that the United States was locked into a worldwide ideological struggle between Christian civilization and Communism, and that the Soviet Union was America's mortal enemy. Then, in response to Clay, Dulles asked rhetorically: Could a united Germany be relied upon to form a part of Christian civilization that would resist Soviet Communism? Dulles thought not. Could a united Germany be achieved without forcing France to go Communist? Again Dulles thought not. And, finally, Dulles asked, "Was a united Germany compatible with a stable and peaceful Europe?" Again, the answer was no. To John Foster Dulles it was absolutely clear that a united Germany was not in America's interest. A united Germany would be inherently unstable, as history so clearly proved. More important, the effort required to achieve German unity would redound to the advantage of the French Communist Party. It would fan the flames of anti-German sentiment in France and drive the French to Communism for safety (the standard State Department rationale at the time). Above all, a united Germany would be too big to be contained in the impoverished confines of postwar Europe. It would be a menace to its neighbors and to itself. Germany could quickly become the master of Europe once again, said Dulles, and in his view that risk was not worth taking.

Instead, Dulles urged that the United States go slow in seeking a quadripartite accord with the Soviet Union. He suggested that as an additional safeguard, the Ruhr be stripped from Germany and placed under international control—a vital element in European recovery, and a further guarantee against a united Germany.

Clay responded with equal force, drawing deeply on his experience as Military Governor. The future of Europe lay in Germany, he argued, not in France. Unless the German people were given some hope for the future, *Germany* would go Communist. Since Molotov's speech in Paris, Communism had made important inroads. Only Secretary Byrnes's visit to Germany and his great speech at Stuttgart had slowed the tide. But the future of Germany hung in the balance. To detach the

Ruhr would be a horrible mistake. Not only would it ensure that Germany would turn eastward, but the Ruhr itself would become a source of continuing tension and unrest. Ultimately, Clay said, it would lead to war or to a total Communist victory in Europe.

The exchange between Clay and Dulles was hot and unpleasant. Both spoke sharply—and each believed intensely in the correctness of his own position. The tension at the meeting was palpable. All of those present were soon aware they were witnessing a historic exchange. American policy hung in the balance. In Clay's view, only Ben Cohen was sympathetic to the argument he had made, but Cohen remained silent. Marshall made it clear he supported Dulles. In Marshall's view, Clay suffered from *localitis*—a problem he said he had encountered frequently during the war whereby local commanders were too involved in their own situation to appreciate what was happening around them. Marshall thought Clay was too deeply enmeshed in the occupation of Germany to understand the global nature of the Communist problem America confronted. The meeting closed with Dulles triumphant. The division of Germany had become a foregone conclusion. Quadripartite government was dead—and with it all hopes of German unity, as well as all hopes of extending Western democracy to the Soviet zone. The vast area between the Elbe and the Oder-Neisse would be abandoned to Communism. The future of Europe, as Dulles and Marshall saw it, lay in a divided Germany, and the fateful decision had been made. Whether even the Ruhr could be salvaged for a truncated Germany was questionable. Clay was isolated and despondent. He was more determined than ever not to accompany the American delegation to Moscow.

Paradoxically, at the very time of his most stinging defeat on Occupation policy at the hands of Dulles and Marshall, Clay was given his fourth star by the War Department and made a full general. He was scheduled to assume command of the European Theater from General McNarney on March 15. Since there were a number of changes he was intent on making, and he preferred to make them as soon as possible, Clay believed that that was reason enough to remain behind. More important, however, he disagreed deeply with the new direction of American policy and wanted to distance himself as much as possible.

The Council of Foreign Ministers convened in Moscow on March

10, 1947. Almost immediately, Clay received a cable in Berlin to come to Moscow as soon as possible to assist in the discussions on Germany. Clay demurred. He received a second cable on March 14, this time from Ben Cohen, informing him that General Marshall desired his presence in Moscow as a matter of urgency. Clay flew from Berlin that afternoon. The fact is, it was Cohen, not Marshall, who badly wanted Clay in Moscow, because he knew that without Clay, Dulles's views on the Ruhr would be unopposed.

Clay was met at the airport by Bedell Smith, who, as U.S. ambassador in Moscow, was host to the American delegation. Since Smith was an old and close friend of General Marshall, his presence, and the inevitable role that he would play, was scarcely reassuring to Clay. Indeed, on the drive from the airport to the embassy, Smith told Clay of the powerful impact Dulles had made. From his own vantage point in Moscow, Smith said, he thought Dulles was correct about the Soviet Union.

As soon as he arrived at the embassy, Clay sought out Ben Cohen, only to have his worst fears confirmed. As Clay recalled years later, "John Foster Dulles was advocating a plan to detach the Ruhr from Germany. General Marshall and General Smith rather liked the idea. I fought it bitterly. So it became a matter of considerable controversy within the American delegation. It never reached the conference because we could never agree on an agenda [with the Russians]. The conference wound up without ever having discussed this particular problem. So we never presented it. But if we had presented it, I'm sure the Russians would have grabbed it. And what kind of Europe you would have today is beyond my comprehension.

"One of the problems was that General Marshall had just come back from China, and he'd had absolutely no time to brief and inform himself about the issues. But after the conference was over, when he came back through Berlin on his way home from Moscow, he had changed completely. And it was then for the first time that he approved what we were doing to restore a reasonable economy in Germany."

Q: How did the issue of detaching the Ruhr from Germany arise?
CLAY: Foster Dulles. He was a member of the delegation [to the Moscow Council of Foreign Ministers], presumably representing the Re-

publican Party. Don't forget, the Republicans controlled both houses of Congress at that time.

"The idea was that without the Ruhr, Germany would be powerless. And by detaching the Ruhr and rebuilding it, Foster believed, you would revive the economy of Western Europe. Without it, you could not. To this there was some merit. But the damage you would have done to Germany is impossible to measure. It certainly would have turned Germany over to the Communists.

"One of the problems was that Mr. Dulles was then in his French phase. He was extremely pro-French at the time. Years later, he and I were sitting beside one another at a Lincoln Day Republican dinner, and he leaned over to me and said, 'Lucius, do you remember how you and I fought to keep them from detaching the Ruhr from Germany?' And he really believed it. As Secretary of State, his thinking had so changed that he couldn't realize, or couldn't remember, that he'd been the principal advocate in 1947 of detaching the Ruhr from Germany. And in fairness to Foster, I don't know what he would have done at Moscow if the conference had actually discussed the Ruhr. Mr. Dulles was a lawyer. He used to put out feelers and premises far beyond what he actually believed. But the fact is, he did want to detach the Ruhr from Germany at that time."

Q: Was Robert Murphy at Moscow?

CLAY: Murphy was there. And he was also in bad odor, because he was as much opposed to detaching the Ruhr as I was. Bedell Smith was for it, because he thought it was probably a good idea to be for whatever Mr. Dulles was for. This was 1947. I don't think anyone was against it except Murphy and me. Everyone else just stood around and let us carry the torch. But fortunately the Russians bailed us out and we never got to it.

The bitter struggle between Clay and Dulles dominated the delegation's deliberations in Moscow. Dulles was determined to use his influence to the fullest and did not hesitate to remind the conferees that the GOP controlled both houses of Congress. If his views were not accorded their just weight, Dulles made it clear that he would have difficulty defending what went on in Moscow when he got back to the United States. Ben Cohen, who did his best to mediate between Dulles and Clay, tried to defuse the situation with a joking reference to the bipartisan nature of U.S. foreign policy, but the fact was that Dulles and Clay were both too intense and too deeply wedded to their convictions to permit any compromise, let alone levity.

Clay was visibly uncomfortable to be with the delegation. According to conference participants, everyone "was aware that Foster Dulles and Bedell Smith were Marshall's fair-haired boys," and Clay's voice had far less impact than when Byrnes had been Secretary. As the meetings dragged on, the tension between Clay and Dulles mounted. On March 22, the four foreign ministers established a working party to explore the German situation further. Composed of Clay, Robertson, Hervé Alphand, and Andrey Vyshinsky, the committee was to prepare a report for the foreign ministers summarizing the areas of agreement and disagreement. When Dulles insisted that Clay make no commitments to the working party without securing the approval of the U.S. delegation in advance, Clay exploded.

According to Charles Kindleberger, who was then chief of the German and Austrian economic affairs section in the State Department, Clay turned white with anger. His eyes flashed as he bitterly lashed out at Dulles. He reminded Dulles that he, Clay, was Military Governor of Germany, the Commander-in-Chief of U.S. forces in Europe, and a full general in the United States Army who had been dealing with Britain, France, and the Soviet Union concerning Germany for two years. It was outrageous that he be subjected to prior censorship. Clay said he would not stand for it.

"Blood was all over the floor," said James Riddleberger, who witnessed the exchange, along with Murphy and Matthews. Clay and Dulles later apologized to each other—"we realized we were making mountains out of molehills"—but the breach at that time was complete.

Two days later, after several sessions of the working group, Clay reiterated his views at Marshall's morning briefing, insisting that the United States could reach an agreement with the Russians on reparations that would salvage German unity under quadripartite control. The result, as Clay had consistently pointed out, would be to extend U.S. influence from the Elbe to the Oder-Neisse. By now, of course, Clay was virtually alone in defending that position. As the historian John Backer has noted, "The winds of history had shifted and a new course had evidently been set in the White House." "Compromise" had become a dirty word. Containment—and with it the division of Germany at the Elbe—was now American policy.

Clay expressed his bitterness in Moscow openly. "The whole matter is poorly run," he complained. "The Secretary and Cohen don't know what they want. They are disorganized and ultimately are going to throw away Germany." Departing from his customary rectitude, Clay frankly told Sokolovsky that he had nothing to do with the change in U.S. policy. He said that the two of them should have settled the matter of reparations the previous November, when they could have.

Clay asked for and received Marshall's permission to return to Germany. "In view of my responsibilities in Germany, I should return as soon as you will release me," wrote Clay. "If needed, I can always return by air on twenty-four hours notice."

Clay was annoyed, distressed, and despondent. He wanted to return to Berlin as soon as possible. "In Berlin, I knew that if I called a press conference people would listen, and my resignation would have some impact," Clay said many years later. "I was worried that Marshall and Dulles were going to submerge our interests to those of France, and I was determined to prevent it.

"When we went back to the next foreign ministers' conference in London that fall, General Marshall would have no part of [Dulles's plan to detach the Ruhr]. Unlike Moscow, General Marshall was very prepared. He was very positive and very assured in London. He had not been [so] in Moscow. And as a matter of fact, he was a little resentful of Mr. Dulles—who was still a delegate. Foster slipped away from the [London] conference and went over to see de Gaulle—who was out of power at that time. And he had a private meeting with de Gaulle. I'm sure General Marshall didn't like it one bit. And so he was very cool to Mr. Dulles throughout the London conference."

Q: Could you describe General Marshall at that time?

CLAY: General Marshall was a man of tremendous dignity. Very calm. Very controlled. He was an aloof man. He was not "Hail fellow well met." He was a very austere person. I never really knew him on a close, personal basis. I'd been in his office on many occasions, and I had great respect for him. I don't know whether I could say I had any affection for him.

"After he retired, I used to see General Marshall quite often at the Business Council, where he was much less aloof and much warmer than he had been when we were both in the service. Indeed, on one occasion he went out of his way to express to me how well I had done in Germany, which was quite a surprise to me. Because I didn't think he felt that way. And I don't think he did at the time."

Q: Could you compare Justice Byrnes and General Marshall in the role of Secretary of State?
CLAY: Mr. Byrnes informed himself in much more detail than General Marshall. He kept himself in touch by taking his own notes. General Marshall confined his comments to relatively brief remarks aimed at principles rather than details. The one big difference was that Secretary Byrnes had been sitting with the Russians and with the British in a period when they were willing to negotiate. In fact, he had just negotiated the satellite peace treaties. General Marshall, on the other hand, arrived to meet the Russians when they were absolutely unwilling to negotiate anything. So I think, in the one case, Mr. Byrnes had hopes he was going to get somewhere. I really believe that after the Moscow [foreign ministers'] conference, General Marshall had no real hope of success.

Shortly after his return to Berlin from the Moscow conference, Clay wrote to Walter Brown of South Carolina, his old friend from wartime Washington. Brown had served with Clay in the Office of War Mobilization and Reconversion and was one of Justice Byrnes's closest associates. Clay told Brown that he was

> shocked when Justice Byrnes resigned and I am afraid I have not had the same heart for my work since. This was particularly true of [the] Moscow [Council of Foreign Ministers], and after being there for two weeks I asked for and received permission to return to my duties here in Germany. Believe it or not, I am still trying to practice the type and kind of democracy which we all believed in and with real hopes for its success if America is patient and fully prepared to support such a program.

But if Marshall and the State Department were displeased with Clay, his alliance with Eisenhower and the War Department was as strong as ever. "I cannot tell you how deeply satisfied I am that you are on the job in that troublesome area," Ike wrote Clay at the height of the Moscow conference. "More and more there is a growing appreciation of your work and of your difficulties. Whenever I talk about you to newspaper people and to individuals on the hill, I find most gratifying reactions." It was a small but important consolation for Clay, who now felt beset by those who sought to achieve European recovery at Germany's expense.

· 24 ·

End of the Wartime Alliance

CLAY RETURNED FROM MOSCOW READY TO RESIGN AS Military Governor if German interests were compromised by Marshall and Dulles. Moreover, he was convinced that when Marshall got back to the United States, "one of the first things he was going to do" was to make Bedell Smith Military Governor of Germany. "The earlier the better," Clay told Marjorie, who was in the Army's Berlin hospital with a painful case of sciatica. For the first time since his early days as a maverick first lieutenant, Clay found himself out of step with those above him. The difference was that this time the future of occupied Germany was at stake.

Even as European Theater Commander, Clay had continuing difficulties with Washington. When the War Department instructed him in the spring of 1947 to increase restitution deliveries from Germany to Western Europe, Clay bluntly refused. "We have stated repeatedly that we want to make Germany a democratic nation," Clay told the War Department. "Nevertheless, we proceed unilaterally with irritating measures which we continue indefinitely."

> If we are to win and hold Germany for Western civilization, we must bring such measures to an end. The American zone has been safely held by democratic parties up to date. All of my recent intelligence reports point to a rapid penetration of communism. If communism does win western Germany, it is obvious our policies in Germany have failed and those of us responsible for the government of Germany will be completely condemned.

"In spite of this," said Clay, "we do not get the support [we need from Washington] in small matters that are important." Clay said he was not going to give the French "a hunt and seizure right" to take property from the U.S. zone. "I am sure that the results would be disastrous. . . . I am not exaggerating the penetration and growth of communism in western Germany. It can win western Germany if we continue to play our cards the way we are."

Clay had not sought his assignment to Germany in 1945. "It was the last job I wanted," he once confessed. But as the task of rebuilding a democratic Germany unfolded before him, Clay was consumed by the challenge. During his own career as a professional soldier, the world had fought two wars against German aggression. The bestiality of Nazism had blighted an entire continent and reduced much of Central Europe to a pile of rubble. The physical and emotional destruction that Clay found in Germany threatened the very survival of an entire people.

As a citizen and as a soldier, Clay embraced Roosevelt's vision for the quadripartite occupation of Germany and continuation of the wartime alliance. His original instructions from the War Department had aimed not only at the demilitarization and de-Nazification of Germany, but at its democratization as well. But from his first days in Germany, Clay had been concerned about the vindictive tone of some of his directives, and about the difficulty of teaching democracy when hunger and economic deprivation stalked the land. He followed the advice of Henry Stimson to be firm with the Germans politically but interpret his economic instructions flexibly. Repeatedly Clay had put his Army career in jeopardy to obtain food for a starving country, and he had pressed ahead with free elections and political reorganization when even his closest advisers thought he was moving too quickly. Clay also believed that he had achieved an effective working relationship with Marshal Sokolovsky, and he blamed the French for the failure to establish a central government. Despite all of the difficulties in the Allied Control Council, the lack of support by his government, and the occasional skepticism expressed at his own headquarters, he could see visible progress in bringing a democratic Germany back into the family of nations.

He now confronted a new situation. The Wannsee conference with Dulles and Marshall—at which Clay had been accused of *localitis*—made it clear that German unity was no longer possible. His brief stay in Moscow had confirmed that cooperation with the Soviet Union in Germany had been written off by Secretary Marshall and those now in charge of U.S. policy. Clay had been too close to the German problem to subscribe to the anti-Soviet charges emanating from Washington, and he knew that all four powers shared the blame for the stalemate that had developed. He was especially troubled that the final compromise on reparations he had worked out with Sokolovsky had been rejected by his government.

One historian has noted that Clay had seen his mission in Germany "in the idealistic light of the closing phases of his country's last crusade for democracy. Cooperation with the Russians in the heart of Europe and a disarmed democratic Germany had seemed to promise many years of peace. But now, after the failure at Moscow, he had no doubt that from here on it would be a different ball game. There would be two Germanies rather than one and American troops would have to remain in Europe indefinitely."

Clay was disheartened, and it was apparent to those who worked with him in Berlin. His gaunt figure was drained by fatigue—Clay, who was ordinarily of slight-to-medium build, had lost thirty pounds in two years, and he continued to survive on a combination of black coffee and strong cigarettes. As usual, he ate a light lunch at his desk, usually no more than a sandwich, and was rarely at home until late in the evening. When Walter Brown wrote and offered Clay "40 acres and a mule" at Brown's South Carolina estate, Clay threatened to take him up on it. "There is one thing about it," said Clay. "My mule must be properly aged before I take over as his ability to pull a plough must be very limited. I am getting down now to where two rows of watermelon, one row of cow peas, and one row of corn look like a big and satisfactory undertaking."

The Moscow meeting of the Council of Foreign Ministers had adjourned without notable success on April 24, 1947. Dulles's proposal to internationalize the Ruhr did not reach the conference table, and the foreign ministers accepted the need for a higher level of German industry, the details of which were to be worked out by the four military governors. When Secretary Marshall and his party stopped briefly in Berlin on April 25, Clay was given new instructions. Marshall told Clay that the unification of Germany was, at best, many years away. In the meantime, Clay was to work with General Robertson to strengthen the bizonal area. Above all, Clay was to increase production to make the British and American zones economically self-sufficient as soon as possible. Marshall remained in Berlin for less than an hour. In keeping with Marshall's style, his instructions to Clay were crisp. Nothing more was said about detaching the Ruhr; Clay took that as a positive sign. He had been given new marching orders. The bizonal area would become the bulwark of America's policy of containment. Clay accepted the change in good spirits. He had fought doggedly for a quadripartite solution to the German question and he had lost. He accepted the new challenge and brought military government into line. He did not know how long he would stay.

Q: And the inclusion of Germany in the Marshall Plan?
CLAY: I had known of the Marshall Plan from the very beginning and had made representation for the inclusion of Germany, which was more or less approved. The Congress sent some very talented, hard-working congressmen over to study the need for Marshall Plan aid in various countries and, indeed, to observe particularly what we had been able to do with the German funds we had received . . . and which we had used for the rehabilitation of Germany.

"I think we showed these congressmen how effective this aid could be. This would particularly include Mr. [Christian] Herter [R., Massachusetts—subsequently U.S. Secretary of State] and Senator [Everett] Dirksen [R., Illinois], who was a congressman then. In fact, when he finally went home, Mr. Dirksen, although he had been very lukewarm on the Marshall Plan in the beginning, became one of its most enthusiastic supporters."

Richard Nixon, who was one of the nineteen members of the House of Representatives to accompany Herter, reports that his visit to Germany in 1947 was "among the most sobering experiences of my life. . . . We found thousands of families huddled in the debris of buildings and in bunkers. There was a critical shortage of food, and thin-faced, half-dressed children approached us not to beg but to sell their fathers' war medals or to trade them for something to eat."

Nixon was profoundly moved by the spirit of children "who would not beg," and he reports that "Clay assured us that the Germans indeed had the strength of spirit they would need to recover. What was missing so far, Clay said, was leadership. Germany had lost a whole generation of potential leaders during the war, and thousands more had been disqualified from leadership positions because of links with the Nazis. He told us Germany would have to develop an entirely new crop of leaders for both the public and private sectors."

While Nixon, Herter, and Dirksen were in Germany, Clay received an urgent message from Under Secretary Draper saying that increasing congressional criticism of U.S. aid programs made it imperative that Clay increase food collections from German farmers. "Where is all the criticism coming from?" Clay asked. "We are doing a good job in [food] collection. Congressional committees here now are seeing problems on the ground. Back seat drivers will always criticize. However, I am convinced our program [is] sound and that militant measures would defeat our efforts. Congressional committees are seeing us as we are. I am not a salesman and if they don't like what they find they will have to say so."

Q: And your difficulties with Averell Harriman?

CLAY: Mr. Harriman is a friend of mine. A very good friend. We had no difficulties except who the ECA [Marshall Plan] representative in Germany should report to. They wanted him to report directly to them: Harriman in Paris and Paul Hoffman in the United States. But I refused that. The ECA representative in Germany had to come under military government and under me.

"In other words, if he came into Germany with money, there wasn't any use of a Military Governor any longer. The man with the money would be in control. Mr. Harriman was very much in opposition to this but he finally accepted it. I am not sure that I convinced him; I think, rather, he accepted my view because of our mutual support over many months for a firm policy in Germany.

"Afterwards—to show you how deeply I felt about this—in 1952, when I went back to Washington at the time of the Korean War, I found that almost every department of government had representatives in Europe, and each one of them was reporting directly to his agency in Washington. I got them all together and worked out a program—practically beat their heads together—a program where they all agreed that all government representatives in Europe had to accept the ambassador as the responsible and chief representative of the United States. If they had any communications with their own departments, the ambassador had to be furnished copies and kept informed at all times of what was going on. Five or six years later, when I was testifying before some congressional committee, I found this arrangement was still in operation. It was called the 'Clay Agreement.' I had no idea that it had been so written up. But it had been circulated to all the departments, and it was the 'Bible.' And I think, no matter what the terms of reference are, it is accepted today that the ambassador is the boss."

For the most part, Clay's new instructions from Marshall facilitated German recovery. For different reasons, Secretary Marshall had embraced Clay's view that the revival of the German economy was essential to Western aims. Clay believed in German recovery in and of itself: a prosperous people were more likely to be a democratic people; if a democratic Germany was America's aim, and it was certainly Clay's aim, economic recovery was essential. And Clay saw this recovery in terms of German unity and quadripartite government, which, he believed, would extend the advantages of democratic prosperity to the Soviet zone.

Marshall and the State Department saw German recovery through the lens of the Cold War. A prosperous *western* Germany would provide a bulwark against Communist expansion, and would facilitate the economic recovery of Western Europe. In everyday operational terms, the two views coincided. But the differences were fundamental, and far-reaching. And the primacy of Marshall's views meant that Germany would be divided.

On May 2, 1947, Clay sent a lengthy letter to Marshall detailing Germany's economic problems. In particular, Clay criticized the trade policies being forced on Germany by the Western Allies—policies that doomed economic recovery. For example, the Dutch and Belgian governments were insisting that Germany use the ports of Rotterdam and

Antwerp exclusively, resulting in high foreign exchange costs, rather than allowing Germany to use its own port facilities in Bremen and Hamburg. The Czechs demanded free use of German railway and port facilities as reparations. The United Nations Relief and Rehabilitation Agency (UNRRA) was demanding similar free transit for its supplies shipped to Czechoslovakia. And despite the severe shortage of young workers in Germany, France was retaining thousands of German POWs in France for labor purposes. These hidden reparations costs, said Clay, were merely passing the cost of supporting Germany on to the American and British governments. "I have tried to point out that Germany is bankrupt and that she cannot re-establish herself on a self-sustaining basis until her debts are finally fixed in amount and she herself permitted to enter into trade relations with other countries unhampered by the curse of her past political mistakes.

"I say this not out of sympathy for Germany and the German people," Clay told Marshall, "but because of the necessity to reduce the present burden on the U.S. and U.K. economies. We can unburden ourselves of this expense only by returning Germany to a satisfactory trading position or by abandoning her to chaos."

Several weeks later, Marshall replied. "You have my sympathy," he told Clay. "It is hard to get people in this country to understand the general nature of the situation in Europe, and in Germany in particular, and the complications which are involved in your particular responsibilities."

Whether Marshall agreed with Clay is unclear. Certainly, Clay was not convinced. "I miss you every day," he wrote Justice Byrnes on May 11. "Every word which you said at Stuttgart became a part of my 'Bible' for Germany. I am apprehensive that it now has little significance in guiding our policy in Germany. It was a living document of hope. *I am not pro-German, but I hope with all my heart that in our political warfare with the USSR we do not forget that here in Germany we have 70,000,000 human beings to remember.* We cannot place Germany in a vacuum while we solve world problems as if it did not exist."

As always, Byrnes was supportive. "I am disturbed by what you say about Germany," replied Byrnes. "I have the impression you did not have a pleasant time at Moscow. From what one of my friends in the party [Ben Cohen?] has told me of your run-in with Dulles, I want to go on record as heartily approving what you did. I would have done the same under the circumstances."

While Clay and General Robertson worked to reconcile U.S. and British policy in the new bizonal organization, the Allied Control Council continued to drift. Minor agreements were reached to repeal various Nazi property laws, but the four military governors proved unable to agree to a joint reduction of Occupation forces. As Clay advised Washington, the Soviets thought each zone should be limited to a hundred thousand troops, "except that the Soviet zone should be allowed an additional one hundred thousand [troops] because of its responsibility for Berlin." Clay sought to compromise with Sokolovsky and accept a ceiling of 140,000 troops for the American zone, giving the Soviets two hundred thousand, providing that "other zone commanders accept reasonable figures." But agreement proved impossible, said Clay, when the British insisted that the forces in each zone should be equal.

> I am of the view [said Clay] that we might have reached agreement if the British had not insisted on the principle of equality. It seems to me that the British are fighting for abstract principle as in fact neither the British nor the Americans are very apt to exceed their present strengths whereas a Soviet ceiling of 200,000 would require a substantial reduction in present Soviet strength.

Clay added that he "found it interesting" that Sokolovsky had asked that the matter remain on the agenda of the Control Council and said that he planned to ask the British to reconsider. But to no avail. By the summer of 1947, it had become painfully clear to Clay that, for all practical purposes, quadripartite government in Germany was dead.

Even though the United States was now committed to reconstructing the Western zones, Clay's difficulties with the French continued. In 1945 and 1946, France had rejected any arrangements in the Allied Control Council that might lead to German unity. After the Moscow conference of foreign ministers, when it became clear that four-power government was receding, Paris focused its opposition on German recovery. While Clay and Robertson worked round-the-clock to increase industrial production in Bizonia, and were on the threshold of concluding a new agreement raising the level of industry, the French launched a diplomatic offensive to scuttle the plan. Clay's first indication came in early July 1947, when he received what appeared to be contradictory instructions from the War Department. On the one hand, Clay was told to increase production so that a revived German economy could contribute to European recovery. On the other, he was told to increase reparations deliveries to Western Europe. Clay called the War Department to task. "I find it difficult to know which instructions to follow," cabled Clay. "Both objectives cannot be accomplished at the same time." Saying he could not dismantle plants and equipment for reparations and increase German industrial production simultaneously, Clay asked which course Washington wanted him to follow. As Clay noted later, Washington appeared to be "carrying water on both shoulders."

On July 11, 1947, Clay received a revised policy directive (JCS 1779) that superseded JCS 1067 and officially incorporated as U.S. policy his early messages to Washington and Byrnes's speech at Stuttgart. Clay was told to move ahead with German recovery. "Your authority as Military Governor will be broadly construed," said Washington. Clay was told to take whatever action he deemed "appropriate or desirable to attain your government's objectives in Germany or to meet military exigencies." It was the type of broad grant of authority that Clay believed in, and as he wrote later, "I accepted this statement at face value."

But at the same time, Clay was told that for political reasons he should defer announcing the new level-of-industry plan he had worked out with General Robertson. Clay was truly perplexed. "I had understood that the United States had a firm policy to increase the industrial level in Germany and to expedite its economic growth," Clay cabled Assistant Secretary of War Howard Petersen in exasperation on July 16. "We are [now] advised that we must not proceed with this increase in view of political implications. . . . To us it would appear that these political implications result from French opposition which it was well known would develop at the time we were instructed to revise the level of industry."

Clay then said he thought that the "political implications" were simply a device "to prevent at all costs economic revival in western Germany. Our Soviet opposites have no such inhibitions, and they are hard at work to prove the advantages of the Communist system in eastern Germany. It seems to me that in western Germany we are completely stymied at present. Frankly, *I am at wits end to do anything progressive in economic rehabilitation in view of our present instructions,* and yet I realize that a psychological shot in the arm is urgent and essential in Germany now."

Clay told Petersen that regardless of his own personal views, he would do "what our Government wants. However, we cannot meet conflicting objectives; nor in the face of uncertainty can our part in Germany be carried out with courage and decision."

Clay received no reply. But a few days later, the Paris press carried reports that Secretary Marshall had written to French Foreign Minister Georges Bidault promising to defer any increase in German industrial production. Clay decided he had had enough. As Military Governor he had been given broad discretionary powers in Germany, only to have the State Department renege on German recovery. He vented his anger in a lengthy teleconference with Petersen.

"I think we are facing disaster in Germany," said Clay, "and I don't like to head a failure which I can do nothing about." Clay told Petersen that if the Paris press reports were correct, "I am asked to execute a policy in which I have no hope to succeed, and this in all conscience I could not do." Clay asked to be called back to Washington so he could bow out quietly.

> To my simple mind this change in U.S. policy would be analogous to having ordered General Eisenhower to hold up when he crossed the Rhine so that the attack could be pushed from the Balkans.
>
> I feel that the State Department wants a negative personality in Germany. As you know, I can carry out a policy whole-heartedly or not at all and there is no question left in my mind but that my views relative to Germany do not coincide with present policies. . . . Request orders calling me back [to Washington] which also authorize shipment of personal belongings.

To this, Petersen wired: "Unthinkable for you to resign at this time when as you correctly analyze we have a major issue to settle—namely, precedence of German recovery plans. I don't believe the issue is lost and you are best man to win it." Clay's response was almost poignant: "Two years have convinced me we cannot have a common German policy with the French. Still I am held responsible for economic debacle in Germany and I can no longer accept that responsibility. Believe me, I understand full well State Department establishes policy and when we who are responsible for execution cannot accept it, we must go. . . . Please make no mistake. When I return, my family and belongings come with me. Sometimes you have to leave a job for someone else to win. I am not in anger or irked. However, I believe decision to defer level of industry most momentous since original Potsdam Agreement and most disastrous."

Once again, Clay's resignation dropped on Washington like a bombshell. Murphy advised Marshall through the State Department's own cable facilities that Clay meant what he said. "I believe that if Clay does retire under these circumstances," said Murphy, "he may feel obliged to make certain public statements of his views and disagreements with what he understands has happened."

Howard Petersen immediately showed a transcript of the teleconference to General Eisenhower. After a discussion with Marshall, Ike cabled Clay to sit tight: Clay's views were being listened to and German recovery was not lost. "I thoroughly understand your sense of frustration and your impatience," said Eisenhower. But "You and I have served too long in this Army to contemplate seriously the laying down of a task simply because things sometimes go at sixes and sevens. . . . Times are too critical for anyone to move out of a post in which he can serve his country's interest. As a final word," Ike told Clay, "please remember that now abide Faith, Hope and Charity, these three, and greater than any is a sense of humor."

Clay's response was predictable. Regardless of his strongly held opinions about Germany, Clay was above all a good soldier. And he prized Eisenhower's friendship more than any other. If the Chief of Staff wanted him to remain, Clay would do so.

"I am not temperamental," Clay replied, "but I do have some firm convictions as a result of two years in Germany." In fact, Clay reminded Eisenhower, those views "differ very little from those we shared prior to your return home": that is, the urgent need for German economic and political recovery in the context of four-power cooperation and a united Germany. Clay recognized that this was no longer possible. "We cannot be aware of critical international situations if we are not kept informed," he said. "You could not have run the Allied

Expeditionary Force if you had been kept in the dark relative to conditions elsewhere." Clay complained bitterly about having to learn about "complete changes in U.S. policy" from the press.

> I have never run out on an unfinished job; nevertheless, it might be a real mistake to continue in a job when it looks as if you no longer have the confidence and support of the agencies responsible for policy.

But Clay concluded the message as Eisenhower had hoped he would. "I value your friendship and good will too much not to accept your advice," Clay said. "If you think that my departure would be running out on the job and failing in my obligation to an Army which has been more than good to me, that is enough to keep me here."

Eisenhower, who had experienced his own share of difficulties with the Combined Chiefs of Staff during the war, and who at one particularly bitter moment in 1944 had narrowly headed off the naming of Sir Harold Alexander to "assist" Ike in command of Allied ground forces, sympathized fully with Clay. "I hope my former telegram did not seem stuffy to you," said Ike. "Naturally I am highly gratified with your reply and you may be sure that I understand your situation."

Perhaps more important, on July 26, 1947, Clay was informed by Secretary of War Kenneth Royall (who had succeeded Judge Patterson the week before) that United States policy toward German recovery had not changed, and that France would not be allowed to sabotage U.S. and British efforts. In a joint telegram to U.S. headquarters in Germany, Royall and Secretary of State Marshall confirmed to Clay "the U.S. government will support vigorously the level of industry agreement reached by you with [General] Robertson and defend it against any suggestions from other nations for modification." Clay was also told that "in view of the recognized urgency of the situation in Germany, it is the desire of this Government that announcement . . . should be made as soon as possible." The only qualification would be a total collapse of democracy in France, which Clay did not think likely. Two days later, in a follow-up message, Royall and Marshall confirmed that "No other country will have any vote, veto or power of decision as to the bi-zonal level of industry." Furthermore, Clay was told that any suggestions from other countries (i.e., France) would be sent to Clay and Robertson for their consideration before Washington acted. The bizonal authorities, in effect, were back in the driver's seat.

For Clay, the victory appeared complete. German recovery would proceed as scheduled. Once again, to the anguish of the Francophiles in the State Department, Clay had prevailed. But it was another costly victory. Clay had once more put his neck in a noose to ensure German recovery. No one had pulled the rope, but whether he could do that again was highly problematic. In fact, Kennan, Matthews, and Acheson urged Marshall to speed up the State Department's takeover in Germany and to replace Clay with someone more tractable. Bedell Smith, already tiring of his Moscow assignment, was the candidate mentioned most frequently.

Clay replied to Secretary Royall on July 28. Unaware that the worst was still to come, Clay told Royall he fully understood that German recovery had to be considered within the context of the European economy. "If reasonable restoration of Germany should lead to fall of democracy in France, it would be serious indeed. Nevertheless, sometimes this risk must be taken as French Government will continue to insist that this will result and no one can prove otherwise except by actual test.

"I still believe we must proceed vigorously with revival of German economy and increase the level of German industry if we are to save Germany from chaos and communism, and that a communistic Germany is almost certain to result in a communistic Europe."

Despite what appeared to be Washington's approval of Clay's policy for German recovery, the issue continued to smolder. And when Secretary Royall visited Clay in Berlin on August 1, a fire storm broke out. Royall had scheduled a press conference in Berlin to reaffirm U.S. support for German recovery. When asked about French objections, Royall replied that he "knew of no agreement . . . to consult with France before promulgation of any plan to raise the level of industry in Western Germany." Royall's comments were fully consistent with the two cables he and Marshall had dispatched to Clay. These cables reflected Washington's response to Clay's threat of resignation, but obviously were inconsistent with Secretary Marshall's contrary statement to Bidault. And it appears that until Royall's statement in Berlin, the French had not been informed that Washington had reneged on its prior commitment to consult with Paris before approving an increase in German industrial production. Clay had objected to that commitment and threatened to resign; Washington decided to back Clay and told him that there would be no French veto; but unfortunately no one bothered to inform the Quai d'Orsay. To Clay, it seemed an unfortunate replay of the Saar crisis of December 1946, with the State Department once again pursuing two contradictory policies. On the one hand, a commitment had been given by Marshall to the French to consult; on the other, Clay was told that there would be no consultation. Royall had let the cat out of the bag, and French reaction was understandable and immediate. "No matter what Washington had pretended to mean," David Schoenbrun reported from Paris, "it meant only one thing in France—priority for the reconstruction of Germany over the reconstruction of France. Foreign Minister Georges Bidault and company almost keeled over with shock [at Royall's remarks] while Maurice Thorez and the Communists chortle those famous last words, 'we told you so.' "

Robert Lovett, who had recently succeeded Acheson as Under Secretary of State, advised Marshall that "the French Government interpreted these reported statements of Secretary Royall as a disavowal of the assurances which had been conveyed by you to M. Bidault in your telegram of July 21st." Lovett's memorandum to Marshall, which was drafted in the European Affairs Division of the State Department, sought to reverse the assurances that had just been given to Clay and to reassert the primacy of France over U.S. Occupation policy in Germany.

Lovett told Marshall that "It is impossible to reconcile Secretary Royall's statement, with previous assurances given to Bidault." Royall's statement "serves to demonstrate the unworkable and, indeed, dangerous nature of any such type of understanding with the War Department on matters affecting U.S. foreign policy." The issue had become a battle for turf in Washington in which the pro-French element at State now tried to take back what Clay had won. According to Lovett, "At the present time, because of the attitude of the War Department, the United States is in an impossible position with regard to the conduct of its foreign policy. We are unable as a result of the present situation to live up to our assurances to the French and are exposing the United States in its relations with France to a justified charge of duplicity and dishonest dealing.

"We feel that this latest incident shows there is no meeting of the minds and that we are now forced to ask for a reconsideration of our understanding with the War Department and to reassert the necessity that the Secretary of State have a right to modify" whatever agreements Clay had made in Germany. Lovett urged Marshall to set aside the arrangement with Clay in favor of French support.

Clay first learned of the State Department's recantation in a teleconference with Royall (now back in Washington) on August 8, 1947. As Royall told Clay: "The frank, perhaps blunt, statement in my Berlin press conference of the fact that there was . . . no agreement to confer with the French on the level of industry has apparently raised a storm in Paris."

Despite the State Department's prior commitment to him, Royall told Clay that Marshall thought a tripartite conference with the British and French was the only way to clear the air. "I have not agreed to these discussions yet but I feel I may have to do so." Royall said that because of Clay's prestige, "I think it most important that you be our representative at the discussions. . . . I also feel that this may be an opportunity to get the level of industry settled and operating sooner than would otherwise be possible."

Clay was appalled. Once again the French had made an end run around military government and had carried the day in Washington. "I can offer no comment at moment as my only feeling is one of helpless futility," he told Royall.

> I have done all that I can to establish a new level of industry. Frankly, and I am not saying this in a spirit of saying I quit because I can't get my way, [but] I can see no hope for the solution of the German problem ahead and feel that my own ability to contribute to it is at an end. . . . You see, Mr. Secretary, the situation here is almost hopeless. We are stopped at every turn with [new] instructions while economic and political conditions in Germany steadily worsen.

Clay said that it was not a matter of prestige. "I can only suggest that State Department proceed as it deems fit, but I would like for it to tell the full story of its instructions to me . . . with respect to the level of [German] industry."

Royall broke off the teleconference with Clay to attend a meeting of the Cabinet. When he returned, and with Marshall's approval, he recommended that Clay attend a quickly scheduled tripartite meeting in London to settle the level of industry in Germany. As Military Governor, Clay would represent the War Department. Clay's cabled reply, which is printed in full, illustrates his despondency.

> After careful and serious consideration, I have no intelligent comment or recommendation which would serve any useful purpose. As you know, as long as I am here I will do my best to carry out any order which I receive from the War Department to the limit of my ability.

The following day, Murphy informed Marshall that "Clay informally tells me that decision [for Clay to attend a tripartite London conference] is not acceptable to him. . . . He spoke with bitterness over what he considers [the] absence of conviction and principle on part of the State Department." Murphy said that Clay intended to cable General Bradley (who had just been named to succeed Eisenhower as Chief of Staff) to request retirement. "On other occasions in the past I have felt that his expressed desire was tempered by a continuing interest in the job to which he has devoted himself so effectively. . . . This time he really seems to have lost interest."

Marshall did not reply to Murphy's cable. But when Lewis Douglas, the U.S. Ambassador in London (who was to chair the level-of-industry talks), cabled Marshall with a similar concern, Marshall observed that it was essentially a matter for the War Department. Nevertheless, he told Douglas that he would have no objection if Douglas contacted Clay and urged him to stay.

Once again, when faced with insistent pleas from America's oldest ally, the State Department had buckled. Using the ammunition provided to him by Kennan and Matthews, Under Secretary Lovett presented the issue to Marshall as one of State Department prerogatives versus War Department intransigence. The troublesome military governor who habitually placed German interests ahead of U.S. global concerns should be repudiated. American Occupation policy must yield to the larger interests of an accommodation between Washington and Paris. And just maybe, thought those in the State Department's European Affairs Division, Clay would resign and they could replace him.

Marshall, in fact, had for some time felt that Clay should be replaced. Among other things, Clay and Eisenhower were too close to make Marshall comfortable (Marshall had come to resent Ike's popularity), and Bedell Smith—who was Marshall's closest military associate—eagerly sought a reprieve from his Moscow outpost. With Smith as Military Governor of Germany, the State Department would no longer be forced to contend with two troublesome military governors (MacArthur was clearly beyond the State Department's control). America's policy in Germany could be subordinated to the interests of Western Europe, and responsibility would be back with the State Department, where Kennan, Matthews, and Lovett believed it belonged.

At Marshall's direction, a conference of the three Western powers occupying Germany was scheduled for London in two weeks. U.S. Ambassador Lewis Douglas would chair the American delegation, and Clay was told to attend on behalf of the War Department. But if Kennan, Lovett, and Matthews had thought their battle was won, they once again underestimated Clay's resourcefulness. While Clay detested having to attend another conference about a matter he thought had been settled, and while he bitterly resented having to play second fiddle to Lewis Douglas, he was able to swallow his pride and fight with such tenacity for the revival of German industry that the London conference eventually placed its seal of approval on the plan Clay and Robertson had negotiated.

But the going was not easy. Eisenhower would soon be replaced by Bradley as Army Chief of Staff, Judge Patterson was no longer Secretary of War, and the entire phalanx of diplomatic Washington was arrayed against Clay. On August 16, less than one week before the London conference was to convene, Clay blew off some steam to William Draper in Washington. Formerly Clay's right-hand man for economic matters, Draper (with Clay's reluctant approval) had become Under Secretary of War when Howard Petersen resigned in early August to return to his Philadelphia banking career. Clay told Draper once again that he was reluctant to go to London, but Draper assured him that only he (Clay) could assure that a proper level for German industry was adopted. "The Secretary [Royall] and I feel very strongly that your presence in London is vital to this country's interests," said Draper. "Without any desire to depreciate [Lawrence] Wilkinson or [Donald] Humphrey [Clay's subordinates for economic matters], you know as well as I do that they are not Lucius D. Clay." Clay replied on the teleprinter:

> I recognize, as you do Bill, that no one can continue in a job if he continually offers his resignation because of his inability to accept conditions. . . . It is of course possible to run Germany from Washington, although what the results would be, only time would show. The fact remains that after two and one-half years . . . I am not willing to accept the responsibility for military government in Germany with operational decisions being made elsewhere. I personally do not believe that the job can be done by anyone except under broad policy directives which permit flexibility in operation and in negotiations, and the present trend is very much the other way.
>
> It is rather humiliating to military government to send its chief representative to London as an adviser in discussing the level of industry in Germany for which he has been responsible for two and one-half years. However, a little humiliation is perhaps good for us and anyway is soon forgotten.

Clay then went on to say that his presence in London would be disastrous from a diplomatic viewpoint, ruminating that he "did not sign up to work for Lew Douglas as much as I like him personally."

Although Clay agreed to attend the meeting in London, he continued to resent his relegation to the role of an adviser to Ambassador Douglas. Clay did not object to a State Department takeover of Occupation responsibility; indeed, he had sought precisely such a changeover since mid-1946. But so long as the War Department was in charge of Germany, Clay felt it was demeaning for the Military Governor to sit in London as an adviser while Occupation policy was being hammered out over his head.

When he was questioned by reporters in Berlin about the significance of the upcoming London meeting, Clay was noncommittal, except to tell Marguerite Higgins of the New York *Herald Tribune* that "it was better if the level of industry plan was accepted by three [powers] and still better if approved by four." (Clay's personal code of Southern chivalry always made it difficult for him to deflect probing questions from female reporters, and he rather liked Miss Higgins.)

On the eve of his departure for London, Clay repeated his misgivings to Draper in Washington. "Have just seen a surprising cable from Lew Douglas to State [Department] saying British Government now claims it has never approved Bizonal agreement [on the level of industry]. This is another instance of British continually reopening agreements which have been made by Robertson and me in Berlin. Lew Douglas likes to run with the ball in open field. I urge once again that British not be allowed to get away with this. . . ."

Clay then sarcastically remarked that perhaps the United States should invite the Russians to the conference, "because Bizonal affair now becomes great international conference. I can't see why Washington doesn't recognize futility of settling specific occupation problems by conference after conference. *It's like Thanksgiving dinner now with the German problem the world's major problem. Everybody wants to be at the table to see they get white meat."*

The London meeting lasted five days. The tension in the American delegation was apparent. Douglas told his State Department colleagues that Clay was a fine soldier but "not good in negotiations—especially with foreigners"—a peculiar comment about the man who had maintained friendly relations with the Russians for two and a half years in Germany and who for four wartime years had handled military Lend-Lease. On his part, Clay told the assembled U.S. diplomats in London that he had suffered all that he could stand. For two years, Washington had not sent him any instructions; now they wanted to control the most minute details of Occupation policy. Mistrust and animosities were mutual. The State Department officials believed Clay could not or would not see America's broader interests—an official echo of Marshall's *localitis* complaint—and Clay thought the diplomats were prepared to sacrifice German recovery to placate French public opinion. "Whenever we go into a conference about Germany," said one disgruntled State Department official, "we first have to negotiate a treaty with General Clay." At the time, Clay took that as a compliment.

In a curious way, the conference proved more successful than Clay had foreseen. The level of industry that Clay and Robertson had agreed upon was adopted; it was agreed that public announcement could be made in Germany immediately, and the three powers noted for the record that increased German production did not imply that priority was being given to the rehabilitation of Germany at the expense of Western Europe. France obtained the appearance of diplomatic victory so important to assuage domestic discontent; Clay (and Robertson) in turn secured French approval to proceed with German recovery.

"Publication of [the new] level of industry has already had profound effects in Germany and I am sure [it] will serve as a spur to general recovery," a delighted Clay cabled Secretary Royall on August 31. "Discussions in London were interesting. Douglas handled the matter well. However, he was helped materially by firm State Department policy instructions, for which we are grateful."

Clay told Royall that if the United States assumed a greater financial responsibility for the bizonal area, it should insist on a proportionate voice in the settlement of economic matters. But he strongly advised that the pattern of rotating the chairmanship between Robertson and himself be retained. "If we have the voice, we do not need the outward evidence," said Clay, "and to change [the rotation] would damage British prestige materially. For long-range goodwill this would be a mistake. We should always leave the British an equal voice in political decisions, and, of course, troop commands should be kept separate."

But when Great Britain threatened to withdraw its troops from Germany unless given preferential financial treatment in Bizonia, Clay balked. "O ye of wavering heart," he told Draper. "We must assume it to be a bluff. . . . I am sure the British will not get out of Germany at any cost.

"Don't let [American] delegation be flustered," said Clay. "I thought we were a poker playing nation. If we stand firm and the British go home we will have time to think out what price withdrawal. If they continue to negotiate, we have won." Four days later, he told Draper that if the British insisted on their ultimatum, "then the British were looking for an excuse to leave Germany, and we are buying a dead pig."

On October 27, Clay repeated his concern about Britain and France to Gordon Gray, who had become Assistant Secretary of the Army following the creation of the Department of Defense (and the abolition of the War Department) under the National Security Act of 1947. Gray had written to Clay for ideas he might incorporate into a speech heralding the defense reorganization. Clay said it was important that the United States should have a somewhat greater voice in strictly financial matters in Germany (since the United States was picking up the tab), but "we should not even suggest that we assume a dominant political voice.

"We need England and France as equal partners and not in a subordinate position. It is in the interest of democracy that both England and France maintain their European prestige . . . and in fact our financial support to these countries has in view maintaining their prestige and leadership."

It was at this time that Clay first sensed a pressure mounting in official Washington to consider a strategic withdrawal from the exposed Western position in Berlin. Seeking to head it off, he told Gray that it was imperative to "emphasize the importance of our remaining in Berlin. Even though Berlin is surrounded by the Soviet zone, we took over a fourth interest and planted the American flag here. *If we leave Berlin, much of our prestige in Germany and in central Europe would go with us."* Clay said the United States should stay, "unless we are forced to move out by an act of aggression or as a result of a peace treaty."

By late 1947, Clay had moved almost 180 degrees. The creation of a vigorous western Germany as a bulwark against Communist aggression had by then captured Clay's imagination. Unification remained remotely possible, but Clay no longer advocated conciliatory treatment of the Soviet Union. As was his habit, Clay did not look back. He threw himself totally into creating the means of effective resistance. Characteristically, Clay never admitted that his attitude toward the Russians had changed. At his regular Berlin press conference on October 28, 1947, Clay announced a new "get tough" policy with the Soviet Union, but he maintained that it was fully consistent with the policy he had been following since 1945. "Under JCS 1067," said Clay, "our policy objectives are to protect democracy and to resist communism. I have no intention of entering into a series of recriminations and charges between the United States and the Soviet Republic. However, I do intend to defend the principles we believe and attack those in which we don't believe, and we certainly don't believe in communism in any manner, shape, form, or fashion."

Asked by Jack Raymond of *The New York Times* if he expected to stay in Berlin, Clay said, "As long as I remain in Germany, I expect to maintain my headquarters in Berlin." Whereupon James O'Donnell of *Newsweek* asked Clay how long he intended to remain in Germany. "Very obviously I will remain in this job to the extent the War Department believes desirable. On the other hand, the War Department will try to meet my request to be retired sometime in 1948." When pressed by O'Donnell as to whether he was retiring from the Army or merely as Military Governor, Clay replied, "Full and complete retirement. I am going catfishing." Clay said he had been in the Army thirty-four years. But he cautioned his listeners that his retirement would not take place immediately: it would probably be at least eight months away, and maybe as much as fourteen. "In other words, there has been no attempt to fix a date, other than not later than the end of the next calendar year [1948]."

When Clay's remarks about responding to Communist attacks were reported, they were regarded generally as a fundamental shift in U.S. policy in Germany. Edward R. Murrow of CBS claimed it was a declaration of "psychological war between the U.S. and USSR for possession of the German mind." As usual when caught off guard, Washington was at a loss. Draper cautioned Clay to hold his fire "until we have an opportunity to comment." But just as Clay had been impatient when Washington blocked his efforts to compromise with the Soviets, he was now impatient with Draper's efforts to restrain him. Clay said he proposed "to attack communism and the police state before the German people, whereas in the past we have confined our efforts to presenting the advantages of democracy." Recent attacks on the American system by Sokolovsky and Colonel Sergei Tulpanov (Sokolovsky's political adviser) "demanded an immediate and public reply. I have made that reply," Clay said. He told Draper:

> We are engaged in political warfare and we might as well recognize it now. Under these conditions we cannot wait for Washington's approval when our adversaries speak to the German public. If I get the Department of the Army into trouble, I will apologize; on the other hand, I shall not let Soviet attacks go unanswered and have both our press and the German people believe that we are afraid to answer. Do not worry that I will become a war monger.

Clay's reply merely heightened Washington's concern. Army Secretary Royall told Clay to stop making policy statements and wait for the Army's instructions. Clay stuck by his guns. "I feel very badly about your message," he told Royall. "However, I must point out that in no way did I consider [my press conference statement] a major change in policy." This time, the State Department evidently agreed with Clay. The fact is, the State Department position had not changed; Clay had, and his tough statement about the Soviets was correctly reported by

Murrow as a change of direction for Clay. As Lovett confirmed to Murphy on November 1, "We agree in principle to the necessity for stepped up propaganda in Germany," but he warned that full coordination was essential.

With the London conference of foreign ministers set to convene in early November, Clay pressed Washington to establish a West German government. Clay cabled Draper:

> If the Council of Foreign Ministers fails to produce an answer for a united Germany, we must have the courage to proceed quickly with the establishment of a government for western Germany. The resentment of the Germans against colonial administration is increasing daily, and those Germans who hate communism . . . will soon lose their positions of leadership with their own people.
>
> Two and one-half years without a government is much too long. While it is true that no German leaders will speak openly for a western Germany, they all realize as do the people that such a government must be formed if the November meeting of the CFM fails to produce a united Germany.
>
> At the risk again of being accused of *"localitis",* I must say with all the sincerity at my command that 42 million Germans in the British and American zones represent today the strongest outpost against Communist penetration that exists anywhere. . . . We cannot and we must not take the risk of losing western Germany and having all of Germany become a satellite of the USSR. As powerful as we are, it would be almost impossible for us to resist communism in the face of a Russo-German agreement. If such an agreement should ever occur, it will be because of our failure in Germany. We can fail in Germany by doing nothing or [by doing] too little to recreate leadership in the German people. It is almost too late.

On the eve of the London conference, General Eisenhower asked Clay for his recommendation on Allied troop strengths in Germany. The Army was under pressure to cut its budget, and Ike asked whether a troop reduction could be negotiated. Clay replied on November 6 that U.S. and British Occupation forces should be fixed at 100,000 each, the French at 60,000, and the Soviets, 150,000. Clay said the United States and British figures were just about in line with present troop strengths, but the suggestion "would reduce Soviet strengths by more than one half. It would allow a Soviet strength in excess of any other occupying power, which is perhaps justifiable in view of the longer border responsibilities which the Soviet troops do have." Clay said the United States did not need 100,000 troops for internal security, but any withdrawal of American troops "would have significant psychological effects, in Germany, as such withdrawal would be widely interpreted as the beginning of our abandonment of Central Europe."

Clay departed for the London meeting of the Council of Foreign Ministers on November 23, not certain what to expect. On the day before, Marshal Sokolovsky had showered his Control Council colleagues with what Clay described to Draper as twenty-five pages of vilification and abuse. "Conditions [in Berlin are] quite taut but I am afraid I am enjoying them." Clay told Draper that he still hoped for a positive outcome in London, "but with no logical reason."

Clay also asked Draper to clarify the date for his retirement from the Army with General Eisenhower, "or perhaps more correctly with General Bradley." He assured Draper that "I am willing to stay until late next year if really desired, but I do not wish to make suggestions that might be too embarrassing to the Chief of Staff in his efforts to reduce the number of four star generals."

The London Council of Foreign Ministers represented the last gasp of the wartime alliance. Between November 25 and December 15, 1947, Molotov, Marshall, Bevin, and Bidault met seventeen times. The treatment of Germany and Austria was the sole subject on the agenda. When it became abundantly clear that no progress could be made, and as Molotov became increasingly abusive, repeating almost verbatim the accusations Sokolovsky had leveled in the Control Council the previous month, Secretary Marshall abruptly terminated the conference *sine die.* The Council of Foreign Ministers, created by the Big Three of Potsdam, had broken up. The wartime coalition had dissolved. "This was the only time I ever saw Molotov wince," Clay said.

> I am sure that all of us present [Clay wrote afterward] recognized that we were now engaged in a competitive struggle, not with arms but with economic resources, with ideas and ideals. It was a struggle in which we desired no territory but were determined that others should not acquire further territory through the use of oppressive power, fear to dull the hearts and distorted information to capture the minds of peoples power-

> less to resist. . . . We knew not how long it would last or what turn it would take.

Clay, of course, was not privy to the State Department's decision to terminate the Council of Foreign Ministers and solidify Germany's division. The Division of European Affairs was now in control of American policy, and the anti-Soviet hostility of the past thirty years found expression under Marshall's leadership. As Bedell Smith, who attended the conference at Marshall's invitation, wrote to Eisenhower from London on December 2, "The difficulty under which we labor is that *in spite of our announced position, we really do not want nor intend to accept German unification in any terms that the Russians might agree to, even though they seem to meet most of our requirements.* . . . However, this puts us in a somewhat difficult position and it will require careful maneuvering to avoid the appearance of inconsistency if not hypocrisy."

Smith's crisp statement to Eisenhower captures the essence of United States policy after Byrnes's departure as Secretary of State: divide Germany and build a strong anti-Communist redoubt in the Western zones. His frank acknowledgment not only that this was contrary to America's avowed policy of promoting quadripartite government and German unity but that the Soviets had indeed met "most of our requirements," sheds important new light on the events leading up to the Berlin blockade and the creation of the West German government in 1949.

If Smith's purpose in writing to Ike was to garner his support for U.S. policy, he did not succeed. "It was indeed nice of you to send me your impressions of the Conference and the obvious difficulties we are having," Eisenhower replied, and he then went on for several pages about unrelated personal matters and mutual friends.

Unlike Smith and Marshall, Clay looked on the failure of the London conference with genuine regret. In one sense, his mission had failed. "To those of us who had started quadripartite government in Germany with determination to make it work, who believed for a few months that it might work, and who had tried to make it work in the face of daily obstruction and frustration, there was a special significance in the results of the London conference. While I recognized the inevitability of the course we had to follow, it was not with exhilaration but with sadness over the failure of a 'noble experiment' that I left Lancaster House when the meeting adjourned."

In December, President Truman submitted the Marshall Plan to Congress. Initial reaction was favorable. In Paris, a Committee of European Cooperation had begun to analyze the economic resources of its sixteen members to determine what each country should accomplish and how much U.S. aid it could expect. Whether Germany would be allowed to participate had not been resolved. Clay, of course, was determined that Germany be included. But those in charge of Marshall Plan aid (Paul Hoffman and Averell Harriman) declined to say what Germany could expect, and certainly did not want the Germans to participate in the initial planning phase. The French, as usual, adamantly opposed the appearance of a German delegation at the planning meetings, and Norway's representative said he still favored the Morgenthau Plan for Germany. As far as Germany's European neighbors were concerned, the war was too recent to contemplate German participation in American largesse.

To circumvent European objections, Clay developed a subterfuge. "My contention was that military government had the right to speak as the government of Germany. Later we would transfer that right to the Germans. So Robertson and I attended the early meetings of the Marshall Plan, and we brought the bizonal ministers along as our advisers. That got them accepted far more quickly than they would have been otherwise."

A more serious problem was the initial Marshall Plan allocation of $364 million to Bizonia—far less than that to countries with much smaller populations, like Belgium and the Netherlands. But after five years in wartime Washington and four years before that as the Corps of Engineers spokesman on Capitol Hill, Clay was accustomed to fighting for government appropriations. The German cause had been his responsibility for almost three years, and he was not prepared to see Germany short-changed in American aid. "Failure in prompt German recovery would have far reaching effects on the recovery of its neighbors," he told Washington in his protest against the meager allocation. "I know this action will bring much international criticism of me, but I have to resist selfish motivation by others so long as we are responsible for Germany. . . . My skin is thick." He eventually won out: at congressional insistence, the German ERP allocation was substantially increased. But Clay lost his battle that Germany be treated as an equal. Marshall Plan aid to Germany was made contingent upon an agreement by German authorities to repay the funds—a provision to which only Germany was subjected. Clay's plea to avoid deliberate discrimination against Germany "even before ECA gets underway" was eloquent but ineffective.

Subsequently, when Bernard Baruch urged Congress to incorporate Germany fully into the Marshall Plan, Clay wrote to express his appreciation. Clay told Baruch that his testimony was "so sound and wise that I could not refrain from writing to you once again to express my very real appreciation for the contribution which you always make in times of national crisis." Clay said that Germany's "prostrate economy must be restored if there is to be a stable Europe."

> Certainly we recognize fully the real apprehension of Germany's neighbors as to their security in the future from German aggression. However, their traditional and well justified fear of German aggression sometimes blinds them to the immediate and overshadowing menace of the Red Army externally and planned revolution internally.

John Hilldring, the Assistant Secretary of State for Occupied Areas, summarized Clay's role in Germany at that time. In an internal State Department memorandum, Hilldring stated that "General Clay has conducted his administration of Germany as though Germany represented the only U.S. interest in Europe. I have nothing but praise for the job Clay has done in Germany. It has been magnificent. But it is not unfair to him to say that he has been far less objective and wise in blending his administration with the equally worthy purposes of the United States in other European countries."

General Clay would have agreed with that assessment—up to a point. Unlike official Washington, Clay believed the future of Europe would be decided in Germany, not France. As Military Governor, he was determined that German interests be protected and that democracy be given a fair chance. He thought he knew how to accomplish that. He was not sure that Washington did.

· 25 ·

Berlin Blockade

> The future of democracy requires us to stay here until forced out. God knows this is not a heroic pose because there is nothing heroic in having to take humiliation without retaliation.
>
> Clay to Bradley, April 10, 1948

CLAY WAS DISAPPOINTED AND DISTRESSED AT THE collapse of the London conference of foreign ministers. He did not know why Marshall had abruptly terminated the meeting—Molotov had been at least as vituperative on occasions in the past—and he recognized that the consequences would be severe. Clay had been deeply committed to German unity. He was confident that the open competition between Western values and Communist regimentation would produce a democratic Germany; that the Germans, when given the choice in open elections, would vote overwhelmingly for liberty and freedom; and that Western democracy could be extended to the Soviet zone. Clay's faith in democracy was genuine. He honestly believed in the competition of ideas, and he was willing to put democracy to the test. In retrospect, it is difficult to say that he was wrong. The inability of Communism to compete on even terms in Germany was initially demonstrated in 1961, when the East German regime closed their open border to the West. It was proved beyond doubt when the German Democratic Republic finally collapsed in the closing days of 1989.

But Clay was virtually alone in holding to that view in 1947. Washington had changed policy. Quadripartite government was dead. The breakup in London provided its obituary. Later Clay would cite that breakup as one of the factors that led to the Berlin blockade. Whether the United States was to blame or the French or the Russians is a moot point. A separate West German state was in the offing, and Clay sought to salvage what he could.

Bevin and Marshall quickly agreed that Clay and Robertson should press ahead with the economic and political reconstruction of the Western zones. Clay was given a green light to proceed with a long overdue currency reform. Gradually, Bizonia's economic council would be converted into the nucleus of a West German government, Germany's foreign trade would be increased, and the French zone incorporated into U.S. and British planning. Clay did not secretly embrace the idea of a "Russian menace" as the means of rebuilding Germany. But when given no alternative, he made the best of it.

Because of the common front being forged against the Soviet Union, Clay's relations with the State Department appeared to improve. "Our work in London has brought us into a very close relationship with State Department personnel concerned with occupation policy," he cabled Draper on December 20. "There appears to be little real difference in our thinking as to the future."

But Clay's political antennae were picking up other distressing signals at London. Both the State Department and the military appeared to be increasingly nervous about the exposed Western position in Berlin. Already the Army staff in Washington, under the direction of Lieutenant General Albert Wedemeyer, was warning of possible Soviet pressure on the city and preparing contingency plans for the evacuation of American dependents. Clay agreed that Soviet pressure on Berlin could be anticipated and that obviously there would be difficulties, but he said that he and Robertson intended to hold out as long as possible. If things became too tough, Clay indicated they would refer the problem to Washington and London. But he and Robertson "would not bring the question up until it developed," he said. Clay told Marshall they "had adequate resources on which to live in Berlin for some time," and stressed the political importance of the Western powers' remaining in the former German capital.

When he returned to Berlin, Clay held a steady course. Public opinion in the United States had changed dramatically in one year. The exhilaration of victory had subsided. Germany increasingly was viewed as a potential ally in the emerging struggle against Communism. More and more pressure was being put on military government, particularly by Congress, to ease up on the Germans. "All of this reminds me of my original prophecy," Clay told Draper on New Year's Eve. "First we would be condemned for softness and then for hardness. I am afraid I am too hard-shelled now to care much about either.

"Hope you can visit us soon. I expect to enjoy the forthcoming year riding in my luxurious train, drinking my extra liquor ration in one of our super luxurious clubs, or perhaps Siberia. Siberia is more attractive. In spite of cynicism, we are grateful for Department [of the Army]'s constant support. . . . Nothing further here, but thanks and goodbye for 1947."

The continued shortage of food in Germany remained Clay's most pressing problem. In Washington, Tracy Voorhees, a prominent New Jersey lawyer, had been put in charge of food supplies for the occupied areas, and all through 1947 there had been a steady increase in grain shipments to Germany. Though food collections in Bizonia lagged behind target figures, Clay firmly rejected the heavy-handed collection measures Washington wished him to employ. "No one believes these measures would work in the long run," Clay told Draper in early 1948. "They might temporarily, but at great expense to anti-communism, which particularly resents Soviet collection methods." Clay said that the British had a large collection team in the field, but actually had collected less food than the Americans.

In Clay's view, a currency reform was the only answer to the food shortage. The Germans had little confidence in the Occupation Reichsmark. Inflation was held in check only by rigorous price and wage controls, and German farmers simply would not bring their crops to market, preferring to hoard and barter them for tangible goods. Clay thought the problem was exacerbated by U.S. insistence that food be distributed based on the work someone performed, without reference to cost, price, or income. "This type of regimentation has never been wholly successful even in Russia," he told Washington. "Under our economic system income has always been a factor in food distribution." Clay said that, short of the most repressive measures, there was no way to change that.

> Large incomes in Germany can still get [black-market] food unavailable to small incomes in spite of all regulations, and enforcement measures can never be wholly successful.
>
> I cannot pull rabbits out of a hat. I still think food collections surprisingly good under existing conditions. In any event, I've done my best in Germany and if it is not enough, then my successor may be able to solve problems beyond me and perhaps he should be sent now to solve them. It is no time in Germany to try drastic strong-arm measures.

For the most part, the Germans were unaware of Clay's resistance to Washington's advice. When addressing the issue in public, Clay always exhorted his German listeners to produce more food and distribute it more equitably. Occasionally he threatened to enforce food collections with the military constabulary, but he never did so. When questioned at a press conference in early 1948 about a wave of strikes protesting food shortages, Clay said the reaction of the workers was totally understandable. So long as they struck in an orderly fashion, he said, it was "a positive demonstration of democracy."

Clay was less charitable when German officials who were employed by the Occupation challenged American motives. Public protest was one thing, insubordination quite another. In early 1948, when Dr. Johannes Semler, Bizonia's economics chief, attacked the United States for sending the Germans "chicken feed" *(Hühnerfutter)* to eat, Clay promptly relieved him. Semler's remarks were addressed to a local CDU rally at Erlangen. Speaking without a prepared text, Semler (whom Clay described to Washington as "the most competent of the German ministers") argued that Allied Occupation policies—which he described at some length—were economically discriminatory and prevented Germany from earning her own keep. Semler's argument had considerable merit, and Clay did not basically disagree. In fact, Clay himself had repeatedly protested to Washington against what he called "hidden reparations," which included selling German exports below market value and the use of German patents, scientific data, and technical know-how without compensation.

Semler unfortunately had been carried away by the momentum of the meeting in Erlangen, and entertained his audience with increasingly sharp sarcasm directed at the United States, such as his infelicitous remark about chicken feed. Semler said that the Americans, instead of sending the Germans wheat, were sending them *Hühnerfutter* to eat, a pejorative reference to corn—which German consumers found less desirable. As a quip to a closed meeting of party functionaries, the remark would not have been odorous, especially in the context of Semler's entire presentation. Unfortunately, it was a public meeting, and the German press seized on Semler's remark about chicken feed, splashing it across their front pages. Clay immediately relieved him. Not for the criticism of Allied policy—that was fair game—but for using the term "chicken feed," and, more important, because of the press coverage the remark received. Clay saw it not merely as an ungrateful criticism of American generosity, but as a serious blow to the good will he was trying to establish for Germany in the United States. The fact that Semler was speaking for the Occupation made it doubly inexcusable.

Reflecting on the episode many years later, Clay evidenced no regret. "Very obviously," he said, "if the United States was bringing food in, and furnishing it to the Germans free of charge, we couldn't have a minister of economics making speeches like that and have him continue as minister. After all is said and done, we were not forgetful for one minute that we were an occupying power. Democracy didn't go so far that we would allow former Nazis to run for office. I don't think we were extending our negative control too much further when we said that a man who had been bitterly critical of the United States—which was feeding Germany for free—could not hold office."

Q: Did you have any doubts?

CLAY: None whatsoever. I would not have removed him if he had not criticized the type and kind of food we were sending. In view of the worldwide food shortage at that time, it was an absolute act of generosity on our part. And to have him call it "chicken feed" was absolutely inexcusable. The Congress would have crucified us when we asked for more money.

To replace Semler as economics minister, Clay named Professor Ludwig Erhard, the rotund Bavarian professor who became the father of West Germany's economic miracle. As was Clay's way, he wrote immediately to General Bradley urging that U.S. food shipments to Germany be stepped up as soon as possible. "We can only emphasize that the 1,800 calorie ration which we have requested is the absolute minimum from which any substantial economic recovery can be expected."

It was while Clay was grappling with the problem of feeding Germany that he was rocked by a blockbuster press release from Washington. On January 8, 1948, Secretary of State Marshall suddenly announced that the State Department would assume full control of the German Occupation on July 1. Clay was dumbstruck. He read the announcement on the wire service news ticker, having had no advance warning. He had not been consulted beforehand.

Clay did not quarrel with Marshall's decision to replace him. But he was deeply hurt that after two and a half years in Germany, his government lacked the simple courtesy to notify him before the public announcement was made. For an officer of Clay's upbringing, this was a rank discourtesy that he could not forget and could but slowly forgive—if he ever did.

"General Marshall's announcement certainly came as a surprise," Clay told Draper in a teleconference immediately afterward. "I had just assured [General Sir Brian] Robertson and the Germans they could definitely expect me to be here until late in the year. Likewise, I had declined certain offers [in American private industry] for the same reason within the last week. Announcement makes it look like I was fired and which perhaps is the case." Clay told Draper that it was now necessary to confirm the date, "as effect of uncertainty will be disastrous to morale and recruitment."

Certainly the Department of the Army was caught off base by Marshall's sudden announcement. Draper told Clay that the matter had come up unexpectedly. The Army had not been informed beforehand, and State had not intended to precipitate the issue at that time. The fact was that since 1945 Clay had urged that the State Department assume responsibility for Germany. In the summer of 1947, he had made plans for retirement at year's end. As recently as November 1947, he had asked that his retirement date be set, and agreed to remain in Germany "only if it is 100 percent desired." At the Department of the

Army's firm insistence, Clay agreed to stay as Military Governor and CINCEUR through 1948. "There is no question as to your preeminent suitability for the task you have," wrote Eisenhower on December 2. Those arrangements presumably had Foggy Bottom's blessing. A State Department press release, issued at that time, announced that the Department "had no present intention to take over responsibility for the administration of occupied areas from the Army," and that the take-over had been indefinitely postponed.

But neither Draper nor Clay was aware of the extent to which the State Department chafed under the Army's control of Germany and Japan. Because of his public stature and possible Republican presidential candidacy, MacArthur was beyond reach. (Galbraith and his State Department associates occasionally joked about the possibility of MacArthur's breaking diplomatic relations with the United States.) But Clay, who was often as obstinate as MacArthur, was in the last analysis a military officer who could be replaced. Robert Lovett and George Kennan, in particular, urged Marshall to remove Clay, and Marshall himself had wearied of Clay's insistence on doing things his way in Germany. But the decisive factor in the Secretary's sudden announcement was Marshall's long and intimate friendship with Bedell Smith. Austere to the point of frostiness in personal relations, Marshall had made a singular exception in the case of Smith. At Fort Benning in the thirties, and later in Washington, the two were close companions, hunting and fishing together when the opportunity permitted. Neither Marshall nor Smith made friends easily. But just as Ike and Clay had formed a relationship that transcended professional responsibilities, so too had Marshall and Smith.

In January 1948, Bedell Smith was still U.S. Ambassador in Moscow. He had been there over two years—a grueling assignment in the best of circumstances, and a particularly demanding one as relations between the United States and the Soviet Union deteriorated. The Moscow winters were dark, the cold was severe, and Smith, not unreasonably, wanted a change. In addition, he longed to be awarded a fourth star, to be a full general in the United States Army—a promotion that had been denied him when the war ended. But above all, Smith longed to be Military Governor of Germany. In 1945, Secretary of War Stimson and John McCloy had rejected him in favor of Clay. But in 1948, with Marshall as Secretary of State, the opportunity beckoned once more. As Ambassador to Moscow, Smith had proved himself a valuable member of America's diplomatic team. He was an able administrator and, unlike Clay, was prepared to follow the State Department's instructions to the letter. The Division of European Affairs at State applauded the change, and Marshall himself welcomed the opportunity to put his old friend back in uniform. From the State Department's perspective, the substitution of Smith for Clay was ideal.

Q: What prompted General Marshall to announce that the State Department was assuming responsibility for the Occupation?
CLAY: I don't know what prompted that. I'd been urging it for a long time, but nobody had listened to me. And when the announcement was made, I was given no warning whatever.

"It was about this time that I got a letter from Bedell Smith saying that he was going to take my place. So I'm sure this had been worked out between General Marshall and General Smith. I don't know whether General Eisenhower was in on it or not. I doubt it. Remember that General Marshall was extremely fond of General Smith. Marshall had been the leading proponent of General Smith's becoming General Eisenhower's chief of staff during the war. When Marshall took over as Secretary of State, Bedell was our ambassador in Moscow. And he'd been in Moscow about as long as anybody wants to stay in Moscow. It was a very dismal place to stay in those days as an American ambassador, and I'm sure he told General Marshall that he wanted to leave and come to Germany. He had not been made a four-star general, and I think he wanted to go back on active duty and get it. Being Military Governor was a four-star rank.

"I'm sure both of them knew I wanted to leave, so I'm sure General Smith's letters to me at this time were an indication of what was happening. But I had not been informed by General Marshall or the War Department. And if the War Department had known, I'm sure they would have informed me immediately."

Q: So this was arranged by General Marshall and General Smith?
CLAY: I believe that was the genesis. I must say that I'd had some very real disagreements with the State Department at the Moscow conference [of foreign ministers] on the question of the Ruhr, and this may have had considerable to do with it. So I wrote to Bedell and said "Yes, we'd be delighted to fix up the house you want, do whatever you want

us to do, and are perfectly ready for you to come." He'd even set a date. Sometime around April or May [1948]. At the time, I wanted to leave. I thought I'd had enough. And frankly, I wasn't getting the support from the State Department that I had had when Mr. Byrnes was there.

Clay and Marjorie began to pack their belongings. At Clay's request, a State Department transition team came to Germany, and preparations for the transfer advanced quickly. Already some of Clay's household goods had been shipped home. There was no real hurry to evacuate the modest bungalow on Im Dol Strasse in which they lived —Smith wanted a much more imposing villa on the Wannsee. Nevertheless, Clay asked to be returned to the United States by April 1 for retirement, and this time the Army approved his request.

Clay thought nothing of it when Justice Byrnes wrote to him shortly after Marshall's announcement to inquire about the circumstances. To Clay, Byrnes's inquiry was a kindly note from an old and dear friend. "Please do not think that I ran out on the job," Clay replied. "I have been anxious to get out for some time as our policies were becoming less and less possible of execution in Germany, and I am therefore glad that it developed as it did. *Nevertheless, the first time I heard of the transfer* [to the State Department] *was in the newspapers and I was not consulted as to the timing desirable for orderly transfer.* I say this to you only because your good opinion will always mean a great deal to me, and I would not have you think I failed in my obligations."

Clay's reply was all Byrnes needed to set in motion one of the most unusual power plays in Washington politics. Stung by the way he himself had been dismissed by President Truman in January 1947, Byrnes was determined that Clay not suffer a similar fate. In fact, as a Washington power broker, Byrnes's capacity for revenge was famous. "I'd rather have any twelve other senators opposing me than having Jimmy Byrnes opposing me," said one high official of the Roosevelt and Truman administrations. Unbeknownst to Clay, and totally without his consent or approval, Byrnes called in his chits in the Senate to block Marshall's plan. First, the Senators from Clay's home state of Georgia were brought in: Walter George, the ranking Democrat on the Appropriations Committee; and Richard Russell, who held a senior post on Armed Services—two of the 1948 Senate's titans. Then Styles

Bridges of New Hampshire, chairman of the Appropriations Committee, and Burnette Maybank of South Carolina, both of whom admired Clay's work in Germany. Sam Rayburn added his influence. By mid-March, Byrnes had secured the necessary commitments to block any nomination to succeed Clay that Marshall might send forward. Marshall apparently had overlooked the fact that the Military Governors of Germany and Japan required Senate confirmation—or else had not anticipated that Byrnes would mobilize the Senate in Clay's behalf.

What makes Byrnes's activity so exceptional is that word of what happened never leaked out. Smith continued to write to Clay through mid-March, asking that certain arrangements be made prior to his arrival, and Clay himself, who knew nothing of what was afoot, continued to pack for his departure. There were no leaks to the press, no public discussion, and not a word uttered on the Senate floor. But Byrnes's efforts paid off. With the State Department already embattled in the Senate over Marshall Plan appropriations and the money for European recovery, Marshall did not want to antagonize the formidable array of senators who supported Clay. Russell, George, Bridges, and Maybank were charter members of the Senate's inner club, and Marshall reluctantly backed off. Clay would remain as Military Governor.

On March 23, 1948, Secretary Royall broke the news to Clay in a "Top Secret—Eyes Only" teleconference. "It is very important that we keep this matter secret until it is released by the President," said Royall. Then another bombshell. According to Royall: *"It was decided yesterday afternoon that State Department will not take over the German occupation."*

Royall told Clay that Marshall proposed to issue a press release to that effect "within the next hour or so" and wanted Clay's approval as to the wording. Once again Clay was caught completely off guard. He approved Marshall's text ("by saying little it tells the story"), and once again agreed to remain in Germany for an indefinite period. "I hope," Royall told him, "and General Bradley [who had recently succeeded Eisenhower as Army Chief of Staff] joins me in this hope, that you will stay on the job at least through the present calendar year. You are urgently needed there."

For years afterward, Clay believed that it was the increased tension in Europe in early 1948—the stepped-up Communist pressure in Italy and France, and the coup in Prague—that led the State Department to pull back. The Department of the Army shared that view. Byrnes's role was never revealed. Marshall's decision was never explained.

Q: And it was Justice Byrnes who intervened with his friends in the Senate to prevent the change?
CLAY: That is what I understand. I don't think General Marshall and General Smith recognized that the appointment as Military Governor required Senate confirmation. But I was never told that officially. I didn't learn about it until years afterward. All I know was that nothing happened. And about that time, we began to get into serious problems with the Russians, and then the blockade came along, and that was it.

Aside from Byrnes's intervention in Clay's behalf, the fact was the international situation *had* deteriorated seriously in the first three months of 1948. It made sense to leave an experienced hand like Clay in Germany—and Smith in Moscow, for that matter. This would have been true if Marshall had reached that decision independently. That it was forced on him meant that Clay's relations with Washington continued to be strained. The State Department recognized they could not relieve him, the Department of the Army did not want to relieve him, and the Congress was firmly on Clay's side. He had become America's proconsul in Germany, with strong political support. Notwithstanding the hopes of Lovett, Marshall, and the European Affairs Division, the direction of Occupation policy had been returned to Berlin.

As Clay saw it, the problems with the State Department had been resolved. There was general agreement that the bizonal economy should be accelerated, that a currency reform—with or without the French—was essential, and that a West German government should be put in place as soon as possible. More important, the hand of military government had been strengthened enormously. The State Department could suggest, but, as with MacArthur in Japan, Clay's word was now law. When France protested the speed with which Clay and Robertson were proceeding to reorganize the bizonal economic council into the nucleus of a West German government, Clay fired off a sharp dispatch to Washington. "It seems always as if France and the Communists take the same position, if for different reasons," he told Royall and Draper. "We can only please the former by doing what the latter want.

"We are in a critical position in Germany and either have to move forward to give the Germans increased responsibility in the Bizonal area to insure their proper contribution to European recovery, or we must move backward to increase our own forces to run a more colonial type of government."

Clay said that "It is difficult to understand how the French expect the Americans and British to discuss with them arrangements which they could protest but in which they have indicated no willingness as yet to participate. In point of fact, we are getting somewhat tired here of always having the finger pointed at us for offending French pride by taking Bizonal actions without French approval, instead of having the finger pointed at the French for wanting to be a partner in planning but independent in operation."

This time Clay's protest was successful. After assuring Paris that the expanded bizonal administration would in no way prejudice the structure of a future German government, Washington told Clay to proceed. Immediately thereafter, he and Robertson issued Military Government Proclamations 7 and 8. These proclamations provided for a two-house legislative assembly, an executive committee responsible to the legislature,* a high court of justice, and a central bank. The lower house of the legislature (the economic council) would be apportioned on the basis of population; the upper chamber (Länderrat) would, like the U.S. Senate, be composed of two representatives from each *Land* government. And, French protests to the contrary, the eventual government of the Federal Republic strongly resembled the bizonal organization that Clay and Robertson had put in place. Germany had moved a massive step toward postwar rehabilitation. One positive side effect, in Clay's view, was that the German people were beginning to speak out on political issues and even to criticize U.S. and British military government. Clay took this as a compliment. For the first time in fifteen years, the Germans felt they could speak out without undue risk. That meant that, regardless of French intransigence, the days of the Occupation were numbered.

For that reason, Clay wanted to press ahead quickly with de-

* Clay had sought an independent executive more along American lines, but, as he advised Draper, parliamentary responsibility was a German tradition. "I doubt very much that we will ever get a German constitutional assembly which will deviate from the only experience they have had. For that reason our insistence on an independent executive is probably wasted effort."

Nazification. Public pressure to end the process was rising in the United States, and Clay opposed curtailing the program until the worst offenders had been brought to justice. In February, the House Appropriations Subcommittee on Foreign Aid recommended a full amnesty for the remaining Nazi offenders. When Clay refused to comply, the full Appropriations Committee chastised military government for disregarding congressional desires. Secretary Royall thereupon instructed Clay "to conclude all denazification trials by the end of April [1948], rather than in May or June as [you have] contemplated." But Clay remained adamant. The de-Nazification phase of the Occupation was coming to an orderly close, said Clay, and he would not be rushed. "I think I know what the German reaction would be," he told Draper, "and stopping [de-Nazification proceedings] would not be good. It would be bowing to criticism in Germany which comes only from the Nazi element." As always when pushed by Washington to take action in Germany that he thought unwise, Clay pushed back. "I would rather lose the military government appropriation than what we stand for in Germany," he told Draper.

Two days later, Clay cabled Draper that the de-Nazification program was on schedule. Each month "leaves a constantly smaller backlog," said Clay, but unfortunately this backlog "contains the really bad actors. A general amnesty would free these bad actors and would really discredit the entire program." But Clay also told Draper he would wind up the program by May 1, except for a few serious cases. He delivered on that commitment. When May 1948 began, 320,000 of the outstanding cases had been tried, reclassified, or dismissed. Only 28,065 remained, and these cases were handled expeditiously. Several weeks later, Clay wrote *finis* to U.S. de-Nazification efforts, dismantled the OMGUS apparatus, and discharged its personnel.

PRESSURE ON BERLIN

The Berlin crisis of 1948 marks the high point of the postwar struggle for Germany. Forty years later, the confrontation between East and West over the future of the isolated city can be seen as the decisive denouement of the Cold War. The Soviet blockade, the amazing Allied airlift launched in response, the Western currency reform, and the subsequent formation of the Federal Republic of Germany provide the important benchmarks in the creation of contemporary Europe. The division of Germany between East and West, the division of Europe between NATO and the Warsaw Pact, and the clear demarcation of the Communist and non-Communist realms trace to that epic struggle waged by the United States, Britain, France, and the Soviet Union over Berlin. That battle marked the end of the wartime alliance. It also heralded the rehabilitation of Germany. Perhaps even more important, the Berlin crisis marked the outer limit of Communist expansion in Europe. The resolute Allied response galvanized the Western nations to stand firm against Communist encroachment: it provided the emotional tonic that was necessary to rejuvenate a dispirited, underfed, war-weary population. In a sense, the successful outcome in Berlin represented the triumph of American and British policy to build a strong anti-Communist bulwark in the Western zones of Germany. In another sense, it represented a decisive display of Western determination and resourcefulness. Finally, it indicated clearly that both East and West preferred the certainty of established frontiers to the risk and uncertainty of military conflict.

Throughout the crisis, Clay doubted that the Soviets wanted war—or were either economically or emotionally capable of fighting one. Along with British Foreign Secretary Ernest Bevin, he insisted that the West stand firm. In fact, at times it looked as if only he and Bevin thought that Berlin could (or should) be held. As Bevin's biographer (Lord Bullock) has written, both Clay and Bevin "believed the Russians were trying out the situation to see how far they could go with impunity." Both "agreed that [the Russians] were more likely to be encouraged by Western readiness to withdraw than provoked by Western determination to stay." In the end, despite continued misgivings in Washington, Paris, and the United Nations, Clay and Bevin prevailed. But as the Duke of Wellington remarked after another epic European struggle, "It was a damned near-run thing."

Berlin, of course, was particularly susceptible to Soviet pressure. With a population of 3.3 million people, Berlin was not only Germany's largest city but its largest industrial center as well. It was not only Germany's political capital, but its commercial, economic, and cultural capital too. Like Germany itself, Berlin was divided into four sectors.

While a four-power Kommandatura (similar to the Allied Control Council for Germany) set policy, each occupying power was ultimately responsible for its own sector. But the major problem was that Berlin was located 110 miles inside the Soviet occupation zone. This allowed the Russians to draw directly on the resources of their zone to supply their Berlin sector with food, fuel, water, and other essentials. The Western powers, on the other hand, were cut off from their zones and could only supply their garrisons (and 2.2 million Berliners living in the Western sectors) if the Russians were willing to make local resources from their zone available and permit unimpeded access to Berlin from the West. With fewer than fifteen thousand Allied troops in the city, Berlin was militarily untenable in the event of war. But the Soviets did not need to go to war to test Allied resolve. The long, exposed supply line between Berlin and the Western zones afforded ample opportunity to apply pressure on the West, and the gradual imposition of the blockade in early 1948 allowed the Russians to gauge the situation at each step along the way.

In January 1948, the Soviet pressure began. Clay and Robertson, acting under the instructions given to them in London, had begun to move quickly to expand Bizonia's political base and strengthen its economy. When the French appeared to hesitate, and then to question Western policy, the Russians decided to test the water. On January 23, Red Army soldiers stopped a British military train en route to Hamburg from Berlin and demanded to inspect two cars filled with German passengers. When the British refused, Soviet officials held the train for eleven hours before returning it to Berlin. American trains were also halted by Soviet inspectors, who insisted on the right to check the identity of individual passengers. This was directly contrary to the oral agreement between Clay and Zhukov in June 1945, as well as a clear departure from the practice of the past two and a half years. Clay and Robertson responded to the Soviet challenge by placing armed guards on the trains to prevent entry. Sporadic Russian attempts to check the trains continued in February and March, and occasionally the Soviets would hold a train for several hours when the train commander refused to allow the Russian inspectors on board.

In retrospect, it appears that the Russian action in January was touched off by Bevin's announcement that British, French, U.S., and Benelux representatives would meet in London shortly to discuss Germany's future. The Russians were well aware of growing French reluctance to join Bizonia, and decided it was an opportune time to test Allied policy. A slight interference with Western traffic to Berlin would accomplish that with little risk. In fact, throughout the months leading up to the complete blockade of all traffic to Berlin in June 1948, Soviet moves were closely tied to Western actions. As the United States and Britain indicated their determination to press ahead with the formation of a West German government, Soviet attempts to deter the Allies became more ominous.

In Berlin itself, the meetings of the Allied Control Council grew tense and testy. The friendly camaraderie of past years evaporated. At the meeting on January 20, Marshal Sokolovsky bitterly accused Clay and Robertson of attempting to establish a separatist German government in Bizonia. Both Clay and Robertson (disingenuously) denied the charge, and Clay proposed to move forward with a quadripartite currency reform for all of Germany if the Russians were willing. When the Control Council met again on February 11, Sokolovsky resumed his attack, claiming that the U.S. and Britain sought to include western Germany in a military and political Western bloc. "This is a dangerous course," warned Sokolovsky.

Neither Clay nor Robertson was deterred. The six-power conference on Germany's future convened on schedule in London in late February; in Frankfurt, the cooperation between U.S. and British authorities on the one hand, and German political leaders such as Konrad Adenauer and Jacob Kaiser of the CDU and Kurt Schumacher of the SPD on the other hand, helped lay the groundwork for a West German government. By now, Clay had become the leading advocate of an independent West Germany. Despite his strong-willed temperament, Clay was above all a good soldier. His orders to expand the political and economic base of Bizonia were clear. Clay accepted and respected that. Equally important, with quadripartite government effectively dead, Clay saw a strong West German government as the most readily available avenue to restore political and economic life in at least three-fourths of Germany. This was a substantial achievement. In fact, Clay's many years in practical politics had taught him that a three-quarters solution was frequently the best that could be obtained. Clay was not worried about the Red Army at this point, but he was decidedly concerned about increased Communist political pressure, which he saw as a prelude to a possible seizure of power. To withdraw from Berlin under those circumstances would, in Clay's view, ensure a Communist takeover in Germany.

But in Paris and Washington, officials were becoming increasingly uneasy. The French government feared a military confrontation with Russia in Germany and a political confrontation with the Communists at home. Washington worried primarily about the exposed position of Berlin. Reflecting the general tenor of public apprehension in the United States, Senator Henry Cabot Lodge, Jr. (R., Massachusetts), wrote to Clay in early March about conditions in Berlin. Was it safe for Americans to remain there? On March 5, 1948, Clay replied that "our security arrangements in Berlin are adequate. In fact, I believe American personnel are as secure here as they would be at home. Berlin is a somewhat isolated area being surrounded by Soviet-controlled territory and this situation does provide a nervous reaction among a few American personnel but such feeling is far from universal." Clay, who lived in Berlin, and whose headquarters was there, said that any increase in the Berlin garrison "would be a complete waste of personnel. Probably no occupation force ever lived under as secure conditions and with greater freedom from serious incidents than do the American forces living in Germany."

Clay's message to Lodge is consistent with his similar messages at that time to the Department of the Army. He saw no reason for alarm. But these messages are totally inconsistent with his famous cable of the same date (March 5, 1948) to Lieutenant General Stephen J. Chamberlin, the Army's director of intelligence (G-2). Clay's cable to Chamberlin— "the most overworked quotation in the literature of the Cold War," in the words of Lord Bullock—came from out of the blue. In a Top Secret message to Washington, Clay told Chamberlin:

> For many months, based on logical analysis, I have felt and held that war was unlikely for at least ten years. Within the last few weeks, I have felt a subtle change in Soviet attitude which I cannot define but which now gives me a feeling *that it may come with dramatic suddenness.*

According to Defense Secretary James Forrestal, Clay's message to Chamberlin hit Washington "with the force of a blockbuster bomb." General Bradley said afterward that it "lifted me right out of my chair." Coming on the heels of the Communist coup in Prague, it provided the proof that U.S. policy-makers needed that military conflict with the Soviet Union was inevitable. Forrestal copied the cable verbatim in his diary, and saw to it that it was widely circulated throughout Washington. Its contents were leaked to *The Saturday Evening Post,* and it helped create a public hysteria that war in Europe was imminent. In fact, Clay's message was especially earthshaking because, almost alone among the upper echelons of the Truman administration, Clay had scoffed at the possibility of war with Russia.

When Clay saw the use to which his message had been put, he was appalled. In Clay's views, the leak to the news media was particularly reprehensible. "The revelation of such cablegram," he told General Bradley, "is not helpful and *in fact discloses viewpoint of responsible commander out of context with many parallel reports."* In his subsequent account in *Decision in Germany,* Clay took pains to dissociate himself from the alarmist interpretation that had been placed on his message. Clay said that the change in attitude he had noticed on the part of the Russians was related to their decision to impose the blockade, not to preparations for war.

Years later, I asked General Clay about the discrepancy between his message to Chamberlin and his many other messages to Washington at that same time. "General Chamberlin came to see me in Berlin in late February [1948]," said Clay. "He told me that the Army was having trouble getting the draft reinstituted, and they needed a strong message from me that they could use in congressional testimony. So I wrote out this cable. I sent it directly to Chamberlin and told him to use it as he saw fit. I assumed they would use it in closed session [of the appropriate congressional committees]. I certainly had no idea they would make it public. If I had, I would not have sent it. But I thought it was important that we rebuild our military forces, and I was glad to give General Chamberlin a message that he could use. Shortly afterwards I remember that Bill Draper asked me in a teleconference to give him a statement he could use before the House Appropriations Committee. I told him I had already sent one to Chamberlin."

As one military historian has pointed out, Clay's cable "was not to be the last occasion on which the American military were to try to influence congressional opinion by an inflated estimate of Soviet intentions and capabilities, but it may well have been the first and most significant." Just as Dean Acheson, Clark Clifford, and President Truman would use the threat of Communism to secure passage of the British loan in 1946, and the Truman Doctrine to support Greece and Turkey in 1947, Clay invoked it on behalf of UMT in 1948. In all fairness, Clay did not envisage how his cable to Chamberlin would be used. On the other hand, he was scarcely a political neophyte. He believed that his cable would be used by the Army for tactical purposes with Congress. He did not foresee that it would be used to frame U.S. policy, nor that it would be made public. Certainly it did not reflect his thinking at the time or the way he saw the situation in Berlin, as his subsequent cable to Bradley made clear. As far as Clay was concerned, he was simply doing Chamberlin a favor. The cable was not sent through normal command channels but to Chamberlin directly. It was the backdoor channel of informality that lubricated the professional Army. In retrospect, Clay should have known better.

The fact was that in Berlin the situation remained tense but not threatening. Marshal Sokolovsky used the March 10 meeting of the Allied Control Council to castigate Clay and Robertson for being "intolerant of genuine democracy," and the Communist press became vitriolic in their denunciations of the Western powers. But Clay and Robertson pressed ahead with the expansion of Bizonia's political role and were well on their way to resolving their outstanding differences on currency reform and reparations deliveries, despite continued resistance by the French. Clay was not worried about the safety of Berlin. But that calm was not shared in Washington and, ironically, Clay's cable to Chamberlin was one source of the anxiety. On March 17, General J. Lawton Collins, the Army's vice chief of staff, initiated a "Top Secret" teleconference with Clay to discuss American dependents in Germany, Austria, and Trieste. "Should they be evacuated because of the danger?" asked Collins.

CLAY: Withdrawal of dependents from Berlin would create hysteria accompanied by rush of Germans to Communism for safety. Withdrawal [of dependents] from [American] zone first would create panic in dependents in Berlin. This condition would spread in Europe and would increase Communist strength everywhere.

COLLINS: We note from Berlin [news] report that Russians are to remove dependents from Berlin and Dresden in May and June. Have you confirmation of this report?

CLAY: Soviet papers have published reports, but this is not verified. It may just be part of "war of nerves." . . .
COLLINS: What if any action toward evacuation of dependents is being taken in British and French zones?
CLAY: None as yet and we are confident we would be advised if any movement was now planned. British and French will follow and not lead us in any program of military significance.
COLLINS: Do you think we should stop further dependents from leaving the U.S. ?
CLAY: From a military view, stoppage desirable, but from political and psychological viewpoints bad. . . . German people would be frightened elsewhere but in Berlin might become hysterical. Neighboring countries would be alarmed and would lose some of their present courage.
COLLINS: One of our considerations is the hostage angle. . . . What is your opinion about reducing or evacuating dependents now abroad?
CLAY: Again, from strictly military viewpoint alone, evacuation is logical but would be ruinous politically. We are here now and must take the consequences. [In the event of evacuation] German people would go into despair and in Berlin into panic. Neighboring countries would be seriously affected and "doubting Thomases" would flock to Red standard.
COLLINS: Should evacuation include civilian employees?
CLAY: You have my answer.

Collins told Clay that Washington had no new information indicating a Soviet military offensive, but wanted to review its plans and obtain Clay's views. Many years afterward, I asked General Clay if he had been worried about the American dependents in Berlin. According to Clay, "Someone in Congress began questioning the wisdom of leaving our dependents in Berlin where they were subject to being captured. That sort of thing. And the War Department [Department of the Army] was all in favor of taking them out. There was some merit in that contention. One was the responsibility of keeping American women and children in an area behind the Iron Curtain that you couldn't possibly defend. Number two was the fact that if you were going to try to supply this area, the fact that you had dependents there added to your supply problem—although, considering the relatively small number of dependents compared to the size of the city, it didn't add that much to the problem. And the public criticism, I think, led to this action by the War Department suggesting that we take our dependents out."

Q: And you objected?
CLAY: It was a problem of morale. Of good faith. I think that if we had started moving our dependents out we would never have had the people of Berlin stand firm. And I think it would have been completely disastrous if we'd pulled our women and children out while we asked the women and children of the Berliners to stay there. It was just that simple. Our dependents were hostages of our good faith.
Q: Did any dependents want to leave?
CLAY: I said to our people, "If any of you are nervous—and I don't want anybody who's nervous about his family around here—you may certainly send them home. But on one condition. You must go with them." None went. I don't think it was a fair decision that I left to them, but I didn't intend it to be.

Three days after Clay's teleconference with Collins, the Allied Control Council in Berlin broke up for good. Sokolovsky, who was presiding, asked Clay and Robertson for the details of the decisions taken by the six-nation conference in London pertaining to Germany's future. Clay replied that the request was reasonable, but that he had to wait for governmental approval before he could comply. Sokolovsky, who apparently had been given his script by the Kremlin beforehand, barely waited for Clay's remarks to be translated before reading a long, prepared statement bitterly attacking the Western powers. "I see no sense in continuing the meeting," Sokolovsky said, and he and the entire Soviet delegation walked out. The Allied Control Council for Germany was dead. As Clay wrote afterward, "An international undertaking which might have contributed to lasting peace had failed. We knew that day as we left the conference room that quadripartite government had broken up and that the split in Germany which . . . had seemed inevitable for some months had taken place."

Q: Was the last meeting of the Control Council a tense one?
CLAY: It was not particularly tense. I think we were discussing something relatively routine when Marshal Sokolovsky went into his diatribe and then got up and walked out. Sokolovsky was not a showman.

He was a very down-to-earth, practical fellow, and I'm sure he was doing what he'd been ordered to do. But he didn't do it with the dramatic trimmings that Molotov used in London. He played it as low-key as one could play such a thing.

Q: Had you expected Marshal Sokolovsky to walk out?

CLAY: I certainly did not expect him to walk out at that meeting, but I can't say that it took me by surprise. It was quite obvious to me that the Control Council was dead, and the question was who was going to walk out first. I was pretty well determined that it was not going to be me. That's a sure way to get a lot of applause, but it's no way to solve a problem.

On March 31, 1948, the Soviets stepped up their pressure on the access routes to Berlin. The six-power conference in London had recessed, the French continued to show signs of reluctance about establishing a West German government, and the Russians may have believed that another warning shot—a more substantial blast—might deter the Western powers from going ahead with their plans for a divided Germany. Claiming that the volume of rail traffic between the Occupation zones and Berlin had become so great that more control was required, the Soviets announced a new set of regulations to supersede the oral agreement about access to Berlin made by Clay, Weeks, and Zhukov in 1945. Under these new regulations, the Soviets asserted their right to check military passengers and their baggage; moreover, no freight shipments from Berlin to the Western zones could be made without Soviet approval. General Robertson objected immediately and, with Bevin's full support, announced that the British would not permit the Russians to inspect their trains. Clay announced that the new Soviet regulations did not accord with previous agreements on Berlin but, unlike Robertson, could not obtain quick approval from Washington to stand firm. In a lengthy, late-afternoon teleconference, Secretary Royall told Clay that because a shooting incident "might precipitate war," they were considering whether President Truman should write Stalin directly. "Another suggestion," said Royall, "is that trains move but that in no event shall there be shooting. What do you think of this?"

CLAY: I would prefer to evacuate Berlin, and I had rather go to Siberia before that. If the Russians want war, we will only defer the next provocation for a few days. For that reason, I do not think either suggestion realistic. I do not believe this means war, but any failure to meet this squarely will cause great trouble.

General Bradley, who continued to be beset by the fear of imminent conflict with the Soviet Union, said afterward that if he had had "any hair on the top of my head," Clay's message "would have stood it on end. I could sympathize with Clay's reaction, but this was neither the time nor place to open fire on the Russians."

Royall told Clay that the Army would have to discuss the matter with the State Department and the President, and asked to resume the teleconference at 9:00 P.M. (3:00 A.M. Berlin time).

When the teleconference resumed that evening, Bradley reluctantly gave Clay the go-ahead. He told Clay that his proposed response to the Soviets "has been carefully studied" by Defense Secretary Forrestal, Royall, and Under Secretary of State Lovett. "It was considered important that no action be taken different from what has been the practice recently. If our action should now provoke war, we must be sure that the fault is not ours."

CLAY: I understand. We are not carrying a chip on our shoulder and will shoot only for self-protection. We do not believe we will have to do so. We feel the integrity of our trains is a part of our sovereignty and is a symbol of our position in Germany and Europe.
BRADLEY: You are authorized to move the trains as you see fit. It is considered important that the normal train guard not be increased and that they carry only the arms normally carried. Furthermore, it is important that the guards not fire unless fired upon. State Department, Secretary of Defense, and the President concur in this reply.
CLAY: I will of course accept and carry out instructions to the letter. I cannot agree that we should not increase guards. I also will instruct guards to open fire only when fire is opened to them. I do not agree that this is a fair instruction to a man whose life may be in danger. Having so stated, you may be assured that your instructions will be followed to the letter.

Bradley asked Clay what the French were doing. Clay replied that the French had answered the Soviet order "about as the British but subsequent action unpredictable. I believe [General Pierre] Koenig will follow us. I am sure Robertson will." Clay said the problem was that the French were still talking about the "German menace," and that "they minimize the Russian problem."

ROYALL: We are sorry that so much chaperonage was necessary but the war danger element made it necessary to consult many people and to compose many views. We believe you were right in referring matter to Department [of the Army]. Our complete confidence and good wishes remain with you.

As Clay wrote afterward, "I thought I detected some apprehension on the part of Secretary Royall and his advisers that a firm stand on our part might develop incidents involving force that would lead to war. Therefore I expressed my opinion that if war were desired by the Soviet government, it would not be averted by weakness."

If Clay and Robertson thought the Russians were bluffing, they quickly learned otherwise. Shortly after midnight on April 1, the Russians stopped two American and two British trains bound for Berlin after the train commanders refused to allow Russian inspectors on board. Clay told Bradley that a fifth train was allowed to proceed by the Soviets when the U.S. train commander "lost his nerve and permitted Soviet representatives to board the train." What would later be known as the "baby blockade" of Berlin, a blockade affecting only the Allied garrisons, had begun. Clay told Washington that he and Robertson had decided not to force the issue and would rely on a limited airlift, which he said would meet all military needs for the immediate future. Clay broached with Robertson the idea of forming an Anglo-American truck convoy in Bizonia and forcing it past the Russian border guards. Robertson demurred. He told London that the Russians could block the highway to Berlin with a few tanks and bring the convoy to a halt, quite apart from the fact that the Russians might get the better of a shooting match.

Bradley offered limited support. He told Clay not to force the matter on the autobahn "without further consultation." Indeed, Washington was becoming even more nervous about the exposed Allied position in Berlin. Clay's cable of March 5 had, of course, contributed to Washington's concern. The Pentagon worried about the feasibility of staying in Berlin, and at the State Department, Marshall and Lovett queried the wisdom of doing so. As doubt increased, it fell to British

Foreign Secretary Ernest Bevin to steady the Western course. Like Clay, Bevin was confident that the Soviet Union did not plan to resort to overt military aggression in Europe. But, also like Clay, he feared that an Allied withdrawal from Berlin would trigger panic in Western Europe, with far-reaching political consequences on which the Soviets would capitalize. From the outset of the Berlin crisis, Bevin set himself firmly against any retreat under pressure and any compromise that smacked of appeasement. As one recent work on the blockade has noted, Bevin's attitude throughout the crisis was conditioned by his reaction to Munich a decade earlier. "From beginning to end, [Bevin] consistently resisted the basic solution proposed by the Russians for lifting the blockade in exchange for a Western lifting of the London Programme" for a West German government. Throughout 1948 and 1949, Bevin gave Clay the support he needed to hold the beleaguered city.

But it was Clay who commanded on the ground. On April 2, he confronted another Washington effort to withdraw American dependents. First, Lieutenant General Albert Wedemeyer, the Army's director of plans and operations (G-3), cabled to ask Clay's opinion about a plan to remove all U.S. dependents and civilian employees from Berlin immediately. Clay replied that the Soviet stoppage of U.S. and British trains was "aimed at driving us from Berlin, and immediate evacuation of dependents would be considered a Soviet success."

As soon as Clay had dispatched his reply to Wedemeyer, Secretary Royall and General Bradley requested a teleconference. "We are receiving many inquiries from Members of Congress as to why we do not evacuate dependents from Berlin," said Bradley. "Evacuation now might be plausible because it would reduce number to be supplied by air. What is your thinking on this subject in view of new situation?"

CLAY: I do not believe we should evacuate now. In emergency, we can evacuate quickly. However, evacuation now would play into Soviet hands and frighten rest of Europe. I propose:

(A) To sit tight.
(B) To let dependents who are nervous go home.
(C) To gradually move unessential [civilian] employees to Frankfurt.

In general, in spite of some imaginative correspondents' reports, our people are calm and continuing their everyday life normally.

Clay warned Bradley that he anticipated that within the next few weeks the Soviets would demand that the Western powers withdraw from Berlin "because of failure of Allied Control Council to govern Germany. I think we should await such demand before making any decision to evacuate noncombatants. Robertson assured me today he would stick with us. French are firm now but not wholly reliable. Finally, there are few dependents here who have any thought of leaving unless required to do so. I wish to emphasize that there is little nervousness here. Our stake is too high and evacuation would deceive no one."

ROYALL: With strong feeling about evacuation of dependents in Congress and elsewhere we will have to consider further what course to follow. . . .
CLAY: Evacuation in face of Italian elections and European situation is to me almost unthinkable. Our women and children can take it and they appreciate import. I cannot overemphasize my fear of consequences. . . .

Despite Clay's remonstrance, Bradley was not convinced. He would not instruct Clay to remove the American dependents from Berlin, but he quietly had his son-in-law, an Air Force officer on duty in Berlin, reassigned to the Pentagon. Bradley's concern typified the fear of conflict with Russia that gripped Washington. As Bradley wrote afterward:

> Lee [Bradley's daughter], Hal and the grandchildren . . . were still in Berlin. If the Russians overran the city and captured them, the personal blow to me might be incapacitating. [Accordingly,] I made the decision to remove them from danger. I asked the Air Force to order Hal to duty in the States. The Air Force willingly consented, assigning Hal to the Air Staff in the Pentagon.

Bradley generously concedes that "Hal was not very happy about being pulled out of the front lines to a Pentagon desk job." But the move scarcely reassured Clay as to Washington's resolve.

As Western plans for a West German government intensified, the Soviets reciprocated with increased pressure on Berlin. On April 9, the Reuters news agency reported from London that the United States had proposed to establish a provisional German government in the three Western zones and hold immediate elections for a constituent assembly preparatory to drafting a West German constitution. Reuters said that Britain, France, and the Benelux countries were actively considering the plan and indicated that quick agreement was likely. The Russians, who had previously halted civilian rail traffic into Berlin from Hamburg and Nuremberg, responded by announcing that all traffic on the remaining rail line between Hannover and Berlin would require additional clearances from the Soviet Military Administration before proceeding. Traffic was not completely stopped, but the Soviets were making it plain that final approval for its passage rested with them.

Once again Bradley sought Clay's opinion. It was now clear that the Soviets would continue to intensify their pressure on Berlin, and Bradley wondered whether it wouldn't be prudent to leave the city completely before being forced out. "We doubt whether our people are prepared to start a war in order to maintain our position in Berlin and Vienna," he told Clay.

The April 10, 1948, teleconference between Bradley and Clay represented the low-water mark of American resolve. The Chief of Staff believed Berlin untenable. He offered Clay a way out. Shouldn't we announce the withdrawal ourselves, asked Bradley, and "minimize the loss of prestige?"

Clay could not be and would not be shaken. He told Bradley that the United States should remain in Berlin unless driven out by force. It was Clay's view—correct, as it turned out—that the Soviet pressure tactics were designed to intimidate the West and deter the Allies, especially France, from pressing ahead with a separate West German government. He warned Bradley that Soviet pressure would continue to intensify, but that it was simply a war of nerves. The United States must stand firm. "Why are we in Europe?" asked Clay.

> We have lost Czechoslovakia. We have lost Finland. Norway is threatened. We retreat from Berlin. . . . There is no saving of prestige by setting up in Frankfurt that is not already discounted. After Berlin will come western Germany, and our position there is relatively no greater and our position no more tenable than Berlin.

> If we mean to hold Europe against communism, we must not budge. We can take humiliation and pressure short of war in Berlin without losing face. If we move, our position in Europe is threatened. If America does not know this, does not believe that the issue is cast now, then it never will and communism will run rampant.

On a separate but related matter, Clay was appalled when Bradley told him that he and Robertson should not bring any German officials with them to the Marshall Plan talks due to convene shortly. If that were the case, Clay said, he would not attend the meeting either. "We spend billions to hold Germany to the west and yet cannot offer one decent gesture. . . . This decision will mean more to communism in Germany than the Berlin situation. . . . Once again, I ask do we have a German policy?"

Clay's plea to remain calm about Berlin stiffened Washington's resolve temporarily. But two weeks later, Wedemeyer once again asked him about evacuating U.S. dependents. The political and psychological disadvantages were understood, said Wedemeyer. Nevertheless, Washington wanted Clay to be ready with contingency plans just in case. At the same time, Bevin again echoed Clay's resolve to remain in Berlin. In a personal message to Marshall on April 30, Bevin said that the Russians were "up to every devilment" in Berlin and Vienna, but that there "could be no question of letting ourselves be forced out of either city." The following week, in a major foreign-policy address to the House of Commons, Bevin told a cheering House that "We are in Berlin as of right and it is our intention to stay there." Great Britain was not about to be panicked by Soviet pressure. Bevin's was the first clear public statement of Western policy from either London or Washington in the bleak spring of 1948, and Clay was grateful for Bevin's support. Unfortunately, the clear resonance of Bevin's statement was garbled by an ill-advised private overture to Moscow made by Bedell Smith at Marshall's direction (and George Kennan's suggestion) on May 4. As the Berlin crisis escalated, Smith told Molotov that the state of American-Soviet relations was regrettable, and that "as far as the U.S.A. is concerned, the door is wide open for full discussion and the composing of our differences." The Soviets published Smith's comments immediately, making all too apparent the gap in Western strategy. The British were firmly against speaking to the Russians until all pressure on Berlin had been lifted; the United States sought to parley in the hope of easing Soviet pressure. Bevin was shocked at the unilateral American turnaround, and asked Ambassador Douglas, "What the hell is going on?" In Berlin, Clay was equally furious, but not surprised. It had been clear to him for the last month that he was holding Berlin by his fingernails.

On the other hand, the six European nations meeting in London showed no inclination to back off from creating a separate government in western Germany. When the talks had recessed in late March, Clay, Robertson, and Koenig had been instructed to find a compromise that would permit the early establishment of a West German government and allow for the integration of the German economy—particularly the Ruhr—with that of Western Europe. As usual, the French had held back. But when Marshal Sokolovsky walked out of the Allied Control Council on March 20, it was apparent even to the French that quadripartite government and German unity were dead. France had the choice of going it alone or of integrating its zone with Bizonia. Since Clay and Robertson had made it abundantly clear that they would press on with the creation of a West German government whether the French participated or not, Paris had little choice but to join. But it was a painful decision for most Frenchmen, and General Koenig was clearly unenthusiastic. Ironically, the road to French participation in Bizonia had been paved by the Soviet walkout from the ACC—just the opposite from what Moscow had sought.

The first signal that France was serious about joining Bizonia came informally. Couve de Murville, the senior French diplomat dealing with Germany, was vacationing on the Riviera following the recess in the London discussions. He called Clay directly and asked if he could come to Berlin to explore their differences. "I grasped the suggestion at once," said Clay. "I sent my plane down to the Riviera to pick him up. He arrived in Berlin on April 6, 1948 for a three-day visit in which he divided his stay between General Koenig and me." Couve de Murville was one of the few Frenchmen with whom Clay worked easily, and one of the very few whom Clay liked. More important, Clay thought Couve de Murville was above the petty bickering that had poisoned U.S.-French relations in Germany. And he thought that between them they could cut a deal.

Clay's intuition proved correct. Up until Couve de Murville's visit to Berlin, the six-power talks had been burdened by excessive detail.

The negotiators, especially the French, had focused on drafting statutory minutiae rather than on the principles that would underlie the new West German government. In his informal talks with Clay, Couve de Murville dismissed the detail and focused on principle. "This convinced me," said Clay, "that we should try a new approach." On the morning of the last day of Couve de Murville's visit, Clay rushed to his headquarters on Kronprinzenallee to dictate a brief eight-point memorandum that he believed would provide the agreed basis for a West German government. By this time, Clay's close working relationship with General Robertson made him confident that the British would go along. In less than a thousand words, Clay laid the foundation for the new German government. When Couve de Murville arrived at Clay's headquarters later in the morning, he read the memorandum and liked it. "I initialed it. He initialed it. And he took a copy back to Paris. From then on out, that was the French position. It had never been their position before."

Clay's brief memorandum, to which Couve de Murville agreed, provided for the election of a constituent assembly no later than September 1, 1948, the drafting of a West German constitution by that assembly, a federal structure for the new government, and the constitutional protection of individual rights and freedoms. According to Clay's draft, after the constitution had been approved by the three occupying powers, it would be submitted to the *Länder* for ratification. The constituent assembly was also charged with drafting an election law, and a new government would be elected thirty days after the constitution was ratified. Except for foreign affairs, the occupying powers would relinquish day-to-day control of Germany to the new government, subject to a very general supervisory authority. But the big breakthrough achieved by Clay and Couve de Murville pertained to those measures to be put into effect immediately. There would be no trizonal government as such, but the occupation policies of the French zone would be brought into line with those of Bizonia. A common currency reform, a coordinated export-import policy, and a common banking system would be established forthwith.

Q: So your meeting with Couve de Murville broke the logjam?

CLAY: It really did. From the beginning, the French were provoked because they weren't asked to Potsdam. And therefore they started off after Potsdam always saying that they weren't required to live under the Potsdam rules. This was number one. Number two, an even greater problem, was that a strong French government did not emerge during this period. It was changing constantly. General de Gaulle was out of power. And I think a lot of Frenchmen still looked to de Gaulle [for direction] rather than [to] the French government. The result was that it was very difficult to get firm, lasting decisions from the French commander [General Koenig], and I am sure that he was having the same trouble getting them from his government. Couve de Murville was the one person who could influence French policy at that time.

Following Couve de Murville's agreement, Clay's memorandum was formally submitted to Robertson and Koenig. The Military Governors approved it, and it was forwarded to the London conference, which reconvened on April 20. It became the basis for the final approval of a West German government, authorized by the six nations in their communiqué on June 6, 1948. When the London conference ended, the establishment of a West German government had become a foregone conclusion. The three Military Governors were instructed to proceed with the currency reform and to set a date for elections to a constituent assembly that would draft a new constitution. The division of Germany between East and West was at hand.

The decision of the London conference to proceed with a West German government and currency reform were companion measures. One could not succeed without the other. The currency reform, which took place only in the three Western zones, divided Germany economically. The London conference set in motion the steps to divide it politically. And both were bitterly opposed by the Soviets.

Q: Was the Russian blockade of Berlin a reaction to the currency reform?

CLAY: By and large, it has always been blamed on currency reform. I don't know how you can tell what really created the final break. Perhaps the fact that the London foreign ministers' conference in 1947 had broken down may have contributed to it. Perhaps the establishment of the bizonal area contributed to it. Perhaps it was currency reform. I don't know. We'd had stoppages before of the trains, and delays and stoppages on the waterways. So the first events by no manner of means necessarily indicated that there would be a blockade of Berlin. It was harassment, and we were not at all sure how deep the harassment would go.

No single action contributed more to Germany's economic recovery than the currency reform undertaken in the three Western zones in June 1948. The original plan to replace Germany's dangerously inflated currency had been drafted in 1946 by officials from the U.S. Treasury and American military government. But quadripartite differences had stalled its adoption. By 1948, with four-power government effectively dead, there was no longer any hesitation on the part of the United States. Clay had advised Washington repeatedly that German recovery remained problematic unless the currency problem was resolved.

Actually, the problem of Germany's excess money supply was of long standing. Under Hitler, the money in circulation in Germany had increased from 5 billion Reichsmarks in 1933 to 70 billion in 1944. Bank deposits had increased from 30 billion to 150 billion, and Germany's debt from 12 billion to 400 billion marks. War damage claims alone exceeded 300 billion Reichsmarks. And at the same time, there were fewer and fewer goods to purchase. In fact, substantial inflation had occurred even before the surrender in 1945, and it continued virtually unabated during the Occupation, stemmed only slightly by rigorous Allied price and wage controls. In 1948, with the existing Reichsmark virtually worthless, German merchants simply refused to sell the goods they possessed, farmers hoarded their crops instead of bringing them to market, and industrial expansion proved to be impossible. Only German diligence and discipline kept people working for the worthless money in which they were paid.

Under the terms of the currency reform as proposed by Clay and Robertson, the German money supply would be reduced by more than 90 percent, the Reich debt would be repudiated, and equalization (burden-sharing) payments would be made to those Germans who had been bombed out or otherwise who had suffered excessive war damage. But for a variety of reasons, the American government rejected military government's equalization plan. It was in essence a tax levy on capital, and Washington wanted no part of that, fearing to set a precedent. Clay and Robertson were instructed to go ahead with the remaining aspects, and bizonal experts were set up in a secret location near Kassel in early 1948 to arrange the details. As finally promulgated, the currency reform provided that all of the old Reichsmarks would be turned in and withdrawn from circulation. Each person was allowed to exchange 60 of the old Reichsmarks for 60 new Deutsche marks immediately. All remaining balances would be frozen. Eventually, conversion of a portion of the frozen balances would be permitted. The overall result was to shrink the German currency supply by 93.5 percent. (Or, said differently, Germans got 6.5 new Deutsche marks for 100 old Reichsmarks.) All outstanding debts were devalued simultaneously, and the government's debt was canceled completely. Finally, the new central bank that Clay and Robertson had created (the Bank Deutscher Länder) would be authorized to control the new currency, and its issue initially limited to 10 billion marks.

Whether France would participate in the changeover was not clear. Initially, following Couve de Murville's agreement, the French government had indicated they would go along. But as relations between East and West deteriorated, the French had become increasingly skeptical of joining a move that they recognized would divide Germany irrevocably. In Clay's view, it was a paradox. For three years, French policy in Germany had thwarted effective four-power control and German unity. Now, in 1948, when Britain and the United States were on the verge of introducing a new currency that would clearly divide the German economy between East and West, the French held back.

Even more disconcerting was the last-minute intervention by Washington to retain the U.S. military conversion rate at 10 cents per Deutsche mark instead of the 30 cents contemplated. The Department of the Army, it appeared, wanted currency reform for the Germans, but it also wanted to retain the financial advantage it had enjoyed when the German currency had been weak. "Your message has hit me like a bombshell," Clay fired back to Draper. "If it is an order, it may necessitate a complete postponement of currency reform." Clay told Draper that a "ten-cent exchange rate would give an undue advantage to occupation personnel and a purchasing power which will be out of line with the prices which will prevail in Germany after currency is stabilized." Clay said he was even more concerned about the effect of Washington's demand on the British and French. "We have consistently led the way in not taking advantage of the German economy," he said, but if the United States now insisted on a 10-cent conversion rate, other countries would seek similar advantages. Above all, said Clay, American companies and businessmen doing business in Germany would still exchange currency at 30 cents to the mark, and this would lead to an inevitable black market as businessmen would try to buy marks from U.S. servicemen who were obtaining the marks at 10 cents. "This should be avoided at all costs."

Two days later, Under Secretary Draper replied on behalf of the Army, saying he was surprised that Washington's demand was a "bombshell" since it represented the "best advice of State, Treasury and Army." But, on reflection, they agreed that Clay was correct and were withdrawing their request.

Q: Could you go into the currency problem?

CLAY: Without question, I think the two most important achievements of military government were the currency reform and the creation of the Federal Republic. But in specifics, without the currency reform, Germany would never have been able to take advantage of the Marshall Plan and would never have had the rapid economic recovery, which was almost miraculous. The currency reform gave Germany a currency which has remained sound since the day of the reform.

"The fact is, I thought we could have had a currency reform a year earlier as a quadripartite matter, and had even had the initial currency secretly printed at that time and moved into Bremen, so that when we were ready, we would have the currency on hand.

"Our only difficulty when we did go ahead was the final approval of our government as to the timing. This applied equally to the British and French. In fact, the French government almost withdrew the final night. We had our trucks loaded and they were on their way with the new currency to the various banks where the exchange was to be made the following morning. My French opposite suddenly arrived at my house [in Berlin] with a statement that the French couldn't go along. They wanted it all called off or there wouldn't be any trizonal merger. It immediately became obvious that he was acting under instructions from his government. It also became obvious that we had to make a decision. So General Robertson and I said, 'Well, that's too bad. You stop the banks in your zone from taking the new currency. We're going ahead.' Period.

"General Koenig conveyed this to his own government, and they had a parliamentary session that night. Apparently they got a vote of approval, because along about midnight the French said they would go along. They had been concerned, I think, that it would create problems with the Russians. Which it did. But quadripartite government was already dead by that time."

Q: Why did the German public have confidence in the new money?

CLAY: There were several reasons. First, I think that they had turned in so much of their old currency for the new that this in itself made it an object of value.

"Second, [Ludwig] Erhard's action in removing economic controls shortly thereafter also helped, because this enabled people to get better prices for their goods than they might have otherwise. Third, the currency reform was a further indication of military government's desire to permit Germany to move ahead economically."

Ludwig Erhard, the Bavarian economics professor whom Clay had named Economics Minister when Semler was dismissed, often took credit for the currency reform. Erhard did lift economic controls shortly afterward, but his role in the currency changeover has been grossly exaggerated. On the afternoon of June 18, 1948, just before the currency reform was to begin, Clay was preparing to call Erhard to inform him, as the first to know on the German side, when Erhard himself came into Clay's office. At this point, only the ten or twenty military government technicians working in secret near Kassel knew the details of the reform, and they were carefully locked away from public contact. Like most Germans, Erhard was aware that such plans were in the air, but he did not know the terms, or the day, or the hour the exchange was to take place. Before Clay could say anything, Erhard brought up the rumors about the changeover. A new currency was being introduced, he said, and he, the Economics Minister, did not know anything about it. Erhard said he had been betrayed.

"I am sorry," said Clay. "The rumors you have heard are true. I had to conceal it from you, but I will gladly talk to you now." Erhard kept his temper under control, and managed to remain calm. He told Clay, "This is a question of honor and dignity. I must resign, Herr General. I have been made a fool of before *dem Deutschen Volk* [the German people]."

"I'm awfully sorry, Professor Erhard," Clay replied. "But if you're going to resign, you had better do it within the next hour. The currency reform will be announced at eight o'clock."

It was late on a Friday afternoon, and the weekend was about to start. Erhard stamped out of Clay's headquarters and had his chauffeur drive him to the Frankfurt radio station [Hessische Rundfunk], where he had a regularly scheduled Friday talk show. When he went on the air, Erhard suddenly announced the currency reform as if he had authored it. It was a virtuoso performance. Erhard claimed complete credit and took full responsibility, and Clay never set the record straight.

"I could not have planned it any better," said Clay many years later. "I called Erhard up the next day and promised I would never reveal the truth of the matter if he didn't." Erhard remained mum, and Clay did not reveal the details until many years after Erhard's death.

The lifting of German price and wage controls was a different matter, one for which Erhard deserves full credit. On May 24, 1948, Clay had advised Draper that "German bureaucratic controls were stifling expansion." Clay said he intended to lift them, and warned Draper to "get ready for the mud." But one month later, Clay had not yet acted. Erhard stepped into the policy vacuum. On his own initiative as bizonal Economics Minister, he simply announced that price and wage controls were terminated. Many years later I asked General Clay if Erhard had the authority to lift the controls.

CLAY: Well, Erhard, who was Economics Minister, simply put out an announcement that all economic controls in the bizonal area were lifted. My British opposite [General Robertson] was over to see me within a very few minutes, protesting the lifting of these controls. And it was quite obvious that since he was representing a country that had won the war and was still living under controls, that he couldn't be in favor of removing them in Germany. Nor could his government. When Erhard came to see me, I chided him for having taken such a step without consultation. He reminded me that we had given him rather broad authority as Economics Minister, and that was it.

"Robertson and I could not veto what he had done unless we both did. It took a unanimous vote between us to veto him. We never had a vote. We just let it go. I think General Robertson felt he had done his duty when he protested. I'm sure that he advised his government that he had protested. I'm sure that his government, in defending its position before the Parliament, pointed out that they had protested."

Q: Were you annoyed at Erhard's action?

CLAY: At first I was a little provoked that he had done this without consultation. Later I realized that if he had consulted with us, we would probably have turned him down. Frankly, out of sympathy with Great Britain, operating under controls and a victor in the war, I would have found it very difficult to have tried to force approval. So, for me, the way it happened was the best way for it to happen.

In the midst of the excitement in June 1948, Clay received an unexpected offer from Washington. On June 2, Draper advised him that the Chief of Engineers, General R. A. Wheeler, was retiring June 30. Was Clay interested in the job? Draper said Secretary Royall was giving Clay the right to refuse it before he recommended anyone else. Clay was touched. "While it was always my highest Army hope, I have a job here which I must stay with. I am honored and grateful but this is my job until the Army no longer needs me. . . . Please give Secretary Royall my deepest thanks."

The teleconference brought Clay bad news as well. Draper said that crusty old John Taber, chairman of the House Appropriations Committee, was holding up Army appropriations until the personnel situation in Germany and Japan was reviewed. Taber thought too many people of marginal qualifications were on the payroll. Draper said Royall had gotten "off the hook" by agreeing to send a personnel expert to Germany to review the situation. Clay was disgusted, but not surprised. "If you're committed, that is that," he told Draper. And then added his usual kicker. "I doubt if I am qualified to hold this job if I am not qualified to gauge the measure of my personnel." So ended the Secretary of the Army's commitment to Congressman Taber.

Clay was well aware that the successful conclusion of the London conference, calling for the formation of a West German government, might precipitate a strong Soviet reaction. When Draper had asked in May about French air capability should the Allied garrisons in Berlin be blockaded, Clay had replied that, while the British could cope, "the

French are in bad shape as they have no air transport worthy of name." Clay said that they had asked for help, but only in general terms. "I doubt my ability to help them except in limited degrees inadequate to their needs. I think we must sit tight and see how the situation develops." On June 2, Clay warned Draper that he should alert the Air Force that the French probably would be requesting help. "London conference may precipitate need quickly," said Clay.

Overall, Clay was pleased with the outcome of the London conference. The arrangement on the Ruhr was not as bad as he had feared, and it finally looked as if the French would go along—thanks to Couve de Murville. "Lew Douglas was the able diplomat and negotiator and I'm afraid I was the tough so-and-so injecting the needle. Don't think I gained any friends but anyway Lew took the injections and did a masterful job in getting an agreement which is much better than I really hoped for."

The United States and Great Britain announced their support for the London program on June 9. But once again France held back. Clay was dismayed. "Until French government has acted," Clay told Draper, "our propaganda machine can only emit rather feeble grunts." Clay wanted Washington to press the French to act quickly. He was especially concerned because the Soviets once again were posing as the popular champion of German unity. "In our effort to gain France, we have let loose political forces in Germany which might lead to a rejection of the constitution. . . . We must recognize that German public opinion becomes of increasing importance in the political struggle for Germany, and that we cannot neglect the reaction of some seventy million Germans.

"I recognize the nature of the French problem," said Clay. "However, I do want to bring to the attention of the responsible authorities in Washington once again that we still have a German problem."

Undoubtedly sensing France's reluctance, and still seeking to deter the Western powers from dividing Germany, the Soviets tightened their pressure on Berlin's supply line. On June 10, Soviet military authorities attempted to remove locomotives and rolling stock from the American sector of Berlin. Clay posted military guards, and the Russians backed off. The following day, the Soviet Military Administration halted all rail traffic (civilian as well as military) into Berlin on the one remaining line that ran through Helmstedt. Twenty-four hours later, they just as suddenly restored it. The Russians were playing a high-stakes game of political brinksmanship. By flexing their muscle, the Soviets hoped to intimidate the French government to keep them from approving the London accords and to deter the Western currency reform as well. Clay told Draper on June 11 that, in case the French refused to ratify the London agreement, he and Robertson were preparing to proceed without them. "While it is our view here that this is within the scope of our present instructions, we would appreciate the State Department being advised in full of this proposal."

At the same time, Clay alerted Washington to the possibility of additional Soviet pressure. Clay said he thought recent Russian efforts were designed to keep France from approving the London accords, rather than to force the West from Berlin. "That move will come when we install separate currency [in West Berlin] if it is to come at all." Clay also said they could not supply the needs of the Berlin population if the rail links to the Western zones were cut.

> Nevertheless, we would propose to remain in Berlin until the German people were threatened with starvation if the Soviets did resort to real extreme tactics. . . . Whether for good or bad, Berlin has become a symbol of the American intent.

As Clay anticipated, the Russians continued to exert pressure. Whether it was to deter the currency changeover or to intimidate the French National Assembly (where approval of the London accords was pending) seemed of little consequence. The two were inextricable. On June 14, the Russians closed the highway bridge across the Elbe River on the autobahn between Berlin and Helmstedt. The Soviet Military Administration claimed that repairs were necessary. Traffic was diverted to a small ferry fifteen miles away.

Curious as it may seem, Clay still was not worried about the Russians. He believed they would continue to tighten the noose around Berlin, but would not resort to direct military action. But he was indeed worried about France, where the shaky Bidault government now found itself under increasing fire in the National Assembly from both the Gaullists and the Communists over the London accords. Passage was anything but assured. If the French government fell, Clay and Robertson were determined to press ahead. But was Washington ready to do so? The reply he received from Draper on June 15 was not encouraging. "It is very important that the French go along with us," Draper told Clay. If the National Assembly rejected the London accords, Washington wanted to review the situation once more before proceeding. The implication was that Clay and Robertson should defer the creation of a bizonal government until further notice. "We will communicate with you immediately," said Draper.

Clay was dumbfounded. After three years of military occupation, the Germans were ready for self-government. If the Western powers didn't provide it, the Russians would. And with the steady Soviet drumbeat for German unity, Clay knew the West must act quickly. The arduous bargaining sessions in London had produced a document Clay could live with. It was a massive step forward in German rehabilitation: the cornerstone of Western Europe's revival and a vital bulwark against further Communist expansion. If U.S. policy had turned mushy, Clay wanted a clarification. As Bevin had asked Marshall earlier, "What the hell was going on?"

"Your message W-83856 is the most disturbing cablegram I have received since I have been in Germany," Clay told Draper. Clay said there had been a rapid deterioration of the political situation in Germany because of failure of the Western powers to act promptly on the London agreement.

> We understand that the French had been advised that we were prepared to go ahead in the Bizonal area, even if the French government could not accept the agreement. . . . French non-acceptance will be interpreted widely as due to their unwillingness to face USSR on the issue.

"We cannot win this way," said Clay. "I THOUGHT WE CROSSED THE RUBICON AT LONDON BUT APPARENTLY WE SAT DOWN IN THE MIDDLE OF THE STREAM." Clay told Draper that Robertson and the British government were still prepared to press ahead, with or without the French. Prompt action would salvage the situation; delay would be fatal. "I await instructions."

If Washington had been wavering, Clay's riposte restored their confidence. "I fear you have misunderstood our cable," said Draper. "Yesterday, Bevin, [Sir William] Strang, and [Ambassador] Douglas all categorically rejected all French proposals to modify or reconsider terms of London Agreement. In case of outright rejection of the London Agreement by the French Government as result of adverse vote in Assembly, you are authorized to proceed with Robertson as stated."

Bevin's role in stiffening Western resolve deserves further comment. The British Foreign Secretary not only refused to consider modifying the London Agreement, but used his vast influence in the international labor movement to bring pressure on French Socialists to support the accord. At the height of the crisis in the National Assembly, Bidault sent Jean Chauvel, the secretary general of the French Foreign Ministry, to London to obtain a number of modifications in the agreement that might make it more palatable to French public opinion. This had been a frequent French bargaining technique, and usually the United States and Britain had given in. This time, London stood firm. Bevin abruptly rejected Chauvel's overtures and, on June 14, had the British Cabinet confirm that Britain and the United States would go ahead with a West German government regardless of what France did. The final vote in the French National Assembly was close. But the Socialists ultimately supported Bidault, and the London Agreement was approved.

In the meantime, Clay and Robertson continued to negotiate the last-minute details of the currency reform with General Koenig. The French held back, awaiting the final vote in the National Assembly. The Soviets also kept the heat on. On June 16, the Russians walked out of the Berlin Kommandatura, the quadripartite body responsible for governing the city of Berlin. The split in the four-power machinery for Germany was now complete. Clay was less concerned about the Russian action than about the failure of the French to agree to the currency reform. Time was running out. Once again, France wanted last-minute concessions. Like Bevin, Clay held his ground. In a late-night teleconference with Washington on June 16, Clay told Draper: "The die is cast. We cannot stop the machinery now. We can only hope the French will not pull out." Clay said that it was evident that the French did not want to agree to a currency reform if they did not accept the London Agreement.

Draper then told Clay that he had just heard that the French government was making the London Agreement a matter of confidence, which meant that Bidault was risking his government on the issue. Clearly, if the London Agreement was approved, the currency issue could be resolved. Draper guessed that Koenig had been told to hold his approval pending the vote.

"I hope you are right," Clay said. "I have a hot press tip that it will be voted tonight with government majority of thirty. That may ease situation. However, I must [anticipate] the worst as we cannot stop."

Although Draper offered to ask Secretary Marshall to intervene directly with Paris, Clay indicated no preference, deferring to Washington's judgment.

In the midst of the teleconference, Clay received word from Lieutenant General Roger Noiret, Koenig's deputy, that he had been given the power to negotiate and was coming to Clay's house at eleven that night. "Perhaps settlement is now possible," Clay said. "In view of this, would like to run now. . . . Pleasant dreams and thanks again."

Clay's instinct proved correct. He and Robertson eventually reached a settlement with Noiret that allowed the currency exchange to take place. But he overestimated Bidault's majority in the National Assembly. When the final vote was taken at midnight, the government survived 300–286.

When the currency reform was announced, the Russians responded by sealing their zonal frontier and slowing (but not stopping) freight traffic to Berlin. The Soviet border closure made good economic sense. Without it, the old Reichsmark, which had become worthless in the West, would flood into the Soviet zone, where it remained legal tender. This would create financial havoc in an economy already suffering from too few goods and too much money. In fact, Clay was not especially worried about the Soviet move. To some degree, he and Robertson had anticipated it. "If they had put in a currency reform and we didn't," said Clay, the border closure "would have been the first move we would have to take." The British said the same thing. The Soviet measures were "exactly what Britain would have followed in the opposite contingency," the Foreign Office told Canadian diplomats in London.

The currency reform in the three Western zones took effect on June 21. The U.S., British, and French sectors of Berlin had been excluded: Clay and Robertson had held back in Berlin, hoping that an agreement could be made with the Soviets that would permit a single currency under quadripartite control for the entire city. But when Marshal Sokolovsky responded on June 22, those hopes were dashed. The Soviets announced their own currency reform, to begin June 24. *All of Berlin,* said Sokolovsky, would be included. He rejected Western demands that the Berlin currency be placed under quadripartite control and announced that, as of June 26, the Soviet-issued Reichsmark would be the only valid legal currency in the entire city, including the Western sectors. This amounted to the economic incorporation of Berlin into the Soviet zone. It gave Soviet authorities exclusive control of Berlin's money supply. More important, the unilateral declaration by Sokolovsky meant that in Soviet eyes, the Western powers no longer had a role in the government of Berlin: a position the Russians had tentatively staked out on June 16, when they left the Kommandatura.

Clay and Robertson reacted immediately. On May 29, the Department of the Army had advised Clay that the State Department did not consider the "use of the Soviet mark as legal tender in the Western sectors to be politically advisable." Now Clay and Robertson asked that the matter of Berlin currency be placed under the Kommandatura. When Sokolovsky again refused, Clay and Robertson, reluctantly joined by General Koenig, announced that the Soviet currency decree was invalid in the Western sectors and introduced their own currency reform, to take effect the following day. To have accepted the Soviet currency as the sole legal tender "would have placed Berlin financially completely in Soviet hands," Clay told Royall immediately afterward.

Perhaps more significantly, while the Military Governors conferred, the Berlin City Assembly, meeting in the old city hall, located in the Soviet sector, and totally without police protection, courageously voted to apply the Soviet currency order only to the Russian sector. The three Western sectors would continue to look to the Western powers for their instructions, said the deputies. Despite intense physical intimidation, and the obvious risk that stand entailed, the Berliners had cast their lot with the West.

The Russian response was immediate. At 0600 hours on June 24, 1948, the Soviets cut the last rail link to Berlin. The flow of electric current from the Soviet sector into the three Western sectors was halted shortly thereafter. Within two days, all highways and canals between Berlin and the Western zones were blocked. The Berlin blockade had begun.

In retrospect, it appears clear that the Berlin blockade represented no preconceived Soviet master plan to force the West from Berlin or to capture a united and dispirited Germany—although both may have been attractive goals. But the Soviets did seek to scuttle the London

Agreement and prevent the formation of a separate West German government. By the gradual application of pressure on Berlin, they did their utmost to deter the French National Assembly from accepting the London Agreement—and came within eight votes of succeeding. The Western currency reform was an essential first step on the road to a West German government. Having lost the battle in Paris, the Russians could not prevent the changeover. As Clay recognized, the Soviets' initial border closure was designed to minimize its effects, not to pressure Berlin. Only later, with their own currency reform, did the Soviets enter that deadly confrontation that brought the Cold War to a climax. By attempting to introduce the East mark as the only recognized currency in Berlin, the Soviets were threatening the Western powers directly. If they gave in, the Russians would control Berlin economically; political control would follow in due course. If the West withdrew, the consequences would be even greater, and a panic flight to Communism by many in western Germany would likely ensue. The only alternative was to stand firm. But in late June 1948, there were few besides Clay, Bevin, and the intrepid Berliners who believed that was possible.

When Marshal Sokolovsky walked out of the Allied Control Council on March 20, Clay had worried that it was preparatory to ordering the Western powers from Berlin. But the Russians never did that. They never escalated the crisis to the point of a final showdown. That convinced Clay that the Soviets did not want war. They were pressing to see how far they could go, but were clearly unwilling to risk actual hostilities.

· 26 ·

Founding of the Federal Republic

> I hold no brief for the Germany of today. I do hold a brief for the Germany of tomorrow. If we mean to restore a democratic Germany which will resist the penetration of communism; if, in fact, we wish to bring that western Germany into the comity of western nations, then we must do it with two hands that offer friendship rather than one hand carrying flowers while the other wields a big stick.
>
> Clay to Lewis Douglas, April 26, 1948

THE BLOCKADE OF ALL LAND ROUTES TO BERLIN caught the West by surprise. Clay feared for the Berliners, but the "baby blockade" in April had reassured him that the Allied military garrisons could be supplied by air. British Foreign Secretary Ernest Bevin shared Clay's view. Both were convinced that Berlin must be held at all costs. But the French were hesitant, and official Washington was virtually paralyzed with fear and uncertainty. As George Kennan reported, "No one was sure how the Russian move could be countered, or whether it could be countered at all. The situation was dark and full of danger."

It was Clay in Berlin and Bevin in London who rallied the Western cause. While official Washington vacillated, His Majesty's Government quickly articulated the Allied position: there would be no withdrawal from Berlin; there would be no Western resort to war—although the possibility of conflict had to be faced; and, perhaps most important, the decision of the six-power London conference to proceed with the formation of a West German government would be implemented quickly.

Bevin's determination to press on with a West German government provided virtually no room for negotiating with the Soviets. Recent Russian statements from Eastern Europe, plus Sokolovsky's rebuff to the Western Military Governors on the Berlin currency question, made it clear that the Soviet Union was primarily concerned with forestalling the formation of a separate West German government. Bevin's position precluded any compromise. That left no alternative but to wait the Russians out.

Bevin's tough stand suited Clay. He opposed any negotiations with the Russians until the supply lines to Berlin were reopened. He remained convinced that the Soviets were both unready and unwilling to go to war. His on-the-spot assessment suggested that a military convoy supported by tanks and artillery could break the blockade and traverse unimpeded the 110 miles through the Soviet zone to Berlin. Clay thought the Russians would not risk a military confrontation, and would simply let the convoy pass without incident. Such a determined show of force, Clay believed, would convince the Soviets that the West meant to stay in Berlin, and the crisis would be resolved.

Robert Murphy agreed with Clay, as did Ernst Reuter, the intrepid Socialist mayor of Berlin. Like Clay, both thought the Russians were bluffing. On June 23, 1948, Clay and Murphy flew to U.S. Army headquarters in Heidelberg to make the necessary preparations for a military movement along the autobahn. Clay would not dispatch the convoy without Washington's approval, but he wanted the necessary staff work completed and the troops assembled so that he could act on a moment's notice. Clay directed General Huebner to prepare plans for a regimental combat team, supported by armor and artillery, to proceed along the autobahn from Helmstedt to Berlin. The task force would number about six thousand men, and would include an engineer battalion with bridging equipment. Clay hoped the British and

French would attach battalion-sized support units, but had no assurances.

To command the task force, Clay selected Brigadier General Arthur Trudeau, an experienced engineer who commanded the First Constabulary Brigade at Wiesbaden. Clay delegated operational control to Huebner and Trudeau. If the task force encountered Russian resistance, Trudeau was authorized to decide whether it was merely token —in which case he could proceed—or full-scale opposition—in which case Clay reserved the decision for himself. General Curtis LeMay, commanding the U.S. Air Force in Europe, was instructed to provide air support. In the event of all-out Russian resistance, LeMay was ready to launch a pre-emptive strike on all Soviet airfields in Germany. "Naturally we knew where they were," said LeMay. "We had observed the Russian fighters lined up in a nice smooth line on the aprons at every place. If it had happened, I think we would have cleaned them up pretty well, in no time at all."

It was Clay's opinion at the time that a determined Western military effort would not be interfered with, and the ground link to Berlin would be reopened. There would be no hostilities unless the Soviets wanted war; if they did want war, it would only be a matter of time in any event. Clay's assessment was based on his own analysis of intelligence reports—which indicated no unusual Soviet troop movements, no efforts to stockpile military supplies, and no indications of tactical preparations. But, more important, Clay saw no indication in Soviet conduct in Germany that the USSR wanted war. "The care with which the Russians avoided measures which would have been resisted with force had convinced me that the Soviet government did not want war," Clay reported. It was Clay's assessment that the Russians believed the West would yield in Berlin rather than risk a military showdown, and were pressing to see how far they could go. For that reason, Clay wanted to call their bluff. It was as much pride as statecraft.

When Clay returned to Berlin, he found his staff divided and Washington dead set against any military operation along the autobahn. Clay himself was the partial author of Washington's trepidation, for his unfortunate March 5 telegram had unnerved the most militant cold warriors. Within the Pentagon, Bradley and the Joint Chiefs believed Berlin militarily indefensible, while Forrestal and Army Secretary Royall thought it was not worth the risk of war to test Russian resolve. Secretary Marshall shared both assessments. In London, Bevin agreed with Clay that the Russians were bluffing, but doubted the wisdom of an armed convoy along the autobahn. Robertson, Clay's British counterpart, shared Bevin's view, believing the Russians could block the convoy just as they had the Western attempt to send military trains across the Soviet zone in April. He warned that a few Russian tanks stretched across the autobahn would force Trudeau's column to shoot or turn back. If Trudeau opened fire, the risk of escalation was inevitable; if Trudeau turned back, an even worse psychological defeat would ensue.

But, like Clay, Bevin was not content to let the situation drift. He believed that Western inaction and indecision were Russia's principal allies. Accordingly, on June 24, Bevin asked Robertson to send his deputy, Major General N. C. D. Brownjohn, to London to report to the Cabinet firsthand. Brownjohn was pessimistic. He did not share Clay's view that Berlin could be held, and said that the city's food supply would be exhausted in less than a month. He doubted whether military trains or an autobahn convoy could get through. As Lord Bullock reports, Bevin was dissatisfied with Brownjohn's report and ordered an immediate study, as a matter of the utmost urgency, on alternative ways of supplying Berlin. In particular, Bevin wanted to know whether the city's population could be supplied by air.

Robertson's headquarters in Berlin tackled the task with gusto. Air Commodore Waite (RAF) quickly concluded that it might be possible to supply the city, at least for a short time, and persuaded Robertson to discuss the matter with Clay. When Robertson first raised the question on June 25, Clay was skeptical. He had already instructed LeMay to begin flying supplies into Berlin from Frankfurt for the U.S. garrison but looked on it as a stopgap measure. Clay had doubts about the technical feasibility of supplying a city of 2.2 million people by air (he remembered Goering's empty pledge to supply von Paulus and the German Sixth Army at Stalingrad), and he was still wedded to the idea of forcing a column along the autobahn. "I am convinced that a determined movement of convoys with troop protection would reach Berlin," he told Washington that day. Clay said that such a military display "might well prevent rather than build up Soviet pressures which could lead to war. Nevertheless, I realize fully the inherent dangers in this proposal since once committed we could not withdraw."

But Clay knew he was riding a dead horse. The plan to send an armed convoy up the autobahn had found no support whatever. He also knew that Bradley and Royall wanted to cut their losses in Berlin, and he suspected that Marshall agreed. On reflection, Clay thought they might accept an airlift, at least on a temporary basis. Bevin was already committed, and Robertson had made arrangements for the Royal Air Force to resupply the British garrison. Within a matter of hours, Clay was converted. The airlift would keep Washington honest. His plan to send an armored column up the autobahn could always be dusted off if the opportunity permitted.

Q: General, do you recall your reaction when the rail line to Berlin was blocked?

CLAY: I was mad as hell. I felt that for this to happen to the United States was absolutely unbelievable. I felt we had to take action. Period.

Q: And you protested?

CLAY: Obviously we made the usual protests.* And I suppose this had been going on for a couple of days before I realized that it was a real blockade. That's when I told Huebner to organize and prepare a combat team to move into Berlin.

Q: And Washington resisted?

CLAY: You must remember that the military people [in Washington] were thinking about this in terms of military decisions. And, militarily speaking, we were in no position to hold our own against the Russians in Germany. They had twenty-five divisions. Including the British and French, we could only muster three. Without the use of our air power, including the atomic bomb, our ability to hold them was limited. The Pentagon did not want to get into this type and kind of situation. This was the time when I thought the decision should have been made by the State Department, not by the military. But, of course, the State Department at that time thought just like the military did. I am quite sure that if we had gone in on the ground, ready to fight, we would not have been stopped, and we might have prevented a Korean War by demonstrating our willingness to fight.

Q: But the military was opposed?

CLAY: I am sure that was General Bradley's position. And he was

* Clay's manner of phrasing this sounded very like Claude Rains's comment in *Casablanca:* "Round up the usual suspects."

advising the President that we did not have the military strength to meet the Russians on a military level. I think that when I wanted to go in on the ground, President Truman was ready to authorize it. This is what I've always been told. But at the last moment, he wanted to have General Bradley's concurrence. He had great respect for General Bradley. General Bradley was from Missouri, and he was the kind of soldier Mr. Truman admired. They spoke the same language. And he didn't get General Bradley's concurrence. But President Truman was ready to approve it. Later on, Washington told me I could send in a combat team provided it went in without ammunition. I thought this was about as foolish a thing as you could possibly try, and I didn't do it. They actually said, "If you choose, you may go in, provided that if you are stopped you withdraw without shooting." I couldn't imagine anything more humiliating.

Q: Wasn't bridging a problem? Suppose the Russians destroyed the bridges?

CLAY: The problem of bridging was one we could have solved. I don't think that was a problem. The real problem was that our people said that if the Russians do resist and start fighting, you're through. You haven't got any reserves, and we haven't got any to send you. Militarily speaking, they were correct. Politically, I think they were wrong.

Q: And the airlift?

CLAY: It was about this time that General Robertson came to see me, and we discussed trying out an airlift. And we started it. Our primary purpose was to show that we could make enough landings to do the job.

Q: The idea originated with Robertson?

CLAY: We were all busy at this time computing what we'd have to bring in, how much tonnage it would require, and so on. And I'd told LeMay earlier to bring in what we needed for our own garrison. But at the time, I thought [the bulk of supplies] should come in on the autobahn. That was my primary concern. But I also recognized that we had to do something. General Robertson came over to my office and told me what he could do in the way of an air supply, how many planes he had under his control, and so on. So I quickly agreed with Robertson, and we put this in motion. I would have to admit that I didn't know whether we could do it or not. Within ten days, I felt we could do it.

Q: Do you recall how you began?

CLAY: I called LeMay (I think Robertson was present) and asked if he could carry coal on his airplanes. He said, "General, we can carry anything," or words to that effect. So I said to him, "You'd better start doing it." Then I said, "I want you to take every airplane you have and make it available for the movement of coal and food to Berlin."

Q: Were there enough planes available?

CLAY: My experts said we needed to deliver forty-five hundred tons of supplies per day. The capacity of a DC-4 was ten tons. So we had to prove that we could fly 450 planes into Berlin each day. That's what we had to prove. But we didn't have enough DC-4s. They were not available in the theater at that time. But we did have a lot of DC-3s and C-47s left over from the war that were just parked at Rhein-Main [in Frankfurt]. So we did it with those DC-3s and C-47s: we proved that we could fly 450 planes into Berlin each day. The tonnage at that point was nothing. The DC-3s only carried two tons. So we were landing only nine hundred tons a day. That would not have kept the city alive. As the DC-4s became available, we substituted them to get the required tonnages.

"In the meantime, we established an Army quartermaster depot in charge of the collection of the food and coal, the packaging of it to load on the planes, and the arrangements to get it to Rhein-Main and bring it to Berlin. These were details with which our people, who had been fighting a war, were quite familiar. They knew what to do and how to do it."

Q: Did this come as a surprise to LeMay?

CLAY: I think it did, yes. Not only did it come as a surprise, but I don't think at that moment he quite realized what he was getting into. He did very quickly, though. It was a very short conversation, really—not more than two or three sentences. Everybody knows LeMay. Tough. Hard-boiled. Down-to-earth. The image he created is one of a tough commander, which he was. But I think it fails to give him credit for a very high intelligence and a very high degree of administrative competence. He's a very able person. Actually, he was promoted [to head the Strategic Air Command] and moved out before the airlift was over.

Q: Was your prewar experience building airports in the CAA a factor in your decision?

CLAY: Possibly. I think more important than that, though, was a visit I made to China in 1943, where I'd seen the movement of goods by air from India over the Himalayas to China. This was General [William H.] Tunner's outfit. And so LeMay brought Tunner over to Germany and put him in charge of the airlift.

Q: And the technical problems?

CLAY: There were a good many technical problems, of course. In the first place, you had the problem of priorities in cargo. This was very important, because you had to get foods that were easily transportable and not too bulky. Packaging was important, because you can't bulk-load airplanes: everything had to be packaged in bags. This was particularly difficult with coal. And you had to develop packing that would hold it. Coal was really our most serious problem, because coal dust is not only deadly to the mechanisms of an airplane but also can be explosive. We even tried to air-drop supplies at one point, but it didn't work. The breakage and loss was too great.

"These were the type of technical problems we ran into. But they were problems that were commonplace to an army that had been fighting a war, just a different magnitude. I used to go out to Tempelhof [the U.S. airfield in Berlin] every day. Not in the sense of adding anything, but when you are in command, you go where the trouble is. I think that is the only way your people know how interested you are and how important you consider this."

Q: Did you think the Berliners would hold out?

CLAY: That was a major concern. The first thing I did after I knew we could land enough airplanes was to send for [Mayor] Reuter. He came in, and I said to him, "Before I go ahead now with my final recommendation, I want you to know this: No matter what we may do, the Berliners are going to be short of fuel. They are going to be short of electricity. I don't believe they are going to be short of food. But I am sure there are going to be times when they are going to be very cold, and feel very miserable. Unless they are willing to take this and stay with us, we can't win this. If we are subjecting them to a type and kind of treatment which they are unwilling to stand and they break on us, our whole lift will have failed. And I don't want to go into it unless you understand that fully, unless you are convinced that the Berliners will take it." And he said without any hesitation, "General, I can assure you, and I do assure you, that the Berliners will take it." [Willy Brandt, Reuter's biographer, accompanied Reuter to his meeting with

Clay. He reports that Reuter did not quite believe the city could be supplied by air, but was determined to resist a Communist takeover, regardless of the costs.]

Q: Could you describe Mayor Reuter?

CLAY: In the first place, he spoke English very well, so I had no problems conversing with him. We did not need interpreters. He was a man of the people. He'd been a Communist at one stage of his life, and he had left the party because he didn't believe in its methods. He had no fear whatever. He was a courageous man. He was a strong man and a forceful speaker. He had the people of Berlin behind him. He had been elected mayor in 1947, but the Russians had vetoed him. I think he was a great man. It was very unfortunate that he died when he did [September 29, 1953], because I think he would have become one of the truly great men of Europe.

"Quite frankly, I had had little contact with him until I called him in on the Berlin matter. I paid very little attention to the details of the Berlin government. This was handled by Colonel [Frank] Howley and the Kommandatura. But I had no problem getting along with Reuter, and we became very good friends after that.

"I remember at the time that it was difficult for us to convince people in the United States that the Berliners could take it. This was one of the questions that Foster Dulles raised. The State Department had asked him to come to Germany and make a report. He and I were not very friendly then, and he was very lukewarm to the airlift. I met him in Frankfurt and I insisted that he come to Berlin. And he came to Berlin and stayed in my house. Colonel Howley was there. I think he wrote in his book that the only thing Dulles and I agreed on was the quality of Rhine wine. But I had Mayor Reuter come. I said to Reuter, 'This is your problem.' And I left the two of them alone. I guess Reuter did as good a job selling him as he did me, because I never heard any more expressions from Dulles that the Berliners wouldn't take it."

Q: What was the War Department's response when you began the airlift?

CLAY: I never asked.

Q: You never asked?

CLAY: No, I never asked permission or approval to begin the airlift. I asked permission to go in on the ground with the combat team, because if we were stopped we'd have to start shooting. This was where the Russians had an advantage in that we would have had to initiate the fighting to get through. But we didn't have to start fighting to get through in the air, so I never asked permission.

"I should add that by July, after the airlift had begun, I was convinced that if we moved a combat team along the autobahn the Russians would let it through. However, in contradistinction to the air, where I went ahead on my own—the only way the airlift could be stopped was by the Russians' using their fighter planes to bring our planes down. But they would have to commit an act of war. If we moved on the ground and they put obstacles in front of us, we had to open up the attack. And therefore I did not want to be put in the position where we opened the attack without approval. So with the ground movement I asked permission. I did not ask permission for the airlift."

Q: And the airlift went smoothly?

CLAY: Nothing of that magnitude goes smoothly. My main problem came after I had proved that we could land 450 planes daily. We needed DC-4s to increase our tonnage. They sent me a handful of DC-4s, but nowhere near enough. And I needed all they had. The Air Force was very much against giving them to me. They said this was our last transport reserve, and if war came we wouldn't have any reserve. President Truman overruled them. He gave the planes to me.

Q: That was in July 1948?

CLAY: No, it was October. I got them when I went back to make a speech at the Al Smith dinner in New York. That's always in October —just before the election. Up to that time, we had been getting the DC-4s piecemeal, but not really enough to do the job. We needed about sixty more. And that was just about what the Air Force had [in reserve]. President Truman gave me those in October, and he overruled the National Security Council to do it.

Q: Could you describe the circumstances?

CLAY: [Robert] Murphy and I were invited to appear before the National Security Council. After we made our presentation and asked for more planes, the President went around the table and asked the various members of the Council what their views were. And there was not one of them in favor of us. I thought we had lost. Then, as we were going out, the President said to me, "Come on in my office." And he said to

Secretary Royall, "You come too." And when I went in he said, "I'm afraid you're very unhappy, General, but don't be. You're going to get your airplanes." And he told Secretary Royall to provide them.

Q: Your opinion of President Truman?

CLAY: Obviously, I had the highest respect for him.

Q: And the Al Smith dinner?

CLAY: It was that evening. I had promised the good Cardinal [Francis Spellman] when he was in Berlin the previous Christmas that I would do this for him. And although it was ten months later and the airlift was on, I felt that I should do it. But I had been in Washington all day. In addition to the meeting of the National Security Council, I had also appeared before committees in the House and Senate. I didn't think I could stay out of Berlin more than forty-eight hours without there being rumors that I wasn't coming back. It was quite a critical period, particularly with the knowledge that I needed airplanes.

"General Eisenhower [then president of Columbia University] asked me to stay with him. But I just couldn't do it. I told him that I would not get to New York until five o'clock, and that I would have to leave for Berlin immediately after dinner.

"Well, I'd hardly gotten to my room at the Waldorf when General Eisenhower walked in. I was still in my shirtsleeves trying to get cleaned up for dinner. He came in and sat with me while I changed clothes and dressed. We had a nice talk, and that was it. But it had been a very hectic day. And, of course, President Truman had authorized me to announce that I was going to get the airplanes that I needed—which I did in my speech that evening. And sitting on my left when I did that was Governor Dewey, who was being greeted by everyone that evening as the next President."

Q: Did you have a preference in 1948?

CLAY: I hate to put anything like this on the record, because Tom Dewey is one of my closest friends. But in 1948 I was very much for President Truman. He had just overruled his National Security Council to give me the airplanes I needed. I would have voted for him for any office in the world.

"Mr. Truman was very decisive. He listened intently to what other people said, but he made his own decisions. I had known him before, in the Senate. And while I had the respect for him that I had for many senators, I never thought of him as one of the great senators. The next thing I knew, he was President. I have great respect for all Presidents. But very quickly I formed a particular respect for him because of his decisiveness—his willingness to take the decisions that involved some risks, but by doing so avoid greater risks later on. I really know nothing about his performance on the domestic front, but I think that in running our foreign policy in the days immediately after the war, that he was very decisive and, indeed, a great President."

Q: Were you personal friends?

CLAY: I can't say that he and I were personal friends. I didn't know him that well. I'd met him on Rivers and Harbors work, and I was often before his committee during the war. But I had not been a personal friend. Nevertheless, he gave me tremendous support in Berlin. Under his leadership we had the formation of the North Atlantic Treaty Organization and the formation and recognition of the West German government.

Q: How does a rather ordinary senator become so effective in the higher office?

CLAY: The office of President calls up the very best in everyone. Moreover, you get the support of experts and information that is not available to anyone else. You have better advice, better information on which to act. Mr. Truman was also a great lover of history. He knew the courageous decisions that had been made in the past, when they had been made, and who were the Presidents that had made them. In other words, I think he had the background and the ability to rise to the occasion. And he was a man of courage. He had no inferiority complex. He was humble, but he had no inferiority complex.

Q: In retrospect, what did the airlift accomplish?

CLAY: If we had withdrawn from Berlin, which we would have had to do without the airlift, I don't think we could have stayed in Europe. I doubt if there would have been a Marshall Plan. I doubt if there would have been a NATO. How can you prove these things? I don't know. But I'm convinced that if we had left Berlin, we would never have had the confidence of the West Germans, or of any of the Western Europeans. I think that if we had pulled out and the Russians had moved in, we would have lost confidence in ourselves. If they had succeeded in that, it would have started a whole chain of events. The airlift prevented them from doing that.

"What were the alternatives? There are always a lot of 'ifs.' '*If* we had been willing to go in on the ground,' '*if* it had worked.' It might have resulted in the Russians' being more willing to negotiate. But that's 'if' thinking.

"However, even if we had gone in on the ground and the Russians had permitted it and our troops had arrived in Berlin, we would have broken the blockade only for the Allied forces, but we would not have broken the blockade for German traffic. And if we were going to keep that route open for German traffic, we either had to take over that highway and guard it, or else the Russians would have to give up on stopping German traffic. This was one of the reasons I was never that sure of going in on the ground, much as I wanted to do so. I wanted to do so for pride. But I don't know what we would have done if we had gone through and the Russians had just let us go through and then had stopped the next group of German trucks that tried to make it.

"I think the reason the airlift was such a spectacular success was not because it was an airlift but because we succeeded in keeping a city of several million people alive over a relatively long period of time. The impressive results were what really counted, and what really made the Europeans believe in us."

On June 26, the airlift began. The first transport planes loaded with food and coal arrived in Berlin. It was a trickle at first. Neither Clay nor Robertson was confident that the meager resources available could sustain West Berlin's 2.2 million citizens indefinitely. But it was the only option available under the circumstances, and both did their utmost to expand the airlift quickly.

It was equally clear that Washington remained hesitant and unsure. On June 25, Clay had been asked by Secretary Royall to explain once more why he had introduced the new Western currency into Berlin. Clay answered abruptly. It was clear that he was fast losing his patience with the Army's timidity—especially in the face of the determined stand that the Berliners and his British allies were taking. "The decision was made," he told Royall, "in view of Soviet declaration that Soviet zone currency under Soviet laws and complete Soviet control would be installed in Berlin. This would have placed Berlin financially completely in Soviet hands." Clay reminded Royall that this information had all been furnished to Washington previously "in a number of cablegrams."

Washington's response was one more teleconference, in which Clay was asked by Under Secretary of State Lovett to clarify the currency situation in Berlin. Specifically, Clay was asked if he would suspend the currency conversion in the Western sectors to allow Soviet currency to circulate. Clay refused.

> We should not confuse currency issue as real issue [Clay told Lovett]. It is a pretext. . . . Issue is western Germany and its part in European recovery. . . . Please remember, emphasize, and never stop repeating that currency in Berlin is not the issue—the issue is our position in Europe and plans for western Germany.

In the face of American indecision, the diplomatic initiative shifted to London. While Washington continued to query Clay about possible compromises, Bevin told the British press on June 26 that His Majesty's Government intended to stay in Berlin, come what may. He followed up with a lengthy personal message that day to Marshall in which he not only urged that the airlift be expanded, but suggested that several squadrons of B-29 bombers (capable of carrying atomic bombs) be dispatched immediately from the United States and stationed in Great Britain—tangible evidence to the Soviets of Western determination to hold Berlin. Had it not been for Bevin's resolute stand, Berlin could easily have been lost that fourth week of June 1948.

On June 28, Bevin reported the Berlin situation to Cabinet. There could be no question of yielding to Soviet pressure, he said—to which there was no disagreement. If the Western powers were forced from Berlin, Bevin said European recovery would be fatally weakened. It was agreed that the airlift should be expanded quickly. Clay's proposal to press through on the ground was rejected: it was too easy for the Soviets to erect effective obstacles. When General Robertson reported that the Russians might deploy barrage balloons in the air corridors to impede the airlift, the Cabinet authorized that they be shot down at once.

In Washington, top-level diplomats and military leaders met with President Truman on the afternoon of June 28. No U.S. statement had yet been issued, and American policy-makers were divided as to whether the United States should try to hold on in Berlin. Bradley reports a scene of shocking confusion. "Everybody was talking at once about a very complicated situation." There was no agreed recommendation, and Truman's views had not been canvassed. But the President quickly resolved the issue. When Under Secretary of State Lovett mentioned the possibility of withdrawal, President Truman briskly interrupted: "We are going to stay. Period." Army Secretary Royall expressed concern and asked skeptically whether the consequences had been thought through. Truman's reply provided the assurance Clay and Bevin needed. "We will have to deal with the situation as it develops," said Truman. "We are in Berlin by the terms of an agreement, and the Russians have no right to get us out by either direct or indirect pressure."

President Truman approved Bevin's suggestion that two B-29 groups be sent to Europe. Lovett summarized the American decision in a cable that evening to Ambassador Douglas in London. Said Lovett, "We stay in Berlin." He said it was agreed that the city would be supplied by air, and U.S. air strength in Europe would be reinforced. "We see advantage in keeping Berlin situation before world attention by every feasible device of diplomatic exchange, publicity and appeal, not excluding ultimate reference of case to UN at appropriate time. We are hopeful war can be avoided by these means."

Bevin and Clay were delighted by Truman's firm response. Clay urged that additional planes for the airlift be dispatched from the United States as soon as possible and that a B-29 squadron be flown to Germany en route to Great Britain. Said Clay:

> We are no longer at a point where we need to fear that the bringing in of reinforcements will influence the Soviet position. They are either bluffing now or they have made up their minds and the currency issue is . . . only a pretext. It is our view here that they are bluffing and that their hand can and should be called now. They are definitely afraid of our air might. Moreover, arrival of aircraft will be deciding factor in sustaining Allied firmness.

Meanwhile, Bevin was pressing Washington for a public statement of support. Thus far, he told Ambassador Douglas, Britain had been carrying the ball alone. It was time for the U.S. position on Berlin to be made clear. It would be a great help, he said, if Marshall "could say something appreciative about the Berlin Social Democrats and their steadfastness" in the crisis. Marshall responded on June 30 with a brief comment that the United States was in Berlin by agreement "and we intend to stay." President Truman restated the position more forcefully in his press conference the following day.

But it was evident from Marshall's reluctant statement that official Washington was not convinced that Berlin could be held. In fact, the contrast between Marshall's brief comment and Bevin's stirring address to the House of Commons that same day made it evident that Western resolve was far stronger in London than Washington. "If the intention is to make trouble for us in Berlin," Bevin told the House, "His Majesty's Government cannot submit to that. We cannot abandon these stout hearted Berlin democrats who are refusing to bow to Soviet pressure." (Marshall had made no reference to the Berliners.) After referring to the steps under way to reinforce the airlift, Bevin paused to give added weight to his words. Then, with all deliberateness, he told the House:

> We recognize that as a result of these decisions a grave situation might arise. Should such a situation arise, we shall have to ask the House to face it. His Majesty's Government and our Western Allies can see no alternative between that and surrender—and none of us can accept surrender.

In a subsequent conversation with Douglas, Bevin repeated that he did not favor opening negotiations with Moscow until the Russians realized that the West intended to stay in Berlin. He also insisted that Washington was not to bypass Clay and Robertson, "but on the contrary, to give them every support and to reinforce their position."

In Berlin, Clay was genuinely thrilled by Bevin's stand. His ringing speech to the House of Commons was the first significant public statement of support that Clay had received, and he was deeply grateful. But Clay's joy was short-lived. It immediately became clear that Washington did not share Bevin's robust determination. No sooner had the text of Bevin's speech come over the news ticker than Clay was informed by Royall that under no circumstances should Clay shoot down Russian barrage balloons in the air corridors "without first obtaining a clearance from the Department [of the Army]."

Clay fired back a sharp reply.

> I fully understand the desire of our government not to start shooting nor to develop an incident that may lead to war. Nevertheless, this situation is one which can be handled only with some power of decision in the theater commander's hands. My British opposite has the requisite authority. I think it is extremely important that we be in a position so that we may act together.
>
> I must, therefore, request that my present discretionary authority not be curtailed. I cannot take the responsibility of requiring our air crews to undertake what may develop into hazardous flights unless I have the authority to take appropriate action.

Clay said that such discretionary authority was essential to the "successful accomplishment of [his] mission," and told Bradley and Royall that if he "couldn't be trusted with such discretionary authority" he should be relieved. Nothing further was heard from Washington, and Clay assumed his discretionary authority had not been curtailed. But at a White House meeting on July 2, General Marshall was decidedly unenthusiastic about sending additional B-29s to Europe. Marshall warned that the decision was provocative and reported that he had asked Douglas to explore the situation once more with Bevin.

Several days earlier, a brief flurry of concern had erupted when Marshal Sokolovsky was unceremoniously arrested in the U.S. sector of Berlin for speeding and detained for over an hour. Soviet military headquarters in Germany was located in the Berlin district of Karlshorst, in the eastern sector of the city. But the senior Soviet officers lived in Potsdam, some thirty miles to the west. The most direct route lay through the American sector, and Russian drivers habitually drove with reckless abandon on their daily trips between Potsdam and Karlshorst. Clay had ordered a crackdown, and one of the first vehicles apprehended was that of Sokolovsky. When his car was stopped, the Russian bodyguards who were following in another car jumped out with their weapons at the ready. The American MP who had made the arrest put his pistol in the pit of Sokolovsky's stomach, and kept him under detention until a U.S. officer arrived—almost an hour later—to identify and release him.

Clay felt badly about the incident, and arranged to visit Sokolovsky to apologize. They had been close friends, and Clay recognized that it was silly to let things get out of hand in Berlin. Afterward he told Washington that Sokolovsky received him "with marked official politeness but with evident restraint. . . . For the first time in the history of our meetings, no refreshments were offered." Clay said that he believed Sokolovsky "is set on his present course but is by no manner of means happy or confident. I was also of the definite impression that he had hoped I was bringing some proposal with me and that he kept waiting for me to offer some proposal [concerning the Berlin situation]."

When Sokolovsky sent a somewhat conciliatory letter to Robertson suggesting that the Berlin problem could be solved, Clay and Bevin were skeptical. The three Western military governors were instructed to meet informally with Sokolovsky to explore the issue, but to refrain from any official commitment. Clay reported to Washington that the meeting had at least clarified Soviet intent: the Berlin currency issue was a ruse. Sokolovsky had indicated "that the technical difficulties [on the transport routes to Berlin] would continue until we abandoned our plans for a West German government."

Nevertheless, it required the best efforts of Clay and Bevin to prevent Washington from rushing headlong into premature negotiations with Moscow. As Bevin's biographer reported, the meeting of the Military Governors with Sokolovsky "had at least served to delay rushing to Stalin as the Americans had wanted, and to bring home to them that the Russians were using the situation in Berlin to try and reopen the entire German question." As usual, Bevin was dead right. "State joins me in compliments on the method of handling the conference," Royall cabled Clay on July 3. "The conference fully confirms . . . the real motives and purpose of the blockade."

On July 10, with the Soviet blockade in full force and with food supplies in Berlin dwindling, Clay urged that additional C-54s (the military version of the DC-4) be dispatched to Europe immediately. Clay told Bradley he realized the airlift was expensive, but a failure to keep Berlin supplied would be even more expensive. Two days later, he repeated his request. "Would appreciate answer soonest to request for additional C-54's. . . . Each day of delay will make our position more difficult. Hence, I urge prompt dispatch of additional C-54's soonest." And in a separate cable that day to Bradley, Clay once again recommended sending a convoy to Berlin along the autobahn: "I am still convinced that the Soviets do not want war. However, they know that the Allies also do not want war and they will continue their pressure to the point at which they believe hostilities might occur." Clay said that despite the inherent risk, he was convinced that the convoy "would get to Berlin and that the technical difficulties would cease to exist."

On July 15, Clay repeated his request to send a task force in on the ground. In an "Eyes Only" cable to Bradley, Clay urged that he be given permission "to proceed with this convoy movement as quickly as it can be arranged here. . . . I also think it important that the two B-29 groups now approved for movement into the U.K. be started at once, as it is my view that they should be in England when this convoy movement is started."

Bradley replied almost instantly. "Future courses of action including possibility of using armed convoys are being carefully considered," he told Clay. "However, we are not yet prepared to reach a firm decision. Decision for such action can obviously be taken only by highest level."

While the Administration anguished over what should be done, Bevin and the British Cabinet made plans for the worst. His Majesty's Government were in no mood to back down. Even Nye Bevan, its most anti-American left-winger, strongly supported Clay. Bevan shared Clay's view that the Russians were bluffing. He argued powerfully in Cabinet for letting Clay push through a convoy, supported by tanks, as the swiftest way of ending the crisis. When the Cabinet decided to support the airlift instead, the Government was determined that it succeed. Prime Minister Attlee and Bevin met with the British Chiefs of Staff on July 9 and agreed that it was prudent to plan on the assumption that war might develop. Robertson was told that in the event of an emergency he was to withdraw to the Rhine, and it was decided to prepare two airfields in the Netherlands for the RAF to use in covering the British withdrawal. Field Marshal Montgomery, Chief of the Imperial General Staff, was dispatched posthaste to Paris, where he reported widespread defeatism and a fear that France once more would be left in the lurch. But neither Bevin nor Attlee nor the British Cabinet was disheartened. Bevin knew the Russians had major military problems of their own. He acknowledged that it might have been a mistake for the Allies to agree to the original zonal arrangements that located Berlin 110 miles inside the Soviet zone, but it would be disastrous to all of Western Europe if they now allowed themselves to be forced out.

In contrast to the determination in London, pessimism reigned in Washington. Even the airlift was questioned. The Assistant Secretary of the Air Force, Cornelius Whitney, told the National Security Council in mid-July that "the Air Staff was firmly convinced that the airlift was doomed to failure." Under Secretary of State Robert Lovett shared that view. He dismissed the airlift as an "unsatisfactory" and "temporary expedient." Forrestal brooded darkly about a deadline in mid-October, when winter weather would ground the airlift. He said that at that time they faced a choice between abandoning Berlin or smashing through by force—a move he believed was destined to fail. The Army staff also pressed for a quick solution. "The only logical decision" was to withdraw from Berlin before defeat became inevitable, the President was told.

But Truman refused to be stampeded. He agreed with Clay that "if we move out of Berlin we [will] have lost everything we are fighting for." He told the NSC that the United States would stay in Berlin "even at the risk of war"—a risk that most of those present believed was far too immediate. The President declined to approve the convoy Clay wanted to dispatch to Berlin, but he authorized expanding the airlift as quickly as possible. Truman reported the confrontation with his advisers in his diary that evening:

> Have quite a day. . . . A meeting with General Marshall and Jim Forrestal on Berlin and the Russian situation. Marshall states the facts and the conditions with which we are faced. I'd made the decision ten days ago to *stay in Berlin.*
>
> Jim wants to hedge—he always does. He is constantly sending me alibi memos. . . .
>
> We'll stay in Berlin—come what may.
>
> Royal[l], Draper and Jim Forrestal come in later. I have to listen to a rehash of what I know already and reiterate my "stay in Berlin" decision. I don't pass the buck, nor do I alibi out of any decision I make.

In London, Bevin was faced with an equally serious bout of pessimism—not from Cabinet or Parliament (which were willing to run whatever risks were required), but from his military commander in Berlin. Unlike Clay, General Robertson began to have serious second thoughts about the airlift. He doubted if Berlin could be supplied much longer. On August 10, Robertson cabled Bevin that it would not be possible to keep Berlin supplied by air through the winter. He told Bevin that it would be better to accept the Russian currency in Berlin rather than risk the failure of the airlift. "I am convinced that in the course of time the Soviets will steal the city from under our noses," said Robertson.

Bevin was appalled. His huge bulk shook with anger. Not only did he disagree with Robertson, but Robertson's cable was so pessimistic that Bevin ordered that it not be circulated in the Foreign Office. According to one of Britain's leading scholars of the airlift, Bevin evidently "thought that the Military Governor's report showed signs of defeatism and appeasement and he feared that these would spread to other British officials and to the public." The Foreign Office told Robertson to remember that "much more than Berlin will be at stake," and that Bevin was prepared "to contemplate serious and even extraordinary measures . . . in order to win the day." As Bevin's biographer has noted, throughout his tenure as British Foreign Secretary, Bevin was determined not to repeat Chamberlain's mistake of appeasing Hitler ten years before. By standing firm in Berlin, Bevin was confident they could avert war.

Bevin reiterated his determination to Washington. As he told Ambassador Douglas, he would rather hold Berlin to the bitter end and be driven out by force than to give way voluntarily. Bevin agreed with Clay that the next two months would be decisive and that it was essential to increase the airlift's capacity before the onset of winter. And he cautioned Douglas to stop worrying over the costs of the airlift: it could not possibly cost as much as one day of war. The Soviet Union wanted to make Germany a Communist satellite, said Bevin. They had failed, and now sought to make the Russian zone (and Berlin) a satellite. Bevin believed that the only way to frustrate Soviet intentions was to hold fast in Berlin.

Clay shared Bevin's determination. Like Bevin, he deplored Washington's tendency to rush into negotiations with the Soviet Union. In a "Top Secret—Eyes Only" cable to Draper on July 19, Clay remonstrated once again against what Washington believed the easy way out: to negotiate with the Soviet Union over the future of Germany. "I am sending this radio [message] to you personally," said Clay, "as I realize that my views and comments go beyond my responsibilities as theater commander."

> I cannot but feel that the world today is facing the most critical issue that has arisen since Hitler placed his policy of aggression in motion. In fact, the Soviet Government has more force immediately at its disposal than did Hitler to accomplish his purpose. Only America can exert the world leadership, and only America can provide the strength to stop this policy of aggression here and now. The next time may be too late. I believe determined action may stop it short of war. It cannot be stopped without the serious risk of war.

Clay reminded Draper that when the Western powers had decided to press ahead with European recovery, "we recognized fully the probabilities of Soviet counter-measures. . . . The very violence of the Soviet reaction now is the proof of the success of our several programs to restore democracy in Europe. Having committed ourselves to a course of action to this end . . . can we afford now to throw it away as we encounter our first major evidence of Soviet resistance?" Any "failure on our part to establish a German government now could only be interpreted as weakness and apprehension on our part. . . . [A] unified Germany can come now only when the balance of power in Europe is restored."

Clay told Draper that Soviet pressure on Berlin was based on one of two premises. Either the Russians sought to retard European recovery by all measures short of war, or they had decided to go to war at this time. But there were no reports of military movements by the Soviets, and no indication that they were preparing for war in Europe. "In other words, they are still bluffing but will continue to do so until it is absolutely evident that their bluff is being called." If the U.S.S.R had decided to go to war—Clay strongly believed that they had not—"a retreat now will merely be followed by pressure elsewhere within a matter of weeks or months. If war is inevitable, the time that we can gain by retreat now is so relatively short that it has little value. The choice before us is a hard choice. However, if we do decide to retreat now, this retreat will not save us from again and again having to choose between retreat and war. With each retreat we will find ourselves confronted with the same problem but with fewer and fewer allies on our side."

Despite Clay's skepticism and Bevin's opposition, Washington pressed to begin negotiations directly with Stalin. Clay thought little would be gained, Bevin believed Washington was forcing the issue, and both feared that progress toward a West German government would be compromised in an untimely effort to reach agreement with the Soviets. Bevin told the State Department's Charles Bohlen that a premature meeting with Stalin before the capability of the airlift had been established would be playing into Moscow's hands.

It was at this point in the crisis that Clay came down with a painful attack of lumbago. He could not move his neck and was able to walk only with great difficulty. There is no doubt that the lumbago was a reflection of the tension that Clay was under and the struggle with Washington that consumed him. Once he was assured that Berlin would not be abandoned, the pain subsided.

On Sunday, July 25, Clay met in Berlin with Bohlen and Ambassador Bedell Smith, who had flown in from Moscow for a round of briefings and discussions prior to making the appeal to Stalin that the State Department desired. At Washington's direction, Clay then flew with Bohlen and Smith to London, where an agreed tripartite submission to Stalin was thrashed out with Bevin and French Ambassador Massagli. Bevin remained unsympathetic to the overture. To ensure that it did not get out of hand, he dispatched his principal private secretary, Frank Roberts, to Moscow to act as Britain's representative. As Clay recalled afterward, he too was not optimistic about the results.

When the three Western representatives in Moscow (Smith, Roberts, and French Ambassador Yves Chataigneau) met with Stalin at 9:00 P.M. on August 2, the doubts that Clay and Bevin shared were confirmed. After initially questioning Western efforts to form a German government, Stalin indicated that the blockade could be lifted provided the Allies accepted Soviet currency in Berlin. The first report of the meeting from Bedell Smith described Stalin as in an extraordinarily amicable and cooperative mood. In Washington, Bohlen thought the outcome "highly satisfactory." But the early optimism evaporated quickly. Clay was shaken when he learned that Smith had proposed to accept Soviet currency as the sole medium of exchange in Berlin without the West's having any control over its issue. "Without such control," Clay informed Bradley, "we would in fact in short order have no real say in Berlin government." Clay was especially disturbed because Smith had not reported the Russian demand. He himself learned of it indirectly, from Roberts's report to Bevin, which had been sent to Robertson. Pursuant to Bevin's instructions, Robertson had shown the report to Clay, who then cautioned Draper against any further concessions in Moscow. "We have gone as far as we possibly can."

> Berlin political leaders frightfully upset at rumor of Soviet currency becoming single currency. If we are voided of all control, they will be at mercy of Soviet Government.

Bevin made the same point to Ambassador Douglas in London. "Bevin does not want to appear 'sticky,' " Douglas told Washington, "but [he] believes strongly that we must stand firmly. He holds tenaciously to the view, (a) that we must not yield on the necessity of quadripartite control of Soviet currency in Berlin or (b) . . . accept quadripartite control of currency in Berlin in consideration for a commitment on our part to postpone the program in western Germany." Douglas said that "Bevin hopes urgently that we will exert every effort to increase the airlift."

The four-power discussions continued in Moscow throughout the month of August. The strong reaction of Clay and Bevin caused the Western negotiators to pull back from major concessions, just as Molotov quickly reneged on Stalin's original proposal. The Soviets believed time was on their side: that the airlift could not supply Berlin once winter weather arrived and flying conditions deteriorated. With the singular exception of President Truman, most in Washington agreed. But Clay and Bevin were by now convinced the airlift would succeed—if given enough planes. Clay worked desperately to increase the daily tonnage. He pressed LeMay and Tunner to reduce turnaround time for the planes and to build up supplies in Berlin before winter. In Berlin, Clay reverted to the Army Engineer of old and ordered a new airfield constructed to handle the increased volume of incoming planes. Thirty thousand Berliners answered his call and with their hands and backs cleared the land, removed the rubble, and graded the runways. Within two months, a new airfield, the site of Berlin's present international airport in the borough of Tegel, was operational. In London, Bevin dug in to prevent unnecessary compromise in Moscow. Both saw Berlin as a trial of strength. It would be won by the side with the stronger nerves.

By the end of August, the negotiations in Moscow had thrashed out what appeared to be the outlines of an agreement. The Western powers agreed to accept Soviet currency as the sole legal tender in Berlin, providing it was under quadripartite control, and the Russians agreed to lift the blockade. It was also understood that a foreign ministers' meeting would be held in due course. The resulting directive was sent to Berlin, where the four Military Governors were instructed to work out the details by September 7—little more than one week away. But the agreement that had been reached in Moscow was more apparent than real. The directive's loose wording papered over fundamental differences as to how the Soviet currency was to be controlled. The Western powers believed it would be regulated by a quadripartite financial commission; the Soviets claimed it would be under exclusive Russian control. The directive permitted both interpretations. As Clay advised Draper on August 30, "I have no hope of reaching a solid argument which protects our position. It seems to me that all this and more was assigned to Bedell to get in Moscow. He did not, so I see no reason why we should hope for more here. It is not Soviet custom to give more in the field than in Moscow."

The three Western Military Governors met daily with Sokolovsky from September 1 to September 8. But no agreement resulted. Clay told Draper that "at no time during these conferences have Soviets agreed to early meetings or to continue meetings for long hours. This, as you know, is not characteristic and can only result from the desire to stall. Moreover, in meetings their attitude is indifferent almost to be contemptuous." Later he told Royall that "Soviet tactics were clever and deceptive with just enough concessions to take the hot fire out of a protest at Moscow."

When the meetings with Sokolovsky concluded, Clay pleaded for more planes. "We must increase airlift very soon to hold our position." He told Bradley that he needed sixty additional C-54s immediately and because of winter weather would require forty-seven more in December "if lift is still continuing at that time." Clay said that would raise the U.S. airlift's capacity to fifty-two hundred tons a day, "which should be our target." In fact, LeMay and Tunner, supported by the RAF, delivered seven thousand tons of supplies to Berlin on September 18. Clay told Secretary Royall "this proves that we can last indefinitely in Berlin and in fact can probably . . . do as much by air as we ever did by rail and highway." And, indeed, by March 1949 the airlift's daily average reached eight thousand tons, and on April 12, 1949, a twenty-four-hour record was set when U.S. and British planes delivered thirteen thousand tons of food and fuel to Berlin.

But in September 1948, the capacity of the airlift was not yet proved. Most American policy-makers remained skeptical. As a result, the failure of the Military Governors to find a solution to the crisis fueled a growing pessimism in Washington. Secretary Marshall told the National Security Council on September 9 (the day after the talks in Berlin had broken off) that in spite of the airlift, time was on the side of the Russians. Bedell Smith in Moscow shared that view. Both believed that Berlin was indefensible and should be disposed of as soon as possible. From Marshall down, Washington officials grossly underestimated the effectiveness of the airlift as well as the determination of the Berliners to resist, both of which were nearly scuttled in the haste to reach an agreement with the Soviets. According to a subsequent RAND Corporation analysis of the 1948 negotiations:

> The West, particularly the United States, seems frequently to have misinterpreted Soviet signals. American newspapermen, and also those professionally concerned with the conduct of U.S. foreign policy, tended to greet each affable expression or minor concession by the Soviets as an indication of a basic change in Soviet foreign policy, without asking whether this affability might have some other meaning. This tendency precluded a full and sober assessment of what the Soviets were trying to accomplish, and it also inhibited any long-term measures by which to affect Communist pressure.

When the talks in Berlin collapsed, the United States sought to renew negotiations in Moscow. Once again Bevin intervened to prevent undue haste. This time, however, Washington saw the Berlin situation as a matter of principle: if the Soviets didn't explicitly agree to the Allies' right to be in Berlin, Marshall and Lovett wanted to break off discussions and go to the U.N. Bevin, with three centuries of British statecraft behind him, recognized that it was a matter of power, not principle. He preferred to continue talking to the Russians, and not force a break until the airlift's success put the Soviets on the defensive. French Foreign Minister Schuman, who had succeeded the prickly Bidault following the latest change of government in France, agreed with Bevin. As he told Marshall, what we want "is not to have the Russians recognize our rights, but to have them raise the blockade." Once again, Bevin prevailed. Marshall reluctantly told Bedell Smith that Allied unity took precedence over U.S. preferences.

On September 14, the Western ambassadors presented Stalin with an *aide-mémoire* blaming the failure of the Berlin talks on Marshal Sokolovsky's refusal to agree on a suitable method for currency control. On September 18, the Soviets replied, accusing the West for the talks' collapse and correctly pointing out that the original Moscow directive to the Military Governors made no explicit mention of four-power currency control. Four days later, the Western powers replied in identical notes delivered to the Kremlin, restating their position and asking the Soviet Union to remove the blockade before negotiations continued.

In Clay's view, there had been no change in the Soviet position for the past six weeks. But during that period, the airlift had proved itself. Clay told Bradley that on Air Forces Day, September 18, the United States and British had landed 861 planes in Berlin, even though for eighteen of the twenty-four hours visibility had been so bad that all of the flights had to rely on instrument landings. "The airlift has proved to me that we can stay here even if we have to make a separate city of the three western sectors. . . . In fact, except possibly for two or three winter months, we can support Berlin better than ever in the past. It will cost considerably more money but relatively only a fraction of what we are now spending to aid Europe and to re-arm to stop Soviet expansion. *Let's do it.*" Bevin shared Clay's enthusiasm. He too believed the tide had turned.

While the negotiations in Moscow were under way, the Soviets stepped up their pressure in Berlin. Marshal Sokolovsky casually told the Military Governors that Russian air maneuvers would take place in the air corridors commencing in mid-September. This was a threat Clay and Robertson took seriously, but Clay warned Sokolovsky that he would have to face the consequences should an accident occur. The result was that Russian fighters stayed clear of Allied aircraft. Meanwhile, in the Russian sector, the Communist-controlled Socialist Unity Party (SED) launched a campaign of intimidation, threats, and physical violence against those Berlin city officials who supported the Allies. Clay believed that the mob violence was a prelude to a Soviet attempt to take over the city's government. As he told Draper on September 6, Soviet tactics in Berlin

> were getting rough. Yesterday, a Communist mob prevented City Assembly [located in the Soviet sector] from meeting. It manhandled three American reporters at the scene. Today, a well-organized mob was on hand again. The deputy mayor [Louise Schroeder] foolishly and without our knowledge, took forty-odd plainclothesmen from Western sectors over to keep order. Uniformed police from Soviet sector under direct orders of Soviet officer started to arrest them. They rushed into offices of the three western liaison representatives [at City Hall], where some are still under siege.* However, Soviet sector police broke into our office and led about twenty of the poor devils off to death or worse.
>
> Pride is a cheap commodity, thank God, or I would never hold my head up. We are being pushed around like we were a fourth class nation. My impulse was to send our military police to restore order. . . . However, I realize the implications and am just taking it for the moment. Still, as we maintain the quiet because of the negotiations, [Soviet] pressure increases. It will culminate, I am sure, in [their] rejection of present city government and probably will result in [Communist] inspired rioting in western sectors.

Clay told Draper that the Communist mob action was so serious that "we cannot fail to intervene soon or lose all prestige. . . . If mob violence continues, I shall advise Soviets that since this is a quadripartite city we will send our military police in to restore order."

Once again Clay's readiness to take action was more than Washington was prepared for. The Pentagon, in particular, was concerned about the possibility of escalation. When shown a copy of Clay's remarks, Bradley quickly queried whether Clay actually contemplated entering the Soviet sector with American MPs.

Clay told Bradley not to worry. "Sometimes I let off steam to Draper which I cannot let off here. I tell him what I would like to do but am not doing." Clay said that

* When the British liaison officer at City Hall asked Robertson for instructions, Robertson called the Foreign Office for advice. According to Lord Bullock, "Bevin personally authorized immediate intervention and the liaison officer had his answer within fifteen minutes" *(Ernest Bevin,* vol. II, p. 593).

> Entry of our MP's into Soviet sector would be in violation of our own position and I do not intend such action which would legalize [Soviet] entry into our sector without advance approval from you. However, conditions could arise which would lead me to such recommendations. You need not fear any precipitate action on our part. We have taken much without it. However, you cannot live surrounded by force and bluff without showing that you have no fear of the first and only contempt for the latter.

The day after Clay spoke, the Berlin city government voted to move from the historic Rathaus, located in the Soviet sector, to temporary facilities in the British sector. On September 9, the people of Berlin rallied in support. Over three hundred thousand Berliners—the largest crowd since the beginning of World War II—jammed the square in front of the blackened ruins of the Reichstag (located in the British sector, near the Brandenburg Gate) to hear Mayor Reuter and other Berlin political leaders denounce Soviet efforts to impose their will on the city. Following the rally, part of the crowd marched into the adjacent Soviet sector, where several youths climbed to the top of the Brandenburg Gate and tore down the Russian flag that was flying there. When others in the crowd began to burn the flag, the Russian guards stationed at the nearby Soviet War Memorial rushed to recover it. The troops opened fire into the crowd, killing two and wounding others. A bloodbath was narrowly averted when the British provost marshal courageously stepped in front of the Russian soldiers and ordered them to cease firing, while British military police worked frantically to restore order. A gentle drizzle dampened tempers, and by evening the crowd had dispersed.

The next day, Clay told Draper "we are in the midst of a dangerous game. Obviously western military government had nothing to do with the anti-Communist demonstration except that British military government issued a permit [for the demonstration to take place]. The huge attendance was I am sure a great surprise even to the Germans and led the German political leaders into inflammatory speeches. . . .

"It was difficult if not impossible for the British to refuse the permit in view of planned Communist mob actions, but to my mind we are playing with dynamite. *Mass meetings directed against Soviet military government can easily turn into mass meetings against other occupying powers,* and can develop into the type of mob government which Hitler played so well to get into power.

"It is an unhappy development which we recognize fully but at the moment do not know what to do. Hence, with probable wisdom, for the moment we are doing nothing."

Clay said that he and Robertson would have "a quiet talk" with Reuter. "We may have to take some action soon [unless we want] a dangerous, habit-forming precedent to repeat itself."

Clay and Robertson had little difficulty persuading Reuter to rein in the demonstrations. The following week, with the airlift tonnage increasing daily, Clay wrote a long, reflective letter to Justice Byrnes. At the time, Clay was not aware of the role Byrnes had played to thwart Marshall's plan to replace him as Military Governor. "I have not written you for some time," said Clay, "because I was so convinced that I would be home during the past summer." Clay brought Byrnes up to date on the currency reform and the swift economic recovery that was taking place in Germany. "Almost overnight hoarded goods appeared on the shelves. . . . Likewise, hoarded goods in manufacturing plants began to move to the stores. Even fruits and vegetables from the farm once more went on sale in the market place. . . . Building activities are evident everywhere. Greater financial support from home, plus a full harvest has made the food outlook better than at any time. The result is that Germany is going back to work, and in western Germany in particular the people on the street visibly have taken a new hold on life."

Clay told Byrnes:

> The Berlin situation is tense although by no manner of means as tense as it is written up in the United States. German political leaders of the more democratic parties have shown outstanding courage in resisting Soviet terroristic tactics and the Communists have been unable to gain Berlin politically. The airlift has been a magnificent success and can keep us in Berlin through the winter.
>
> I do not know how much longer I am to be here. I had planned to be gone by now and have been waiting for some time for a sufficient period of stability in our relations with Russia to again request my retirement. Nevertheless, while Berlin is still under siege, I cannot ask for retirement.

While the Russians were acting to complete the division of the Berlin city government (and the incorporation of the Soviet sector into the Russian zone), the Western powers were moving to bring the Berlin question before the United Nations. But after two months of intense negotiations, the Security Council remained deadlocked. Winter was about to begin, and the Soviets still believed time to be on their side. The Allies, on the other hand, were growing increasingly confident that Berlin could be held. The airlift had galvanized Western resistance. A public-opinion poll in October indicated that 86 percent of the Berliners believed the city could be supplied by air for the foreseeable future. Only 45 percent had thought that in July. Eighty-three percent now believed the United States was the superior military power and that it would prevail over Russia if war did come. Almost unanimously (98 percent), the Berliners thought the West was doing the right thing by remaining in Berlin. In his *Memoirs,* U.N. Secretary General Trygve Lie noted that as the success of the airlift increased, the Western powers became less ready to make concessions. In particular, Lie mentions Dr. Philip Jessup, the U.S. ambassador to the U.N., who visited Berlin in late October and saw the airlift in operation. From that point on, according to Lie, Jessup was convinced that the West would prevail. In fact, at Clay's urging, Jessup spoke over the German radio network on October 31, informing the Berliners of the negotiations at the United Nations and assuring them that the United States was determined to stay in Berlin.

The following day, Clay took the initiative once more. He announced that food rations in Berlin would be increased by 20 percent. Fats and sugars, which had been in desperately short supply for years, would be augmented significantly. The new ration for the Berliners would be two thousand calories—more than anywhere else in Germany. The "doubting Thomases" had their answer.

In Washington, Clay's stature rose significantly. *Time* magazine already had devoted two covers to Clay, *Newsweek* followed suit, and *Fortune* ran a glowing article on the airlift in its November 1948 issue. General Bradley, who had been among the most skeptical in the Pentagon, wrote that "Clay's brainchild, the airlift, worked out far better than anyone dared hope" and called Clay "a logistical genius." More important, President Truman was firmly on Clay's side. He recognized what Clay had accomplished. As Truman wrote afterward, reflecting on Clay's visit to Washington in October, "General Clay placed before us an account not only of the technical achievement of the airlift but also of the effect our action in Berlin had on the German people. They had closed ranks and applied to the task of reconstruction with a new vigor. It had turned them sharply against communism. Germany, which had been waiting passively to see where it should cast its lot for the future, was veering toward the cause of the Western nations."

On October 13, Clay once more raised the matter of his retirement, telling the Department of the Army that he could not leave while Berlin was still under siege. "I hope this will cause no problem to the Department," said Clay, who was not especially surprised when Draper replied that it was essential for Clay to remain in Berlin until the blockade was lifted. But he was genuinely taken aback (and a little flattered) when the Army asked him if he would consider taking over the occupation of Japan when MacArthur retired. According to Draper, "The Command in Japan at that point will badly need your background in occupation problems, in currency reform, in the curbing of inflation, and in increasing industrial production. Your assignment to Japan would represent an ideal solution from the point of view of the Army and the American people when General MacArthur retires." Clay replied:

> I appreciate the Japan suggestion but it calls for a fresher person than myself. I definitely want to retire if and when I can leave this assignment gracefully. However, I cannot now voluntarily leave with Berlin still in blockade as to do so would be running out. I have no way to foretell when relative stability will occur here *vis-à-vis* Russia, but when that moment arrives . . . I am ready to call it a day.

Clay's periodic difficulties with the State Department continued, but he seemed to dismiss them as increasingly irrelevant. After three and a half years in Germany, Clay had come to consider the State Department bureaucracy—Kennan, Matthews, and Bohlen—only slightly less pernicious than the French. Both, he believed, wanted to scuttle German recovery. When State suggested in November that Clay was placing German interests ahead of the broader concerns of Western Europe (the issue again involved control of the Ruhr), Clay bluntly told Washington that he had *"seen much of this 'broad interests' theory which resolves itself into our refusal to place into effect certain measures desired by junior officials of State Department which were never approved by higher authority and sent to me as instructions."* As Military Governor, Clay always insisted on calling the shots in Germany. Washington could relieve him if it wished, but he consistently refused to take staff recommendations as instructions. The chain of command ran from Clay through General Bradley and Secretary Royall to President Truman. Their orders were followed by Clay to the letter. But in the absence of direct instructions from them, Clay believed that his authority was complete. And as Robert Lovett once remarked with considerable understatement, Clay "rather insisted on it."

But Clay lost his battle to equalize war damage losses among the German population. Early Allied policy had encouraged Clay to press ahead with German equalization measures. But when the legislation was finally passed by the Bizonal Council in December 1948, Washington ordered Clay to delay its approval. Clay protested sharply. "More and more," he told Army Secretary Royall, "I am beginning to feel that we are continually being placed out on a limb which is being sawed off behind us." Although the British and French were prepared to approve the equalization measure, it appears that the U.S. Treasury Department was once again concerned that it was, in effect, a tax on capital: a redistribution of German wealth. That sent shivers through the Truman administration. Draper told Clay that Washington's view was firm, and that while the change might be embarrassing to Clay personally, he was instructed to defer approval and to allow a future German government to take responsibility. Clay sounded off to Draper, as he often had done in the past: "I shall of course carry out the order on equalization; which will greatly damage military government's prestige as it makes [our] word meaningless. When I have done so, I shall request relief."

This time, Clay was not just blowing off steam. On January 5, 1949, he wrote Bradley and asked that a date be fixed for his retirement. Clay told Bradley that he had been reluctant to leave so long as Berlin was under siege. For better or worse, said Clay, "I have become associated in the German mind with our determination to remain in Berlin." But the airlift had proved itself, he said, and "most of us exaggerate our personal contribution and importance to any given situation. Perhaps this is what I have been doing."

Despite the airlift's success and what appeared to be a complete victory over the Russians, Clay was deeply distressed by what he saw as the dangerous drift in U.S. policy since the 1948 election. Clay told Bradley that America's policy toward Germany appeared to be changing, and he did not think the change was a wise one. He was particularly unhappy that so little progress had been made in creating a strong West German government and integrating that government into Western Europe. He had begun to fear that Washington wanted to occupy Germany indefinitely. In particular, he was concerned about the State Department's "Program for Germany," a document drafted by George Kennan and the policy planning staff in November that had proposed that Germany be neutralized and argued strongly against establishing a separate West German government. "It may well be that these measures have all been in the interest of our foreign policy as a whole," Clay told Bradley, "but they are at the expense of a successful administration of Germany." Curiously, by 1949 Clay and Kennan had shifted positions. Kennan, who in 1947 had urged Germany's division and the termination of quadripartite government, now touted neutralization and German unity. Clay, who in 1947 had opposed Germany's division and had advocated compromise with the Soviet Union to make four-power government a success, by 1949 had become the principal advocate of a separate West German government and its linkage with the West. Clay told Bradley:

> As a soldier, I am of course subject to your orders even [as] to retirement if you still consider conditions to be tense or if in any way my retirement could bring discredit to the Army. Nevertheless, I now feel definitely that it is in the best interests of the Army that I be permitted to retire. . . .
>
> I shall leave the Army with great regret, with life-long appreciation for the opportunity it has given me to serve, and with an abiding faith in its personnel and purpose.

After almost four years in Germany and numerous resignations over policy differences in the past, Clay's request for retirement scarcely caught Washington by surprise. Clay firmly believed that the celebrated architects of Cold War containment were purchasing Allied unity at Germany's expense. He also thought that Washington wanted to manage the details of German policy from Foggy Bottom. It was bad policy as well as bad organization, and Clay had had enough. But once again the Army needed Clay. The Pentagon did not buy Kennan's proposal to withdraw all military forces from Germany. More important, though the airlift was a success, the battle of Berlin was far from won. "I think it would be harmful for your resignation to be announced at this particular time," Secretary Royall told Clay two days later, "as it might lend some color to propaganda that we are relaxing our firm policy toward Russia." Royall said that President Truman was replacing Marshall and Lovett for his second term (due to begin January 20, 1949), and that Dean Acheson was returning to the Cabinet as Secretary of State. Royall would see Acheson promptly "and try to determine whether State will give Army more leeway or less leeway in policy decisions" in Germany. He asked Clay to reconsider.

The sudden news that Marshall and Lovett were leaving caused Clay to pull back. He saw a glimmer of hope that his plans for a West German government might be achieved, and he told Royall that he did not want to embarrass the Army with an abrupt departure. Both agreed that the timing of his resignation, should it occur, had to be such as to avoid undermining German morale by indicating a lack of continuity in U.S. policy. Clay agreed to think about it.

Clay had been caught by surprise at the news of Marshall's and Lovett's departure. He was not confident that Acheson completely agreed with him about the proper direction of German policy, but he was certain that Marshall and Lovett did not. He also thought that Marshall's departure would mean a stronger stand in Berlin. The Army would have less compunction about arguing military strategy with Acheson, and Clay could influence, if not control, the Army's policy. Above all, Acheson would require some time to settle in. That would give Clay the time he needed to prod the Germans into action on a new constitution.

When Clay replied to Secretary Royall on January 10, he already had decided to take advantage of the change at State. "When I requested retirement," Clay told Royall, "General Marshall had not submitted his resignation." Clay said that under the changed circumstances he would "prefer to defer" the timing of his retirement "until the new Secretary of State has taken office." Clay stressed that he did not want his retirement to be controversial. Nevertheless, "four years here have given me some very real convictions [about Germany] and I would be unsuccessful in administering a policy which was really in conflict with those convictions."

Bradley was now firmly on Clay's side. He understood what Clay had accomplished in Germany, and he now understood the odds Clay had been working against. So did President Truman. On February 3, 1949, Truman told *New York Times* publisher C. L. Sulzberger that he was so pleased with what Clay had accomplished that he was going to leave him in charge in Germany as long as Clay wanted to stay. Truman said he had decided not to transfer responsibility to the State Department.

Clay took advantage of Marshall's departure at State to press ahead with the currency reform in Berlin. Since late June, the new West mark and the Russian East mark had been circulating side by side, both recognized as legal tender for official purposes, although the street value of the East mark had slipped to 5-to-1 in black-market trading. The currency issue in Berlin had originally been central to negotiations to lift the blockade. But as it became increasingly apparent that the airlift would succeed, and as Soviet attention focused more and more on dividing the city administratively, Clay pressed to make the West mark the sole legal tender in the Western sectors. In some respects, Clay was yielding to the pressure of Mayor Reuter and other Berlin leaders who insisted that such a move would encourage the embattled Berliners: it would link West Berlin economically to the Western zones of Germany, and facilitate the city's economic recovery. For the same reason, Clay knew the British were lukewarm about the possibility and the French were distinctly hostile. Paris wanted to take no step that might tie Berlin to a new West German state. Nevertheless, Clay wanted the three Western powers to act in concert and urged Washington to bring pressure on Britain and France, declining the Army's suggestion that he act unilaterally in the American sector. "I believe that the French would like to pull out of Berlin," he told Bradley, and a unilateral currency changeover by the United States "might give them the opportunity."

Once again it was the link between the Berlin Social Democrats and Bevin that turned British policy. In early February, Reuter visited London (the first German political leader to be publicly received since World War II) and convinced Bevin of the need to tie West Berlin to the West German economy. As Clay informed Washington on February 9, after Reuter's visit, "London's views have changed. British now express their readiness to make West currency legal tender in Berlin. This is a real step forward." After a month of prodding and cajoling, France was eventually brought into line, and on March 20, 1949, the three Western Military Governors announced that from that date on, the West mark would be the sole legal tender in West Berlin. In effect, the division of the city was now complete. As Mayor Reuter announced, the currency changeover "means the definite recognition that Berlin belongs to the West."

By the spring of 1949, it was clear that the Soviet blockade of Berlin had failed. The Allied airlift had galvanized Western resistance, and public opinion had turned decisively against the Soviet Union. Within the Eastern bloc, Marshal Tito abruptly announced Yugoslavia's defection from the Comintern. Plans for a North Atlantic Treaty Organization were proceeding. In effect, Communism in Europe had been thrown on the defensive.

At that point, Stalin appears to have decided to end the confrontation in Berlin. Rather than risk military action to disrupt the airlift, he preferred to accept a limited defeat. The city of Berlin had been divided, the Russian hold on the Eastern zone of Germany was as tight as ever, and perhaps, in good Leninist fashion, it was time to retrench and consolidate. The first evidence of a change in Soviet strategy occurred in January 31, 1949, when Stalin granted an interview to the American journalist Kingsbury Smith of the International News Service (INS). Smith's questions to Stalin were submitted beforehand in writing, and the Kremlin made public Stalin's replies.

One of Smith's questions dealt with the situation in Berlin. If the Western powers deferred the establishment of a West German state pending a new meeting of the Council of Foreign Ministers, would the USSR be prepared to lift the blockade? Stalin replied that under those conditions, "the Soviet Government sees no obstacles to lifting the transport restrictions" to Berlin.

On first reading, Stalin's answer caused little jubilation in the West. Bevin in particular had little interest in delaying the formation of a West German government. He was convinced that there was no hope of the blockade's being lifted in the foreseeable future. Clay shared that view. But in the State Department, Stalin's reply was analyzed with great care. The wish may have been father to the thought, but Acheson observed that Stalin had made no mention of the Berlin currency question as a precondition to settlement. This marked the first time since June 1948 that the blockade had not been tied to the currency question, and Acheson was heartened. With President Truman's approval, Philip Jessup, the U.S. ambassador to the U.N., was instructed to find out from the Russian delegation at the United Nations whether Stalin's omission of the currency question had been "accidental."

On February 15, Jessup struck up a conversation in the delegates' lounge with his Soviet opposite, Jacob Malik, and casually inquired whether there was "anything new in Premier Stalin's reply" to Kingsbury Smith. Jessup called Malik's attention to the fact that Stalin "had said nothing about the currency question." Malik confessed he didn't know whether that was significant, but agreed to find out.

Exactly one month later, Malik invited Jessup to the Park Avenue headquarters of the Soviet U.N. delegation and told him that Stalin's omission of the currency matter was "not accidental." As Jessup told the State Department, "The [Soviet] interpreter had the translation of this formal message already typed out in English and read it off."

From that point on, the Jessup-Malik discussions at the U.N. were conducted in great secrecy. The State Department perceived "a new Soviet attitude" and instructed Jessup to explore the possibility of a settlement in Berlin. Clay was not informed that the discussions were under way; in London, Bevin remained deeply skeptical. He insisted that in any communication with Malik, Jessup was to state explicitly that the preparations for a new West German government would continue regardless of the outcome in Berlin. In fact, Bevin refused to allow the conversations to proceed until a firm agreement had been reached with Acheson and French Foreign Minister Schuman about the future German government. Bevin simply refused to trade a unified western Germany for the Soviet's removal of the blockade. If Clay was cut out of the loop, Bevin was as resolute as ever.

When it became abundantly clear to the Soviets that the future West German government was not negotiable, Stalin yielded. On May 5, a four-power statement announcing that the blockade would be lifted on May 12 was released simultaneously in Washington, London, Paris, and Moscow. Eleven days thereafter, the statement said, a new meeting of the Council of Foreign Ministers would convene in Paris. Germany and Berlin would be discussed, but the Western powers had made it clear that they would press ahead with the formation of a West German government in Bonn. The formula that was announced on May 5 allowed the Russians to save face. A meeting of the Council of Foreign Ministers would indeed take place; the question of Germany would indeed be discussed. But it was patently clear that Western plans would not be delayed. In effect, the blockade would be lifted without condition. The city of Berlin was split, the West mark would remain the sole currency in the Western sectors, and normal transportation between Berlin and the Western zones would be resumed. In effect, the victors from World War II had resolved their differences. Berlin, Germany, and Europe would remain divided. The future of Germany had been settled. The basic interests of East and West had been accommodated. That accommodation, Dean Acheson observed at the time, was "dealing sensibly with . . . established fact."

Clay first learned of the Berlin settlement from press reports on April 29. The following day, Assistant Secretary of the Army Tracy Voorhees cabled the text of the agreement to Clay for his comments. Clay was stunned and resentful that he had been kept in the dark about the Jessup-Malik discussions, but told Voorhees it looked like a complete victory. "The inherent danger is the well-known tendency of democracies to rest on their laurels." But Clay said he foresaw little danger on the access routes to Berlin. "There is one important thing to remember. The blockade was broken by airpower, and the airpower should be maintained in full until the Council of Foreign Ministers has completed its deliberations."

Although Clay had been caught by momentary surprise, he had been aware for some time that Soviet policy was in flux. On March 29, Marshal Sokolovsky had been recalled to Moscow and replaced by General of the Army Vassily Chuikov, who had commanded Red Army forces during the Battle of Berlin in 1945. When queried about the change, Clay told Washington that Sokolovsky's recall was "most probably the promotion of a capable man. Certainly he was not an extremist against the U.S." Sokolovsky was appointed deputy Soviet defense minister and later became the Russian equivalent of chairman of the Joint Chiefs of Staff. His book on military policy, published in 1963, was considered the definitive work on Soviet strategy when it appeared.

When Chuikov arrived in Germany two weeks later, he sent Clay a personal letter to announce his appointment. Clay informed Washington that he considered "Soviet courtesy of this type so unusual that I attach significance to it as a possible preliminary move to a settlement" in Berlin.

By early 1949, the issue of Clay's retirement had assumed major symbolic dimensions. Clay was exhausted and wanted to leave, but he felt honor bound to stay in Berlin until the blockade was lifted. A premature departure would undermine German morale. What looked like a clear victory could quickly fall apart. More important, from Clay's view, was the new West German government. The German leaders in the Parliamentary Council were still bitterly divided on a number of contentious constitutional issues, and the Allies had failed to agree on the terms of the so-called Occupation Statute that would specify their residual power. Clay had no illusions that reaching agreement would be easy, but he recognized that he was in the best position to steer both the Germans and his fellow Military Governors to timely compromise. Clay was now conscious of the historic role the Occupation had played in Germany, and he wanted to ensure that a new West German government was established under the best possible circumstances.

While the professional State Department chafed under Clay's sometimes imperious ways, the Army and President Truman now gave him unwavering support. Bradley and Royall were unstinting in their generous recognition of Clay's accomplishments and pressed him to stay on until victory was assured. Even George Kennan now grudgingly conceded that Clay's presence in Germany was pivotal. On January 27, 1949, Royall requested that Clay time his retirement to coincide with the "approval of German constitution by the Military Governors"—an event that would terminate the Occupation.

Clay declined to give Royall a firm commitment. He recognized that difficult negotiations lay ahead and did not want to surrender his highest trump card—namely, the coercive effect that his threat of resignation could bring to the proceedings. He told Royall that he could not make "any good estimate of date constitution will result," but suggested that if he did stay, it would be best that he leave before German elections took place.

The next day, in a teleconference, Clay asked Draper for his personal advice. "Can you tell me frankly if there is any real importance to my continuance here? I do not have any feeling of Government support and I see every day deviations from policy and concessions made [to the British and French] by people who know nothing of the problem. For my self-respect, I feel strongly I should go very quickly."

Draper told Clay that what appeared to be a lack of support in Washington was due mainly to the fact that Acheson had not yet settled in as Secretary of State. But he urged Clay to stay on. "In my opinion you are badly needed until the present problems [relating to a West German government] with the British and French are solved."

Clay acceded, saying, "I do not want another day, and stay only because I do not [wish to] create any possible embarrassment to anyone or above all to our policy—whatever it may be."

The fact is, negotiations over the proposed West German government were going badly. In London, diplomatic discussions with Britain and France over the Occupation Statute had produced a proposal that would allow any of the three powers a perpetual veto on German legislation. Clay was scathing in his criticism. He told Draper that, if the Allies insisted on retaining that much authority, the new German government "would become a laughing stock to all Germans. We must remember that we are dealing with human beings.

"Given this document with its Rube Goldberg procedures . . . the task of administering Germany [would be] worse than any affliction suffered by Job, and even his patience would not suffice."

Clay insisted that the Occupation Statute be short and concise, dealing with principles, not details, and that the Germans be afforded as much leeway as possible. "After all," Clay told Tracy Voorhees, "these 45 million Germans may be human beings who love their country." If the United States gave in to French demands for an absolute veto, the resulting West German government would be a travesty. "It will be difficult to obtain German enthusiasm for a government which promises democracy and at the same time the western powers say we do not trust you to make this government democratic."

As Washington began to plan for Clay's retirement, the complications multiplied. Secretary Acheson was reluctant for the State Department to assume responsibility for the Occupation, and the Army could not arrive at a suitable candidate to be Clay's replacement. Since Clay was not only Military Governor but also commander-in-chief of U.S. forces in Europe (CINCEUR), it was fast becoming an in-house battle for promotion. In mid-February, General Eisenhower, still president of Columbia University, called Clay unexpectedly and urged him to provide a name to Bradley as soon as possible. Clay was mystified by Ike's call and asked Draper what was happening. Clay thought Eisenhower wanted him to endorse Mark Clark, but wasn't sure. "Damned if I know whether I am supposed to endorse [Clark] or the opposite," he told Draper in a teleconference. "If you can find out discreetly, and if my recommendation would carry any weight, I would go all out for him over our friend in Moscow [Bedell Smith]."

Draper told Clay that Clark had been suggested by the Army but had been turned down by the State Department. "Your friend in Moscow has begged off on account of health with full concurrence of Pentagon." Draper said that State "for some reason" wanted General John Hull, but that Albert Wedemeyer, Matthew B. Ridgeway, and Thomas T. Handy were still in the running. All of this left Clay mystified. "Sorry to have bothered you on what now seems unimportant," he told Draper, and wished him well on his impending retirement as Under Secretary.

With Draper gone, Clay's messages to Washington grew increasingly pessimistic. He was dismayed that he and Robertson and Koenig were unable to resolve their differences over the inclusion of the French zone in Bizonia, and genuinely alarmed at the diplomatic talks in London over the proposed Occupation Statute. "At present," he told Voorhees, "the tripartite meetings of the Military Governors are a duplicate of quadripartite meetings, with Koenig taking the part of Sokolovsky. . . . It is difficult to expect West Germans to move ahead vigorously when the three governments which have authorized their constitution appear hopelessly deadlocked."

"For nine months no progress has been possible toward Trizonal government . . . because of French appeals [to Washington and London]. Governments do not reject appeals but rather arrange conferences. . . . Thank God I will be out of it soon, for to think that a government can be run on an appeal basis makes it sound like a police court. Once our country stood for the rights of people. Perhaps we should give the Germans no rights. If so, let us not go through the pretense. . . . I predict that within six months of such an agreement, complete failure will result. . . . What a price to pay for a French zone that cannot sustain itself. [We] obtain a partner who may be essential to our European program, but who enters the partnership in Germany for sabotage only."

Clay was especially critical of the talks in London concerning the Occupation Statute and repeatedly urged their cancellation. He always resented discussions elsewhere pertaining to his responsibilities in Germany and doubted both the wisdom and the competence of those to whom the talks had been entrusted. "Lew [Douglas] is a grand person," Clay told Voorhees, "but he likes to be liked and is always [an] eager beaver to reach agreement in which everyone is happy." Clay objected to "piecemeal solutions which are defeating our German objectives" and warned that there would be no West German government unless a broad comprehensive agreement could be reached.

In fact, there were some in Washington who wanted to back away from a West German government completely. Kennan had presented to Acheson his revised plan for a neutralized Germany on March 9, though telling the new Secretary of State he thought it was probably too late for the United States to change its position regarding a West German government and that he doubted it was feasible to reach an accord with the Soviets by which all four powers would withdraw from Germany. Acheson said he was sorry to hear that—indicating that Washington was indeed wavering and confused about the future of Germany. In fact, Acheson wondered aloud whether the decision to establish a West German government was the official policy of the U.S. government or simply "the brainchild of General Clay."

Robert Murphy, who had returned to Washington from Berlin, acquainted Acheson with the developments leading to the decision of the London conference in June 1948 to press ahead with a West German government. Murphy assured Acheson that it was indeed a government decision, and had been backed strongly by Bevin and General Marshall.

The Pentagon once again attacked Kennan's proposals. Clay thought it was "totally impractical" to withdraw Allied forces from Germany. It would be "turning the show over to Russia and the Communists without a struggle." Bradley and Secretary of Defense Louis Johnson (who had succeeded Forrestal at the end of February) strongly agreed. Bradley argued that the policy planning staff's proposals would compromise the entire Western position in Europe and surrender the initiative to the Red Army. Clay added that this was "suicidal." He said: "We have won the battle [for Germany], but under [Kennan's] proposal [we] are writing an armistice as if we had lost the battle."

The Pentagon leaked Kennan's plan to James Reston of *The New York Times,* and the resulting column by Reston administered, in Kennan's words, "a spectacular *coup de grâce*" to the proposal. The result was to establish a sub-Cabinet committee on Germany composed of representatives from State, Defense, and the National Security Council,* under the chairmanship of Robert Murphy. Under Murphy's skillful leadership, Acheson was converted to the idea of a strong West German government, and soon became one of its leading advocates. When a new draft policy statement emphasizing U.S. commitment to a strong West German government integrated into Western Europe was sent to Clay for comments on April 2, Clay had nothing but the highest praise. "As a statement of policy . . . I have not one word of criticism. . . . [It] is a splendid document and makes a logical explanation of why we support Germany. I can only offer my congratulations to all who participated in it."

The first week of April 1949 marked a decisive shift in American policy. Acheson had come to the conclusion that Clay was correct about the danger of piecemeal negotiations and had shut down the discussions in London. "My first impression on going over the material prepared in London," Acheson wrote afterward, "was one of despair. The papers were tremendously complex and totally incomprehensible. . . . It was literally unthinkable to [the diplomats in London] to discard the whole substance of their expertise. But this had to be done."

The result was that when the three Western foreign ministers (Acheson, Bevin, and Schuman) met in London in April, most of the outstanding questions were settled quickly. The "comprehensive agreement" Clay asked for was concluded. The principal task of the foreign ministers was to sign the North Atlantic Treaty and establish the footing of a collective Western defense structure. This helped satisfy French concerns about the possibility of future German aggression. The foreign ministers then reached agreement on trizonal fusion in Germany and the Occupation Statute. As an elated Voorhees cabled Clay, the Army's policy had been vindicated. "There is a strong argument for charging the Army with the child's paternity. Whether this baby just born is legitimate or illegitimate, here it is." Secretary Royall told Clay,

* Murphy and Kennan from State, Richard Bissel from the NSC (CIA), and Albert Blum and Tracy Voorhees from Defense.

"I am intensely proud of the Army's accomplishment and of your personal achievement in making today's achievements possible. As Secretary of the Army, and for myself personally, I express to you our profound gratitude."

Q: How did you get the ball rolling for a German government?
CLAY: Obviously, with the blockade taking place, the overwhelming presence of Russia had created a desire in West Germans to move quickly and create a government for the additional strength it would provide—particularly a government that was supported by the Allied powers.
Q: So the blockade provided an impetus to proceed?
CLAY: The blockade provided an impetus. The currency reform also provided an impetus, because it established a common currency throughout the three Western zones and really created a single economy. And it was very difficult to operate a single economy unless you had a central government. All of these things acted to bring the Basic Law [the West German constitution] more nearly to fruition. And I must admit that in every way possible short of direct interference, I was certainly using whatever influence I had to speed them up, because I wanted the Basic Law completed before I left Germany.
Q: Did you feel any pressure from the Germans to create a West German government?
CLAY: The initial pressure was from us, not from them. But they saw the point very quickly. You could not get a fully restored German economy without a German government. But we used our influence indirectly. We had certain things we told them from the beginning we would reserve to ourselves. One was that we would not allow too powerful a central government. We didn't attempt to define what a too-powerful central government would be. But we did say we would not accept one that was too powerful. We left it to them to work that out.
Q: Did you use the airlift as leverage?
CLAY: Utterly ridiculous. I never used any pressure or threats of any type or kind, except my own opinions of how their actions would be interpreted by their own people.

"The political leaders in West Berlin—Mayor Reuter and Otto Suhr [CDU]—weren't too anxious to incorporate Berlin into the Federal Republic. They were very concerned that this might rule Berlin out as the future capital of a united Germany. They also recognized [that] the safety in the four-power agreements with respect to Berlin might be abrogated by joining West Berlin with West Germany. They were not eager for it. And, of course, none of the West Germans were eager for it. I was in favor of it. But the British and French were not, and neither was the American government."

Q: At the time of the Basic Law, were you concerned about creating a government for only part of Germany? For the fact that you were dividing Germany?

CLAY: The die was cast by then. The Germans were understandably more concerned about it than we were. That's why they called it a Basic Law. They were very careful in their designation so it wasn't something final. If there was a united Germany, they expected to rewrite the constitution and to give the East Germans a hand in its preparation. This was a fundamental point with them.

"At the time, there was no way to get a united Germany. I tried for four years and couldn't do it. Time and time again we offered to hold elections, but the Russians would never agree to elections under the terms and conditions we thought would guarantee free elections. So we never held them. We had no choice. If we were going to establish a German government, we could only establish it in the Western zones."

Q: And the Russian response?

CLAY: It is difficult to categorize Soviet policy in 1948 and 1949. I really don't think they had a firm policy. They did not want to give up East Germany until they had consolidated their position in Eastern Europe. East Germany was obviously a buffer for them. After they had finished taking over and consolidating Eastern Europe, then and only then did they move to establish and build up East Germany. I don't think at any time did they have any real expectation of taking over West Germany militarily. I think they did feel they were going to be successful with the Communist party gaining political power in other countries of Western Europe, and that this would accomplish over time the same purpose of bringing all of Europe under Communist control.

Q: Did your frequent role as spokesman for the Germans bother you?

CLAY: I think you've got to remember two or three things. In many respects, I was the toughest of the Military Governors. I was certainly far tougher than my British and French associates with respect to de-Nazification and war crimes. In addition to that, our country was footing the bill—not the British government or the French government—it was our country. It was our primary insistence and urging that got the [German] economy going. Therefore, I think it was only logical that we were working to get a German government, because I don't care how centralized you may be, you can't have unity of opinion among three Military Governors. Only a German government could provide the direction the economy needed. It is remarkable that we got along as well as we did, particularly the British and ourselves. If we hadn't, I don't know what would have happened. We probably would have had even greater chaos than we did.

Q: What do you believe was the major shortcoming of the Basic Law?

CLAY: The new central government didn't really have as much power as the Germans wanted. We had insisted on that, but in the end it didn't really have as much power as I thought it should have either. The question of the relative power of central versus state [*Land*] government was a major question throughout. I think it was fundamentally a political issue. The Socialists were much more in favor of a strong central government than the Christian Democrats. I don't think either party understood federalism in the sense that we understand it. It is a living thing. Its meaning varies. It is remarkable the changes that have taken place under our Constitution as the more rapid communications of the modern world have intruded. We have constantly increased the power of our national government as compared to our states. I think the German Basic Law provides for stronger states' rights than we do.

Q: What was your position on government support for parochial schools?

CLAY: I didn't care. I had no position, except that I didn't think it should become so divisive [an issue as] to defeat the Basic Law. I told them that we had the same problem in the United States and had never learned to resolve it. Of course, it is not a federal problem with us. But we haven't solved it by any manner of means. And the Germans haven't solved it either. What they did do was to eliminate it as a constitutional problem in the Basic Law.

Q: Are there any particularly American aspects in the Basic Law?

CLAY: The idea of judicial review [the authority of a supreme court to declare acts of the legislature and executive unconstitutional] is one we were constantly talking and preaching. As a matter of fact, we wanted a more powerful executive than they were willing to have. We couldn't get it. But we wanted it. They didn't want a strong executive and therefore didn't have one.

"The only way I tried to influence the constitutional convention [Parliamentary Council] was by advising them of my views through Dr. [Carl J.] Friedrich and various others of my staff who were in constant touch with the convention. I won't say that Professor Friedrich was my only representative, but I certainly stayed in very close touch with him. I'd gotten him over [from Harvard] because not only was he an expert on constitutional law, in addition to that he was fluent in the German language and thoroughly familiar with the troubles of the Weimar Republic and could help avoid some of the mistakes it made. Dr. [Edward] Litchfield [later president of the University of Pittsburgh] was another. And in these informal discussions we made no bones about what we meant by federalism or judicial review. I think that indirectly we influenced the Basic Law, far more than we would have if we tried to dictate it. If we had tried to dictate the Basic Law, the convention would have adjourned. There wouldn't have been any constitution.

"I'm sure that [Lord] Strang and Robertson were urging a parliamentary-style government, while we were urging a presidential-congressional type. So long as we did this informally and never took official positions, I think it was fine. But I never had any expectation that we would get a government elected for a fixed term, like our Congress and the President. It wasn't the German tradition. I did hope that we would get a president with some power, like France's de Gaulle [in the Fifth Republic]. That makes government possible, even with fragmented parties."

Q: But judicial review was accepted?

CLAY: Yes. But you must remember the Germans had quite a number of scholars of constitutional law. Very knowledgeable people like Carlo Schmid [of the SPD]. So there was no absence of knowledge about forms of government when they met.

"The same for the 'constructive' vote of no confidence. If they have a vote of no confidence in Parliament, it doesn't require the resignation of the Chancellor unless they have determined a successor before the vote is taken. This was adopted to satisfy our desires for a more powerful executive. By instituting this particular procedure, they gave the Chancellor a more assured tenure. And he became more of an executive force than he would have been as merely the head of a parliamentary majority."

Q: And the Occupation Statute?

CLAY: There were certain problems in the Occupation Statute involving the retention of Allied rights in certain industries, which the Germans deemed excessively harsh and were very unhappy with. So was I—I had done all I could to modify them. Fortunately, the Germans went ahead anyway. I say "fortunately" because the provisions were never enforced. And then in 1955 the Germans were given sovereignty.

"I was also disturbed about the length of the text [of the Occupation Statute]. But the interesting thing about it was that as we were getting into those last negotiations on what constituted armaments and what didn't, the British insisted that German shipbuilding was the great danger and the French claimed that chemical-dye plants were the greatest danger. And I presume that both did represent a threat, in the sense that each was convertible, to the building of warships in one case and ammunition in the other. But you couldn't help being faintly aware that they were two important industries in the respective countries. We didn't have too much concern about it except to please the British and French. And we did recognize that theirs was the greater danger from German rearmament."

Q: Were you under rigid instructions from Washington as to what to accept and what not to accept?

CLAY: I wasn't under any instructions from Washington except on the reserved powers. Those were rigid. Otherwise I was completely free. In fact, I didn't have any instructions. At the last minute, the government sent over Ambassador Murphy and the Defense Department sent over Goldthwaite Dorr to be my advisers, but they didn't have any instructions either.

Q: And your conclusions about the Basic Law?

CLAY: I still had some doubts as to whether we would have a strong enough government. I don't know whether we would have if the Germans hadn't been fortunate enough to have as their first Chancellor a very strong man. Adenauer was strong enough to give the central government the power to act.

Q: Did you get to know Adenauer? Or [Kurt] Schumacher [leader of the SPD]?

CLAY: Not very well. Adenauer had been mayor of Cologne, in the British zone, and of course I knew of him. One of the interesting things is that the British relieved him as mayor because they thought he was too old. That was in 1945. Twenty years later he was still Chancellor of Germany! But he was a very strong individual, and I must say that if he had been the head of a state government and not Federal Chancellor, I don't know how the situation in Germany would have developed.

Q: And Schumacher?

CLAY: Schumacher was a genuine survivor from Nazi imprisonment and the re-creator of the Social Democratic Party. He had also led the fight to prevent the SPD from combining with the Communists. A great speaker. Fanatic in his beliefs, particularly his belief in the Socialist party. He was intense: a very difficult man at times. But certainly one you had to respect.

"Both Adenauer and Schumacher came from the Rhineland, from the Ruhr—the political heart of Germany. Bavaria, with its particularism and separatism, had never been a political arena for Germany as a whole. Adenauer had very little national stature until he came out of the constitutional convention. Schumacher had more stature than Adenauer because he was the leader of a very old and active party. The CDU was actually formed during the Occupation. And if it hadn't combined with the CSU in Bavaria, it would not have been a strong party."

Q: Why do you believe the Basic Law has proved to be so durable?

CLAY: I think there are several factors. One, the German people were really interested in having a stable government. Two, a very strong and able Chancellor. Three, a very strong and able opposition, so that the Chancellor's strength did not lead to dictatorship. Fourth, the development of a very inquisitive free press. Fifth, the rapid improvement in the economy, which made people more content than they otherwise might have been. All of these, combined with the early acceptance of Germany back into the family of nations, which restored a certain pride, gave the German government a very exceptional stability.

"I know it has always been said about the Germans that they have been too concerned with stability to take much of an interest in politics. But with two very active political parties and a very active press, I don't think those conditions apply anymore."

Q: In retrospect, what has been America's most lasting contribution to postwar Germany?

CLAY: That is a very hard question to answer. Certainly, when we went in [in 1945], the British had every opportunity to take the lead in Germany, because the Germans have always looked up to the British. But the British were unable to exercise that leadership because they didn't have the economic strength to support it. And, secondly, they had their own problems at home. They were tired, and they were unable to rise to the occasion even though they had very competent men in Germany. They simply didn't have the support. We did. We had the ability to feed Germany and help it in its efforts to re-establish itself.

"Obviously, if you went back to the Germans, they'd tell you the Marshall Plan was the thing that contributed most. I would say that the Marshall Plan was a spectacular success in Germany because of the successful currency reform that preceded it—the most successful currency reform in history. That was an American contribution, and a very good one.

"And then I think there is the federalism in the German Basic Law. That has now gained hold. And there is the stability of the government, which to a considerable degree is a result of our influence. I don't say we did it. But I think that as a result of our influence and our standing, and in spite of the fact that we'd been accused of all manner of excesses, I think there was a deep respect for Americans as a decent people who wanted to help others. We don't carry deep-seated revenge or hatred. I think all of those things combined to create a very high standing for America in Germany. Maybe I'm biased, but I think the American occupation of Germany was appreciated more by the Germans than by the Americans."

Q: How did you feel when you left Berlin?

CLAY: A little emotional. But I hadn't thought about it, really. We were pretty busy up to the last moment. I left on a Sunday. And it was our habit to have a Sunday parade on the parade grounds just across from military government headquarters. I put it into effect. We had it every Sunday. Rotated the troops, but there was always a parade on Sunday and often I would go to it.

"So I arranged my departure to take place after one of these parades. And it became rather emotional, because to my surprise there were literally thousands of Berliners there. And they lined the streets from the parade ground to Tempelhof [four and a half miles]. So it was rather an emotional departure.

"I landed in Newfoundland, where I was told that I was to speak to both the Senate and the House the next day. So I started writing speeches. I wasn't told about it until Newfoundland."

Q: What were your plans after retirement?

CLAY: I wasn't coming back to anything. I knew I was coming back to retire, so I came back and put in for my retirement. General Bradley asked me if I would stay on. If I had known the Korean War was going to come along in a year or so, I probably would have. But I didn't know that, so I said, "No, I'm getting out." And I got out. [Clay was fifty-one—fifty-two according to Army records.]

"I'll never forget it. We were staying at Fort Myer at the time, and they had the usual retirement party—Secretary of the Army, the Chief of Staff, and whatnot come up with the band, and they give you a last salute as you come out of your quarters. They put you in a car, the guns boom, and off you go. And after you drive through the gate you're all through.

"My wife and I got on the airplane to come to New York, and we literally knew only this: that we were going to spend a few weeks at Cape Cod."

Q: You did not wish to remain on active duty?

CLAY: I would have had ten or twelve more years of service, but I couldn't see where the challenge would be. As I said, I didn't visualize the Korean War, and they had already selected General [J. Lawton] Collins to be Chief of Staff.

"When you run the occupation of a country, and when you've done it for four years, you've had about as much as you want for a while in the way of responsibility and challenge. On the other side of the picture, going back into a peacetime, routine Army life didn't seem very interesting or rewarding. Remember that in 1949 we were down to a minimum military strength. We hadn't formed NATO, and there wasn't anything in sight that looked very challenging.

"The job in Germany, after all, was a very powerful one. I don't think we abused it, but it was very difficult to find a job where I had the same degree of responsibility and challenge. So I decided it was time to get out. The minute I heard the blockade was lifted, I asked to be relieved.

"I felt reasonably sure that a German government was going to be formed, and I felt that my movement out would precipitate it. Which it did. I also did not feel that under any circumstances should the man who had been Military Governor stay after a German government was formed. Mr. [John J.] McCloy followed me, but as High Commissioner, not Military Governor. I may have been wrong. Brian Robertson stayed, and it apparently caused him no problems or trouble. I thought that the military Occupation should be separated from the next phase."

Q: But you had no offers from private industry?

CLAY: I had no offer. Nobody knew I was leaving. I had no idea what I was going to do. Some of the newspapers wrote that I was going to go back to Georgia and go catfishing. I think that is about what I wanted at that time. I wasn't looking for anything to do just then. I was just looking for rest and a relief from responsibility for a while.

· Book Four ·

THE MILITARY INDUSTRIAL COMPLEX

· 27 ·

General of Industry

"Unshaken, unseduced, unterrified," he has guarded well the forward citadel of freedom.

Doctor of Laws
Harvard University, 1949

FOR CLAY, THE OCCUPATION OF GERMANY WAS A tragic international failure, and a significant personal success. Wartime harmony had given way to Cold War rivalry. But an independent West German state was in the offing, and Berlin had been defended successfully. If competition with the Soviet Union was inevitable, Clay had reversed the odds in the West's favor.

The distinguished journalist Walter Lippmann, an early critic of military government, wrote that Clay had emerged from Germany as "one of the strongest American personalities of our time." Former Secretary of War Robert Patterson said that Clay "has given us such an example of skillful achievement and fearless devotion to duty that it would be hard to find the like of him in our history," while

The New York Times hailed him as "Viscount Clay of Berlin." The scientist Vannevar Bush, who had worked with Clay in wartime Washington, lauded him as one of the great military men America had produced. "He has performed a tough job for the country, under harassing circumstances, with steadiness of purpose and great dignity. We owe him much." And in a moving personal letter, General Bradley called Clay "a great soldier and statesman whose contribution to the peace of the world will be increasingly recognized in the years to come."

Above all, Clay prized the note he received from Eleanor Roosevelt, who wrote to tell him that "I think you have done a wonderful piece of work for which all of us should be deeply grateful." Clay was touched by Mrs. Roosevelt's concern. "I do not know how you always find the time to be so thoughtful of others," he replied. "I am most grateful for your letter, because President Roosevelt started me on my task in Germany. I like to think that he would not have been disappointed, and your letter helps me think so."

Clay had been one of the staunchest supporters of FDR's policy of accommodation with the Soviet Union. He worked diligently to make quadripartite government in Germany a success, and he blamed the French, not the Russians, for its initial failure. Almost alone among the upper echelons of the Truman administration, Clay believed that a lasting accord could be reached with the Soviet Union. He worked easily with Marshals Zhukov and Sokolovsky and regarded both with affection and respect. When the policies of their governments permitted, Clay had little difficulty reaching agreement with them on complicated issues. In fact, the trust between Clay and Sokolovsky had become so great by 1947 that they usually relied on only one interpreter for their meetings.

When American policy abruptly changed in the spring of 1947, Clay dutifully shifted gears to adjust. Under the leadership of Secretary of State Marshall, the United States turned its back on German unity, stressing instead the development of a strong West German state as a bulwark against Communist expansion. At first, Clay believed that the United States was selling Germany short: that German unity would extend Western influence into the Soviet zone and bring it into the Western orbit. But he soon realized that Washington was uninterested. Clay thereupon seized the opportunity that the Cold War afforded to restore the economy and political structure of the three Western zones.

Clay saw his primary task as one of leading a stable, democratic Germany back into the family of nations. And the three-quarters of Germany represented by the Western zones was a massive step in the right direction. But Clay was not a dedicated cold warrior, and he genuinely regretted Germany's division. By 1949, he was able to blame it on Soviet intransigence, and in particular on the failure of Russian authorities to accept all-German elections on Western terms. He defended the freedom of Berlin against Communist assault, and would not be bluffed by Soviet pressure. When Washington grew timid, Clay stood firm. What some saw as recklessness, Clay viewed as determination. And when many in official Washington counseled compromise and even withdrawal from Berlin, Clay held out and single-handedly launched the airlift. The tide of the Cold War turned. Clay, along with Ernest Bevin and President Truman, had been one of the principal architects of victory.

As Military Governor, Clay was the antithesis of pomp and pretension. He operated with a small personal staff, and rejected the trappings of high office. His lightning-swift replies to cables and queries from Washington were usually written in longhand using a No. 2 lead pencil across the face of the incoming message. When he traveled on inspection trips, he had standing orders against martial displays, and he quickly rebuked any subordinate who laid on police escorts that blew whistles, rang sirens, and scattered civilians. If Clay ran out of cigarettes at a press conference, he would bum a smoke from the reporter who happened to be closest. His beguiling, dedicated concept of American virtue rejected nepotism, carpetbagging, and profiteering. In the rubble and dislocation of 1945, when visitors and dependents were not permitted in Germany, he refused to have his son Frank's wedding moved to London so that Marjorie and the bride's mother could attend. Those privileges were not available to other officers in the Occupation; Clay would not bend the rules for his family. When his nephew Herbert Clay, Jr., an Army major working in the OMGUS economics section, sought to shed his uniform and remain in the same job as a civilian with higher pay, Clay ordered him back into the Army immediately. He disapproved the award of a Distinguished Flying Cross to his son Lucius, Jr., a major in the Army Air Force stationed in Germany—not because "June" did not deserve one, but because Clay thought it would smack of favoritism. And before he departed from Berlin in 1949, he wrote a personal check for $7,000 to the owner of the Dahlem bungalow in which he had lived for four years, ostensibly to pay for the host's wine he had consumed.

Curiously, Clay spoke no German, and had little contact with the German population. Official dealings were conducted at arm's length. Clay did not mix socially. He feared that Germans he became friendly with would be tagged collaborators. (At the beginning of the Occupation, learning that many professional men in Germany were customarily addressed as "Doctor," Clay took to addressing virtually all male Germans in this fashion, and kept it up the entire time he was there.)

Don Humphrey, who succeeded William Draper as Clay's economics adviser, wrote that Clay ruled Germany "by his intelligence, his energy, and the vehemence of his convictions, not by his rank. [He] lived and operated in a goldfish bowl. He never cloaked his remarks in the anonymity of the uniform or sought protection in the privilege of rank. He took responsibility, he answered criticism, and when necessary, slugged it out—with or without gloves." Humphrey cites Clay's intensity, his mastery of detail combined with a profound sense of the larger values involved, and, above all, his utter selflessness as the keys to his success. "The post he held for four years was among the most trying and thankless jobs in history. Lesser men would have come home under the criticism thrown at Clay. No one outside of the President carried a greater load of responsibility. The support he gained he made for himself. . . . It is Clay the man, not Clay the General, who was so intimately identified with every aspect of the German occupation."

Without any particular empathy for the Germans, Clay established, directed, and defended an Occupation against those who variously sought vengeance, chaos, or exploitation. When he arrived in Germany in 1945, his instructions were essentially negative. Clay worked tirelessly to reverse the Carthaginian tone of those directives and to put Germany back on its feet. He struggled against a *vae victis* mood in Allied capitals in order to preserve Germany's cultural treasures, to guard its patents and scientific achievements, and to prevent its industrial plant from being dismantled. He devoted himself to ensuring that a defeated Germany received at least its fair share of American grain and food products in a Europe on the verge of starvation.

In the absence of explicit instructions from the War Department, Clay made policy in Germany. The result was friction and frequent controversy with the State Department—which Clay believed was intent on sacrificing German interests to those of France and Germany's smaller neighbors. Unlike the Francophile professionals in Foggy Bottom, Clay recognized early on that European recovery could not be purchased at Germany's expense. He differed from official U.S. thinking in 1945 when he stressed that it was France, not the Soviet Union, that was resisting German unity. In May 1946, Clay halted reparations deliveries from the American zone, hoping to bring France into line. When that failed, he proposed a bizonal merger with the British—a halfway house to German unity. When Russian Foreign Minister Molotov captured the propaganda initiative in Germany in the summer of 1946 with promises of quick recovery, it was Clay who insisted on a swift Western response, and helped to draft Secretary Byrnes's famous speech in Stuttgart that set a new tone for the American Occupation.

Clay moved Germany quickly in the direction of free elections, an uncensored press, and educational reform. He established the Free University in Berlin on his own authority and beat back staff efforts to control in detail what Germans could do and how they could do it. Clay put together an outstanding team in military government. But he relied on his staff to carry out his instructions, not to formulate policy independently. Clay loyally carried out his de-Nazification orders and refused to be called off from punishing the worst offenders when the mood in Washington changed. That did not prevent him from standing up to public pressure when he believed the evidence in such trials warranted a commuted sentence or a lesser punishment—as in the case of Ilse Koch. He reached a viable compromise in November 1946 with Marshal Sokolovsky on the tangled issue of reparations, only to have his government cast it aside. He reached another compromise with French diplomat Couve de Murville in 1948, thus securing the success of the six-power London conference that paved the way to a West German government. He successfully resisted the internationalization of the Ruhr and pressed for quick upward revision of Germany's level of industry. In early 1949, he broke the deadlock over trizonal fusion and the Occupation Statute in a secret meeting with French Foreign Minister Robert Schuman in Paris. When German political leaders balked at the final compromises needed to bring the Basic Law into effect, he intervened again to force a timely compromise. Above all, it was Clay who discarded military advice that Berlin could not be held, and put together the massive Allied airlift that reversed the momentum in the Cold War struggle for Western Europe.

After four years, Clay's departure from Germany in 1949 brought an outpouring of emotions. Agreement had been reached on the Basic Law; the West German government stood in the wings; the Russian blockade had been broken; and the effects of the currency reform were already taking hold. West Germany was on the road to a full and complete recovery. The bitter struggles against overpowering odds seemed a thing of the past.

On May 12, 1949, three days before his final leavetaking, Clay attended his last review as CINCEUR at the Army's major training area at Grafenwöhr. Eleven thousand men of a revitalized First Division marched past their commander-in-chief in perfect military order. Sixty Thunderbolt fighters of the 86th Fighter Wing flew over, spelling out a gigantic "C L A Y" as the last regiment passed in review.

The following day, with the blockade lifted and traffic to Berlin moving normally, the city celebrated. Schools and businesses shut down, and a special session of the Berlin City Assembly commemorated the airlift and the retiring Military Governor. With all of western Germany's political leaders in attendance, Mayor Reuter spoke of the forty-eight American and British airmen who lost their lives in crashes during the airlift. As he spoke, all of those present rose to their feet in a moment of tribute. SPD leader Franz Neumann then read the names of those who had died, and the assembly voted unanimously to rename the broad plaza in front of the Tempelhof airfield "Platz der Luftbrücke" (Plaza of the Airlift) in their honor. Reuter concluded the ceremony with a ringing tribute to Clay.

> In our great struggle in the summer of the past year, we called on the world for help. The world heard our cry.
>
> We are happy to have here in our midst as a guest the man who . . . took the initiative in organizing the airlift at that time. The memory of General Clay will never fade in Berlin. We know for what we have to thank this man [prolonged stormy applause, the members rising], and we take advantage of this hour in which he bids farewell to Berlin to say that we will never forget what he has done for us.

On Saturday, May 14, Clay's last full day in Berlin, he symbolically laid protocol aside and paid a personal visit to Reuter in the Mayor's office at the Berlin city hall. It was Clay's way of showing his own appreciation to Reuter and to the Berliners, with a simple gesture of respect he knew they would understand: the Military Governor calling on a German politician. The next day, it was Clay's turn to be surprised when a half-million Berliners lined the streets in cheering affection to see him off. Tears streamed down Clay's cheeks as he and Marjorie waved goodbye from the steps of the Air Force transport that waited to fly them home.

After an overnight stop in Newfoundland, Clay arrived in Washington the morning of May 17. He was met by General Bradley and whisked immediately to the White House, where President Truman decorated him with the military's highest peacetime decoration, the Distinguished Service Medal. From there, Clay went to Capitol Hill, where he addressed each of the two houses. For Speaker Rayburn, it was a friendship of many years come to a glorious fruition. Normally undemonstrative and taciturn, Rayburn bubbled over with enthusiasm as he confessed to a cheering House of Representatives that "I never had more pleasure in my life in presenting anyone than I do in presenting our distinguished guest today . . . who is as able as any man I ever met, in the Army or out."

Consistent with Clay's style, his remarks were brief. His speech lasted fifteen minutes. "It is impossible to forget, and it is difficult to forgive," he reminded the House. "One has only to revisit Buchenwald or Dachau to remember the extreme cruelty of the Nazi regime. I saw in Berlin the spirit and soul of a people reborn. It may, indeed, be the spirit that lights the flame of freedom in Germany that may grow through the years. . . . Today, they need the helping hand of the freedom-loving democratic people of the world."

In the Senate, Clay was introduced by another old friend, Vice President Alben Barkley, who reminded the Senators that Clay's father had served in that body for thirteen years. Clay was deeply moved. He told the Senate that as "a soldier [who] returns home after having tried to do his duty, it is difficult to find the words to express the deep gratification which he holds in his heart."

> Sunday, two days ago, I watched my last retreat in Berlin. I watched our flag being lowered in the full knowledge that it would be raised again on the following morning. I felt that in these four years it had become a symbol of firm justice and not oppression, of a rule of law but not

> arbitrary law, and that it had become to millions of people not of our land the same symbol of freedom and of the dignity of man that it is to us.

Again Clay spoke for fifteen minutes. As in the House, he was interrupted frequently by applause. He had memorized both speeches beforehand and spoke without notes. Two years later, almost to the day, another American proconsul would address Congress using some of the same words. But MacArthur spoke in bitterness and rancor: as a general relieved of command by his commander-in-chief. For MacArthur, the political arena beckoned. By contrast, Clay spoke in triumph. His policies in Germany had been vindicated. And the last thing he wanted was a new career in public life.

From Washington, Clay went to New York. There he was given the traditional ticker-tape parade through lower Manhattan. Once more, close to half a million people turned out to see the hero of Berlin. From New York, he went to Marietta and another glorious homecoming. The tiny square was jammed with eight thousand townsfolk as Clay, standing in the shadow of his father's statue, was embraced by Georgia's political establishment. The Daughters of the American Revolution unveiled a plaque honoring Clay, placed opposite his father's image. A week later, his retirement processing complete, Clay and Marjorie left Fort Myer for Cape Cod. He knew that he wanted to write a report to the American people about his trusteeship in Germany. He had no job offers, no publishing contract, and an annual retirement income of $9,000. His net assets amounted to slightly more than $3,000 in a family savings account. After thirty-four years in the Army, having served as the head of all military procurement activities in World War II and spent four years as Military Governor of Germany, Clay was close to broke.

"It is hard to know what to do," Clay wrote to Ike on June 18. "Retired pay and retired activities do not suffice in themselves. I cannot enjoy the public lime-light so I have about come to the conclusion to find a small business to join and go commercial in a relatively quiet way."

Q: What are the prerogatives of a retired four-star general?
CLAY: None. Absolutely none, other than his retired pay.
Q: How did you view the Army at your retirement?

CLAY: Everything that has ever happened to me, everything that I have achieved has come as a result of my military service. I wouldn't give it up. I would have given anything to have had combat, but I didn't worry about it too much. I had interesting things to do, I had friendships and comradeship, and I thought it was a very worthwhile life.

"When I left in 1949, the services were beginning to recover from the tremendous letdown in 1945. They had not only let down in 1945, but they had great surpluses of weapons that were becoming obsolete. And yet they had very little money to develop new weapons. In addition, the Army had gone through two very trying experiences. One was the separation of the air forces out of the Army. The other was the abolition of the War Department and the creation of the Department of Defense. All of this left the Army in a rather trying period in 1949."

Q: Your speeches to Congress—you delivered them without notes.

CLAY: Until 1965, I never read a speech. I would write it out and more or less memorize it. But I was given only a couple of hours' notice that I had been invited to address Congress, so I didn't have any time to work on [the speeches]. I just went over and over in my mind what I wanted to say. But I have never made a speech that I did not write myself.

Q: Did you have any desire to run for office in 1945?

CLAY: No. I'm not a politician. I'm not a "hail fellow well met" and I would not do very well in the political arena. It had been suggested. Many wanted me to run for governor of Georgia. But I wasn't the least bit interested.

Clay was besieged by friends and well-wishers who wanted him to seek Georgia's Democratic nomination for governor. Both Senator George and Senator Russell urged him to run, and Ralph McGill, the crusading editor of the Atlanta *Constitution,* kept up a steady fusillade of editorial commentary touting Clay's candidacy. From all over the state, citizens wrote offering their support. William Tutt, an attorney in the small town of Elberton, told Clay in language more colorful than most that "Georgia has been in the relentless clutches of predatory politicians for more than twenty years. It has sunk to such depths of degradation that only a man of the highest character can lift it from the slime of factional politics."

Clay was honored and a little amused by such requests, but made it abundantly clear that he was not a candidate. "I have a deep conviction," he wrote Tutt, "that officers in the regular Army, whether active or retired, have no place in public life." Clay consistently applied that standard to himself. He always made an exception where General Eisenhower was concerned.

Clay also declined to be considered for the presidency of the University of North Carolina, and rejected a proposal that he head the newly organized New Jersey Turnpike Authority at a salary of $20,000. Fred Searles, president of Newmont Mining, and Ferdinand Eberstadt, the New York investment banker with whom Clay had worked during the war, offered to back Clay financially "in anything you want to undertake on the basis of an arm's length deal." But Clay had no such plans at that time and politely declined the overture.

Q: The book you wrote at Cape Cod—*Decision in Germany.*

CLAY: About six months before I left Germany, I wrote the draft for the book. I wrote it in the airplane, on the train, wherever I was going. I wrote it while I still had access to the documents. I had the secretary of our General Staff [in Berlin] review the documentation. Every statement in it is documented—if you can get access to the documents.

"I was trying to write an account of military government that would stand up in the light of history—even if it were textbookish in character. And so, when I came back [in 1949], I was approached by any number of people to publish it. And while I was at the Cape getting ready to make a decision, Mr. [Douglas] Black [of Doubleday] and Mr. [William] Robinson of the *Herald Tribune* came up to see me. They were there, and so I said 'OK.' I'm not sure that it was the best decision to publish with Doubleday, but I did. They had published General Eisenhower's book [*Crusade in Europe*], and he recommended them strongly. Then they gave me Walter Kerr [of the *Herald Tribune*] to help me in reorganizing the book, and to re-edit it with me—the book itself was already written. Then it was published in serial form in the *Herald Tribune,* and then as a book by Doubleday."

Q: And your days at the Cape?

CLAY: This was literally the first vacation we had had since Pearl Harbor. We were staying at my sister-in-law's, but I had rented a house across the street where I did all of the writing. I've written a great deal. Not books, but cables, memoranda, letters, and so writing has always been part of my life. At the Cape we were pushing to get it out while it was still important news. I wrote all morning, and usually for a couple of hours after lunch. I usually tried to quit around three o'clock and go for a swim. But I was ordinarily writing from eight till about twelve, and then from one to three.

Clay received a $55,000 advance from Doubleday. Unlike Eisenhower and Bradley, who took advantage of a favorable IRS ruling to treat their income from *Crusade in Europe* and *A Soldier's Story* as capital gains, Clay paid straight income tax on the proceeds.

Q: Did you think about treating the income as a capital gain?

CLAY: Yes, but I was writing about my government service. I saw no reason to profit from that. I wish I could have, because the advance put me into a very high tax bracket at the time.

Clay had a similar response when Chuck Skinner, head of GM's Oldsmobile division, provided him with a new Oldsmobile. Skinner had been in charge of military production for Clay in World War II and was an old friend. He had the car ready when Clay arrived from Germany. "The car is yours as long as you want it," said Skinner. Clay appreciated Skinner's thoughtfulness, but insisted on paying full price for the car. Still, "It saved our lives," he wrote Skinner on May 29.

Clay finished *Decision in Germany* in three months. Walter Kerr provided useful advice, but apparently never wrote a word. As Kerr later told E. J. Kahn of *The New Yorker,* "General Clay welcomed me graciously, and conferred with me amiably off and on for about six weeks, but he never let me get in a written word."

As Clay intended, *Decision in Germany* is a weighty account of his proconsulship. "As case material for the historian, the book is invaluable," wrote Sebastian Haffner in *The Observer.* There are no kiss-and-tell revelations. The difficulties Clay experienced with Washington in 1946 and 1947 are glossed over, almost without comment, and his friction with Marshall and Bedell Smith is scarcely mentioned. Clay thought it was "unbecoming" to reveal policy differences with those for whom he worked, and it was not until many years later that Professor John Gimbel, in a series of scholarly books and articles, revealed the split between Clay and Washington as to how Germany should be treated. Clay did discuss in a gingerly fashion his problems with Washington at the time of the blockade. But he was generous in his assessment of the motives of those involved, and, considering when it was written, especially fair in his treatment of Marshals Zhukov and Sokolovsky. As more than one British reviewer noted, Clay seemed to think more of his Russian counterparts than he did of the uptight British and difficult French representatives in Germany.

That summer, Clay was awarded four honorary degrees. On June 1, Columbia University, with General Eisenhower as president, bestowed Doctor of Laws degrees on both Clay and Bradley. "The Columbia commencement turned out to be fairly dramatic," said Clay. "General Eisenhower presented the awards. He presented the first degree to General Bradley and said what a pleasure it was to give this award to his war comrade with whom he'd been so closely associated in the drive across Europe. Then he gave mine to 'an old and dear friend' whom he'd known for many years. By that time he was crying, and Bradley was crying, and I was crying—and I think most of the audience was crying too. It was not quite that bad, but it was very emotional."

On June 6, wearing civilian clothes, Clay joined West Point's graduating class for its final dinner at the Academy. The following day, he spoke at the commencement. In language more militant than was his custom, Clay told the cadets that "those forces intent upon destroying freedom should be recognized as enemies and treated accordingly." The following week, it was Rutgers; on June 21 and 23, Yale and Harvard bestowed their degrees.

At Yale, Clay shared the podium with John McCloy and the architect Eero Saarinen. Yale President Charles Seymour spoke out against the growing clamor to purge universities of leftist thought and rejected the idea of a loyalty oath for Yale's faculty. "We shall permit no hysterical witch hunt," said Seymour. "Yale will continue to defend American political ideals by positive and imaginative measures, not a rear guard action." As an exemplar of American ideals, Dr. Seymour turned to Clay. "To him, as much as to any single man, the world is indebted today for the fact that the West can still carry on its struggle for human rights and that America yet battles for the liberty of man. Soldier and administrator, proconsul of democracy in a crisis of history, Yale University confers upon you the degree of Doctor of Laws. . . ."

At Harvard, Clay was again the center of attention. Senator Henry Cabot Lodge, Jr. (class of '24), was chief marshal as 3,067 graduands received their degrees from President James B. Conant. Clay was cited by Harvard as a soldier and statesman. " 'Unshaken, unseduced, unterrified,' " said Harvard, "he has guarded well the forward citadel of freedom." The quotation was from Book V of Milton's *Paradise Lost:*

> So spoke the seraph Abdiel, Faithful found
> Among the faithless, faithful only he;
> Among innumerable false, unmoved,
> *Unshaken, unseduced, unterrified,*
> His loyalty he kept, his love, his zeal;
> Nor number, nor example with him wrought,
> To swerve from truth, or change his constant mind,
> Though single. From amidst them forth he passed,
> Long way through hostile scorn, whilst he sustain'd
> Superior, nor of violence feared ought;
> And, with retorted scorn, his back he turn'd
> On those proud towers, to swift destruction doomed.

As Clay had anticipated, the job offers came quickly. "I was offered the executive vice presidency of General Motors, and then of IBM. And I was offered the job of president of several of our very large trade associations. I turned them all down. For two or three reasons. One, I wanted to live in a small city. Two, I wanted to work for a small corporation, not a big one. I'd been working in a big organization for a long time, and I wanted a change. And three, I did not want to be in a position where I had to deal and negotiate with the Defense Department. I did not think that was appropriate."

Q: But many retired military officers go to work for defense contractors.

CLAY: It may be right for them. I did not think it was right for me. I thought it was unbecoming of a professional Army officer to do that. I did not see how you could be a major grantor of contracts one minute, and then work for those getting the contracts the next minute. I still don't.

"There were also a couple of foundations that made offers. The American Heritage Foundation had gone to General Eisenhower and asked him to try to get me to head it. And the board of directors had assured him that they would underwrite the financing. Well, when I went to see them, it was very obvious that the only way you could continue in business was to raise money every year. And if the president didn't go out and raise money, the president wouldn't have a job. Because there wouldn't be any money to pay him. And I didn't want any part of that.

"The Health Information Foundation, which also approached me, was a good deal more certain. But I wasn't sure I was in sympathy with it. It was supported by the pharmaceutical companies. They were under attack at the time, and they were very anxious to create a foundation that would disseminate information about why they did certain research and all this, that, and the other. I didn't like that either."

Q: Didn't General Eisenhower ask you to become Dean of Engineering at Columbia?

CLAY: I never attached any great importance to it. He may have attached more importance to it than I did. I could not imagine for one minute Columbia University with two retired generals running it.

In the autumn of 1949, with *Decision in Germany* completed, Clay accepted an offer to become chief executive of the Eucusta Paper Corporation, a small, privately owned company near Asheville, North Carolina, that manufactured cigarette paper. As a two- or sometimes three-pack-a-day smoker for over forty years, Clay saw no disqualifying health issue, and the salary of $40,000 (more than four times his Army retired pay) seemed attractive.

Q: Eucusta Paper was a small company, and Asheville, North Carolina, was a small city. Did you like it?

CLAY: Well, within two months after I joined the paper company, it was bought by Olin, which is a very large corporation, and I resigned at that point. Olin was, and still is, a very large defense contractor. I did not want to work for a defense contractor. It was as simple as that.

"Eucusta Paper had been a family-owned business, and like all family-owned businesses it presented certain difficulties. Mr. Straus, the owner, had wanted to get out and enjoy his success—until I got there. Then he wasn't so anxious to get out. Which is normally the case.

"But Eucusta Paper was in a virtual monopoly position. They were just about the only manufacturer of the paper cigarettes are made from. They had the complete confidence of the tobacco companies, and from a business standpoint they were in an ideal position. I don't think I would have been happy there in the long run. However, that is not why I left. I resigned because the company was bought by Olin."

Q: Did you have another offer?

CLAY: No. I didn't know what I was going to do. The first few weeks after I resigned from the paper company and had nothing to do, I was bored to death. From December [1949] until April [1950], I simply lived down there. I led more or less a retired life. There were certain board meetings that I would come up to in New York, and that was about it.

"Frankly, it was not a very pleasant interlude. We had a very lovely home in Asheville, which is a beautiful part of the country. We lived in the Biltmore forests. A surprising number of Army officers who had retired and whom I had known before were living there. But we didn't enter into their activities very much. The Army people down there were retired. Their life centered around golf and bridge. I wasn't ready for that."

Q: But you soon became the chief executive of Continental Can Company?

CLAY: It really came out of the blue. I had gone up to New York in April [1950] on behalf of the Crusade for Freedom [the fund-raising arm of the National Committee for a Free Europe] to help raise money. I had a dinner meeting scheduled with Henry Ford, Jr., and the Ford Motor people at the University Club. I was staying at the Carlton Hotel. About three o'clock that afternoon, I got a telephone call from Sidney Weinberg of Goldman, Sachs. I'd worked with Sidney during the war. [Weinberg had been deputy director of the War Production Board.] He wanted me to go with him to see Carle Conway, who was chairman of the board of Continental Can.

"So Weinberg picked me up and took me over to meet Mr. Conway. That was at Continental Can's headquarters, on Pershing Square. And on the way he told me that they were looking for a new chairman, who could also become the chief executive officer.

"When I met Mr. Conway, he was particularly interested about my ideas on decentralization. He felt that the company was too centralized. When I left, he told me that he was having a dinner for his board of directors at the University Club, and he asked if I could join them.

"I said, 'I can't. I have a dinner engagement of my own [with

Henry Ford].' And I told him about it. I always found it curious that both dinners just happened to be at the University Club that evening. Mr. Conway said that their dinner was half an hour earlier, and he asked me to stop by for cocktails before dinner. He said, 'I want you to meet our board.'

"So I went to the meeting. Then I left and went downstairs to my dinner party. As we were finishing dinner, I got a note from Mr. Conway that said, 'Please come back up.' I went back up, and his board was still there. They were having an after-dinner drink, and I joined them. We chatted for a while—talked about decentralization, organization, and various topics like that. As we were leaving, Mr. Conway and Mr. Weinberg asked me if I would join the board for lunch the next day at the Recess Club. And I said I would.

"Well, I joined the board for lunch, and we walked back to Continental Can, where the board was meeting directly after lunch. They asked me to come up and wait. 'We won't be more than a few minutes at this board meeting, and then we'll take you to your hotel.'

"So I went up with Sidney Weinberg and Mr. Conway, and I sat in Mr. Conway's office while he went into the board meeting. About three minutes later, he walked back in and said, 'You've just been elected chairman of the board. Will you come in and take over the rest of the agenda?' So I walked in and took over the agenda, and I was the new chairman of the board and chief executive. That's how it happened. It was that fast and that simple.

"About a week or two later, the financial vice president came in to see me, and he said, 'General, we're making out our paychecks and there is nothing in the minutes as to what you are being paid. What are you supposed to be paid?' I said, 'I haven't the slightest idea. We never discussed it.' So I had to wait until the next meeting of the board to have my pay established."

Clay's wait was justified. The Continental Can board apparently liked what they saw, because Clay's salary was set at $96,000 plus stock options, and within three years was raised to $150,000. That was in 1953, when the President of the United States earned $75,000 and a new eight-cylinder Pontiac cost $2,100. Reflecting on his remuneration, Clay said, "I've never discussed salary with anyone. In the Army, it was fixed. I didn't discuss it with the paper company, I never mentioned it with Mr. Conway, and when Bobby Lehman asked me to take over the direction of Lehman Brothers [in 1963], I never discussed it. I think it's usually best that way. If the people you're working for like you, and like what you're doing, they are going to see that you are well compensated. Probably better than if you set a price on it yourself."

Clay became chairman of the board and chief executive officer of Continental Can Company the afternoon of Thursday, April 5, 1950. He moved into Carle Conway's corner office at Pershing Square and began to familiarize himself with the company. Not until that evening, back at the Carlton Hotel, did he call Marjorie in North Carolina and tell her the news. "She didn't know a thing about it until I called her up and told her that I had accepted it. It happened that fast."

The next day, Clay took Continental Can's airplane and flew down to Asheville, where he picked up Mrs. Clay and a few clothes. "She came back with me and we stayed at the old Ritz-Carlton Hotel. I went back to work while she went out to look for an apartment. Of course, we'd moved so many times in the Army that the art of moving was not unknown to her. So I don't think she was too surprised that we were moving, except maybe about the speed.

"She found an apartment at 1040 Fifth Avenue. We rented it at first, but when it went cooperative we had to buy it. We lived there until we went back to Berlin [in 1961]."

Q: General, were you concerned that you didn't know anything about the can business?

CLAY: No. One thing you learn in the Army is that you never know what you're going to be called on to do. I couldn't believe that running Continental Can Company would be any more difficult to master than being Military Governor of Germany. And I didn't think that being Military Governor could be any more difficult than being made responsible for military production in World War II. And I had no experience whatsoever in the supply field when that happened. In the Army, you were assigned a job and you did it. Period.

Q: The offer to head Continental Can came to you while you were in New York on behalf of the Crusade for Freedom. Could you go into that?

CLAY: Yes. I had come back from Germany with the view that we needed foreign broadcast facilities that were independent from the government. We had tried this out with RIAS [Radio in the American Sector] in Berlin, and it was very successful in broadcasting our message. I felt we could do the same thing. I talked about this with the State Department, and found that Ambassador [Joseph C.] Grew and a couple of others had the same thought and were working to get something established.

"The Crusade for Freedom was a fund-raising effort. We cast a 'Freedom Bell' to install in the Berlin city hall. It was a replica of the Liberty Bell in Philadelphia. We sent it on tour across the United States to raise money and signatures, and then sent it back to Berlin to be installed. And it became a very meaningful symbol of freedom to Berlin."

Clay's 1949 sponsorship of the Crusade for Freedom, Radio Free Europe, and Radio Liberty marked a sharp departure from his attitude in 1946, when he objected vigorously to the establishment of such facilities in Munich as inimical to the purposes of four-power government. The Berlin blockade, the airlift, and the successful establishment of the West German government partially explain Clay's shift. In any case, his rapid ascent in the business world, his new social life in New York, his membership in the Business Advisory Council, and his first-hand experience in dealing with the Russians quickly placed him in the forefront of those who advocated a militant anti-Communism. The political differences between him and John Foster Dulles receded. This was not because Dulles had changed his view. Clay had.

As the 1950s progressed, Clay took less of a role in foreign policy. Although he continued to raise money for Radio Free Europe, he played no part in its direction. But in the fall of 1950, he returned to Berlin for the installation of the Freedom Bell in the tower of the Schöneberg Rathaus (West Berlin's city hall). Once again more than five hundred thousand Berliners greeted him. As a token of their appreciation, Mayor Reuter announced that the broad avenue that runs in front of U.S. headquarters in Berlin, previously known as Kronprinzenallee, would be renamed Clayallee in the general's honor.

The history of Radio Free Europe and the Crusade for Freedom is a tangled affair, caught up in the Cold War and émigré politics. RFE in Munich provides an important source of intelligence about matters in

Eastern Europe, and it offers to those who live behind the Iron Curtain a voice of Western information and culture. But its role as a private, nongovernmental entity was always questionable, and as Clay later acknowledged, "There was always some government money in it." When the role of the CIA in funding Radio Free Europe and the Crusade for Freedom was revealed in the late 1960s, Clay returned temporarily to become chairman of its board of directors. By that time, Clay was well past his Cold War advocacy, but he did not believe he could turn down a request from an organization he had helped to found. In 1974, with the organization back on an even keel, Clay quietly resigned.

Clay was temperamentally much happier in 1951 when he joined with Eleanor Roosevelt to oppose passage of the McCarran-Walter Immigration Act, one of the most restrictive immigration measures in American history. "Mrs. Roosevelt contacted me and asked me if I would join the opponents," said Clay. "I did not always agree with Mrs. Roosevelt, but I always, *always* thought of her as a truly great American. And on this issue I was particularly concerned, knowing the tremendous number of deserving refugees still in Central Europe. And unless the McCarran Act was defeated, we would be cutting them off from the United States. I thought that that was just about as foolish as anything I could think of." Clay remained concerned about the plight of refugees, and devoted considerable time to fund-raising activities in their behalf. (In 1974, he became chairman of the American Committee to Assist the United Nations Commissioner for Refugees when Arthur Goldberg resigned.)

At Continental Can Company, Clay took charge quickly. His first task was to disperse "Concan's" overly centralized operations, and as he told *Forbes* magazine, "to instill a spirit of dignified disrespect for the way things are done now." Within one month, Clay had inspected each of the company's sixty-four installations scattered across North America. As in Germany, he gave the plant manager twenty-four hours' notice, and had each manager meet him at the airport, to give him a briefing on the way to the plant. "It's a fascinating business," Clay said later. "You get to the point where you walk into one of these plants and when you hear the clang of tin plate it sounds like organ music."

At first Clay was slightly overwhelmed by the opulence of the corner office he took over from Carle Conway. He told Conway that he would prefer a smaller one, but Conway insisted the office went with the position. "For twenty-five years, that office has been the seat and symbol of authority at Continental Can," he told Clay. Shortly afterward Clay was asked how he wanted the office redecorated. He said it was fine as it was. On being pressed to have it fixed up to suit his personal tastes, Clay said he would handle it himself. The only change Clay made in thirteen years was to install the autographed photographs of President Truman, General Eisenhower, and Ernest Bevin.

Q: After you became head of Continental Can, did the company's share of business with the government increase?
CLAY: No. I would say there was very little change. During World War II, we had made a few defense components—parts for proximity fuses and that sort of thing. And in the Korean War, we took on one of these projects at our plant in Baltimore and, I think, performed it very satisfactorily. I doubt if we made any money on it. I rather expect we lost on it. If anything, I lost money for Continental Can in this field. This was taken on as a public service, because I felt that we had to do something. Then, when I went down to Washington to help Mr. [Charles E.] Wilson [run the economy during the Korean War], I wouldn't let Continental do any business with the government at all.

In 1950, when Clay became chairman of Concan, the company had been waging an uphill struggle to overtake the American Can Company ("Canco"), its older and larger rival. Between them, the companies controlled over 90 percent of the can-making business in the United States, with sales of well over $1 billion (1950). But Concan was distinctly number two.

Competition between American and Continental had always been intense. According to *Forbes,* it was "the hottest commercial rivalry since Macy met Gimbel." American Can had been founded through the amalgamation of a number of smaller companies in 1901 by William B. Leek, the "tin plate king," and for several years enjoyed a virtual monopoly. But in 1905, Edwin Norton of Norton Tin Can & Plate, one of the original can-makers who had joined to form American, broke away and set up the Continental Can Company in Syracuse, New York, with an initial capital of $500,000 and one can-making machine. In 1921, when Carle Conway, a son-in-law of Edwin Norton, came into Continental, the company was about one-quarter the size of American. Conway was a natural-born salesman and industrialist, and by 1950, when Clay arrived, Continental had pulled up to about 71 percent of American's gross sales. But Conway recognized that the company was too centralized to expand effectively: too much authority was concentrated in Conway's own hands. Concan simply had outgrown its organization, which was why Clay was mandated in to reorganize and decentralize.

Conway and Weinberg had not talked to Clay about the shipping bottleneck at Cherbourg he had broken in 1944, but Clay initially employed much the same strategy at Concan. He loosened the knot at the New York headquarters, where operational control was concentrated, and created a series of autonomous divisions (metal, fiber drums, paper containers, crown and cork, flexible packaging). Soon, Clay had "everybody thinking he was his own boss." Clay retained final policy control, but all operational decisions were transferred to the divisions. Each plant manager became responsible for profit, budgeting, and programming. It was the way Clay preferred to operate in the Army, and it quickly paid dividends at Concan. In fact, Clay told a U.S. business magazine that he saw little difference between business and the Army, except "the test in business is more immediate. It's that little figure in the lower right corner that you have to watch."

As a result of Clay's strategy of delegation, executive morale at Concan quickly improved. In 1955, *Fortune* magazine reported "a noticeable stretch in the stature of Continental people." More important, the new, decentralized structure enabled Clay to expand Concan quickly. So long as Continental restricted itself to tin cans, Clay felt they would inevitably trail American. The answer was to diversify—to expand into other packaging fields and convert Continental into a broad, balanced packaging company. Clay also beefed up Concan's research division. The aluminum can (now standard in the packaging industry), aerosol cans for food products, frozen-concentrate cans, sterile milk in paper cartons, and flexible plastic containers of all descriptions emerged from Continental's research-and-engineering division.

By 1956, Concan's earnings surpassed American's for the first time. In 1959, after nine years with Clay at the helm, Continental's sales had increased 172 percent—exactly twice that of Canco in the same period —and it had indeed become the most diversified enterprise in the packaging field. *Forbes* attributed Concan's success to its extraordinary ability to tailor its product to fit the needs of a diverse group of customers. "For every product that is packaged," said Clay, "there is one most suitable package against which other forms of packaging can compete only at a disadvantage." Continental's plants multiplied to 145—each of which Clay inspected at least once a year. In 1956 alone—a year of record profits—Continental acquired glassmaker Hazel-Atlas, the papermaking company Robert Gair, and crown-making White Corp. Clay later was forced to divest Altas, but through a series of mergers and acquisitions in the 1950s, Continental catapulted into undisputed first place in the packaging industry.

Clay delegated and decentralized, but he ran Continental Can directly, "not just 100 percent—about 106 percent," in the words of a Concan executive quoted by *Time.* Or, as Clay himself told an overflow audience of fourteen hundred at the Harvard Business School in 1954, "All my life I have heard of the executive who has so cleaned his desk that he has no details to worry about, and can devote all of his time to what is called long-range planning." Clay said the only executives of that type that he knew of "have long lost their ability either to administer or to think. The executive who is really interested in the growth of his company . . . must do his thinking at home or on weekends because his spare working hours will be occupied in seeing young executives who come to see him or in going to see those who do not."

Q: Could you describe your philosophy of management at Concan?

CLAY: I don't know that I have a philosophy, really. There are so many different ways of managing, and there are so many different ways that are successful, and so many that fail, that I don't really know if there is a proper way. Everybody who achieves the responsibility of a manager has his own philosophy of management. Some men run a show through fear. Some run a show through sheer ability. Some because they inspire affection and determination. There isn't any science of management. It is an art. And nobody can write the rules.

"I will say one thing. I didn't want the people who were working for me to come and ask my advice, and then I'd give it to them and not have them follow it. If they acted on their own without seeking my advice, that was perfectly all right. But if they came to me and asked my advice, this was like asking, What do you do? I delegated responsibility and expected the people to whom I delegated it to make the decisions. If they had a problem on which they didn't want to make a decision, and they came to me and asked my advice and I gave it to them, I expected them to follow it. But I wanted people to take responsibility. And sometimes you need a little cunning and artifice to stimulate the will to accept responsibility and the courage to exercise authority.

"I've been very fortunate in that for many, many years I've had responsibilities of substantial magnitude. When I was a lieutenant in the Chief of Engineers' office on the Rivers and Harbors desk, we were dealing with $400–500 million a year. And while I had none of the legal responsibility, I had much of the actual responsibility. I have really never worked for anybody that didn't let me take all of the responsibility that I would take. And I think that was my theory of management in the Continental Can Company: to give the people in the Continental Can Company the opportunity to take all of the responsibility they were willing to take. That would be the only way I could express any philosophy of management I might have had. To find among the people around you those that are willing to take responsibility, to get rid of those who are not willing to take responsibility, and for those who are willing to take responsibility, to give them all that they are willing to take.

"This was true in Germany to a lesser degree, because the people in Continental Can Company had had far more experience in the canning business than I had. But as far as military government was concerned, I was at least equal to the expert. I undertook more detail [work] in military government than I would have had to do in any ordinary job."

One of those young Continental Can executives who did take responsibility, and many years later followed Clay as chairman and CEO, was Ellison Hazard. "You never conducted a normal conversation with General Clay," said Hazard. "We all called him 'General,' and it was a very straightforward—almost military—relationship. Either he was telling you something he wanted you to know, or you were telling him something you wanted him to know. But there was no easy, relaxed intercourse."

Q: You undertook many public activities when you were chairman of Continental Can.

CLAY: My philosophy is that if you are occupying a prominent position in the business community, then you have a public responsibility as well. You have to undertake at least your share. Maybe I went beyond that.

"I don't think Continental Can Company had any such philosophy when I went in. They do now. Plant managers are encouraged to take a role in community affairs. In fact, I spent a good deal of time to encourage that. I even went so far as to say that if anyone wanted to run for office, we'd be glad to give them a leave without pay while they ran and take them back if they didn't win. We even had one or two takers—and they didn't belong to my political party either."

Q: Were you concerned about the impact of Continental Can's operations on the ecology?

CLAY: When I was in Continental Can Company, we spent a great deal of money to eliminate odors and acids in our [smoke]stacks. This was particularly true in connection with our lithograph activities. I worked with the experts in this field to install the catalysts to do this. So we had been moving into this field in the 1950s. We recognized that it was a problem. We also recognized a problem at our paper mills. And we spent substantial sums at these mills to improve the conditions that were there when we acquired them. I don't mean by that that we had gone as far or as fast as the ecologists would like, but we had recognized the problem and spent a great deal of money in this respect.

"Now, on the other side of the picture—just to talk about some of these things—I built a dam on the Red River. And it certainly destroyed the scenic effects, whatever they were, of what I considered a very ugly river. And it created in its place a great water reservoir in which thousands of people boat, swim, and find recreation. Well, I happen to think that this was in the interest of ecology.

"I think it would be fine in the interest of bird life, in the interest of scenery, to let the Mississippi River flood every year. But the United States can't afford to let the Mississippi River flood every year. We can't afford to give up that ground. We've got to control it.

"I have no sympathy for the people who think we should have

buffalo still roaming on the plains. My God, those plains where the buffalo roamed fed the entire world after World War II. I love nature and have a great affection for it. But I don't believe in being a damn fool about it.

"What is environmental compatibility? Maybe that is the phrase. When I was a young boy, in my hometown of five or six thousand people, we had no water supply. Everybody had wells. Most of the people had outhouses. There was no sewage system, and if you had one it just emptied out into some back pasture. Today all of that has been eliminated. But so have the open fields. And so have the streams. Nevertheless, for the health and survival of the human species, the present environment is a whole lot better than when it was a beautiful wide-open area. Somewhere along this concern, we've got to have common sense."

By 1959, Concan's sales exceeded $1.1 billion, and earnings stood at an all-time high. Wall Street touted Clay as one of American's leading industrialists. Sidney Weinberg of Goldman, Sachs called Clay "the same old son of a bitch he was in the Army, and he still produces the same outstanding results."

Q: General, the Eisenhower administration brought suit against Continental Can for a number of antitrust violations. Did your friendship with the President and Attorney General [Herbert] Brownell come into play?

CLAY: Well, if it did, it didn't work. As a matter of fact, I've always believed that if General Eisenhower hadn't been President and Mr. Brownell hadn't been Attorney General, we never would have lost Hazel-Atlas.

"I think they bent over backwards to bring suits against us, to push us into the corner, to do everything they could. I think they went overboard on it, to tell you the truth. And I'm not sorry that they did. Appearances are important. But the fact remains that I suspect very much that had it not been for my relationship with them, Continental Can would have never had an antitrust suit on Gair. The Kennedys closed that one out. Not the Eisenhowers and Brownells—the Kennedys. And I think Bobby Kennedy closed it out because he didn't think he had a case."

In 1956, when Concan was indicted, the Eisenhower administration put more than lip service behind the ideas of honesty, integrity, and even-handedness. When former Attorney General Herbert Brownell was asked about the antitrust suits against Continental Can, he said that he made the decision to bring action "without consulting General Clay—which was hard for both of us. It was a very unpleasant experience for me," said Brownell, "because by that time General Clay was one of my closest friends. The recommendations were made by the career people [in the Department of Justice]. I instructed them to be meticulous in handling it according to the ordinary procedures. It was too bad to happen to a friend, and I've always felt that General Clay felt he had been made a goat because he was a friend."

Clay's relations with organized labor at Continental Can also deserve comment, principally because in Germany he was occasionally criticized for opposing labor's interests. The work force at Concan was represented by the United Steelworkers, whose president at the time was David McDonald. The steelworkers' chief negotiator was Arthur Goldberg, and as Clay recalled, "Our negotiations were tough and very difficult. However, once we had reached an agreement, McDonald and Goldberg carried it out. And while I think they were awfully tough and they made us pay, they never condoned wildcat strikes, they never condoned slowdowns on the job, and I have a great deal of respect for them."

In fact, it was Continental Can under Clay's leadership that granted the steelworkers the first guaranteed annual wage in U.S. history. "If I may be so bold as to brag," McDonald told *The New York Times,* "nothing like this has ever before been achieved in American labor-management negotiations."

Clay was scarcely settled at Continental Can in 1950 when the Korean War erupted. In early July (little more than a week after North Korean forces streamed across the 38th parallel), New York Governor Thomas E. Dewey called him and asked him to head the state's civil defense program.

Q: How well did you know Governor Dewey?

CLAY: Well, I met him for the first time at the Al Smith dinner in 1948. I had seen him a time or two after that, but I'd only been in New York a couple of months at that point and I had not formed a friendship with him—which I did very quickly. Shortly after I took on the civil defense job, my wife and I went out and spent the weekend with them at their farm in Pawling. Then we became closely involved in the Eisenhower campaign [in 1952], golf companions, and very close friends. But it really started with the civil defense job.

Clay and Dewey were very similar and hit it off immediately. They were approximately the same age, short to medium height, shared a common small-town upbringing, dressed well, spoke clearly, and enjoyed more or less the same things. Through their individual ability, they had climbed to the top of two very competitive professions. They shared a common interest in American national security, but, more important, viewed most problems through a common lens. Dewey shared Clay's fierce opposition to Communist expansion. Like Clay, he also believed strongly in American civil liberties. For example, when the Queens GOP boss Frank Kenna urged Dewey to move against alleged Communists on Columbia's faculty (including Charles and Mary Beard), Dewey angrily rebuked him. Lists of "alleged Communists," said Dewey, always made him suspicious. Clay agreed completely.

Clay and Dewey were alike in other ways. Both had razor-sharp minds, and both were ruthless with those who did not measure up. Though Clay at that time was still a nonvoting Democrat and a loyal supporter of President Truman, while Dewey was a leader of the Republican Party, both men shared a common high standard of personal and public integrity. They were soon speaking to each other in the shorthand of mutual understanding.

Q: But you had just become chief executive of Continental Can. Could you accept Governor Dewey's offer [to head civil defense]?

CLAY: I told him I would take it on a part-time, nonpaying basis if I could select a full-time assistant to be with me—to which he quite readily agreed.

"We were given a small appropriation—not very much, a couple of hundred thousand dollars. We took over an old loft building [at 124 East Twenty-eighth Street] and made it into offices, which made quite a hit with the Governor since I'm sure he was afraid we would require elaborate and beautiful offices. Then I got Larry Wilkinson [Clay's former deputy for financial affairs], who was then with Dillon-Reed, to come with me as a full-time assistant. We built up a small staff and proceeded to build up a civil-defense plan: basically, the designation of evacuation routes in the event of an air strike, marking them adequately and setting up a communications center to ensure that we had continual communications in the event we did have an air strike. All of the planning steps. It was my contention that basically this was what we needed: a plan that could go into effect when necessary rather than actually trying to put something into effect that would not only be expensive but also very soon would be obsolete. So most of our expenditures were on planning, with the exception of marking roads and highways as air defense routes and the designation of some air raid shelters. And that was about it. I tried to avoid doing foolish things, and I think we did. Very soon we were recognized as having the most effective program in the United States. But it was a program that involved very little expenditure."

As civil defense chairman, Clay spent four afternoons a week at the Twenty-eighth Street headquarters. At first he traveled in a sleek chauffeur-driven state limousine Dewey had made available in lieu of compensation. After using the car for several weeks, Clay discovered that Albany was charging its upkeep and the salary of the driver to the civil defense budget. Clay chose not to raise the issue and possibly embarrass Dewey. Instead, he quietly sent the car back to the state motor pool.

Clay was under no illusion as to the efficacy of civil defense. In the event of atomic attack, midtown Manhattan would be flattened. The casualties would be enormous. Even in the unlikely event of sufficient warning, Clay concluded that it would take more than an hour to empty some of New York's larger skyscrapers. "All that can really be done is to make the best use of available resources, in order to minimize the effect of an attack on areas not directly hit," Clay told *Time* magazine—whose cover he graced for the fourth time.

At the end of December 1950, with the war in Korea going badly and the possibility of a much larger war looming, Congress established the Defense Production Agency to coordinate the nation's economy. President Truman tapped GE's Charles E. Wilson to head the agency. Wilson had been the principal deputy chairman of the War Production

Board in World War II and was an old hand at industrial organization. To assist him, Wilson looked to two other old hands from wartime Washington: Clay and Sidney Weinberg.

According to Clay, "Sometime in December, Sidney Weinberg invited me to 'Twenty-One' to have dinner with Charles Wilson. And during the course of the dinner, Mr. Wilson said that the President had asked him to come down [to Washington] to head up the Defense Production Agency—that had just been established. And he wanted Mr. Weinberg and me to go with him. Obviously, as far as I was concerned, there was only one answer I could give. I said yes. I knew Wilson. He had been [Donald] Nelson's deputy [in World War II], and I'd seen a lot of him at that time. And I had a great deal of respect for him. After I came to New York, I saw him a couple of times socially."

Q: But you were still head of Continental Can?

CLAY: The job in Washington was to be nonpaid. Technically, I was a special assistant to Mr. Wilson. But I gave up the active direction of Continental Can Company. I was placed on leave of absence with pay.

"When I went down there, Mr. Wilson wanted me to be the executive director [of the DPA], but I turned that down. I simply undertook to organize his office—as I had done for Justice Byrnes. We worked with the Secretary of Labor on manpower contracts, and Anna Rosenberg did that. And then with the Secretary of Commerce on priorities, and we brought Fred Searles down for that. And I think overall it was effective. But after I got down there and got into it, I became convinced that the Korean War was not of sufficient size and magnitude to really require any special effort on the part of the American economy. We were not really in a national emergency. A friend of mine loaned me his house, and I lived in Washington Mondays through Thursdays, spent Fridays at the Continental Can Company, and the weekend at home."

Q: What were your relations with President Truman?

CLAY: Our offices were in the old State, War, Navy Building [now the Executive Office Building], next to the White House. But Mr. Wilson was the man in charge, and he saw far more of Mr. Truman than I did. Whenever I saw him, my relations were always pleasant and friendly. I didn't really see enough of the decision-making in the Korean War to make a comparison with World War II, but my own experiences with President Truman were of a man who never hesitated to make decisions. I have a tremendous admiration for President Truman.

"Mr. Wilson, by virtue of his job, was a member of the National Security Council. He asked me to attend when he was not there, and I refused to do it. I refused for two reasons. In the first place, I had a complex about a former soldier being in this job. But, secondly, I don't like attending meetings as a substitute. I think when you do, you don't know what to say. You're not speaking for yourself, and in debate you don't know what the fellow for whom you're substituting might have said. So I think it is an impossible position."

Q: Were you still in Washington when General MacArthur was relieved?

CLAY: No, I was back in New York by that time. My only comment was that the President and the military establishment should not have allowed him to stay [in Japan] for so long. It could have been done earlier and more gracefully, just on the grounds of his age and the time he had been away from the United States. It should never have been allowed to get to such a controversial stage.

Q: Were you a Republican at that time?

CLAY: If so, I didn't know it. I hadn't really become a voting citizen at that time.

"But after I went down to Washington in the Korean War, and with the greatest respect for Mr. Truman, I came out with the conclusion that the Democrats had been in power too long and that we needed a change. We needed to throw out a lot of people and get a lot of new people in, and a lot of new ideas and new thoughts. And that was when I became a Republican."

Q: Did you think these new ideas would come from the Republican Party?

CLAY: I can't say I thought they would come from the Republican Party, but it was a cinch that if the Democrats had stayed in there wasn't any possibility of getting a fresh look at government.

"Through the years up to that point, my political associations were almost entirely with the Democratic Party. But then I went out to get the Republican nomination for General Eisenhower, because I didn't think Senator [Robert A.] Taft [R., Ohio] could win. I felt he was too much identified as a conservative. I don't think he was—but he was so identified. And that he couldn't win. This was the whole basis of our effort to persuade General Eisenhower to run for President.

"I have great respect for Senator Taft. He was my sponsor for the honorary degree at Yale. But at the same time, I didn't believe it was possible for him to rally the country around him and create a new style in government. His image was such that he would only have had the support of the extreme right, and he could not be elected. I still think that. If he had won the nomination, I think we would never have had a Republican President in 1952.

"Actually, I'm not too sure General Eisenhower wasn't even more conservative than Senator Taft. But his image wasn't. Plus the fact that Eisenhower had a background of having come up the hard way. Senator Taft was the son of a former President, and it was difficult to know whether he could understand some of the problems that General Eisenhower might understand. But there is no use nominating a presidential candidate you're afraid you can't elect.

"Of course, the people who were for Taft still maintain that any Republican could have been elected in 1952. I just don't believe that. Look at 1948, when everyone thought Governor Dewey was going to win. Eisenhower had a very tough opponent against him in 1952—a very able campaigner—Governor [Adlai] Stevenson. And it was closer than most people realize."

· 28 ·

Electing a President

> Lucius's father and my grandfather served together in the United States Senate. And Lucius had become absorbed in politics at a very early age. In Eisenhower's 1952 campaign, it was Lucius who called the shots. I was there because they needed a front man.
>
> Henry Cabot Lodge, Jr.

ONCE CLAY WAS SETTLED AT CONTINENTAL CAN, HIS international standing and growing business acumen made him a sought-after candidate by various boards of directors: the interlocking network of American business that has fascinated insiders and outsiders alike. In 1950, Clay became a member of the Business Advisory Council, the top-drawer group of business executives sponsored by the Commerce Department whose annual conclaves at Sea Island and White Sulfur Springs bring together the leaders of America's private sector. By 1951, he was a member of the boards of directors of Marine Midland Trust, General Motors, the Lehman Corporation, and

Newmont Mining. General Motors elevated him to its powerful financial-policy committee the following year. American Express and Metropolitan Life extended board membership to Clay in 1953, General Aniline and Film (GAF) and United States Lines the following year. In 1958, he was made a trustee of Columbia-Presbyterian Medical Center (where he headed a new fund drive), the National Fund for Medical Education, and the Sloan Foundation.

These directorships did not come from out of the blue. Many of the heads of these firms, such as Fred Searles of Newmont Mining, or John Hancock and Robert Lehman of Lehman Brothers, had worked closely with Clay during the war. Others knew him by reputation, either from wartime Washington, Berlin, or the Korean mobilization. His reputation as a chaos-into-order man of global standing made him an ideal associate for firms that wanted to stiffen management. In due time, Allied Chemical, Chase Manhattan, and Standard Brands utilized Clay's services. Clay devoted considerable time to his growing extracurricular responsibilities, gilding his impressive credentials within the business community. The words "General Clay is calling" were usually sufficient to get the busiest government or corporate official on the line. Harold Boeschenstein, long-time chairman and chief executive officer of Owens-Corning Fiberglas, said that "Lucius was a driven man. He was an autocrat by nature. If we lived in an earlier age, he would have been a baron or a duke. He would have been a benevolent one, but he would have been an autocrat nonetheless."

Socially, Clay joined the elite at Links, Blind Brook, The Creek, the University, and the Cloud clubs, as well as Eastward Ho! Country Club on Cape Cod. But his membership in Washington's Army and Navy Club always took precedence, a holdover from a career to which he acknowledged he owed everything. Later Clay was admitted to Pinnacle, Cypress Point, the Augusta National, and Bohemian Grove: all-male bastions of the American business establishment.

Marjorie basked in the affluent glow of Clay's success but, as an Army wife, usually kept both feet squarely on the ground. She still cooked in the heavy aluminum utensils she had bought when Clay was a first lieutenant in Pittsburgh in 1932.

Shortly after moving into their spacious duplex at 1040 Fifth Avenue, Mrs. Clay affixed three small windshield decals in the shape of Army mules to the elevator door on the private landing they shared with another family. She had done this wherever they lived. To Marjorie, the Army mules stood "for my three Army mules: Lucius, Lucius Junior, and Frank"—and posh Fifth Avenue was no exception. Two or three days later, the mules were mysteriously removed and the elevator door repainted. She replaced the decals on the door, where they remained until the apartment was sold when the Clays returned to Berlin in 1961.

When Clay assumed the chairmanship of Continental Can and moved to New York, he and Marjorie quickly renewed their friendship with the Eisenhowers. Ike and Mamie were not-so-comfortably ensconced in the rambling presidential mansion at Columbia, built by McKim, Mead, and White for Nicholas Murray Butler in 1912. Mamie especially enjoyed Marjorie's company, but Clay had his hands full at Concan, and for a variety of reasons maintained more distance. In the summer of 1950, Ike wrote Clay to complain they were not seeing enough of each other. "We always have several good bottles of whiskey on hand, if you want to stop by," said Eisenhower.

In fact, Eisenhower and Clay continued to be very close, and were destined to become much more so. It was not only their long, friendly association and the affection their families shared. Eisenhower respected Clay's business and political judgment. In 1950, Ike was America's reigning military hero, the popular esteem he enjoyed equaling that of Pershing in the 1920s or Grant after the Civil War. But Eisenhower's experience in U.S. politics was limited, and his familiarity with the business world was nil. He admired Clay on both counts. From Eisenhower's perspective, Clay's knowledge of American politics was encyclopedic. Although Ike had served briefly as Chief of Staff after returning from Europe in 1945, he had never become involved in domestic politics. On the other hand, most of Clay's military career had been devoted to Washington politics. He knew not only the leading personalities in the executive and legislative branches, but also their voting records and the unspoken underlying issues. If a politician had a hidden agenda, Clay usually had some inkling. In Ike's view, Clay was a walking dictionary, a man who could translate the arcane language of partisan politics: an essential need for someone so basically nonpartisan as Eisenhower. Ike also admired Clay's leading role in American business. Professional military officers sometimes look longingly at the business world, and in Ike's view, no ex-soldier had achieved more success than Clay.

In the past, Eisenhower had consulted Clay about his own political plans, and the two had often discussed politics. In 1945, Clay had urged Eisenhower to get out of Germany and return to the United States because he thought Ike's image would be tarnished if he remained. "I did so on the grounds that no matter what might happen, he was a political personage," said Clay. "He couldn't avoid it. I don't think that necessarily related to his running for President, but it didn't rule it out."

In January 1948, when a boomlet for Eisenhower erupted in the Democratic Party, Eisenhower showed Clay the text of a letter he intended to send to New Hampshire, taking himself out of the Democratic primary. Ike wanted Clay's advice. "When he showed me the letter, it was no great surprise," said Clay. "In the first place, I knew that he was a Republican. He told me at that time that if he were going to run for President, he wouldn't consider doing it as a Democrat. That he would do it as a Republican. That was when he wasn't contemplating either. Nevertheless, there was no question in his mind that he was a Republican. So I knew that he was a Republican. A very undemonstrative, and probably nonvoting, Republican. I don't know when General Eisenhower first voted, but I'm sure he never voted until he established residency in New York [as president of Columbia]."

Q: That was also when you first voted? After you moved to New York?

CLAY: Yes. In the days when I first went into the Army, you couldn't vote by absentee ballot in Georgia. In addition to that, my state for a long time excluded the insane, convicted felons, and members of the Regular Army from voting.

"This was true in much of the South. If you'll remember, Governor Tilden, the Democratic candidate, lost the presidential election [in 1876] because the federal troops were marched to the polls in Georgia to vote for Mr. [Rutherford B.] Hayes. Georgia was one of the states where the federal occupying forces constituted the balance, and Hayes was elected. In any event, I had never voted until I came to New York, and I doubt if General Eisenhower had either."

Q: Was there any talk of General Eisenhower running for President when you moved to New York in 1950?

CLAY: Not that I know of. The first I heard was in the fall of 1951, when Governor Dewey called me and asked me to come down to his apartment at the Roosevelt. That was in September 1951. Now there had been an earlier Eisenhower movement started by Senator [Frank] Carlson of Kansas and the Republican state chairman of Kansas, Harry Darby, but it really hadn't gotten off the ground.

"I never did anything about [Eisenhower's candidacy] until that meeting with Tom Dewey. There were only four of us: Dewey, Mr. [Burdell] Bixby [the Governor's secretary], Mr. [J. Russell] Sprague [Republican national committeeman from New York], and myself. It was around dinnertime. I think we went down for dinner. The Governor said that as things now stood, Senator Taft was going to be the Republican nominee, and he couldn't possibly be elected. And that if we didn't get somebody with greater voter appeal to run, we would have a continuation of the Democratic administration—which he felt needed to be changed. So did I. It had been in power much too long.

"The only man that could change this, who did have the popular appeal, said Dewey, was General Eisenhower. Dewey said he understood that I was a great friend of the general's, and did I think he would run?

"I said, 'I don't know. But I am sure that he will not run unless he is sure that there is a strong demand for him to run, an effective organization, and, I would add, although I'm not sure that he would, that there be every chance for it to be reasonably financed.' I said that if I could be convinced of those factors, I think it would be the right thing for him to do, and I would be prepared to do everything I could to get him to run. That was our initial meeting, and that's about where it ended."

Q: When did you decide you were a Republican?

CLAY: My decision that I was a Republican was also my decision that I was going to do my utmost to get General Eisenhower to run for the Republican nomination. I had no party affiliation until then, although by family background I was a nominal Democrat.

"I don't think I even reported that first meeting [with Governor Dewey] to General Eisenhower. But that meeting led to a second meeting [on November 10, 1951], where others were present: Herb Brownell, Senator [James] Duff [of Pennsylvania], Senator Lodge, and our original group. And at this meeting we made the decision that we had to start afresh. That the old Eisenhower movement under Carlson and Darby, no matter how sincere it was, had lost its energy, and we had to make a new start. So we looked for the type of popular public figure that we thought would be helpful on this, and this is when we asked Cabot Lodge to become our front manager."

Henry Cabot Lodge, Jr., the handsome young senator from Massachusetts, was the ideal front man for the Eisenhower forces. Grandson of his distinguished namesake, who had been the scourge of Woodrow Wilson and the League of Nations, Lodge had established impressive credentials as a liberal Republican. But his family name gave him entrée to the conservative wing of the party as well. And in the autumn of 1951, his re-election to the Senate seemed assured.

"Every pimple must have a head," said Lodge, "and so I became the head of this group. We would meet every ten days at the Commodore. All of these men knew what to do. I was simply out in front. Herb Brownell was the planner and thinker. I was the front man, talking to the press, the delegates, the public. But in those early stages, Clay was the key figure. Except for Lucius, none of us had talked to Eisenhower. I was the first [to do so], and I didn't go over until April [1952]. And Lucius set that up.

"But Clay kept a very low profile. He didn't want the public to see his hand. Nonetheless, he was extremely helpful behind the scenes. Lucius is terrifically blunt. In a rough-and-tumble political fight when you're dealing with so many spineless people who're sitting on the fence waiting to see who's going to win, a man like Clay is extremely useful. He scared some people to death.

"Tom Dewey's influence was tremendous too. Like Clay, Dewey had to stay under cover because he was *persona non grata* to the right wing. He said, 'I'm going to subordinate myself to you. I'll not make a speech or write an article without your approval.' And for the life of me, I didn't want him making speeches or writing articles. And Dewey took it wonderfully. He was completely selfless. But his presence had a tremendously invigorating effect."

The most serious problem the Clay-Dewey-Brownell cabal confronted in November 1951 was that Eisenhower's intentions remained a mystery. General Eisenhower had taken a leave of absence from Columbia and returned to active duty January 31, 1951, at President Truman's request, becoming the first head of NATO's military forces. As supreme commander in Europe, Eisenhower could take no political stand that might compromise his military position. The issue was further complicated by Eisenhower's delicate relations with President Truman, who was not only Ike's commander-in-chief but the most likely Democratic contender in 1952. The result was that Eisenhower kept his own counsel.

Nevertheless, and regardless of the enthusiasm and expertise that Clay, Dewey, and Brownell had assembled, nothing definitive could be done without at least a wink from Eisenhower. It fell to Clay to discern Eisenhower's plans, and he flew secretly to Paris in mid-November. But even with Clay, Ike played his cards close to his chest. "The sum and substance of our talk," Clay recalled, "was that I could say [when I returned to New York] that I had reason to believe that if the movement generated enough public support, that we *might* have a candidate. It wasn't a green light, but it wasn't a red light either. And in my own mind, I thought he would run—although he hadn't said that.

"Sometime later that month, General Eisenhower returned to Washington, and I had breakfast with him at his hotel, primarily to get him to be very careful to avoid making any public statement which indicated that he might not be receptive to an invitation to run. And I'm afraid he was about ready to say that and take himself out of the race. I believe he was under tremendous pressure at NATO, and he thought it might help if he took himself out of the race. At that time, NATO was his primary concern, and I was very worried that he might say he wasn't receptive. We had not yet had enough time for the movement to really jell. But by that time I was confident that we would jell. So my whole purpose in that visit to Washington was to ensure that General Eisenhower didn't say anything that would take him out of the picture.

"In the meantime, we had been moving along with our organization. We knew which Republican national committeemen would support us, who wouldn't, and where our strength would come from. By that time, we were beginning to really create an organization under Mr. Brownell. Theoretically, the manager was Senator Lodge. In reality, Mr. Brownell was in charge.

"We very quickly set up an 'Eisenhower for President' financial campaign under Harold Talbott [later Secretary of the Air Force]. There is very little written on this period. Mr. Brownell and Mr. Dewey and myself are the only three that know about it. And we don't always agree. Governor Dewey, before he died, was writing a book about it. He called me a half a dozen times to verify one or another detail.

"After that second meeting at the Roosevelt, we met many times. At Governor Dewey's suite, and not too much later, we decided to set up offices over in the Commodore Hotel. Brownell did that. But all during this period, there were frequent meetings between the three of us, and frequent telephone calls. And I would say that while others were added to our entourage, up until the time of the convention it was to the three of us that General Eisenhower looked for his advice and counsel. After the nomination, it was a different story. But up to the nomination, it was to the three of us that he looked.

"We selected Mr. [Paul] Hoffman for the 'Citizens for Eisenhower' movement. Eisenhower was very fond of Hoffman, but Mr. Hoffman's political judgment and shrewdness was zero. I think I could say this without trying to overestimate my part in it. But I was the only person accepted by [General Eisenhower] and accepted by the people who wanted to give him the nomination. I was a representative of both sides. In other words, if I said to Dewey and Brownell, 'This is what General Eisenhower will do or will not do,' it was never questioned. On the other hand, whatever I would say to him as representing the views of the people behind the campaign, he never questioned. He might not accept it, but he never questioned it. So, in this particular period, I was the go-between.

"Another group of advisers was that around Cliff Roberts [of the investment firm of Reynolds & Company]. But their advice was less valuable. In fact, at one meeting, they had about made up their minds to advise General Eisenhower that it was too late, that he might be defeated, and what a tragedy that would be. And I said, 'I thought you people knew General Eisenhower. If you think it would be a tragedy for him to run and be defeated, if he looks at this later and decides he didn't run because of our advice, I think you will be creating a much greater tragedy. The point is, we need him. The country needs him. And I think we badly need a change of parties. I don't believe General Eisenhower is going to decide whether he is going to run or not on the basis that there's no question of his being elected.' And so I don't think that they advised him not to run.

"But I didn't have too much to do with these other groups. I really was working with Dewey and Brownell. If General Eisenhower was going to be elected, it had to be through the Dewey-Brownell-Darby-Duff group of people, who were political professionals and knew what they were doing. It couldn't be done by this very fine, really wonderful group of American businesspeople who didn't know any more about politics than I did. But I was learning fast. At least I had good instructors: Tom Dewey and Herb Brownell."

In early December 1951, Clay sent Eisenhower a brief memorandum detailing the state of the campaign and the complications caused by Eisenhower's role as supreme commander. Clay also pointed out some organizational problems. Senator Duff, he said, was "full of ego and determined to be anointed." Duff did not like Lodge; Lodge "could not stand Duff." Dewey was doubtful about both Duff and Lodge, and no one trusted Stassen. Clay noted the dates of the upcoming state conventions, and the problems they were having in attracting delegates if those delegates could not be sure that Ike was a candidate. In the 1950s, delegates to political conventions were party professionals —and professionals did not want to be kept dangling.

As Eisenhower's biographer, Stephen Ambrose, reports, Clay's letter made Ike's head swim. Nevertheless, he replied immediately. "I must say that while I have very little time to devote to the kind of exhaustive thinking that was responsible for the memorandum," he told Clay, "I instinctively find myself in agreement with it." Nevertheless, Eisenhower said: "Time and time again, I have tried to make clear that the American Military Commander of the Allied Forces in Europe cannot possibly allow his own actions or words to inspire partisan argument in America. To my mind, this would be close to disloyalty."

Eisenhower was walking a tightrope. He told Clay that "Our Friend" (their code for Governor Dewey) wanted him to make a positive statement defining his political status by January 15, 1952. "Even to contemplate such a thing makes me extremely uneasy, although I have in the past admitted to Our Friend that my family ties, my own meager voting record, and my own convictions align me fairly closely with what I call the progressive branch of the Republican Party."

To Clay and Dewey, Ike was still waffling, and the difficulties were increasing daily. Eisenhower was torn between his duty to NATO and what Clay perceived as his growing interest in the presidency. But Ike wanted more tangible evidence of a groundswell of public support. On the other hand, Clay, Dewey, and Brownell needed Ike's blessing to make the groundswell materialize. Four days before Christmas, Clay wrote Eisenhower and explained the predicament.

Clay's letter brought the reality of practical politics home to Eisenhower. He could not encourage the effort by Clay and Dewey on his behalf so long as he remained in Paris, but he didn't want to discourage them either. "Your letter has just come to my desk and it disturbs me so much that I am putting everything else aside to answer immediately," Eisenhower wrote Clay on December 27, 1951. Ike tried to reassure Clay as to his intent. "Only yesterday I was asked to name the personality in the United States who was best acquainted with me and my methods, and who also had a wide acquaintanceship with people of substance at home. [The question had been put to Eisenhower by William Robinson, publisher of the New York *Herald Tribune* and a frequent bridge-playing companion.] Without hesitation, I gave your name. This came about in connection with the discussion as to who was best qualified to act as an intermediary between me and the 'pros', since direct communication between us could obviously be embarrassing."

Eisenhower's answer reassured Clay that Ike intended to run. In fact, Eisenhower invited Clay to Paris ("I hope you are going to find it possible to make a business trip in this direction"), and the two established a code system to cloak their subsequent messages. Clay's telegrams to Eisenhower at NATO were to be addressed to Colonel Robert Schultz, Ike's military aide, and signed "Shelley," for Edna Shelley, Clay's secretary at Continental Can. Similarly, Eisenhower's messages for Clay would be addressed to Shelley and signed "Schultz." Personal letters were frequently hand-carried between Paris and New York by pilots on TWA.

To help Clay explain his seeming coyness to others, Eisenhower cited the applicable Army regulations that governed him:

> A[rmy] R[egulation] 600-10. 18. Election to, and performance of duties of public office. —a. Members of the Regular Army, while on active duty, may accept nomination for public office, provided such nomination is tendered without direct or *indirect* activity or solicitation on their part. [Eisenhower's emphasis.]

"In view of this," said Ike, "I hope you find it possible to forgive any seeming slight of which I have been guilty. I assure you that it was unintentional."

As far as Clay was concerned, Eisenhower was now committed. On his own responsibility, Clay authorized Lodge to enter Ike in the New Hampshire GOP primary, and on January 6, 1952, Lodge wrote to Governor Sherman Adams in Concord that Eisenhower was a Republican in sympathy with "enlightened Republican doctrine." "Clay got the information, and I wrote the letter," said Lodge, assuming that Clay had cleared it with Ike. The following day, when Eisenhower was questioned by newsmen in Paris, he issued a statement that Lodge had given "an accurate account of the general tenor of my political convictions and of my Republican voting record." But the fact is, Clay had forced the issue—just as he had done so many times in Germany. Despite what Lodge thought, Clay had, in fact, not contacted Eisenhower for approval. He simply took the responsibility on himself, just as he had when he launched the airlift, and told Lodge to go ahead. Ike could repudiate Clay if he wished. But Eisenhower responded just as Clay had hoped he would. He issued a public statement that permitted Lodge to go ahead. Privately, he sent a sharp rebuke to Clay for his temerity. Clay could live with that.

Q: When did General Eisenhower finally tell you that he would run?

CLAY: Well, I can tell you that exactly, because the day that he really made that decision was the day that King George VI was buried [February 16, 1952].

"I went over to the funeral as one of President Truman's representatives. But the principal reason I went was to see General Eisenhower. It was much easier to see him in England, and would create less talk than if I went to see him in Paris. This was at his suggestion. After the funeral, I went out to the house of one of Eisenhower's aides—British General [Sir James] Gault. And it was there that he made the irrevocable decision to run. And I came back with it. Before that, he had not made a final decision. At that stage of the game, we felt we had to know and that by the first of June he would have to declare. So I went over to give him this story, and to tell him that unless he was willing to declare, that we were all working in an effort that would not mean anything."

Q: Weren't there several others who went over to see Eisenhower at that time? George Allen, and Sid Richardson, the Texas oilman?
CLAY: Well, they were there.
Q: They didn't go with you?
CLAY: No sir.

"They were staying with Eisenhower down at General Gault's. Actually, I was quite taken aback to find them there, because I didn't want to talk freely in front of them. I pressed General Eisenhower all I could for a definite answer, and he still didn't want to give one. In fact, he got quite angry with me for insisting. So I said, 'Well, there is nothing more I can do,' and got up to leave. He followed me out and said, 'Let's don't leave things on this note.' And then he took me into a small cloakroom by the entrance, and that was when he finally said that he would run."

Clay's meeting with Eisenhower at General Gault's was the final moment of decision. In effect, Clay gave Eisenhower an ultimatum: if he wanted to be President, he had to say so. Probably only Clay could have posed the issue so directly. Then again, Clay was a poker player, and this he always had been.

Q: Did you feel that General Eisenhower wanted to run?
CLAY: No. I think he had very mixed emotions.

"He wasn't being coy, because he knew that the [Republican] party wasn't going to go out and give him the nomination on a platter. Nobody ever gets it that way, and he knew that. Eisenhower was no fool. I think it was more like this: He knew that he had a tremendous standing in America, but that if he entered into a political contest he could lose the nomination, in which case his standing would be greatly lowered. Or he could lose the election, in which case it would be lowered even more. Therefore, in a personal sense, what did he have to gain? On the other hand, he really and truly had a feeling that if there was a chance, you just didn't have the right to say you wouldn't do it. There was some ambition mixed with this, and there were some other things. The fact remains, this was really a very simple man in a lot of ways.

"But there is no question in my mind but that he was tremendously influenced by the position which he held in public esteem—which he understood and appreciated. He was also influenced by the fact that what right did a man who had been given this much respect and affection have to say no? This sounds like an oversimplification, but I really think these were the things that played on his mind."

Q: Was General Eisenhower reluctant to leave NATO?

CLAY: That may have been part of his consideration, but I don't think it was his principal concern. When he said that he had made up his mind to run, he said he would resign as quickly as he could as commanding general of NATO. In addition, he said he would resign his commission as a General of the Army. Don't forget that General of the Army [a five-star rank] is a lifetime appointment: you never retire. I thought it was interesting that he wanted to resign from the Army not because he was going into a presidential campaign but because, so long as he was a soldier, he felt he could not resign from his post at NATO. He felt very strongly that a soldier could not decline to serve at whatever post his commander-in-chief had given him. So the only way he could leave NATO was to resign his commission. Then, having cast the die, he would come home by the first of June and would be available for the campaign.

"I don't think it was a calculated delay on his part, because every day that he delayed made our task more difficult. There wasn't any question about what we were willing to do, but our ability to do it got less and less. Politicians don't like to be kept sitting on a rail. Before we even entered the race, Mr. Taft had a tremendous number of votes. We were operating against a man who had been running for a long, long time. So our ability was limited by time."

By January 1952, the Taft forces were far out in front. Senator Taft had been bested by Dewey for the GOP nomination in 1944 and 1948, and had been running ever since. Taft stood for the flinty Republicanism of the Midwest, and was a bitter critic of big government in all of its forms—including large military expenditures and foreign aid. He opposed sending U.S. troops to Europe in 1949, and from the beginning was skeptical of President Truman's intervention in Korea. A January 1952 NBC poll of the delegates to previous Republican conventions put Taft well ahead. In addition, the Taft supporters had captured the key posts for the Chicago convention that summer. Speaker Joe Martin (R., Massachusetts), a strong Taft backer, would preside over the convention itself, while other pro-Taft men would chair the rules, credentials, and platform committees. Dewey and Clay professed not to be worried—Dewey observed that winter promises (i.e., the commitments many delegates had made to Taft) often dissolved in the June heat—but they were being made increasingly nervous by Eisenhower's refusal to announce formally. "God damn it," Clay exploded at one meeting of the steering group. "We've been telling this man we can do this and we can do that—but the time has come when we have to call on him to do it."

Q: Was this why you organized the "We Want Ike" rally in Madison Square Garden? To bring pressure on Eisenhower?

CLAY: I wasn't for the Madison Square Garden rally. I thought it was a lot of damn foolishness. But it did have a real effect in persuading General Eisenhower to announce. Miss [Jacqueline] Cochran, the famous aviator [and wife of financier Floyd B. Odlum], went over with a report. She had the movies of the rally, and it was a highly emotional thing, and somehow or another it really affected General Eisenhower. To me it was simply a planned demonstration. To think that twelve or fifteen thousand people in Madison Square Garden indicated a national tidal wave seemed pretty foolish to me. But I arranged for Jacqueline Cochran to see Eisenhower, and I was really amazed at the lift it gave him. It was really a relatively unimportant thing, except for the effect it had on him.

Q: And this was genuine?

CLAY: Well, when you're at that stage of the game, you have all of the things that you are weighing that say no and all of the things that you are weighing that say yes, and I suppose it doesn't take much to tip the scales.

"As I said, I was very lukewarm about it. But after they decided to have it, let me assure you that we made damn sure that Madison Square Garden was filled. We brought people in from all over.

"And later, when it came time for the New Hampshire primary, we sent Tom Stephens [Governor Dewey's aide] up to New Hampshire to help [Governor] Sherman Adams with the campaign. I remember talking to the Governor on the telephone, and he was a great strength to us. It was because of his conduct of the campaign in New Hampshire that we actually selected him to be General Eisenhower's floor manager at the convention.

"But what the hell, let Lodge have the credit. He was the manager. The fact is, I think General Eisenhower gave him the credit. But the real brains behind the Eisenhower election was Herb Brownell. And the political strength was Tom Dewey.

"But Dewey—and rightfully so, because he was afraid that it would look like he was trying to get control [of the party] in an indirect way—Dewey was a big enough man to do all of this very much in the background. But there wasn't a major move made or major conference held in which we didn't go to Tom Dewey. And he had still a great deal of national strength in the Republican party."

Q: Do you think General Eisenhower knew the role Governor Dewey played?

CLAY: Not really. He never really knew the role that anybody played. In fact, if you read his memoirs, he gives most of this credit to Cabot Lodge. But, hell, it was all Brownell. And I had all I could do to keep Lodge from gumming up the works. He was an excellent front man. Period.

Dewey shared Clay's assessment. "Cabot Lodge had no experience in this area," Dewey wrote afterward. "He had great charm and great intelligence, but this wasn't a field in which he had much experience." In fact, although Clay had obtained Eisenhower's personal commitment to run, it was Dewey who smoked him out publicly. On the heels of Eisenhower's smashing primary victory in New Hampshire, Dewey leaned on Brownell to take a more active role in the delegate hunt. Clay arranged for Brownell to fly to Paris incognito and spend the day with Eisenhower at NATO. "General Clay got a ticket for me on TWA," said Brownell. "I traveled under an assumed name. I spent a day with General Eisenhower, at which time we made arrangements for him to come back to the United States and be a candidate."

But despite his commitment to Clay, and now to Brownell, Ike continued to hold back on making a public announcement. He wanted to remain in Europe as long as possible. Dewey, Clay, and Brownell grew increasingly frustrated. But Eisenhower kept them waiting. "I keenly realize," he wrote Dewey on March 18, "that I am of no particular help in all the matters of policy and decision with which you people are continuously faced. But I feel . . . that as long as I am performing a military duty and doing it with all my might, I am possibly providing as much ammunition for your guns as I could in any other way."

Eisenhower was not being indecisive. He had his own ideas about strategy and was following his own game plan. Ike may have been "a simple man in many ways," as Clay suggested, but he could also be a very subtle, cunning, and complex one. He was keeping the final decision in his own hands.

By mid-April, with still no formal announcement from Ike, Dewey and Clay were becoming desperate. Brownell was running into increasing difficulty corralling delegates, and a number of important state primaries had to be entered. If Ike did not announce his intentions quickly, Taft's lead would be insurmountable. Clay devised a stratagem to force Ike's hand, and Governor Dewey became his eager accomplice. The ruse centered on General Douglas MacArthur, who had recently been named the convention's keynote speaker. At the age of seventy-two, MacArthur was barnstorming across America, whipping up a torrent of rhetorical frenzy over his dismissal by President Truman. Even to an unbiased observer, it was clear that MacArthur was hoping to ignite a wave of popular support that would sweep the convention and give him the Republican nomination. That would set the stage for a final reckoning in November with the man who had relieved him. It was certainly a plausible scenario, and Clay, at wit's end over Ike's refusal to announce, decided to take advantage of it.

Having served in Manila in MacArthur's small prewar headquarters, Clay was intimately familiar with the cordial dislike Eisenhower felt toward MacArthur (which MacArthur just as cordially reciprocated). Clay knew that the one thing Eisenhower could not tolerate would be for MacArthur to wrest the Republican nomination away from him. When he apprised Governor Dewey of the situation and of the animosity that existed between Ike and Mac, Dewey needed no coaxing. The campaign, he thought, hung in the balance. On April 6, the Governor wrote to Eisenhower in longhand (no copy was ever kept) that unless Ike gave an immediate signal to his supporters, General MacArthur might well sweep the convention. Clay forwarded the letter to Eisenhower on the next TWA flight to Paris. It was hand-carried by the pilot, Captain Robert Nixon, and delivered to Eisenhower's aide when the plane landed at Orly.

Finally, Clay and Dewey had found the right button. As Clay

anticipated, Eisenhower rose to the bait. On April 12, 1952, three days after Dewey's letter arrived, Eisenhower asked to be relieved of his NATO command. A White House press release, issued immediately afterward, announced that General Eisenhower would return to the United States on June 1. Eisenhower had thrown his hat into the ring.

Q: When General Eisenhower returned from Europe, did you accompany him on his speaking tour?
CLAY: No. I didn't want to be seen to be part of this thing. I don't think very many people knew I was involved. It wouldn't have done any good to see a lot of old soldiers hanging around.

Nevertheless, Clay remained intensely active in the campaign. Brownell reports that he met with Clay every day during the preconvention period. "Clay was so close to Eisenhower that people felt he could always get Eisenhower's concurrence to any program that he recommended. And it was an accurate appraisal. That was very helpful to me as campaign manager.

"Clay would also meet with key delegations, key delegates, key Republicans around the country. He was a man of action and he was very forceful with these people. It was remarkable to me that he understood the political system so well. He knew what made politicians tick. So it wasn't as though it was a general coming in to order civilians around. He made friends with these people, these delegates, and it was tremendously helpful.

"General Clay has a keen mind, a strong, analytical mind. He would have made a fine lawyer. He was also severe in his criticisms. He never pulled his punches. If you call us an executive committee of three [Dewey, Brownell, and Clay], we were never at a loss to find out where he stood on any matter. But he was also very fine about accepting another person's judgment. He evidently had confidence in Governor Dewey and me, and he would accept our judgment when he thought we knew more about it than he did."

At the convention itself, Clay stayed with Eisenhower at the Blackstone. Dewey headed the New York delegation and spent much of his time bringing wayward delegates into line. But Brownell was the quarterback calling the plays. As Clay recalled, Brownell was at the Stevens. "He was operating very much in the background. But he had an elaborate network of young people working as liaison with each of the state delegations, and he was absolutely on top of the situation. We had a tough job. The Taft forces controlled everything. That turned out to be one of their problems. They were overconfident.

"The first issue before the convention was the seating of the delegates—the acceptance of their credentials. And several of the state delegations were contested. We had delegations from Georgia and Texas pledged to General Eisenhower. The Taft people had rival delegations. And the Taft people wouldn't compromise. They wanted both delegations of Taft supporters seated, with nothing for us. The result was a floor fight on the seating of the Georgia and Texas delegations. Our first victory was to get television coverage of the fight. This got public opinion completely behind General Eisenhower, and it had a lot of influence on the delegates. Because there was no question that the sentiment in Georgia and Texas was for General Eisenhower. But the Eisenhower forces had been steamrolled [in the state conventions]. Judge [Elbert P.] Tuttle argued our case from Georgia, and we won it on television. The people were appalled at what the Taft forces had done. When the vote was taken and we won those two contests, and our delegates, not the Taft delegates, were seated, we knew we were in."

Despite the loss of Georgia and Texas, Taft was still well ahead of Eisenhower in the informal vote count. The day before the balloting, an Associated Press poll showed Taft leading Eisenhower 533 to 427. The Eisenhower strategy—as devised by Brownell—was to hold enough state delegations behind "favorite sons" to deny Taft the nomination on the first ballot. That strategy centered on holding Minnesota behind perennial candidate Harold Stassen and, most important, California behind Earl Warren. If Taft could be stopped on the first ballot, Brownell, Dewey, and Clay believed that Eisenhower could pull enough votes on the second ballot to win.

Two days before the balloting, General Eisenhower had what Herbert Brownell believed was an ileitis attack. "I guess General Clay and I were the only ones outside of Mrs. Eisenhower and Milton [Eisenhower] who knew about it," said Brownell. "The delegates did not know. General Eisenhower was in extreme pain in his suite there at the Blackstone. And he got up and got dressed and went out and had a press conference, and then went back to bed. It was one of the greatest performances I ever saw in my life. That was the type of thing that General Clay and I had to make decisions on—as to how it should be handled."

Clay recognized that Eisenhower was ill at the convention but did not think it was serious. "I'd known General Eisenhower for a long time, and he had some very bad eating habits. And he could get some very acute stomach pains. Maybe it was a forerunner of the ileitis attack, but I doubt it. Obviously, his nerves were at a very high tension. He was keeping what for him were very strange hours. I think it was just a stomach cramp. I never attached any importance to it. That's par for that type and kind of situation."

Q: Did Eisenhower's victory on the first ballot come as a surprise?

CLAY: No, although it was very close. The New York vote came as a surprise. When Governor Dewey answered the roll call and announced that New York was voting ninety-two for Eisenhower and only four for Taft, we knew we had won. [The Taft forces had claimed they would get eighteen votes in New York.] Brownell immediately sent word to the floor not to hold anything back. We were going for broke on the first ballot. Sherman Adams, who was our floor manager, got word to Warren Burger in the Minnesota delegation, and Minnesota switched from Stassen to Eisenhower and that put us over the top. General Eisenhower always gave the credit to Stassen, but Stassen tried to stop the shift until the very end. It was Warren Burger and some others who took the Minnesota delegation to Eisenhower.

Q: And California?

CLAY: We didn't know what California would do. We knew Senator Nixon was for us, but Senator [William] Knowland was for Taft. All we wanted was for Governor Warren to stay in and not release his votes on the first ballot. We were more concerned about denying the California vote to Taft than getting it ourselves.

Q: Did you watch the roll call with General Eisenhower?

CLAY: Yes. Herb Brownell and Milton [Eisenhower] were there too. Mrs. Eisenhower was lying down in the bedroom. She was not feeling well.

Q: Did General Eisenhower follow the count closely?

CLAY: No, surprisingly. I think he was more confident than anyone in the room. Or less concerned—let's put it that way. Because Brownell and I were terribly concerned, particularly when we got down to Wisconsin [on the roll call] and we were still not over the top, and we had thrown in all of our reserve strength. Then Minnesota switched and everything was fine.

"We were all sitting around in Ike's room at the Blackstone. It was a period of great tension for all of us. But General Eisenhower, at least outwardly, displayed very little concern. I think when Minnesota broke, Brownell and I hugged each other before we even congratulated General Eisenhower. But within five or ten minutes he made the decision that he was going across the street [to the Hilton] and see Senator Taft. That was his decision—nobody suggested it to him. And Brownell and I went with him.

"Actually, Senator Taft could not have been more gracious. And neither could General Eisenhower. As far as those two were concerned, it was a gracious meeting. Around the Taft camp, there was an air of tremendous disappointment, even some bitterness. But not between Taft and Eisenhower.

"By that time, there was a tremendous crush [in the hotel]. Everybody wanted to see the new nominee. We went down the back elevators. The lobbies of both hotels were jammed. And we really just had to fight our way through. I'm not even sure we had much of a police escort, because this was all decided on the spur of the moment and no time was wasted. There was no Secret Service escort in those days."

According to Brownell, "General Eisenhower was completely flabbergasted by the whole process. He'd never seen anything like it. He didn't know how we knew what was going to happen. So Clay and I were the first ones to celebrate [when Minnesota switched], and then we went over to shake hands with Eisenhower. He said, 'That was an awfully close call, wasn't it?'

"But Eisenhower was certainly the calmest person in the room. I never could understand how he didn't have some feelings inside of him, but he was either an awfully good actor or else he was awfully calm. Of course, that's one thing when you're managing a presidential campaign: you can't let the candidate know how close it may be, because the candidate has to concentrate on public relations and problems of that kind. It would be very distracting to him to know all of the headaches that you have in dealing with the various state delegations—every one of which has a selfish point of view and a different motive for acting as they do."

Aside from the nomination of General Eisenhower, it was the 1952 Republican convention in Chicago that chose Richard Nixon to be Ike's running mate and catapulted him to national office. I asked General Clay how Nixon was selected. Clay responded that: "General Eisenhower did not want to dictate whom he wanted for Vice President. He did say that he wanted a young man who could attract young people, who was a veteran, and there weren't very many who fitted his description."

In fact, Nixon was selected as Ike's running mate by Brownell, Clay, and Dewey. As Brownell recalls, "We had dinner the evening before with General Eisenhower in his suite in the Blackstone. I told him that we would have to select the Vice President the next day and that we would like to get his ideas. Eisenhower was clearly surprised, and he said, 'Well, I thought the convention had to do that. I didn't realize that that was for me to decide.'

"For old political pros, that was quite a shocker. General Eisenhower genuinely didn't realize that the choice was up to him. I said, 'Yes, sir, General, that is true insofar as the balloting is concerned, but I am sure that the delegates will look to you exclusively for a recommendation.'

"Well, Eisenhower thought about that for a while, and it seemed to satisfy him. So I said that if he would give us his choice, I would convey it to the key leaders of the party—that he wouldn't have to bother about the mechanics. That we would see that the selection was done smoothly at the convention.

"So General Eisenhower went over a list of people. He mentioned the people he had confidence in, mostly businesspeople—the president of General Electric [Charles Wilson], the president of American Airlines [C. R. Smith]—that sort of thing. People who Eisenhower believed had great executive ability. And so I said, 'General, these are all fine men, and I'm sure they would make excellent Vice Presidents, but we really need a name that would be recognizable to the average delegate on the floor, someone they can relate to.'

"Eisenhower nodded, and so I kept talking. I told him what I thought the key principles were: In view of his [Eisenhower's] age, we wanted a young man. We hopefully wanted someone from the West, someone with political experience, to balance the ticket. I went over the necessary qualifications for a Vice President, and I said that General Clay and Governor Dewey and I had talked it over and that, unless he expressed a preference otherwise, we would recommend Senator Nixon of California to him. He thought for a moment, said he had met Senator Nixon, and that he would be guided by our advice. Then he told us to clear Nixon's name with the other leaders of the party. And that was it.

"Well, we had already called a meeting for the next day in my office. Both General Clay and Governor Dewey attended. We had selected ahead of time the people we felt were entitled to be there. There were about twenty people. I opened the meeting as chairman, and I said that if anybody considered themselves a candidate for Vice President, they should absent themselves from the discussion. Well, when you've got a group of politicians together to determine a Vice President and ask them if they want to stay or get out on the remote chance that they might be considered if they got out, nobody left. And this really left only Nixon. Lodge was there. And he didn't leave.

"We discussed various candidates for a while. Somebody [Senator H. Alexander Smith of New Jersey] wanted to offer the nomination to Taft. We all thought that he wouldn't take it, but that he was entitled to the offer, so somebody was sent out to make the suggestion to him. And as we suspected, he wasn't interested. Taft suggested that we consider Senator [Everett] Dirksen of Illinois, but that was impossible because of his vicious attack at the convention on Governor Dewey. Then, as the discussion drifted on, several other names were mentioned but fell flat; then Governor Dewey mentioned Nixon, and it soon became unanimous. I went back into my office with Clay and Dewey to call Nixon and tell him. I have a photograph of that. And Clay and Dewey are listening on the phone with me."

Nixon's selection was not the product of an accidental coin flip. Though he did not fully realize it at the time, Nixon was crucial to Eisenhower's convention strategy. California had seventy delegates committed to Governor Earl Warren on the first ballot—enough to throw the convention either way. No one knew what Governor Warren would do, and Taft had powerful supporters in California, including Senator Knowland, the Republican leader in the Senate. Nixon became Ike's "fifth column," assigned to undermine Warren and lead a second-ballot move to Eisenhower. As Lodge recalled, "We had some very practical thoughts about Nixon. We needed a counter to Taft in California, and Nixon was it. It was Nixon's role to keep California from going to Taft. I approached him on the Senate floor, well before the convention, and asked him if he would be interested in the vice presidency. 'Who wouldn't?' he said. Not very elegant, but that's what he said."

But it was Clay and Dewey who cut the deal with Nixon. After Lodge's overture, Dewey invited Nixon to be the principal speaker at the annual GOP fund-raising dinner in New York. Afterward he invited Nixon up to his suite for a nightcap, along with Clay and Brownell. When Dewey suggested the vice presidency, Nixon indicated he would be "greatly honored."

Clay's recollection of the meeting differs, but not significantly. "We indicated to Mr. Nixon the type and kind of person that General Eisenhower would want in government. But I don't think we were trying to distinguish between a Cabinet post or the vice presidency. In other words, we made no commitment."

Q: But you were for him?

CLAY: Well, he had a fine name among most Republicans as a result of the disclosures in the Alger Hiss–Whittaker Chambers case. He was from a critical area: California. He was young, vigorous, and appealing. I was very much for him. So were Dewey and Brownell. There is no question as far as Dewey, Brownell, and Clay were concerned, that he was the man we wanted, and we knew General Eisenhower considered him acceptable.

When Brownell called Nixon with the news of his selection, Nixon's close friend William Rogers was present. Rogers reports that Nixon was "surprised as hell," leading Dewey's biographer to report that Nixon was apparently as good an actor as he was a politician. At that point in the convention, Dewey and Brownell were in total control, and Nixon's name was ratified by acclamation.

Q: Did you take an active role in the campaign itself?

CLAY: Not much. Obviously, I was raising money and that sort of thing, but I did not participate in the campaign because I would have been of no value to it. Don't forget, I was still running the Continental

Can Company, Governor Dewey was governor of New York, and Herb Brownell was busy in his law practice [at Lord, Day, and Lord]. So we basically left it to Sherman Adams, Tom Stephens [later President Eisenhower's appointments secretary], and Leonard Hall. And Lodge. Major problems would come back to us in New York, but the day-to-day details we left to Adams and Stephens.

Q: And your relations with Senator Taft?

CLAY: Very fine. As a matter of fact, right after the convention he went up into the Thousand Islands [on the St. Lawrence River] for a vacation, and I called him on the telephone to say how much General Eisenhower hoped he could count on him for advice and consultation. And he was very warm, very friendly. He did all he could. And that was a lot.

Q: Was General Eisenhower an active, vigorous campaigner?

CLAY: Yes and no. He got on that train and went all across the country making appearance after appearance. And he got better at it every day. When he first started out at Abilene, he wasn't very good at it. But he improved every day. Amongst other things, he really liked people, and I think people recognized it. I think this was his great contribution: his ability to make people know that he liked them.

Q: In his memoirs, General Eisenhower seemed offended that people were for *him* rather than what he stood for.

CLAY: Ha! I think this was true right to the end. The American people took him for what they wanted Americans to be. I don't think they really cared much about what he stood for. They felt he was honest and decent and upright. Which he was.

"Most of Eisenhower's campaign staff had been with Governor Dewey in New York—Leonard Hall, Jim Haggerty, Tom Stephens. Haggerty later became his press secretary, and Stephens his appointments secretary. They went with Eisenhower on the campaign train. They were professionals. Very astute. Sherman Adams became the campaign manager because of the fine work he had done at Chicago."

Q: Could you explain why General Eisenhower did not come to General Marshall's defense during the campaign, after he had been attacked [as "an eager front man for traitors" and "a living lie"] by Senator William Jenner [R., Indiana] and Senator McCarthy [R., Wisconsin]?

CLAY: In my view, the most unfortunate aspect of that episode was a remark that President Truman made which led to a great deal of unnecessary bitterness between him and General Eisenhower. It was very difficult for General Eisenhower to forgive President Truman. Here was the question of Senator Jenner being opposed to General Marshall and attacking him bitterly while running for re-election as a Republican in a state where General Eisenhower was scheduled to appear at a rally. The question was whether the Jenner people should have been allowed to appear at the rally. But I don't know what you could have done to prevent them from attending. You would really have created a chasm in the Republican Party. Jenner was the candidate of the Republican Party in Indiana.

"The question came all the way back to us in New York. And we felt that Eisenhower had to do it: that he had to appear with Jenner. Nobody would have thought anything about it if President Truman hadn't grabbed onto it. Mr. Truman was doing that politically, but he was also doing that out of an almost unbelievable worship that he had for General Marshall. But General Marshall apparently took no offense. Later he stood in the stands with General Eisenhower during the inaugural review.

"Of course, General Eisenhower couldn't understand President Truman's partisanship, because he wasn't partisan himself. He took what Mr. Truman was doing for political reasons as a personal attack. I don't think President Truman ever intended it that way, but it certainly created a lot of unnecessary bad feeling."

Clay's elliptical defense of Eisenhower suggests that he did not consider the former Secretary of State immune from sharp partisan attack. Marshall was no icon for Clay, and though he personally detested Jenner and McCarthy, his long exposure to political life had left him with an exceedingly thick skin when it came to personal abuse. Equally important, the concern of the Eisenhower strategists at that moment was to get Taft's disgruntled supporters back into the fight (most had been sitting on their hands since the convention). To snub Jenner and his supporters seemed akin to shooting yourself in the foot with the old guard. (Later, in the 1970s, Clay headed the fund-raising efforts for the Marshall Library at VMI, and he left his personal papers to the Marshall Foundation after his death.)

The most serious issue to erupt during the 1952 campaign was the revelation by the New York *Post,* on September 16, of a secret $18,000 expense fund maintained by Senator Nixon and raised from contributions by wealthy Californians. The fund was used by Nixon to pay for office expenses, Christmas cards, travel, and related items that exceeded Nixon's senatorial allowance. The story was initially dismissed by the Eisenhower campaign as Democratic smear tactics, but the "Nixon Fund" quickly took on a life of its own. When the New York *Herald Tribune* and *The Washington Post* called for Nixon's repudiation, the issue assumed crisis proportions. Clay and Dewey were concerned with controlling the damage, and both were appalled that Nixon's indiscretion might wreck the ticket. Eisenhower's principal speechwriter, Emmet John Hughes, reports that Clay was particularly "angry and vehement, for he felt a particular responsibility—and disenchantment—as one who had urged upon Eisenhower . . . the choice of Nixon as his running mate."

In some respects, Clay and Dewey were the financial conscience of the Eisenhower campaign. Despite their intense competitiveness, both were instinctively repelled by anything that smacked of personal impropriety. And in their personal conversations, both thought that Nixon should be jettisoned. "I never spoke to Mr. Nixon about it," said Clay. "Governor Dewey did speak to him, but I personally don't know whether Governor Dewey asked him to withdraw. It is possible that he did. I've always been accused of suggesting that Mr. Nixon withdraw. The only thing that I did was to call General Eisenhower. There were no telephones on board. We got word to the train somehow, and General Eisenhower got off the train at some way station [Jefferson City, Missouri], and talked to me from a phone booth. And I asked him not to say anything or issue any statement [about Nixon]. I said, 'Herb Brownell is on his way to Cincinnati to sit down with you and to dope out the right strategy.' And to please say nothing until he had talked to Herb Brownell. And it was that night in Cincinnati that General Eisenhower agreed not to make any decision until Mr. Nixon's [television] speech. Which turned out to be the proper strategy."

Eisenhower clearly shared Clay's initial displeasure at the disclosure of the Nixon Fund and was deeply distressed at the political damage it might cause. That view was shared by virtually all who accompanied Eisenhower on his campaign train. (California's Senator Knowland was frequently mentioned as a possible replacement.) But Eisenhower had agreed to provide Nixon with thirty minutes of television time to tell his side of the story, and the Republican National Committee dutifully purchased it for $75,000. Nixon's speech was to be on Tuesday night. Brownell met with Eisenhower in Cincinnati on Monday.

Brownell recalls that his meeting with Eisenhower "was a long one. It ended somewhere around midnight. At the conclusion, Eisenhower asked me to join the campaign officially—which I did. But in our discussion, I urged General Eisenhower not to ask for Nixon's resignation, but to wait for his speech. And that unless something unexpected developed, he should ask Nixon to stay on the ticket. By contrast, I think both General Clay and Governor Dewey may have wanted to ask Nixon to get off the ticket. But I had come to the conclusion that it would cause too much confusion. We would appear indecisive. So I urged General Eisenhower to wait."

Nixon's television defense was one of the most remarkable speeches in American political history. By turns maudlin and moving, it triggered an outpouring of support that ensured Nixon's survival. "I watched Nixon's speech at home on television," said Clay. "I thought it was so corny that it would be an immediate flop. I went downstairs to get a newspaper. I found the elevator man was crying and the doorman was crying, and I knew then that I was wrong."

When the votes were counted on election day, Eisenhower had easily defeated Adlai Stevenson. Brownell, Clay, and Dewey had been correct. The struggle against Taft for the nomination had been the most difficult part. By mid-October, it had become clear that the GOP was on its way to a smashing victory—fueled by public dissatisfaction with the war in Korea, allegations of Communist infiltration at home, and corruption in high places: K^1C^2 in the formulation of Republican stalwart Karl Mundt of South Dakota. When the votes were tallied, Eisenhower had carried all but nine states and defeated Stevenson 442 to 89 in the Electoral College. Eisenhower's coattails carried the GOP to control of both the House and the Senate: the last time the Republicans would control the House in the twentieth century.

Eisenhower departed immediately for two weeks of relaxation and recuperation at his favorite resort, the Augusta National Golf Club. He entrusted Clay and Brownell with the responsibility of putting together the Administration that would take office on January 20. "We were told to consult with a representative of the Taft forces [Thomas Coleman, GOP national committeeman from Wisconsin], but he wasn't much interested and never showed up. So Brownell and I were a committee of two," said Clay.

Q: What instructions did General Eisenhower give you and Brownell? What type of person did he say he was looking for?
CLAY: He didn't give me any [instructions]. I think he had enough confidence in our judgment to know that we were going to try to find men of high caliber. After all, he didn't give us the power of decision: ours was the power of recommendation. And we recommended to him several names for almost every office, stating our reasons and our preferences. In each case, he made the final decision.

The first member of the new Eisenhower team turned out to be Brownell himself, although formal announcement of Brownell's appointment was not made until several weeks later. The second was Joseph Dodge to be director of the Bureau of the Budget (as the Office of Management and Budget was then styled). Dodge, who was president of the Detroit Bank, had worked with Clay in Army Service Forces in World War II and later served as financial adviser to Clay in Germany and then to MacArthur in Japan. "We invited Mr. Dodge to come down to New York the night of the election and to be there when the election was over," said Clay. "And General Eisenhower asked him that night to become head of the Budget. Because the first thing a President has to do is get control of his budget."

The job of White House Chief of Staff was equally critical. Clay had recommended Brownell to Eisenhower, and on the afternoon of election day, Ike invited Brownell up to Columbia for a chat. "He was living at the President's home up on Morningside Heights," said Brownell. "When I got there, he was up on the top floor painting, which I had never seen a candidate do on election day. And General Eisenhower said, 'How do we start?'

"I said, 'Well, you're going to be elected easily.' So we made arrangements for him to go down to [election headquarters at] the Commodore and receive the returns that night. Then he turned to me and told me how he intended to set up the White House staff. He'd evidently been doing quite a bit of thinking about it. And he said he wanted me to become chief of staff. I told him that my principal interest in life was to be a lawyer and I wanted to continue in the law.

So he went on painting, and finally he turned around and said, 'You want to be a lawyer?'

"I said, 'Yes.'

"He said, 'How about being Attorney General?'

"So I was quite overwhelmed by that. I said, 'It certainly meets my job description. The only problem would be financial.'

"I went back to my office to see how much money I had. And I called up General Clay before I told my wife. I told him what had happened and asked him how much it would cost me to live in Washington. He was delighted, and he told me exactly. Well, I figured I had just enough to last four years. Then I went home and talked to my wife, and she agreed that I should take it. So I went back up to Columbia and told General Eisenhower that I would take it."

According to Clay, Brownell had insisted throughout the campaign that he did not want to go into the government. But when General Eisenhower asked, he agreed.

Q: Did you consider joining the Administration?

CLAY: Nope. No. As a matter of fact, I had a commitment from General Eisenhower that he wouldn't ask me. This was for several reasons. First, I told him, "I don't believe that you should have Army officers in prominent positions in your Administration." To some degree, he violated that by letting Bedell Smith be the Under Secretary of State. But that was at Foster Dulles's earnest solicitation.

" 'A second reason is that I think I can be of more service to you if I'm not in your Administration. You're going to need somebody that you can feel free to call on to do things that you couldn't feel free to do if he was working for you. And I think in this way I can probably be more helpful to you than otherwise.

" 'In the third place, I don't want it even to be thought that I worked for you in this election because I was looking for public office.' "

The most important Cabinet post to be filled was that of Secretary of State. John Foster Dulles was the obvious choice. "We were already committed to Dulles," Clay recalled, "and we scarcely discussed any other candidates. Certainly, no serious consideration was given to anyone else. I believe that [British Foreign Secretary] Anthony Eden was coming to New York, and we wanted to have that appointment settled and in place."

Q: And your earlier differences with Mr. Dulles?
CLAY: We had no differences by that point. That was all water under the bridge.

Despite Clay's assurance, tangential evidence suggests that both he and Eisenhower leaned initially toward their old friend John J. McCloy as Secretary of State. But McCloy's Republican credentials were somewhat in doubt (he had worked too long for FDR and Truman), and Brownell, strongly supported by Dewey, urged that he be bypassed, at least initially, in favor of Dulles. Brownell and Dewey accurately pointed out that Dulles had helped to bring the Republican Party back from its isolationist stance and into the twentieth century, and that it was important that his service be recognized. Later, if Ike wished to change, he could do so. Both Clay and Eisenhower immediately accepted the wisdom of that argument.

The remaining Cabinet selections were made while the President-elect was in Georgia. Clay and Brownell flew down to Augusta on Sunday, November 9, in a Continental Can Company plane, and landed at a private airstrip to avoid reporters. Clay was attending a regular meeting of the blue-ribbon Business Advisory Council at Sea Island, while Brownell joined Ike at Augusta. At Sea Island, Clay met informally with the leaders of corporate America. Names of possible appointees were discussed freely. "I remember having a drink with Lucius and Sidney Weinberg," said Paul Cabot, head of the First Boston Corporation. "We were suggesting names for various Cabinet positions, and Lucius had a definite opinion about everyone: Good or bad. Yes or no. No qualification whatever. Finally, I blew up. I said, 'Jesus Christ, Lucius, there's a word "maybe" in the English language. Don't you ever use it?' "

After Dulles's selection as Secretary of State and Brownell as Attorney General, the two principal positions in Eisenhower's Cabinet to be filled were Defense and Treasury. Clay quickly seized on two fellow members of the Business Advisory Council who were with him at Sea Island. For Secretary of Defense, Clay tapped Charles E. Wilson ("the other Wilson"), the bluff, ebullient head of General Motors, rumored to be the highest-paid executive in America in 1952 at $201,000 a year. "President Eisenhower had thought for a while of giving it to the chairman of Chrysler [Kaufman T. Keller]," said Clay. "And while I thought very well of him, I said [to President Eisenhower], 'If you are going to go to the business world for the Secretary of Defense, why not go to the biggest business we have?' That seemed to make sense to him, so that's why we went to Mr. Wilson. We felt that Defense was probably the most difficult administrative job in government, and here was the man with certainly as wide an administrative experience as any man in the United States. As a result of the Defense reorganization [in 1947], we had created this huge department, and it seemed to me that its first need was to be established on a sound administrative basis. Which it had not been up to that time. That may not have been the right decision, but in spite of all the things that happened, I think Mr. Wilson set up a pretty fair administrative structure in the Defense Department."

Q: And you approached Mr. Wilson?

CLAY: Yes. We were all down at Sea Island. Mr. Wilson asked for a few hours to think it over, and I asked him to treat the offer as extremely confidential, because if he did not accept we did not want it to be known, because this makes whomever you ask next look like he was second choice.

Q: And Treasury?

CLAY: After I talked to Mr. Wilson, I went after Mr. [George M.] Humphrey, who was president of M. A. Hanna [& Company] in Cleveland [a large conglomerate involved in iron and steel production, banking, and plastics]. Mr. Humphrey may have been suggested by Sidney Weinberg. Certainly Mr. Weinberg thought highly of him, as did I. Mr. Humphrey was a man who had a great deal of experience in the financial world. He was both a lawyer and a financier. And he looked awfully good to me.

"I had met Mr. Humphrey when I was in Germany. He had been appointed by President Truman [in 1948] to look into the reparations question. And we were in considerable disagreement at that time. But I formed a great respect for his fairness and his ability. It was not because we were operating on the same wavelengths. We were not. He wanted to cancel all reparations. It did not seem to me that such a course was consistent with the commitments we had made when we founded the bizonal and, later, trizonal governments. And he couldn't understand that.

"In any event, he said he wanted to think about the offer as well, and, just as with Mr. Wilson, I asked him to treat it confidentially. A few hours later, I went back to Mr. Wilson's room, and to my surprise I found Mr. Humphrey sitting there. Mr. Wilson had immediately asked Mr. Humphrey for his advice. Mr. Humphrey did not disclose to Mr. Wilson that he had been asked to become Secretary of the Treasury. Unlike Mr. Wilson, he treated [the offer] as it should have been treated. Shortly thereafter, Mr. Wilson told me he would accept, and then, somewhat later, Mr. Humphrey did too."

Q: Did you make a mistake recommending Mr. Wilson for Defense?

CLAY: I think that Mr. Wilson was a hell of a lot better as Secretary than his successor from Ford [Robert McNamara]. I had known him when he was running General Motors, and I had high respect for him and his executive ability. I think he brought in good people to help him.

"I think he made a serious mistake in not becoming involved in foreign policy. He saw the Defense Department primarily as a management job. He didn't seem to appreciate fully that the armed services are an instrument of foreign policy, or that our force structure must reflect our foreign policy.

"Also, I've always believed that he was never quite able to live down his maladroitness with his tongue when he appeared at his confirmation hearings.* I think he should have sold his stock in General Motors. Of course, it represented quite a loss to him [to have to sell at that time]—several million dollars. And at that point, I think you stop and think a little bit about what you are giving up."

Q: General Eisenhower did not know either Mr. Wilson or Mr. Humphrey?

CLAY: I believe that is correct. But that was not too important. In the

* When asked about possible conflict of interest, Wilson replied, "I cannot conceive of [a conflict] because for years I thought what was good for our country was good for General Motors, and vice versa." It was that seeming insensitivity that set the tone for Wilson's tenure as Secretary of Defense, many people replaying the quote as "What's good for General Motors is good for our country."

Army, you rarely know the people you're assigned to work with beforehand. General Eisenhower was remarkably gifted in bringing people from a variety of backgrounds together and forging them into a successful team. In some respects, that may have been his greatest talent. What he wanted were people who were exceedingly competent and on whom he could rely to run their departments. And he relied on us, Mr. Brownell and me, to assemble them. We didn't go into this extended search in which you have elaborate committees and staff people play such an important role. Brownell and I knew most of these people first-hand. We made some mistakes but, in retrospect, I think the Eisenhower administration looks very good.

Q: And the other Cabinet posts?

CLAY: Arthur Summerfield of Michigan had become national chairman of the Republican Party, so he seemed a natural to become Postmaster General. Traditionally, that post was held by the party chairman, Mr. [James] Farley or Mr. [Robert] Hannegan.

"We picked Governor [Douglas] McKay of Oregon to be Secretary of Interior. Our first choice had been Governor Arthur Langley of Washington, but he had just been elected to a new four-year term, and he declined. We recommended Ezra Taft Benson for Agriculture. We considered both Congressman [Clifford] Hope and Senator [Frank] Carlson of Kansas, but we wanted someone from further west. Benson was from Utah, he was not too partisan, and he had a record of agricultural reform. He was also strongly recommended by Senator Taft. Neither Brownell nor I knew him, but we thought it was a good idea for party unity to have at least one [person] recommended by Taft in the Cabinet. Benson was also one of the twelve elders of the Mormon Church, and I think President Eisenhower rather liked that. And, overall, I think Benson did a pretty good job.

"The most difficult post was Labor. We were thinking about appearances at that point, and we wanted a little more diversity. If possible, we wanted someone from the AFL. Finally, someone recommended Martin Durkin, who was president of the plumbers and steamfitters union. He was a Democrat, a Catholic, and he had a good record. We thought it was a good idea to have a Catholic in the Cabinet. But it was a tragic mistake. He had a brain tumor, and was never able to function effectively. And he and General Eisenhower simply did not hit it off. He resigned during the first year, and was replaced by James P. Mitchell, who had headed our section on labor relations in Army Service Forces during the war and who proved to be an excellent appointment."

Q: Didn't Harold Stassen of Minnesota want to be Secretary of Labor?

CLAY: He was never in our minds. Mr. Stassen was appointed later by President Eisenhower to be on the White House staff, but I assure you it was not on my recommendation.

Q: Were the other Cabinet recommendations made by you or Mr. Brownell?

CLAY: They were made by both of us. We never had any disagreements. We trusted one another's judgment. Sometimes he knew people in one area, sometimes I did. But there was never any friction. Never.

Q: Were you consulted by President Eisenhower on the war in Korea?

CLAY: Only in a very general way. But if we learned any lesson from the Korean War, we should have learned that limited war makes no sense. [General] Max Taylor sold this [doctrine of limited war] to the Kennedys, and they bought it as something they thought would be less risky. General Eisenhower did not believe in limited war. When he came into office, I think the reason the Korean War ended was that the Russians and Chinese were not at all sure that he would not use nuclear weapons to bring it to an end. And so they agreed to an armistice. One of the reasons Eisenhower was so successful in avoiding war was that he had made up his mind that there were certain circumstances under which he would use nuclear weapons. I'm not sure they were fully defined in his own mind. But he wasn't going to get involved in fighting a ground war in Asia. Period. And if we were going to fight there, he was going to use nuclear bombs if necessary. And I believe the Russians understood that. They thought he would. And so I think General Eisenhower, with all of the military decisions he had made, knew what he would do. He was not reckless. He rejected advice that he use nuclear weapons at Dien Bien Phu. But he always kept that possibility open. And he was therefore willing to have a smaller defense establishment than we've been willing to do ever since.

As soon as Eisenhower's Cabinet was picked, Clay began to put some distance between himself and the President-elect. He did not accompany Ike to Korea and after the inauguration made it a practice never to call the White House. If Eisenhower wished to consult Clay—which he did from time to time—Clay was invited to the family quarters "after duty hours," or to join the President on a fishing trip to Colorado, or to have breakfast in the White House.

"Ike and Lucius were very, very close," said GOP Chairman Leonard Hall. "They understood each other instinctively. Not only had they worked together for many years, but they spoke the same language. Not just Army lingo. They were on the same wavelength. There was an unspoken rapport between them. When Ike had a serious problem, he talked to Lucius. Ike gave him a free hand to pick the Cabinet. He trusted Lucius's judgment. And Lucius picked his conferees in the business world. He didn't consult with the [Republican] National Committee. He and Brownell sent the names over to us after the selections had been made, but it was only a courtesy. They didn't ask for our advice; they told us these were the Cabinet appointees. And it was the same thing at the sub-Cabinet level. Eisenhower delegated full authority to his Cabinet members to staff their own departments. The National Committee was not involved.

"But, strange as it may sound, we politicians always got along with Clay. Neither he nor Ike were politicians. But we could communicate with Clay. Whenever we wanted something from General Eisenhower—whenever we would want him to do something of a political nature—and it was going to be difficult to convince him, we always brought Lucius in. 'Sure, I'll ask him,' Clay would say. 'The most he can do is throw me out of his office. He's done that before.' "

Tom Stephens, Eisenhower's appointments secretary, added that "Clay was one of the very few people who would disagree with Eisenhower. Politely, but firmly. Very few Cabinet members could do that, not even Dulles. 'Yes sir.' 'No sir.' They were in the chain of command, and they were good at their jobs. But Clay, by Christ, if he disagreed with the President, he would tell him so. And Eisenhower respected that.

"On the other hand, Lucius wasn't a fellow who would drop by to see the President very much," said Stephens. "Not that he didn't want to. But he was busy, and he realized that the President of the United States was busy too. Take a guy like George Allen. He was there every week. He was a bridge player. It was recreation for the President. But Lucius wasn't a bridge player."

Clay made an exception to his policy of not calling the White

House when he thought the situation sufficiently serious. "I was one of the few who talked frankly to the general," said Clay. "And the general always appreciated it, although he used to get mad as hell sometimes. But he'd get over it very quickly. Then he'd say, 'You're the only one around here who gives me hell.' But I wouldn't have been useful to him any other way. And I didn't want anything. There wasn't a damn thing that he could give me, so I didn't have any problems.

"Don't forget that when I was his deputy for military government, we were governing an entire country. We were trying to rebuild a government in an occupied country where there had been a complete collapse of government. So this business of talking over a full range of governmental issues was something that had become rather a habit with us."

One area where Clay intervened was to arouse Eisenhower to the dangers of the 1953 Bricker Amendment to the Constitution—a long-treasured scheme by states'-rights conservatives to emasculate the President's powers in foreign affairs. Sponsored by Senator John Bricker of Ohio, a white-thatched Republican conservative, the Bricker Amendment would have given Congress the power to annul executive agreements made by the President with foreign countries. An equally controversial provision specified that treaties could not become law in the United States without additional congressional legislation to bring them into effect. The move for the amendment was fueled partially by the bitter reaction to wartime agreements made by President Roosevelt with Churchill and Stalin, particularly the agreement at Yalta concerning the future of Eastern Europe; and partially by states'-rights reaction to a series of Supreme Court decisions upholding the supremacy of international agreements over state laws. When the amendment was initially introduced by Senator Bricker in January 1953, sixty-two senators were listed as co-sponsors, and a groundswell of public support made passage appear imminent. The American Bar Association, the U.S. Chamber of Commerce, the Veterans of Foreign Wars (VFW), and the American Legion, not to mention the Daughters of the American Revolution, rallied to the cause. With the notable exception of *The Washington Post* and *The New York Times,* most of the press did as well. Even General Eisenhower appeared unconcerned, although it would be his powers as President that would be curtailed.

Secretary of State Dulles alerted Eisenhower to the danger, but as late as December 1953, Ike appeared undecided. At first he expressed some sympathy for what the supporters of the Bricker Amendment intended. Eisenhower had a civics-textbook view of American government. He genuinely believed that Congress, not the President, was the policy-making arm, and he thought that FDR and Truman had pressed presidential powers too far. After Dulles's repeated warnings, he sought unsuccessfully to cajole Bricker into a compromise. That too proved to be a hesitant signal, since Bricker assumed Eisenhower's efforts at conciliation meant that he supported the plan. In fact, even after Ike became concerned about the potential dangers of the amendment, he hesitated to risk an open break with Bricker and his supporters in the GOP. "Can't we find a way to avert a head-on collision over this darn thing?" he plaintively asked his Cabinet earlier that autumn. The problem was that only the aroused opposition of Eisenhower himself could defeat the amendment, and Ike was reluctant to intervene.

Clay followed the public debate closely. "I was opposed to the restrictions it imposed on the President," said Clay. "I thought it would be ruinous to our conduct of foreign policy. But at that point, I was watching from the sidelines. The White House staff always got a little edgy whenever I got involved, so I tried to be very careful not to get involved.

"In any event, one day late in 1953, John W. Davis, the distinguished constitutional lawyer [of Davis, Polk, Wardwell, Sunderland and Kiendl], called me. Davis was held in awe by most of the legal profession. I knew him, but not well. He had been the Democratic nominee for President in 1924 against Mr. Coolidge, and I know that, had it not been for his age, General Eisenhower wanted to name him Chief Justice when Mr. [Fred M.] Vinson died [in September 1953]. Well, Mr. Davis told me how concerned he was with the Bricker Amendment and how he and Professor [Edward S.] Corwin at Princeton were organizing a committee to fight it: the Committee for Defense of the Constitution, I think it was called. And he wanted to know whether I would become co-chairman with them. And so I joined them. We set up a small staff and enlisted a broad cross-section of prominent Americans to help us. People like former Supreme Court Justice [Owen J.] Roberts, Dean Griswold at Harvard Law School, Jack McCloy, Henry Wriston, Averell Harriman, and so on. And we mounted a public campaign against the Bricker Amendment. Actually, the lawyers did most of the work.

"But very quickly we recognized that President Eisenhower was the key to this thing. So I arranged for Mr. Davis and Professor Corwin to have a private dinner with General Eisenhower in the family quarters of the White House. That was in January 1954. And it was a very good meeting. The President held a great respect for John Davis. And I think that we may have strengthened his resolution."

Whether Clay's dinner convinced Ike is unclear. But two days after meeting with Davis and Professor Corwin, the President waded into the fight with both feet. "I am unalterably opposed to the Bricker Amendment," he wrote Senate Majority Leader Knowland on January 25: "Adoption of the Bricker Amendment by the Senate would be notice to our friends as well as our enemies abroad that our country intends to withdraw from its leadership in world affairs."

But if Eisenhower was now committed, it was still an uphill struggle. The President began to lobby influential senators, while Clay intervened "with Dick Russell [of Georgia] and a few others." When the final vote was taken in the Senate on February 26, the Administration won by one vote. Sixty senators, including minority leader Lyndon Johnson, voted for an amended version of the Bricker Amendment (known as the "George substitute," named for Senator Walter F. George of Georgia). Thirty-one senators, one more than the necessary one-third, voted against. The Bricker Amendment had failed by the narrowest of margins.

The second important time Clay intervened during Eisenhower's first term was to organize the interstate highway program and steer it successfully through Congress. One of the eternal curiosities of American politics is the proclivity of "conservative" presidents to launch breathtakingly bold experiments. Franklin Roosevelt was elected in 1932 with a pledge to balance the budget and curtail federal expenditures. Within one hundred days, the New Deal had embarked on a gigantic program of Keynesian recovery. In foreign policy, it was the anti-Communist Richard Nixon who opened American contacts with China, and Ronald Reagan, the spokesman for right-wing conservatives, who improved relations with the Soviet Union. Perhaps it is not that surprising that the fiscal conservatives of the Eisenhower era launched the most massive public works project in American history and totally reshaped the transportation structure of the United States, helping, literally, to pave the way for three decades of economic expansion.

When Eisenhower terminated the Korean War, reduced the size of the military establishment, and curtailed defense expenditures, an inevitable economic downturn ensued. Arthur Burns, then head of the President's Council of Economic Advisers, Treasury Secretary Humphrey, Gabriel Hauge, and others on the White House staff urged President Eisenhower to commence a variety of domestic projects, including a massive highway program, to accelerate the economy. Eisenhower was reluctant to undertake any program that involved substantial deficit financing, but accepted the argument of his advisers that an expansion of public works activity might be useful. In particular, Eisenhower leaned toward a highway program, preferably financed by drivers' tolls, that would link America's major cities. "I had seen the superlative system of German *Autobahnen,*" said Eisenhower, "and recognized then that the United States was behind in highway construction. In the middle of the 1900's I did not want us to fall still further behind."

But Eisenhower worried about uncontrolled federal spending and was reluctant to entrust initial planning for the program to government bureaucrats. In addition, such an undertaking would require broad public and business support. A special presidential commission, composed of distinguished Americans, seemed a natural solution. Certainly, it was one Eisenhower felt comfortable with. In that context, it is not surprising that Ike turned to Clay. "Call General Clay," he told Sherman Adams, when Adams inquired about the commission's membership.

"Sherman Adams called me down [to Washington]," said Clay. "This was in August 1954. We had lunch with the President, and they were concerned about the economy. We were facing a possible recession, and he wanted to have something on the books that would enable us to move quickly if we had to go into public works. He felt that a highway program was very important. So he asked me if I would head a committee to make a study to recommend what should be done. That was the genesis of the President's Advisory Committee on a National Highway Program."

Q: You selected the committee?

CLAY: I selected the committee. If we were going to build highways, I wanted people who knew something about it. It was a small committee: Steve Bechtel of Bechtel Construction Company; Sloan Colt, the president of Bankers Trust; Bill Roberts, head of Allis-Chalmers; and Dave Beck of the Teamsters.

Q: That's a pretty loaded committee.

CLAY: Of course. That's why I picked them. They knew what the highway system was all about.

"Steve Bechtel had more experience in the construction field than anyone in America. He wasn't involved in road building, but he had a comprehensive knowledge of the construction industry. Bill Roberts built construction equipment; he knew what the problems were there. Mr. Colt was experienced in finance. We had to determine how we wanted to finance this, and so his experience was invaluable. And Dave Beck of the Teamsters certainly had an interest in highways, and he gave us labor representation. He was a damn good committee member."

Q: Did you have any difficulty getting men of that stature to serve?

CLAY: None whatever. They recognized that this was an important undertaking and they wanted to be part of it.

Q: And at the time, you were a director of General Motors?

CLAY: Yes. I also knew what highways were about and how important they were. Highways were not unpopular then. They were not disturbing the ecology. The demand from everyone was for more and better highways. The real problem was, how did you bring this demand together so that you'd have a unified system? Therefore, we came up with the interstate highway system. I know that is now under attack in some quarters. But in my opinion, it was absolutely essential to the continued growth of America.

"It was very evident that we needed better highways. We needed them for safety, to accommodate more automobiles. We needed them for defense purposes, if that should ever be necessary. Not only for moving troops and supplies, but for the evacuation of population centers in case of possible attack. And we needed them for the economy. Not just as a public works measure, but for future growth. Our road system in 1954 was simply inadequate. And it was also evident that these new and better highways should be so connected to provide routes from somewhere to somewhere. Therefore, the interstate concept. As a matter of fact, we found that this concept was already well developed within the old Bureau of Public Roads, and we built on that."

Q: In retrospect, do you have any second thoughts as to how the program might have been improved?
CLAY: In the original program, we did not include provisions for expressways through cities. That was added later. It greatly increased the cost of the program, and it is these expressways that are not very popular today. So I think we might have paid more attention to the bypassing of cities. Although, there again, a city doesn't want to be bypassed either. I'm not really sure what the answer is with relation to our big cities and the freeways. However, I am sure that the interstate system was well designed. It is proving that in the way it has served our transportation needs ever since.

On January 12, 1955, the President's Committee on Highways released its report. It called for an expenditure of $101 billion over ten years, and forty-one thousand miles of divided highways linking all U.S. cities with a population of more than fifty thousand. The public response was overwhelmingly favorable. As recommended by Clay, the interstate program represented the largest public works undertaking by the U.S. government in peacetime history. Its cloverleafs and parkways changed the face of America, and aside from the serious ecological problems that manifestly were insufficiently considered, it provided the nation with a transportation net superior to those of most other industrialized countries, including even Germany.

Clay recommended that the program be initially financed with a $20-billion bond issue at 3 percent interest. The measure (known as the Federal Aid Highway Act) passed the Senate in 1955, but lost massively in the House—largely over the question of financing (the Democrats wanted the money to come directly from the Treasury, with no bond issue). In 1956, a revised measure, paid for primarily by a 4-cent-per-gallon tax on gasoline, passed both Houses easily and was signed into law by President Eisenhower on June 29. The resulting Highway Trust Fund, supported by the gasoline tax, kept the system solvent. But as it continued to generate money into the 1970s and 1980s (at a rate of $6 billion annually), considerable clamor arose about alternative uses, particularly for urban mass transit. Clay took no part in those discussions. His task had been to design and create a national highway net. Which he had. "When something is over, it is over," Clay often said, partially anticipating Yogi Berra's *bon mot.* After the interstate program was passed by Congress, Clay had left the transportation field to others. In later years, he had mixed feelings. He was deeply committed to America's economic development, but recognized the problems the automobile created. There were no easy answers.

The Bricker Amendment controversy and the interstate highway program were exceptions. For the most part, Clay stayed away from Washington during the Eisenhower years and concentrated on running Continental Can. "I did my best to keep my relations with General Eisenhower on a completely personal basis. I didn't want to be a Colonel House [Woodrow Wilson's mentor] or a Harry Hopkins. I would have completely destroyed my friendship if I'd tried to be one. And I never had anything like that in mind."

Max Rabb, who was White House counsel during the Eisenhower years (and President Reagan's eight-year ambassador to Italy), said that if Clay had any faults it was that he did not intervene with Eisenhower as much as he should have. "That's the worst thing I could say about [Clay]. He didn't want to press anything in the White House because he thought we on the staff might resent it. In fact, he had considerable money in the bank with us. It was important that Eisenhower got word from the outside, from outside government, and Clay was one who could give it to him. Certainly there was nothing pernicious in Clay's influence. Quite the contrary. I can't recall that he ever asked for anything. And he had a certain old-school dignity about him, not a stuffed-shirt dignity. Clay was someone you could like as well as respect. And, unlike many military people, he could be flexible; he could innovate. He was a very strong man who could disguise his strength.

"An interesting little sidelight on this era," said Rabb, "is to compare the roles of General [Alfred] Gruenther, General Clay, and General Smith. They all had a different relation [with the President]. Gruenther was as sharp as he could be, but his relation with Eisenhower was purely personal. He was one of the few that would be brought in to play bridge. But he would never cross that line; he would never discuss business unless the President wanted to. Bedell was at the opposite end. He would see the President only on business, never pleasure. He would be called in only on immediate State Department matters. [Smith was Under Secretary from 1953 to 1954.] Clay was in between. He was a close personal friend of the President, but they frequently discussed business. Clay was an important part of the American community, a part of the establishment. His general advice on basic questions was important. And he had considerable influence on Eisenhower. Don't forget, Clay had become extremely successful in the business world, and Eisenhower greatly admired business success. Maybe a little more than most. But all presidents admire success.

"All three of them [Gruenther, Clay, and Smith] were dedicated to Eisenhower. He could lean on them. But they were all different. I don't recall a single incidence during that period when they were all together. And I'm sure that Bedell's appointment [as Under Secretary] came despite Clay."

But, as Rabb noted, Clay was devoted to Eisenhower—and believed deeply in his presidency. It was a personal, not a partisan, commitment. And, once again, it was Clay who levered Ike into running for re-election in 1956. "We all knew that in the final push to get General Eisenhower to commit himself, it was Lucius who would have to bell the cat," said Republican Chairman Leonard Hall.

Clay was acutely aware of Eisenhower's reluctance to run for re-election. Only with great difficulty had Brownell been able to convince Ike to remove from his Inaugural Address in 1953 a statement that he would not seek a second term. Clay also worried that Eisenhower would delay any announcement too long, and other GOP candidates would throw their hats into the ring. Clay knew Ike's style: to delay a crucial decision until the last possible moment. So Clay began the assault early. On November 18, 1954, two weeks after the congressional midterm elections, Clay called on Eisenhower for a long chat. The President recorded the conversation in his diary. "A drive to force from me a commitment that I be a candidate for the Presidency in 1956 has suddenly developed into a full-blown campaign," Ike wrote.

> Clay approached the matter circumspectly and even in roundabout fashion [said Eisenhower], but when he once got on the real purpose of his visit, he pursued his usual tactics, aimed at overpowering all opposition and at settling the matter without further question.

Eisenhower told Clay that it was wrong to focus on a single individual: the policies of progressive Republicanism were "far bigger than any one individual. Here we parted company," the President wrote.

> Clay said, "I am ready to work for you at whatever sacrifice to myself because I believe in you. I am not ready to work for anybody else that you can name." He also insisted that he and his friends needed now the assurance that I would not "pull the rug out from under them." This is exactly the phrase they used on me in 1951, and I well know how such a foot in the door can be expanded until someone has taken possession of your whole house.

Once again, Eisenhower kept his own counsel. As Clay knew all too well, Ike could not be rushed. It was one of the secrets of the President's management style: he would hold the decision in his own hands and let his supporters dangle. Perhaps even more important, Eisenhower was genuinely reluctant to run for a second term.

Clay was not disheartened. "He didn't throw me out," Clay told Leonard Hall afterward. He took that as a positive sign. For the next year, Clay waged a discreet but continual campaign to pressure Eisenhower into a commitment. It was part game and part hunt, another minuet of political courtship.

In late summer 1955, Eisenhower invited Clay to go fishing in Colorado: "easy fishing in a small stream and with full opportunity to do nothing but sleep if you want to," wrote Ike. Eisenhower said he enjoyed the opportunity "to talk over a lot of things with someone who has no axe to grind and in whose loyal friendship I have complete confidence. That is all there is to it—but you can see how important it is to me."

Clay accepted Ike's invitation, and the two spent an enjoyable week in the Rockies. But Clay's efforts to inveigle a commitment from Eisenhower underwent a severe setback in September 1955, when the President suffered a major heart attack while in Colorado.

Q: Were you with General Eisenhower in Colorado at that time?

CLAY: No. As a matter of fact, I was in the hospital having an ulcer operation. But I had been there with him for a weekend of golf. And while we were out there playing golf, I realized I was pretty sick. The fact is, I couldn't eat anything and was really sick as a dog. I got in the airplane and came home.

"It was my own fault. I never took any time for recreation over a period of ten or fifteen years. I guess that catches up to you eventually, although I didn't think so at the time. I knew I had ulcers when I got back to New York that night. I called Sidney Weinberg. I asked him if he knew the name of a stomach surgeon. I didn't even have a doctor at that time. Sidney was on the board of Columbia-Presbyterian Hospital. He called me back and said, 'A Dr. Milton Porter is on his way down to see you at your apartment.' Well, Dr. Porter came down to see me, and I said, 'I wish you'd arrange for me to go into the hospital. I've got to have an operation for ulcers.' He thought I was crazy. But after he examined me, he wanted me to come right in. I told him I had a board meeting the next day, but I'd come up right after the board meeting. Which I did. And a couple of days later, they operated on me. Took out four-fifths of my stomach. It's a rough operation, really. You feel like you've been run over by a ten-ton truck.

"It was while I was in the hospital General Eisenhower had his heart attack. I was very shocked. I went down to Tucson to recuperate, and just after I got there [Sherman] Adams called me up and said, 'Come up here to see him. He wants to see you.' So I went up. And it was quite a trip for someone in my condition."

Eisenhower's heart attack made the President more reluctant than ever to announce his candidacy for a second term. Brother Milton Eisenhower cautioned Ike against running, as did his son John, his daughter-in-law Barbara, and his old friend George Allen. Eisenhower's personal physician, Dr. Howard Snyder, and heart specialist Paul Dudley White withheld judgment. Like Clay, Eisenhower had an iron constitution. He returned from Denver's Fitzsimmons Army Hospital to Washington six weeks after his attack, and walked off the presidential airplane and down the ramp at National Airport to the cheers of an unexpected welcoming party that included all of the members of the Cabinet, the diplomatic corps, a number of senators and congressmen, and former President Herbert Hoover. Eisenhower returned to the White House and held his first full Cabinet meeting on November 22 —exactly two months from the date of the heart attack.

Still, Eisenhower made no campaign commitment. In early December 1955, GOP chairman Leonard Hall visited Eisenhower at his Gettysburg farm to discuss the nomination. "I chatted with him, and he was really low," said Hall, "the way most men are after they have heart attacks. Finally, I said to him, 'Chief, the Cabinet members have all been up here to see you, and when asked by the newspapermen whether they talked any politics with the President, they were able to say no.'

"I said, 'If I go out of here and meet these newspapermen and say I haven't talked politics with you, they'll call me a damned liar.'

"So I said, 'Let's talk about what I will say.'

"Ike said, 'Len, you go out and say what you think you should say.' That was the way he operated. Ike was a fellow who could delegate. He would give you tremendous leeway. He wanted you to take the initiative," said Hall.

"So I went out and said to the press that the ticket was going to be Ike and Dick.

"George Allen told me later that he was with the President when my statement came over the ticker. He said Ike put on a little grin and said, 'Damnit, I didn't tell Len to say that.' But that was the way Ike worked."

Eisenhower's style of broad delegation was equally apparent when Clay called on him the day after his meeting with Leonard Hall. Clay, who knew the style well, told Ike that he would soon be meeting with various groups of Republican leaders. Clay said he was going to tell these groups that if his health permitted it, Eisenhower intended to run again, that the President felt it was his duty to do so to prevent the "old crowd" from returning to the White House. Once again, Clay gave Eisenhower the opportunity to rein him in. When the President did not, Clay promptly scheduled a series of meetings, first at the Links Club on East Sixty-second Street in New York, then at Attorney General Brownell's home in Washington. Like a trusted deputy, Clay was bringing the troops into line. The meetings were attended by all of the original Eisenhower loyalists: Governor Dewey; former Governor Dan Thornton of Colorado; Paul Hoffman; William Robinson of the *Herald Tribune;* Tom Stephens; W. Alton Jones, chairman of Cities Service; Charles S. Jones, president of Richfield Oil; Fred Gurley, president of the Atchison, Topeka & Santa Fe; and other Clay associates from the business world—the financial kingpins of the GOP.

But despite the best efforts of Clay and Leonard Hall, Eisenhower still made no public announcement. It looked suspiciously like a rerun of 1952, when Ike held out at NATO. In early February, Eisenhower checked into Walter Reed Army Hospital in Washington for a series of examinations. Afterward Dr. Paul Dudley White announced that, "Medically the chances are that the President should be able to carry on an active life satisfactorily for another five to ten years." White added that if Eisenhower ran, he would vote for him. But Ike still made no commitment.

Eisenhower went from Walter Reed down to Treasury Secretary Humphrey's Georgia plantation for some quail hunting. He still made no announcement concerning his plans. He returned to the White House on February 25. Three days later, he called Clay at Continental Can, just before lunchtime. "He called me up," said Clay, "and he said, 'Please come down here for dinner tonight and spend the night with us.' Actually, Mrs. Clay and I were supposed to be in Houston, Texas, for dinner that night. We were going on a little fishing trip down in New Mexico the following day.

"Well, I knew that when he called up personally there was something involved, so I said, 'Of course, except we can't spend the night. We'll have to leave and go on to Houston.' So I called Houston, canceled out on the dinner, and told them we'd get in about five o'clock in the morning. I don't think our host ever forgave us. Anyway, this was more important. At least, I thought so.

"So we went down to the White House, and we had dinner. And after dinner we went upstairs into the front hall, which was used as the general's sitting room. And he said he was going to make the decision that night as to whether or not he was going to run again. He said he had waited until his health was all right, and he was now satisfied that there was not an immediate health problem. Obviously, he had to take that into consideration.

"He said, 'I can't get Mamie to express herself.'

"She said, 'No, I certainly am not going to say one word. It is your decision. If you don't do it and are unhappy because you didn't do it, it's got to be your unhappiness. If you do it and it breaks your health down, that has to be your decision too.' And she stuck right by that.

"Finally, he said, 'OK. I have to do it. I'll run again. I'm going to run again.'

"Then we went downstairs and saw a movie. Afterward Marjorie and I got on the plane and went on down to Houston. Now I'm not trying to say that he called me down there to help participate in his decision. I've always believed that he had already made his mind up, even though he had not told anybody, and that because of my closeness to him and the part that I had played in his first nomination, he wanted to give me the privilege of being there and knowing what he was going to do before it was announced.

"My opinion was that he had to run again, that he would have been very unhappy if he didn't, and that he would never forgive himself if he didn't. That had been my opinion all along. He knew that. There was no question in his mind where I stood. As a matter of fact, if he had not run again, I think his life would have been miserable."

The following day, February 29, 1956, President Eisenhower told a special news conference that he intended to run. "I have reached a decision," he told the press. "If the Republican National Convention asks me to run, my answer will be positive, that is, affirmative." Clay breathed a big sigh of relief.

Clay played no role at the 1956 Republican convention. Eisenhower's nomination was assured, and although Clay was decidedly unenthusiastic, Nixon appeared to have the vice presidency locked up. "I don't think there was any real animosity, but there was a group around Ike who felt Nixon shouldn't run again," said Leonard Hall. "Lucius was one of them. We met out there in San Francisco—Lucius, Herb Brownell, myself, and Tom Stephens—and Lucius was arguing that there should at least be a candidate against Nixon for the nomination."

Clay recalled talking "to two or three would-be vice presidential candidates," but said, "Nixon had it completely sewed up. I thought that unless there was a race it would be a pretty dead convention. But the only trouble was that the only man who wanted to make it a race [Harold Stassen] didn't have any votes. And I made no effort to support him."

Clay always alleged that his opposition to Nixon in 1956 was based solely on his desire to enliven the convention. It is not convincing. As old pro Leonard Hall observed, "I've been in this game a good many years, and you don't play with the vice presidency just to make the convention interesting. I would have to come to the conclusion that Clay and the others were opposed to Nixon. No one ever said, 'We don't want Nixon.' No one ever said that. But there were enough rumors, and meetings, and so forth, out of which you could draw that conclusion." That was apparently Nixon's view as well. In his book *Six*

Crises, Nixon labeled Clay with one of the worst epithets in his vocabulary. He called him a "Democrat."

When Eisenhower's second term ended, Clay and Marjorie remained on the same intimate terms with the Eisenhowers that they had known since Manila. Their visits were less frequent, but Clay was always available when Eisenhower called. By 1960, Clay had, in fact, become a Republican. But he remained lukewarm about Nixon and took no part in the 1960 election, except to raise money for the GOP campaign.

Despite Clay's prominent role in the Republican Party, his political judgments continued to be personal rather than partisan. He adored Eisenhower but never warmed to Nixon. Tom Dewey was one of his closest friends, but he admired President Truman enormously. Ernest Bevin and Ernst Reuter, the great Socialist leaders of postwar Europe, were in a class by themselves. So too was Walter Reuther, with whom Clay had worked closely during the war. Clay enjoyed Acheson and Harriman, but had little use for the isolationist right wing of the GOP. He tolerated Dulles, but worshipped Mr. Stimson. Marshall he could take or leave, depending on the circumstances: the Chief of Staff was one thing, the Secretary of State quite another. McCarthy and Jenner he despised; Harold Stassen he did not respect. All in all, a balance sheet of considerable political sophistication.

· 29 ·

Back to Berlin

> In the hierarchy of Berlin heroes, General Clay ranks two steps higher than say, Frederick the Great.
>
> Norbert Muhlen, *National Review,* 1962

THE ELECTION OF JOHN KENNEDY IN 1960 MARKED A renewed emphasis on Cold War competition. The Russians had beaten the United States into space, the *Sputnik* scare in 1957 dramatizing Soviet scientific achievement; a supersophisticated U-2 American spy plane had been shot down over the Soviet Union on the eve of the 1960 Paris summit; and Fidel Castro had launched a Communist challenge to the United States less than ninety miles from Key West. The psychological initiative in the East-West struggle appeared to have shifted. Eight years of peace, prosperity, and international stability under Eisenhower seemed to many thoughtful critics to cloak a pervasive complacency and conceal a fundamental erosion of Western power. Kennedy spearheaded the effort to revitalize America, and the 1960 election focused on alleged U.S. military deficiencies: the "missile gap" and the Eisenhower administration's excessive reliance on a strategy of "massive retaliation." To Kennedy and a new stable of defense intellectuals, that strategy left the United States no choice but surrender or nuclear annihilation.

Upon taking office, Kennedy embarked on a program to expand American conventional forces and provide a means for fighting limited wars below the nuclear threshold. Whereas Eisenhower had categorically rejected the idea of military conflict except to ensure national survival, the Kennedy team saw limited war as an essential instrument of United States policy. The Kennedy approach rested on a much more aggressive view of East-West relations. Whereas Eisenhower, and even Dulles, had been content to defend the status quo, JFK sought to regain lost ground. Cuba presented the first opportunity. And while it was true that Cuba had gone Communist while Eisenhower had been President, it was also true that Cuba was an exception. The fact was, the international situation was not as bleak as Democratic campaign rhetoric suggested.

It is true that the Russians had been first into space, but America's scientific lead was overwhelming; the "missile gap" with the Soviet Union was more apparent than real; and in the crucial struggle for Central Europe, the forces of democracy were on a roll. This was particularly true in Germany, where the Federal Republic had become the economic wonder of the world. In East Germany, by contrast, Communism creaked along, unable to establish either its political or its economic *bona fides:* a basket case of postwar exploitation. That distinction is important. Because after trying and failing to reverse the situation in Cuba with an ill-fated landing at the Bay of Pigs, the Kennedy administration succumbed to an unrelenting pessimism that colored its approach to what was, arguably, an entirely different situation in Europe.

When Clay left Germany in 1949, the Federal Republic had just been founded. Postwar recovery had just begun. The effects of currency reform and Marshall Plan aid had not yet kicked in. In an objective sense, the difference in living standards between the three Western zones and the Soviet zone was not that great: all of Germany was more or less destitute.

But the years after 1949 were years of impressive growth in West

Germany. Under Adenauer's stern tutelage, political democracy took root. The economy prospered. And refugees from the Soviet zone flocked west to participate. By 1961, some 3.5 million East Germans (18 percent of the population of the German Democratic Republic) had fled across the open border in Berlin to ask for asylum and resettlement in the Federal Republic. Those refugees helped fuel West Germany's economic miracle. For the most part, they were young professionals and skilled craftsmen: a trained German work force that could be plugged into an expanding economy. Their families provided an essential source of population growth in a society stung by wartime casualties and a low postwar birth rate. By contrast, the loss of these 3.5 million citizens exacerbated the economic retardation of East Germany. Many had been trained in East German schools and apprentice programs. Others enjoyed prewar skills, crafts, and professions. All were essential to an economy already overtaxed by large, nonproductive police and military commitments.

That was only one of East Germany's problems. Since 1945, the Soviet Union had systematically exploited its German satellite. The initial pillage by the Red Army was replaced by the massive dismantlement of plants and equipment. That yielded in time to the skimming of limitless reparations from East German current production. A top-heavy administrative structure, feckless central planning, and excessive reliance on Communist doctrine doomed individual initiative and plunged the GDR into a consumer's nightmare. Basic, everyday commodities were perpetually in short supply, and on the open market the East German mark traded at four, sometimes five, even six to one West German mark. An ill-conceived land reform in 1945, which broke up the Soviet zone's large farms into small holdings of less than ten acres, doomed agricultural economies of scale and made what had been prewar Germany's breadbasket a net importer of grain and meat. Even worse, the Communist regime, which enjoyed a certain historic legitimacy, lost whatever popular support there might have been and became a pliant tool of the Soviet occupation. In international affairs, East Germany (much more so than Poland, Hungary, or Czechoslovakia) was viewed as the illegitimate offspring of Soviet expansion, and the Western powers refused to grant it diplomatic recognition. The cumulative effect of these factors led to a pervasive psychological malaise in the GDR. Everything conspired to get worse. And as things did get worse, more and more people packed their bags and fled west. It was a vicious circle. The worse things got, the more people left; and the more people left, the worse things became. By the late 1950s, the very future of the German Democratic Republic was in peril.

Walter Ulbricht, the Communist leader of East Germany, recognized that he could do little about Soviet exploitation or Western hostility. But he could stop the outpouring of refugees through Berlin. If the border could be controlled and the population exodus curtailed, Ulbricht argued that the German Democratic Republic could find its feet. Ulbricht's preference was to eliminate the Western military presence in Berlin and bring the entire city under Communist control. But, failing that, a border closure between East and West Berlin would serve much the same purpose.

Ulbricht was a clear thinker. The situation in Berlin was anomalous: a curious relic from World War II. In 1961, the city was still technically under four-power occupation. There were two city governments: one in the three Western sectors for "West Berlin"; one in the Soviet sector for "East Berlin." But one could move about freely in the city, and the Allied presence was largely symbolic. West Berlin was effectively integrated into the Federal Republic of Germany, some 110 miles to the west, while East Berlin was the capital of the GDR. And in most respects, the two parts of the city reflected their attachments. West Berlin was a bustling, prosperous outpost of Western life, East Berlin a drab shadow of Communist inefficiency. The contrast was striking. To many observers, it exemplified the difference between East and West—between communism and democracy.

Since the blockade, West Berlin had been a beacon of hope behind the Iron Curtain: a shining symbol of the Western way of life. More important perhaps, it was also a testament to Western determination to resist Communist expansion, to stand firm in the face of Soviet threats and intimidation. Clay and the airlift had assumed mythic stature. The West Berliners relished their role as a front-line city in the struggle for democracy and trusted the Western powers, particularly the United States, to protect them.

By the same token, West Berlin was a bone in East Germany's throat. The open border between the two sections of the city allowed the citizens of the GDR to sample freely the good life in the affluent West. Many East Berliners worked in West Berlin, often in menial jobs.

But their pay in West German marks more than compensated for their apparent decline in status: a good waiter in West Berlin earned more in purchasing power than most doctors in East Berlin.

Even more serious, however, was the escape hatch that West Berlin provided. Citizens of East Germany could travel freely to East Berlin and then walk or take public transportation over to West Berlin. It was a simple matter of going crosstown. There were no systematic police controls, no customs checks, and in many places the border wasn't even marked. In that respect, Berlin was an open city. No other Communist country had to confront an open border, and the effect on East Germany was clearly catastrophic.

Once in West Berlin, the would-be refugee had only to report to one of several West German reception centers where he and his family would be processed quickly, flown out (usually that same day) to the Federal Republic, and resettled. West German citizenship was automatic. A new job, an apartment, and rapid integration into West German life was more or less assured. For the refugee, despite the wrenching emotional toll of leaving one's home and one's friends, it was a relatively simple process. And by 1961, the tide of refugees had become a flood: as many as thirty thousand East Germans were reporting monthly in West Berlin and asking for resettlement.

Quite obviously, the problem posed by the open border in Berlin was one of long standing. It did not erupt overnight. In 1958, Soviet leader Nikita Khrushchev had challenged the Western military presence in the city and demanded the immediate withdrawal of Allied troops. Eisenhower faced Khrushchev down. Isolated incidents on the access routes between West Germany and West Berlin in 1959 and 1960 reflected a growing tension, but in the end, the Eisenhower administration left office with the basic situation in Berlin unchanged.

Initially, the Kennedy administration took a pugnacious stand concerning Western rights in Berlin. During the election campaign, JFK had stoutly defended the Allied presence in the city, and Berlin's implicit role as a conduit for East German refugees. On March 10, 1961, the State Department stated unequivocally that no concessions would be made in Berlin to shore up the Communist regime in East Germany. Secretary of State Dean Rusk suggested that whatever crisis there had been since Khrushchev's 1958 ultimatum appeared to have eased.

But the optimism of the New Frontier took a heavy hit at the Bay of Pigs in early April, and Chairman Khrushchev quickly sensed an opportunity to rectify the border problem in Berlin while the United States was on the defensive. At a hastily scheduled summit meeting in Vienna, the blustery Khrushchev rattled Kennedy's nerve, threatening to conclude a separate peace treaty with East Germany which he claimed would terminate Western rights in Berlin. Kennedy and his entourage were shaken. The reality of JFK's inaugural pledge to "bear any burden" appeared to strike home. In his report to the American people on the Vienna conference, the President said that his meeting with Khrushchev not only had been "a very sober two days," but that "our most somber talks had been on Berlin." The President and his advisers, most of whom were unfamiliar with the evolution of the situation in Berlin, prepared for the worst. In some respects, it was a repeat of Washington's reaction to the events leading up to the Berlin blockade of 1948. The farther one was removed from the scene, the more exaggerated the danger became. The State Department warned the Bonn government (which was in the midst of an election campaign) against any provocative measures concerning Berlin; the President announced a quick buildup in U.S. conventional forces; the size of the military draft pool was doubled; and seventy-one Air Force reserve units were alerted for a possible call to active duty.

As Khrushchev's threats sank in, the Kennedy administration began to fear that Berlin was the flashpoint that could ignite a general nuclear war. Berlin was not a minor guerrilla conflict in some remote, far-off jungle. It was the United States and the Soviet Union in immediate confrontation. The campaign rhetoric about limited war as an instrument of policy seemed tragically naïve when a global conflagration was in the offing.

The Kennedy team, which had instinctively rejected the Eisenhower doctrine of deterrence based on massive retaliation, had been spooked. The President reread Barbara Tuchman's *The Guns of August,* a sparkling analysis of how Europe blundered into World War I. Hugh Sidey reported in *Time* magazine (which later chose JFK as the Man of the Year for 1961) that the President had become moody and withdrawn, that he often fell into deep thought in the midst of festive occasions with family and friends. Supposedly, he sat up late in the White House brooding about the dangers of war.

Suddenly, American policy on Berlin began to waffle. To the consternation of de Gaulle, Adenauer, and British Prime Minister Harold Macmillan, Washington sought to open immediate negotiations on Berlin with the Russians. While General de Gaulle disdainfully reminded Kennedy that "a calm reliance on the status quo will serve to emphasize that the war tension [concerning Berlin] is created solely by Mr. Khrushchev," the United States thrashed about for a means of settling what had now become a serious crisis. By any standard, Berlin was certainly a crisis for East Germany and the Soviet Union. It had become one for the West because of American indecision. As in 1948, Washington was mesmerized by the view that Berlin was not worth the risk of war. Senate Majority Leader Mike Mansfield (D., Montana) publicly questioned whether the United States should remain in Berlin.

To American policy-makers in 1961, the problem in Berlin quickly reduced itself to the open border between East and West. To that extent, they agreed with Khrushchev and Ulbricht. So long as East Germans could come freely into West Berlin and ask for asylum, the situation in the GDR would continue to deteriorate. A popular uprising could not be ruled out. Soviet military intervention seemed inevitable. As seen from the New Frontier, that spark could set off a nuclear holocaust as each side matched the other, tit for tat. If one pursued that logic, the answer seemed clear: allow the East Germans to close the border to West Berlin.

All summer, the stream of refugees had been increasing. The condition of East Germany's limping economy had gone from bad to worse. Elements of the housing industry reported a shortfall of 78 percent from normal production quotas. Many consumer goods were being turned out at less than a third of the required rate, and the East mark had plummeted to eight-to-one on the open market in West Berlin. On the weekend of August 6–7 alone, more than four thousand East Germans had reported to jammed reception centers in West Berlin to ask for resettlement. The Germans had an expression for it: *Torschlusspanik*—a panic to get out before the door was shut. By virtually any measure, the German Democratic Republic was coming apart, and urgent action was necessary to stop the hemorrhaging.

In late July, the Kennedy administration tipped its hand. In a nationwide television address, President Kennedy pledged U.S. determination to remain in Berlin. But he coupled that pledge with an offer "to remove any actual irritants [to the Soviet Union] in West Berlin"—a veiled reference to the refugee reception centers. More important, whenever the President referred to Berlin in his speech, he used the term "West Berlin," suggesting that the United States was concerned only with its rights in the Western sectors, that the quadripartite status of the *entire* city was being written off. Major General Albert Watson, the U.S. commander in Berlin at the time, later reported that as he listened to Kennedy's speech, he underlined *West* Berlin whenever the President mentioned it. Fourteen times, he counted. To Watson, the message was clear. Later that week, Senator J. William Fulbright, chairman of the Senate Foreign Relations Committee and a close personal friend of JFK, stated on "Meet the Press" that he didn't understand why the East Germans hadn't already sealed the border to West Berlin, since he thought they had the right to do so. When President Kennedy was asked to comment on Fulbright's remarks, he pointedly declined the opportunity to dissociate himself.

In other words, by mid-August 1961, Washington had come to the conclusion that the continued refugee exodus from East Germany was in no one's interest. It was draining the GDR and threatening to destabilize the precarious balance between East and West in Central Europe. The concomitant risk of nuclear war suggested that it was essential to allow the East Germans to close the border. The Kennedy administration's concern focused on the situation in the GDR. No one had considered the possible ramifications of a border closure on West Berlin, or on the morale and well-being of the 2.2 million Berliners who lived there. Or, for that matter, of the ultimate effect that writing off the quadripartite status of Berlin would have on European (particularly West German) confidence in American leadership. It may have been an unspoken tribute to the steadfastness of the West Berliners, but in their rush to defuse the Communist refugee problem, the Kennedy administration took their support for granted. It was a tragic oversight of youth and inexperience, and it quickly converted what had been primarily an East German and Soviet problem into a severe crisis of Western confidence. In some respects, the prestige of the United States in Western Europe has never recovered.

When the East Germans finally moved to close the border between East and West Berlin in the predawn hours of Sunday, August 13, 1961, the Allied powers were caught by tactical surprise, but little more.

Ulbricht was doing what Washington intended: East Germany was moving unilaterally to cut off the flow of refugees. Under their standing orders, the Allied military garrisons in Berlin did nothing to interfere. U.S. troops remained in their barracks. As seen from Washington, the crisis had eased. There would be no popular uprising in the GDR, no intervention by the Soviets, and no necessity to consider a Western military response. The Administration breathed a collective sigh of relief. "This is Khrushchev's way out of his predicament," Kennedy told his appointments secretary Kenneth O'Donnell. "It's not a very nice solution but it's a hell of a lot better than a war."

But it quickly became obvious that Washington had misjudged the situation. The border was closed, the refugee exodus had been stopped, but in West Berlin fear and panic gripped the population. After thirteen years in the front lines of the Cold War, the West Berliners could not understand why the Western Allies had done nothing to prevent the border closure. All Sunday, they watched in disbelief as the despised East German Vopos (for "Volkspolizei," or People's Police) systematically sealed the border between East and West Berlin with flimsy barricades made of barbed wire. In their view, the pitiful East Germans were being allowed single-handedly to destroy the four-power status of Berlin and to nullify a solemn agreement made by the occupying powers in 1945. If the West, particularly the United States, did not have the gumption to stand up to the tottering Ulbricht regime, what hope did they have that Washington could be relied upon against Soviet encroachment, when the risk would be manifestly greater?

More important, the tragic human consequences of the border closure were sinking in: families divided, friends and loved ones separated, workers shut off from their employment. It was exactly as if Chicago or Los Angeles suddenly were divided in two, with no contact between the two halves permitted. Daily life for many Berliners was more than disrupted: it would never be the same. On Monday, three hundred thousand West Berliners rallied in front of their city hall to demand action. Mayor Willy Brandt, a logical successor to the intrepid Reuter, wrote President Kennedy urging that the United States reassert four-power responsibility in Berlin. U.S. Ambassador Walter Dowling cautioned the State Department that the situation was deteriorating quickly.

At first, the anguished reports of fear and panic in West Berlin were disbelieved by the State Department. In a dispatch from Washington, *The New York Times* reported that the Kennedy administration had rejected suggestions from the West German government for strong countermeasures. Ambassador Dowling was told curtly that Washington was in charge. His messages were pigeonholed as a predictable example of "Berlinitis." Mayor Brandt's impassioned plea was likewise dismissed as a shabby election trick, by a "mere mayor," to score points in the West German election. Not until former CBS correspondent Edward R. Murrow, the head of the United States Information Agency (and an old Berlin hand from the days of the Occupation), sent back dire warnings from the beleaguered city did Washington begin to take seriously the extent of the crisis that had developed. Murrow was a trusted friend of the President and he was able to communicate with JFK directly. He told Kennedy straight out that the United States had misplayed the situation badly and that the "psychological climate" in Berlin was deteriorating quickly. It was not enough simply to say that West Berlin would be protected; a positive demonstration was urgently required. Murrow urged immediate U.S. action to restore confidence.

Kennedy was determined not to reopen the question of the East German border closure. That move, he was convinced, had been essential. But he recognized the new, unanticipated crisis in West Berlin to be critical and, as Murrow suggested, sought a positive response: a symbol, some positive demonstration of American resolve. In his letter, for example, Mayor Brandt had suggested that General Clay be returned to Berlin to take charge. After thirteen years, Clay was still the savior of Berlin and the most tangible example of American determination to hold the city against Communist aggression. As Norbert Muhlen observed in the *National Review,* Clay's status in the hierarchy of Berlin heroes was two steps higher than Frederick the Great, and if anyone could restore confidence, it would be Clay.

On Thursday, August 17, as West Berlin shoppers stripped bare the well-stocked shelves of the city's markets, and savings deposits plummeted as frightened citizens withdrew their money, Kennedy discussed with Dean Rusk, and later with Dean Acheson, the possibility of sending Clay to Berlin on an official visit. Both were enthusiastic. In Acheson's view, "When you don't have a policy, and don't know what to do, then it helps to send someone like General Clay back there [to Berlin] to restore morale."

Clay had been following the situation in Berlin closely. Despite his continuing responsibilities at Continental Can, he always kept in close touch with German affairs. As the refugee exodus swelled during the summer, he became concerned, but was reluctant to speak out. Clay did not disagree entirely with the need to stop the outflow from the GDR, but he was especially sensitive to what the reaction to such a stop would likely be in West Berlin. By 1961 a prominent Republican—and a dutiful supporter of Richard Nixon in the 1960 election—Clay did not believe that it was his place to offer unsolicited advice to the new Administration. But when the border was closed on August 13, and no Western response was forthcoming that might have reassured the Berliners, Clay became worried. On Tuesday, August 15, he wrote to General Maxwell Taylor at the White House to say that he considered the situation in West Berlin to be very serious and volunteered to help in any way he could. "I got a telephone call from General Taylor almost immediately," said Clay. "He told me that he had shown my letter to the President, and that the President had appreciated it very much and would be in touch with me."

Q: But you had not been a supporter of Kennedy?
CLAY: No. But I was a supporter of President Kennedy once he was elected. I don't mean by that I would have voted for him. But I have supported every President in the execution of American foreign policy. I don't think you can have more than one foreign policy in the country, and that is the President's.

Nevertheless, Clay's prominent role in the GOP, and particularly in the Eisenhower administration, posed an immediate political problem for the White House. To call on Clay in a moment of extreme crisis in Berlin appeared to be an admission that the Kennedy team was unable to handle the situation. More seriously, it might suggest that the old war-horses of Ike's time had been correct after all, and that Kennedy was in over his head in dealing with the Russians. It was a serious dilemma. On the one hand, the panic in West Berlin was virtually out of control—and there was little question but that Clay could provide the necessary calming effect. On the other, the domestic political cost of turning to Clay could be incalculable.

By Thursday evening, the White House had found a solution. Kennedy would send Vice President Johnson to Berlin as his special envoy, and Clay would accompany him. As Vice President, Johnson would head the party and occupy center stage, but it was Clay's presence that would reassure the Berliners. It was a balanced ticket. The Administration would retain control, Johnson's Democratic credentials were beyond doubt, and Clay would symbolize the appropriate bipartisan resolve. The U.S. media would focus on Johnson; the German press would concentrate on Clay. It was a response worthy of the best tradition of American diplomacy.

Thursday evening, Kennedy called Johnson away from a dinner party and asked him to fly to Berlin the next night as the President's special representative. Johnson was initially reluctant. He knew nothing of foreign policy and thought it might be too dangerous. But as Johnson usually did in such times, he called Speaker Rayburn for advice. Rayburn told Johnson to go but advised him to take Clay along. Rayburn did not know what the White House had planned, but he told Johnson that he should not go to Berlin without someone who knew something about the situation. Clay was the best man, Rayburn said. Friday morning, Rayburn called Clay in New York and told him what he had done. "Obviously, I couldn't do anything about it until the President asked me to go," said Clay. "But very quickly I got a phone call asking me if I would come to the White House for a conference. I went down to the White House through the side entrance and went upstairs. The President shook hands with me and told me he was sending Vice President Johnson to Berlin, and he asked me if I would accompany him. I said, of course, that I would."

Q: Had you met President Kennedy before?

CLAY: President Kennedy may have visited Berlin as a congressman, but I don't remember it. I only remember that his sisters came and went out on a picnic lunch with Bob Murphy's daughters and they all got arrested by the Russians on one of the islands in the Wannsee that was in the Russian zone. It didn't cause any difficulty. I didn't even know about it. Mr. Murphy didn't want me to know about it, so he didn't tell me until years later.

Q: When President Kennedy asked you to go to Berlin with the Vice President, was there any doubt as to whether you should accept?
CLAY: No. Not at all. I could never refuse a request from the President.
Q: But the political implications?
CLAY: I am an American. If the President asks me to do something, and it's in my power, I'm going to do it.

"After the President asked me to go, he took me into the upstairs study, where there was a meeting assembled, twenty or so people—Vice President Johnson, Secretary Rusk, Mr. [Charles] Bohlen, Mr. [McGeorge] Bundy, Mr. [Ted] Sorensen, Mr. [Pierre] Salinger, people from Defense, the military, General Taylor—really quite a large meeting. The President asked my opinion about sending military reinforcements to Berlin. I told him I was very much in favor of it. General Taylor and General [Lyman] Lemnitzer [Chairman of the Joint Chiefs of Staff] were opposed. They thought we were putting too many eggs into one basket. There were some pros and cons [discussed], and President Kennedy decided that this would be done. That reinforcements would be sent. And it was a very effective move.

"The question of timing was also discussed. The President decided that every effort would be made to get the troops to arrive in Berlin so that the Vice President could greet them personally. Some [advisers] felt that this was adding unnecessary irritation and provocation. But the President made the decision that this would be done, and it turned out to be a very important part of the Vice President's visit."

Kennedy's decision to send a U.S. battle group to Berlin along the autobahn marked a sharp departure from the position the Administration had taken thus far. As Clay noted, JFK was prepared to take a firm stand when the situation required. Clay's own strong views undoubtedly helped, since Kennedy could assume that Clay was speaking for Eisenhower and the Republican Party when he urged that the reinforcements be sent overland. As in 1948, the President's military advisers dissented. To Maxwell Taylor and Lyman Lemnitzer, sending more troops to Berlin would recklessly deplete the thin line of American troops stretched across the NATO central front in West Germany: an unwise deployment that would be unreasonably provocative and invite Soviet retaliation on the exposed access routes to Berlin.

For a moment, Clay thought he was listening to a rehash of the arguments used by the Pentagon in 1948 when he wanted to break the blockade. But this time, the situation in West Berlin was if anything more critical. An immediate show of force was required to restore confidence in American leadership. The entire Western position in Germany—the fruits of fifteen years of hard work against bitter odds—threatened to come unraveled. Clay was at his most forceful during the White House meeting and won JFK's support. As in 1948, the President overruled his military advisers. Kennedy ordered that the U.S. battle group be dispatched to Berlin across the 110 miles of autobahn stretching through the Soviet zone. Clay thought it was a courageous decision. And it led to a curious rapport between him and the young President. Kennedy admired Clay's advocacy and decisiveness: his ability to move swiftly through bureaucratic resistance. Clay appreciated the President's willingness to take responsibility and make tough decisions. Clay thought JFK was learning and growing in stature, just as Truman had done.

Q: Do you recall President Kennedy's attitude?

CLAY: I formed the clear impression that the President had made up his mind that we were going to be firm in Berlin. Certainly he hoped to display sufficient firmness to restore the morale of the West Berliners. I believe that he hoped to convince the Russians that any further steps they might take would be very dangerous. I also felt that he did not want to go further than that at that time; that he did not want to take any action of an aggressive nature—to remove the Wall, for example. That he hoped the actions he was taking would convince the Russians of the firmness of his position, so that we would not have any further retrogression of the Berlin situation.

"In other words, it was a rather sober judgment of the responsibilities that were involved. On the whole, he was on middle ground amongst those who were advising him. There were many who would have liked him to be more aggressive, and there were others who didn't even think that we should send in more troops—that the Russians would regard it as a hostile act."

Q: Could you contrast President Kennedy's handling of the crisis to what President Eisenhower might have done?

CLAY: In General Eisenhower's case, he probably would not have had a conference. He would have talked to his advisers separately. Then, if he had decided to send the Vice President to Berlin, he would have called him in and told him to go.

"I'm not being critical. There were two different methods. But the method of having a group of people sit around and talk and then making the decision, which was the method President Kennedy was employing at that time, was obviously a little different from the way I made decisions or had experienced decision-making in the White House previously. The only times I saw President Truman, for instance, he made the decisions. I will always remember the National Security Council meeting in [October] 1948 when Mr. Truman listened as each member expressed his views. But he didn't try to get a consensus. He listened, but then he decided. In fact, he overruled what appeared to me to be the consensus [pertaining to reinforcing the airlift].

"I won't say that President Kennedy was trying to get a consensus either. But if I had been Secretary of State—I don't know whether I want this on the record or not—I would not want to sit down at a conference of presidential staff members and other advisers who would argue against me. When the Secretary of State does that, he drops himself to their level."

The White House conference broke up shortly after 7:00 P.M. on Friday. Press Secretary Pierre Salinger announced that Clay and Vice President Johnson would be leaving that evening for Berlin, and that President Kennedy had ordered that the U.S. garrison in Berlin be reinforced. "An Army battle group of approximately 1500 men will proceed by way of the Helmstedt-Berlin autobahn, arriving on Sunday."

At six o'clock Saturday morning, the battle group President Kennedy had ordered to Berlin began to roll. The First Battle Group of the 18th Infantry regiment, stationed at Mannheim, West Germany, moved out for the three-hundred-mile motor march along the West German autobahn from Mannheim to Frankfurt to Kassel, and then along the Harz Mountains to Braunschweig, near the East German border. Not since 1945 had a U.S. military convoy moved in Germany under battle conditions. But the 18th Infantry, under Colonel Glover S. Johns, were combat-ready and prepared for an uncertain reception. The convoy would bivouac near Braunschweig for the night, enter the GDR at Helmstedt early Sunday morning, and arrive in Berlin shortly after twelve noon. General Bruce C. Clarke, the U.S. Army commander in Europe, established his command post at Helmstedt Saturday afternoon. He was in direct contact with the White House. West German police cleared the autobahn in front of the troop column. Shortly after midnight, the last vehicle of the 18th Infantry closed in Braunschweig for the night.

As the 18th Infantry moved toward Braunschweig, Vice President Johnson's plane landed in Bonn—a courtesy call on Chancellor Adenauer, who was in the midst of a bitter West German election campaign against Mayor Brandt. As the head of the West German government, Adenauer fully expected to accompany Johnson and Clay to Berlin. But to take Adenauer along might appear to be a political endorsement. To refuse to take him would be an even worse personal slight. In Clay's view, it was a no-win situation. In the end, Washington had decided that Adenauer should not be invited to join Clay and Johnson, and for a brief period U.S.–West German relations suffered a sharp decline. According to Clay, "The decision not to ask Chancellor Adenauer to accompany us to Berlin was made at our conference at the White House. I don't know whether it was the right decision. It was made on the grounds that there was an election in West Germany, and Adenauer and Brandt were running against each other. To take Adenauer with us to Berlin could be construed as a political endorsement. That at least was the basis of the decision. And that is why he wasn't taken.

"As a matter of fact, it fell to Mr. [Charles] Bohlen and myself to let the Chancellor know that he was not to go on the trip. He was furious. He had assumed he was going with us. He was all set and ready to go."

Q: Did you concur in the decision?

CLAY: I think if it had been up to me, which it was not, I would have had *both* Brandt and Adenauer meet us in Bonn and then taken both of them with us to Berlin. But I'm talking now after the fact. Certainly, Adenauer was very unhappy. He never blamed Bohlen and myself. He knew damn well that we hadn't made the decision.

"I think one of the problems at that time was really and truly because of the great age difference between President Kennedy and Chancellor Adenauer. I don't think they ever really had confidence and trust in each other. I'm sure that Adenauer looked on Kennedy as a young and inexperienced man. He'd been accustomed to dealing with Dulles and General Eisenhower. And he never really reached a degree of compatibility with President Kennedy. That was one of the problems in 1961. How did you reconcile this tremendous difference in age? It was extreme age [Adenauer was eighty-five] looking on what it thought was extreme youth [Kennedy was forty-four]. Conversely, it was youth wondering if you could trust the judgments of a man as old as Adenauer. And I don't think either one of them ever recognized that this chasm existed."

Clay and Johnson landed at Tempelhof airport in Berlin shortly after 2:00 P.M. Saturday, to begin a frenzied celebration of American resolve. Despite his initial misgivings, Johnson was overwhelmed at the reception. "When we arrived in Berlin, the only thing we saw was crowds," said Clay. "Thousands and thousands and thousands on thousands, wherever we went. Of course, Brandt had seen to that, and the Vice President's route was known and advertised. It was really a tremendous outpouring of people. And it had a tremendous impact. Nobody believes a Berlin welcome until they've seen it."

Q: And Vice President Johnson?
CLAY: Vice President Johnson was not very aware of the situation in Berlin. At that time, he had not had much experience in foreign policy. This was a new venture for him. Bohlen and I gave him as much background as we could on the airplane going over. And he handled himself damn well. Of course, he was an old pro. He did particularly well in Berlin, especially when he got out of the car and mixed with the crowd. It was very effective.

Johnson was in his element in Berlin. The enormous turnout worked as a tonic on him. As Johnson responded, the Berliners responded. His presence was electric. The signs of demoralization and fear began to vanish. Clay stood in the background. Then the Berliners caught sight of him, and the cheering became even greater. Ordinary citizens looked at one another and nodded knowingly. General Clay would not be here, they seemed to say, unless everything was going to be all right.

At the Berlin city hall, another massive crowd, and another masterful performance by LBJ. In what was perhaps the finest speech of his political career, Johnson departed from a carefully prepared text to place American honor squarely on the line. Quoting extemporaneously from the Declaration of Independence, Johnson reassured the Berliners: "To the survival and the creative future of this city, we Americans have pledged, in effect, what our ancestors pledged in forming the United States: our lives, our fortune, and our sacred honor."

Clay spoke briefly. He did not want to upstage the Vice President, whose words, Clay thought, were just what the situation required. The ovation Clay received was tumultuous. "Here stands the man," said Brandt, "who helped save our lives then. Today he is back among us." Clay blushed at the outpouring of affection. His words quietly evoked the triumph he shared with the Berliners: "I want to say how wonderful it is to see proud and still-free looks on the faces of the people of West Berlin. Thanks to your courage, with the support of my own countrymen and the support of all freedom-loving people, what we started together twelve years ago we will finish together and Berlin will still be free."

When Clay finished, the Berlin police band broke into an emotional playing of "The Star-Spangled Banner," followed by the "Deutschland Lied" and "Berliner Luft"—the city's unofficial anthem. A magnificent hush had settled over the vast crowd. From inside the bell tower of the Rathaus, the Freedom Bell, dedicated by Clay in 1950, commenced its toll. The sound of the bell, in the eerie quiet of 350,000 massed people, was a sound Clay never forgot. For the Berliners, it had been a magnificent day. The panic eased.

On Sunday, the psychological advantage was pressed home. Shortly before 1:00 P.M., the first elements of the 18th Infantry rolled into Berlin. The passage through the Soviet zone had been uneventful. Johnson and Clay were on hand to greet them—from the same reviewing stand from which Clay and General Omar Bradley had welcomed the 2nd Armored Division in 1945. Johnson told the troops that they were a symbol of America's determination to remain in Berlin "no matter what course things run."

Never has an occupying army been so joyously received. As the truck column made an unprecedented tour of the city, up the broad sweep of Clayallee, down the glittering Kurfürstendamm, back through the winding streets of the American sector, thousands of Berliners turned out to cheer and throw flowers at the American GIs. Colonel Johns called it the most emotional reception since the liberation of Paris. When Clay and Johnson left Berlin the next morning, the crisis had eased. West Berlin morale had been stabilized, at least temporarily. Without challenging the East German border closure, the United States had demonstrated its intent to protect the Western sectors. Clay was pleased that he had been helpful. On Monday night he was back in New York, and on Tuesday morning, back at his desk at Continental Can.

Q: General, what caused the morale in West Berlin to deteriorate so quickly after the Wall was built?

CLAY: No one had any authority to act. One of the problems was that there had been a very long period when nothing of any consequence happened in Berlin. And during that period, the chain of command had changed substantially.

"When Mr. McCloy succeeded me [in 1949], he sent General [Maxwell] Taylor up to Berlin and he gave him almost plenary powers. But when Taylor left, those powers were never again given to the commander in Berlin. Another increase in the chain of command came with the establishment of NATO. This moved the [U.S.] Army commander down a step. When I was the Army commander, I also commanded all American forces in Europe: Air Force, Navy, anything that was in Europe. But with NATO, that became the NATO commander's job. And in 1961, it was [General Lauris] Norstad. And that was a problem, because Norstad couldn't make a decision as the U.S. commander without making it as the NATO commander, and none of the European nations wanted [to take] any action in Berlin. So he was being pulled back all of the time by the fact that he was wearing a NATO hat.

"Remember, when I was in Berlin [from 1947 to 1949], I was the commanding general of all of U.S. forces in Europe. And when it came to this type and kind of decision, I was there and I made the decisions. The night that the Wall was put up, the chain of command was from a major general in Berlin—and then only after a meeting with the other Allied commanders—to the American Army commander in Heidelberg, and from Heidelberg to Norstad in Paris, before it ever went to Washington. The State Department man [in Berlin] could do better. He could wire direct to the State Department. But the military commander had to go through his long chain of command. And he was only a major general. By the time they could have a meeting of the Allied commanders, and then have a meeting with Mayor Brandt, and then get their recommendations off, the battle was already lost. By the time they got word to the government, it was the next day. And then, by the time our government consulted with the various ambassadors, the Wall was up. Finished. The job was not stopping them at that point; it was tearing it down—which was a very much more difficult task."

Q: Couldn't the American commander in Berlin [Major General Albert Watson] have taken action on his own initiative the night the Wall went up?

CLAY: Not if he followed his orders.

Q: Couldn't he have ordered U.S. troops to the sector boundary?

CLAY: Not if he followed his orders. He had to get authority all the way back this long chain of command to make any kind of demonstration with his troops.

"If he had followed his orders. Now, you always have a right as a commander, if you deem it essential for the protection of your troops, to do whatever you think is necessary. You do that taking the full consequences for your actions. But I don't think anything could have been done that night in Berlin unless it had been done unilaterally by the American commander. There wasn't any possibility that the British or French were going to do anything. So, if he had to make that decision, he would have had to do it by himself. And from all I have learned, at that particular time Mayor Brandt didn't want anything done either. He was too concerned about the situation to run the risks that were inherent in any such action. I'm not being critical.

"I think the real diagnosis of what was happening on August 13 came too late. That was that the Wall had been put up by East German troops, and that the Russians never did show up. To me that would have been very significant—if I had known it in time. But if your intelligence services didn't give you that information in time, and in Berlin they didn't, you wouldn't even know that."

Q: Was there a breakdown in intelligence?

CLAY: I don't know. I can't tell you how much the commanding general in Berlin knew. They claim to have been taken by surprise. I've heard rumors that some of our operatives [in East Berlin] had given some indication of the border closure. But I don't know. There was no [way] in which I could find out. It would be between the CIA and the military commander. I'm sure it wasn't picked up by military intelligence.

Q: Did you report to President Kennedy when you returned from Berlin?

CLAY: I did not report to President Kennedy after that trip. I think Vice President Johnson did.

"I know that shortly afterward I flew back down to Washington at Mr. Johnson's request, and then with 'Chip' Bohlen went down to the Senate, where the Vice President had gathered ten or twelve Senate leaders, and he asked Bohlen and me to give them our impressions.

"My own view was that the problem in Berlin was over. That the damage had been done, if you want to put it that way. The Wall was erected and I didn't think there would be any additional pressures. I felt that the East Germans and Russians would feel that they had already accomplished more than they had expected, and that they were now going to rest on their laurels for a while. But I was concerned with what the effect might be on Berlin morale. Obviously, our visit had done a good deal to restore Berlin morale, but whether it was enough I had no way of knowing."

The problem was not over, however. The East Germans wasted little time before they pressed their advantage in Berlin. First they began replacing the flimsy barbed-wire barriers that had initially been put up with formidable concrete-and-steel barriers: the Wall began to take shape. Houses on the border were evacuated, their doors and windows sealed. On August 21, the GDR announced that the number of crossing points for those in the West wishing to enter East Berlin was being reduced from twelve to seven. These were subsequently reduced to three. There were no crossing points for those in the East who wished to go west. The East German order was accompanied by a new decree banning all persons in the West from approaching the Wall. A hundred-meter no-man's-land—on West Berlin territory—was proclaimed, which the East Germans said they would enforce. Three days later, several U.S. Army buses were held up for two hours when they tried to enter East Berlin—a further attempt by the Ulbricht regime to undermine the quadripartite status of the city.

When the West failed to respond to these increased Communist restrictions, morale in West Berlin took another nosedive. According to *The New York Times,* policy-makers in Washington viewed the East German crackdown "as merely an extension of the Communist barricades between the two parts of Berlin . . . that did not affect Western vital interests." But in West Berlin, Allied inaction was seen as weakness in the face of a continuing East German assault, and Berliners anticipated that the encroachment would continue until the Allies forcefully brought it to a halt. In August 1961, however, there seemed no inclination in Washington, London, or even Paris to do that. Washington, in particular, was still mesmerized by the fear of nuclear war over Berlin. Secretary of State Rusk worried publicly about a major conflict "touched off by some PFC on the border." Senate Majority Leader Mike Mansfield called for quick negotiations with the Soviet Union to settle the crisis. And the White House again rejected West German proposals for stepped-up countermeasures.

By the end of August, a panic flight from West Berlin had begun. Citizens were pulling up stakes and moving west. Real-estate values in the Western sectors plummeted. For the first time in memory, apartments stood vacant. Morale had hit rock bottom. A Communist takeover was feared to be imminent. Chancellor Adenauer, still in a heated election campaign with Mayor Brandt, challenged Kennedy to take action. Western reverses in Berlin were leading to a dangerous revival of neutralist sentiment throughout Germany, Adenauer said. In the face of continued Allied inaction, the public had begun to question whether Germany should have joined NATO. The elderly chancellor told Washington that if the United States did not begin to defend its position in Berlin, a desire for an accommodation with the Soviet Union, perhaps even a neutral role between East and West, could become a serious factor in West German politics.

With the West German election less than three weeks away, Adenauer's stark letter hit Washington with the force of an Arctic blizzard. Der Alte, despite his age difference with Kennedy, was the most formidable anti-Communist in public affairs—the patriarch of Germany's postwar recovery and its attachment to the West. If Adenauer feared neutralism and a possible realignment of West German foreign policy, it had to be taken seriously.

President Kennedy intervened directly. Unlike many who rode into office with the New Frontier, JFK sensed that a new crisis of leadership had erupted in Berlin. If he didn't quickly assert presidential authority, a further erosion of the U.S. position would inevitably take place. Richard Nixon, speaking out publicly for the first time since his defeat in 1960, had begun to criticize Kennedy's "Hamlet-like psychosis" whenever action was required, and the GOP was girding for congressional midterm elections. It was certain that Berlin would become a major issue unless the decay was halted quickly.

To the visible discomfiture of the State Department and the White House staff, Kennedy once again called Clay in New York. Would the general go back to Berlin and take charge? JFK showed little hesitation about overruling his diplomatic advisers. Clay was not only a prominent Republican, but the revered hero of the blockade. His return would restore Berlin morale and possibly protect the Administration from partisan attack.

Q: President Kennedy called you?

CLAY: Yes. He called me and asked me to come down to see him. He was concerned, as I was, about the morale in Berlin, and he wanted me to go back as his personal representative to demonstrate once more the seriousness with which he viewed the situation.

"Anyway, I went down to the White House, where we had a brief conference. It was very interesting, because President Kennedy had written a letter in which he said he was sending me to Berlin as his personal representative with the rank of ambassador, and added into it a paragraph that stated that I would be fully and completely responsible for all decisions in Berlin during the period that I was there. When I went back a day or two later, all set to go, he rather embarrassingly said to me that 'The State Department is very unhappy about the last paragraph. They think this is cutting Ambassador [Walter] Dowling [U.S. ambassador to West Germany] and the State Department to pieces, and they would like to take it out. What do you think about it?'

"I said, 'Mr. President, I don't really care. If I have access to you if I need it, I would expect to have your approval or disapproval. If it was a matter of serious import, I would get in touch with you to find out. So I don't really care.'

"A little later on, I was sorry I said that. But not because of the

State Department. My problems over there came from the military chain of command rather than the State Department: U.S. Army headquarters in Heidelberg and NATO headquarters in Paris. Both.

"I don't blame the State Department for objecting. I think they were right. I never visualized, however, having a problem with the military. Because I didn't realize until I got over there how the broad delegations of authority that I had given to my subordinates had all been taken away, and they were all operating on the end of a telephone. This wasn't true in my day and time. And it was really too bad. In point of fact, the NATO commander [Air Force General Lauris Norstad] had never even visited Berlin at that time. I think that was for political reasons—because all of NATO wasn't involved in Berlin. But on the other hand, when he was wearing his American hat, he was the commander of U.S. forces in Berlin. He did visit it after I had rather pointedly called his attention to this omission. And I'm not being critical. Because this is where these two hats that the NATO commander wears sometimes conflict."

Q: And you believe that the failure to delegate authority to those in command was part of the problem?

CLAY: Obviously, the more restricted your subordinates are, the more necessary it is to exercise tight control from above. I don't happen to believe in that type and kind of control. And I think the situation in Berlin was particularly difficult when there were two commanders whose approval had to be obtained, not just one—the U.S. Army commander in Heidelberg *and* the NATO commander in Paris.

"I've always believed that the commander on the spot has to have enough leeway to take timely action when necessary. And the government has to be able to repudiate those decisions when they are wrong. You just can't pass everything back to the White House. In point of fact, sometimes it's desirable for government to repudiate an action in the field—even if they bring the commander home and secretly give him a decoration.

"In my view, two things have led to this present situation: the telephone scrambler and nuclear weapons. Obviously, only one person, the President, can make the decision to employ nuclear weapons. But the elaborate communications system devised to ensure that is being used to conduct day-to-day operations abroad. I can remember when an ambassador was an important official. He's not today. Just like everyone else, he's on the end of a telephone to Washington. When I went back to Berlin [in 1961], I even had a scrambler device in my car. If necessary, I could have talked directly to the President from there. I didn't, because I don't believe you call the President on matters clearly within your responsibility.

"At the time of the airlift, it wasn't possible to call the President. We had a scrambler device then. The trouble was that it would scramble, but it would not unscramble. We also had a coded teleprinter, but it was hooked into the Pentagon, and President Truman wasn't about to go over to the Pentagon to hold a teleconference with you. Sometimes the Secretary of State might be there, but by the time you wrote everything out for transmission, it might take several hours to conduct the conversation."

Q: But wasn't one of the advantages of your returning to Berlin the fact that you could pick up the telephone and talk directly to the President?

CLAY: It was not as much of an advantage as you might think. You don't call the President of the United States unless it is a very serious and very real emergency. It's fine to say that you have the right. But you don't utilize that right, or you soon would outwear your welcome. It really had to be a pretty serious matter before I called the President. On several occasions, he called me. In fact, I'm sure that he called me more than I called him.

"I always tried to go through Rusk. And Rusk almost invariably would say, 'Well, I agree with you, but you call the President and tell him.' And this was really quite a surprise to me, because I was trying to go through channels, but the channels didn't want me to. Whenever something serious occurred, no one wanted to make a decision. They all wanted me to talk to the President."

Q: That would not have been the case with Mr. Acheson or Mr. Dulles?

CLAY: That's for damn sure.

Q: When you returned to Berlin as President Kennedy's special representative, did you continue to run Continental Can?

CLAY: No sir. I absolutely turned the company over to Mr. [Thomas] Fogarty [senior vice president] and went on my way. I was still chairman, but I was on leave, and I took no role whatever in the company. Mr. Fogarty used to send me reports in Berlin. I read them, but I never made any comments. As far as I was concerned, he was running the company.

Q: How long did you expect to stay?

CLAY: I had no idea. I was going to stay until I felt satisfied that the immediate loss of morale and the economic slowdown in Berlin were over.

Q: What was Mrs. Clay's reaction to your going over?

CLAY: All of this took her a great deal by surprise. Particularly the decision we took then to move, to give up our apartment in New York, and to change our whole method of living. It was a major change in her life, but there is no better soldier than Mrs. Clay. She's always gone where I went, and there has never been any question of that, really.

Q: Why did you decide to give up the apartment on Fifth Avenue?

CLAY: I don't know why, really, except it was a big apartment—there was always the problem of help—and we thought we were probably coming back [from Berlin] to retire, at least in a very short time, from Continental, and we would be leaving New York. So this seemed the right time to close down the apartment. That's what we did. If I had known that we were going to stay in New York another ten years, we never would have done it.

With the appointment of Clay as President Kennedy's special representative, the defense of Berlin had come full circle. The man who had saved the city in 1948 was being asked to return and re-establish Western resolve. It was a symbolic appointment, nothing more. Clay was no longer the military proconsul of a defeated country. Washington had emphasized that his appointment would not offset the existing command structure. General Norstad in Paris, and General Bruce C. Clarke, the career officer who commanded the U.S. Army at Heidelberg, both resented his coming. The State Department worried that Clay was not aware of the realities of nuclear war and that his presence would further complicate the already complicated administrative setup. Clay's job was to report, recommend, and advise. He would have no command function.

Clay viewed his appointment in much the same way: he would be President Kennedy's man in Berlin but, more important, a hostage to American good faith. It is a reflection of what Don Humphrey once called Clay's utter selflessness that he gave up his responsibilities as head of one of America's largest corporations to undertake a task that hinged on his prestige more than his judgment: front man for an Administration whose policy was unsure. Clay never worried about the bureaucratic chain of command, and was certainly not intimidated by those who held power. His link to authority was the President, and he was fully aware of the political clout that he carried.

Clay arrived in Berlin on September 19, 1961, two days after the West German election. (Adenauer was returned as Chancellor, but with a much smaller, 242–190 majority over Brandt's SPD.) He was treated to another of Berlin's massive receptions: thousands of people lined the eleven-mile route, often three and four deep, between Tempelhof and his new quarters at the Berlin Command's Wannsee guest house (site of the fateful conference with Marshall and Dulles on the eve of the Moscow Council of Foreign Ministers in 1947). For the Berliners, Clay was their personal talisman. The general's return was a touching reunion. It was also a guarantee of American determination.

Q: How did you set about to restore West Berlin morale?

CLAY: In the first place, I think the Berliners felt confident that I wouldn't have come if I hadn't had confidence that the United States was prepared to stay in Berlin.

"Then, I started a movement to encourage further American investment in Berlin—with some degree of success. We made much out of everything that happened. For example, I got General Motors to start a small plant there, making spare parts. It didn't amount to very much, but it was new and something different, and it *was* a General Motors plant. Of course, this all helped.

"Third, I insisted that when the Russians began to harass us, that we harass back. If they began to hold up our military vehicles when they went into East Berlin, I insisted that we hold up the Russian vehicles when they went into West Berlin. Mainly, this was to do what I thought was very important: to prove that our presence in Berlin was something between the United States and the Russians—not the East Germans.

"I also sent American troops to patrol the sector boundary. There had been several incidents in which it was alleged that East Germans had crossed over into our sector to pick up people who had fled. I put patrols out with orders that if anyone got across into the American sector, no one was to be allowed to come and take them back. All of these steps, I thought, would help show the Berliners that we were not going to give in."

Q: Did you believe the autobahn access to Berlin was endangered?

CLAY: It very definitely was. That is why I started the practice of sending convoys in and out all of the time. It was later stopped, but I think it was a damn foolish thing to stop.

"The reason I took these actions was to restore Berlin morale. Not that I expected these actions in themselves to achieve any miracles. But I wanted the people of Berlin to know that we weren't afraid, that we were willing to prove that we were not afraid by taking these actions. I don't think this point was ever really understood, either by the military chain of command or in Washington.

"General Watson [the Berlin commander] understood it. He was chagrined that he had allowed the Wall to be built in the first place—which wasn't his fault. I guess I encouraged him to be sufficiently aggressive so that he was in hot water from time to time with both Clarke and Norstad. But in the long run, I don't think it hurt him. [Watson was promoted to lieutenant general in 1965.] In fact, I think it helped him. If he hadn't taken these actions I prodded him into taking, he would have gone down in history as the general who allowed the Berlin Wall to be built."

Q: How did you fit into the Berlin command structure?

CLAY: I don't know how to answer that. To the extent that General Watson and Mr. [Allan] Lightner [the State Department political adviser] were permitted by their respective superiors, I had full and complete cooperation. I did not have very good cooperation from the military high command, primarily Paris [General Norstad]. Army headquarters in Heidelberg simply refused to take a part and turned it over to Paris.

Q: Do you have any regrets about going back to Berlin in 1961?

CLAY: I can't say it was a very happy situation. On the other hand, I believe I helped Berlin by going back. And that was the only reason I went. When I left [in May 1962], the morale of the city was infinitely better than when I went there. If so, I accomplished my purpose. God knows, I had nothing to gain by going back. But if I had refused, I would have felt guilty the rest of my life.

Q: And your support from President Kennedy?

CLAY: The President was all right. Every time I went to the President, I got support. But I got none from the military people. None whatsoever.

"It taught me one thing. That is, I don't think we should ever be in a position where the NATO commander is also the senior American commander in Europe. I don't think that it was possible for Norstad to be anything but a NATO commander. And I don't think NATO should be making American decisions. In American matters, the chain should run from an exclusively American general to Washington."

Q: But wasn't General Norstad also the commander of British and French troops in Berlin?

CLAY: It did not work that way, however. The British communicated directly with London. We were the only people who had to go through NATO. The British didn't go through NATO; the French didn't go through NATO. Only we.

"There has always been an American NATO commander. And when that commander was General Eisenhower, his influence was such that it didn't represent a problem. He did not have to satisfy the NATO countries, as his successors have had to.

"I don't know how you can do it. I never had any confidence that if I sent a message to Norstad, that it was an American message. In other words, after the message got to Paris, I never knew who saw it. It could have been transmitted to the British and French governments before it got to our government. Or at least at the same time. It was a very unsatisfactory relationship.

"Clarke, to his credit, recognized that he was just an additional cog in the machine. He couldn't make any decision without getting Norstad's approval. And it made him mad as hell that he couldn't make any decisions. So he got out. He told Watson to report directly to Norstad."

Q: Did that improve things?

CLAY: Not really. The problem was Norstad. For example, Norstad ordered Clarke to stop the autobahn patrols. He sent Clarke up to break it to me gently that he'd been ordered to stop the patrols. Silliest damn order I'd ever heard. So far as Norstad is concerned, I don't think he was capable of handling anything. But that is just a personal opinion.

Q: Shortly after you returned to Berlin, you set off a bombshell by saying, "West Germany finally must recognize the existence of two German states."

CLAY: That wasn't what I said. It was a bombshell the way it was reported. This was supposed to have been an off-the-record discussion, and one of the British correspondents broke it.

"At that time, the roadblocks [on the autobahn to Berlin] were manned by Russians. I was asked, if we came up one morning and found that we were being stopped by East Germans instead of by Russians, did I think this would be a cause for military action. And I deliberately said no, that I didn't believe it would be. And I don't think so today. But it was so misinterpreted that when it became public—because it wasn't supposed to have been made public—I took steps to say that I wasn't making any policy declarations, that they had to come out of Washington. I never did know what Washington's views on it were. I never heard."

One of Clay's first direct actions after he arrived in Berlin was to fly by Army helicopter across East German territory to the isolated West Berlin enclave of Steinstücken, a tiny village of 191 inhabitants on the outskirts of the American sector. A mapmaker's nightmare, Steinstücken was one of twelve tiny pieces of territory that were part of West Berlin but were physically separated from the city by an intervening stretch of East Germany—sometimes only a few yards. Following the construction of the Wall, the residents of Steinstücken had been virtually imprisoned. It had been ten years since an American official had visited the village, and many residents had given up hope of ever being reunited with West Berlin. In addition, an East German refugee was in hiding there—a continuing invitation to the East German Volkspolizei to go in and search the village. Clay was informed about the plight of the village upon his arrival, and suggested to General Watson that he send a patrol to punch a hole through to Steinstücken. But when Watson asked for permission, General Clarke in Heidelberg refused, and Norstad agreed with him. Despite the tonic effect such a move would have on West Berlin morale, both considered it provocative.

Clay was annoyed but not dissuaded. Steinstücken was the most vulnerable part of West Berlin, and Clay was determined to see it secured. In Clay's view, precisely because of the exposed position of Steinstücken, it was the best place to allay the fears of the West Berliners. He suggested to Watson that he send a helicopter to the village instead. That too was turned down by Heidelberg and Paris. Clay thereupon ordered a helicopter for his personal use and instructed the pilot to fly him to Steinstücken. "They could not refuse to give me a helicopter," said Clay. "I had the authority to call for one for my own travel. So I did." The flight was unprecedented. Clay had regained the initiative.

The East German border guards took aim at Clay's helicopter, but held their fire. Clay spent a total of forty-five minutes in the village, chatted individually with numerous citizens, and visited publicly with the mayor in the shopfront window of the mayor's grocery. "I brought the refugee out with me when I left," said Clay, "and had Watson assign a regular Military Police detachment over there."

Clay's dramatic flight to Steinstücken captured West Berlin's imagination. The East Germans attacked the flight as a provocative violation of GDR sovereignty. The British protested to Washington that Clay was too reckless. Clay ignored the fuss. A vital first step had been taken to reverse the erosion of the Western position. Clay was doing what he did best: seizing the initiative when others feared the consequences. When Clay made a routine trip to the Kurfürstendamm the next afternoon, he was mobbed by a massive throng of cheering Berliners. The worst, they knew, was over.

Q: In October, you deployed U.S. tanks at Checkpoint Charlie?

CLAY: The East Germans were trying to insist that they had the right to inspect the identity papers of Allied personnel going to East Berlin. This was a direct violation of all of the agreements that had established the quadripartite status of Berlin. Since 1945, members of the Occupation forces could move freely throughout all of Berlin. If we had permitted the East Germans to interfere with this, it would have really destroyed West Berlin morale. Because we would have been letting the East Germans, not the Russians, exercise the sovereignty over Berlin that we claimed resided in the four powers.

"The issue arose when the East German border guards stopped Mr. Lightner [the U.S. political adviser] and asked to see his passport. While this doesn't seem very important to us back here [in the United States], it was of tremendous importance to our position in Berlin that we not let the East German government compel our Occupation personnel to present passports to them for inspection. To do so would have implied that we recognized their right to control whether we could enter the Russian sector. In effect, we would have undermined our whole legal position to be in Berlin—which was based on the quadripartite status of the city."

Q: Did you arrange to have Mr. Lightner cross into East Berlin to test the issue?

CLAY: No. Mr. Lightner had gone over to the opera. He'd been doing this for years. He went in his own car. The East German guards allowed him in, but on his return they stopped his car and they demanded that he show his credentials to them. He refused. So they refused to open the barrier to let him through.

"I didn't know anything about it until I got a telephone call. Lightner had a telephone in his car. He had called in his problem, and they immediately called me. I suggested to General Watson that he send a military patrol to the crossing point and bring Mr. Lightner and his car out. Which he did. The East Germans at that point made no effort to stop them. So we had reasserted our right to pass through their checkpoint without submitting to their controls.

"At this point, I felt it was essential that we force the Russians to show up and take responsibility. Thus far, the Russians were trying to propagate the myth that the East Germans had erected the Wall and that the Russians were not involved. That the four-power status of Berlin was dead. And so, after we had extracted Mr. Lightner, we brought up four tanks and several armored cars [to the checkpoint] to underline our intent. The Russians responded immediately and brought up four tanks to their side of the checkpoint; then we brought up six more tanks to our side; the Russians brought in six more. And to the outside world it looked like a very exciting thing: ten Russian tanks on one side of the Wall and, a hundred yards away on the American side, ten American tanks laid up, all with their guns pointing directly at one another.

"But these were Russian tanks, not East German tanks. It was obvious that the Russians did not trust the East Germans in this situation. As soon as they did that, I was no longer concerned. The Russians had come out of hiding, and I was sure they were not going to do anything. But we had proved our point. The Russians were in charge. We were not going to have to deal with the East Germans. And that was the whole purpose.

"Nevertheless, as we were sitting there in the command room in Berlin, about 11:00 P.M., I was told that Mr. [McGeorge] Bundy was on the telephone and wanted to speak to me. But when I picked up the phone, I recognized the President's voice immediately. By that time, he had received the AP news dispatches and whatnot, and so he called me. I explained the situation to him, and I told him that I thought we had reached a stalemate and that we had accomplished our mission. I said, 'It is very interesting, because we've got ten tanks on our side, and they've got ten on their side.' Then I said, 'I've got to change my figures. I've just been told that the Russians have twenty more tanks coming up, which would give them exactly the total number of tanks that we have in Berlin. So we'll bring our twenty [tanks] up.' I said, 'Don't worry about it, Mr. President. They've matched us tank for tank. This is further evidence to me that they don't intend to do anything. They've moved in now because they are afraid it will get out of hand, and they don't want it to do that. What we've done is to prove that the Russians are still in charge.'

"He said, 'Well, that's all right. Don't lose your nerve.'

"I said, 'Mr. President, we're not worried about losing our nerve over here. What we're worried about is whether you people in Washington are losing yours.'

"Then he said, 'I've got a lot of people here that have, but I haven't.' And that was the end of the conversation."

Once again Clay had scored an impressive victory over the East Germans. While official Washington muttered nervous misgivings, and Britain protested what it called "foolish posturing over an essentially minor issue," Clay had punctured the myth of East German sovereignty over East Berlin. When the going got rough, the Russians had intervened, and Clay counted it an exercise well done. The West Berliners took renewed heart, the confrontation at Checkpoint Charlie became legend, and Clay's personal stock rose even higher. Clay might make U.S. officials in Washington nervous, but those in Berlin rejoiced that he was there. Howard Trivers, the political officer in the U.S. Mission, said, "Had it not been for General Clay's presence in Berlin when Mr. Lightner was stopped, the American military and civilian authorities would have been obliged [by Washington] to crawl back ignominiously."

Just as in 1948, Clay felt the President of the United States was far more determined to hold fast in Berlin than his advisers. "But above all," said Clay, "I was sure that he was not going to let the situation deteriorate. I had complete confidence that in a real emergency we would get approval from the President to act.

"Actually, in the whole time I was there, I had his support on all of my recommendations with the exception of one. At one point, the Russians began to buzz our [commercial] airplanes and were doing this several times a day in the air corridors. I wanted to send our fighter aircraft into the air corridors daily in response, and I wanted to start flying [both fighters and commercial aircraft] above the ten-thousand-foot limit.* I believed that it was essential to the long-term survival of Berlin that this ten-thousand-foot limitation in the air corridors be destroyed. That is a ridiculous limitation for jet aircraft. And this seemed to me the right time and place to destroy it. We actually had our fighters set up in the air and ready to go in. But the President did not agree to send them. I felt that we should have taken advantage of the opportunity the Russians gave us. Norstad was very, very much against it, and I never got the President to move on it."

Gradually, through the winter of 1961–62, the spirit of West Berlin revived. The number of families moving to West Germany declined, and the balances in West Berlin savings accounts—perhaps the most accurate barometer of tension in the city—began to recover. Clay's continued presence in the city had a calming effect. Paul Davies, senior partner at Lehman Brothers, one of the many American investors whom Clay invited to Berlin, reported going to the opera with General Clay. "It was truly extraordinary," said Davies. "We got into our seats after the lights went down. The audience knew General Clay was there, but there was no commotion. When the opera was over, everyone applauded. Then—I've never seen anything like it—the whole audience rose to their feet and turned to Clay's box and applauded him. And the applause went on and on. It was amazing, and I guess it reflected their confidence and affection."

By Christmas, Clay thought Berlin morale had recovered sufficiently so that he could depart. Although his relations with the State

* The 1945 quadripartite air-control agreement specified that all aircraft flying in the three air corridors to Berlin would be limited to ten thousand feet.

Department had not improved, and Generals Clarke and Norstad continued to view his presence in Berlin as subversive to their authority, the onset of diplomatic discussions between Secretary Rusk and Russian Foreign Minister Gromyko gave him the opportunity to bow out gracefully.

"I wrote to the President," said Clay, "and told him I thought it was time to come home. He called me on the telephone immediately and said he appreciated the fact that things had quieted down and that I was probably right, but that he would be most appreciative if I would stay on a few months longer. I told him that I'd gone over to Berlin to be helpful and I wasn't going to leave as long as he wanted me to remain, and that I would stay a few months longer.

"In March he wrote me and said that he was sending General [Maxwell] Taylor over to see me. Taylor came over and asked me whether I thought there was any use in me staying any further, and I told him that I was convinced there wasn't. So I gave him a letter resigning, which he gave to the President. The President then wrote me to come to Washington to talk to him about it, because he wanted to figure out a way of doing it that wouldn't alarm the people in Berlin.

"I came back and told the President I wanted to leave, and he was very understanding about it. I said, 'I think it would be nice if you let me get back to Berlin and notify Mayor Brandt before any announcement is made.' Brandt was going to have the opportunity to tell the Berlin people about it. To which the President agreed completely. But that day, one of those errors came up which so frequently come up at press conferences. Somebody asked the President about my leaving, and he announced that I had resigned. It was a little embarrassing, especially for Mayor Brandt. The President told me he hadn't meant to do it and that he was very sorry. But it was done."

When announcement of Clay's departure hit Berlin on the morning of April 11, a minor panic ensued. Disbelief quickly turned to fear and a renewed sense of despair. Berlin was being forsaken once again, it appeared. There were turbulent scenes at newspaper kiosks, with angry Berliners berating the hapless vendors—the purveyors of such disturbing news. Clay was a symbol, and his impending departure, if true, seemed an ill-omen in those troubled times. "We are sold to the Russians, but not yet delivered," as one Berliner put it.

The best efforts of Mayor Brandt and the Berlin press corps failed to stem the growing apprehension. Not until Clay himself returned the following day and made a reassuring public statement was confidence restored. Clay told the Berliners matter-of-factly that the crisis was over, that his job was finished, and that he thought he could be of more help to the city in Washington than in Berlin. Clay's calm tone soothed frayed nerves. So great was his stature among the Berliners that no one questioned his statement. No further explanation was sought. "After all," it was said, "we can't expect General Clay to stay here forever." Or, in the *Galgenhumor* (gallows humor) for which Berliners were famous, "At least now we'll know when things are *really* bad, because then General Clay will come back."

Q: General, just for the record, did you ever recommend that we tear down the Wall?

CLAY: No. After I had been in Berlin about a month, I wrote to the President about Berlin and its problems. I told him then that I thought it was much too late for us to do anything about the Wall, that it had become such an issue that I did not believe that we could tear the Wall down then without armed conflict. I think we might have stopped the Wall from being built that night [August 13, 1961]. Unfortunately, due to the indecision among the Allies, even the indecision in Brandt's mind as well, there were no positive recommendations. And by the time all of this reached the President, it was already too late. In my opinion, we had missed the timing on tearing the Wall down.

Clay's final appearance in Berlin was at a gigantic May Day rally on the Platz der Republik in front of the burned-out hulk of the old German Reichstag. For the CEO of Continental Can Company, an appearance at a German May Day rally might seem out of character. But Clay accepted Mayor Brandt's invitation without hesitation: part of the mystical bond that linked him to Berlin. When news that Clay would attend the rally was announced, the East Germans notified Brandt that it was a "provocation" they could not permit. That was all the encouragement the West Berliners needed. The largest crowd in postwar German history, 750,000—one out of every three Berliners—turned out to pay homage to Clay and West German President Heinrich Lübke. When East Berlin loudspeaker trucks on the other side of the Wall tried to drown out the speakers' comments, the mood of the crowd turned ugly. West Berlin police restrained those who wanted to climb the Wall. As Clay observed later, the East Germans didn't realize what they could have triggered with their sound trucks. "No one can say what might happen when a crowd of seven hundred thousand people gets out of hand."

Clay left Berlin on May 2, 1962. He had accomplished his mission. True to his code of professional service, he never complained publicly about what he thought was a failure of will on the part of his government. Clay did what he had hoped to do: he restored the confidence of West Berlin that it would not be forsaken. Dean Rusk, who had frequently been unnerved by Clay's actions, soon came to the conclusion that Clay had served the cause of peace far better than he had imagined at the time. For the young policy-makers of the New Frontier, Clay had demonstrated that it wasn't necessary to let aggressors have their own way. Clay held steady in Berlin, while others figured out how to proceed.

Eventually, the border closure led to a stabilization of East-West relations in Germany. The German Democratic Republic did find its feet, at least temporarily, and, thanks to Clay, West Berlin learned to live with the situation. In 1972, the United States, the Soviet Union, France, and Great Britain formally agreed to Germany's division in the so-called Berlin Accords of that year. The GDR was granted formal diplomatic recognition, the quadripartite status of Berlin was reaffirmed, the Soviet Union undertook to guarantee free access to West Berlin, the city of East Berlin was acknowledged to be the capital of the German Democratic Republic, and both German states were admitted to the United Nations. In a curious way, the Berlin Wall facilitated that accord. But the cost had been substantial. The human toll of families divided at that time cannot be measured. The damage to American prestige has been enduring. And as subsequent U.S. involvement in Vietnam and elsewhere around the world suggests, the lessons of delegation, responsibility, and decisiveness had not been learned.

· 30 ·

Wall Street Banker

I would say you would have to color Clay a Rockefeller Republican.

Leonard Hall,
Republican National Chairman

CLAY RETURNED TO NEW YORK IN MAY. HE MADE A brief report to President Kennedy, and immediately retired as the operating head of Continental Can. Under Clay's leadership, Concan had become the dominant firm in the packaging industry, its 1962 sales exceeding $1.4 billion. Perhaps even more important, Clay's management style had developed a leadership cadre at Concan that soon became a model for American industry. Broad delegation of authority and decentralized operating control quickly became buzz words at the nation's business schools. When Clay departed for Berlin in September 1961, he did not worry about Continental's future: the team he had put together was fully capable of running the company in his absence.

"I gave up the chief executive's job [at Concan]

when I went to Berlin, and I had no intention of taking it back," said Clay. "I had a year before retirement, and I intended to retire, and I did retire. I had a number of boards and enough activity to keep me reasonably busy. I remained chairman of the executive committee at Continental Can, but Mr. [Thomas] Fogarty continued to run the company. Continental Can provided me with an office and a secretary, as it does for all of its past chief executives. Outside of the various boards I served on—and I was on quite a number at the time—I don't think I had anything else in mind. That's about as far as I had planned at the time."

Clay was officially sixty-five (actually sixty-four) and in robust health. He looked more like a senior business executive than a retired Army officer, his eagle-sharp features softened by weekends of golf and sailing off Cape Cod. Clay was still exceptionally trim and fit—he still continued his daily practice of one-armed pushups, an old trick that he had learned many years ago at West Point and which had astounded Zhukov and Sokolovsky in 1945. Many thought he looked to be in his early fifties.

Clay had no regrets about his decision to retire. "I think it is important for people to move on," said Clay. "Running an industrial company requires a considerable amount of physical ability if you are going to be a company leader. You've got to get out and visit the plants and know what's going on. You've got to have a certain amount of physical stamina and endurance. The same is true in the Army. It's not because of lack of mental ability. It is because in commanding troops in war, you never know when you're going to be called on in the middle of the night for decisions, or just when and where. And the weather. And the elements. You've got to have physical stamina if you are going to be able to make the decisions that have to be made. We found sixty-four much too old for field commanders in World War II. We found that our division commanders generally ought to be around fifty. I made it very obvious at Continental Can that there was no chance of my remaining after sixty-five. I put the rule in that required mandatory retirement."

Q: Mr. Carle Conway had been older than sixty-five.

CLAY: That's right. That's one of the reasons I put the rule in.

Q: Were you tempted to back off?

CLAY: No sir. I can't take positions like that and then back away from them. It would be absolutely out of character if I did.
Q: Would you apply this rule to government as well?
CLAY: You have a little different situation in government. So many of the jobs are jobs that last only for the duration of one Administration. There the question of age insofar as succession is concerned is not as important as it is in industry. The civil service usually does not fill Cabinet and sub-Cabinet positions. By and large, to get the exceptional person, you can forget the age limits. But, there again, I think you are better off with a government that is composed of men and women of reasonable age and physical ability as well as mental activity. But it is not the same question of morale that you have in the military service or industry.

"Mr. Stimson, for example, was a man of such outstanding stature that his appointment [as Secretary of War], even at his age [seventy-four], was never criticized. And he was a tower of strength. Now, if he hadn't had a General Marshall, and vice versa, whether they would have been able to function so well is something I don't know. Mr. Stimson did function. He functioned magnificently. Although he only put in a relatively few hours a day.
Q: The image of President Eisenhower is that he also only put in a few hours a day.
CLAY: Yes, but that's just ridiculous. He worked long and hard, but he never let his mind get cluttered up by details or by making other people's decisions.

"I know very well that in the early stages of the game, when members of his own Cabinet would come to him with problems, he'd say to them, 'That's your own problem.'

"He went down to his office in the White House early. He had breakfast very early. That's an old Army trait. He went to bed relatively early and was up early, and I think by and large handled his mail before most people were coming to work.

"I was always at Continental Can early. Around eight o'clock. It represents a problem, because all of a sudden you realize that when you go down at eight o'clock your principal subordinates feel that they've got to be down there too. And so they're breaking their necks to come in from the country and whatnot, and you practically have to order them not to. I still go down to the office at eight. I do my mail and whatever else I have to do that requires my own personal attention. And I like to be free after nine-thirty or ten o'clock so that I can take any telephone calls or meet or see anybody that wants to see me."

Q: And boards of directors? You were on quite a number.

CLAY: I have always advocated, and in fact I led the way, to a retirement age for directors as well. I did this at General Motors and at the Metropolitan Life Insurance Company. At General Motors, we fixed the age at seventy. At Metropolitan, at seventy-two. So I've always believed in a retirement age for board members.

"There are arguments both ways. The principal argument for not having an age limit is that you have directors who are experienced, know the affairs of the company, and, as long as they are alert and mentally capable, it is very difficult to replace them with anybody that would bring as much knowledge and background to the deliberations of the board. This would be fine if it did not involve the necessity for selection. And it becomes awfully difficult if at some stage of the game you want to retire director Smith because he's no longer alert, but you want to keep director Jones. The only way that you can really resolve that problem is by having a firm retirement age, so that people can't stay on who have lost their mental alertness.

"Now I don't know the age at which you lose your mental alertness. I've seen it happen to people shortly after they reached seventy, and I've seen people still mentally alert at eighty. But I think that as a general rule, between seventy and seventy-two you have a period in which experience compensates for age and you are getting a better director, and that after that your director is not going to be as good. So I think that in the general interest of boards, it is better to have a fixed retirement age."

Clay kept in touch with the situation in Berlin after he returned to New York, but was more or less confident that the worst was over. He went back briefly to speak at the July 4 celebration in West Berlin in 1962—a promise he had made to Mayor Brandt—and was consulted from time to time by President Kennedy about the Berlin situation. It was merely a courtesy, Clay thought, but nevertheless he had formed a genuine liking for JFK. "He had a brilliant mind," Clay once told Richard Scammon. "He listened well, he asked pointed questions, and it was exhilarating to be with him because you don't run into that type of mind too often."

On his part, Kennedy had formed something of a fascination for Clay, especially for his high standard of professional rectitude. When the President's subordinates carped at Clay's vigorous actions in Berlin, Kennedy sympathized with the general's tendency to act without waiting for instructions. Kennedy himself had inserted General Maxwell Taylor into the White House as a lever with the cumbersome Joint Chiefs of Staff, and Clay served JFK's purpose as a blunt instrument of presidential policy in Berlin. As Kennedy observed to Ted Sorensen, General Clay was "a conservative Republican doing a good job on a thankless assignment and staying publicly loyal under a Democratic administration." Arthur Schlesinger, Jr., wrote afterward that Clay's "stout-hearted leadership [in Berlin] left a valuable precedent."

In fact, by the summer of 1962, Clay had become one of JFK's favorite Republicans. Where the President could despair at the unresponsiveness of the government's bureaucracy, he saw Clay as a swashbuckling, hard-driving executive who could get things done and who did not care whose toes he stepped on. To Kennedy, the military leadership he inherited from General Eisenhower (with the possible exception of Admiral Arleigh Burke, Chief of Naval Operations) was as colorful as a bucketful of fog. Clay and Maxwell Taylor, on the other hand, were cut from different cloth. In the argot of the New Frontier, they had charisma and vigor. The fact that Clay was extremely close to General Eisenhower was an added advantage. By dealing with Clay, the Kennedy administration invoked Ike's implicit support without asking the former President directly.

In the fall of 1962, at the height of the Cuban missile crisis, President Kennedy called Clay once again to enlist his support. "The President said that he was afraid Mr. Khrushchev was getting sticky and that he was going to give him an ultimatum that day with respect to taking the missiles out of Cuba. He said, 'I hope you're going to be around over the next five or six days where if I need you I can get you.' As a matter of fact, I was going to Spain on a shooting trip, which I had to call off. I found out subsequently that he called Jack McCloy, who was in Europe, and asked him to come home. Well, the crisis passed over. Mr. Khrushchev accepted the ultimatum and it was all over."

Late that autumn, President Kennedy asked Clay to undertake a review of America's foreign-aid program. "The President just called me up—I think it was probably in November 1962—and asked me if I would form a committee to study the problem. So I went down to see him, and he told me that he was very much concerned with the aid program, that he knew there was a great deal of opposition to it in Congress and he thought he was going to have a great deal of difficulty getting it through. He said he would like to have it examined carefully by a group in which the Congress might have some confidence. I agreed to undertake the job, and we sat down to figure out who to put on the committee."

Q: Why did President Kennedy ask you to head the study?
CLAY: I don't know why the President wanted me. Partially, I am sure, because I was a Republican, and he may have thought that this would help with the Republican Party. But, actually, at that time I was an Eisenhower man rather than a Republican. Also, perhaps he felt that the public had some confidence in me. But it never occurred to me to ask why. I've been asked by various Presidents to do these things, and I've always said yes. I guess I'm completely unable to say no to a President. I never ask the reason why.
Q: And your position on foreign aid in 1962?
CLAY: I would be the last person in the world to be against foreign aid, because without the aid to occupied countries, we could not have maintained life in Germany immediately after the war. It was also quite apparent to me that unless we gave aid to Germany, we would have a Germany on relief indefinitely. So it took very little to convince me of the importance of the Marshall Plan.

"Now whether we spent too much too fast, or more than was necessary, I think this could be argued for many, many years and nobody would really know the answer. But the Marshall Plan saved Western Europe. It gave it a chance to get on its feet. Then we extended the idea far too broadly, I think, to countries that were not equipped to use the aid. The sophisticated European countries knew how to use the aid and the money and the help that we gave them to revive their economies, and they did. But then we began to give it to countries that did not have that capability, and it became just a dole in many, many instances. The money that we gave in the long run didn't even maintain good will, because whenever you cut it back or stopped it, you made more enemies than you had friends when you started it. So I think that we went too far in giving aid to countries that were not prepared for it, that did not have the sophistication to use the aid.

"So in our committee we tried to make a distinction between the kind of aid that we thought was dcsirablc and the kind of aid we did not believe desirable. Furthermore, we accepted and recognized that we could not afford to cut drastically. So our program, which was definitely a slowdown program, was not to slow it down materially that first year, but over a three-year period. The Agency for International Development (AID) had made numerous three-year commitments, and we did not think that we should force AID to run out on those commitments. So what we wanted was a slowdown in the amount of money made available, but making that slowdown primarily effective in those countries that didn't know how to use the money."

Q: But you and President Kennedy picked the committee?

CLAY: Yes. We tried to pick people who had some basic knowledge of foreign aid. Primarily to save time. Which accounted for the heavily Republican composition of the committee. But I don't think they were Republicans in a partisan sense. We simply had to rely on the previous eight years to get people who were experienced.

"Interestingly enough, the people President Kennedy thought he could count on for the most support were the people we had the greatest difficulty with, although I don't think the President ever knew that. I think he thought that Gene Black [former president of the World Bank] was his great ally. But Gene Black was completely opposed to aid to underdeveloped countries. And yet I think he let the President believe right up to the very end that he was on the President's side in all this. I never could understand that.

"After we finished the report in draft form, I told the committee I would like very much to send it over to the President and get his reaction, that I didn't want to confront him with a report that he had had no opportunity to read or comment on. There was some disagreement about this, but the committee finally agreed to do so. So we sent a rough draft over to the President through Mr. [David] Bell [head of AID]. The President thought some of the wording was a little harsh, so I went over it with him. Finally, I suggested, and he agreed, that Mr. [McGeorge] Bundy come over and appear before the committee with suggestions as to how we might alter the language. Not the substance, but the language.

"Mr. Bundy came over to try to get us to soften the language a bit. I had the whole committee there for that, because I wasn't going to take on that responsibility. We also worked very closely with Mr. Bell. I can't say he agreed with us, but he made everything available to us. And I thought Mr. Bell was one of the most able administrators AID had had.

"The committee didn't recommend a total aid figure. That was one of the troubles. We stayed away from figures in the report. We said that there was too much being spent, but that it ought not to be cut immediately, because that would be inconsistent with our commitments. Congressman [Otto] Passman [D., Louisiana, chairman of the House Appropriations Subcommittee on Foreign Aid] interpreted this as a recommendation for a drastic cut in the President's program. Which it was not. So I went to work to try to save his program—by testifying and by writing letters to some twenty newspaper editors asking for their support. I tried to assure them that the report was not intended to be used for what it was being used for [by Mr. Passman], although I'm not too sure how much support I would have had from my committee. Mr. McCollum, Mr. Phleger, and Mr. Lovett were pretty much against foreign aid. Then we had Dean Mason from Harvard, and he wasn't so enthusiastic about foreign aid for the underdeveloped countries either. Mr. Meany dissented from the report, but he never attended a committee meeting. He never listened to any of the testimony."

Q: Did he send a representative?

CLAY: He offered to send a representative, but we didn't allow representatives. If we had, everybody there would have sent a representative. I have great respect for George Meany. He is a broad-gauged labor statesman. But the value of his dissent was lost to some extent because he had not been to any of the committee meetings.

Clay went public to help the President's cause. He told *U.S. News & World Report* that "foreign aid is an essential part of the foreign policy of this country. It is a necessary tool in accomplishing our foreign policy objective." Clay said that over the years the total amount of assistance would decline, but that some foreign aid would always be required. Arthur Schlesinger later observed that Clay had been stung by the attacks on President Kennedy's program and felt an obligation to help out. In the end, Congress passed a foreign-aid package of $3.2 billion in 1963, over $1 billion less than the President had requested.

At Christmas 1962, while Clay was still involved with the foreign-aid problem, he received what was undoubtedly the most unusual request of his long career. Shortly after 6:00 A.M. on Christmas Eve, Attorney General Robert Kennedy called him in New York. Clay was already at Butler Air Terminal at LaGuardia, ready to board a Continental Can Company plane for Washington. He and Marjorie planned to spend Christmas with their son Frank's family in Arlington. Frank was an Army colonel at the time and stationed at the Pentagon.

The Attorney General had Clay paged at the airport. When Clay picked up the phone, Robert Kennedy told him of a last-minute snag that had developed in releasing the prisoners that Fidel Castro had been holding since the ill-fated landing at the Bay of Pigs. Supposedly, they were to have been released in Havana on December 23, so that they could spend Christmas in Miami with their families. But Castro was holding up the release, Kennedy said, until he got an additional $3 million. "We've got to act today," Clay recalled Kennedy as saying, "or there are going to be a lot of disappointed people in Miami on Christmas." Kennedy asked Clay if he would help.

Clay agreed immediately. "We had already paid a ransom—if you want to call it that—in terms of medicines and other supplies worth considerably more," said Clay. "But it seems that a promise of $3 million in cash had been made by some of the refugees, and Castro was demanding that this also be paid. Well, whether it was blackmail or not, it was a question of what you were going to do in the interest of humanity. So I told Bobby that 'I'm on my way to Washington now, and I'll stop by your office as soon as I get there.' "

At eight-fifteen, Clay was in Kennedy's office at the Department of Justice. Kennedy had initially thought of providing the money himself, but because of his official position, that was not possible. He had then tried Boston's Richard Cardinal Cushing, but Cushing could come up with only $400,000. Red Cross Vice President Robert Shea, who was working as the U.S. negotiator with Castro, suggested to Kennedy that he call Clay. "We told him that if he wanted to raise that much money that quickly," said Shea, "he needed someone like Clay, who could get on the telephone and say, 'John, I've got you down for fifty thousand,' and the only response would be 'Yes, sir.' "

As Robert Kennedy hoped, Clay quickly provided the money. After discussing the situation briefly with Kennedy and his staff, Clay recognized that the only way he could raise $3 million in the few hours that were available would be for him personally to advance the entire amount, hoping that he could raise the necessary funds afterward to cover his advance. It was the type of lightning response Clay was famous for. He did not have $3 million, and he had no guarantee that he would ever be reimbursed. But without hesitation he immediately put his personal credit on the line. That Robert Kennedy was one of the most partisan of Democrats did not bother Clay in the least. In fact, Clay liked Bobby and admired his toughness. For Clay, it was not an issue of partisanship. The Attorney General of the United States had asked for his help in an emergency. It was as simple as that.

From Kennedy's office, Clay called his friends Peter Grace and Felix Larkin of the Grace National Bank in New York. Both had to be routed out of their homes on Long Island. Clay asked if they would honor a personal note from him for $3 million. Larkin said that the limit they could go on a personal loan was $2 million, but they would help Clay get the other $1 million from another bank.

"We weren't really given any assurance that we would be paid back," reports Larkin, "except for the fact that Kennedy and Clay were involved. Our confidence that we would be paid back was based on our confidence in General Clay. This was a loan in the old-fashioned banking tradition of the Mellons and the Morgans, based on the man rather than on looking to what assets he had, what collateral he could pledge, what mortgages you could take. We simply had confidence he could raise the money. It is an interesting facet of General Clay: the respect he's held in, the repute he has, our confidence in him, so to speak."

To cover the remaining $1 million, Larkin called officials at First National City Bank in New York. Would they honor another personal note from General Clay for $1 million? They said they would. In less than two hours, Clay had provided the money. The problem remained of how to get it to Castro, since no U.S. bank did business in Cuba. Assistant Attorney General Louis Oberdorfer suggested the Royal Bank of Canada, which had a branch in Havana. Nicholas Katzenbach, the deputy Attorney General, then called Montreal. The Royal Bank agreed that as soon as the money could be deposited at their office in New York, they would pay it out to Castro in Havana.*

On the strength of General Clay's word, the Grace Bank, now working with the First National City Bank, agreed to transfer the entire amount immediately. "Then we found out we didn't have a note," said Clay. "So Larkin dictated his note over the telephone, and we typed it out and I signed it. The money went on through, and the transfers were all going through, and I decided I'd better by a damn sight get ready and raise some money. By then it was about one o'clock. So, instead of spending Christmas Eve with my grandchildren, I was on the telephone in Bobby Kennedy's office from one o'clock until six o'clock raising money.

"Finding people on Christmas Eve is very difficult. Fortunately, with a White House operator, you get a very high degree of cooperation from everybody, and by six o'clock that night I had commitments of over a million dollars. At that time, I felt reasonably safe, and I decided there wasn't any use trying any more at six o'clock Christmas Eve. So I went to my son's house and told him I was in hock for $2 million."

Christmas Day, President Kennedy called Clay at his son's house to thank him for arranging the prisoners' release. "I'll never forget it," said Frank Clay. "There was my father leaning on Pat's ironing board talking to the President of the United States about whether Walter Reuther and George Meany were going to contribute."

In February 1963, at the age of sixty-five, Clay began his third principal career: as investment banker and managing partner of Wall Street's hallowed firm of Lehman Brothers. Once again the offer came from out of the blue. "Bobby Lehman called me up one day in January or February and asked if he could come up to see me. I had been on the board of the Lehman Corporation, of which Lehman Brothers was the manager, for some time. He came up to see me and he said, 'We'd like it very much if you'd come down here as a senior partner in Lehman Brothers.' It just was that simple, really.

* Castro was paid $3 million in Canadian currency. Under prevailing exchange rates, that amounted to $2.925 million U.S.

Washington, D.C.
December 24, 1962

we
Sixty (60) days after date, I promised to pay to the (to be initialled)
order of the Grace National Bank, One Million Nine Hundred
Twenty Five Thousand dollars ($1, 925, 000) for value received
with interest from the date hereof at the rate of 4 1/2% per annum
until paid.

Committee of Cuban Families

by Lucius D. Clay
Authorized representative

Promissory Note for Repatriation of Cuban Prisoners

Washington, D. C.
December 24, 1962

Dear Mr. Grace:

In accordance with the telephone conversations which I and others had with you from Washington this morning, the Cuban Families Committee has borrowed from the Grace National Bank and signed a promissory note for $1,925,000.00 to be used in the repatriation of Cuban prisoners and to be deposited with the Royal Bank of Canada as agreed.

Both myself and the others who were in the conversation are pledged to raise the full amount of the loan and to repay it within 60 days.

May I add that your action has made possible the happy reunion at Christmas of these prisoners who have been imprisoned since the Bay of Pigs.

I can assure you that our actions are approved by our Government.

Sincerely,

Lucius D. Clay
Authorized Representative
Committee of
Cuban Families.

Mr. J. Peter Grace, Jr.
9 Hanover Square
New York, New York

Clay's Letter to the Bank

"I thought about it for a few days, talked to a few friends about it, and signed up. You wouldn't believe it, but at the time I accepted we hadn't even talked money. There was never any bargaining. After I got down there and saw the partners' agreement they had set up for me to sign, it was obviously a very liberal one. But there had been no negotiations. It sounds naïve, but that's the way it happened."

Q: What were your duties at Lehman Brothers?
CLAY: I was made a senior partner. There were three other senior partners at the time; I became the fourth. Bobby Lehman wanted to take a less active role, so I was made chairman of the executive committee when I went down there. The work was piling in and they needed a reorganization. They'd had a rotating chairmanship of the executive committee, and obviously that didn't provide for complete coordination, so Bobby asked me if I would take over the chairmanship of the executive committee and try to get them organized to handle the increasing volume of business. And this I did. Or tried to do.

"I gave up the chairmanship as soon as I could, for several reasons, primarily because I've always felt that the running of a business is not a job for an older man; it is a job for younger men.

"I think that I'm one of the few people at Lehman Brothers who in the ten years that I have been there has turned back consistently on his percentage of income. Three times since I've been there, I've reduced my percentage of the profit of Lehman Brothers voluntarily, because I just don't think that older people ought to stand in the way of young people. Everything in a banking house is on a percentage basis. Your partnerships are on a percentage basis. And obviously the senior partners have a larger percentage of the profit. And I think that it is very important that the senior partners give up a substantial proportion of their percentage of participation, so that it can be transferred to younger partners. Otherwise there is no room for younger partners to grow."

Q: But what did Lehman Brothers want with a retired general in 1963?
CLAY: I don't know. I never found out. I never knew what the Continental Can Company wanted with one either. But I'm probably the only man on Wall Street that ever conducted a currency reform. I'm probably the only one down there that ever put in a national bank

reform. I know I'm the only one that ever established a government. I think I probably had four years of financial experience in Germany that was deeper than that of the people who work and live on Wall Street.

Q: And your job as a partner?

CLAY: The basic job of a partner is to develop clients for the firm, and then use the expertise of the firm in solving the problems of your client. There wasn't any presumption of any business I might bring. Continental Can was already there. I've brought them in a number of customers over the years. But there was no way of knowing that when I went down. Chase Manhattan was one that I brought in. I was on the board there for a while. But I had to get off when I went down to Lehman Brothers because of the law that you can't be on the board of a commercial bank and of an investment bank at the same time. I don't think it was entirely out of friendship that Chase Manhattan came. They originally selected three firms. One of them had to drop out because they were representing another bank, and that left two of us, Lazard Frères and Lehman Brothers. And Chase said, "Because our old director is on the board, Lehman will be our leading manager." And that is the way it happened.

Q: At that time, wasn't there considerable rivalry and bitterness between Lehman Brothers and Goldman, Sachs?

CLAY: Yes. But as a matter of fact, I didn't even realize at the time that this bitterness existed. It arose before my time. And I think it was extremely bitter.

"At one time Goldman, Sachs and Lehman Brothers had operated almost as a unit. Goldman, Sachs were the actual underwriters, and Lehman Brothers provided the capital. And all of their underwriting was done together. The initial underwriting of Sears-Roebuck, for example, had been a joint venture. Then they had a big blowup, in the late twenties. And the feeling that was generated in that blowup I think lasted as long as Bobby Lehman and Sidney Weinberg were alive."

Q: Did it affect your friendship with Sidney Weinberg?

CLAY: It did indeed. He never forgave me for joining Lehman Brothers. Why I don't know. And I was terribly sorry, because Sidney was a very dear friend and I had great respect for him. I was completely taken aback when this happened. I didn't have any expectation that our friendship was going to end like this.

After the initial reorganization at Lehman Brothers, Clay took a less active role in the firm's affairs. He participated in its activities, used his influence as circumstances required, but left the direction of the firm increasingly to younger men.

But Lehman Brothers gave Clay an attractive vantage point from which to continue his public activities. Clay cherished the ethic of public service. As he once told an audience of potential donors to the American Red Cross, "The road to democracy is not a freeway. It is a toll road on which we pay by accepting and carrying out our civic responsibilities." Clay deeply believed that. And he devoted his last years to public endeavors.

One of Clay's favorite projects was the construction of a new medical center for Columbia-Presbyterian Hospital in New York. Clay's only experience with the inside of a hospital was when Dr. Milton Porter had removed four-fifths of his ulcerated stomach in 1955, and Clay had formed a strong bond with Presbyterian. When he was asked in 1965 to head the construction fund drive, he quickly accepted. By 1969, Clay had raised $63 million, and would eventually raise over $100 million for new facilities on Washington Heights. Clay became vice president of the board of trustees, but devoted himself primarily to raising money.

As a private institution, Columbia-Presbyterian conformed to Clay's vision of free-enterprise America. As he wrote to donors in 1969:

> Our physicians and nurses are dedicated to serving humanity, and the hundreds of new physicians and nurses trained at Presbyterian Hospital each year carry its century old tradition of excellence to all parts of the nation. I believe their humanitarian commitment, supported by private philanthropy . . . represents one of the finest expressions of public responsibility in a free society.

Another of Clay's interests was Tuskegee Institute in Alabama, the black agricultural college founded by Booker T. Washington in 1881. The fund drive Clay headed there in the mid-sixties generated more than $60 million for new facilities and more faculty. "Mr. [Bayard Foster] Pope [of Marine Midland Trust], who was an old friend of mine," said Clay, "asked me to join him on the board. I knew about Tuskegee. I'd been at Auburn on ROTC duty [in 1921], and Auburn is just a few miles away. So I knew quite a bit about Tuskegee, and I was happy to serve."

Q: Is there a future for black colleges in the South?
CLAY: This was a question that raised a considerable number of problems, particularly with our ability to raise funds for Tuskegee.

"My answer is that at the moment we need all of the colleges we have. There seem to be some signs now that the numbers are tapering off, but the demand for space in colleges has exceeded the spaces available for some time, so we can't afford to give up any colleges. Second, a great number of students that come to Tuskegee are not really ready to go to a university. Many would be perhaps so unable to cope with the atmosphere in a university that they would get an inferiority complex that might last with them forever. This is particularly true today, when your better students, your top black students, get into the major universities; they are sought out now. But the young black who has come from a restricted background needs the kind of school like Tuskegee to bring him out. So I think it is very important that they be maintained.

"At a black institute like Tuskegee, such students don't have to feel inferior. That is one of the real problems at the university level, where, for a variety of reasons, but mainly because of his own lack of a cultural background, he could very easily develop either a militant attitude or an inferiority complex. I think that unless he is a very gifted student, he is probably better off getting his initial education at Tuskegee than he would be, say, at the University of Alabama.

"There is very little graduate work at Tuskegee as of now. Perhaps in a few years this will have to be corrected; we will have to go further. The fact is, I don't even like to say what Tuskegee's future might be ten or twelve years from now. But at the moment it is badly needed for the purpose it serves."

Q: Has the caliber of the student at Tuskegee fallen off in the face of active recruitment from colleges elsewhere?
CLAY: I would hesitate to answer. Probably, as far as the entering class is concerned, it has. However, there are a tremendous number of students who enter Tuskegee barely making the grade and that turn out to have damn good potential.

"A little over 50 percent are from Alabama. Just under 50 percent are from elsewhere. I have great confidence in Tuskegee, which has had a series of very remarkable black presidents. [Robert R.] Moton and [Frederick D.] Patterson and [Luther H.] Foster have been the three presidents who have contributed tremendously to the development of Tuskegee Institute. It really started out as a manual high school. Agriculture is not as important as it once was in the curriculum, but they still have a very fine program, particularly in their veterinary program—which is one of the better ones in the South."

It was at Tuskegee in 1968 that Clay had his first experience with student radicals. "I went down for a board meeting," said Clay. "The board usually met on Saturday, and we would go down on the Friday before. That Friday night, there was beginning to be some student activity around the guest house where we stayed. And by Saturday, when we went into the board meeting, a student committee had met and put in its demands. There were quite a collection of students, and all of the exits to the administration building were blocked. We couldn't get out of the building.

"I told President Foster that I was flying home Saturday evening. Period. So Saturday afternoon I went down about five o'clock, and all of the doors were barred. I tried to get out through the kitchen doors, and they were blocked. However, out of the blue, three or four very big, very husky young black men came up and said, 'Let's get the general out.' They opened the door and out I went. That's all I know about it. They held the rest of them there through Sunday, and they finally called the sheriff and even the National Guard to secure their release. But I had already left. So I don't have any idea as to just what happened. I really didn't know how I got out. But I did."

When Clay told President Foster that he planned to leave that afternoon, Dr. Foster quietly made arrangements for Clay's departure. "General Clay is not a man to fool with," said Foster. "I knew he meant what he said. If the Russians couldn't blockade him in Berlin, I knew he was not going to let the students block him here. So I went into my office and called our football coach. I told him that I wanted him to have as many of his players as he needed at the kitchen door at five o'clock, and that they were to take General Clay out. I said the rest of us would stay here until it was over.

"I was concerned because General Clay worked very hard for Tuskegee," said Foster, "and we were proud to have him on our board. He had grown up in a different time, but he understood and supported the changes that were taking place."

Clay took no role in the 1964 election. Hamilton Fish of New York began a brief movement to draft Clay for the GOP nomination, but Clay tried to disabuse him of the idea. "I assure you that I never encouraged it," said Clay. "I never felt that it had any meaning. I never took it seriously." After Barry Goldwater's stinging defeat at the hands of Lyndon Johnson, Clay was approached by the GOP's leadership to become chairman of the Republican Finance Committee to return the party to solvency.

"The GOP was in bad shape after the disastrous 1964 presidential campaign," said Clay. "It was financially in bad shape; I think it was at its lowest ebb. Ray Bliss [Republican national chairman] had gone in to try to reorganize the party, but he couldn't do it without money. Tom Dewey came over to see me with George Champion. And they asked me if I would take on the task. I thought about it, and I decided that if you belonged to a party and it was in trouble and they thought you could help, then that was the only time that you couldn't say no. So I took it on. I can't give you any other logical reasons, because at my age [Clay was sixty-seven] it was a very unusual and difficult thing to do. But I did it. And I'm glad I did it.

"I not only put the party back in solvency, but by the time Mr. Nixon was nominated in 1968, we had a very substantial sum of money in the treasury—over a million dollars. While that was nothing for a major campaign, it was a very unusual thing for a political party to go into a presidential campaign with a surplus. We had a surplus."

Q: You resigned as GOP fund chairman after Mr. Nixon was nominated at the 1968 convention?

CLAY: I had made it very clear that I was not going to stay to be the fund-raiser in a presidential campaign. I didn't go in it for that. I went into it when the party was down and out to do my part to contribute to its rebuilding and with no expectation of carrying on in a presidential campaign. I was too old, among other reasons. And besides, that belongs to the young and the ambitious.

Q: You did not support Mr. Nixon?

CLAY: There was never a question of my being against Mr. Nixon. I simply felt that as a Republican we had better vote-getters. I could have been just as wrong as I could be. In any event, he got elected. But I felt we had better vote-getters.

"After George Romney [of Michigan] withdrew from the race, I made a visit to Governor Rockefeller to urge him to run. That doesn't mean I was against Dick Nixon. But I didn't think that he was a vote-getter. And I felt that we were much surer of winning the election with someone else. But I sort of lost my confidence in Romney about the time that he lost it too. And I did go to see Governor Rockefeller to urge him to run. But I also said that, 'As long as I am chairman of the finance committee, I will not take a public position.'

"Governor Rockefeller then announced that he was going to run, and then he withdrew. Then he went back into it again. I figured a long time on what to do, because I knew that he was too late when he went back in the second time. But I had made a commitment to him, and I felt I had to live up to it. So I did. And I supported him."

Former GOP Chairman Leonard Hall attributed Clay's resignation as finance chairman to Nixon's nomination. "Clay was a Rockefeller Republican," said Hall, "and he never thought much of Nixon. Probably it went back to 1952 and the 'Checkers' thing. But Lucius did quite a job for the party as finance chairman. I recall that he had threatened to resign six or seven times. Lucius says that quite frequently when he takes a job. He can say 'I resign' quicker than anyone I know. But usually he doesn't. And he's a great asset to have on your side in a fight."

Clay did help raise money for Nixon's campaign, but not as finance chairman, and he took no active role in the election. In the 1970s, he was called on by the President whenever German issues arose, and, with John McCloy and Dean Acheson, formed an informal bipartisan triumvirate to counsel Nixon on the Berlin Accords. When Radio Free Europe came under attack for using secret funds from the CIA, Clay briefly accepted its chairmanship to steer it into calmer waters. When the Federal National Mortgage Association (Fanny May) became a publicly held corporation in 1970, Clay was elected its first chairman (defeating Nixon appointee Sherman Ungar). "I agreed to take it on for an important transition period," said Clay. "When I went down there and an election took place, I did not realize that there had been a fight in the board and that Mr. Ungar was in active competition for the chairmanship. If I'd realized that, I wouldn't have touched it with a ten-foot pole. But I'd gone too far then, so I went ahead. And I became Fanny May's first chairman. But only for its transition into a private company."

Throughout his life, Clay was always an easy mark for the tough jobs that others shunned. Mayor John Lindsay appointed him to head New York City's development corporation to revitalize the city's flagging industry. When Arthur Goldberg ran for governor of New York, he asked Clay (his old bargaining opponent at Continental Can) to take his place as head of the American Committee to Assist the United Nations Commissioner for Refugees, the Aga Khan. Later Clay served as a member of New York City's Charter Revision Commission. In addition, he twice headed the national fund drive for the American Red Cross, three times for the Arthritis and Rheumatism Foundation, and on a quiet personal level raised the money to pay Sherman Adams's debt to the IRS when the former White House Chief of Staff ran afoul of the tax laws in the 1960s. Altogether, Clay helped raise over $750 million for charitable purposes (including the GOP)—which is probably an all-time record for personal fund-raising, if records were kept in such matters.

In 1973, at the age of seventy-five, Clay retired from Lehman Brothers—well before the carnage that ultimately brought down the House of Lehman. He and Marjorie retained an apartment at the Carlton House on Madison Avenue, but spent most of their time on Cape Cod at the old rambling house—known in East Chatham as "Square Top," for the shape of its roof—that they had bought in the 1950s. Clay enjoyed the Cape, and Marjorie did even more so. Their seven grandchildren were in regular attendance each summer.

By 1973, Clay's robust health was failing. His massive consumption of cigarettes and black coffee was taking its toll. Although his mind remained crisp, his body became frail. He was racked with emphysema. He died in his sleep in his bedroom at Square Top on April 17, 1978. Three days later, he was buried with full military honors in the cadet cemetery at West Point. Clay's grave stands in the front rank, overlooking the Hudson River. He is flanked by General George Goethals, a fellow Engineer who built the Panama Canal, and Air Force Colonel Edward H. White, the first American astronaut to walk in space, who perished in the Apollo capsule fire at Cape Canaveral. Clay's tombstone is modest: his name, his rank, and the fact that he was Military Governor of Germany and commander of U.S. forces in Europe. At the foot of the grave, buried flush with the ground, is a small marble tablet placed there by the citizens of Berlin:

WIR DANKEN
DEM BEWAHRER
UNSERER FREIHEIT

We thank the defender of our freedom.

APPENDIX

JCS 1067

[Extract]

April 1945

Directive to Commander in Chief of United States Forces of Occupation Regarding the Military Government of Germany

1. The Purpose and Scope of this Directive:

This directive is issued to you as Commanding General of the United States forces of occupation in Germany. As such you will serve as United States member of the Control Council and will also be responsible for the administration of military government in the zone or zones assigned to the United States for purposes of occupation and administration. It outlines the basic policies which will guide you in those two capacities after the termination of the combined command of the Supreme Commander, Allied Expeditionary Force. . . .

PART I
General and Political

2. The Basis of Military Government:

a. The rights, power and status of the military government in Germany are based upon the unconditional surrender or total defeat of Germany.

b. Subject to the provisions of paragraph 3 below, you are, by virtue of your position, clothed with supreme legislative, executive, and judicial authority in the areas occupied by forces under your command. This authority will be broadly construed and includes authority to take all measures deemed by you necessary, appropriate or desirable in relation to military exigencies and the objectives of a firm military government. . . .

3. The Control Council and Zones of Occupation:

a. The four Commanders-in-Chief, acting jointly, will constitute the Control Council in Germany which will be the supreme organ of control over Germany in accordance with the agreement on Control Machinery in Germany. For purposes of administration of military government, Germany has been divided into four zones of occupation.

b. The authority of the Control Council to formulate policy and procedures and administrative relationships with respect to matters affecting Germany as a whole will be paramount throughout Germany. You will carry out and support in your zone the policies agreed upon in the Control Council. In the absence of such agreed policies you will act in accordance with this and other directives of the Joint Chiefs of Staff.

c. The administration of affairs in Germany shall be directed towards the decentralization of the political and administrative structure and the development of local responsibility. To this end you will encourage autonomy in regional, local and municipal agencies of German administration. The German economic structure shall also be decentralized. . . .

4. Basic Objectives of Military Government in Germany:

a. It should be brought home to the Germans that Germany's ruthless warfare and the fanatical Nazi resistance have destroyed the German economy and made chaos and suffering inevitable and that the Germans cannot escape responsibility for what they have brought upon themselves.

b. Germany will not be occupied for the purpose of liberation but as a defeated enemy nation. Your aim is not oppression but to occupy Germany for the purpose of realizing certain important Allied objectives. In the conduct of your occupation and administration you should be just but firm and aloof. You will strongly discourage fraternization with the German officials and population.

c. The principal Allied objective is to prevent Germany from ever again becoming a threat to the peace of the world. Essential steps in the accomplishment of this objective are the elimination of Nazism and militarism in all their forms, the immediate apprehension of war criminals for punishment, the industrial disarmament and demilitarization of Germany, with continuing control over Germany's capacity to make war, and the preparation for an eventual reconstruction of German political life on a democratic basis.

d. Other Allied objectives are to enforce the program of reparations and restitution, to provide relief for the benefit of countries devastated by Nazi aggression, and to ensure that prisoners of war and displaced persons of the United Nations are cared for and repatriated.

5. Economic Controls:

a. As a member of the Control Council and as zone commander, you will be guided by the principle that controls upon the German economy may be imposed to the extent that such controls may be necessary to achieve the objectives enumerated in paragraph 4 above and also as they may be essential to protect the safety and meet the needs of the occupying forces and assure the production and maintenance of goods and services required to prevent starvation or such disease and unrest as would endanger these forces. No action will be taken in execution of the reparations program or otherwise which would tend to support basic living conditions in Germany or in your zone on a higher level than that existing in any one of the neighboring United Nations. . . .

6. Political Activities:

   a. No political activities of any kind shall be countenanced unless authorized by you. You will assure that your military government does not become committed to any political group. . . .

PART II
Economic

General Objectives and Methods of Control

You will assure that the German economy is administered and controlled in such a way as to accomplish the basic objectives set forth in paragraphs 4 and 5 of this Directive. Economic controls will be imposed only to the extent necessary to accomplish these objectives, provided that you will impose controls to the full extent necessary to achieve the industrial disarmament of Germany. Except as may be necessary to carry out these objectives, you will take no steps (a) looking toward the economic rehabilitation of Germany, or (b) designed to maintain or strengthen the German economy. . . .

German Standard of Living

You will estimate requirements of supplies necessary to prevent starvation or widespread disease or such civil unrest as would endanger the occupying forces. Such estimates will be based upon a program whereby the Germans are made responsible for providing for themselves, out of their own work and resources. You will take all practicable economic and police measures to assure that German resources are fully utilized and consumption held to the minimum in order that imports may be strictly limited and that surpluses may be made available for the occupying forces and displaced persons and United Nations prisoners of war, and for reparation. You will take no action that would tend to support basic living standards in Germany on a higher level than that existing in any one of the neighboring United Nations and you will take appropriate measures to ensure that basic living standards of the German people are not higher than those existing in any one of the neighboring United Nations when such measures will contribute to raising the standards of any such nation. . . .

Source: Press release, U.S. Department of State, October 17, 1945.

NOTES

Preface

PAGE	
x	"this remarkable man": McCloy interview, Milbank, Tweed, Hadley, and McCloy, New York, N.Y., 19 February 1971.
xii	Clay's papers as Military Governor: Jean Edward Smith, *The Papers of General Lucius D. Clay, Germany 1945–1949,* 2 vols. (Bloomington: Indiana University Press, 1974). (Hereinafter cited as *Clay Papers.)*

Introduction

PAGE	
1	"the fiery type of fellow": Lovett interview, Brown Brothers, Harriman, New York, N.Y., 4 May 1971.
2	"one of the most skillful politicians ever": John Kenneth Galbraith, "The Decline of American Power," *Esquire,* March 1972, p. 83.
2	Pétain on West Point: Quoted in T. Bentley Mott, "West Point: A Criticism," *Harper's,* March 1934, pp. 478–79.
3	"He was quite sure": Lovett interview.
3	"bolshevik": Clay's Army efficiency report, 16 June 1920.
4	"Lucius always kept his eye": Harriman interview, Georgetown (Washington, D.C.), 22 June 1971.
5	"General Motors or U.S. Steel": James F. Byrnes, *All in One Lifetime* (New York: Harper & Bros., 1958), p. 272.
5	"The most able fellow": U.S. Congress, Senate Committee on the Judiciary, Internal Security Subcommittee, *Morgenthau Diary (China)* (Washington, D.C.: Government Printing Office, 1965), vol. 2, p. 1129.
6	"Ruling over enemies": *Look,* 12 September 1945.
6	"city of the dead": Lucius D. Clay, *Decision in Germany* (Garden City, N.Y.: Doubleday, 1950), p. 21.
6	"the Civil War was always with us": Clay interview. All quotations from General Clay, unless otherwise identified, are from JES interviews. These are on file at Columbia University and the Eisenhower Library.

7 "a Communist on 1500 calories": CC-2124, Clay for Echols and Petersen, 27 March 1946, in *Clay Papers,* pp. 183–85.

7 "not much different from election measures": CC-2135, Clay for War Department, 20 April 1946, in *Clay Papers,* pp. 256–58.

8 "cultivated, taciturn, polished, and clear": Reinhold Maier, *Ende und Wende* (Stuttgart: Wunderlich, 1949), p. 392.

8 Clay's message to Royall: TT-2150, Clay to Royall, 21 April 1949, in *Clay Papers,* pp. 1121–24.

9 "Clay was a pleasure to work for": McLean interview, Leahy Clinic, Boston, Mass., 24 May 1971.

9 General Robertson's comments: Cited (without attribution) in E. J. Kahn's "Profile" of General Clay, "Soldier in Mufti," *The New Yorker,* 13 January 1951, p. 29. Clay (in good humor) attributed the remark to Robertson.

11 "Lucius was an autocrat": Boeschenstein interview, Owens-Corning Fiberglas, New York, N.Y., 16 February 1971.

11 Hazard's remarks: Ellison Hazard interview, Continental Can Company, New York, N.Y., 12 December 1970.

11 "Clay had tremendous self-discipline": Boyd interview, Copper Range, New York, N.Y., 22 March 1971.

13 "arrogant, stubborn, opinionated": Cabot interview, First Boston Corporation, Boston, Mass., 12 December 1970.

BOOK ONE: THE EARLY YEARS

1: *The Clays of Georgia*

PAGE

17 Description of Senator Clay's election comes from reports carried in all Georgia newspapers, 5–17 November 1896. Originally, the Speaker of the U.S. House of Representatives, Charles F. Crisp, had been chosen to succeed General Gordon. But Crisp died before the Georgia Legislature could confirm the choice, and Clay was chosen in his stead. Upon Clay's election, the Atlanta *Constitution* (17 November 1896) noted: "Steve Clay was a poor farm boy, the son of a poor farmer, and from the day he was eight years old and first went to the fields on his father's farm to do his share . . . he has known what work has meant."

18 Concerning the Clay genealogy, the most complete treatment was written by Hon. Zachery Smith and Mary Rogers Clay, *The Clay Family* (Louisville, Ky., 1906). L. W. Rigsby, of the Georgia Clays, has pulled together some remaining family archives. These

were published by him as "The Georgia Branch of the Virginia Clays and Their Celebrated Cousins," *Home and Family,* 4 July 1926. A genealogical chart of "The Colonial Clay's of Virginia and Some of Their Descendants 1443–1943" was compiled by Clifford Charles Clay of Atlanta, 1943. Together with other useful papers, it is on file in the Clay Genealogical Folder, Georgia Department of Archives & History, Atlanta. *The Clay Family Quarterly,* published irregularly by G. R. Clay, P.O. Box 35254, Houston, Tex. 77035, is interesting but not especially useful. In the same category are the autobiographies of Brutus Junius Clay and Cassius Marcellus Clay, Lincoln's ambassador to Russia. General Clay's immediate family have little in the way of family archives. From his cousins in Atlanta and elsewhere I have obtained numerous newspaper clippings, scrapbooks, and recorded interviews. These are noted in the Acknowledgments.

18 Concerning Pearce Clay's plantation, Rigsby (citing contemporary records) describes it as "a little kingdom within itself. Cabins surrounded the homestead, populated with slaves, and the farm was teeming with industry; farming operations, shops for repairing tools, and sheds wherein thread was spun and woven into cloth. His cribs were well supplied with grain and his hogs, cattle and colts roamed over the range. His loom house always had a supply of cloth to satisfy the needs of his slaves, as well as the members of the family." (L. W. Rigsby, pp. 49–50.)

18 Relations with south Georgia Clays: Little love is lost between the aristocratic Clays of south Georgia and those of Cobb County. L. W. Rigsby, family historian of the south Georgia Clays, reports: "[Senator] Steven Clay . . . admitted that W. M. Clay, his grandfather, and David Clay were brothers [sons of Pearce Clay], so I have been informed. . . . However, Polliticians [sic] are given to claiming kin with those who can vote and it is possible that if such an admission was made that it was made for political effect. Yet there is some evidence to justify the investigation." (Letter to Miss Ruth Blair, 13 September 1924, Clay Genealogy Folder, Georgia Department of Archives & History.)

19 Will Clay: The description of Will Clay was provided by his great-granddaughter Zaida Clay Walsh, and his great-grandson Eugene Herbert Clay in personal interviews with the author; and by Louise Frix, a granddaughter living in Atlanta. Ms. Frix kindly made available to the author her extensive scrapbooks of the Clay family.

19 Clay & Blair: The Marietta legal firm of Clay and Blair was well known throughout Georgia—Clay the barrister who presented the cases, Blair the solicitor who prepared them. An advertisement

in the Marietta *Journal,* 14 December 1893, stated: "A. S. Clay & D. W. Blair, Attorneys at Law—Marietta, Georgia, Rooms 1 and 2 on left over Wash White's store. We give our entire attention to the practice of the law. Promptness is our Motto. Collection a specialty."

20 Democratic-Populist struggle: The best general survey of Georgia politics in the era of A. S. Clay remains C. Vann Woodward's *Origins of the New South, 1877–1913* (Baton Rouge: Louisiana State University Press, 1951). Also useful are Robert P. Brooks, *The Agrarian Revolution in Georgia, 1865–1912,* Bulletin No. 639 (Madison: University of Wisconsin, 1914); E. M. Banks, *The Economics of Land Tenure in Georgia* (New York: Columbia University Press, 1905); Dewey W. Grantham, Jr., *Hoke Smith and the Politics of the New South* (Baton Rouge: Louisiana State University Press, 1958); Alex M. Arnett, *The Populist Movement in Georgia* (New York: Columbia University Press, 1922); C. Vann Woodward, *Tom Watson: Agrarian Rebel* (New York: Macmillan, 1938). The best brief history of Georgia is E. Merton Coulton, *Georgia: A Short History* (Chapel Hill: University of North Carolina Press, 1933). Lucian Lamar Knight, *A Standard History of Georgia and Georgians,* 6 vols. (New York and Chicago: Lewis, 1917), is less useful. Mrs. W. H. [Rebecca] Felton, *My Memoirs of Georgia Politics* (Atlanta: Index Co., 1911), is delightfully written by the widow of a Georgia congressional colleague of Clay. V. O. Key's *Southern Politics in State and Nation* (New York: Knopf, 1949) remains indispensable to a student of Southern politics in any era.

20 Senator Clay and Tom Watson: In 1906 Clay interceded with President Theodore Roosevelt in Watson's behalf in a patronage dispute in Georgia. In a "PERSONAL & CONFIDENTIAL" letter to Watson (11 September 1906), Clay pledged his cooperation in the removal of John M. Barnes as postmaster of Thomson, Watson's hometown. "I will surely do by you as I believe you would by me in similar circumstances," Clay wrote. "I resisted his appointment to the best of my inability. . . . I felt certain that I would succeed but I was turned down through the influence of prominent Republicans in Georgia.

"Certainly, I will not stand by and see such an indignity heaped upon you if I can prevent it. The President will not return to Washington before the first of October. I suggest that you write Mr. Hardwick [U.S. congressman from Georgia, T. W. Hardwick] and I will go with him to Washington as soon as the President returns. Experience has taught me that much more can be accomplished in this way than by writing. However, I will do as you suggest. Please write me immediately. Yours very truly, A. S. Clay" (Tom Watson Papers, University of North Carolina).

21 "We should be broad and liberal": Clay's interview in *The New York Times* is in the issue of 26 March 1902, p. 1. For information concerning Senator Clay's congressional record, I consulted contemporary issues of the Atlanta *Constitution,* the Atlanta *Journal,* the *Marietta Journal, The Washington Post,* and *The New York Times.* The *Congressional Record* (1897–1910) records his activities on the Senate floor. The "Hearing of the Select Committee on Woman Suffrage," 60th Cong., 1st Sess., is Senate Doc. 409 (Washington, D.C.: Government Printing Office, 1908).

21 denunciation of U.S. imperialist claims: Senator Clay sharply attacked American involvement in the Pacific and U.S. imperialism generally. Said he in his maiden speech to the Senate: "When the present war with Spain began, we declared to the civilized world that it was not to be a war of conquest. The freedom and independence of Cuba was the clearly expressed purpose of the war. . . . We have apparently abandoned our original purpose, and are seeking to acquire by conquest Puerto Rico and the Philippine Islands, to annex Hawaii, and the next step will be to seize Cuba. . . . The argument made in favor of the annexation of these islands [Hawaii] thus far is to enable us to capture the Philippine Islands. The answer to that argument is that we have no business to capture the Philippine Islands. . . . Heretofore we have avoided any complications liable to involve us in trouble with foreign powers. We have endeavored to live in peace with the world and have been content to carry on friendly commerce with all nations. We have acted toward them as we would have them act toward us. This course has enabled us not only to become great and powerful, but happy, prosperous, and peaceable, and has given us a country that challenges the admiration of the world" *(Congressional Record,* vol. 31, pt. 7, 55th Cong., 2d Sess., 27 June 1898 [Washington, D.C.: Government Printing Office, 1898], pp. 6350–54).

21 "Clay was diligent": *Memorial Addresses on the Life and the Character of Alexander S. Clay,* 61st Cong., 3rd Sess. (Washington, D.C.: Government Printing Office, 1911). Biographical notes on the senator are few and far between. The best are contained in W. L. Northern, *Men of Mark in Georgia,* vol. 4 (Atlanta: Caldwell, 1908), pp. 39–44; and *Memoirs of Georgia,* vol. 1 (Atlanta: Southern Historical Association, 1895).

22 Senator Clay and Theodore Roosevelt: Senator Clay twice invited Mr. Roosevelt to Marietta: once in 1901, when he was Vice President (declined), once as President in 1905 (accepted). The first

invitation, written the year Roosevelt became Vice President, invited him to speak at a 4 July Chautauqua in Marietta. Wrote Clay, "I sincerely hope that you may be so situated as to accept this invitation and visit Georgia. I shall expect you to be my guest while here and I feel sure that in no section of our common county would you find a more royal welcome than here. . . . Yours most cordially, A. S. Clay" (4-page handwritten letter, March 26, 1901, in the Papers of Theodore Roosevelt, Manuscript Division, Library of Congress).

23 Collapsed on Senate floor: *The New York Times,* 17 February 1908, p. 1.

23 Senator Clay's last will and testament was recorded 9 September 1910 (Cobb County Record Book 3, p. 144). After bequeathing his estate to his wife for life and then equally to their children, Clay stated: "I desire that my funeral be a plain and simple one, and the monument over my grave to be also plain and simple, giving the date of my birth and death, and public positions I have held. I expressly desire to teach simplicity in every step taken after my death. Observation teaches me that useless extravagance on funeral occasions deprives the living of their just rights."

2: *Marietta Boyhood*

PAGE

25 Clay was born: Reference to General Clay's birthdate, 23 April 1898, was carried in the Marietta *Journal,* 28 April 1898. According to the *Journal:* "Senator A. S. Clay arrived home Friday evening just in time to be greeted by the arrival of a fine son at his home." (When I tried previously to corroborate Clay's official, 1897 birthdate, I found only reference to a gala party given by General Clay's mother two days after the supposed birth [Marietta *Journal,* 29 April 1897].) In fact, Clay's birthdate showed considerable elasticity. The Force School in Washington, D.C., for example, had it recorded as 23 April 1896 (letter to JES from Jacobeth P. Novak, director, Department of Pupil Personnel Services, Public Schools of the District of Columbia, 22 July 1970). Clay's certificate attesting the false birthdate, signed by his mother, is on file in the Office of Old Military Records, U.S. Archives (30 June 1915).

26 The Clay home: This house on Atlanta Street in Marietta is still standing, although it is no longer in the Clay family, having been sold shortly after Mrs. Clay's death in 1940. The last Clay property in Marietta was sold 25 April 1942, six months prior to the location in Marietta of the Bell bomber plant—an important fact,

perhaps, since Clay was instrumental in having the Bell plant located there. See chap. 11.

26 "Some say he was murdered": Eugene Herbert Clay, Jr., interview, Columbus, Ohio, 1 June 1971.

27 Herbert Clay's death was handled gingerly: General news reports were carried in the Atlanta papers, 23 June and 24 June 1923.

27 Frank Butner Clay: Reports of Lieutenant Frank Clay's affliction can be found in the Atlanta *Constitution,* the Atlanta *Journal,* and the Marietta *Journal,* 18–23 January 1915.

28 Evelyn Clay: Evelyn Clay's tragic attempt to live on her father's reputation forty years after his death is partially documented in a series of letters to President Truman, 1948–52, Harry S. Truman Papers, Truman Library, official file 2188, Independence, Mo.

29 "Momma Clay was old-fashioned": Zaida Clay Walsh interview, Atlanta, Ga., 16 June 1971.

29 "She was very bitter about the North": Eugene Herbert Clay, Jr., interview.

31 Georgia Tech: A letter (23 August 1971) to the author from A. L. Bastock, Jr., director of registration and records, Georgia Institute of Technology, reports that Clay "did come to Georgia Tech, but was told he was too young to enroll. He stayed a few days and went home. He was never enrolled and for this reason does not appear on the school records."

31 "independence to the Philippine Islands": Clay's high-school debate was reported in the Marietta *Journal,* 29 May 1914.

3: West Point

PAGE

34 The records of Clay's appointment to West Point, his nomination papers, and his final efficiency report are on file in the Division of Old Military Records, U.S. Archives. His class standing was reported annually in the *Official Register of the Officers and Cadets, United States Military Academy* (West Point: United States Military Academy Printing Office, 1915–18). *The Register of Graduates and Former Cadets of the United States Military Academy,* published annually by the West Point Alumni Association, was useful in locating many of General Clay's classmates.

34 Clay's West Point record: The archives at West Point contain little material on the Class of June 1918. Aside from two letters written prior to his entry, Clay's file was empty. Also, there is no individual record of the demerits he incurred. A day-by-day search of the "skin lists" revealed the following infractions: "Lights burning during breakfast" (14 September 1916); "Floor not properly swept" (8 December 1916); "Throwing food in front of mess hall

—4 demerits" (4 May 1916); "Book of fiction on table" (13 March 1916). Clay's promotion to cadet supply sergeant is contained in USMA Special Order 180, para. 1, 30 August 1917; his demotion to private in Special Order 249, para. 2, 1 December 1917.

34 "Lucius was a nonconformist": Casey interview, Naples, Fla., 16 December 1969.

34 the Military Academy's reputation: The best contemporary account of West Point is still Stephen E. Ambrose, *Duty, Honor, Country: A History of West Point* (Baltimore: Johns Hopkins Press, 1966). Also useful were T. Bentley Mott, "West Point: A Criticism," *Harper's,* March 1934; Colonel S. E. Tillman, "A Review of West Point's History," *Journal of the Military Service Institution of the United States,* January–June 1916, pp. 184–96.

34 "West Point is not a subject for reform": General Hugh Scott, *Some Memories of a Soldier* (New York: Century, 1928), p. 420.

35 "forty years behind the times": Peyton March quoted in Edward M. Coffman, *The Hilt of the Sword: The Career of Peyton C. March* (Madison: University of Wisconsin Press, 1966), p. 186.

35 Like Grant and Eisenhower: General Grant's classic account is in *Personal Memoirs of U. S. Grant* (New York: Charles L. Webster, 1885), vol. 1, pp. 35–43. Said Grant, "I did not take hold of my studies with avidity, in fact I rarely ever read a lesson the second time in my entire cadetship. I could not sit in my room doing nothing. There is a fine library connected with the Academy from which Cadets can get books to read in their quarters. I devoted more time to these, than to books relating to the course of studies. Much of the time, I am sorry to say, I devoted to novels, but not those of a trashy sort. I read all of Bulwer's then published, Cooper's, Marryat's, Scott's, Washington Irving's books, Lever's, and many others that I do not now remember." For Eisenhower's comments, see Dwight D. Eisenhower, *At Ease: Stories I Tell My Friends* (Garden City, N.Y.: Doubleday, 1967), pp. 3–26.

36 "never taught to write at VMI": Reported in Forrest C. Pogue, *George C. Marshall: Education of a General* (New York: Viking, 1963), p. 47.

39 MacArthur as Superintendent: MacArthur's role as Superintendent is described most recently in Ambrose, *Duty, Honor, Country,* pp. 261–83; William Manchester, *American Caesar* (Boston: Little, Brown, 1978), pp. 116–41; D. Clayton James, *The Years of MacArthur, vol. 1, 1880–1914* (Boston: Houghton Mifflin, 1970), pp. 259–94; Douglas MacArthur, *Reminiscences* (New York: McGraw-Hill, 1964), pp. 77–84.

41 "red tape methods": *The New York Times,* 9 May 1920. "The graduates of West Point," wrote Eliot, "did not escape, with few

exceptions, from the methods they had been taught and drilled in during peace. The methods of fighting were in the main new, and the methods of supply and accounting ought to have been new. The red tape methods prescribed to the regular army in peace . . . were very mischievous all through the actual fighting and remain a serious impediment to the efficiency of the War Department to this day."

41 Pétain's critique: Quoted in Mott, "West Point," *Criticism,* pp. 478–79.

4: The Training of a Bolshevik

PAGE

43 Fort Humphreys: In 1933, the name of Fort Humphreys was changed to Fort Belvoir, the traditional name for the Fairfax estate. It remains the seat of the Corps of Engineers. For a description, see Major James A. Dorst, "Ft. Humphreys and Historic Belvoir," *The Military Engineer,* vol. 15, no. 82 (1923), pp. 332–34.

46 Leslie R. Groves: Brigadier General Richard H. Groves generously provided me with a copy of his father's (Lieutenant General Leslie R. Groves's) manuscript dealing with life at Camp Humphreys.

46 final efficiency report: All of Clay's efficiency reports were made available to me by the adjutant general at General Clay's direction.

48 Clay's publications: Lucius Dubignon Clay, "The Engineer ROTC Camp of 1921, at Camp Humphries [sic], Va.," *The Military Engineer,* vol. 12, no. 72 (1920), pp. 488–92. Clay published regularly as a junior officer. His article on the problems of ROTC was published the next year: "Popularizing ROTC Instruction," *The Military Engineer,* vol. 13, no. 79 (1921), pp. 230–32. The Engineer training regulations written by Clay were: TR 445-235, *Portable Footbridges;* TR 195-30, *Explosives and Demolitions;* TR 195-5, *Principles of Field Fortifications;* and TR 445-215, *Stream Crossing Expedients.* Also, "Portable Footbridges of Kapok Pillows," *The Military Engineer,* vol. 15, no. 82 (1923), pp. 137–38.

49 "I was terribly impressed": Maxwell Taylor interview, Washington, D.C., 25 July 1971.

50 Dion Williams: On 8 April 1924, Marine Commandant Williams wrote: "The services of Lieutenant Clay were particularly valuable, during the night of January 5th, 1924, he worked all night instructing our men in the erection of the Pontoon Bridge, and was otherwise of the greatest assistance to our Engineer Company. . . ."

50 landing on Culebra Island: Clay's account of the exercise is in his article "With the Marines on Culebra Island," *The Military Engineer,* vol. 16, no. 86 (1924), pp. 147–48.

50 Clay's last efficiency report at Humphreys, written by Major James Dorst, described him as "One of the best young officers in the service. Exceedingly energetic and capable. He works far better on his own initiative. Mercurial in temperament and very sensitive to criticism."

50 On his work as instructor at West Point, see Lucius D. Clay, "Some Observations as an Instructor," *The Military Engineer,* vol. 20, no. 3 (1928), pp. 216–18.

50 A useful work on West Point in the twenties is Colonel Roger Nye, "The USMA in an Era of Educational Reform," unpublished Ph.D. dissertation, Columbia University, 1966. Also useful are Stephen E. Ambrose, *Duty, Honor, Country: A History of West Point* (Baltimore: Johns Hopkins Press, 1966), and D. Clayton James, *The Years of MacArthur,* vol. 1, 1880–1941 (Boston: Houghton Mifflin, 1970).

52 providing Marjorie with a sizable income: Because of a family quarrel, John McKeown left all of his considerable estate to Marjorie, effectively disinheriting her sister. Mrs. Clay promptly divided the inheritance equally with her sister.

53 Clay's law school request: The date of Clay's letter to the adjutant general was 8 August 1929. The letter remains a part of Clay's official 201 File.

53 Duty in Canal Zone: For an impression of Engineer training in the Canal Zone in the twenties and thirties, see Capt. F. H. Kohloss, "Engineer Training in Panama," *The Military Engineer,* vol. 26, no. 149 (1934), pp. 357–60.

53 "I took over B Company": Colonel Charles "Chesty" Ward, a West Point classmate who succeeded Clay as commander of B Company, 11th Engineers, writes: "B Co., 11th Engineers was an excellent company. The NCO's were a very superb group. Most of those under General Clay were there under me. They were a stabilizing element that carried over from officer changes. . . . Discipline was not a serious problem. . . . There was a serious depression affecting civilian employment and most soldiers were happy to be in the Army. The state of readiness was excellent for the Army in those days" (letter to JES, 8 December 1970).

53 11th Engineers: The most complete unit history of the 11th Engineers was prepared by the office of the Chief of Military History, Organizational History and Honors Branch, 9 February 1953. Histories of the exploits of the 11th Engineers in World War I include Van Tuyl Broughton, *History of the Eleventh Engineers* (New

York: Little and Ives, 1926); *Company C, Eleventh Engineers: A History* (Indianapolis: Hollenbeck Press, 1919); *Welcome Home* (New York: Klebold Press, 1919).

54 U.S. military action in Panama: Pursuant to the 1903 treaty between the United States and Panama, now superseded, American forces in the Canal Zone were permitted to intervene in Panama in cases of rebellion or civil disorder.

55 "a real revolution": The Panamanian revolution toppling Arosemena was spearheaded by the Accion Comunal, a liberal group headed by H. Arias, who quickly became president. A running account was carried in *The New York Times,* 3–5 January 1931. Colonel Lippincott's early warning, combined with the fact that Arias was then Panamanian ambassador in Washington, suggests that the United States was more than a disinterested bystander.

55 efficiency reports: In Clay's final efficiency report in Panama, Major Pier Focardi, Caples's successor, wrote, "Close personal supervision of all details, obtaining promptly desired results and keeping his men in the highest morale makes him a superior troop officer." Brigadier General C. D. Roberts, the commanding officer at Fort Davis, gave Clay a similar rating: "An accomplished, highly efficient and hard working officer. Has unusual executive ability and capacity of getting along with those with whom he is working and getting work done without friction."

55 "to cause the necessary surveys . . .": 4 Stat. L. 22(1824).

56 Vang Construction Company: Clay was reported to be a three-goal polo player for the Vang Construction Company team. When I asked Clay if this was a conflict of interest, he said, "My God, it wasn't against the law to play golf or polo with the people you did business with."

56 Clay in Pittsburgh: Details of Clay's stay in Pittsburgh from Styer interview, Coronado, Calif., 20 April 1972.

5: Muddy Waters

PAGE

59 Corps of Engineers: One of the best volumes on the Corps of Engineers remains Arthur Maass's *Muddy Waters: The Army Engineers and the Nation's Rivers* (Cambridge, Mass.: Harvard University Press, 1951). Also valuable but narrower in scope is William Leuchtenburg's *Flood Control Politics* (Cambridge, Mass.: Harvard University Press, 1953), a case study of flood control in the Connecticut Valley, 1927–50. For a detailed study of the development of the civil functions of the Corps of Engineers, see W. Stull Holt, *The Office of the Chief of Engineers of the Army,*

Service Monographs of the United States Government, No. 27 (Baltimore: Institute for Government Research, 1923). The case contra is made by Arthur E. Morgan, *Dams and Other Disasters* (Boston: Sargent, 1971). Among official publications, the *Annual Report of the Chief of Engineers* provides a wealth of detail about the functions of the Corps, as do the annual *Hearings* of the respective House and Senate committees dealing with Corps activities. During Clay's time in the Chief's office, these were the Committee on Appropriations, the Committee on Rivers and Harbors, and the Committee on Flood Control in the House; and the Committee on Appropriations and the Committee on Commerce in the Senate. See also Lenore Fine and Jesse Reminton, *The Corps of Engineers: Construction in the United States* (Washington, D.C.: Government Printing Office, 1972).

60 one president . . . vetoed: On 5 October 1978, President Carter did veto a $10.16-billion omnibus public-works bill (H. Rept. 95-1490) that contained $2.63 billion for the Corps of Engineers. But Carter's veto proves the point. The final compromise measure that was enacted that year (H.J. Res. 1139) contained $2.63 billion for the Corps of Engineers.

60 "Clay was terribly industrious": Edgerton interview, Washington, D.C., 12 December 1971.

62 "the WPA program . . . set up under Harry Hopkins": Harry Hopkins's appointment calendar at the Franklin D. Roosevelt Library (Hyde Park) reveals that Clay and General Markham offered their services to Hopkins on Friday, 19 January 1934 (4:30 P.M.). They paid a second call on Hopkins, presumably to discuss the matter further, on Monday, 22 January 1934 (2:45 P.M.). Clay's initial reference to the WPA should be to the CWA (Civil Works Administration), which was formed in November 1933 under Hopkins. It was superseded by WPA in early 1935. Ickes's attitude toward the Corps of Engineers is detailed at great length in *The Secret Diary of Harold L. Ickes* (New York: Simon and Schuster, 1951–53), especially vols. 1 and 2. Also see Ickes's foreword to Maass's *Muddy Waters.*

69 Clay and Rayburn: Rayburn's close friendship with Clay is amply attested in a collection of personal letters in the Sam Rayburn Papers at the Sam Rayburn Library, in Bonham, Texas. In 1957, by then a prominent Republican, Clay wrote Rayburn nostalgically of their association in the thirties. "In changing from a life-long and home-trained Democrat to work for General Eisenhower's election, somehow I felt a little embarrassed to visit you, particularly as so often you had let me sit in on Democratic Councils. What I am really trying to say is that on my next visit to

Washington, I would like very much to pay my respects again," wrote Clay (10 April 1957). Rayburn replied warmly: "It has been a long time since I have had any touch with you, and I have been wondering why—remembering how close we were for several years. I have thought all the time that probably the reasons you gave in your letter were what had prevented your calling me and letting us get together as we had in times past. It would not have been embarrassing to me at any time to have seen you" (17 April 1957).

71 Concerning the Corps's failure to protect the environment, see especially Elizabeth Drew, "Dam Outrage: The Story of the Army Engineers," *The Atlantic,* July 1970.

73 Clay and General Markham: The relation between Clay and General Markham, who did not object to being corrected in public by this junior officer, is revealed in the *Hearings* before the Senate Appropriations Committee on the War Department Appropriation Bill, 1937 (5 March 1936), 74th Cong., 2nd Sess. (Washington, D.C.: Government Printing Office, 1936), pp. 163–99: *Senator Chavez [D., New Mexico]:* How many engineers have you out there? *General Markham:* I do not remember the figures. I would have to get that. I would say possibly 20 or 30. *Captain Clay:* Including the administrative board and the office force, we have out there right now approximately 150, I would say. *General Markham:* Of all grades? *Captain Clay:* Yes, sir. *Senator Chavez:* How many do you expect to employ at the peak? *General Markham:* I cannot tell you for the moment. We would have to look that up in the office. *Captain Clay:* I think it will run about 3,000. *General Markham:* About 3,000.

74 "Captain Clay is scheduled for detachment": U.S. Congress, House Committee on Appropriations, *Hearings on the War Department Civil Functions Appropriations Bill for 1938,* 75th Cong., 1st Sess. (Washington, D.C.: Government Printing Office, 1937), pp. 91–92.

74 "you didn't belong in the Corps of Engineers": A copy of Clay's speech to the 1971 Engineer Dinner was provided to the author by Brigadier General Richard H. Groves, Corps of Engineers.

74 "the most devious bastards": Groves interview, Washington, D.C., 26 June 1971.

6: Ike and Mac and Mr. Sam

PAGE

78 Clay and Eisenhower: Lieutenant William Lee (later Brigadier General Lee, USAF), who taught Clay and Eisenhower to fly in the Philippines, kept a diary of that period, which is on file at the

Eisenhower Library. Entries relating to General Clay run from 5 February 1938 to 7 April 1938. Lee throws an interesting light on the Clay-Eisenhower relationship in his entry of Wednesday, 23 March 1938: "I worked awhile at Camp Murphy this morning. Col. Eisenhower was out for a while . . . and took a [airplane] ride with Jew Lewis. He saw a tractor that I wanted to buy for use on grading the flying field in operation and I think he is in favor of buying it, but doesn't want to buck Capt. Clay unless he has to. Capt. Clay is opposed to buying it and has some good reasons."

81 MacArthur's difficulties: MacArthur's 1939 difficulties in the Philippines are recorded in D. Clayton James, *The Years of MacArthur* (Boston: Houghton Mifflin, 1970), vol. 1, pp. 526–38; Frazier Hunt, *The Untold Story of Douglas MacArthur* (New York: Davis-Adair, 1954), pp. 183–93; Theodore Friend, *Between Two Empires: The Ordeal of the Philippines, 1929–1946* (New Haven: Yale University Press, 1965), pp. 190–94; James K. Eyre, *The Roosevelt-MacArthur Conflict* (Chambersburg, Pa.: Craft Press, 1950), pp. 28–33; J. Woodward Howard, Jr., *Mr. Justice Murphy: A Political Biography* (Princeton: Princeton University Press, 1968), pp. 104–9. MacArthur did not mention Quezon's disaffection in his *Reminiscences* (New York: McGraw-Hill, 1964). On the other hand, Eisenhower (*At Ease: Stories I Tell My Friends* [Garden City, N.Y.: Doubleday, 1967]) provides sufficient information for the informed reader to draw his own conclusions: "President Quezon seemed to ask for my advice more and more. He invited me to his office frequently. This was partly because of the office hours General MacArthur liked to keep. . . . Because I was the senior active duty officer [MacArthur found himself retired], my friendship with the President became closer. Our conversations became broader and deeper. They were no longer confined to the defense problem. Taxes, education, honesty in government, and other subjects entered the discussions and he seemed to enjoy them."

83 a reluctant Harold Ickes: Ickes, no friend of the Corps of Engineers or of Sam Rayburn, reports the incident in his diary, Sunday, 22 December 1935: "More complications with reference to the Red River project in Congressman Sam Rayburn's district in Texas. I think I have related [Nov. 28, 1935] that the President promised several million dollars for this and then after Rayburn had announced that fact, he was unable to find where the money was to come from. Finally, Rayburn came to me in distress, although he had pretty much opposed everything I have ever wanted on the Hill. . . . I took this up with the President and he said to refer it to the National Resources Committee. That I

did, and an adverse report came back, which I sent to the President. . . . Generally speaking, I have always opposed grants of money for preliminary surveys unless we have definitely decided to go ahead with the projects. . . . Colonel McIntyre talked it over with Hopkins and me the other day and we decided to recommend $150,000. This did not go at all well with Rayburn, and at Cabinet meeting . . . the President told me to call in Mr. Delano and General Markham and, in effect, tell them that he wanted them to recommend an allocation of $500,000 for the survey. . . . This is just one example of many of what seems to me a very bad way of handling public business under the work-relief appropriation."

83 Construction activities: The Corps of Engineers' archives for the Denison project are at the GSA records storage area in Suitland, Maryland (Records Group 77). Copies of the Clay-Rayburn correspondence, for the most part job requests and land-appraisal inquiries from Denison constituents, are on file at the Sam Rayburn Library in Bonham, Texas. In addition, information about working with Clay on the dam provided in Sverdrup interview, St. Louis, Mo., 21 June 1971.

85 Oklahoma legislature had previously granted: Chap. 29, Sec. 1, Sess. of Laws of 1907, carried forward in the *Oklahoma Statutes of 1931* as Sec. 10053.

85 Oil extraction: Oil was discovered in 1939 by the Pure Oil Company in the area to be flooded by the Denison Dam. The record of Clay's Washington conference with the representatives of Pure Oil is reported in a memorandum to the Chief of Engineers, 1 April 1940. His proposal to return to the original grantor those mineral rights vested before discovery of the so-called Cumberland Field is contained in two letters to the Chief of Engineers, 23 March and 11 April 1940. This was approved by Assistant Secretary of War Louis Johnson, 17 April 1940. By 1943, the Cumberland Field was producing one million barrels daily.

85 To head off Phillips's opposition: The complete text of Governor Phillips's inaugural attack on the Denison Dam is reprinted in the Durant *Daily Democrat,* 10 January 1939. Clay's confidential memorandum of his 22 July 1939 meeting with Phillips is among the papers in Records Group 77, as is the lengthy Phillips-Woodring (Stimson) correspondence.

At the same time that Phillips was importuning against the dam, Sam Rayburn and Oklahoma Senators Josh Lee and Elmer Thomas kept up a steady flow of telegrams to Woodring supporting the project. Phillips's suit against construction *(Oklahoma* v. *Atkinson, et al.)* was filed in the U.S. District Court for the

Eastern District of Oklahoma on September 9, 1940. Arguments on defendant's motion to dismiss were heard by a three-judge panel on 28 October 1940, with the court (speaking through Judge Walter A. Huxman) requesting that both parties submit briefs on the questions raised, "including the jurisdiction of the court to entertain the suit and the constitutionality of the [1938 Flood Control] Act" (letter, Robert H. Jackson to Henry L. Stimson, 9 November 1940 in Henry L. Stimson Papers, Yale University, New Haven, Conn.). The court's judgment dismissing the suit was rendered 25 January 1941 (Civil Action 348).

85 "The Governor was indignant": Clay's confidential memorandum, dated 27 July 1939, is on file at the Washington National Records Center, Record Group 77.

85 Engineer Department: In its civil works activity, the Corps of Engineers is generally referred to as the U.S. Engineer Department (USED).

86 "If a suit is brought": letter, Clay to Rayburn (27 August 1940). Rayburn Papers, Sam Rayburn Library, Bonham, Texas.

86 Clay's role in Denison: For a useful collection of newspaper clippings about the Denison Dam I am indebted to Arthur A. Phillips of Denison, who generously granted me access to his scrapbooks of that period. Otis K. Higginbotham, resident engineer at the dam, provided me with detailed information concerning the dam's environmental effect. Claude Easterly, editor of the Denison *Herald,* who covered the dam's construction as a reporter, answered numerous letters of mine with helpful information. "My beat included Clay's office," wrote Easterly, "and I had regular contact with him. In my many years of newspapering, I have found some who gauged their cooperation with newspapermen . . . according to the size and prestige of the newspaper they represented. . . . Nothing even suggesting this attitude was ever hinted by Clay. Like others here, I soon came to appreciate him as obviously an . . . executive of great ability and also as a considerate and friendly person. He was warm and personable and at the same time firm and purposeful. He could be both without infringing on either. . . . I invariably found Clay more receptive and cooperative than some lesser personalities I have encountered along the way" (27 July 1971).

87 ordered to Washington: Mrs. Clay retained several letters from the period, including one from W. L. Peterson, president of the State National Bank of Denison. "Not even the shock that I received when I fell in the bathtub," wrote Peterson, "equalled the shock and surprise that almost stunned me when I heard that you were being transferred to Washington" (30 September 1940).

7: B-17s on the Runway

PAGE	
93	meeting with LaGuardia: Colonel R. Joe Rogers interview with General Clay, 8 November 1972. U.S. Army Institute for Military History, Carlisle, Pa.
93	Lovett on LaGuardia: Lovett interview, Brown Brothers, Harriman, New York, N.Y., 4 May 1971.
93	Washington was a bustling boom town: For a colorful, first-hand description of life in Washington before and during World War II, see David Brinkley, *Washington Goes to War* (New York: Knopf, 1988).
97	Trip to Brazil: Clay left Washington for Brazil 2 January 1942. He returned 23 January and recommended an additional expenditure of $2.7 million for airfield improvements. He also suggested that several detachments of Army mechanics and communications specialists be put at each airfield, and that emergency shipments of ammunition and machine guns be shipped to northeastern Brazil to permit air crews and Brazilian Army troops to defend the fields against possible fifth column attack (letter, Candee and Clay to CG, GHQ, 23 January 1942, cited in Stetson Conn and Byron Fairchild, *The Framework of Hemisphere Defense* [Washington, D.C.: Government Printing Office, 1960], pp. 311–12.) In his report, Clay described the situation in Brazil as follows: "We find in Rio much 'solidarity,' Good Neighborliness, and a willingness to concede the importance of the defense of N. E. Brazil, but practically no inclination to do anything concrete in the matter. The Brazilians agree that the area should be defended and say that they will seek our air units, or even ground forces, when attack becomes imminent. In the mean time, they will gladly permit the conversion of commercial fields into military airports and the installation of other facilities and improvements by us while they furnish the ground transportation" (letter to CG, GHQ, 27 January 1942). At the time Clay left for Brazil, the Army was preparing to send a force of fifteen thousand men to Brazil, if necessary to defend the supply route to Britain (Plan LILAC). Clay's visit, plus the continuing efforts of the U.S.-Brazil Joint Military Board, made such a venture unnecessary—assuming that it could have been mounted in early 1942, which is highly unlikely.
97	Pan American: In November 1939, Pan American had been made the agency of the United States government under the defense airport program for the construction and improvement of airports in the Caribbean, Central America, Brazil, and Liberia. Panair dos Brasil, a Pan American subsidiary, had undertaken to build the bases at Belém and Natal. Other bases were built in Cuba, Haiti,

the Dominican Republic, and Venezuela. (A consolidated brief on the Agreements and Contracts Constituting the Airport Development Program is in Air Transport Command, Plans Division Files: History, South Atlantic Div., pt. I, pp. 75–87.)

BOOK TWO: WARTIME WASHINGTON

8: Director of Materiel

PAGE

103 years of neglect: Memo, AC of S WPD for C of S, 25 September 1940. See also Annual Report of the Chief of Staff (Douglas MacArthur) in *Annual Report of the Secretary of War to the President, 1933*. During the interwar years, appropriations for the War Department averaged $339 million annually. These funds provided for all War Department activities except the civil works of the Corps of Engineers: i.e., pay and subsistence of the Army, support of the National Guard and ROTC, operation of arsenals and storage depots, War Department overhead, training, and procurement. See Mark S. Watson, *Chief of Staff: Prewar Plans and Preparations* (Washington, D.C.: Government Printing Office, 1950), pp. 15–56; R. Elbertson Smith, *The Army and Economic Mobilization* (Washington, D.C.: Government Printing Office, 1958), pp. 38–71; John D. Millet, *The Organization and Role of Army Service Forces* (Washington, D.C.: Government Printing Office, 1954), pp. 18–22.

104 equipment outdated: In fiscal year 1939, the Army spent $84 million for new equipment—an amount equal to that spent for radio tubes in 1944 (memorandum, Clay to Operations Council, WPB, 7 July 1944, Clay Desk Files, Hq. ASF, Director of Materiel, 1942–45, National Archives).

104 Mauborgne . . . complained in 1940: Chief Signal Officer for Chief of Staff, 20 February 1940, National Archives.

104 "without a taint of scandal": Henry L. Stimson Diary, 11 December 1940, Manuscript Collection, Yale University, New Haven, Conn.

104 Research and development: 76th Cong., 3d Sess., House of Representatives, Subcommittee of the Committee on Appropriations, *Hearings,* "Military Establishment Appropriation Bill for 1941," pp. 4–8. As late as February 1940, General Marshall argued against replacing the Army's antiquated 75mm howitzers with new 105s because the cost of replacing the six million rounds of 75mm ammunition on hand would be "difficult to justify" (House Appropriations Committee, 76th Cong., 3d Sess., *Hearings,* "Mili-

tary Establishment Appropriation Bill for 1941" [testimony of 23 Feb. 1940], pp. 4–5; Senate Committee on Military Affairs, 76th Cong., 1st Session, *Hearings* on HR 3791, pp. 285–97).

104 Neutrality Act: 49 *Stat.* 1081.

105 "defense, not aggression": Memorandum, DC of S (Embick) for AC of S G-4 (Spalding), 9 May 1938. National Archives.

105 Army's meager research funds: In fiscal year 1939, the Army's total budget for research and development amounted to $5 million —one four-hundredth part of the funds later spent to develop the first atomic bomb. See Watson, *Chief of Staff;* p. 32.

105 "needless expenditures": In cutting the Army's research-and-development budget from a modest $9 million, General Spalding (AC of S G-4) remarked, "The amount of funds allocated to Research and Development in former years is in excess of the proper proportion for the item in consideration of the rearmament program" (memo, AC of S G-4 for C of S, 30 October 1936, subject: Research and Development for FY 1939). In late 1937, when the chief of ordnance requested an additional $500,000 to speed development of an antitank weapon capable of penetrating modern armor, General Embick again refused the request (memo, DC of S for AC of S G-4, 3 November 1937, subject: Increase in Research funds). Cf. memo, AC of S G-4 for C of S, 8 February 1939, subject: Army Research and Development.

105 Vannevar Bush: Bush eventually took his offer to President Roosevelt, who quickly embraced it. For Bush's offer, see Memo, Ex. Off. Mil. Div. of OC of Engineers to AC of S WPD, 6 April 1939, subject: Basic Research for National Defense. See also James P. Baxter, *Scientists Against Time* (Boston: Little, Brown, 1946); Vannevar Bush, *Pieces of the Action* (New York: Morrow, 1970), pp. 30–37.

105 "I could not get excited": Quoted in Walter Isaacson and Evan Thomas, *The Wise Men* (New York: Simon and Schuster, 1986), p. 171. Also see George F. Kennan, *From Munich After Prague* (Princeton: Princeton University Press, 1968), pp. 80–87.

106 King George to Roosevelt: Edgar B. Nixon, ed., *Franklin D. Roosevelt and Foreign Affairs,* vol. 3 (Cambridge, Mass.: Harvard University Press, 1969), p. 234.

106 FDR's fireside chat: William Stevenson, *A Man Called Intrepid* (New York: Harcourt, Brace, Jovanovich, 1976), pp. 315–316.

106 weapons orders through Morgenthau: Roosevelt's gambit was revealed in January 1939, when a new-model bomber crashed during a test flight at Los Angeles Municipal Airport. Among those killed was an official of the French Air Ministry, Paul Chemidlin, whom the Douglas Aircraft Company at first identified simply as

"Smithin, a company mechanic." When asked about the incident the following day by the Senate Military Affairs Committee, General H. H. Arnold replied that "Chemidlin was out there under the direction of the Treasury Department, with a view of looking into possible purchase of planes by the French Mission." Morgenthau confirmed Arnold's testimony, whereupon Woodring and Craig publicly criticized the President for maintaining two arms programs: the official, War Department program, and the unofficial one, under the Treasury. (When General Craig sought to return to active duty during the war, President Roosevelt appointed him head of the board reviewing applications for direct commissions in the Army.) For reports of the Chemidlin affair, see *The New York Times,* 27–29 January 1939.

107 Stimson's new team: Elting E. Morison, *Turmoil and Tradition: A Study of the Life and Times of Henry L. Stimson* (New York: Atheneum, 1964), pp. 417–18; Watson, *Chief of Staff,* p. 337. When told by the Army brass that they could not justify production orders beyond those needed to equip a four-million-man Army, McCloy exploded: "You may be bound by that," he said, "but that doesn't impress me. The President has announced that we will become the arsenal for democracy. We are out to top Germany in peace or in war" (meeting in the DC of S's office, 24 January 1941, C of S files, notes on conference, binder 8). For a recent treatment of McCloy and Lovett, see Walter Isaacson and Evan Thomas, *The Wise Men* (New York: Simon and Schuster, 1986).

107 "so full of dead wood": Lovett interview, Brown Brothers, Harriman, New York, N.Y., 30 March 1971.

107 still remarkably unprepared: "Logistics in World War II," *Final Report of the Army Service Forces* (Washington, D.C.: Government Printing Office, 1948), pp. 16–18.

107 Three weeks after Pearl Harbor: Forrest C. Pogue, *George C. Marshall: Ordeal and Hope, 1939–42* (New York: Viking, 1966), pp. 159–60; Watson, *Chief of Staff,* pp. 343–46; General Albert C. Wedemeyer, *Wedemeyer Reports* (New York: Henry Holt, 1958), pp. 65–67. Cf. Paul A. C. Koistinen, "The 'Industrial Military Complex' in Historical Perspective," *Journal of American History,* vol. 56 (March 1970), pp. 819–39; Adam Yarmolinsky, *The Military Establishment* (New York: Harper & Row, 1971), pp. 55–56.

107 Under the National Defense Act of 1920, Army responsibility for procurement and industrial mobilization was lodged in the office of the Assistant Secretary of War. The position of Under Secretary, created December 16, 1940, carried over these powers. I have used the term "Under Secretary" throughout.

107 M-Day plans: See especially Albert A. Blum, "The Birth and Death of the M-Day Plan," in Harold Stein, ed., *American Civil-Military Decisions* (Montgomery: University of Alabama Press, 1963), pp. 61–96.

108 In preparing his reorganization plan, Marshall specifically directed that Under Secretary Patterson not be informed (notes on conference in ODC of S, 5 February 1942). Indeed, as it was originally formulated, Marshall's plan ran contrary to the statutory responsibility of the Under Secretary under the National Defense Act of 1920. Goldwaithe Dorr, special adviser to Mr. Stimson, believed this was not an "intentional design," but reflected "the inadvertence of a group of officers who did not know much about the supply side of the Army" (Dorr memorandum, pp. 14–15, cited in Millet, *Army Service Forces,* p. 33). Thus, Somervell and Dorr modified Marshall's original draft, restating the statutory responsibility of the Under Secretary. Patterson, when confronted with a *fait accompli,* decided he could work out the details informally with Somervell, although Harold Smith, Director of the Bureau of the Budget, was sufficiently concerned to ask the President to protect the Under Secretary by defining his power. Otherwise, Smith believed, "the proposed arrangement could easily result in purchase and procurement work being insulated from the top civilian side of the Department" (memo, Director, Bureau of the Budget, quoted in O. L. Nelson, *National Security and the General Staff* [Washington, D.C.: Infantry Journal Press, 1946], p. 851; D.A. Cir. 59, 2 Mar 1942. Sec. 7e).

108 Services of Supply: The Services of Supply, designated Army Service Forces on 12 March 1943, was modeled after Pershing's Services of Supply, which was set up as an independent command in the AEF in 1918. See Johnson Hagood, *The Services of Supply* (Boston: Houghton Mifflin, 1927); James G. Harbord, *The American Army in France* (Boston: Little, Brown, 1936). Clay always referred to the organization as the "Services of Supply," and in the interest of clarity, I have used that term throughout.

108 "I'm tired of hearing Drum beat the drum": Noel F. Bush, "General Drum," *Life,* 16 June 1941, p. 96.

110 Marshall on postwar reorganization: Marshall believed that the post–World War II reorganization of the War Department, particularly the reassertion of the power of the independent branch chiefs, was designed to prevent "a man like Somervell" from attaining power again (Forrest C. Pogue, *George C. Marshall,* vol. 2, pp. 297–98).

112 ruthless energy: See John D. Millet, *The Works Progress Administration in New York City* (Chicago: Public Administration Ser-

vice, 1938); Arthur W. MacMahon, et al., *The Administration of Federal Relief Work* (Chicago: Public Administration Service, 1941). Of the seven men who preceded Somervell as head of the WPA in New York, including the formidable General Hugh ("Iron Pants") Johnson, one had died from overwork, several had quit in disgust, and the others had been beaten by the job. But Somervell turned the New York WPA operation into a model district: he kept upward of 203,000 men (more or less) usefully employed, inaugurated thousands of projects, and poured over $10 million monthly into a faltering economy. He successfully avoided involvement in the feud between Mayor LaGuardia and Robert Moses, easily out-generaled Communist radicals who sought to discredit the WPA, and when confronted by a militant sit-in simply locked up the toilets and went home.

Charles J. V. Murphy once described Somervell as "all lace and velvet and courtliness on the outside, fury and purposefulness within" ("Somervell of SOS," *Life,* 8 March 1943, p. 86). See also "The SOS," *Fortune,* September 1942, p. 68.

112 "Styer complemented Somervell perfectly": Lutes interview, Army-Navy Club, Washington, D.C., 11 December 1971.

113 "without a drop": Aurand interview, Army-Navy Club, Washington, D.C., 11 December 1971.

113 "I'll promote him": Somervell's description of his conference with Marshall, as related by Clay to JES.

114 the United States produced: *U.S. Army in World War II, Statistics,* Procurement, 9 April 1952 draft, prepared by Richard H. Crawford and Lindsay F. Cooke under the direction of Theodore E. Whiting; cited in R. Elberton Smith, *The Army and Economic Mobilization* (Washington, D.C.: Government Printing Office, 1958), p. 25.

116 Gasoline pipeline: See memorandum for the Chief of Engineers (from Clay), 5 June 1942, subject: Gasoline Pipe Line Equipment for Bolero, Clay Papers, Army Service Forces, National Archives, Washington, D.C.

9: America's Victory Program

PAGE

118 State of the Union message: "These figures, and similar figures for a multitude of other implements of war," said Roosevelt, "will give the Japanese and Nazis a little idea of just what they accomplished in the attack at Pearl Harbor. And I rather hope that all of these figures . . . will become common knowledge in Germany and Japan" *(The Public Papers and Addresses of Franklin D. Roosevelt, 1942* [New York: Harper & Bros., 1950], p. 32).

119 "the production people can do it": Quoted in Robert Sherwood, *Roosevelt and Hopkins: An Intimate History* (New York: Harper & Bros., 1948), pp. 273–74.

119 Beaverbrook estimated: Letter, Lord Beaverbrook to the President, 27 December 1941; Lord Beaverbrook, memorandum for the President of the United States, 29 December 1941.

119 "reasonably certain": W. H. Harrison to Donald Nelson, 20 January 1942. In a slightly revised form, this memorandum is War Production Board doc. 2, January 20, 1942; cited in Civilian Production Administration, *Industrial Mobilization for War* (Washington, D.C.: Government Printing Office, 1947), pp. 279–80.

119 "indices of balanced production": Memo, Somervell for C of S, 7 January 1942, subject: Effect of President's Directive of 3 January, cited in Richard M. Leighton and Robert W. Coakley, *Global Logistics and Strategy, 1940–1943* (Washington, D.C.: Government Printing Office, 1955), p. 199.

119 War Munitions Program: Army Service Forces, *Annual Report,* 1943, p. 18; Civilian Production Administration, *Industrial Mobilization,* p. 274; R. E. Smith, *Economic Mobilization,* p. 142.

120 program came as a shock: Leighton and Coakley, *Global Logistics,* p. 199.

120 "balance": Planning Papers, 6 January 1942, sub: Victory Program, WPD 4494, Office of Modern Military Records, National Archives. (Hereinafter cited as OMMR/NA.)

121 "could not be accomplished by 1943": Memo, Eisenhower (AC of S War Plans Div) for Marshall, 20 February 1942, subject: Victory Program, OMMR/NA.

121 "It is of little use": Memo, Adm. King for SN, 19 February 1942, subject: Priority of Production of Material, OMMR/NA.

121 Nelson's comment: As stated in memo, Clay to Somervell, 12 March 1942, subject: Advisability of Adjustment of the Presidential Objectives, Clay Papers, Army Service Forces, National Archives.

122 "instructions of The Commander in Chief": Memo, Somervell to Clay, 8 March 1942, Clay Papers, ASF.

122 reductions in presidential objectives: Memo, Clay to Somervell, 12 March 1942, subject: Advisability of Adjustment of the Presidential Objectives, Clay Papers, ASF.

122 if the targets . . . were to be met: Memo, Clay to Somervell, 12 March 1942, subject: Presidential Objectives for 1942 and 1943, Clay Papers, ASF.

122 Eberstadt . . . gave board approval: Memo, Eberstadt to Patterson and Somervell, 25 March 1942, subject: Proposed Readjustment Program, Clay Papers, ASF.

123 messages from the joint tank committee: Advance Copy of Findings of US-British Tank Committee, March 1942, Clay Papers, ASF.

123 "increase the fire power": Memo, Somervell (Clay) to Patterson, 26 March 1942, subject: Balanced Production Program for 1942 and 1943, Clay Papers, ASF.

123 memorandum of agreement: "Thus [wrote Clay], it included 46,523 units of tank-type equipment (including 24,703 tanks, 8940 armored cars, and 12,880 self-propelled artillery mounts) . . . together with 52,384 guns, including antiaircraft and antitank weapons mounted on tank chassis" (memorandum of agreement between the Under Secretary of War and the Chairman of the War Production Board, 29 March 1942, Clay Papers, ASF).

123 "I shall request the Services": Nelson to Roosevelt, 30 March 1942, Clay Papers, ASF.

124 "clearly a matter of major policy": Nelson to Roosevelt, 31 March 1942, Clay Papers, ASF.

124 Marshall to FDR: Letter, April 1942, Clay Papers, ASF.

126 Letter to Nelson: Roosevelt to Nelson, 1 May 1942, Clay Papers, ASF.

10: Lend-Lease

PAGE

131 "We have to deal with big leaguers": Quoted in Lt. Gen. Maurice A. Pope, *Soldiers and Politicians: The Memoirs of Lt.-Gen. Maurice A. Pope, C.B.M.C.* (Toronto: University of Toronto Press, 1962), p. 234. Pope was chief of the Canadian Joint Staff Mission in Washington.

131 intensified the Allies' demands: Edward R. Stettinius, *Lend-Lease: Weapon for Victory* (New York: Macmillan, 1974), pp. 129–36; Letter, Maj. Gen. James H. Burns to President, 23 July 1941. General Burns's summary of Soviet requirements as known at the end of August 1941 is in his memorandum to the Chief of Staff, 31 August 1941. FDR's approval is contained in memo, President for SW, 31 April 1941: Richard M. Leighton and Robert W. Coakley, *Global Logistics and Strategy: 1940–1943* (Washington, D.C.: Government Printing Office, 1955), pp. 97–99.

131 over 80 percent: Memo, Maj. Gen. Robert C. Moore for C of S, 30 June 1941, subject: Schedule of Items Which Can be Trfd to Other Countries; memo, AC of S WPD for AC of S G-4, 28 June 1941, subject: Comments on TRF Program of W D Under Def Aid (with General Marshall's handwritten approval); memo, McCloy for Exe Off DDAR, 12 July 1941.

132 "could not . . . assume the responsibility . . .": Robert E. Sher-

wood, *Roosevelt and Hopkins: An Intimate History* (New York: Harper & Bros., 1948), p. 472. See also M. A. Gwyor, *Grand Strategy* (London: H.M. Stationery Office, 1964), vol. 3, p. 397.

132 "the whole trouble with Foreign Aid": Memo, Somervell for Clay, 27 July 1942. Cf. Memo, Aurand for Somervell, 24 June 1942, subject: Army Supply Program.

132 resented the subordination: On leaving the division in mid-July 1942, Aurand suggested that it should be returned to the general supervision of the assistant secretary of war (memo, Aurand for Clay, 18 June 1942, subject: Plan of ID in Orgn.). See also Leighton and Coakley, *Global Logistics,* p. 262.

133 Combined Production and Resources Board: White House press release, 9 June 1942; memo, Roosevelt to Nelson, 9 June 1942; minutes of the War Production Board, WPB, *Documentary Publication No. 4* (Washington, D.C.: Government Printing Office, 1946), p. 94. The official history of the period prepared by the Bureau of the Budget describes the role of the CPRB as one of conferring and devising plans rather than allocating resources. See U.S. Bureau of the Budget, *The United States at War* (Washington, D.C.: Government Printing Office, 1946), p. 131.

133 the British . . . saw the new board: According to the War Department's official history, the new structure "came to resemble closely the blueprint the British had brought to Washington in December 1941" (Leighton and Coakley, *Global Logistics,* p. 257).

133 raised [Nelson's] status: Civilian Production Administration, *Industrial Mobilization for War* (Washington, D.C.: Government Printing Office, 1947), p. 225.

133 Clay . . . objected heatedly: John Fennelly, *Memoirs of a Bureaucrat: A Personal Story of the War Production Board* (Chicago: October House, 1965), pp. 115–16.

134 "report through me": The Procurement Division, which handled all of the contract work for the Services of Supply, was also originally set up on a par with Clay's Division of Requirements and Resources. Headed by Brigadier General Charles D. Young, former vice president of the Pennsylvania Railroad, the Procurement Division's functions also overlapped Clay's. Colonel Albert J. Browning, the former head of production for the War Production Board, whom Clay had inveigled to join the Services of Supply, went to see Somervell to request that the division be put under Clay. According to Browning's reasoning, you couldn't separate the production and contracting functions. Somervell agreed, the Procurement Division was placed under Clay, and General Young, "a fine old gentleman who couldn't adjust to the pace and tempo

of wartime Washington," was allowed to go back to private life (SOS GO 6, 15 April 1942; SOS GO 24, 20 July 1942).

134 Army Supply Program: According to the Army's official history, once Clay took over, "improvement in the handling of Lend-Lease at the operating level was rapid. . . . There were certain intangible changes resulting from the fact that Lend-Lease was placed under new management and integrated into an organization for the supply of the Army. . . . Aurand had been the ablest defender of the Lend-Lease principle within the War Department and was a far more convinced advocate of the common pool theory than Somervell or Clay. They recognized the importance of Lend-Lease as an instrument of coalition warfare as well as Aurand, but their experience and orientation was toward supplying the U.S. Army first, and they tended to subordinate Lend-Lease to this end. They preferred direct action within the confines of the SOS staff to the involved deliberations of combined committees. In sum, the new management adopted a more national outlook, aimed at preventing foreign raids on the U.S. supply pool." (Leighton and Coakley, *Global Logistics,* pp. 264–66.) See also memo, Clay to Franks, 20 August 1942; memo, Franks for Chiefs of Supply Services, 8 September 1942, subject: Responsibilities of Chiefs of Supply Services for Accomplishing Aid to United Nations.

134 "Lucius was always so goddamned direct": Harriman interview, Georgetown, Washington, D.C., 22 June 1971.

138 "would unduly delay the Protocol": Memorandum for Mr. Hopkins, 21 May 1943, subject: Russian Protocol, Clay Papers, ASF.

138 steam shovels and cranes: Letter, Rudenko to Clay, 8 September 1944, Clay Papers, ASF.

138 "Let's try to do this": Letter (draft), Edgerton to Rudenko, 15 September 1944, Clay Papers, ASF.

138 "importance of cranes and shovels": Memo routing slip, Clay to Edgerton, 33137, n.d., Clay Papers, ASF.

138 "Canadian guard": Quoted in Pope, *Soldiers and Politicians,* pp. 234–35.

138 "running out of rubber": For an analysis of the deficiencies in the U.S. rubber program, see House doc. 836, 77th Cong., 2d Sess., 10 September 1942, *The Rubber Situation.* See also Eliot Janeway, *The Struggle for Survival* (New Haven: Yale University Press, 1951), pp. 340–46; U.S. Bureau of Budget, *United States at War,* pp. 293–97; Civilian Production Administration, *Industrial Mobilization,* pp. 377–79.

140 "change the insignia on my shoulder": Letter, Clay to Colonel (later Lieutenant General) Samuel D. Sturgis, Jr., Chief of Engineers, 1953–56, Clay Papers, ASF.

140 "doomed to stay in Washington": Letter, Clay to Casey, 20 November 1942, Clay papers, ASF.

141 Operations Analysis: Memorandum for the Deputy Chief of Staff (McNarney), subject: Operations Analysis, 13 September 1942, Clay Papers, ASF.

11: The Battle of Washington

PAGE

144 "I can't delegate it": FDR speaking to the Commerce Department's Business Advisory Council, 23 May 1940. See also *The Public Papers and Addresses of Franklin D. Roosevelt, 1941* (New York: Harper & Bros., 1950), pp. 60–69. For a lively discussion of this period, see James MacGregor Burns, *Roosevelt: The Soldier of Freedom, 1940–1945* (New York: Harcourt Brace Jovanovich, 1970), pp. 50–56.

144 succession of temporary agencies: In August 1939, Roosevelt authorized appointment of the big-business-dominated War Resources Board: Edward R. Stettinius (U.S. Steel), Walter S. Gifford (AT&T); John Lee Pratt (General Motors); General Robert Wood (Sears-Roebuck); Karl T. Compton (MIT); Harold G. Moulton (Brookings); and John Hancock of Lehman Brothers—a close associate of Bernard Baruch. When appointment of the board was announced, industrialist Cyrus Eaton wired FDR in disgust that "one of these financial camels might pass through the needle's eye of middle western public opinion, but hardly the whole herd."

The WRB was succeeded on 30 May 1940 by the National Defense Advisory Commission—a throwback to the Advisory Commission to the Council of National Defense in World War I, and representing big business, big labor, and several distinguished public representatives: William Knudsen, Sidney Hillman, Stettinius, Leon Henderson, Chester Davis, Ralph Budd, and Harriet Elliot. The NDAC yielded the following year to Office of Production Management (OPM)—Knudsen, Hillman, Stimson, and Knox—and the Office of Price Administration and Civilian Supply (OPA) under Leon Henderson, which again were partially superseded by the Supply Priorities and Allocations Board (SPAB) under Vice President Henry Wallace, with Donald Nelson as executive director.

144 Nelson was delegated full power: Executive Order 9024, 16 January 1942.

144 "It took Lincoln three years . . .": Letter, Frankfurter to Roosevelt. Max Freedman, *Roosevelt and Frankfurter: Their Correspondence, 1928–1945* (Boston: Little, Brown, 1967). A former vice president for sales of Sears-Roebuck, Nelson was sent to Washing-

ton in 1940 by General Robert Wood to assist Henry Morgenthau in handling British and French defense purchases. "General Wood called me into his office and gave me the news that he had 'sold me down the river,' " wrote Nelson (Donald Nelson, *Arsenal of Democracy* [New York: Harcourt, Brace, 1946], p. 67).

144 the preparedness pecking order: On 17 May 1940, Nelson was appointed acting director of procurement in the Treasury Department; on 27 June 1940, coordinator of national defense purchases under the National Advisory Council; then head of the Priorities Division of the Office of Production Management, and, finally, executive director of the Supply and Priorities Allocation Board in late 1941.

144 "Donald Nelson was a compromiser": Boeschenstein interview, Owens-Corning Fiberglas, New York, N.Y., 16 February 1971.

145 Nelson . . . began to dissipate the authority: "As interpreted and executed by me," wrote Nelson later, "it was not the one-man job conceived by the President when the Board was created. The economic power vested in me at that time was potentially greater than that ever held by any other civilian, except a wartime President. The record will show that of my own initiative I shed controls and authorities not directly germane to my principal function . . . as rapidly as I could" (*Arsenal of Democracy,* pp. 171–72).

145 Nelson's reputation suffered: "Many years later, Nelson came to see me at Continental Can," said Clay. "He was trying to sell a patent. And he was a pathetic case. He wasn't taken back by Sears-Roebuck after the war, and he just gradually deteriorated and went downhill."

145 basic task of the War Production Board: According to the Nelson-Patterson agreement, 12 March 1942, the WPB was to "exercise general direction over the war procurement and production program," while the Services of Supply, "in accordance and compliance with the policies and directives of the War Production Board, carries on its supply functions of research, design, development, programming, purchase, production, storage, distribution, issue, maintenance and salvage." The agreement, said Clay in retrospect, "worked very well for quite a few *days.*"

145 responsibility was sometimes murky: See Memorandum and replies, A. C. C. Hill, Jr., to Donald Nelson, W. L. Batt, W. M. Harrison, Sidney Hillman, Houlder Hudgins, J. S. Knowlson, Gerard E. Lambert, Stacey May, Robert Nathan, John Lord O'Brien, 9 April 1942, WPB file 721-11.

146 "scheduling controversy": For general treatments of the scheduling controversy, see Committee on Public Affairs, *Industrial Mo-*

bilization for War, pp. 505–19; John D. Millet, *The Organization and Role of Army Service Forces* (Washington, D.C.: Government Printing Office, 1954), pp. 220–26.

146 Kuznets's proposal: Memorandum, Simon Kuznets to the Planning Committee, WPB, 31 August 1942. See also John E. Brigante, *The Feasibility Dispute: Determination of War Production Objectives for 1942 and 1943* (Washington, D.C.: Committee on Public Administration Cases, 1950), p. 71.

147 Somervell's reply: Memo, Somervell to Nathan, 12 September 1942, quoted in full in Brigante, *Feasibility Dispute,* pp. 82–83.

147 Nathan's answer: Millet, *Army Service Forces,* p. 216. Curiously, Brigante, who seeks to illustrate the balanced "tone" of Nathan's reply (in contrast to Somervell's), inexplicably omits Nathan's "ostrich-like" reference *(Feasibility Dispute,* pp. 84–85).

147 Clay shot back: Memo, Clay to Somervell, 5 October 1942, subject: Planning Committee doc. 151. (Italics added.)

150 "nothing but the closest working relations": Weiner interview, Washington, D.C., 11 December 1971.

151 Production Executive Committee: In addition to Clay for the Services of Supply (as Somervell's representative), the PEC included Vice Admiral S. M. Robinson, Major General Oliver P. Echols (Army Air Forces), Rear Admiral R. A. Davidson (Bureau of Naval Aeronautics), Rear Admiral Howard L. Vickery of the Maritime Commission, and Ferdinand Eberstadt.

151 "jurisdictional battles": Letter, Clay to Wilson, 24 November 1942, Clay Papers, ASF.

153 "by faulty organization": Henry L. Stimson Diary, 7 July 1943, Manuscript Collection, Yale University, New Haven, Conn.

153 "half a ton of bricks": Bruce Catton, *The War Lords of Washington* (New York: Harcourt, Brace, 1948), p. 203.

153 "compose [your] former differences": Letter, FDR to Stimson and Nelson, 28 November 1942. Nelson's highly personal account of the controversy *(Arsenal of Democracy,* p. 385) quotes the following conversation with FDR:

" 'Don, I understand you are in a fight with the Army again.'

" 'Yes, Mr. President, I am,' I said. 'I am in a life-or-death struggle with the Army over the scheduling of components, and I'm going to win it, because otherwise we can't reach these production goals. . . .'

"The President said, 'Well, I'll be glad to help you.'

" 'Mr. President, if you please, I'll fight this through myself,' I said. 'All I ask of you is don't help the other fellow.' "

In view of FDR's subsequent instructions to Secretary Stimson and Nelson "to compose [your] former differences," plus the increasing role Justice Byrnes was playing in mobilization planning, Nelson's account should be read very skeptically.

153 conciliatory letter: Nelson to Stimson, 26 November 1942. Cf. Nelson, *Arsenal of Democracy,* p. 386.

153 Forrestal's congratulatory letter: Forrestal to Clay, 15 December 1942, Clay Papers, ASF.

155 Bell bomber plant: Robert Lovett, then Assistant Secretary of War for Air, recalls that the reason the Bell bomber plant "went into Marietta was that it was an area with a large population of first-class Anglo-Saxon farmers with not much to do in the way of farming. They were men with a mediocre amount of education, but a good farm boy from that area could take any kind of machine apart and put it back together again. He had to in order to live on his farm. So you had a good basic labor force. And when they opened the doors, the plant was flooded with them. They are very unique people in that part of the country. When they take a job, they acquire a strong sense of loyalty to the company. They don't want an outsider from New York telling them when to strike. If they want to strike, they'll damn well strike on their own. These were the essential, convincing arguments [for Larry Bell]. Of course, it didn't do any harm to have the chairman of the Senate Appropriations Committee from Georgia [Walter George], or the Congressman who was approaching seniority on the House Military Affairs Committee [Carl Vinson]. That's just a fact of life you take into account" (Lovett interview, Brown Brothers, Harriman, New York, N.Y., 4 May 1971).

155 "I had no financial interest": The grantor-grantee index in the office of Recorder of Deeds in Marietta (Cobb County) reveals that the last piece of property owned by the Clays was sold in March 1942—eight months before the Bell plant went in.

155 "But I did have an interest in the town": In September 1944, Clay wrote to his childhood chum "Rip" Blair, who was then Marietta's mayor, that "we hear nothing but fine things of the way that you and Marietta have responded in the solution of the many problems which inevitably develop from a huge industrial expansion, and you have every reason to be proud" (Clay Papers, ASF).

156 Clay to Truman Committee: Records of Hqs., ASF: Director of Materiel, 12 April 1943, subject: Production.

156 compel industry to renegotiate contracts: The leading case is *Lichter* v. *United States,* 334 U.S. 742 (1948). Said Justice Burton, speaking for the Court, "The constitutionality of the conscription of manpower for military service is beyond question. The constitutional power of Congress to support the armed forces with equipment and supplies is no less clear and sweeping. The mandatory renegotiation of contracts is valid, *a fortiori.*"

158 "forceful, persuasive, and bright as hell": Cabot interview, First Boston Corporation, Boston, Mass., 12 December 1970.

160 "I had hoped that . . .": Letter, Clay to Connolly, 20 June 1943, Clay Papers, ASF. "I certainly hope that events will materialize so that I can again have the pleasure of serving under you in the field and away from the uselessly developed headaches of Washington," Clay went on to say.

161 "We have progressed too far . . .": Memo, Clay to C/S ASF (Styer), 6 August 1943, subject: Memorandum of 29 July 1943—Study of Duplication of Procurement, Clay Papers, ASF.

161 For details of Somervell's plan, see Millet, *Army Service Forces,* pp. 406–7.

161 "stirring up a hornets' nest": Stimson Diary, 21 September 1943, Manuscript Collection, Yale University, New Haven, Conn.

161 Marshall would command the cross-Channel attack: Robert E. Sherwood, *Roosevelt and Hopkins: An Intimate History* (New York: Harper & Bros., 1948), pp. 758–60; Henry L. Stimson and McGeorge Bundy, *On Active Service in Peace and War* (New York: Harper & Bros., 1950), pp. 436–43; Forrest C. Pogue, *George C. Marshall: Organizer of Victory, 1943–1945* (New York: Viking, 1973), pp. 277–78.

162 moving their belongings: Katherine T. Marshall, *Together: The Annals of an Army Wife* (Atlanta: Tupper & Love, 1946).

162 sought to build Somervell up: *Congressional Record,* 22 September 1943, p. A4286. When a Nazi propaganda broadcast from Paris subsequently announced that "General George C. Marshall, the U.S. Chief of Staff, has been dismissed," and that President Roosevelt had assumed command, Marshall passed the report to Hopkins with a scribbled note: "Dear Harry: Are you responsible for pulling this fast one on me? G.C.M." When Hopkins showed the note to Roosevelt, FDR scribbled a penciled reply on the bottom: "Dear George—Only true in part—I am now Chief of Staff *but* you are President." *FDR* (Sherwood, *Roosevelt and Hopkins,* p. 761).

165 Clay to Styer: Memo, Clay to Styer, 16 November 1943, subject: Planning for Production Rescheduling, Clay Papers, ASF.

165 "your speech to the House today": Letter, 9 December 1943, Sam Rayburn Papers, Rayburn Library, Bonham, Texas.

165 "a close and friendly relationship": Memo, Clay to Director, Production Division, ASF, 6 December 1943, subject: Resumption of the Production of Civilian Products. Under Secretary Patterson was somewhat startled by the conciliatory tone of Clay's directive and warned that "anxiety to assist the civilian agencies in resuming civilian production may lead to concessions that should not be made" (memo, Patterson to Clay and Echols, 19 December 1943,

Clay Papers, ASF). See also Committee on Public Administration Cases, *The Reconversion Controversy* (Washington, D.C.: CPAC, 1950), pp. 34–38.

166 Role of Production Executive Committee in reconversion: See Millet, *Army Service Forces,* pp. 226–28; Committee on Public Administration Cases, *Reconversion Controversy,* pp. 34–38.

166 "If Lucius Clay had been in charge": Nathan interview, Washington, D.C., 12 March 1971.

166 "The undersigned has served": Letter, Clay to Somervell, 20 December 1943, subject: Assignment to Field. (This letter, with Somervell's reply, was retained by Clay and is now in JES's possession.)

167 Somervell to Clay: 1st Endorsement, 21 December 1943.

12: Saving the Taxpayer from Chiang Kai-shek

PAGE

169 "hopeless and blue": Letter, Clay to Colonel L. J. Sverdrup (GHO, S.W. Pacific), 28 February 1944, Clay Papers, ASF.

169 reconversion battle approached a climax: See Committee on Public Administration Cases, *The Reconversion Controversy* (Washington, D.C.: CPAC, 1950), p. 56.

169 "peace jitters": Memorandum for the Secretary of War, written 21 July 1944, subject: Production Difficulties, Clay Papers, ASF.

169 "There is a public psychology . . .": Quoted in Committee on Public Administration Cases, *The Reconversion Controversy,* p. 87.

170 "not opposed to reconversion": U.S. Congress, Senate, Special Committee to Investigate the National Defense, *Third Annual Report,* pp. 207–10. See also U.S. War Production Board, *Development of the Reconversion Policies of the War Production Board,* pp. 43–48, 92–102.

170 "General Clay's report of shortages": Washington *Post,* 22 August 1944.

170 caused little regret: Cf. Bruce Catton's comment to Sterling Green of the Associated Press: "Nelson has been kicked right square in the groin" (Bruce Catton, *The War Lords of Washington,* Greenwood Press, Westport, Conn., p. 276).

170 ". . . little good in Washington": Henry L. Stimson Diary, 24 August 1944, Manuscript Collection, Yale University, New Haven, Conn.

170 "you are a schlemiel": U.S. Congress Senate, Committee on the Judiciary, Internal Security Subcommittee, *Morgenthau Diary (China)* (Washington, D.C.: Government Printing Office, 1965), vol. 2, p. 1265.

171 "selling razor blades": Quoted in Barbara Tuchman, *Stilwell and*

the American Experience in China (New York: Macmillan, 1970), p. 479.

171 "DONALD NELSON LEAVING . . .": Cable, Lutes to Somervell, 19 August 1944, Clay Papers, ASF.

173 Madame Chiang's entourage: U.S. Congress, *Morgenthau Diaries (China),* vol. 2, pp. 641–64; John Morgan Blum, *From the Morgenthau Diaries, Years of War: 1941–45* (Boston: Houghton Mifflin, 1967), p. 107.

173 reverse Lend-Lease: Letter, Stimson to Roosevelt, written 22 May 1944, with enclosure: Résumé of Chinese Exchange Situation, 19 May 1944, Clay Papers, ASF.

173 "we've got to depend": Elliott Roosevelt, *As He Saw It* (New York: Duell, Sloane & Pearce, 1946), p. 154. The Leahy quote is from William D. Leahy, *I Was There* (New York: Whittlesey House, 1950). "Our one great objective was to keep China in the War," Roosevelt told Stalin at Tehran (Robert E. Sherwood, *Roosevelt and Hopkins: An Intimate History,* New York: Harper & Bros., 1948, p. 778).

174 "grave consequences": Cable, Chiang to FDR, 9 December 1943, quoted in Charles Romanus and Riley Sunderland, *Stilwell's Command Problems* (Washington, D.C.: Government Printing Office, 1956), pp. 74–75.

174 "This looks good": Blum, *From the Morgenthau Diaries,* vol. 3, pp. 111–12.

174 "our principal concern": Memo, Somervell (Clay) to Morgenthau, 3 January 1944, Clay Papers, ASF. (Clay consistently misspelled Stilwell [Stillwell]).

174 "regardless of exchange rates": Cable 19415, written 10 January 1944, Clay Papers, ASF.

175 "Progress is being made": Cable 87, Gauss (Adler) for Morgenthau, 13 January 1944.

175 "Nothing could be more conducive": Blum, *From the Morgenthau Diaries,* vol. 3, pp. 113–14.

175 "a speedy decision": Cable, Clay to Stilwell, n.d. (probably 15 January 1944), Clay Papers, ASF.

175 "look out after themselves": Cable, Gauss to Sec. State, 16 January 1944.

175 "go jump in the Yangtze River": U.S. Congress, *Morgenthau Diary (China),* vol. 2, pp. 1022–23.

175 "I am mad as hell": Ibid., p. 1024.

175 "very dissatisfied": Ibid., p. 1028.

176 "at a slow pace": Ibid., p. 1031.

176 cost of the airports . . . astronomical: Clay memo, 22 December 1943, Clay Papers, ASF.

176 "money down a rat hole": Conference, Bell, White, Hiss, Clay, 19

January 1944, in U.S. Congress, *Morgenthau Diary (China),* vol. 2, pp. 1030–33.

176 told to work out a new exchange rate: Cable, Marshall to Stilwell, 20 January 1944. After the cable was cleared with Stilwell and Ambassador Gauss, Roosevelt's reply was sent to Chiang, on 26 January 1944. To remedy objections made by the U.S. mission in Chungking (Cable, Gauss to Sec. State, 25 January 1944), the fourth paragraph of the original draft was changed to read as follows: "*Furthermore,* since you say your government is not in a position to continue any direct maintenance of American troops in China, including such maintenance as well as construction, [we are] prepared to place to your account the U.S. dollar equivalent of any Chinese funds made available under general arrangements that will be suggested by General Stilwell and the Ambassador." (Italics added.) Use of the word "*Furthermore*" proved to be a major mistake, since the Chinese immediately took the paragraph to mean *in addition* to the monthly $25 million. This was not the intent of its framers. See *infra.*

176 "GM into tailspin": Cable, Stilwell to War Department, 27 March 1944, Clay Papers, ASF.

177 "ridiculous": Cable, Hearn to Clay, 12 February 1944, Clay Papers, ASF.

177 firm stand was essential: Transcript of meeting, 14 February 1944, in U.S. Congress, *Morgenthau Diary (China),* vol. 2, pp. 1054–55.

177 "the United States must reduce": Memo, Somervell (Clay) to Marshall, written 14 February 1944, subject: Exchange Policy with China, Clay Papers, ASF.

177 exchange rate of 100:1: U.S. Congress, *Morgenthau Diary (China),* vol. 2, pp. 1058–60.

177 quick fix: Cable 4557, For Stilwell from Clay signed Marshall, 20 February 1944, Clay Papers, ASF.

177 $1.2-billion premium: Memorandum for the Secretary of War, 18 February 1944, subject: Expenditures in China, Clay Papers, ASF.

178 "most expensive theater of the war": Cable, Gauss to Sec. State, 24 February 1944.

178 "unable to see any advantage": Cable 4642, Clay to Hearn, 29 February 1944 (probably sent 1 March 1944), Clay Papers, ASF.

178 "a hundred yards away from the White House": U.S. Congress, *Morgenthau Diary (China),* vol. 2, pp. 1090–91. Clay also prepared for Stimson's signature a letter to the President detailing the chronological sequence of the China negotiations (written 22 May 1944). "An excellent account," Morgenthau told Roosevelt (ibid., p. 1136).

178 "the most able fellow": Ibid., p. 1129.

179 "biggest and best equipped army": Conference, Bretton Woods, N.H., 10 A.M., 16 July 1944, in ibid., p. 1166.

179 "for the maximum possible 'take' ": Memorandum, Clay to Somervell, 17 July 1944, subject: Exchange Conference, Clay Papers, ASF.

179 "best we can do": Blum, *From the Morgenthau Diaries,* vol. 3, p. 289.

179 "man who helped the most": U.S. Congress, *Morgenthau Diary (China),* vol. 2, 1388.

180 "can not be minimized": Memo, Somervell (Clay) to Chairman, WPB, written 23 October 1944, subject: Production of Ammunition, Clay Papers, ASF.

181 move his bloated Com Z: Stephen E. Ambrose, *The Supreme Commander* (Garden City, N.Y.: Doubleday, 1970), p. 488; Captain Harry Butcher, *My Three Years with Eisenhower* (New York: Simon and Schuster, 1946), pp. 227–29.

181 The French subsequently complained: Forrest C. Pogue, *The Supreme Command* (Washington, D.C.: Government Printing Office, 1956), pp. 322–23.

181 Ike flew into a rage: Aurand interview, Army-Navy Club, Washington, D.C. Major General Robert Crawford, Ike's G-4, recommended on 18 September 1944 that SHAEF exercise "a considerably greater measure of supervision over Lee's headquarters than seems to be contemplated by existing orders" (Pogue, *Supreme Command,* p. 268).

182 "definite impression": Cable, Eisenhower (Personal) from Marshall, 18 October 1944.

182 "trust that General Clay": Cable, Eisenhower to Marshall, October 20, 1944.

182 "I am taking off": Letter, Clay to Brig. Gen. Thomas E. Farrell, 25 October 1944, Clay Papers, ASF.

183 "do a bang-up job": Letter, Eisenhower to Somervell, 30 October 1944.

185 "*New Yorker* 'Profile' ": E. J. Kahn, "Profile," *The New Yorker,* 13 January 1951, p. 29.

185 "more than deserved the Bronze Star": Letter, Lee to Somervell (handwritten), 25 November 1944.

186 one round per gun per day: Roland Ruppenthal, *Logistical Support of the Armies* (Washington, D.C.: Government Printing Office, 1959), vol. II, pp. 248–55.

186 the McCoy Board: Officially, the War Department Procurement Review Board: Major General (ret.) Frank McCoy, Major General (ret.) C. L. Williams, Brigadier General (ret.) William E. Gilmoore, and Mr. M. J. Madigan, OUSW.

187 "General Clay has been especially selected": Cable, Eisenhower to Marshall, 20 November 1944.

187 "the crossing of the Rhine": Cable, Eisenhower to Marshall, 22 November 1944.

13: Deputy Director of War Mobilization

PAGE

189 Office of War Mobilization: For general information, see especially Herman Miles Somers, *Presidential Agency: OWMR* (Cambridge, Mass.: Harvard University Press, 1950). For the Act itself, see 78th Cong., 2nd Sess., PL 458, 3 October 1944.

189 "risk prolonging the war": *Newsweek,* 19 February 1945, p. 52.

189 "initiative was with Byrnes": Letter, Somervell to Eisenhower, 12 December 1944.

190 authorized to act in Byrnes's name: *The New York Times,* 7 December 1944.

190 "Clay was a very logical choice": Boeschenstein interview, Owens-Corning Fiberglas, New York, N.Y., 16 February 1971.

190 creeping "militarism": E.g., John Fischer, "The Army Takes Over," *Harpers,* vol. 190 (May 1945), p. 484.

190 "no man more capable than Clay": James F. Byrnes, *Speaking Frankly* (New York: Harper & Bros., 1947), p. 47.

190 "He'd then gone to the Supreme Court": Byrnes was appointed to the Court by FDR in the summer of 1941 to fill the vacancy caused by the resignation of Justice McReynolds of Tennessee, the last of the "four horsemen" of the conservative apocalypse. Byrnes stepped down from the Court little more than a year later (October 1942) to become FDR's "assistant president" for the home front. During the year Byrnes served on the Court, his voting record suggests a slightly conservative bias, although his record on civil rights and civil liberties strongly resembled that of Hugo Black. But Byrnes lacked a reflective judicial temperament and was not a serious legal scholar. He far preferred the more active challenges of political life. His role on the Court, reflecting his experience as Senate Majority Leader, was as a conciliator and negotiator rather than as a spokesman for a particular viewpoint. In addition, Byrnes, who did not have a strong legal background, could sometimes be casual about his votes. When Justice Murphy circulated his draft Opinion for the Court in *Seminole Nation* v. *United States,* 316 U.S. 286 (1942), Byrnes scribbled his concurrence on the draft: "You are a good Indian so I follow you," he told Murphy.

193 "too goddamned independent": Lovett interview, New York, N.Y., May 4, 1971.

194 would not be too sticky: See letter, Stimson to Byrnes, 19 December 1944.

194 principle . . . would be preserved: Memo, Dorr to Patterson, 20 December 1944, Subject: Conference with General Clay re: Manpower.

194 The Byrnes compromise: OWMR Press Release, 9 December 1944.

194 "coaxing people to take war jobs": Memo, Patterson for Stimson, 21 December 1944, subject: Manpower.

194 joint appeal to President Roosevelt: Byron Fairchild and Jonathan Grossman, *The Army and Industrial Manpower* (Washington, D.C.: Government Printing Office, 1959), p. 238.

195 "The Lord hates a quitter": President Franklin D. Roosevelt, *State of the Union Message,* 6 January 1945, House doc. 1, 79th Cong., 1st Sess. (Washington, D.C.: Government Printing Office, 1945).

195 "using a shillelagh": House Committee on Military Affairs, 79th Cong., 1st Sess., *Hearings on HR 1119* (Washington, D.C.: Government Printing Office, 1945), p. 166.

195 "Quack medicine": *The Pilot,* 21 January 1944.

195 Patterson abruptly switched: Statement of Robert P. Patterson, 10 January 1945, House Committee on Military Affairs, *Hearings on HR 1119,* pp. 3–34.

195 "In my absence": Letter, Byrnes to Clay, 22 January 1945.

196 ". . . you are a general, aren't you? . . .": Clay's restatement to JES of his meeting with Secretary Stimson, in interview.

196 Clay's role in manpower dispute: The engaging naïveté of academicians is illustrated in the official history of the home front prepared under the auspices of the Committee of Records of War Administration, chaired by Pendleton Herring. "The ability of the military agencies to press for manpower legislation," it states, "was strengthened at this time by the presence of General Clay (formerly head of the Army Service Forces' Production Division) as Deputy Director of OWMR, while the position of the War Manpower Commission was weakened by the absence of its Chairman on a European trip" *(The United States at War* [Washington, D.C.: Government Printing Office, 1946], p. 453).

198 "The President . . . favored the construction": Memorandum, 9 January 1945, quoted in Somers, *Presidential Agency,* p. 125.

198 Smith . . . issued an immediate reclama: Memorandum, Smith to Roosevelt, 17 January 1945.

198 "I am inclined to support": Somers, *Presidential Agency,* p. 126.

198 "a blistering memo": Memo, Searles to Clay, 24 February 1945.

14: Selection of a Proconsul

PAGE	
201	McCloy quote: McCloy interview, Milbank, Tweed, Hadley, and McCloy, New York, N.Y., 19 February 1971.
202	one of the ablest men: U.S. Congress, Senate Committee on the Judiciary, Internal Security Subcommittee, *Morgenthau Diary (China)* (Washington: Government Printing Office, 1965), vol. 2, p. 1129.
202	"one of the most skillful politicians": John Kenneth Galbraith, "The Decline of American Power," *Esquire,* March 1972, p. 83.
202	On September 4, 1944: According to the minutes, the high commissioner "should be an official of high political ability and considerable prestige who can speak with authority for this Government in all matters where a common policy must be worked out with the U.K. and the U.S.S.R."
203	"people like General Electric": U.S. Congress, Senate Committee on the Judiciary, Internal Security Subcommittee, *Morgenthau Diary (Germany)* (Washington, D.C.: Government Printing Office, 1965), vol. 1, pp. 573–74.
203	distrust of Robert Murphy: Ibid., p. 524.
203	"question of the high commissioner . . ." and "find a spot for him": Ibid., pp. 536–37. Roosevelt approached Byrnes about the position on 10 June 1944, but apparently made no follow-up (Roosevelt MSS, PSF 50, Hyde Park).
203	"touché": U.S. Congress, *Morgenthau Diary (Germany),* p. 536. For Stimson's report of the same meeting, see Henry L. Stimson Diary, 6 September 1944, Yale University, New Haven, Conn.
204	"So far as Patterson is concerned": U.S. Congress, *Morgenthau Diary (Germany),* pp. 573–74.
204	"looking very tired": Ibid., pp. 588–89.
204	Hopkins . . . interested in the job: Ibid.
204	"Oh God, it was terrible": Ibid., pp. 604–6.
204	"I have been assuming . . .": Ibid.
204	Byrnes abruptly declined: Letter, Byrnes to Roosevelt, 13 September 1944, Roosevelt MSS, PSF 50, Hyde Park.
204	"same kind of job": U.S. Congress, *Morgenthau Diary (Germany),* vol. 1, pp. 604–6.
204	"he wants it for himself": Ibid., p. 623.
205	Morgenthau's plan: U.S. Department of State, *Foreign Relations of the United States: The Conference at Quebec, 1944* (Washington, D.C.: Government Printing Office, 1972), pp. 360–63.
205	"I know Hopkins so well": U.S. Congress, *Morgenthau Diary (Germany),* vol. 1, p. 623.
205	Morgenthau's lunch with Patterson: Ibid., pp. 648–50.

206 "military man": Stimson Diary, 27 September 1944.

206 "the President . . . seemed to like the idea": U.S. Congress, *Morgenthau Diary (Germany),* vol. 1, p. 678.

206 initiative should come from Eisenhower: Stimson Diary, 13 October 1944.

206 Patterson "was a little tempted to try it": Ibid., 16 October 1944.

207 "The Army has plenty of officers": Memorandum for the Secretary of War, 17 October 1944 (SECRET), in Henry L. Stimson Papers, Manuscript Collection, Yale University, New Haven, Conn.

207 "Eisenhower should do the choosing": Stimson diary, 19 October 1944.

207 "in the hands of the generals": U.S. Congress, *Morgenthau Diary (Germany),* vol. 2, pp. 1064–65. Frank Coe, former professor of economics at the University of Toronto, headed the Treasury's international division. In 1948, he fled to China, where he remained until his death in 1981.

207 McCloy to Eisenhower: Letter, 25 October 1944 (SECRET), Dwight D. Eisenhower Papers, Eisenhower Library, Abilene, Kansas.

207 Eisenhower to McCloy: Letter, 1 November 1944, ibid.

208 Smith to Hilldring: Letter, 6 November 1944, ibid.

208 Patterson drafted a telegram: Cable to the President (not sent), 15 February 1945, Stimson Papers.

209 "Justice Roberts seemed to be the best man": Stimson Diary, 19 February 1945.

209 If it had to be a civilian: Memorandum, 2 March 1945, re: Man for Germany, Stimson Papers.

209 Patterson lacked "worldly wisdom": "Notes after conference with the President," March 1945, ibid.

209 "You will break Jimmy Byrnes' heart . . ." and "Clay for the soldier . . .": Ibid. Cf. James F. Byrnes, *Speaking Frankly* (New York: Harper & Bros., 1947), p. 47.

210 McCloy to interdepartmental committee: H. Freeman Matthews (chairman), Robert Murphy, James Riddleberger, Philip Mosely, Emile Despres, and Edmund Gullion, all of State; Captain W. H. Vanderbilt, Navy; and McCloy *(Foreign Relations, 1945,* vol. 3, p. 442.

210 "Lucius Clay may become available": letter, Eisenhower to Somervell, 14 March 1945 (SECRET—EYES ONLY), Eisenhower Papers FWD-17848.

210 Account of Stimson's meeting with his advisers is from Stimson Diary, 14 March 1945. Stimson talked to Connolly later that day. "I had a long and satisfactory talk with him," wrote Stimson, and "I thought well of him."

211 "Byrnes was very nice about it": Ibid., 16 March 1945.

211 *"Heil McCloy":* McCloy interview.

212 "I'll take care of the boss": Ibid. McCloy's reference to Clay's page-boy experience was without foundation—an embellishment, perhaps—but reflected Clay's familiarity with Congress.

212 Morgenthau entered the conversation: U.S. Congress, *Morgenthau Diary (Germany),* vol. 2, p. 1121.

212 Byrnes had a long talk with Roosevelt: Byrnes, *Speaking Frankly,* p. 47. See also memorandum for the President, 27 March 1945, James F. Byrnes Papers, Clemson University, Clemson, S.C. "I repeat," wrote Byrnes, "that General Clay is the most efficient, all-round man I have found in the departments"—suggesting that Byrnes may have been backing Clay as his successor.

212 first informed Clay: Lucius D. Clay, *Decision in Germany* (Garden City, N.Y.: Doubleday, 1950), pp. 1–2; cf. Robert D. Murphy, *Diplomat Among Warriors* (Garden City, N.Y.: Doubleday, 1964), pp. 248–51. Murphy is incorrect that Byrnes was the primary force behind Clay's appointment. As Clay once advised the author, "It came from Colonel Stimson. Of that, I'm sure" (interview, 14 December 1970).

213 Desire for combat: Clay, *Decision in Germany,* pp. 1–4.

214 McCloy left Washington: Stimson Diary, 29 March 1945.

214 [McCloy] anticipated heavy going: McCloy interview.

214 "We have had so much vacillation": Stimson Diary, 31 March 1945.

215 German gold horde: Murphy, *Diplomat Among Warriors,* p. 293; Murphy interview, Owens-Corning Fiberglas, New York, N.Y., 23 February 1971; McCloy interview.

215 "ran into a little roughneck": McCloy interview.

215 Eisenhower . . . quickly grasped McCloy's point: The issue of Clay's independence from the SHAEF General Staff was partially settled on 29 April 1945, when Eisenhower promulgated a directive drafted by Clay on "The Relationship of Deputy Military Governor and the U.S. Group Control Council (Germany) to the Theater Staff." See also Clay, *Decision in Germany,* p. 108; *Foreign Relations, 1945,* vol. 3, pp. 930–40; Dwight D. Eisenhower, *Crusade in Europe* (Garden City, N.Y.: Doubleday, 1948), pp. 434–35.

216 "able and forceful character": DON642, J.S.M., Washington, to A.M.S.S.O., 31 March 1945, British Public Record Office, 7.0 3.71 49036 7094.

217 Daniel Bell: Letter, Clay to Morgenthau, 4 April 1945, *Clay Papers.* See also U.S. Congress, *Morgenthau Diary (Germany),* vol. 2, p. 1108.

217 On the conservative nature of the foreign service, see, among others, Martin Weil, *A Pretty Good Club: The Founding Fathers of the U.S. Foreign Service* (New York: Norton, 1978), pp. 15–84; Waldo Heinrichs, *American Ambassador: The Life and Times of Joseph L. Grew* (Boston: Little, Brown, 1966), pp. 22–98. In February 1937, *Harper's Magazine* reported that "The overregard for social privilege, the association with the diplomatic corps of other countries, the mingling with the expatriates of the 'American colony' . . . serve to create a foreign service with scant regard for democratic movements and little respect for members of those races customarily dismissed by Anglo-Saxons as inferiors" (Hubert Herring, "The Department of State," *Harper's,* February 1937).

217 Hopes State Department will remain neutral: Reported by Robert Bendinik, managing editor of *Nation,* as quoted in Weil, *A Pretty Good Club,* p. 103.

BOOK THREE: GERMANY

15: Ike's Deputy

PAGE

224 Relation of military government to Army staff: For Clay's memorandum to Eisenhower defining the role of military government, see *Clay Papers,* pp. 4–5. An excellent analysis of the significance of Clay's move to a military government separate from the Army is provided in John Gimbel, "Governing the American Zone of Germany," in Robert Wolfe, ed., *Americans as Proconsuls: United States Military Government in Germany and Japan, 1944–1952* (Carbondale: Southern Illinois University Press, 1984), pp. 92–102.

231 Joseph Dodge, president of the Detroit Bank, served on Clay's wartime staff in the Army Service Forces and became his financial adviser in Germany. Later he served as director of the Bureau of the Budget under President Eisenhower.

231 Brigadier General William Draper, an investment banker with Dillon, Reed, also had served on Clay's wartime staff in ASF and became his economic adviser in Germany. Later he became Under Secretary of the Army.

235 "went back to Washington in November": For a report of Clay's conversation in Washington, see the résumé prepared by Major General Hilldring, 3 November 1945, in *Clay Papers,* pp. 111–17.

238 "direct to the homes of the German people": Clay to McCloy, 26 April 1945, in *Clay Papers,* pp. 7–8.

16: Withdrawal from the Russian Zone

PAGE

249 European Advisory Commission: The EAC was established by Churchill, Roosevelt, and Stalin at the Tehran Conference, 1 December 1943. Composed of diplomatic representatives of the United States, Great Britain, and the Soviet Union, and meeting in London, the EAC was instructed to prepare plans for the occupation of Germany and Austria. See U.S. Department of State, *Foreign Relations of the United States—The Conferences at Cairo and Tehran, 1943* (Washington, D.C.: Government Printing Office, 1961), pp. 596–604.

252 "a powerful lever": British Foreign Office, Reconstruction Department U2738/20/70; Cf. Winston Churchill, *Triumph and Tragedy* (Boston: Houghton Mifflin, 1953), pp. 448–49; British Chiefs of Staff COS (45) 102nd mtg. See also David Eisenhower, *Eisenhower at War* (New York: Random House, 1986), pp. 740–50.

252 to negotiate "directly": See especially David Eisenhower, *Eisenhower at War.*

252 "not going to risk . . . World War III": Omar N. Bradley, *A Soldier's Story* (New York: Henry Holt, 1951), p. 544.

252 "grave misunderstandings": Forrest C. Pogue, *The Supreme Command: United States Army in World War II: The European Theater of Operations* (Washington, D.C.: Government Printing Office, 1956), pp. 446–47.

252 "simplest possible": Cable, Eisenhower to Deane, Alfred D. Chandler, Jr., and Stephen Ambrose, eds., *The Papers of Dwight David Eisenhower: The War Years* (Baltimore: The Johns Hopkins Press, 1970), pp. 2613–14.

252 "all on the side of the Soviets": Cable, Eisenhower to Marshall, in ibid., p. 2615.

253 CCS instructed Eisenhower: Ibid.

253 "communism and democracy": See Captain Harry Butcher, *My Three Years with Eisenhower* (New York: Simon and Schuster, 1946), p. 855; cf. David Eisenhower, *Eisenhower at War,* p. 813.

253 Clay strongly resented the impediments: For an extensive survey of alternative zones of occupation being considered by the British Foreign Office, see the excellent study by Tony Sharp, *The Wartime Alliance and the Zonal Division of Germany* (Oxford: Clarendon Press, 1975), pp. 145–49.

253 "It's got to work": *Time,* 25 June 1945; OMGUS 435-43, consolidated daily journal, office staff secretary, 16 May 1945.

254 "should remain a military consideration": Memo, Brig. Gen. George A. Lincoln for Gen. Hull, 13 April 1945, subject: Military Contacts With the Russians, quoted in Pogue, *Supreme Command,* pp. 465–66.

254 Truman to send Churchill: As Truman advised Churchill, "Our State Department does not believe that the matter of retirement of our respective troops to our zonal frontiers should be used for bargaining purposes" (quoted in Chester Wilmot, *The Struggle for Europe* [New York: Harper & Bros., 1952], p. 696). See also William D. Leahy, *I Was There* (New York: Whittlesey House, 1950), p. 410.

254 draft message to Stalin: Harry S. Truman, *Year of Decisions* (Garden City, N.Y.: Doubleday, 1956), p. 214; Herbert Feis, *Churchill, Roosevelt, Stalin: The War They Waged and the Peace They Sought* (Princeton: Princeton University Press, 1967), p. 634.

254 Eisenhower to Truman: Cable, quoted in Truman, *Year of Decisions,* p. 215.

254 Churchill remained adamant: Sharp, *Wartime Alliance,* pp. 144–45; Churchill, *Triumph and Tragedy,* pp. 517–18; Truman, *Year of Decisions,* pp. 214–16.

254 dispatched Harry Hopkins: *FRUS: Conference of Berlin (Potsdam), 1945* (Washington, D.C.: Government Printing Office, 1960), vol. 1, pp. 4, 8, 11.

255 "in any real hurry": Cable, Eisenhower to Marshall, quoted in Truman, *Year of Decisions,* p. 300.

255 "could not carry out": Feis, *Churchill, Roosevelt, Stalin,* p. 77; see also Jean Edward Smith, *The Defense of Berlin* (Baltimore: Johns Hopkins Press, 1963), p. 73.

255 British . . . suggested a compromise: Feis, *Churchill, Roosevelt, Stalin,* p. 139; Sharp, *Wartime Alliance,* p. 151.

255 Protocols on zonal boundaries: For texts, see Beate Ruhm von Oppen, ed., *Documents on Germany Under Occupation, 1945–1954* (London: Oxford University Press, 1955), pp. 29–37.

255 Montgomery's instructions: The instructions are summarized in Viscount Montgomery, *The Memoirs of Montgomery of Alamein* (Cleveland: World Publishing Co., 1958), p. 338.

255 Clay to Washington: Clay (signed Eisenhower) to Combined Chiefs of Staff, 2 June 1945, in *Clay Papers,* p. 17.

256 Joint Chiefs of Staff . . . replied: Quoted in Truman, *Year of Decisions,* p. 301.

256 "profound misgivings": *FRUS Potsdam,* vol. 1, p. 92.

257 Commanders-in-Chief signed the Declaration: The three documents signed that day (all drafted by the European Advisory Commission) were the Declaration with Regard to the Defeat of Germany and the Assumption of Complete Authority with Respect to Germany by the Governments of the United Kingdom, the United States, the USSR, and the Provisional Government of the French Republic; the Statement of the four powers relating to zones of occupation; and their Statement pertaining to the control

machinery in Germany. For texts, see Oppen, ed., *Documents on Germany,* pp. 29–37.

258 "the question of withdrawal": FWD 23724, Clay (signed Eisenhower) to Joint Chiefs of Staff, 6 June 1945, in *Clay Papers,* p. 18; see also Feis, *Churchill, Roosevelt, Stalin,* p. 141.

258 Murphy's report: *FRUS 1945,* vol. 3, pp. 330–32. See also Clay, *Decision in Germany,* pp. 20–23.

258 For documentation pertaining to Hopkins's visit to Moscow, see *FRUS Potsdam,* vol. 1, pp. 24–62. See also Robert Sherwood, *Roosevelt and Hopkins: An Intimate History* (New York: Harper & Bros., 1948), pp. 887–913.

259 Hopkins's cable to HST: Quoted in *Clay Papers,* pp. 21–22.

260 "unable to delay the withdrawal": Quoted in Truman, *Year of Decisions,* p. 303.

260 Churchill promptly conformed: According to Admiral Leahy, chief of staff to the President, "Churchill's action in agreeing to our withdrawal was entirely unexpected. . . . [It] indicated to me that the great Englishman was not in vigorous health. It was not in his nature to give up so easily" (Leahy, *I Was There,* p. 382).

260 "lasting peace in Europe": Churchill, *Triumph and Tragedy,* pp. 605–6. For the Truman-Churchill-Stalin cables, see *FRUS 1945,* vol. 3, pp. 135–37; *FRUS Potsdam,* vol. 1, p. 107; Truman, *Year of Decisions,* pp. 303–5; Churchill, *Triumph and Tragedy,* pp. 606–8.

17: Access to Berlin:

PAGE

266 agreement to begin the withdrawal: *FRUS, 1945,* vol. 3, pp. 133–37.

267 Marshall's message: *FRUS, Potsdam,* vol. 1, pp. 131–32.

267 "I have requested General Antonov": Cable, Deane to Marshall, as quoted in Harry S. Truman, *Year of Decisions* (Garden City, N.Y.: Doubleday, 1956), p. 307.

267 "free access for our troops to Berlin": Radio message, Deane to SHAEF, in ibid., pp. 229–30; *FRUS, Potsdam,* vol. 1, pp. 131–32.

267 Clay provided the U.S. military mission: *FRUS, 1945,* vol. 3, pp. 358–61; Herbert Feis, *Between War and Peace: The Potsdam Conference* (Princeton: Princeton University Press, 1960), pp. 146–47; Jean Edward Smith, *The Defense of Berlin* (Baltimore: Johns Hopkins Press, 1963), pp. 81–82.

268 drawn up by the American delegation: Philip E. Mosely, *The Kremlin in World Politics* (New York: Random House and Knopf, 1960), pp. 186–87.

268 Winant "vehemently" objected: Robert D. Murphy, *Diplomat Among Warriors* (Garden City, N.Y.: Doubleday, 1964), pp. 284–86.

268 Strang shared that view: For an indispensable summary of the EAC discussions, see Tony Sharp, *The Wartime Alliance and the Zonal Division of Germany* (Oxford: Clarendon Press, 1975), pp. 92–94.

268 Bremerhaven: CCS 320/26, 27; *FRUS, 1944,* vol. 1, pp. 340–41. Sharp, *Wartime Alliance,* pp. 90–92.

268 November 14 amendment to the Protocol: According to the final text of the November 14, 1944, amendment:

> For the purpose of facilitating communication between the South-Western Zone and the sea, the Commander-in-Chief of the United States forces in the South-West Zone will: **(a)** exercise such control of the ports of Bremen and Bremerhaven and the necessary staying areas in the vicinity thereof as may be agreed hereafter by the United Kingdom and United States military authorities to be necessary to meet his requirements; **(b)** enjoy such transit facilities through the North Western Zone as may be agreed hereafter by the United Kingdom and United States military authorities to be necessary to meet his requirements.

(See *FRUS: The Conferences at Malta and Yalta—1945* [Washington, D.C.: Government Printing Office, 1955], pp. 121–23.)

268 Fedor Gousev: Quoted in Sharp, *Wartime Alliance,* pp. 97–98.

269 Clay's meeting with Zhukov: For the text of Clay's memorandum discussing this meeting, see *Clay Papers,* pp. 26–35.

274 "the responsibility . . . was mine": Lucius D. Clay, *Decision in Germany* (Garden City, N.Y.: Doubleday, 1950), p. 26.

274 "is honest about it": Margaret Truman, *Harry S. Truman* (New York: Morrow, 1972), p. 546.

18: General Clay and the Russians

PAGE

278 "We in Berlin": Dwight D. Eisenhower, *Crusade in Europe* (Garden City, N.Y.: Doubleday, 1948), p. 475.

278 "he saved his country": Clay's interview with Albert Moffett, WCVE-TV, 18 May 1976, North Chatham, Mass., Marshall Research Foundation Oral History.

278 "I am somewhat optimistic": Letter, 16 June 1945, in *Clay Papers,* pp. 23–24.

279 "It is difficult to predict": Letter, Clay to McCloy, 29 June 1945, in ibid., pp. 35–45.

279 feature article on Soviet forces: *The Grouper* (U.S. Group, Control Council, Berlin), vol. 1, no. 8 (1 September 1945), p. 5.

279 "A prompt initiation": Alfred D. Chandler and Stephen Ambrose, eds., *The Papers of Dwight David Eisenhower: Occupation, 1945* (Baltimore: Johns Hopkins Press, 1978), pp. 198–99. Subsequently, Eisenhower wrote to Brigadier General Paul Thompson that he was "somewhat disturbed . . . that American soldiers are judging our Russian allies too much upon external appearances. . . . I hope that we can do something toward indoctrinating our own people so that they may understand something of what the Russians have been through. . . . The Russians have contributed mightily to the winning of this war. They have produced good soldiers and brilliant generals and, moreover, they are a naturally friendly race" (ibid., p. 257).

279 Zhukov "most friendly": Ibid., p. 228.

279 "especially on the part of the Russians": Letter, Clay to McCloy, 3 September 1945, in *Clay Papers,* pp. 62–68. (Italics added.)

280 "The whole purpose": Memorandum, Eisenhower to Clay, in Chandler and Ambrose, eds., *Eisenhower Papers,* pp. 521–27. As Eisenhower wrote Henry Wallace on 28 August 1945, "I am convinced that friendship—which means an honest desire on both sides to strive for mutual understanding—between Russia and the United States, is absolutely essential for world tranquility. Moreover, I believe that most of the Russians I have met share this conviction" (Wallace MS Diary, vol. 35, University of Iowa).

280 "Marshal Zhukov was particularly affected": Memorandum, Clay to Eisenhower, in Chandler and Ambrose, *Eisenhower Papers,* p. 545.

281 "every firm commitment": Eisenhower, *Crusade in Europe,* p. 474.

281 On the anti-Soviet views of the foreign service, see especially Martin Weil, *A Pretty Good Club: The Founding Fathers of the U.S. Foreign Service* (New York: Norton, 1978), pp. 1–219, and the sources cited therein. See also Fraser J. Harbutt, *The Iron Curtain: Churchill, America, and the Origins of the Cold War* (New York: Oxford University Press, 1987), pp. 154–56.

282 "the most persistent effort": RG 59, H. Freeman Matthews files, Box 1, folder M, National Archives, cited in John Gimbel, *The Origins of the Marshall Plan* (Stanford: Stanford University Press, 1976), p. 22.

283 Clay's November 1945 State Department conference: Major General John Hilldring's memorandum of the discussions, in *Clay Papers,* pp. 111–117. Those in attendance included William L. Clayton, Willard L. Thorp, H. Freeman Matthews, Seymour J.

Rubin, James W. Riddleberger, Charles P. Kindleberger, and John de Wilde.

284 the French were saving the United States: Clay, *Decision in Germany,* p. 131.

284 Patterson to Byrnes, 21 November 1945, in *FRUS 1945,* vol. 3, pp. 908–9. (Italics added.)

284 "gravely disturbed": Patterson to Acheson, December 28, 1945, in *FRUS 1945,* vol. 3, pp. 922–23.

284 McCloy's comments: John J. McCloy, "American Occupation Policies in Germany," *Proceedings of the Academy of Political Science,* vol. 21 (1946), p. 550.

284 Echols's testimony is in U.S. Senate, Special Committee Investigating the National Defense Program, *Hearing,* 80th Cong., 1st Sess., April 5, 1946, p. 25797.

285 Petersen's remarks: Speech by Howard Petersen to Chamber of Commerce, Columbus, Ohio, June 24, 1946, ASW 350.001, Box 12, R.G. 107, National Archives.

285 vesting and marshaling of German external assets: Clay to Hilldring, 25 January 1946 (CC22138); Clay to Hilldring, 8 February 1946 (CC22380); Clay to Hilldring, 9 February 1946 (CC22881); Clay to Hilldring, 17 February 1946 (CC23226); Clay to Hilldring, 18 February 1946 (CC23277); all in *Clay Papers,* pp. 149–51ff.

285 restitution of looted property: See, for example, CC21041, Clay to Hilldring, 29 December 1945, reprinted in *Clay Papers,* pp. 140–41.

285 reparations claims: CC19295, Clay to Hilldring, 23 November 1945; Clay to Hilldring, 28 November 1945; both in *Clay Papers,* pp. 123–26.

285 "Patents belong to Germany as a whole": CC5824, Clay to Echols, 27 May 1946, in *Clay Papers,* pp. 223–24. Clay's protest was to no avail. For the London Accord on Treatment of German Owned Patents, 27 July 1946, see *TIAS,* No. 2415.

285 Protest on Radio Liberty: CC1697, Clay to War Department, 12 August 1946; see also CC2948, Clay to War Department, 2 September 1946; both in *Clay Papers,* pp. 249–50, 261. Again, Clay lost. See Acheson to Byrnes, 21 August 1946, *FRUS, 1946,* vol. 5, pp. 687–89.

286 Kennan's celebrated cable: Kennan to Byrnes, 22 February 1946, *Foreign Relations of the United States, 1946,* vol. 6, pp. 696–709. For analysis, see especially C. Ben Wright, "Mr. 'X' and Containment," *Slavic Review,* vol. 35, no. 1 (March 1976), pp. 12ff; John Lewis Gaddis, "Containment: A Reassessment," *Foreign Affairs,* vol. 55 (July 1977), pp. 873–87; Daniel Yergin, *Shattered Peace:*

The Origins of the Cold War and the National Security State (Boston: Houghton Mifflin, 1977), pp. 167–71.

286 request from Matthews: Matthews to Kennan, 13 February 1946, Records of the Department of State, filed with 861.00, National Archives.

286 Kennan on the verge of resigning: George F. Kennan, *Memoirs 1925–1950* (Boston: Little, Brown, 1967), pp. 290–93.

Byrnes was apparently not impressed with Kennan's analyses. When Matthews drafted a reply to Kennan for Byrnes's signature that commended Kennan for "a splendid piece of analysis," Byrnes penciled out the passage and substituted a simple "thanks" (draft of Byrnes to Kennan, 27 February 1946, filed with 861.00, National Archives). By contrast, Matthews himself cabled Kennan, "I cannot overestimate its [Kennan's cable's] importance to those of us here who are struggling with the problem." It is not clear whether Matthews was referring to communism or Byrnes. (Matthews to Kennan, 25 February 1946, filed with 861.00, National Archives).

286 Kennan's telegram was circulated: Byrnes objected strongly to circulating Kennan's cable, although Matthews and Forrestal thought otherwise and ensured it got wide circulation throughout the military services, the State Department and the White House. See Minutes of the Committee of Three (Byrnes, Patterson, and Forrestal), 28 February 1946, Records of the Department of State, filed with 811.0200, National Archives.

286 Murphy's cable: Murphy to H. Freeman Matthews, Director, European Affairs Division, Department of State, 3 April 1946, Records of the Department of State, 861.00, National Archives. The German historian Wolfgang Krieger points out that Kennan's "long telegram" "bears striking resemblance" to the British analysis of that period ("Was General Clay a Revisionist?," *Journal of Contemporary History,* vol. 18 [1983], p. 171). See also Rolf Steininger, "Die britische Deutschlandpolitik in den Jahren 1945/46," *Aus Politik und Zeitgeschichte,* 1981–82, no. 2 (9 January 1982), pp. 28–47.

289 For Lippmann's attack on Kennan, see especially Ronald Steel, *Walter Lippmann and the American Century* (Boston: Little, Brown, 1980), pp. 433ff. For Kennan's reply to Lippmann, see *FRUS 1946,* vol. 6, pp. 721–23.

289 report produced in Research and Analysis Branch: "Capabilities and Intentions of the Soviet Union as Affected by American Policy," Robinson for Bohlen, 10 December 1945, SD 711.61/12-1045, National Archives.

290 "I was being upbraided": John H. Backer interview with George

Kennan, reported in Backer, *Winds of History: The German Years of Lucius DuBignon Clay* (New York: Van Nostrand, 1983), pp. 148–49. The late Dr. Backer, who worked for military government, and who wrote several excellent books on the period (see Bibliography), drew heavily on the JES interviews with General Clay for *Winds of History.* At the time Backer wrote, the interviews were closed, but with my permission he was granted full access. Backer's portrait of Clay's German years is sympathetic, and on most points he and I are in substantial agreement.

291 "Kennan is all theory": John H. Backer interview with Marjorie Clay, cited in ibid.

291 "an impressionist, a poet": Quoted in Walter Isaacson and Evan Thomas, *The Wise Men* (New York: Simon and Schuster, 1986), p. 436.

291 Kennan deplored popular government: A useful recent summary of Kennan's attitude toward democracy is provided in ibid., pp. 171–78. For more detailed analysis, see David Mayers, *George Kennan and the Dilemmas of U.S. Foreign Policy* (New York: Oxford University Press, 1988), pp. 64–78; Barton Gellman, *Contending with Kennan* (New York: Praeger, 1985), pp. 83–105; Ben C. Wright, "George F. Kennan: Scholar-Diplomat," Ph.D. dissertation, University of Wisconsin, 1972, pp. 24–26, 129–32; and Kennan's own *Memoirs,* pp. 87–141, 185. For his attitude toward the Nazis, see especially George F. Kennan, *From Prague After Munich* (Princeton: Princeton University Press, 1968), pp. 80–87.

291 "Clay did not welcome interference": John Kenneth Galbraith, *A Life in Our Times* (Boston: Houghton Mifflin, 1981).

292 Eisenhower queried all military commanders: WX-95097, War Department cable, 20 July 1946. Eisenhower's cable was designed to elicit corroborating material for the bellicose memorandum on Soviet policy then under preparation for President Truman by Clark Clifford and George Elsey. Clay's benign assessment of Soviet behavior was all but ignored. See Yergin, *Shattered Peace,* pp. 241–44; Richard M. Freeland, *The Truman Doctrine and the Origins of McCarthyism* (New York: Knopf, 1972), pp. 56–57. For the text of the Clifford-Elsey memorandum, see Arthur Krock, *Memoirs: Sixty Years on the Firing Line* (New York: Popular Library, 1968), pp. 419–82.

292 "difficult to place blame on Soviets": Clay to McNarney, 23 July 1946, in *Clay Papers,* pp. 243–44. It was apparent to Secretary of Defense Forrestal that Clay's perception of Soviet activity differed fundamentally from his own. When Clay told Forrestal on 16 July 1946 that "the Russians did not want a war and that we should find it possible to get along with them," Forrestal thought that

Clay was nearing a mental breakdown. "He [Clay] runs the risk of blowing up entirely," Forrestal wrote Secretary of War Patterson —a comment that may reveal more about Forrestal's mental condition than Clay's (both quotes in Walter Millis, ed., *The Forrestal Diaries* [New York: Viking, 1951], pp. 182–83).

292 Clifford-Elsey Report: For the full text, see Krock, *Memoirs,* pp. 422–82. Margaret Truman helps put the memo in perspective in *Harry S. Truman* (New York: Morrow, 1972), p. 347.

293 "It was from General Clay in Berlin": Symington to Truman, "Interview with General Clay," 26, 29, 30 July 1946, Harry S. Truman Papers, Truman Library, Independence, Mo.

293 American zone was closed to Soviet entry: On leaving Germany in 1945, General Eisenhower had delivered what one State Department functionary described as "valedictory instructions to get along with the Russians" (861.5048/11-2546, Heath to Riddleberger, 26 November 1945, State Department papers. See also Eisenhower to Zhukov, 6 December 1945, box 118, Eisenhower Papers.

293 Clay on bias of interpreters: Clay was especially concerned because he feared that the Foreign Service officers assigned to Berlin sometimes allowed their anti-Soviet prejudices to intrude into their translations. As a result, he quickly discarded Murphy's assistants and began to employ German civil servants. "I want an interpreter who is thinking of absolutely nothing except how to put somebody's words into exactly the same words in English," said Clay. Demaree Bess, "American Viceroy in Germany," *Saturday Evening Post,* May 3, 1947, p. 146.

294 "thanks to the diplomatic genius": Symington, "Interview." See also John Morton Blum, ed., *The Price of Vision: The Diary of Henry A. Wallace, 1942–1946* (Boston: Houghton Mifflin, 1973), pp. 609–10.

294 "the old 'red scare' ": Letter, Clay to Dodge, 25 July 1946, Joseph Dodge Papers, Detroit Public Library, Detroit, Mich.

294 "step backward in teaching democracy": See Acheson to Murphy, 16 August 1946, and the reference cables cited therein, in *FRUS 1946,* vol. 5, pp. 732–33; CC2135, Clay for War Department, 20 August 1946, in *Clay Papers,* pp. 256–58.

294 "little evidence of Communist gains": CC2135, 20 August 1946.

19: War Crimes Trials

PAGE

296 International Military Tribunal: The International Military Tribunal grew out of the 30 October 1943 Moscow Declaration on Atrocities issued by Eden, Hull, and Molotov (for text, see Beate

Ruhm von Oppen, ed., *Documents on Germany Under Occupation, 1945–1954* [London: Oxford University Press, 1955], pp. 2–3); ratified at the San Francisco Conference of the United Nations; and brought into effect by a quadripartite agreement signed in London, 8 August 1945. For text of quadripartite agreement, see ibid., pp. 50–58.

296 United States undertook additional trials: The authorization for American military government to conduct war crimes trials came originally from Ordinance No. 2 (Military Government Courts) issued by SHAEF as soon as Allied troops entered Germany (for text, see ibid., pp. 11–13). The U.S. tribunal at Nuremberg was established 18 October 1946 (three weeks after the IMT handed down its verdict on 30 September 1946), by U.S. Military Government Ordinance No. 7. For text, see U.S. Department of State, *Germany, 1947–1949: The Story in Documents,* pp. 112–16.

297 trials at Dachau: The Army courts at Dachau were established under the Judge Advocate General in 1945 to hear cases involving crimes against U.S. military personnel and atrocities in concentration camps captured by the U.S. Army. The last case at Dachau concluded 30 December 1947. For a report of the proceedings, see Legal and Judicial Affairs (Cumulative Review) OMGUS Report No. 38, p. 10. See also Earl F. Ziemke, *The U.S. Army in the Occupation of Germany: 1944–1946* (Washington, D.C.: Office of Military History, 1975), pp. 392–95.

300 German generals write the histories: Originally organized under Colonel S. L. A. Marshall, chief historian of the European Theater of Operations, the German generals selected for the project were assembled first at Versailles, then Enclosure 20 at Allendorf, in Hesse. They were placed under the command of Generaloberst Franz Halder, a former chief of the General Staff, and put to work writing histories for use in the U.S. Army Historical Program. After they were released from prisoner-of-war status in July 1947, many continued to work full- or part-time under General Halder. The program terminated in 1959.

300 Treatment of German prisoners: In late 1948, Clay, along with Generals Koenig and Robertson—the three Western Military Governors—grew concerned about the conditions at Spandau prison, where the six remaining major war criminals were held. The prison itself was located in the British sector of Berlin, but under quadripartite control. Each of the four occupying powers supplied a governor and an equal number of guards. Decisions were made by unanimous agreement among the four governors. The Soviet governor, whose interpretation of the regulations was much harsher than that of his Western colleagues, consistently

vetoed efforts to provide special food to the prisoners who suffered from diabetes, and additional food to those suffering from anemia. As Clay advised Washington, "the prisoners were rapidly deteriorating" (CC-7667, Clay [personal and EYES ONLY for (Gordon) Gray], 6 February 1949, in *Clay Papers,* pp. 1005–6). Consequently, Clay, Robertson, and Koenig requested permission from their governments to operate Spandau on a tripartite basis, excluding the Russians (CC-6877, Clay for DA [TOP SECRET], 5 November 1948, in *Clay Papers,* pp. 913–17). But the British and French governments refused. The French government was also loath to take any action that French public opinion might interpret as coddling top-level Nazi prisoners (CC-6877, Clay for DA, 26 November 1948, in *Clay Papers,* p. 937). As a result, Clay decided to act unilaterally. On 2 December 1948, he instructed the American prison governor to treat the prisoners in a more humane manner. Clay told Washington that his action was "supported by the French and British" military. He said that the Nazi war criminals presented a difficult problem. He did not believe that they should be treated better than normal German criminals. On the other hand, "these prisoners receive far worse care than that afforded criminals in U.S. prisons. It is a standard which will become associated with our name." Clay wondered whether they should be transferred to the United States, "as a U.S. obligation" (CC-7667, *supra). Clay Papers,* pp. 1005–06.

301 "death sentence of Ilse Koch": After commuting Koch's sentence, Clay did reply to some of the criticism in the United States. On 27 September 1948, he advised Helen Kirkpatrick of the New York *Post* that he reviewed every death sentence handed down, and had approved nineteen death sentences stemming from conditions at Buchenwald. "In these reviews, I must base my actions on the evidence . . . not on the public reputation of the individual" (35813, Clay to DA, 27 September 1948, in *Clay Papers,* p. 881). The furor did not die down, however. When Army Secretary Royall questioned Clay about the commutation (W-89988), Clay took full responsibility. "I may have made many errors of judgment in my findings and I may make more in the cases still pending. Nevertheless, each decision is made with the utmost sincerity of conviction based on my study of the data before me. If attack there is, it should . . . be levelled at me. I am sorry to have brought the Army under attack, but decisions of this type cannot be political. They are, and cannot be other than, decisions of conscience" (CC-6162, Clay personal for Royall, 2 October 1948, in *Clay Papers,* pp. 888–89). See also CC-7674, Clay for DA, 7 February 1949, in which Clay reminded Washington that

"crimes against German nationals [which Koch did indeed commit] have not been included in war crimes. Therefore, she has not been tried on these charges." Clay said he had asked the Minister-President of Bavaria to consider bringing charges against her for such crimes *(Clay Papers,* pp. 1007–8). In 1949, Ilse Koch was indeed tried by German authorities in Bavaria and sentenced to life imprisonment on two counts of "incitement to murder" of Buchenwald prisoners. She committed suicide in prison in 1967.

301 "Those tried for the Malmédy Massacre": On 3 March 1949, Army Secretary Royall instructed Clay "to hold up any executions . . . in Malmédy case . . . until further notice from here" (W-84947). For Clay's response, see his cables CC-8010, 12 March 1949, in *Clay Papers,* pp. 1042–45; CC-8054, 17 March 1949, in *Clay Papers,* pp. 1054–56; CC-8095, 21 March 1949, in *Clay Papers,* pp. 1059–61ff.

301 Rejects Vatican appeal: CC-7142, Clay for Draper, 21 December 1948, in *Clay Papers,* p. 962.

302 "must make me seem ghoulish": CC-8181, Clay for Voorhees, 29 March 1949, in *Clay Papers,* p. 1062.

306 Telford Taylor's comments: Telford Taylor interview, Columbia University Law School, New York, N.Y., 14 March 1972.

20: Saving Germany's Art Treasures

PAGE

309 "the greatest single art collection": Notes of Secretary Stimson's trip to Germany kept by Colonel William H. Kyle, Manuscript Collection, Henry L. Stimson Papers, Yale University, New Haven, Conn.

310 Stimson applauded Clay's plan: Ibid.

312 secured Truman's oral approval: *FRUS 1945,* vol. 2, pp. 933ff.

312 "held in trusteeship": *FRUS Potsdam,* vol. 2, pp. 923–24. (Italics added.)

312 "be subject to future Allied discussions": Ibid., pp. 922–23.

313 "I am apprehensive": CC-14167, Clay (signed Eisenhower) for War Department, 7 August 1945, in *Clay Papers,* pp. 57–58.

313 essential that a public announcement be made: Clay for War Department, 4 September 1945, in *Clay Papers,* p. 68.

313 "not readily identifiable": For text of joint press release, see cable, Byrnes to Clay, 24 August 1945 (State Dept. #342), in *FRUS 1945,* vol. 2.

314 "preserve them for the German people": Letter, Clay to McCloy, 21 September 1945, in *Clay Papers,* pp. 83–84. (Italics added.) The following week, Clay requested permission to propose that the

Allied Control Council oversee the return of German art objects to their proper zones, and that no further removal from Germany take place without ACC approval. No action was taken on Clay's request.

315 "I feel very strongly": CC-18900, Clay (Personal) for Hilldring, 14 November 1945, in *Clay Papers,* pp. 117–18.

315 War Department authorized him: W-83352, War Department cable, 15 November 1945. See *Clay Papers,* p. 118 (endnote).

315 In October of the following year: W-81664, War Department cable, 2 October 1946, in Lucius D. Clay Papers (Germany), National Archives, Washington, D.C.

316 "difficult to justify their return": CC-4908, Clay Personal for Echols, 4 October 1946, in *Clay Papers,* p. 268.

316 On the State Department takeover of the Occupation, see *The New York Times,* 9 January 1948. See also Chap. 24.

316 "arrange return of German paintings": CC-3050, Clay (EYES ONLY) for Draper, 31 January 1948, in *Clay Papers,* pp. 551–52.

316 "controversy in the Art World": W-95402, War Department cable, 6 February 1948. See *Clay Papers,* p. 552 (endnote).

317 "no longer a valid objection": CC-3111, Clay (EYES ONLY) for Draper, 6 February 1948, in *Clay Papers,* p. 555.

317 "retain and display": See headnote, *Clay Papers,* pp. 627–28.

317 "refused the Army's request": W-99355, Department of the Army cable. See *Clay Papers,* pp. 627–28 (headnote).

317 "how [could] a United States Senator": CC-3853, Clay (Personal) for Draper, 13 April 1948, in *Clay Papers,* pp. 627–29.

319 intent of National Gallery: CC-3719, Clay (EYES ONLY) for Noce, 4 April 1948, in *Clay Papers,* pp. 617–18.

319 "as a tangible German appreciation": W-99355, Department of the Army cable. See *Clay Papers,* p. 634 (headnote).

319 "My views are unchanged": 73134, Clay (Personal) for Draper, 20 April 1948, in *Clay Papers,* p. 634.

320 teleconference: TT 9402, 23 April 1948, in *Clay Papers,* pp. 634–37.

21: Clay Takes Control

PAGE

329 "equally available to all occupying powers": CC-19233, Clay for War Department (TOP SECRET), 21 November 1945, in *Clay Papers,* pp. 121–22; see also CC-20342, Clay Personal for Hilldring (TOP SECRET), 13 December 1945; *FRUS 1945,* vol. 3, pp. 1129–30.

331 POW training school: Clay for War Department, 7 October 1945, in *Clay Papers,* pp. 97–98.

331 "like the labor practices employed by Hitler": Clay for War De-

partment, 28 November 1945, in *Clay Papers,* pp. 125–26. Cf. *FRUS 1945,* vol. 3, pp. 1424–25.

332 "taking the thought of German scientists": CC-7783, Clay (Personal) for Noce, 22 January 1947, in *Clay Papers,* pp. 305–6.

335 "I never saw a marked military orientation": Whipple interview, New York, N.Y., 6 March 1971.

342 De Gaulle rejected key portions: Ministère des Affaires Etrangères, *Documents français relatives à l'Allemagne,* pp. 7–11.

342 De Gaulle to Truman: *FRUS, 1945,* vol. 4, pp. 661ff.

342 Clay openly condemned the French action: Lucius D. Clay, *Decision in Germany* (Garden City, N.Y.: Doubleday, 1950), p. 110.

342 "Russians and British are in full agreement": Clay for War Department, 24 September 1945, in *Clay Papers,* pp. 84–85. For the French position, see *FRUS 1945,* vol 3, pp. 871–77.

343 Koenig formally advised the ACC: *Documents français,* p. 16.

343 "Any real progress appears impossible": Clay for War Department, 4 October 1945 (not sent), in *Clay Papers,* pp. 90–91.

343 "We've made little progress": Letter, Clay to McCloy, 5 October 1945, in *Clay Papers,* pp. 91–97.

344 specially convened meeting of State Department officials: Résumé of meeting at State Department, prepared by Maj. Gen. Hilldring, 3 November 1945, in *Clay Papers,* pp. 111–17.

344 Clay's views: Clay, *Decision in Germany,* p. 110.

345 *"The situation here has not improved":* Letter, Clay to Russell, 15 December 1945, in *Clay Papers,* p. 137.

345 *"French position . . . is not understandable":* CC-21041, Clay (Personal) for Hilldring, 29 December 1945, in *Clay Papers,* pp. 139–41.

346 For the Byrnes-Caffery exchange, see *FRUS 1946,* vol. 5, pp. 403–4, 498, 509–51.

346 "failure of the French to look ahead": CC-22247, Clay (Personal) for Hilldring, 28 January 1946, in *Clay Papers,* pp. 151–52.

347 "The Communist Party has made": CC-23470, Clay for Hilldring, 22 February 1946, in *Clay Papers,* pp. 165–66.

347 "all shipments of wheat . . . will be discontinued": CC-2931, Clay (signed McNarney) for Byrnes and Anderson (TOP SECRET), 11 April 1946, in *Clay Papers,* pp. 189–90.

347 "unwise to exert such direct pressure": *FRUS 1946,* vol. 5, p. 540n.

348 "The Communist Party in Germany": Memorandum, Clay for Byrnes, [n.d.] April 1946, in *Clay Papers,* pp. 191–202. Cf. *FRUS 1946,* vol. 5, pp. 541–42.

349 "It's the first step" and "as a personnel reservoir": TC-5756, 1 March 1946, in *Clay Papers,* pp. 168–75.

350 "job of de-Nazification": Reference is to the Law for Liberation

	from National Socialism and Militarism. For text, see James Pollock and Meisel, *Germany Under Occupation* (Ann Arbor: Wahr, 1947), p. 179.
351	"the French answer was their usual statement": CC-4277, Clay (Personal) for Echols, 2 May 1946, in *Clay Papers,* pp. 203–4.
351	"zones represent airtight territories": CC-5797, Clay for Chief of Staff (Eisenhower), 26 May 1946, in *Clay Papers,* pp. 212–17.
353	"Not to the Russians": Text, Clay press conference, 27 May 1946, in *Clay Papers,* pp. 218–23.
353	"The Russians are tough horse-traders": Arthur L. Mayer, "Winter of Discontent," *The New Republic,* 10 March 1947, p. 19. For a more extensive analysis that places Clay's cutoff in context, see John Gimbel, "On the Implementation of the Potsdam Agreement: An Essay on U.S. Postwar German Policy," *Political Science Quarterly,* vol. 87, no. 7 (June 1972), pp. 242–72, especially pp. 250ff.
353	Rostow's comments: W. W. Rostow to Charles Kindleberger, 10 June 1946, in Walt W. Rostow, *The Division of Europe After World War*, vol. 2, *1946* (Austin: University of Texas Press, 1981), pp. 138–48.
354	"We have always been good friends": Demerey Bess, "American Viceroy in Germany," *The Saturday Evening Post,* 10 May 1947, p. 78.
354	Russians seriously protested: *FRUS 1946,* vol. 2, pp. 846–57.
354	"State Department functionaries": John Gimbel, "The Origins of the Marshall Plan," paper delivered to the first German Conference on the Origins of the Marshall Plan, Essen, Germany, 3 June 1978. See also Gimbel's *The Origins of the Marshall Plan* (Stanford: Stanford University Press, 1976), pp. 98–140, especially pp. 127–40.

22: Coping with Crises

PAGE	
357	"The death rate": Letter, Clay to McCloy, 5 October 1945, in *Clay Papers,* pp. 91–97.
358	"1380 calories to 1145": CC-22247, Clay (Personal) for Hilldring, 28 January 1946, in *Clay Papers,* pp. 151–52.
358	"and far below any minimum standard": CC-23681, Clay (Personal) for Hilldring, 27 February 1946, in *Clay Papers,* pp. 166–67.
358	"adversely affect quadripartite control": CC-1033, Clay (Personal) for Hilldring, 6 March 1946, in *Clay Papers,* pp. 177–78.
359	"The reduced ration": CC-1530, Clay (Personal) for (Brigadier General Robert Ward) Berry [Civil Affairs Division], 16 March 1946, in *Clay Papers,* pp. 178–80.

360 "Clay . . . has asked me for his relief": Letter, McNarney for Eisenhower, 18 March 1946, in *Clay Papers,* pp. 180–81.

360 in his memoirs: Lucius D. Clay, *Decision in Germany* (Garden City, N.Y.: Doubleday, 1950), p. 265.

360 "until the next harvest season": CC-2124, Clay (Personal) for Echols and (Assistant Secretary of War Howard) Petersen, 27 March 1946, in *Clay Papers,* pp. 183–85.

361 Red Army had provided sufficient rations: Hans Adler, "The Postwar Reorganization," *Quarterly Journal of Economics,* vol. 63, no. 3 (August 1946), p. 333; Manuel Gottlieb, *The German Peace Settlement and the Berlin Crisis* (New York: Paine Whitman, 1960), p. 58.

361 Situation in Soviet zone: Wolfgang Friedmann, *The Allied Military Government of Germany* (London: Stevens, 1947), pp. 192–94, 202; John P. Nettl, *The Eastern Zone and Soviet Policy in Germany: 1945–1950* (London: Oxford University Press, 1951), pp. 162–65.

361 seeks Hoover's assistance: CC-2124, 27 March 1946.

361 Clay credits President Hoover: Clay, *Decision in Germany,* p. 267.

362 "The physical condition . . . is deteriorating": CC-5315, Clay (Personal) for Echols, 18 May 1946, in *Clay Papers,* pp. 207–8.

362 tripartite team: "Combined Nutrition Survey of Settled Areas in British, French, and U.S. Zones of Germany," 22 May 1946, OMGUS Collection, National Archives.

362 "rickets is becoming prevalent": CC-5692, Clay (Personal) for Echols, 24 May 1946, in *Clay Papers,* p. 212.

362 "three weeks' supply": TT-8096, teleconference with Petersen, 13 May 1947, in *Clay Papers,* pp. 354–63.

363 "The child feeding program": Clay, *Decision in Germany,* p. 268. See also Louis Lochner, *Herbert Hoover and Germany* (New York: Macmillan, 1960), pp. 179–81; William Y. Elliott, "The Control of Foreign Policy in the United States," *Political Quarterly,* vol. 20, no. 4 (October-December 1949).

364 "the Russians have set up": Letter, Clay to McCloy, 5 October 1945, in *Clay Papers,* pp. 91–97.

365 "policy coordination will be your job": Heinz Guradze, "The Länderrat: Landmark of German Reconstruction," *Western Political Quarterly,* vol. 3 (1950), p. 191.

365 "quickly at local levels": Letter, Clay to McCloy, 16 September 1945, in *Clay Papers,* pp. 74–82.

365 "enjoyed teasing": Clay, *Decision in Germany,* p. 88.

366 "the General's speeches were concerned . . .": Guradze, "The Länderrat," p. 196.

368 He flatly refused: Louis Wiesner, *Organized Labor in Postwar Germany,* p. 214.

369 "principles of complete political neutrality": CC-2135, Clay for War Department, 20 August 1946, in *Clay Papers,* pp. 256–58.

369 "the development of a skin": Letter, Clay to Maier, 12 February 1947, in *Clay Papers,* pp. 310–12.

370 hands-off attitude: John Backer, *Winds of History: The German Years of Lucius DuBignon Clay* (New York: Van Nostrand, 1983), p. 219. See also Leonard Krieger, "The Inter-Regnum in Germany: March-August 1945," *Political Science Quarterly,* vol. 64, no. 4 (December 1949).

371 question of Germany's western frontier: Byrnes to Clay, *FRUS 1946,* vol. 5, pp. 501–3.

372 went along with Byrnes's strategy: Clay, *Decision in Germany,* pp. 124–30; Alan Bullock, *Ernest Bevin: Foreign Secretary 1945–1951* (New York: Norton, 1983), pp. 265–69.

372 "General Robertson and I": Clay, *Decision in Germany,* p. 132.

373 Clay's instructions from Washington: *FRUS 1946,* vol. 5, p. 649, n. 12.

373 Byrnes, in a personal letter to Bidault: Clay, *Decision in Germany,* p. 133.

373 "defeats the purpose of quadripartite government": State, 2998, Clay (signed Murphy) for Byrnes, 27 December 1946, in *Clay Papers,* pp. 288–89.

373 Acheson announced: *The New York Times,* 28 December 1946.

373 "would like to be recalled immediately" and "wholly warranted": TT-1228, 28 December 1946, in *Clay Papers,* pp. 290–91.

374 "If we condone": CC-7514, cable to Petersen, Clay (EYES ONLY-TOP SECRET) for Petersen, 29 December 1946, in *Clay Papers,* p. 292.

374 "I am disturbed about it": Byrnes to Clay, *FRUS 1946,* vol. 5, pp. 657–58.

374 "I cannot feel hurt": CC-7530, Clay (EYES ONLY) for Petersen, 31 December 1946, in *Clay Papers,* p. 293.

374 "Regardless of embarrassment": Cable, Clay (signed Murphy) for Byrnes, 31 December 1946, in *Clay Papers,* p. 293.

375 Free University of Berlin: The definitive treatment of the founding of the Free University is provided in James F. Tent, *The Free University of Berlin: A Political History* (Bloomington: Indiana University Press, 1988). See especially pp. 92–112 and the references cited therein.

376 "took my breath away": Herman B. Wells, *Being Lucky: Reminiscences and Reflection* (Bloomington: Indiana University Press, 1980), p. 310.

376 requests retirement: CC-7029, Clay for McNarney, 15 June 1946, in *Clay Papers,* p. 230.

376 "My stated reasons": CC-7038, Clay (EYES ONLY) for Echols, 17 June 1946, in *Clay Papers,* pp. 230–31.

377 "McNarney's combat record": Robert Murphy, *Diplomat Among Warriors* (Garden City, N.Y.: Doubleday, 1964), pp. 291–92; Backer, *Winds of History,* pp. 205–6.

378 Molotov . . . proclaimed: Bullock, *Ernest Bevin,* p. 283; Beate Ruhm von Oppen, ed., *The Documents of Germany Under Occupation, 1945–1954* (London: Oxford University Press, 1955), pp. 144–47.

379 For Clay's July 19 draft, see *Clay Papers,* pp. 236–43.

381 Petersen strongly agreed: *Clay Papers,* p. 237, note 2.

381 "to consider and report": Backer, *The Winds of History,* p. 218; also see John Gimbel, *The American Occupation of Germany* (Stanford: Stanford University Press, 1968), p. 80.

381 "I don't know what our policy is": CC-1378, Clay for (Brigadier General George F.) Schulgen (Civil Affairs Division), 7 August 1946, in *Clay Papers,* pp. 247–48.

382 "denazification by Germans": Clay for Hilldring, 13 August 1946. Clay did not send this cable. "File. Not used," he wrote in pencil at the top *(Clay Papers,* p. 251).

382 "We are fearful": W-97164, 12 August 1946, in Lucius D. Clay Papers (Germany), National Archives, Washington, D.C.

383 G-2 criticism: USFET (G-2) memorandum to C/S, subject: "German Denazification Boards," Dec. File 014.3, Box 15, OMGUS records, National Archives.

384 "His criticism is largely destructive": Clay to McNarney, December 26, 1946, Doc. File 014.3.

384 "With all due respect": Clay for Hilldring, 15 August 1946 ("File. Not used. LDC"), in *Clay Papers,* pp. 252–53.

384 "in the waste basket": Letter, Clay for Patterson, 17 August 1946, in *Clay Papers,* pp. 254–55.

385 "I am sorry I bothered you": Letter, Clay for Byrnes (handwritten), 19 August 1946, in *Clay Papers,* p. 255.

386 repeated his desire to resign: Letter, Clay for McNarney, 21 August 1946, in *Clay Papers,* p. 259.

386 "Clay is still indispensable in Germany": Letter, Smith to Eisenhower (handwritten), 23 August 1946, in Walter Bedell Smith Papers, Eisenhower Library, Abilene, Kansas.

386 Eisenhower wrote Clay: Letter, 27 August 1946, in *Clay Papers,* p. 263.

386 ". . . serious mistake for me to continue": Letter, Clay to Eisenhower, 8 September 1946, in *Clay Papers,* p. 263.

386 Byrnes's speech at Stuttgart: For the text of Byrnes's speech, see Department of State *Bulletin,* September 15, 1946, pp. 496ff.

387	Galbraith's comments: Letter, Galbraith to JES, March 28, 1988.
390	"increasing disregard for Allied authority": S-5217, (Lieutenant General Clarence) Huebner for War Department, 8 October 1946, in *Clay Papers,* p. 272.
390	"Obviously the German people": Clay (Personal) for Huebner, (n.d.), October 1946, in *Clay Papers,* pp. 272–73.
390	"detailed comment to the constitutional assemblies": CC-2418, Clay for War Department, 23 August 1946, in *Clay Papers,* pp. 260–61.
391	"The constitutional assemblies": CC-3554, Clay (Personal) for Echols, 15 October 1946, in *Clay Papers,* pp. 270–72.
392	"take the matter up with the Secretary of War": CC-5536, Petersen for Rusk, 15 October 1946, in *Clay Papers,* p. 272 (endnote).
392	"the Bible for our actions": *The New York Times,* 10 October 1946, p. 8.
394	reparations question with the USSR: Memorandum, Clay for Byrnes, (n.d.) November 1946, in *Clay Papers,* pp. 279–84.
394	one of the most far-reaching: Backer, *Winds of History,* p. 237.

23: CINCEUR

PAGE	
397	"an aggregation of homesick Americans": Raymond Daniell, *The New York Times,* 16 December 1946.
397	"how to pick up a Fräulein": Russell Hill, *Struggle for Germany* (New York: Harper & Row, 1947), p. 117.
397	definitely would seek retirement: Letter, Clay for McNarney, 21 August 1946, in *Clay Papers,* p. 259.
398	Eisenhower's response: Letter, Eisenhower for Clay, 27 August 1946, in *Clay Papers,* p. 263 (endnote).
398	"We want you to take over": Quoted in JES interview with General Clay, Chatham, Mass., 2 January 1974.
398	"Please do not take this letter": Louis Galambos, ed., *The Papers of Dwight D. Eisenhower: The Chief of Staff* (Baltimore: Johns Hopkins Press, 1978), vol. 8, pp. 1362–63.
399	"during my entire service": Letter, Clay to Petersen, 16 December 1946. Clay Collection, George C. Marshall Library, VMI, Lexington, Va.
400	"could find no fault": Ibid., p. 1363.
401	blemish on the United States: Oliver J. Frederiksen, *The American Military Occupation of Germany, 1945–53* (Darmstadt: HICOG, 1953), pp. 39–41.
402	"He would go down to the company": John Backer interview with Richard Hallock, 5 April 1981.
404	"directed the transfer of Negro soldiers": 39556, cable, Clay for DA, 21 April 1949, in *Clay Papers,* pp. 1119–20.

405 bizonal merger accepted by the British: See Alan Bullock, *Ernest Bevin: Foreign Secretary 1945–1951* (New York: Norton, 1983), pp. 279–86.

405 final arrangements for the merger: *FRUS 1946,* vol. 2, pp. 965 ff; vol. 5, pp. 635–42. For text, see *TIAS,* no. 1575; 61 stat. (pt. 3), 2475.

406 "full speed ahead with a political merger": *FRUS 1947,* vol. 2, pp. 968–69.

407 "Douglas's book": Air Marshal Sir Sholto Douglas [Lord Douglas of Kirtleside], *Combat and Command* (New York: Simon and Schuster, 1963). Of Clay, Douglas said, "I found him one of the most able and clear-thinking of all the American commanders I came to know. He was immensely experienced and shrewd, and was not afraid of having to stand on his own feet, and he was the most active of all the Military Governors in Germany" (p. 759).

407 Sir Brian Robertson: Following his service as military governor and later high commissioner for Germany, Robertson became commander-in-chief of British forces in the Middle East (1950–53), and from 1953 to 1961 chaired the British Transport Commission.

407 General Koenig: Born in Alsace in 1898, Pierre Koenig was the same age as Clay. Koenig did not attend Saint-Cyr, the French military academy, but had been promoted from the enlisted ranks in World War I. He served in the Foreign Legion, and was a captain when World War II began. After fighting a last-ditch defense in Normandy, he was one of the last French officers to flee to England in 1940, and was promoted to colonel by de Gaulle. Sent to Africa, he defended the desert oasis of Bir Hacheim for sixteen days in 1942, surrounded by Rommel's Afrika Korps. In that capacity, Koenig rejected seven separate demands from Rommel that he surrender, and eventually led three-quarters of his original garrison through German lines to safety. The surrender ultimatum that Rommel sent to Koenig on 3 June 1942 was framed, and it hung above General de Gaulle's desk throughout the remainder of the war. (Clay's statement that Koenig was an out-and-out Gaullist may have been an understatement.) After his service as Military Governor, Koenig twice served as French minister of defense, and in his last years was president of the French-Israeli Solidarity Committee. He died on 2 September 1970.

408 "happened to visit Mr. Schuman": For Ambassador Caffery's report, see *FRUS 1949,* vol. 3, pp. 115–118.

408 Tripartite Agreement: For text, see *Germany, 1947–1949,* pp. 88–92.

410 problems of Bizonia: CC-8766, Clay for Draper, 11 April 1947, in *Clay Papers,* pp. 333–34.

410 "would destroy the political gains": CC-8933, Clay (Personal) for Noce (TOP SECRET), 28 April 1947, in *Clay Papers,* pp. 341–42.

411 At Potsdam: *FRUS Potsdam*, vol. 2, pp. 439–40; Joseph Davies Journal, 28 July 1945, Library of Congress.

411 Moscow Council in December 1945: *FRUS 1945,* vol. 2, pp. 736, 740–41, 757, 776, 805–6.

412 "loitering around Munich": Arthur Vandenberg, *The Private Papers of Senator Vandenberg* (Boston: Houghton Mifflin, 1952), pp. 247–249. Also see Joseph E. Davies Journal, 22 May 1945, Davies MSS, box 17, Library of Congress.

412 "As far as Mr. Byrnes was concerned": Acheson Manuscripts, box 64, Harry S. Truman Library, Independence, Mo. See also Charles Bohlen, *Witness to History 1929–1969* (New York: Norton, 1973), pp. 248, 256–59; Theodore Achilles oral-history interview, Truman Library.

412 The views of the State Department's Russian experts are treated at length by Daniel Yergin in *Shattered Peace: The Origins of the Cold War and the National Security State* (Boston: Houghton Mifflin, 1977), pp. 17–41.

412 "The career U.S. Foreign Service Officer . . .": Walter Bedell Smith, *My Three Years in Moscow* (Philadelphia: Lippincott, 1950), p. 30.

412 "sort of patronized": Clay interview with Colonel R. Joe Rogers, 8 November 1972. U.S. Army Military History Institute.

413 "if that continues": *FRUS 1946,* vol. 10, p. 681.

414 U.S.-Soviet relations slipped: Robert J. Donovan, *Conflict and Crisis: The Presidency of Harry S. Truman, 1945–1949* (New York: Norton, 1977), pp. 266–67.

414 "my place is in Germany": Clay to Petersen, R.G. 165, file WDSCA 014, National Archives, Washington, D.C.

415 "Was a united Germany": John Foster Dulles Papers, 7 March 1947, Princeton University Library, Princeton, N.J.

415 The description of the Wannsee conference is from Clay interview, 6 June 1973.

416 meeting closed with Dulles triumphant: John Foster Dulles, *War or Peace* (New York: Macmillan, 1957), pp. 102–3. See also Donald W. Pruessen, *John Foster Dulles, The Road to Power* (New York: Free Press, 1982), pp. 325–30, 335–45.

416 On Clay's reluctance to go to Moscow, see Lucius D. Clay, *Decision in Germany* (Garden City, N.Y.: Doubleday, 1950), p. 146.

417 Smith on Dulles: See Smith, *My Three Years,* pp. 211–15.

418 Dulles determined to use his influence: Kindleberger to John de Wilde, 17 March 1947, Kindleberger Papers.

419 "Marshall's fair-haired boys": John Backer interview with Don Humphrey, Clay's economics adviser, 9 September 1978.

419 established a working party: *FRUS 1947,* vol. 2, p. 276.

419 "Blood was all over the floor": John Backer interview with James Riddleberger, 6 August 1981.

419 "mountains out of molehills": Clay, *Decision in Germany,* p. 149.

419 "The winds of history": Backer, *Winds of History: The German Years of Lucius DuBignon Clay* (New York: Van Nostrand, 1983), p. 214.

420 "The whole matter is poorly run": Clay to Sokolovsky, Kindleberger to John de Wilde, 24, 29 March 1947, Kindleberger Papers.

420 "I can always return": Memorandum, Clay for Marshall, 31 March 1947, in *Clay Papers,* p. 332.

421 "shocked when Justice Byrnes resigned": Letter, Clay to Brown, 21 April 1947, in *Clay Papers,* pp. 340–41.

422 "how deeply satisfied": Eisenhower to Clay, 19 April 1947, in Galambos, ed., *Papers of Dwight David Eisenhower,* vol. 8, pp. 1650–51.

24: End of the Wartime Alliance

PAGE

423 "one of the first things": Colonel R. Joe Rogers interview with Clay, New York, N.Y., 24 January 1974.

423 "The earlier the better": John Backer interview with Mrs. Marjorie Clay, 12 July 1981.

423 "irritating measures": Clay to Noce, 14 April 1947, in *Clay Papers,* pp. 336–38.

425 "a different ball game": John H. Backer, *Winds of History: The German Years of Lucius DuBignon Clay* (New York: Van Nostrand, 1983), p. 238.

425 "My mule": Letter, Clay for Brown, 21 April 1947, in *Clay Papers,* pp. 340–41.

426 Clay was given new instructions: Lucius D. Clay, *Decision in Germany* (Garden City, N.Y.: Doubleday, 1950), p. 124.

427 "among the most sobering experiences": Richard Nixon, *Leaders* (New York: Warner Books, 1982), pp. 136–37.

427 "I am not a salesman": TT-8529 (TOP SECRET), 13 September 1947, in *Clay Papers,* pp. 426–29.

429 "Germany is bankrupt": Letter, Clay to Marshall, 2 May 1947, in *Clay Papers,* pp. 346–49.

429 "You have my sympathy": *FRUS 1947,* vol. 2, p. 931.

429 "I miss you every day": Letter, Clay to Byrnes, 11 May 1947, in *Clay Papers,* pp. 351.

430 "I would have done the same": Letter, Byrnes to Clay, 20 May 1947, James F. Byrnes Papers, Clemson University Library, Clemson, S.C.

430 Minor agreements: Control Council Laws 44, 45, 47, and 48 (1947). See Clay, *Decision in Germany,* pp. 470–71, n. 13.

430 troop strengths: CC-9374, 1 June 1947, in *Clay Papers,* pp. 367–68. Cf. CC9324, Clay's cable to Washington of 1 June 1947, with his later description in *Decision in Germany,* pp. 154–55, which placed a Cold War veneer on Sokolovsky's action. For Robert Murphy's cable to the State Department, see *FRUS 1947,* vol. 2, pp. 871–73.

430 quadripartite government was dead: Clay, *Decision in Germany,* pp. 155–57.

431 contradictory instructions from the War Department: WX-81354. See *Clay Papers,* p. 381 (headnote).

431 "Both objectives cannot be accomplished": CC 9790, 6 July 1947, in *Clay Papers,* pp. 381–82.

431 "carrying water on both shoulders": CC 9906, Clay (EYES ONLY) for Petersen, 16 July 1947, in *Clay Papers,* p. 383.

431 JCS 1779: For text, see U.S. Department of State, *Germany 1947–1949: The Story in Documents* (Washington: Government Printing Office, 1950), pp. 33–41.

431 "at face value": Clay, *Decision in Germany,* p. 238.

431 "I had understood": CC-9906, Clay (EYES ONLY) for Petersen, 16 July 1947, in *Clay Papers,* pp. 383–84. (Italics added.)

432 "I think we are facing disaster" and "Unthinkable for you to resign at this time": TT 8362, 24 July 1947, in *Clay Papers,* pp. 385–88.

433 "obliged to make certain public statements": *FRUS 1947,* vol. 2, pp. 1008–9.

433 "Faith, Hope and Charity": W-82808, Eisenhower to Clay, 25 July 1947, in *Clay Papers,* p. 389.

433 "I am not temperamental": CC-1046, (EYES ONLY—TOP SECRET), Clay to Eisenhower, 28 July 1947, in *Clay Papers,* pp. 389–90.

434 Eisenhower had experienced difficulties: See David Eisenhower, *Eisenhower at War* (New York: Random House, 1986), pp. 482–553.

434 "I hope my former telegram": W-83185, Eisenhower to Clay, 1 August 1947.

434 "the U.S. government will support vigorously": W-82897, Marshall and Royall to Clay and Murphy, 26 July 1947, in *FRUS 1947,* vol. 2, pp. 1009–10.

434 "No other country": 28 July 1947, in *FRUS 1947,* vol. 2, pp. 1010–11.

435 "result in a communistic Europe": CC 1047, Clay to Royall (EYES ONLY—TOP SECRET), 28 July 1947, in *Clay Papers,* pp. 390–91.

435 Royall's press conference: New York *Herald Tribune,* 1 August 1947.

435 Marshall's contrary statement to Bidault: On 21 July 1947, Marshall advised Bidault that, "In order to give time for a full consideration of the views of the French Government, the United States Government will suspend further announcement of the proposal for the revised level of industry in Germany until the French Government has had a reasonable opportunity to discuss these questions with the United States and United Kingdom Governments" (*FRUS 1947,* vol. 2, pp. 1003–4).

436 " 'we told you so' ": Quoted in Backer, *Winds of History,* p. 322.

436 "the French Government interpreted": *FRUS 1947,* vol. 2, pp. 1014–16.

437 "The frank, perhaps blunt, statement": TT 8404 (TOP SECRET), 8 August 1947, in *Clay Papers,* pp. 394–97.

437 "I can offer no comment": Ibid.

438 "to the limit of my ability": TT 8404 (TOP SECRET), 8 August 1947, in *Clay Papers,* pp. 394–97.

438 "he seems to have lost interest": *FRUS 1947,* vol. 2, pp. 1019–20.

438 Marshall told Douglas: Ibid., p. 1027, n. 75.

438 Marshall felt that Clay should be replaced: Lovett interview, Brown Brothers Harriman, New York, N.Y., 4 May 1971.

439 "your presence in London is vital": TT8429, 16 August 1947, in *Clay Papers,* pp. 401–6.

440 "still better if approved by four": New York *Herald Tribune,* 22 August 1947.

441 "It's like Thanksgiving dinner": TT-8442, teleconference, 20 August 1947, in *Clay Papers,* pp. 407–10. For the text of Douglas's cable about which Clay complained, see *FRUS 1947,* vol. 2, pp. 1042–44. On 21 August Acting Secretary of State Lovett replied that any substantive changes in the bizonal agreement should be negotiated between Clay and Robertson. "We [are] relying on Clay's judgment," said Lovett (*FRUS 1947,* vol. 2, pp. 1045–46).

441 The London meeting: For the text of the final communiqué of the Tripartite Talks Relating to the Level of Industry, see *Department of State Bulletin,* September 7, 1947, pp. 467–68; Beate Ruhm von Oppen, ed., *Documents of Germany Under Occupation, 1945–1954* (London: Oxford University Press, 1955), pp. 238–39.

441 "not good in negotiations": George R. Jacobs, private papers, quoted in Backer, *Winds of History,* p. 251.

442 "Douglas handled the matter well": CC 1460 (TOP SECRET), 31 August 1947, in *Clay Papers,* pp. 415–16.

442 "O ye of wavering heart": TT 8663 (TOP SECRET), 24 October 1947, in *Clay Papers,* pp. 441–46: TT 8711, 15 November 1947, in *Clay Papers,* pp. 495–500.

442 "buying a dead pig": CC 2106, Clay to Draper (TOP SECRET), 28 October 1947, in *Clay Papers,* p. 449.

442 "We need England and France": CC 2103, Clay for Gray, 27 October 1947, in *Clay Papers,* pp. 446–48.

443 "get tough" policy: Clay, Berlin press conference, 28 October 1947, in *Clay Papers,* pp. 451–59.

444 "until we have an opportunity": W-89344, Draper for Clay (TOP SECRET), 29 October 1947.

444 "to attack Communism": *The New York Times,* 26 October 1947.

444 "We are engaged in political warfare": CC-2134, Clay for Draper (TOP SECRET), 30 October 1947, in *Clay Papers,* pp. 459–60.

444 wait for the Army's instructions: W-89510, Royall for Clay (TOP SECRET—EYES ONLY), 31 October 1947.

444 "I feel very badly": CC-2160, Clay for Royall and Draper (TOP SECRET—EYES ONLY), 1 November 1947, in *Clay Papers,* pp. 463–64.

445 "We agree in principle": *FRUS 1947,* vol. 2, pp. 895–96. For Murphy's cable, see ibid., pp. 893–95.

445 "If the Council of Foreign Ministers fails": CC-2167, Clay for Draper (TOP SECRET—EYES ONLY), 3 November 1947, in *Clay Papers,* pp. 475–76.

445 Eisenhower asked Clay: WX-89500, Eisenhower for Clay, in *Clay Papers,* p. 492.

445 "would reduce Soviet strengths": SX3741 (TOP SECRET), Clay for Eisenhower, 6 November 1947, in *Clay Papers,* pp. 492–93. For Clay's recommendations to the Council of Foreign Ministers pertaining to Germany, see *Clay Papers,* pp. 479–90.

446 "Conditions quite taut . . .": CC 2371, Clay for Draper (TOP SECRET), 21 November 1947, in *Clay Papers,* pp. 502–8.

446 London Council of Foreign Ministers: For the proceedings of the conference, see *FRUS 1947,* vol. 2, pp. 676–829.

446 "now engaged in a competitive struggle": Clay, *Decision in Germany,* p. 348.

447 "we really do not want": The original of Smith's letter is filed (10 December 1947) in the Dwight D. Eisenhower Papers at the Eisenhower Library, Abilene, Kan. It is extracted in Louis Galambos, ed., *The Papers of Dwight David Eisenhower: The Chief of Staff* (Baltimore: Johns Hopkins Press, 1978), vol. 9, p. 2130, n. 1.

447 "It was indeed nice of you": *Papers of Dwight David Eisenhower,* vol. 9, pp. 2129–30.

448 The French adamantly opposed: CC 3752, 7 April 1948, in *Clay Papers,* p. 619.

448 initial Marshall Plan allocation: Clay, *Decision in Germany,* p. 217.

448 "My skin is thick": TT-1113, 30 August 1948, in *Clay Papers,* pp. 790–96.

449 "even before ECA gets underway": CC 4178, 5 May 1948, in *Clay Papers,* p. 646.

449 Baruch urged Congress: *The New York Times,* 16 February 1948.

449 "so sound and wise": Letter, Clay to Baruch, 2 March 1948, in *Clay Papers,* p. 563.

449 "far less objective and wise": Hilldring to Saltzman, 10 November 1947, B.G. 59, File 110, 271/11-1047, National Archives.

25: Berlin Blockade

PAGE

451 "Our work in London": CC2642, Clay personal for Draper, TOP SECRET, 20 December 1947, in *Clay Papers,* pp. 501–2.

451 warning of possible Soviet pressure: According to Wedemeyer's memo to the Secretary of the Army, the Russians could impose "administrative difficulties, in the expectation that the resulting inconveniences will influence the withdrawal of allied forces" (2 January 1948, ABC 387 Germany [12-18-43], sec. 4-I).

452 Clay's concern about Berlin: Memorandum of conversation: Bevin, Marshall, Clay, Robertson, Douglas, Murphy, Roberts, 18 December 1947, in *Clay Papers,* pp. 514–18. See also *FRUS 1947,* vol. 2, pp. 827ff. See also CC2855, Clay for DA, 13 January 1948, in *Clay Papers,* pp. 541–47.

452 "my original prophecy": TT8919, Clay-Draper, 31 December 1947, in *Clay Papers,* pp. 522–24.

452 "No one believes": TT8950, Clay-Draper (TOP SECRET), 9 January 1948, in *Clay Papers,* pp. 529–33.

453 "I cannot pull rabbits": CC2852, Clay (EYES ONLY) for Draper, 13 July 1948, in *Clay Papers,* pp. 539–40.

453 "a positive demonstration of democracy": *The New York Times,* 30 July 1948.

453 For a treatment of the Semler affair, see John Gimbel, *The American Occupation of Germany, 1945–1949* (Stanford: Stanford University Press, 1968), pp. 191–93.

453 "the most competent of German ministers": CC2822, Clay to Noce, 9 January 1948, in *Clay Papers,* p. 528.

454 Semler entertained his audience: The text of his speech at Erlangen, 4 January 1948, is contained in OMGUS Records, 150-3/3, National Archives.

455 "the 1800 calorie ration": 29560, Clay to Bradley, 18 March 1948, in *Clay Papers,* pp. 583–84.

455 "makes it look like I was fired": TT89504, Draper-Clay (TOP SECRET), 9 January 1948, in *Clay Papers,* pp. 529–33.

455 Draper told Clay: Ibid.

455 "only if it is 100 percent desired": TT8761, Clay-Draper (TOP

SECRET), 22 November 1947, in *Clay Papers,* pp. 505–08. Eisenhower wrote Clay that he also hoped Clay would remain in Germany until December 31, 1948, "a feeling that I know is shared by the Secretary of the Army and Bill Draper" (Louis Galambos, ed., *The Papers of Dwight D. Eisenhower: Chief of Staff* [Baltimore: Johns Hopkins University Press, 1978], vol. 9, p. 2094). The State Department press release was dated 17 October 1947.

456 Robert Lovett and George Kennan: Lovett interview, Brown Brothers, Harriman, New York, N.Y., 4 May 1971. See also the internal correspondence between Kennan and Bohlen in the files of the Policy Planning Staff, boxes 31–33.

456 Marshall himself had wearied: John H. Backer, *Winds of History: The German Years of Lucius DuBignon Clay* (New York: Van Nostrand, 1983), pp. 206–7.

457 Smith as Clay's replacement: The Department of the Army was kept in the dark about Marshall's plans. For Clay's message to Draper informing him that Smith was coming to Germany, see TT9205, 12 March 1948, in *Clay Papers,* pp. 574–78.

457 Smith's letter to Clay: Handwritten, from Moscow, dated 8 March 1948. Clay collection, George C. Marshall Library, VMI, Lexington, Virginia.

458 "Please do not think": Letter, Clay to Byrnes, 13 February 1948, in *Clay Papers,* pp. 561–62.

458 Byrnes had been dismissed by President Truman: Indicative of the ill-will between the two, in June 1949, speaking at the Washington and Lee University commencement in Lexington, Virginia, Byrnes bitterly castigated Truman's domestic program. The President dashed off a note to Byrnes in which he said, "I now know how Caesar felt when he said, '*Et tu, Brutus.*' " Byrnes immediately replied, "I am no Brutus, I hope you are not going to think of yourself as Caesar, because you are no Caesar" (quoted in Margaret Truman, *Harry S. Truman* [New York: Morrow, 1972], p. 426).

458 Byrnes was determined: As was Byrnes's habit, no written record was kept of his activities in Clay's behalf. The narrative of events was provided by General Clay from information volunteered to him in the 1950s by Justice Byrnes.

458 "I'd rather have any twelve other senators": Paul Appleby, Davies Diary, 30 April 1945, quoted in Martin Weil, *A Pretty Good Club: The Founding Fathers of the U.S. Foreign Service* (New York: Norton, 1978), p. 230.

459 Clay to remain as Military Governor: TT9247, Royall, Bradley, Noce and Clay (TOP SECRET—EYES ONLY), 23 March 1948, in *Clay Papers,* pp. 596–97. (Italics added.)

460 Senate confirmation: Clay himself had been confirmed by the Senate, 27 March 1947 *(The New York Times,* 28 March 1947).

460 "France and the Communists": TT8960 (TOP SECRET), 12 January 1948, in *Clay Papers,* pp. 535–39.

460 "We are in a critical position": Clay, *Decision in Germany* (Garden City, N.Y.: Doubleday, 1950), pp. 179–80.

461 "We are getting somewhat tired": CC2840, Clay for Draper (TOP SECRET), 12 January 1948, in *Clay Papers,* p. 534.

461 Proclamations 7 and 8: For texts and an organizational chart of the new bizonal structure, see U.S. Department of State, *Germany, 1947–1949: The Story in Documents* (Washington, D.C.: Government Printing Office, 1950), pp. 466–79.

462 The House subcommittee's recommendation of amnesty is discussed in Clay, *Decision in Germany,* p. 259.

462 "I would rather lose the . . . appropriation": TT9205, Draper-Clay (TOP SECRET), 12 March 1948, in *Clay Papers,* pp. 574–78.

462 "leaves a constantly smaller backlog": CC3499, Clay to Draper, 14 March 1948, in *Clay Papers,* pp. 578–79.

462 Clay wrote *finis:* See William E. Griffiths, "The Denazification Program in Germany," Ph.D. thesis, Harvard University, pp. 500–552.

463 Concerning the significance of the Berlin crisis, see especially Daniel F. Harrington, "The Berlin Blockade Revisited," *International History Review,* February 1984, pp. 88–112.

463 Bevin's view: Alan Bullock, *Ernest Bevin: Foreign Secretary 1945–1951* (New York: Norton, 1983), pp. 371ff; see also Avi Shlaim, "Britain, the Berlin Blockade and the Cold War," *International Affairs,* 1984, pp. 1–14.

464 The events of January 1948 are discussed in CC2840, Clay for Draper (TOP SECRET), 12 January 1948, in *Clay Papers,* p. 534; CC2864, Clay for Draper (EYES ONLY—TOP SECRET), 13 January 1948, in *Clay Papers,* pp. 543–44; CC2889, Clay for Draper (SECRET), 16 January 1948, in *Clay Papers,* pp. 545–46.

464 Red Army soldiers stopped a train: Great Britain, Foreign Office, *An Account of Events Leading Up to a Reference of the Berlin Question to the United Nations* (London: H.M. Stationery Office, 1948), p. 15.

464 Bevin's announcement: For the text of Bevin's statement, see Beate Ruhm von Oppen, ed., *Documents of Germany Under Occupation, 1945–1954* (London: Oxford University Press, 1955), pp. 264–68.

465 meeting on January 20: Clay, *Decision in Germany,* p. 350.

465 For Clay's position on quadripartite currency control, see TT9079,

10 February 1948, and CC3178, 12 February 1948, both TOP SECRET for Draper, in *Clay Papers,* pp. 558–61.

465 not worried about the Red Army: As Clay advised the Department of the Army on 3 March 1948, "I have considered the Communist threat to all of Europe much more immediate and serious than the threat of physical war. If this Communist threat succeeds there would be no need for Russia to make war" (CC3378, 3 March 1948, in *Clay Papers,* p. 564).

466 "our security arrangements in Berlin": CC3408, Clay to Army Legislative Liaison (for Lodge), 5 March 1948, in *Clay Papers,* pp. 566–68.

466 "the most overworked quotation": Bullock, *Ernest Bevin,* p. 572, n. 2.

466 *"with dramatic suddenness":* Clay to Chamberlin, 5 March 1948, in *Clay Papers,* pp. 568–69.

466 "a blockbuster bomb": Walter Millis, ed., *The Forrestal Diaries* (New York: Viking, 1951), p. 387. Cf. George F. Kennan, *Memoirs 1925–1950* (Boston: Little, Brown, 1967), p. 400.

466 "lifted me right out of my chair": Omar N. Bradley and Clay Blair, *A General's Life* (New York: Simon and Schuster, 1983), p. 477.

467 *The Saturday Evening Post:* D. Robinson, "They Fight the Cold War Under Cover," *The Saturday Evening Post,* 20 November 1948.

467 scoffed at the possibility of war: Clay, *Decision in Germany,* p. 354.

467 "The revelation of such cablegram": CC7137, Clay to Bradley (TOP SECRET), 20 December 1948, in *Clay Papers,* pp. 961–62. (Italics added.)

467 took pains to dissociate himself: Clay, *Decision in Germany,* pp. 354–55.

467 "Bill Draper asked me": The Department of Defense declined to declassify Clay's teleconference with Draper of mid-March 1948.

467 "was not to be the last": Michael Howard, "Governor General of Germany," *Times Literary Supplement,* 19 August 1974, p. 970, n. 7.

468 "Should they be evacuated": TT9218, Collins-Clay (TOP SECRET), 17 March 1948, in *Clay Papers,* pp. 579–83.

470 "I see no sense" and "the split in Germany": Clay, *Decision in Germany,* pp. 356–57.

471 For text of the new Soviet rail regulation, see *Clay Papers,* pp. 600–601.

471 "might precipitate war": TT9286, Clay-Royall teleconference (TOP SECRET), 31 March 1948, in *Clay Papers,* pp. 600–604.

472 "open fire on the Russians": Bradley, *A General's Life,* p. 478.

472 "not carrying a chip on our shoulder": TT9287, Clay-Bradley teleconference (TOP SECRET), 31 March 1948, in *Clay Papers,* pp. 604–7.

473 "I thought I detected some apprehension": Clay, *Decision in Germany,* p. 359.

473 not to force the issue: CC3681, Clay for Royall (TOP SECRET), 1 April 1948, in *Clay Papers,* p. 607.

473 Robertson demurred: Robertson to Foreign Office, 2 April 1948. Quoted in Avi Shlaim, *The United States and the Berlin Blockade, 1948–1949: A Study in Crisis Decision-Making* (Berkeley: Univ. of California Press), p. 4.

473 Bradley offered limited support: W98748, Bradley for Clay (TOP SECRET), 1 April 1948.

474 "From beginning to end": Shlaim, "Britain, Blockade and Cold War," p. 3. Sir Winston Churchill, now out of office and leader of the Opposition, not only supported Bevin, but suggested to U.S. Ambassador Lewis Douglas that the Allies threaten to launch a nuclear war against Russia if the Soviet Union did not withdraw from Berlin and eastern Germany *(FRUS 1948,* vol. 2, pp. 895–96).

474 Wedemeyer cabled: WX98818, Wedemeyer to Clay (TOP SECRET), 2 April 1948.

474 "aimed at driving us from Berlin": CC3688, Clay to Wedemeyer (TOP SECRET), 2 April 1948, in *Clay Papers,* p. 611.

474 "Evacuation now might be plausible": TT9300, Clay-Royall-Bradley teleconference (TOP SECRET—EYES ONLY), 2 April 1948, in *Clay Papers,* pp. 613–15.

475 "Lee, Hal and the grandchildren": Bradley, *A General's Life,* p. 481.

476 April 10, 1948, teleconference: TT9341, Bradley-Clay (TOP SECRET—EYES ONLY), 10 April 1948, in *Clay Papers,* pp. 621–25.

477 Wedemeyer once again asked: W80366, Wedemeyer to Clay (TOP SECRET), 27 April 1948. For Clay's reply, see *Clay Papers,* pp. 640–42.

477 "up to every devilment": Bevin *aide mémoire* handed to Secretary Marshall, 30 April 1948, in *FRUS 1948,* vol. 4, pp. 842–49.

477 "our intention to stay there": Quoted in Bullock, *Ernest Bevin,* p. 554.

477 George Kennan's suggestion: Kennan, *Memoirs,* pp. 346–47.

477 "the door is wide open": *FRUS 1948,* vol. 4, pp. 834–57.

478 "What the hell is going on?": Bullock, *Ernest Bevin,* p. 558.

478 "I grasped the suggestion": Clay, *Decision in Germany,* pp. 397–98.

479 brief eight-point memorandum: For the text of Clay's April 1948 memorandum, see ibid., pp. 398–400.

480 communiqué on June 6, 1948: For the final text, see U.S. Dept. of State, *Germany, 1947–1949*, pp. 75–88.

480 proceed with the currency reform: For the terms and text of the law on currency reform, see von Oppen, ed., *Documents of Germany*, pp. 292–94.

482 10 cents per Deutsche mark: W83287, Draper to Clay (TOP SECRET), 5 June 1948.

482 "Your message has hit me": CC4593, Clay to Draper (TOP SECRET), 6 June 1948, in *Clay Papers*, pp. 669–70.

483 "State, Treasury and Army": W83389, Draper to Clay (TOP SECRET), 8 June 1948.

484 Clay's conversation with Erhard as reported by James O'Donnell in Backer, *Winds of History*, pp. 227–28.

485 "German bureaucratic controls": CC4425, Clay to Draper (TOP SECRET—EYES ONLY), 24 May 1948, in *Clay Papers*, p. 658.

486 "until the Army no longer needs me": TT9558 (TOP SECRET—EYES ONLY), 2 June 1948, in *Clay Papers*, pp. 662–64.

487 "no air transport worthy of name": 73255, Clay to Draper (SECRET), 7 May 1948, in *Clay Papers*, pp. 649–50.

487 "Lew Douglas was the able diplomat": TT9558, 2 June 1948.

487 "rather feeble grunts": CC4624, Clay to Draper (TOP SECRET), 9 June 1948, in *Clay Papers*, pp. 672–73.

488 high-stakes game of political brinksmanship: CC4678, Clay to Noce (CONFIDENTIAL), 12 June 1948, in *Clay Papers*, pp. 676–77.

488 "appreciate the State Department being advised": CC4650, Clay for Draper (TOP SECRET), 11 June 1948, in *Clay Papers*, pp. 674–75.

489 "important that the French go along": W83856, Draper to Clay (TOP SECRET), 15 June 1948.

489 "most disturbing cablegram I have received": FMPC-175, Clay (EYES ONLY) for Draper (TOP SECRET), 15 June 1948, in *Clay Papers*, pp. 678–79.

489 "I fear you have misunderstood": W84027, Draper to Clay (TOP SECRET), 17 June 1948.

490 Bevin's role: Bullock, *Ernest Bevin*, p. 566.

490 "The die is cast": TT9623, Clay-Draper (TOP SECRET—EYES ONLY), 16 June 1948, in *Clay Papers*, pp. 680–86.

491 "first move we would have to take": Minutes, OMGUS staff meeting, 19 June 1948, quoted in Harrington, "Berlin Blockade Revisited," p. 96.

491 "exactly what Britain would have followed": Robertson to St. Laurent, 23 June 1948, William L. Mackenzie King Papers, Ot-

tawa, quoted in Harrington, "Berlin Blockade Revisited," p. 96, n. 20.

491 Sokolovsky responded: For text, see von Oppen, ed., *Documents of Germany,* pp. 295–300.

492 "use of the Soviet mark": W82922, 29 May 1948, in *Clay Papers,* pp. 675–78.

492 "Berlin . . . completely in Soviet hands": CC48880, Clay (Personal) for Royall (TOP SECRET), 25 June 1948, in *Clay Papers,* pp. 697–98.

26: Founding of the Federal Republic

PAGE

494 Bevin shared Clay's view: Avi Shlaim, "Britain, the Berlin Blockade and the Cold War," *International Affairs,* 1984, p. 5.

494 "The situation was dark": George F. Kennan, *Memoirs 1925–1950* (Boston: Little, Brown, 1967), p. 421.

495 Recent Russian statements: von Oppen, *Documents on Germany Under Occupation,* pp. 300–8.

495 precluded any compromise: Shlaim, "Britain, the Berlin Blockade and the Cold War," p. 4.

495 tough stand suited Clay: Lucius D. Clay, *Decision in Germany* (Garden City, N.Y.: Doubleday, 1950), p. 374.

495 For Murphy and Reuter's views, see Robert Murphy, *Diplomat Among Warriors* (Garden City, N.Y.: Doubleday, 1964), pp. 314–15.

495 The task force: John Backer interview with General Arthur Trudeau, 14 August 1978, cited in John H. Backer, *Winds of History: The German Years of Lucius DuBignon Clay* (New York: Van Nostrand, 1983), p. 249.

496 "We had observed the Russian fighters": General Curtis E. LeMay, *Mission with LeMay* (Garden City, N.Y.: Doubleday, 1965), pp. 411–12.

496 "Soviet government did not want war": Clay, *Decision in Germany,* p. 374.

496 found his staff divided: W. Phillips Davison, *The Berlin Blockade: A Study in Cold War Politics* (Princeton: Princeton University Press, 1958), p. 104.

497 Brownjohn was pessimistic: Cabinet minutes, (48), 43rd conclusions, minute 3, 25 June 1948, cited in Shlaim, "Britain, the Berlin Blockade and the Cold War," n. 10.

497 Bevin was dissatisfied: Alan Bullock, *Ernest Bevin: Foreign Secretary 1945–1951* (New York: Norton, 1983), p. 575.

497 "I am convinced": CC 4875, Clay (EYES ONLY) for Draper, 25 June 1948, in *Clay Papers,* pp. 696–97.

506 asked by Secretary Royall: W-84649, Royall for Clay (TOP SECRET), 25 June 1948.

506 "The decision was made": CC-4880, Clay (Personal) for Royall (TOP SECRET), 25 June 1948, in *Clay Papers,* pp. 647–98.

507 "currency in Berlin is not the issue": TT-9677 (TOP SECRET), 26 June 1948, in *Clay Papers,* pp. 704–7.

507 Bevin told the British press: For text of statement, see *FRUS 1948,* vol. 2, p. 922.

507 message that day to Marshall: Ibid., pp. 921–26.

507 Bevin reported to the Cabinet: CM 44 (48), in Bullock, *Ernest Bevin,* p. 576.

507 "Everybody was talking at once": Omar N. Bradley and Clay Blair, *A General's Life* (New York: Simon and Schuster, 1983), p. 479.

508 "We are going to stay": Walter Millis, ed., *The Forrestal Diaries* (New York: Viking, 1951), pp. 454–55.

508 "We stay in Berlin": *FRUS 1948,* vol. 2, pp. 930–31.

508 Clay requests planes: CC 4910, Clay (EYES ONLY) for Draper, 27 June 1948, in *Clay Papers,* pp. 707–8. Clay subsequently informed Washington that for operational reasons LeMay preferred that the B-29s be based in England rather than Germany (C-4914, 28 June 1948, in *Clay Papers,* p. 709).

508 "could say something appreciative": Bullock, *Ernest Bevin,* p. 577.

509 "and we intend to stay": Wolfgang Heidelmeyer and Günter Hindwicks, eds., *Documents on Berlin, 1943–1963* (Munich: Oldenbourg Verlag, 1963), p. 67.

509 On Truman's press conference, see *Public Papers of the Presidents of the United States: Harry S. Truman, 1948* (Washington, D.C.: Government Printing Office, 1964), pp. 391–94.

509 "His Majesty's Government cannot submit": House of Commons, 30 June 1948, in Bullock, *Ernest Bevin,* p. 578.

509 "give them every support": *FRUS 1948,* vol. 2, pp. 936–38.

510 "without first obtaining a clearance": W-84975, Royall to Clay (TOP SECRET), 30 June 1948.

510 "my present discretionary authority": FMPC-271, Clay (EYES ONLY) for Bradley and Royall, 1 July 1948, in *Clay Papers,* pp. 711–12.

510 Marshall warned: Millis, ed., *Forrestal Diaries,* pp. 457–58.

510 On Clay's apology to Sokolovsky, see Clay, *Decision in Germany,* pp. 372–73.

511 "with marked official politeness": CC-4924, Clay (EYES ONLY) for Royall, 28 June 1948, in *Clay Papers,* pp. 709–10.

511 "technical difficulties would continue": CC 5027, Clay for Royall and Bradley (TOP SECRET), 3 July 1948, in *Clay Papers,* pp. 722–24.

511 "reopen the entire German question": Bullock, *Ernest Bevin,* p. 579.

511 "State joins me": WX-85244, Royall for Clay (TOP SECRET), 3 July 1948. When the Western protest was finally delivered to Moscow on July 6, it dealt only with a settlement in Berlin; formation of a German government was not questioned. For text of protest, see Beate Ruhm von Oppen, *Documents of Germany Under Occupation, 1945–1954* (London: Oxford University Press, 1955), pp. 581–88.

511 On July 10 Clay urged: CC-5109, Clay for Bradley (TOP SECRET), 10 July 1948, in *Clay Papers,* p. 730.

511 "Would appreciate answer": CC-5131, Clay for DA (TOP SECRET), 12 July 1948, in *Clay Papers,* p. 736.

511 "the Soviets do not want war": CC-5118, Clay for Bradley (TOP SECRET), 10 July 1948, in *Clay Papers,* pp. 733–35.

512 "to proceed with this convoy movement": FMPC-336, Clay for Bradley (TOP SECRET), 15 July 1948, in *Clay Papers,* pp. 739–40.

512 "only by highest level": W-85820, Bradley for Clay (TOP SECRET), 15 July 1948.

512 For Nye Bevan's views, see Michael Foot, *Aneurin Bevan: A Biography, vol. 2: 1945–1960* (London: David Poynter, 1973), pp. 229–30.

512 Montgomery was dispatched: Bullock, *Ernest Bevin,* p. 580.

513 "airlift was doomed to failure": Bradley to Royall, 17 July 1948, CD 6-2-9 folder 1, RG 330, cited in Daniel F. Harrington, "The Berlin Blockade Revisited," *International History Review,* February 1984, pp. 88–112.

513 "unsatisfactory . . . temporary expedient": Memo for the President, 16 July 1948, box 220, President's Secretary's File, Truman Library, cited in Harrington, "Blockade Revisited," p. 99.

513 "The only logical decision": Maddocks to Bradley, 28 June 1948, P & O 092TS Hot File, RG 319, cited in Harrington, "Blockade Revisited," p. 101.

513 Truman's diary: Margaret Truman, *Harry S. Truman,* (New York: Morrow, 1972), p. 15.

514 Robertson's pessimism: FO 371/70506/C6531, Robertson to Foreign Office, 10 August 1948, cited in Shlaim, "Britain, the Berlin Blockade and the Cold War," p. 10.

514 "Soviets will steal the city": FO 371/70508/C6670, Robertson to Strang, 11 August 1948, cited in Shlaim, "Britain, the Berlin Blockade and the Cold War," p. 11.

514 "defeatism and appeasement": Shlaim, "Britain, the Berlin Blockade and the Cold War," p. 10.

514 "even extraordinary measures": FO 371/70506/C6531, Foreign

Office to Robertson, 12 August 1948, cited in Shlaim, "Britain, the Berlin Blockade and the Cold War," pp. 10–11.

514 not to repeat Chamberlain's mistake: Bullock, *Ernest Bevin,* pp. 583–84.

514 make Germany a Communist satellite: FO 371/70507/C6611/s/G, Bevin to Sir Oliver Franks (Washington), 11 August 1949, cited in Shlaim, "Britain, the Berlin Blockade and the Cold War," p. 11.

514 "I am sending this radio": CC-5222, Clay for Draper (TOP SECRET—EYES ONLY), 19 July 1948, in *Clay Papers,* pp. 743–46.

516 Bevin to Bohlen: Charles E. Bohlen, *Witness to History 1929–1969* (New York: Norton, 1973), pp. 279–80; Bullock, *Ernest Bevin,* pp. 586–89; Clay, *Decision in Germany,* pp. 368–72.

516 Clay not optimistic: Clay, *Decision in Germany,* p. 369.

516 first report of the meeting from Bedell Smith: Millis, ed., *Forrestal Diaries,* pp. 440–41. See also Ambassador Smith's two cables to Washington, 3 August 1948, *FRUS 1948,* vol. 2, pp. 999–1007.

516 Clay was shaken: TT-9890, Clay–Royall, Bohlen, et al. (TOP SECRET), 3 August 1948, in *Clay Papers,* pp. 748–52.

516 "no real say": CC-5432, Clay for Bradley and Royall (TOP SECRET), 4 August 1948, in *Clay Papers,* pp. 752–53.

517 "as far as we possibly can": TT-1010, Clay-Draper (TOP SECRET), 7 August 1948, in *Clay Papers,* pp. 755–63.

517 "to appear 'sticky' ": Douglas to State, quoted by Draper in TT-1010, 7 August 1948.

518 For text of the Moscow directive, see *FRUS 1948,* vol. 2, pp. 1085–87, *et seq.*

518 "not Soviet custom": TT-113, Clay-Draper (TOP SECRET), 30 August 1948, in *Clay Papers,* pp. 790–96.

518 from September 1 to September 8: Clay's daily reports of the negotiations are reprinted in *Clay Papers,* pp. 796–849. For Ambassador Murphy's reports, see *FRUS 1948,* vol. 2, pp. 1099–140.

518 "indifferent almost . . . contemptuous": TT-1182, Clay–Royall, Draper and Bradley (TOP SECRET), 8 September 1948, in *Clay Papers,* pp. 845–49.

518 "Soviet tactics were clever": TT-1162, Clay-Draper (TOP SECRET), 6 September 1948, in *Clay Papers,* pp. 829–35.

518 "We must increase airlift": CC-5895, Clay for Bradley and LeMay (TOP SECRET), 10 September 1948, in *Clay Papers,* p. 852.

518 "we can last indefinitely": TT-1271, Clay-Royall (TOP SECRET), 19 September 1948, in *Clay Papers,* pp. 866–77.

519 Marshall told the National Security Council: Harry Truman, *Years of Trial and Hope* (Garden City, N.Y.: Doubleday, 1956), p. 128.

519 Smith shared that view: Clay, *Decision in Germany,* p. 376; Truman, *Trial and Hope,* p. 126.

519 RAND Corporation analysis: Davison, *Berlin Blockade,* p. 194.

519 as a matter of principle: *FRUS 1948,* vol. 2, pp. 1140–44.

519 Bevin recognized: Bullock, *Ernest Bevin,* p. 593.

520 "to have them raise the blockade": Minutes of meeting between Bevin, Marshall, and Schuman, Paris, 21 September 1948, in *FRUS 1948,* vol. 2, pp. 1177–80.

520 Marshall told Bedell Smith: *FRUS 1948,* vol. 2, pp. 1147–49.

520 *aide-mémoire:* For text, see *FRUS 1948,* vol. 2, pp. 1163–65.

520 the Soviets replied: Ibid., pp. 1166–73.

520 Western powers replied: Ibid., pp. 1180–81.

520 no change for the past six weeks: TT-1271, Clay-Royall (TOP SECRET), 19 September 1948, in *Clay Papers,* pp. 866–77.

520 "we can support Berlin better": CC-6050, Clay for Bradley (TOP SECRET), 23 September 1948, in *Clay Papers,* p. 878.

520 Bevin shared Clay's enthusiasm: See, for example, the discussion of Bevin's views in Bullock, *Ernest Bevin,* p. 606.

521 "a Communist mob": TT-1162, Clay-Draper (TOP SECRET), 6 September 1948, in *Clay Papers,* pp. 829–35.

521 Bradley quickly queried: TT-1182, Clay–Royall, Draper, Bradley (TOP SECRET), 8 September 1948, in *Clay Papers,* pp. 845–49. See also CC-5872, Clay for Draper and Bradley (TOP SECRET), 8 September 1948, in *Clay Papers,* pp. 843–45.

521 "I let off steam to Draper": CC-5872, ibid.

522 "a dangerous game": CC-5909, Clay For Draper (TOP SECRET), 11 September 1948, in *Clay Papers,* pp. 856–57. (Italics added.)

523 "Germany is going back to work": Letter, Clay for Byrnes, 18 September 1948, in *Clay Papers,* pp. 858–60.

524 early Berlin public opinion: OMGUS Public Opinion Survey 141, 4 October 1948, reported in Anna J. Merritt and Richard J. Merritt, *Public Opinion in Occupied Germany* (Urbana: University of Illinois Press, 1970), p. 261.

524 subsequent Berlin opinion: OMGUS Public Opinion Survey 147, 17 November 1948, reported in Merritt and Merritt, *Public Opinion,* pp. 267–68.

524 Western powers became less ready: Trygve Lie, *In the Cause of Peace* (New York: Macmillan, 1954), pp. 203, 210.

524 Jessup visited Berlin: Clay, *Decision in Germany,* p. 387; *Berlin Tagesspiegel,* October 31, 1948.

524 food rations increased: Frank Howley, *Berlin Command* (New York: Putnam, 1950), p. 230.

524 "Clay's brainchild": Bradley, *A General's Life,* pp. 480–81.

525 "General Clay placed before us": Truman, *Trial and Hope,* p. 130.

525 "The Command in Japan" and "I am ready to call it a day": TT-1406, Clay-Draper (TOP SECRET), 13 October 1948, in *Clay Papers,* pp. 896–900.

525 State suggested in November: State 1841, cited in *Clay Papers,* pp. 925–26.

526 "*desired by junior officials*": CC-6772, Clay for (Colonel George A.) Lincoln (special assistant to the Secretary of the Army), 18 November 1948, in *Clay Papers,* pp. 925–27. (Italics added.)

526 "rather insisted on it": Lovett interview, Brown Brothers, Harriman, New York, N.Y., 4 May 1971.

526 "out on a limb": CC-7128, Clay for Royall, 20 December 1948, in *Clay Papers,* p. 959.

526 instructed to defer approval: W-81787, Draper for Clay. See *Clay Papers,* pp. 959–60.

526 "I shall request relief": CC-7194, Clay for Draper (TOP SECRET—EYES ONLY), 26 December 1948, in *Clay Papers,* p. 968.

526 asked that a date be fixed: CC-7304, Clay for Bradley (TOP SECRET), 5 January 1949, in *Clay Papers,* pp. 973–75.

527 "Program for Germany": For text, see *FRUS 1948,* vol. 2, pp. 1325–38.

528 "I think it would be harmful": TT-1803, Royall-Clay (TOP SECRET), 8 January 1949, in *Clay Papers,* pp. 977–79.

528 "When I requested retirement": CC-7362, Clay for Royall and Bradley (TOP SECRET), 10 January 1949, in *Clay Papers,* p. 980.

529 Truman was so pleased: C. L. Sulzberger, *A Long Row of Candles: Memoirs and Diaries, 1934–1954* (New York: Macmillan, 1969), p. 432.

529 "the French would like to pull out": FMPC 186, Clay for Bradley (TOP SECRET), 15 January 1949, in *Clay Papers,* pp. 986–87.

530 "London's views have changed": CC-7703, Clay for DA, 9 February 1949, in *Clay Papers,* p. 1011.

530 "a real step forward": CC-7716, Clay for DA (TOP SECRET), 11 February 1949, in *Clay Papers,* p. 1012.

530 the West mark would be the sole legal tender: FMPC-598, Clay for DA (TOP SECRET), 17 March 1949, in *Clay Papers,* p. 1045. For the text of the military governors' statement, see *Clay Papers,* pp. 1045–47.

530 "Berlin belongs to the West": Quoted in Davison, *Berlin Blockade,* p. 263.

530 "the Soviet Government sees no obstacles": The text of Kingsbury Smith's question and Stalin's reply is reprinted in Jean Edward Smith, *The Defense of Berlin* (Baltimore: Johns Hopkins Press, 1963), p. 128.

531 Jessup was instructed: See Truman, *Trial and Hope,* pp. 130–31;

Dean G. Acheson, "On Dealing with the Russians: An Inside View," *The New York Times Magazine,* 12 April 1959, pp. 27, 88–89.

531 "Premier Stalin's reply": For Jessup's report of the conversation, see *FRUS 1949,* vol. 3, pp. 694–95. See also Jessup, "Park Avenue Diplomacy: Ending the Berlin Blockade," *Political Science Quarterly,* vol. 87, no. 3 (1972), p. 377.

531 "not accidental": *FRUS 1949,* vol. 3, pp. 695–98.

531 Bevin simply refused to trade: Ibid., pp. 709–12. See also Bullock, *Ernest Bevin,* pp. 666–69.

531 blockade would be lifted: Department of State press release, 5 May 1949, quoted in Harrington, "Blockade Revisited," p. 111.

532 "dealing sensibly": Acheson press conference, 23 June 1949. State Department press release 484.

532 Voorhees cabled the text to Clay: TT-2171, Voorhees for Clay (TOP SECRET), 30 April 1949, in *Clay Papers,* pp. 1134–37.

532 "blockade was broken by airpower": CC-8467, Clay for Voorhees (TOP SECRET), 1 May 1949, in *Clay Papers,* pp. 1137–38. See also Clay, *Decision in Germany,* p. 390.

532 "promotion of a capable man": TT-2066, Clay–Lt. Gen. Haislip (TOP SECRET), 30 March 1949, in *Clay Papers,* pp. 1063–66. Marshal Sokolovsky's book *Soviet Military Strategy,* trans. Herbert Dinerstein, Leon Goure, and Thomas W. Wolfe for the RAND Corporation (Englewood Cliffs, N.J.: Prentice-Hall, 1963), was described by Hanson Baldwin as "remarkably realistic, objective, and on the whole fairly factual. . . . The first detailed public exposition and discussion of Russian Communist military policies and strategic concepts in almost four decades" (*The New York Times,* 16 June 1963).

533 "Soviet courtesy of this type": FMPC-787, 13 April 1949, in *Clay Papers,* p. 1107.

533 "approval of German constitution": W-83229, Royall to Clay (TOP SECRET), 27 January 1949, in *Clay Papers,* p. 993.

533 leave before German elections: CC-7579, Clay for Royall, Draper, and Bradley (TOP SECRET), 28 January 1949, in *Clay Papers,* pp. 993–94.

534 "I should go very quickly": TT-1865, Clay-Draper (TOP SECRET), 29 January 1949, in *Clay Papers,* pp. 994–98.

534 "Rube Goldberg procedures": CC-7725, Clay for Voorhees (TOP SECRET), 11 February 1949, in *Clay Papers,* pp. 1013–15.

534 "these 45 million Germans": TT-2012, Clay-Voorhees (TOP SECRET), 17 March 1949, in *Clay Papers,* pp. 1047–54.

535 "Damned if I know": TT-1945, Clay-Draper (TOP SECRET), 21 February 1949, in *Clay Papers,* pp. 1024–26.

535	"taking the part of Sokolovsky": TT-2012, 17 March 1949.
535	"sound like a police court": FMPC 680, Clay for Voorhees (TOP SECRET), 29 March 1949, in *Clay Papers,* p. 1063.
536	"Lew is . . . an eager beaver": TT-2012, 17 March 1949.
536	"piecemeal solutions": CC-8121, Clay for Voorhees (TOP SECRET), 24 March 1949, in *Clay Papers,* p. 1061.
536	"the brainchild of General Clay": *FRUS 1949,* vol. 3, pp. 102–5.
536	"suicidal": As quoted in David Mayers, *George Kennan and the Dilemmas of U.S. Foreign Policy* (New York: Oxford University Press, 1988), pp. 147–48.
537	"spectacular *coup de grâce*": Ibid.; Kennan, *Memoirs,* p. 444.
537	Murphy's skillful leadership: See TT-2012, 17 March 1949.
537	new draft policy statement: See TT-2077, Voorhees et al., Clay (TOP SECRET), 2 April 1949, in *Clay Papers,* pp. 1068–81.
537	"I have not one word of criticism": Ibid.
537	"one of despair": Dean G. Acheson, *Present at the Creation* (New York: Norton, 1969), p. 290. See also *FRUS 1949,* vol. 3, pp. 175–86.
537	"legitimate or illegitimate": W-86840, Voorhees to Clay (TOP SECRET), 8 April 1949, in *Clay Papers,* pp. 1101–2.
538	"our profound gratitude": TT-2104, Voorhees, et al.–Clay (TOP SECRET—EYES ONLY), 8 April 1949, in *Clay Papers,* pp. 1100–1101.

BOOK FOUR: THE MILITARY INDUSTRIAL COMPLEX

27: *General of Industry*

PAGE	
549	"strongest American personalities": Walter Lippmann, *New York Herald Tribune,* 6 May 1949.
549	"hard to find the like of him": *The New York Times,* 6 May 1949.
550	"Viscount Clay": Ibid., 18 May 1949.
550	"We owe him much": Letter, *The New York Times,* 10 May 1949.
550	"a great soldier and statesman": Letter, Bradley to Clay, 15 June 1949. Original in JES's possession.
550	Mrs. Roosevelt to Clay: Clay collection, Marshall Library. General Clay's reply is filed with Mrs. Roosevelt's letter.
551	orders against martial displays: John Backer interview with Richard Hallock, 5 April 1981, cited in John H. Backer, *Winds of History: The German Years of Lucius DuBignon Clay* (New York: Van Nostrand, 1983), p. 291.
551	Herbert Clay, Jr.: Demaree Bess, "An American Viceroy in Germany," *The Saturday Evening Post,* 10 May 1947.

551 disapproved the award: Lucius D. Clay, Jr., interview, Washington, D.C., 15 December 1969.

551 check for $7,000: John Backer interview with Edloe Donnan, 27 October 1981, cited in Backer, *Winds of History,* p. 283.

552 "with or without gloves": Don Humphrey, Epilogue, in Backer, *Winds of History.*

554 review . . . at Grafenwöhr: *The New York Times,* 13 May 1949.

554 Reuter's speech: Jean Edward Smith, *The Defense of Berlin* (Baltimore: Johns Hopkins Press, 1963), p. 130.

555 "as able as any man": *Congressional Record* 1453–54, 17 May 1949, 81st Cong., 1st Sess.

555 "One has only to revisit Buchenwald": Ibid., p. 6454.

555 "Sunday, two days ago": Ibid., pp. 6426–27.

556 "It is hard to know": Letter, Clay to Eisenhower, 18 June 1949, President's Personal File, Eisenhower Library, Abilene, Kansas.

557 "Georgia has been": Letter, William Tutt to Clay, 20 May 1949. Original in JES's possession.

558 "no place in public life": Letter, Clay to Tutt, 29 May 1949. Clay's copy in JES's possession.

558 declined University of North Carolina: Correspondence between Judge E. Earle Rives and Clay, May 1949, in JES's possession.

558 rejected New Jersey Turnpike Authority: Correspondence between Robert Goetz and Clay, May 1949, in JES's possession.

558 "in anything you want to undertake": Letters, Searles to Clay, 9 April 1949; Eberstadt to Clay, 16 April 1949. Originals in JES's possession.

559 "The car is yours": Letter, Skinner to Clay, 12 May 1949. Original in JES's possession.

559 "It saved our lives": Letter, Clay to Skinner, 29 May 1949. Clay's copy in JES's possession.

559 "General Clay welcomed me": E. J. Kahn, "Soldier in Mufti," *The New Yorker,* 13 January 1951, pp. 30–31.

559 "As case material for the historian": *The Observer,* 3 September 1950.

559 Gimbel revealed the split: See especially John Gimbel, *The American Occupation of Germany, 1945–1949* (Stanford: Stanford University Press, 1968).

560 more than one British reviewer: See, for example, *The Scotsman,* 30 August 1950; Glasgow *Herald,* 28 August 1950.

560 "recognized as enemies": *The New York Times,* 8 June 1949.

560 "no hysterical witch hunt": Ibid., 22 June 1949.

561 " 'Unshaken, unseduced, unterrified' ": Ibid., 24 June 1949.

561 "retired military officers": At the time, General Brehon Somervell headed Koppers Co.; Joseph T. McNarney was president of Con-

solidated Vultee Aircraft Corp. (Convair); Admiral Ben Moreell ran Jones-Lauchlin Steel Corp.; Clay's West Point classmate Pat Casey headed Schenley Labs; Douglas MacArthur later headed Remington Rand; and General Bradley became chairman of Bulova.

567 "spirit of dignified disrespect": "Concan Finds a General," *Forbes,* 15 March 1959, p. 17.

567 "clang of tin plate": "Lucius D. Clay: General of Industry," *Time,* 21 December 1959, p. 70.

568 "since Macy met Gimbel": "Concan Finds a General," p. 15.

569 "figure in the lower right corner": Ibid., p. 19.

569 "a noticeable stretch": Robert Sheehan, "Continental Can's Big Push," *Fortune,* April 1955, p. 124.

570 "For every product": "Concan Finds a General," p. 15.

570 "not just 100 percent": "Clay: General of Industry," p. 70.

570 "All my life": *Business Week,* 19 June 1954, pp. 136–37.

571 "You never conducted a normal conversation": Hazard interview, Continental Can Company, New York, N.Y., 12 December 1970.

574 "without consulting General Clay": Brownell interview, New York, N.Y., 7 April 1971.

574 "If I may be so bold": *The New York Times,* 14 August 1958.

575 lists of "alleged Communists": Cited in Richard N. Smith, *Thomas E. Dewey and His Times* (New York: Simon and Schuster, 1982), p. 577.

576 "All that can really be done": *Time,* 2 October 1950.

28: Electing a President

PAGE

581 "Lucius was a driven man": Boeschenstein interview, Owens-Corning Fiberglas, New York, N.Y., 16 February 1971.

582 "several good bottles of whiskey": Letter, Eisenhower to Clay, 5 August 1950, DDE Personal File, Eisenhower Library, Abilene, Kansas.

585 "Every pimple": Lodge interview, Beverly, Mass., 5 March 1971.

588 "full of ego": Letter, Clay to Eisenhower, 7 December 1951, DDE Personal File.

588 made Ike's head swim: Stephen E. Ambrose, *Eisenhower* (New York: Simon and Schuster, 1983), vol. 1, p. 519.

588 "find myself in agreement with it": Letter, Eisenhower to Clay, 19 December 1951, DDE Personal File.

589 explained the dilemma: Clay to Eisenhower, 21 December 1951, DDE Personal File.

589 "Your letter has just come": Letter, Eisenhower to Clay, 27 December 1951, DDE Personal File.

590 "Clay got the information": Lodge interview.
590 sharp rebuke to Clay: Letter, Eisenhower to Clay, 8 January 1952, PPF.
593 "God damn it": Quoted in Richard N. Smith, *Thomas E. Dewey and His Times* (New York: Simon and Schuster, 1982), p. 582.
593 Jacqueline Cochran's visit: For a description of the effect on Eisenhower of Jacqueline Cochran's presentation, see Ambrose, *Eisenhower,* pp. 523–27. Moved to tears by the film and Miss Cochran, Eisenhower told her to have Clay come to Paris as soon as possible.
594 "Cabot Lodge had no experience": Thomas E. Dewey interview, Columbia Oral History Project, quoted in R. N. Smith, *Thomas E. Dewey,* p. 582.
594 "General Clay got a ticket": Brownell interview, Lord, Day, and Lord, New York, N.Y., 7 April 1971.
594 "I keenly realize": Cited in R. N. Smith, *Thomas E. Dewey,* p. 584.
595 Dewey wrote to Eisenhower in longhand: Ibid., pp. 585–87.
596 "Clay was so close to Eisenhower": Brownell interview.
597 "only ones . . . who knew about it": Ibid.
599 "Eisenhower was . . . flabbergasted": Ibid.
600 "We had dinner": Ibid. For Governor Dewey's role, see R. N. Smith, *Thomas E. Dewey,* pp. 596ff.
602 "practical thoughts about Nixon": Lodge interview.
602 Clay and Dewey cut the deal: As reported in R. N. Smith, *Thomas E. Dewey,* p. 596.
602 "surprised as hell": R. N. Smith interview with William Rogers, in ibid., p. 597.
604 left his personal papers to the Marshall Foundation: On 1 October 1979, Mrs. Clay acceded to a request from the Marshall Foundation and presented Clay's papers covering the period 1950–78 to the Marshall Library at VMI. They deal with Clay's time at Continental Can and Lehman Brothers, as well as a collection of photographs from Clay's time in Germany. As the Marshall Library correctly notes, "General Clay apparently reviewed his papers periodically and destroyed portions of them" (Marshall Library description of Clay collection, Marshall Foundation, Lexington, Va.)
605 "angry and vehement": Emmet John Hughes, *The Ordeal of Power* (New York: Atheneum, 1963), p. 21.
606 "I urged General Eisenhower to wait": Brownell interview.
607 " 'How do we start?' ": Ibid.
609 McCloy as Secretary of State: In 1965, Professor Richard Challener of Princeton University interviewed General Clay for the

Dulles Oral History Project at Princeton's Firestone Library. The reference to McCloy does not appear in the recorded interview, but Professor Challener reports that Clay told him the story—after ensuring that Challener's tape recorder had been turned off (JES discussion with Professor Challener, Berlin, Germany, 5 June 1989).

609 " 'Don't you ever use it?' ": Cabot interview, First Boston Corporation, Boston, Mass., 12 December 1971.

614 "Ike and Lucius": Hall interview, Garden City, New York, 4 April 1971.

614 "Eisenhower respected that": Stephens interview, New York, N.Y., 21 March 1971.

615 Bricker Amendment: U.S. Congress, Senate, 2nd Sess., S.J. Res. 1 (1954).

615 Supreme Court decisions: *Missouri* v. *Holland,* 252 U.S. 416 (1920); *United States* v. *Belmont,* 301 U.S. 324 (1937); *United States* v. *Pink,* 315 U.S. 203 (1942).

616 "over this darn thing?": As quoted in Hughes, *Ordeal of Power,* p. 143.

617 "I am unalterably opposed": *Presidential Papers, Dwight D. Eisenhower, 1954* (Washington, D.C.: Government Printing Office, 1958), p. 273.

618 "superlative system of German *Autobahnen* . . .": Dwight D. Eisenhower, *Mandate for Change, 1953–1956* (Garden City, N.Y.: Doubleday, 1963), p. 548.

618 "I selected the committee . . .": See Clay's memorandum for the President, 30 August 1954, Dwight D. Eisenhower Papers, Eisenhower Library. Clay's comment concerning Dave Beck suggests that he believed Beck had been the victim of a Justice Department vendetta. Beck was originally indicted on 17 February 1960 for accepting gratuities in violation of the Taft-Hartley Act. He was acquitted on that charge 2 November 1962. But in the interim, he was indicted and convicted for filing two incorrect income-tax returns. It would be accurate to say that Clay thought highly of Beck, notwithstanding his conviction.

621 "That's the worst thing": Rabb interview, New York, N.Y., 4 May 1971.

622 "have to bell the cat": Hall interview.

622 "A drive to force from me": Eisenhower, *Mandate for Change,* pp. 567–68.

623 "easy fishing in a small stream": Letter, Eisenhower to Clay, 15 July 1955, PPF.

624 "I chatted with him": Hall interview.

625 meeting with various . . . Republican leaders: Robert J. Dono-

van, *Eisenhower: The Inside Story* (New York: Harper & Bros., 1956), pp. 400–401.

626 "Medically the chances are": Ibid., pp. 402–3.

627 "If the Republican National Convention": Eisenhower, *Mandate for Change,* p. 575.

627 "who felt Nixon shouldn't run again": Hall interview.

628 called him a "Democrat": Richard M. Nixon, *Six Crises* (Garden City, N.Y.: Doubleday, 1962), p. 162. For Nixon's more detailed account, see his *Memoirs* (New York: Grosset & Dunlop, 1978), pp. 168–76.

29: Back to Berlin

PAGE

630 Democratic campaign rhetoric: For Kennedy's campaign comments on Berlin, see *The New York Times,* 14 October 1960. See also Jean Edward Smith, *The Defense of Berlin* (Baltimore: Johns Hopkins Press, 1963), pp. 228–29.

633 State Department stated unequivocally: *The New York Times,* 11 March 1961.

633 Dean Rusk suggested: Ibid., 7 February 1961.

634 Khrushchev rattled Kennedy's nerve: For the Soviet *aide-mémoire* of 4 June 1961, see Smith, *Defense of Berlin,* pp. 222–23.

634 "a very sober two days": *The New York Times,* 7 June 1961. As Professor Stanley Hoffmann of Harvard has recently pointed out, it is unclear "why Kennedy treated Khrushchev's ultimatum on Berlin in 1961 so much more dramatically than Eisenhower did in 1958." The implication of Professor Hoffmann's observation is that the 1961 Berlin crisis was as much the result of American perception as Soviet action. See Stanley Hoffmann, "Do Nuclear Weapons Matter?," *New York Review of Books,* 2 February 1989, p. 29.

634 Hugh Sidey reported: *Time,* 2 January 1962. See also Hugh Sidey, *John F. Kennedy: President* (New York: Atheneum, 1963).

635 de Gaulle: *The New York Times,* 21 June 1961; 13 July 1961. See also Smith, *Defense of Berlin,* pp. 235ff.

635 Adenauer: *The New York Times,* 12 June 1961.

635 Macmillan: Ibid., 15 July 1961.

635 "a calm reliance on the status quo": Ibid., 8 August 1961.

635 Mansfield publicly questioned: Ibid., 15 June 1961.

636 "irritants in West Berlin": *Public Papers of the Presidents: John F. Kennedy, 1961* (Washington, D.C.: Government Printing Office, 1962), pp. 533–40.

636 Watson underlined *West* Berlin: Watson interview, Washington, D.C., 22 July 1971.

636 Fulbright stated on "Meet the Press": *The New York Times,* 3 August 1961. Fulbright apparently overlooked the explicit agreement made by Clay and Zhukov, 7 July 1945, that provided for freedom of movement throughout the entire city of Berlin. That agreement had never been challenged by the Soviets, even during the blockade of 1948–49. See Lucius D. Clay, *Decision in Germany* (Garden City, N.Y.: Doubleday, 1950), p. 28. Cf. Fulbright's subsequent comments on 12 August 1961, when he acknowledged that free movement between East and West Berlin was protected by four-power agreement *(The New York Times,* 13 August 1961).

636 JFK asked to comment: *Public Papers of the Presidents: John F. Kennedy,* p. 557.

637 "This is Khrushchev's way": As quoted in Norman Gelb, *The Berlin Wall* (New York: Simon and Schuster, 1988), p. 213.

637 Brandt wrote President Kennedy: See Smith, *Defense of Berlin,* pp. 282–83.

637 Dowling cautioned the State Department: Gelb, *Berlin Wall,* pp. 219–20.

638 dispatch from Washington: *The New York Times,* 16 August 1961.

638 by a "mere mayor": *The Washington Post,* 17 August 1961; *Evening Star* (Washington, D.C.), 18 August 1961.

638 "psychological climate": Smith, *Defense of Berlin,* pp. 285–86.

638 higher than Frederick the Great: Norbert Muhlen, "The Wall: One Year Later," *National Review,* 28 August 1962, p. 134.

638 "When you don't have a policy": Acheson interview, Covington and Burling, Washington, D.C., 6 August 1971.

643 "approximately 1500 men": *The Washington Post,* 19 August 1961.

650 "Western vital interests": *The New York Times,* 24 August 1961.

650 For a detailed summary of the events of August 1961, see Smith, *Defense of Berlin,* pp. 252–304.

650 Mansfield called for quick negotiations: *The Washington Post,* 26 August 1961; *Evening Star* (Washington, D.C.), 27 August 1961.

650 Adenauer . . . challenged Kennedy: *The New York Times,* 29 August 1961. See also Samuel H. Barnes et al., "The German Party System and the 1961 Federal Election," *American Political Science Review,* vol. 56 (1962), pp. 899–914.

651 "Hamlet-like psychosis": London *Times,* 24 July 1961.

654 Norstad resented: Norstad interview, New York, N.Y., 14 April 1974.

654 Clarke resented: Clarke interview, Arlington, Virginia, 13 June 1974.

654 State Department worried: Statement of Ambassador Martin Hillenbrand, quoted in Gelb, *Berlin Wall,* p. 246.

658 Clay's news conference remarks: See Smith, *Defense of Berlin,* pp. 310–11.

658 exclave of Steinstücken: For a detailed analysis of the West Berlin exclaves, see Honore M. Catudal, Jr., "Steinstücken: The Politics of a Berlin Enclave," *World Affairs,* vol. 134 (Summer 1971), pp. 51–61. See also Honoré Catudal, *Kennedy and the Berlin Wall* (Berlin: Berlin Verlag, 1980).

659 The British protested: See especially George Bailey, "The Gentle Erosion in Berlin," *The Reporter,* 26 April 1962, pp. 15–19.

661 "crawl back ignominiously": Quoted in Gelb, *Berlin Wall,* p. 253.

662 "It was truly extraordinary": Davies interview, Lehman Brothers, New York, N.Y., 11 March 1971.

663 "sold . . . but not yet delivered": *The New Yorker,* 26 May 1962, p. 117.

664 *Galgenhumor:* Norbert Muhlen, "The Wall: One Year Later," *National Review,* 28 August 1962, p. 134.

30: Wall Street Banker

PAGE

666 "a Rockefeller Republican": Hall interview, Garden City, N.Y., 4 April 1971.

667 "various boards I served on": When Clay retired as the operating head of Continental Can in 1962, he continued to serve on the boards of Chase Manhattan Bank, Continental Can (chairman of executive committee), General Motors (financial-policy committee), Lehman Corporation, United States Lines, Metropolitan Life Insurance Company, American Express, Central Savings Bank, Columbia-Presbyterian Hospital, Sloan Foundation, National Fund for Medical Education, and the American Red Cross.

667 one-armed pushups: Having been given a demonstration, I can personally attest that Clay was still doing one-armed pushups not only when he retired from Continental Can, but when he retired from Lehman Brothers ten years later.

669 "He had a brilliant mind": Richard M. Scammon interview with General Clay, 1 July 1964, John F. Kennedy Library.

670 "a conservative Republican": Theodore C. Sorensen, *Kennedy* (New York: Harper & Row, 1965), p. 595.

670 "stout-hearted leadership": Arthur Schlesinger, Jr., *A Thousand Days: John F. Kennedy in the White House* (Boston: Houghton Mifflin, 1965), p. 403.

671 Clay committee to review foreign aid: Actually, The Committee to Strengthen the Security of the Free World. In addition to Clay, the committee included Robert Anderson (Treasury secretary under Eisenhower); Eugene Black (former president of the World

Bank); Clifford Hardin (chancellor of the University of Nebraska); Robert Lovett (former Secretary of Defense); Edward S. Mason (former dean at Harvard); L. F. McCollum (president of Continental Oil); George Meany (president of the AFL-CIO); Herman Phleger (former legal adviser to the State Department as well as to Clay, earlier, in Berlin); and Howard A. Rusk, M.D. (a close personal friend of President Kennedy).

672 rough draft of the committee report: The Clay committee reported on 23 March 1963 (Washington, D.C.: Government Printing Office, 1963).

673 "foreign aid is an essential part": *U.S. News & World Report,* 8 April 1963, p. 43.

674 Clay had been stung: Schlesinger, *A Thousand Days,* p. 342.

674 Negotiations with Castro: Actual negotiations with Castro were conducted by Brooklyn attorney James B. Donovan, who the year before had arranged the exchange of Soviet spy Colonel Rudolph Abel for U-2 pilot Francis Gary Powers. Havana negotiating sessions were scheduled exclusively at midnight—Castro's choice. To back up Donovan, Assistant Attorney General Oberdorfer and Shea flew nightly from Washington to Coral Gables, where a secret command post was established, and were back at their Washington desks the next morning. Shea and the Red Cross were involved because Castro insisted on the fiction that he was dealing with the Red Cross—not the U.S. government, which of course he did not recognize, and vice versa (Shea interview, American Red Cross, Washington, D.C., 8 July 1971).

675 "only response would be 'Yes, sir' ": Shea interview.

675 "Kennedy and Clay were involved": Larkin interview, Grace National Bank, New York, N.Y., 21 May 1971.

676 Justice Department's role: Attorney General Kennedy carefully dissociated the Justice Department from the prisoner venture. My query to Attorney General John Mitchell, 29 June 1971, drew the laconic reply from Deputy Attorney General Richard Kleindienst: "A search of the Department's files did not reveal any information regarding the matter you described in your letter" (n.d.).

676 "I'll never forget it": Frank B. Clay interview, McLean, Va., 12 July 1971.

679 Lehman Brothers and Goldman, Sachs: According to Robert Lovett, when Clay went with Lehman Brothers it was a move akin to defecting to the Russians in the eyes of Sidney Weinberg (Lovett interview, Brown Brothers, Harriman, New York, N.Y., 4 May 1971).

680 "The road to democracy is not a freeway": Quoted in letter to JES from R. N. Kerst, vice president, Columbia-Presbyterian Medical Center, 19 May 1971.

680 "Our physicians and nurses": Clay to donors, Columbia-Presbyterian, October 1969. Copy in JES's possession.

682 "General Clay is not a man to fool with": Foster interview, Tuskegee Institute, Tuskegee, Ala., 17 June 1971.

684 "never thought much of Nixon": Hall interview.

685 On the carnage at Lehman Brothers, see Ken Auletta, *Greed and Glory on Wall Street: The Fall of the House of Lehman* (New York: Random House, 1986).

BIBLIOGRAPHY

Primary Sources

UNPUBLISHED PAPERS

Joseph E. Brown Papers, Georgia Department of Archives, Atlanta, Georgia
James F. Byrnes Papers, Clemson University Library, Clemson, South Carolina
Cadet Archives, U.S. Military Academy, West Point, N.Y.
Alexander S. Clay Papers, Georgia Department of Archives, Atlanta, Georgia
Lucius D. Clay, Military Service Records, Adjutant General, Washington, D.C.
Lucius D. Clay Papers (Army Service Forces), National Archives, Washington, D.C.
Lucius D. Clay Papers (Germany), National Archives, Washington, D.C.
Lucius D. Clay Papers (1950–78), Marshall Foundation, Lexington, Virginia
Clay Family Papers (courtesy of Louise Frix), Atlanta, Georgia
Joseph Dodge Papers, Detroit Public Library, Detroit, Michigan
Walter Dorn Papers, Columbia University, New York, N.Y.
John Foster Dulles Papers, Princeton University Library, Princeton, N.J.
Dwight D. Eisenhower Papers, Eisenhower Library, Abilene, Kansas
James V. Forrestal Papers, Princeton University, Princeton, N.J.
John B. Gordon Papers, Georgia Department of Archives, Atlanta, Georgia
Leslie R. Groves Papers (courtesy of Richard M. Groves), Washington, D.C.
Herbert Hoover Papers, Hoover Library, West Branch, Iowa
Harry Hopkins Papers, Roosevelt Library, Hyde Park, N.Y.
William D. Leahy Diary, Library of Congress, Washington, D.C.
Isidore Lubin Papers, Roosevelt Library, Hyde Park, N.Y.
Douglas MacArthur Papers, MacArthur Memorial Archives, Norfolk, Virginia
Robert Patterson Papers, Library of Congress, Washington, D.C.
Sam Rayburn Papers, Rayburn Library, Bonham, Texas
Franklin D. Roosevelt Papers, Roosevelt Library, Hyde Park, N.Y.
Theodore Roosevelt Papers, Manuscript Division, Library of Congress, Washington, D.C.
Hoke Smith Papers, University of Georgia, Athens, Georgia
Walter Bedell Smith Papers, Eisenhower Library, Abilene, Kansas
Henry L. Stimson Diary and Papers, Manuscript Collection, Yale University, New Haven, Connecticut
Harry S. Truman Papers, Truman Library, Independence, Missouri
Tom Watson Papers, University of North Carolina, Chapel Hill, North Carolina

INTERVIEWS

JES with General Clay

Interviews marked with an asterisk [*] have been transcribed but not edited, and are on file with the Oral History Research Office of Columbia University and the Eisenhower Library, Abilene, Kansas.

December 6, 1969, Lehman Brothers, 1 William St., New York, N.Y.
January 3, 1970, Lehman Brothers, 1 William St., New York, N.Y.
*September 23, 1970, Lehman Brothers, 1 William St., New York, N.Y.
*October 5, 1970, 220 E. 66th St., New York, N.Y.
*October 12, 1970, 220 E. 66th St., New York, N.Y.
*November 9, 1970, 220 E. 66th St., New York, N.Y.
*November 16, 1970, 220 E. 66th St., New York, N.Y.
*November 23, 1970, 220 E. 66th St., New York, N.Y.
*November 30, 1970, 220 E. 66th St., New York, N.Y.
*December 6, 1970, 220 E. 66th St., New York, N.Y.
*December 9, 1970, 220 E. 66th St., New York, N.Y.
*December 14, 1970, 220 E. 66th St., New York, N.Y.
*January 4, 1971, 220 E. 66th St., New York, N.Y.
*January 9, 1971, 220 E. 66th St., New York, N.Y.
*January 14, 1971, 220 E. 66th St., New York, N.Y.
*January 27, 1971, 220 E. 66th St., New York, N.Y.
*January 29, 1971, 220 E. 66th St., New York, N.Y.
*February 5, 1971, 220 E. 66th St., New York, N.Y.
*February 9, 1971, 220 E. 66th St., New York, N.Y.
*February 11, 1971, 220 E. 66th St., New York, N.Y.
*February 19, 1971, 220 E. 66th St., New York, N.Y.
*February 25, 1971, 220 E. 66th St., New York, N.Y.
*March 3, 1971, 220 E. 66th St., New York, N.Y.
*March 9, 1971, 220 E. 66th St., New York, N.Y.
*March 13, 1971, 220 E. 66th St., New York, N.Y.
*March 18, 1971, 220 E. 66th St., New York, N.Y.
*March 30, 1971, 220 E. 66th St., New York, N.Y.
*April 1, 1971, 220 E. 66th St., New York, N.Y.
*April 17, 1971, 220 E. 66th St., New York, N.Y.
*April 20, 1971, 220 E. 66th St., New York, N.Y.
*April 29, 1971, 220 E. 66th St., New York, N.Y.
*May 11, 1971, Carlton House, Madison Ave., New York, N.Y.
*August 2, 1971, East Chatham, Mass.
December 26, 1971, Carlton House, Madison Ave., New York, N.Y.
June 6, 1973, Carlton House, Madison Ave., New York, N.Y.
June 2, 1974, East Chatham, Mass.

Others with General Clay

Richard D. Challener, for the Dulles Oral History Project, Firestone Library, Princeton University, March 12, 1966
Richard M. Scammon, for the John F. Kennedy Library, July 1, 1964
Harold Kanarek, for the Historical Division of the Office of the Chief of Engineers, Washington, D.C.
Colonel R. Joe Rogers, for the U.S. Army, Military History Institute, Carlisle Barracks, Pennsylvania, 1972
Albert Moffet, WCVE-RV, for the George C. Marshall Library, Lexington, Va., May 18, 1976
James Riddleberger, for the Truman Library, Independence, Mo., 1972

Others by JES

Dean G. Acheson (Covington and Burling, Washington, D.C.), August 6, 1971
Margaret Allen (Alexandria, Va.), July 24, 1971
Lieutenant General Henry Aurand (Army-Navy Club, Washington, D.C.), December 11, 1970
Mrs. Rip Blair (Marietta, Ga.), December 13, 1969
Harold Boeschenstein (Owens-Corning Fiberglas, New York, N.Y.), February 16, 1971
James Boyd (Copper Range, New York, N.Y.), March 22, 1971
Willy Brandt (Berlin, Germany), July 16, 1960
*Herbert Brownell (New York, N.Y.), April 7, 1971
Paul Cabot (First Boston Corporation, Boston, Mass.), December 12, 1970
James Carmichael (Marietta, Ga.), December 13, 1969
Major General Hugh J. Casey (Naples, Fla.), December 16, 1969
Eugene Herbert Clay, Jr. (Columbus, O.), June 1, 1971
Major General Frank B. Clay (McLean, Va.), July 12, 1971
General Lucius D. Clay, Jr. (Washington, D.C.), December 15, 1969
Benjamin Cohen (Washington, D.C.), May 8, 1971
Judge James J. Daniell (Atlanta, Ga.), December 18, 1969
Paul Davies (Lehman Brothers, New York, N.Y.), March 11, 1971
Edloe Donnan (St. Louis, Mo.), June 3, 1971
Goldwaithe Dorr (New York, N.Y.), April 18, 1971
Eleanor Lansing Dulles (Berlin, Germany), August 2, 1976
Richard Durkee (New York, N.Y.), April 11, 1971
Lieutenant General Glen Edgerton (Washington, D.C.), December 12, 1971
Milton Eisenhower (Baltimore, Md.), May 9, 1971
George Elsey (Washington, D.C.), July 11, 1971
Judge Charles Fahy (Washington, D.C.), June 26, 1971
President Luther H. Foster (Tuskegee Institute, Tuskegee, Ala.), June 17, 1971

Professor Carl J. Friedrich (Toronto, Canada), October 19, 1975
Brigadier General Richard H. Groves (Washington, D.C.), June 26, 1971
General Alfred Gruenther (Washington, D.C.), July 24, 1971
Leonard Hall (Garden City, N.Y.), April 4, 1971
W. Averell Harriman (Georgetown, Washington, D.C.), June 22, 1971
Ellison Hazard (Continental Can Company, New York, N.Y.), December 12, 1970
Brigadier General Frank Howley (New York, N.Y.), February 25, 1971
Alan Oakley Hunter (New York, N.Y.), May 20, 1971
Philip Jessup (New York, N.Y.), May 21, 1971
Felix Larkin (Grace National Bank, New York, N.Y.), May 21, 1971
General Curtis LeMay (Newport Beach, Calif.), April 21, 1972
Senator Henry Cabot Lodge, Jr. (Beverly, Mass.), May 5, 1971
*Robert A. Lovett (Brown Brothers, Harriman, New York, N.Y.), May 4, 1971
Lieutenant General LeRoy Lutes (Army-Navy Club, Washington, D.C.), December 11, 1971
*John J. McCloy (Milbank, Tweed, Hadley, and McCloy, New York, N.Y.), February 19, 1971
Donald McLean (Boston, Mass.), May 24, 1971
Morgan McNeil (Marietta, Georgia), December 12, 1969
*Robert Murphy (Owens-Corning Fiberglas, New York, N.Y.), February 23, 1971
Robert Nathan (Washington, D.C.), March 12, 1971
General Lauris Norstad (New York, N.Y.), April 14, 1974
Dr. Milton Porter (New York, N.Y.), May 25, 1971
*Max Rabb (New York, N.Y.), May 4, 1971
Filemon Rodriguez (New York, N.Y.), August 26, 1971
Robert Shea (American Red Cross, Washington, D.C.), July 8, 1971
Edna Shelley (Mrs. R. S. Gates) (St. Louis, Mo.), June 3, 1971
Charles Skinner (East Chatham, Mass.), May 24, 1971
Thomas Stephens (New York, N.Y.), March 21, 1971
Lieutenant General (ret.) Wilhelm D. Styer (San Diego, Calif.), April 20, 1972
Major General Richard Sverdrup (St. Louis, Mo.), June 4, 1971
General Maxwell D. Taylor (Washington, D.C.), July 25, 1971
Brigadier General Telford Taylor (Columbia University Law School, New York, N.Y.), March 14, 1972
Francis L. Turner (Washington, D.C.), July 2, 1971
Zaida Clay Walsh (Atlanta, Ga.), June 16, 1971
Langhorn Washburn (Washington, D.C.), July 1, 1971
Colonel Charles Ward (Greenwich, Conn.), March 26, 1970
Lieutenant General Albert Watson (Washington, D.C.), July 22, 1971
Joseph Weiner (Washington, D.C.), December 11, 1971
Dr. Herman Wells (Bloomington, Ind.), March 8, 1976

Major General William Whipple (New York, N.Y.), March 6, 1971
Lawrence Wilkinson (New York, N.Y.), March 15, 1971

OFFICIAL PUBLICATIONS

Berlin Magistrat. *Berlin Neuaufbau: Das erste Jahr.* Berlin: Ein Rechenschaftsbericht des Magistrats der Stadt Berlin, 1946.

Berlin Senat. *Berlin: Behauptung von Freiheit und Selbstverwaltung, 1946–1948.* Berlin: Heinz Spitzing Verlag, 1959.

———. *Berlin: Facts and Figures.* Berlin: Berlin Press and Information Agency, 1959.

———. *Berlin: Kampf um Freiheit und Selbstverwaltung 1945–1946.* Berlin: Heinz Spitzing Verlag, 1961.

———. *Berliner Schicksal 1945–1952.* Berlin: 1952.

Berlin Statistisches, Landesamt. *Statistisches Jahrbuch Berlin.* Berlin: Kulturbuch-Verlag, 1960.

Byrnes, James F. *Restatement of United States Policy in Germany: Address by the Secretary of State Delivered in Stuttgart, Germany, September 6, 1946.* State Department Publication 2616. Washington, D.C.: Government Printing Office, 1946.

German Democratic Republic. *Memorandum of the Government of the German Democratic Republic on the Berlin Question.* Berlin: 1959.

German Federal Republic. *The Bulletin: A Weekly Survey of German Affairs.* Bonn: Press and Information Office, 1952–89.

———. *The Flight from the Soviet Zone.* Bonn: Ministry of Exiles, Refugees, and War Victims, 1959.

———. *Four Power Conference in Berlin, 1954: Speeches and Documents.* Berlin: Press and Information Office, 1954.

———. German Information Center. *Berlin: Crisis and Challenge.* New York: 1962.

———. *Germany Reports.* Wiesbaden: Press and Information Office, 1953.

———. Ministry of All-German Affairs. *Die Flucht aus der Sowietzone und die Sperrmassnahmen des Kommunistischen Regimes vom 13. August 1961 in Berlin.*

———. *The Soviet Zone of Germany.* Cologne: Ministry of All-German Affairs, 1960.

Great Britain. *An Account of Events Leading Up to a Reference of the Berlin Question to the United Nations.* London: H.M. Stationery Office, 1948.

———. *Berlin and the Problem of German Reunification.* London: British Information Services, 1961.

———. *Conference of Foreign Ministers at Geneva, 1959.* London: H.M. Stationery Office, 1959.

———. *Documents About the Future of Germany.* London: H.M. Stationery Office, 1959.

———. *Selected Documents on Germany and the Question of Berlin 1944–1961.* London: H.M. Stationery Office, 1961.

International Military Tribunal. *Trial of the Major War Criminals Before the International Military Tribunals.* 42 vols. Nuremberg: 1947–49.

———. *Trial of the Major War Criminals Before the International Military Tribunals.* 15 vols. Washington, D.C.: Government Printing Office, 1951–1952.

Union of Soviet Socialist Republics. *Stalin's Correspondence with Churchill, Attlee, Roosevelt and Truman, 1941–1945.* New York: Dutton, 1958.

United Nations. *Demographic Yearbook–1960.* Statistical Office, Department of Economics and Social Affairs. New York: 1960.

U.S. Army. *Berlin.* Berlin: Public Information Office, Berlin Command, 1954.

U.S. Congress. *Congressional Record.* Washington, D.C.: Government Printing Office, 1949–63.

U.S. Congress, House of Representatives. *Special Study Mission to Berlin.* Committee Print, Committee on Foreign Affairs. Washington, D.C.: Government Printing Office, 1959.

———. *Terminating the State of War Between the United States and the Government of Germany: Report to Accompany H.J. Res. 289.* Committee on Foreign Affairs. Washington, D.C.: Government Printing Office, 1951.

U.S. Congress, Senate. *Administration of National Security: Basic Issues.* Committee on Government Operations. Washington, D.C.: Government Printing Office, 1963.

———. *Berlin in a Changing World.* Report of Senator Mike Mansfield, et al., to the Committee on Foreign Relations. Washington, D.C.: Government Printing Office, 1963.

———. *Documents on Germany, 1944–1959.* Committee Print, Committee on Foreign Relations. Washington, D.C.: Government Printing Office, 1959.

———. *Interlocking Subversion in Government Departments* (The Harry Dexter White Papers). Committee on the Judiciary. Washington, D.C.: Government Printing Office, 1956.

U.S. Congress, Senate, Committee on the Judiciary, Internal Security Subcommittee. *Morgenthau Diary (China),* 2 vols. Washington, D.C.: Government Printing Office, 1965.

———. *Morgenthau Diary (Germany),* 2 vols. Washington, D.C.: Government Printing Office, 1965.

———. *The Soviet Union and the Berlin Question.* Moscow: 1948.

U.S. Department of State, *Berlin: City Between Two Worlds.* Washington, D.C.: Government Printing Office, 1960.

———. *Berlin, 1961.* Washington, D.C.: Government Printing Office, 1961.

———. *The Berlin Crisis: A Report of the Moscow Discussion, 1948.* Washington, D.C.: Government Printing Office, 1948.

———. *Department of State Bulletin.* Washington, D.C.: Government Printing Office, 1958–63.

———. *Documents on German Foreign Policy, 1918–1945.* Ser. D. 12 vols. Washington, D.C.: Government Printing Office, 1948–62.

———. *Foreign Relations of the United States: The Conference at Quebec, 1944.* Washington, D.C.: Government Printing Office, 1955.

———. *Foreign Relations of the United States: Conference of Berlin (Potsdam), 1945.* 2 vols. Washington, D.C.: Government Printing Office, 1960.

———. *Foreign Relations of the United States: The Conferences at Cairo and Tehran, 1943.* Washington, D.C.: Government Printing Office, 1961.

———. *Foreign Relations of the United States: Council of Foreign Ministers.* 1946, Vol. 2. Washington, D.C.: Government Printing Office, 1970.

———. *Foreign Relations of the United States: Diplomatic Papers.* 1941, Vol. 1. Washington, D.C.: Government Printing Office, 1958.

———. *Foreign Relations of the United States: Diplomatic Papers.* 1941, Vol. 4. Washington, D.C.: Government Printing Office, 1956.

———. *Foreign Relations of the United States: Diplomatic Papers.* 1942, Vol. 1. Washington, D.C.: Government Printing Office, 1960.

———. *Foreign Relations of the United States: Diplomatic Papers.* 1942, Vol. 3. Washington, D.C.: Government Printing Office, 1961.

———. *Foreign Relations of the United States: Diplomatic Papers.* 1945, Vol. 3. Washington, D.C.: Government Printing Office, 1964.

———. *Foreign Relations of the United States: Diplomatic Papers.* 1946, Vol. 5. Washington: Government Printing Office, 1969.

———. *Foreign Relations of the United States: Diplomatic Papers.* 1947, Vol. 2. Washington, D.C.: Government Printing Office, 1972.

———. *Foreign Relations of the United States: Diplomatic Papers.* 1948, Vol. 2. Washington, D.C.: Government Printing Office, 1973.

———. *Foreign Relations of the United States: Diplomatic Papers.* 1949, Vol. 3. Washington, D.C.: Government Printing Office, 1974.

———. *Germany 1947–1949: The Story in Documents.* Washington, D.C.: Government Printing Office, 1950.

———. *Making the Peace Treaties, 1941–1947.* Washington, D.C.: Government Printing Office, 1947.

———. *Nazi Conspiracy and Aggression.* 10 vols. Washington, D.C.: Government Printing Office, 1946.

———. *Occupation of Germany, Policy and Progress, 1945–1946.* Washington, D.C.: Government Printing Office, 1947.

———. *The Soviet Note on Berlin: An Analysis.* Washington, D.C.: Government Printing Office, 1959.

———. *Toward the Peace: Documents.* Washington, D.C.: Government Printing Office, 1945.

U.S. Office of Military Government, U.S. Sector, Berlin. *A Four Year Report: July 1, 1945–September 1, 1949.* Berlin: 1949.

U.S. Office of Military Government for Germany. *Military Government Information Bulletin.* Berlin: 1945–49.

BOOKS

Acheson, Dean G. *Present at the Creation.* New York: Norton, 1969.
Adenauer, Konrad. *Memoirs, 1945–1953.* Chicago: Regnery, 1966.
Almond, Gabriel. *The Politics of German Business.* Santa Monica: RAND Corporation, 1955.
———. *The Struggle for Democracy in Germany.* Chapel Hill: University of North Carolina Press, 1949.
Ambrose, Stephen. *Eisenhower and Berlin, 1945.* New York: Norton, 1967.
———. *The Supreme Commander.* Garden City, N.Y.: Doubleday, 1970.
———. *Duty, Honor, Country: A History of West Point.* Baltimore: Johns Hopkins Press, 1966.
Amgress, Werner T. *Stillborn Revolution: The Communist Bid for Power in Germany.* Princeton: Princeton University Press, 1963.
Armstrong, Anne. *Berliners: Both Sides of the War.* New Brunswick: Rutgers University Press, 1973.
———. *Unconditional Surrender: The Impact of the Casablanca Policy on World War II.* New Brunswick: Rutgers University Press, 1962.
Arnett, Alex M. *The Populist Movement in Georgia.* New York: Columbia University Press, 1922.
Auletta, Ken. *Greed and Glory on Wall Street: The Fall of the House of Lehman.* New York: Random House, 1986.
Backer, John H. *The Decision to Divide Germany: American Foreign Policy in Transition.* Durham, N.C.: Duke University Press, 1978.
———. *Priming the Germany Economy: American Occupational Policies, 1945–1948.* Durham, N.C.: Duke University Press, 1971.
———. *Winds of History: The German Years of Lucius DuBignon Clay.* New York: Van Nostrand, 1983.
Balabkins, Nicholas. *Germany Under Direct Controls.* New Brunswick, N.J.: Rutgers University Press, 1964.
Balfour, Michael, and Mair, John. *Four-Power Control in Germany and Austria, 1945–1946.* New York: Oxford University Press, 1956.
Banks, E. M. *The Economics of Land Tenure in Georgia.* New York: Columbia University Press, 1905.
Barnet, Richard J. *Roots of War.* Boston: Beacon Press, 1969.
Baxter, James P. *Scientists Against Time.* Boston: Little, Brown, 1946.
Bennett, Lowell. *Berlin Bastion.* Frankfurt: Friedrich Rudl, 1951.
Berle, Beatrice B., and Jacobs, T. B., eds. *Navigating the Rapids, 1918–1971: From the Papers of Adolf A. Berle.* New York: Harcourt Brace Jovanovich, 1973.
Best, Gary Dean. *Herbert Hoover: The Postpresidential Years, 1933–1964,* 2 vols. Stanford: Stanford University Press, 1983.

Betts, Richard K. *Soldiers, Statesmen, and Cold War Crises.* Cambridge, Mass.: Harvard University Press, 1977.
Bialer, Seweryn, ed. *Stalin and His Generals.* New York: Pegasus, 1969.
Blum, John Morgan. *From the Morgenthau Diaries: Years of War, 1941–45.* Boston: Houghton Mifflin, 1967.
———, ed. *The Price of Vision: The Diary of Henry A. Wallace, 1942–1946.* Boston: Houghton Mifflin, 1973.
Bohlen, Charles E. *The Transformation of American Foreign Policy.* New York: Norton, 1969.
———. *Witness to History 1929–1969.* New York: Norton, 1973.
Bradlee, Benjamin C. *Conversations with Kennedy.* New York: Norton, 1975.
Bradley, Omar N. *A Soldier's Story.* New York: Holt, 1951.
Bradley, Omar N., and Blair, Clay. *A General's Life.* New York: Simon and Schuster, 1983.
Brandt, Willy, and Löwenthal, Richard. *Ernst Reuter: Ein Leben für die Freiheit.* Munich: Isar Verlag, 1958.
Brinkley, David. *Washington Goes to War.* New York: Knopf, 1988.
Brooks, Robert P. *The Agrarian Revolution in Georgia, 1865–1912.* Bulletin No. 639. Madison: University of Wisconsin, 1914.
Broughton, Van Tuyl. *Company C, Eleventh Engineers: A History.* Indianapolis: Hollenbeck Press, 1919.
———. *History of the Eleventh Engineers.* New York: Little and Ives, 1926.
Bullock, Alan. *Ernest Bevin: Foreign Secretary 1945–1951.* New York: Norton, 1983.
Bundy, McGeorge. *Danger and Survival.* New York: Random House, 1989.
Burns, James MacGregor. *Roosevelt: The Soldier of Freedom, 1940–1945.* New York: Harcourt Brace Jovanovich, 1970.
Bush, Vannevar. *Pieces of the Action.* New York: Morrow, 1970.
Butcher, Captain Harry. *My Three Years with Eisenhower.* New York: Simon and Schuster, 1946.
Byrnes, James F. *All in One Lifetime.* New York: Harper & Bros., 1958.
———. *Speaking Frankly.* New York: Harper & Bros., 1947.
Cate, Curtis. *The Ides of August: The Berlin Wall Crisis of 1961.* New York: Evans, 1978.
Catudal, Honoré. *Kennedy and the Berlin Wall.* Berlin: Berlin Verlag, 1980.
Chandler, Alfred D., and Ambrose, Stephen, eds. *The Papers of Dwight D. Eisenhower,* vols. 1–9. Baltimore: Johns Hopkins Press, 1970–78.
Charles, Max. *Berlin Blockade.* London: Allan Wingate, 1959.
Christen, Peter. *From Military Government to State Department.* Munich: OMG Bavaria, 1950.
Chuikov, Marshal Vasili I. *The Fall of Berlin.* Translated by Ruth Kisch. New York: Holt, Rinehart and Winston, 1968.
Churchill, Winston S. *Closing the Ring.* Boston: Houghton Mifflin, 1951.
———. *The Grand Alliance.* Boston: Houghton Mifflin, 1950.
———. *The Hinge of Fate.* Boston: Houghton Mifflin, 1950.

———. *Triumph and Tragedy.* Boston: Houghton Mifflin, 1953.
Civilian Production Administration. *Industrial Mobilization for War.* Washington, D.C.: Government Printing Office, 1947.
Clark, Delbert. *Again the Goosestep.* Indianapolis: Bobbs, Merrill, 1949.
Clark, General Mark. *Calculated Risk.* New York: Harper & Bros., 1950.
Clay, Lucius D. *Decision in Germany.* Garden City, N.Y.: Doubleday, 1950.
———. *Germany and the Fight for Freedom.* Cambridge, Mass.: Harvard University Press, 1950.
Clements, Kendrick A., ed. *James F. Byrnes and the Origins of the Cold War.* Durham, N.C.: Carolina Academic Press, 1982.
Cline, Ray S. *Washington Command Post: The Operations Division.* Office of the Chief of Military History, Department of the Navy. Washington, D.C.: Government Printing Office, 1951.
Coffman, Edward M. *The Hilt of the Sword: The Career of Peyton E. March.* Madison: University of Wisconsin Press, 1966.
Cohen, Stephen F. *Rethinking the Soviet Experience: Politics and History Since 1917.* New York: Oxford University Press, 1985.
Coles, Harry, and Weinberg, Albert. *Civil Affairs: Soldiers Become Governors.* Washington, D.C.: Office of the Chief of Military History, 1964.
Collier, Richard. *Bridge Across the Sky.* New York: McGraw-Hill, 1978.
Committee on Public Administration. *The Reconversion Controversy.* Washington, D.C.: CPAC, 1950.
Condit, Kenneth W. *The History of the Joint Chiefs of Staff, 1947–1949.* Wilmington: Michael Glazier, 1979.
Conn, Stetson, and Fairchild, Byron. *The Framework of Hemisphere Defense.* Washington, D.C.: Government Printing Office, 1960.
Connally, Tom. *My Name Is Tom Connally.* New York: Crowell, 1954.
Corbett, Percy E. *War Aims and Postwar Plans.* London: Royal Institute of International Affairs, 1941.
Coulton, E. Merton. *Georgia: A Short History.* Chapel Hill: University of North Carolina Press, 1933.
Curry, George. *James F. Byrnes.* New York: Cooper Square, 1965.
Davis, Franklin. *Come as a Conqueror.* New York: Macmillan, 1967.
Davis, Lynn Ethridge. *The Cold War Begins: Soviet-American Conflict over Eastern Europe.* Princeton: Princeton University Press, 1974.
Davison, W. Phillips. *The Berlin Blockade: A Study in Cold War Politics.* Princeton: Princeton University Press, 1958.
Deane, John R. *The Strange Alliance: The Story of Our Efforts at Wartime Cooperation with Russia.* New York: Viking, 1947.
de Gaulle, General Charles. *The War Memoirs of Charles de Gaulle.* New York: Simon and Schuster, 1959–60.
Deutsch, Harold C. *New Crisis on Berlin.* Toronto: Canadian Institute of International Affairs, 1959.
Dobney, Frederick J., ed. *The Papers of William Clayton,* 2 vols. Ph.D. dissertation, Rice University, 1970; microfilm 1974.

Donner, Jörn. *Report from Berlin.* Bloomington: Indiana University Press, 1961.

Donovan, Frank. *Bridge in the Sky.* New York: McKay, 1968.

Donovan, Robert J. *Conflict and Crisis: The Presidency of Harry S Truman, 1945–1949.* New York: Norton, 1977.

———. *Eisenhower: The Inside Story.* New York: Harper & Bros., 1956.

Dulles, Eleanor L. *Berlin: The Wall Is Not Forever.* Chapel Hill: University of North Carolina Press, 1967.

———. *John Foster Dulles: The Last Year.* New York: Harcourt, Brace & World, 1963.

———. *The Wall: A Tragedy in Three Acts.* Columbia: University of South Carolina Press, 1972.

Dulles, John Foster. *War or Peace.* New York: Macmillan, 1957.

Eden, Sir Anthony. *Facing the Dictators: The Memoirs of Anthony Eden, Earl of Avon.* Boston: Houghton Mifflin, 1962.

Edinger, Lewis. *Kurt Schumacher.* Stanford: Stanford University Press, 1965.

Ehrman, John. *Grand Strategy.* Vol. 5, *August 1943–September 1944.* London: H.M. Stationery Office, 1956.

———. *Grand Strategy.* Vol. 6, *October 1944–August 1945.* London: H.M. Stationery Office, 1956.

Eisenhower, David. *Eisenhower at War.* New York: Random House, 1986.

Eisenhower, Dwight D. *At Ease: Stories I Tell My Friends.* Garden City, N.Y.: Doubleday, 1967.

———. *Mandate for Change, 1953–1956.* Garden City, N.Y.: Doubleday, 1963.

———. *Crusade in Europe.* Garden City, N.Y.: Doubleday, 1948.

Eyre, James K. *The Roosevelt-MacArthur Conflict.* Chambersburg, Pa.: Craft Press, 1950.

Fairchild, Byron, and Grossman, Jonathan. *The Army and Industrial Manpower.* Washington, D.C.: Government Printing Office, 1959.

Feis, Herbert. *Between War and Peace: The Potsdam Conference.* Princeton: Princeton University Press, 1960.

———. *Churchill, Roosevelt, Stalin: The War They Waged and the Peace They Sought.* Princeton: Princeton University Press, 1967.

———. *From Trust to Terror: The Onset of the Cold War, 1945–1950.* New York: Norton, 1970.

Felton, Mrs. W. H. [Rebecca]. *My Memoirs of Georgia Politics.* Atlanta: Index Co., 1911.

Fennelly, John. *Memoirs of a Bureaucrat: A Personal Story of the War Production Board.* Chicago: October House, 1965.

Ferrell, Robert H. *The American Secretaries of State and Their Diplomacy: Marshall.* Vol. 15. New York: Cooper Square, 1966.

———, ed. *Off the Record: The Private Papers of Harry S. Truman.* New York: Harper & Row, 1980.

Fine, Lenore, and Remington, Jesse. *The Corps of Engineers: Construction in the United States.* Washington, D.C.: Government Printing Office, 1972.

Fisher, Ruth. *Stalin and German Communism.* Cambridge, Mass.: Harvard University Press, 1948.

Fitzgibbon, Constantine. *Denazification.* London: Joseph, 1969.

Flechtheim, Ossip K., ed. *Die Deutschen Parteien seit 1945.* Cologne: Haymanns, 1955.

———. *Die KPD in der Weimarer Republic.* Offenbach: Bollwerk, 1948.

Foot, Michael. *Aneurin Bevan: A Biography,* vol. 2: *1945–1960.* London: David Poynter, 1973.

Fredericksen, Oliver. *American Military Occupation of Germany, 1945–53.* Darmstadt: HICOG, 1953.

Freedman, Max, ed. *Roosevelt and Frankfurter: Their Correspondence, 1928–1945.* Boston: Little, Brown, 1967.

Freeland, Richard M. *The Truman Doctrine and the Origins of McCarthyism.* New York: Knopf, 1972.

Friedmann, Wolfgang. *The Allied Military Government of Germany.* London: Stevens, 1947.

Friedrich, Carl J. *American Experiences in Military Government in World War II.* New York: Rinehart, 1948.

Friend, Theodore. *Between Two Empires: The Ordeal of the Philippines, 1929–1946.* New Haven: Yale University Press, 1965.

Gablentz, O. M. von der. *The Berlin Question and Its Relations to World Politics, 1944–1963.* Munich: Oldenbourg Verlag, 1964.

Gaddis, John L. *Strategies of Containment.* New York: Oxford University Press, 1982.

———. *The U.S. and the Origins of the Cold War, 1941–47.* New York: Columbia University Press, 1972.

Galbraith, John Kenneth. *A Life in Our Times.* Boston: Houghton Mifflin, 1981.

Gardner, Lloyd C. *Architects of Illusion: Men and Ideas in American Foreign Policy, 1941–49.* Chicago: Quadrangle Books, 1970.

Gelb, Norman. *The Berlin Wall.* New York: Simon and Schuster, 1988.

Gellman, Barton. *Contending with Kennan.* New York: Praeger, 1985.

Gillen, J. F. J. *American Influence on the Development of Political Institutions.* Karlsruhe: HICOG, 1950.

Gimbel, John. *The American Occupation of Germany, 1945–1949.* Stanford: Stanford University Press, 1968.

———. *A German Community Under American Occupation: Marburg, 1945–52.* Stanford: Stanford University Press, 1962.

———. *The Origins of the Marshall Plan.* Stanford: Stanford University Press, 1976.

Golay, John Ford. *The Founding of the Federal Republic of Germany.* Chicago: University of Chicago Press, 1958.

Gottlieb, Manuel. *The German Peace Settlement and the Berlin Crisis.* New York: Paine Whitman, 1960.

Grant, Ulysses S. *Personal Memoirs of U.S. Grant.* 2 vols. New York: Charles L. Webster, 1885.
Grantham, Dewey W., Jr. *Hoke Smith and the Politics of the New South.* Baton Rouge: Louisiana State University Press, 1958.
Greenfield, Kent R., ed. *Command Decisions.* Office of the Chief of Military History, Department of the Army. Washington, D.C.: Government Printing Office, 1960.
Gross, Franz. "Freedom of the Press Under Military Government in Western Germany, 1945–49." Ph.D. dissertation, Harvard University, 1952.
Hagood, Johnson. *The Services of Supply.* Boston: Houghton Mifflin, 1927.
Halberstam, David. *The Best and the Brightest.* Greenwich, Conn.: Fawcett Publications, 1972.
Hanrieder, Wolfram F. *West German Foreign Policy, 1949–1963: International Pressure and Domestic Response.* Stanford: Stanford University Press, 1967.
Harbord, James G. *The American Army in France.* Boston: Little, Brown, 1936.
Harbutt, Fraser J. *The Iron Curtain: Churchill, America, and the Origins of the Cold War.* New York: Oxford University Press, 1987.
Hardeman, D.B., and Bacon, Donald C. *Rayburn.* Austin: University of Texas Press, 1987.
Henkin, Louis. *The Berlin Crisis and the United Nations.* New York: Carnegie Endowment for International Peace, 1959.
Herz, Martin. *Beginnings of the Cold War.* Bloomington: Indiana University Press, 1966.
Hill, Russell. *Struggle for Germany.* New York: Harper & Row, 1947.
Holborn, Hajo, ed. *American Military Government.* Washington: Infantry Journal Press, 1947.
Holt, W. Stull. *The Office of the Chief of Engineers of the Army.* Service Monographs of the United States Government, No. 27. Baltimore: Institute for Government Research, 1923.
Hoover, Calvin B. *Memoirs of Capitalism, Communism, and Nazism.* Durham, N.C.: University of North Carolina Press, 1965.
Howard, J. Woodward, Jr. *Mr. Justice Murphy: A Political Biography.* Princeton: Princeton University Press, 1968.
Howley, Frank. *Berlin Command.* New York: Putnam, 1950.
Hughes, Emmet John. *The Ordeal of Power.* New York: Atheneum, 1963.
Hull, Cordell. *Memoirs.* 2 vols. New York: Macmillan, 1948.
Hunt, Frazier. *The Untold Story of Douglas MacArthur.* New York: Davis-Adair, 1954.
Ickes, Harold L. *The Secret Diary of Harold L. Ickes,* 3 vols. New York: Simon and Schuster, 1951–53.
Issacson, Walter, and Evan Thomas. *The Wise Men.* New York: Simon and Schuster, 1986.

James, D. Clayton. *The Years of MacArthur,* vol. 1, *1880–1941.* Boston: Houghton Mifflin, 1970.

Janeway, Eliot. *The Struggle for Survival.* New Haven: Yale University Press, 1951.

Jonas, Manfred. *The United States and Germany: A Diplomatic History.* Ithaca, N.Y.: Cornell University Press, 1984.

Jones, Joseph M. *The Fifteen Weeks (February 21 to June 5, 1947).* New York: Viking, 1955.

Kaden, Albrecht. *Einheit oder Freiheit? Die Widergründung der SPD 1945–1946.* Hannover: Dietz, 1964.

Kecskemeti, Paul. *Strategic Surrender: The Politics of Victory and Defeat.* Stanford: Stanford University Press, 1958.

Keller, John W. *Germany, the Wall and Berlin: Internal Politics During an International Crisis.* New York: Vantage, 1964.

Kennan, George F. *From Prague After Munich.* Princeton: Princeton University Press, 1968.

———. *Memoirs 1925–1950.* Boston: Little, Brown, 1967.

Key, V. O. *Southern Politics in State and Nation.* New York: Knopf, 1949.

Khrushchev, Nikita. *The Soviet Stand on Germany.* New York: Crosscurrents Press, 1961.

Kimball, Warren F., ed. *Swords or Ploughshares? The Morgenthau Plan for Defeated Germany 1943–46.* Philadelphia: Lippincott, 1976.

Klimov, Gregory P. *The Terror Machine: The Inside Story of the Soviet Administration in Germany.* New York: Praeger, 1953.

Knight, Lucian Lamar. *A Standard History of Georgia and Georgians.* 6 vols. New York and Chicago: Lewis, 1917.

Korb, Lawrence J. *The Joint Chiefs of Staff: The First Twenty-five Years.* Bloomington: Indiana University Press, 1976.

Kormann, John. *U.S. Denazification 1944–50.* Bad Godesburg: HICOG, 1952.

Krieger, Wolfgang. *General Lucius D. Clay und die amerikanische Deutschlandpolitik, 1945–1949.* Stuttgart: Klett-Cotta, 1987.

Krisch, Henry. *German Politics Under Soviet Occupation.* New York: Columbia University Press, 1974.

Krippendorff, Ekkehart, ed. *The Role of the United States in the Reconstruction of Italy and West Germany, 1943–1949.* Berlin: John F. Kennedy Institute, 1981.

Krock, Arthur. *Memoirs: Sixty Years on the Firing Line.* New York: Popular Library, 1968.

Kuklick, Bruce R. *American Foreign Economic Policy and Germany, 1939–46.* Ph.D. dissertation, University of Pennsylvania, 1968.

———. *American Policy and the Division of Germany: The Clash with Russia over Reparations.* Ithaca, N.Y.: Cornell University Press, 1972.

LaFeber, Walter. *America, Russia, and the Cold War 1945–75.* 3rd ed. New York: Wiley, 1976.

Leahy, William D. *I Was There.* New York: Whittlesey House, 1950.
Legien, Rudolf. *The Four Power Agreements on Berlin: Alternative Solutions to the Status Quo?* Translated by Trevor Davies. Berlin: Carl Heymanns Verlag, 1960.
Leighton, Richard M., and Coakley, Robert W. *Global Logistics and Strategy, 1940–1943.* Washington, D.C.: Government Printing Office, 1955.
LeMay, General Curtis E. *Mission with LeMay.* Garden City, N.Y.: Doubleday, 1965.
Leonhard, Wolfgang. *Child of the Revolution.* Chicago: Regnery, 1958.
Leuchtenburg, William. *Flood Control Politics.* Cambridge, Mass.: Harvard University Press, 1953.
Lewis, Harold O. *New Constitutions in Occupied Germany.* Washington, D.C.: Foundation for Foreign Affairs, 1948.
Lie, Trygve. *In the Cause of Peace.* New York: Macmillan, 1954.
Lippmann, Walter. *The Cold War: A Study in U.S. Foreign Policy.* New York: Harper and Row, 1947.
———. *U.S. War Aims.* Boston: Little, Brown & Co., 1944.
Litchfield, Edward H., et al. *Governing Postwar Germany.* Ithaca, N.Y.: Cornell University Press, 1953.
Lochner, Louis. *Herbert Hoover and Germany.* New York: Macmillan, 1960.
Maass, Arthur. *Muddy Waters: The Army Engineers and the Nation's Rivers.* Cambridge, Mass.: Harvard University Press, 1951.
MacArthur, Douglas. *Reminiscences.* New York: McGraw-Hill, 1964.
MacMahon, Arthur W. et al. *The Administration of Federal Relief Work.* Chicago: Public Administration Service, 1941.
Maier, Charles S. *The Origins of the Cold War and Contemporary Europe.* New York: Watts, 1978.
Maier, Reinhold. *Ende und Wende.* Stuttgart: Wunderlich, 1949.
Manchester, William. *American Caesar.* Boston: Little, Brown, 1978.
Mander, John. *Berlin: Hostage for the West.* Baltimore: Penguin Books, 1962.
Marshall, Katherine T. *Together: The Annals of an Army Wife.* Atlanta: Tupper & Love, 1946.
Martin, James Stewart. *All Honorable Men.* Boston: Little, Brown, 1950.
Matloff, Maurice. *Strategic Planning for Coalition Warfare, 1943–1944.* Office of the Chief of Military History; Department of the Army. Washington, D.C.: Government Printing Office, 1959.
Mayers, David. *George Kennan and the Dilemmas of U.S. Foreign Policy.* New York: Oxford University Press, 1988.
McDermott, Geoffrey. *Berlin: Success of a Mission?* New York: Harper & Row, 1963.
McInnis, Edgar; Hiscocks, Richard; and Spencer, Robert. *The Shaping of Postwar Germany.* London: Dent, 1960.
McLelland, David S. *Dean Acheson: The State Department Years.* New York: Dodd, Mead, 1976.

Merkl, Peter H. *The Origins of the West German Republic.* New York: Oxford University Press, 1963.

Merritt, Anna J., and Merritt, Richard L. *Public Opinion in Occupied Germany.* Urbana: University of Illinois Press, 1970.

Messer, Robert L. *The End of an Alliance: James F. Byrnes, Roosevelt, Truman, and the Origins of the Cold War.* Chapel Hill: University of North Carolina Press, 1982.

Middleton, Drew. *The Struggle for Germany.* London and New York: Allan Wingate, 1950.

Miller, Lynn M., and Pruessen, Roland W., eds. *Reflections on the Cold War.* Philadelphia: Temple University Press, 1974.

Miller, Merle. *Plain Speaking: An Oral Biography of Harry S. Truman.* New York: Putnam, 1973.

Millet, John D. *The Organization and Role of Army Service Forces.* Washington, D.C.: Government Printing Office, 1954.

———. *The Works Progress Administration in New York City.* Chicago: Public Administration Service, 1938.

Millis, Walter, ed. *The Forrestal Diaries.* New York: Viking, 1951.

Milward, Alan. *The Reconstruction of Western Europe, 1945–51.* Berkeley, Calif.: University of California Press, 1984.

Montgomery, John. *Forced to be Free.* Chicago: University of Chicago Press, 1957.

Montgomery, Viscount. *The Memoirs of Montgomery of Alamein.* Cleveland: World Publishing Co., 1958.

Morgan, Arthur E. *Dams and Other Disasters.* Boston: Sargent, 1971.

Morgan, Roger. *The United States and West Germany, 1945–1973: A Study in Alliance Politics.* London: Oxford University Press, 1974.

Morgenthau, Hans. *Germany and the Future of Europe.* Chicago: University of Chicago Press, 1951.

Morgenthau, Henry J. *Germany Is Our Problem.* New York: Harper & Bros., 1945.

Morris, Eric. *Blockade: Berlin and the Cold War.* London: Hamish Hamilton, 1973.

Morrison, Elting E. *Turmoil and Tradition: A Study of the Life and Times of Henry L. Stimson.* New York: Atheneum, 1964.

Mosely, Philip E. *The Kremlin in World Politics.* New York: Random House, 1960.

Murphy, Robert. *Diplomat Among Warriors.* Garden City, N.Y.: Doubleday, 1964.

Nelson, Daniel J. *Defenders or Intruders: The Dilemmas of U.S. Forces in Germany.* Boulder, Colo.: Westview Press, 1987.

———. *A History of U.S. Military Forces in Germany.* Boulder, Colo.: Westview Press, 1987.

———. *Wartime Origins of the Berlin Dilemma.* University, Ala.: University of Alabama Press, 1978.

Nelson, Donald. *Arsenal of Democracy.* New York: Harcourt, Brace, 1946.
Nelson, O.L. *National Security and the General Staff.* Washington, D.C.: Infantry Journal Press, 1946.
Nettl, John P. *The Eastern Zone and Soviet Policy in Germany: 1945–1950.* New York: Oxford University Press, 1951.
Neumann, William L. *Making the Peace: 1941–1962.* Washington, D.C.: Foundation for Foreign Affairs, 1950.
Nicolson, Harold. *Diaries and Letters,* 1945–1962. Edited by Nigel Nicolson. London: Fontana, 1971.
Nixon, Edgar B., ed. *Franklin D. Roosevelt and Foreign Affairs.* 3 vols. Cambridge, Mass.: Harvard University Press, 1969.
Nixon, Richard M. *Memoirs.* New York: Grosset & Dunlap, 1978.
———. *Six Crises.* Garden City, N.Y.: Doubleday, 1962.
Northern, W. L. *Men of Mark in Georgia.* 4 vols. Atlanta: Caldwell, 1908.
Notter, Harley A. *Postwar Foreign Policy Preparation: 1939–1945.* Department of State. Washington, D.C.: Government Printing Office, 1949.
Nye, Colonel Roger. *The USMA in the Era of Educational Reform.* Ph.D. dissertation, Columbia University, 1966.
Opie, Redvers. *The Search for Peace Settlements.* Washington, D.C.: Brookings Institution, 1951.
Oppen, Beate Ruhm von, ed. *Documents of Germany Under Occupation, 1945–54.* London: Oxford University Press, 1955.
Padover, Saul. *Experiment in Germany.* New York: Duell, Sloan and Pearce, 1946.
Paterson, Thomas G. *Containment and the Cold War: American Foreign Policy Since 1945.* Reading, Mass.: Addison-Wesley, 1973.
Payne, Robert. *The Marshall Story: A Biography of General George C. Marshall.* New York: Prentice-Hall, 1951.
Peterson, Edward N. *The American Occupation of Germany.* Detroit: Wayne State University Press, 1977.
Plischke, Elmer. *Berlin: Development of Its Government and Administration.* Historical Section, Office of the U.S. High Commissioner for Germany. Bonn, 1952.
Pogue, Forrest C. *George C. Marshall.* 4 vols. New York: Viking, 1963–85.
———. *The Supreme Command: United States Army in World War II: The European Theater of Operations.* Washington, D.C.: Government Printing Office, 1956.
Pollock, James, ed. *German Democracy.* Ann Arbor: University of Michigan Press, 1955.
———. *Germany Under Occupation.* Ann Arbor: Wahr, 1947.
Pollock, James K., and Lane, John C., eds. *Source Materials on the Government and Politics of Germany.* Ann Arbor: Wahr, 1964.
Pope, Lt. Gen. Maurice A. *Soldiers and Politicians: The Memoirs of Lt.-Gen. Maurice A. Pope, C.B.M.C.* Toronto: University of Toronto Press, 1962.

Pounds, Norman J. G. *Divided Germany and Berlin.* Princeton: Van Nostrand, 1962.

Ratchford, B. U., and Ross, William D. *Berlin Reparations Assignment.* Chapel Hill: University of North Carolina Press, 1947.

Riess, Curt. *Berlin 1945–1953.* Berlin: Non-Stop Bücherei, 1954.

Robson, Charles B., ed. *Berlin: Pivot of German Destiny.* Chapel Hill: University of North Carolina Press, 1960.

Rodnick, David. *Postwar Germans.* New Haven: Yale University Press, 1948.

Rogow, Arnold A. *A Victim of Duty: A Study of James Forrestal.* London: Rupert Hart-Davis, 1966.

Romanus, Charles, and Sunderland, Riley. *Stilwell's Command Problems.* Washington, D.C.: Government Printing Office, 1956.

Roosevelt, Eleanor. *This I Remember.* New York: Harper & Bros., 1949.

Roosevelt, Elliott. *As He Saw It.* New York: Duell, Sloane & Pearce, 1946.

Rosenburg, Arthur. *The Birth of the German Republic 1871–1918.* London: Oxford University Press, 1931.

Rosenburg, Jerry Philip. *Berlin and Israel 1948: Foreign Policy Decision-Making During the Truman Administration.* Ph.D. dissertation, University of Illinois, Urbana-Champaign, 1977.

Rostow, Walt W. *The Division of Europe After World War II: 1946.* Austin: University of Texas Press, 1981.

Rottmann, Joachim. *Der Viermächte-Status Berlins.* Bonn: Bundesministerium für Gesamtdeutsche Fragen, 1959.

Ruppenthal, Roland. *Logistical Support of the Armies,* vol. 2. Washington, D.C.: Government Printing Office, 1959.

Salomon, Ernst von. *Fragebogen.* New York: Doubleday, 1955.

Schaffer, Gordon. *Russian Zone: A Record of the Conditions Found in the Soviet Occupied Zone of Germany During a Stay of Two Weeks.* London: Allen and Unwin, 1947.

Schaller, Michael. *Douglas MacArthur: Far Eastern General.* New York: Oxford University Press, 1989.

Schlesinger, Arthur M., Jr. *A Thousand Days: John F. Kennedy in the White House.* Boston: Houghton Mifflin, 1965.

Schmitt, Hans A., ed. *U.S. Occupation in Europe After World War II.* Lawrence: Regents Press of Kansas, 1978.

Schnick, Jack. *The Berlin Crisis, 1958–1962.* Philadelphia: University of Pennsylvania Press, 1971.

Scott, Hugh. *Some Memories of a Soldier.* New York: Century, 1928.

Sharp, Tony. *The Wartime Alliance and the Zonal Division of Germany.* Oxford: Clarendon Press, 1975.

Sherwood, Robert E. *Roosevelt and Hopkins: An Intimate History.* New York: Harper & Bros., 1948.

Shlaim, Avi. *The United States and the Berlin Blockade, 1948–1949: A Study in Crisis Decision-Making.* Berkeley: University of California Press, 1983.

Sidey, Hugh. *John F. Kennedy: President.* New York: Atheneum, 1963.
Smith, Gaddis. *Dean Acheson.* New York: Cooper Square, 1972.
Smith, Jean Edward. *The Defense of Berlin.* Baltimore: Johns Hopkins Press, 1963.
———. *The Papers of General Lucius Clay, Germany 1945–49,* 2 vols. Bloomington: Indiana University Press, 1974.
Smith, R. Elberton. *The Army and Economic Mobilization.* Washington, D.C.: Government Printing Office, 1958.
Smith, Richard N. *Thomas E. Dewey and His Times.* New York: Simon and Schuster, 1982.
Smith, General Walter Bedell. *Eisenhower's Six Great Decisions.* New York: Longmans, Green, 1950.
———. *My Three Years in Moscow.* Philadelphia: Lippincott, 1950.
Smith, Zachery, and Clay, Mary Rogers. *The Clay Family.* Louisville, Ky.: privately published, 1906.
Snell, John L., ed. *The Meaning of Yalta.* Baton Rouge: Louisiana State University Press, 1956.
———. *Wartime Origins of the East-West Dilemma over Germany.* New Orleans: Hauser, 1959.
Sokolovsky, Marshal Vassily D. *Voennaia Strategiia.* Moscow: Voenizdat, 1968.
Somers, Herman Miles. *Presidential Agency: OWMR.* Cambridge, Mass.: Harvard University Press, 1950.
Sorensen, Theodore. *Kennedy.* New York: Harper & Row, 1965.
Speier, Hans. *Divided Berlin.* New York; Praeger, 1961.
———. *From the Ashes of Disgrace: A Journal from Germany, 1945–1955.* Amherst: University of Massachusetts Press, 1981.
Stanger, Roland J., ed. *West Berlin: The Legal Context.* Columbus: Ohio State University Press, 1966.
Steel, Ronald. *Walter Lippmann and the American Century.* Boston: Little, Brown, 1980.
Stein, Harold, ed. *American Civil-Military Decisions.* Montgomery: University of Alabama Press, 1963.
Stettinius, Edward R. *Lend-Lease: Weapon for Victory.* New York: Macmillan, 1974.
Stevenson, William. *A Man Called Intrepid.* New York: Harcourt Brace Jovanovich, 1976.
Stimson, Henry L., and Bundy, McGeorge. *On Active Service in Peace and War.* New York: Harper & Bros., 1950.
Stolper, Gustav. *German Realities.* New York: Reynal & Hitchcocks, 1948.
Strang, William Lord. *Home and Abroad.* London: André Deutsch, 1956.
Stützle, Walther. *Kennedy und Adenauer in der Berlin Krise.* Bonn: Friedrich-Ebert Stiftung, 1973.
Sulzberger, C.L. *A Long Row of Candles: Memoirs and Diaries, 1934–1954.* New York: Macmillan, 1969.

Taylor, Maxwell. *Swords and Plowshares.* New York: Norton, 1972.

Taylor, Telford. *Sword and Swastika.* New York: Simon and Schuster, 1952.

Tent, James F. *The Free University of Berlin: A Political History.* Bloomington: Indiana University Press, 1988.

Trivers, Howard. *Three Crises in American Foreign Affairs and a Continuing Revolution.* Carbondale: Southern Illinois University Press, 1972.

Truman, Harry. *Year of Decisions.* Garden City, N.Y.: Doubleday, 1956.

———. *Years of Trial and Hope.* Garden City, N.Y.: Doubleday, 1956.

Truman, Margaret. *Harry S. Truman.* New York: Morrow, 1972.

Tuchman, Barbara. *Stilwell and the American Experience in China, 1911–45.* New York: Macmillan, 1970.

Tunner, Lt. Gen. William. *Over the Hump.* New York: Duell, Sloane and Pearce, 1964.

Tuso, John and Anna. *The Berlin Blockade.* London: Holder & Staughton, 1988.

U.S. Bureau of the Budget. *The United States at War.* Washington, D.C.: Government Printing Office, 1947.

Vandenberg, Arthur H., Jr. *The Private Papers of Senator Vandenberg.* Boston: Houghton Mifflin, 1952.

Wallich, Henry C. *Mainsprings of the German Revival.* New Haven: Yale University Press, 1955.

Warburg, James. *Germany: Bridge or Battleground?* New York: Harcourt, Brace, 1947.

Ward, Patricia Dawson. *The Threat to Peace: James F. Byrnes and the Council of Foreign Ministers, 1945–1946.* Kent, Oh.: Kent State University Press, 1979.

Watson, Mark S. *Chief of Staff: Prewar Plans and Preparations.* Washington, D.C.: Government Printing Office, 1950.

Wedemeyer, General Albert C. *Wedemeyer Reports.* New York: Henry Holt, 1958.

Weil, Martin. *A Pretty Good Club: The Founding Fathers of the U.S. Foreign Service.* New York: Norton, 1978.

Wells, Herman B. *Being Lucky.* Bloomington: Indiana University Press, 1980.

Wheeler-Bennett, John W., and Nicholls, Anthony. *The Semblance of Peace: The Political Settlement After the Second World War.* New York: St. Martin's Press, 1972.

White, W. L. *Report on the Germans.* New York: Harcourt, Brace, 1947.

Williams, Francis. *A Prime Minister Remembers: The War and Post-War Memoirs of the Rt. Hon. Earl Attlee.* London: Heinemann, 1961.

Willis, F. Roy. *France, Germany, and the New Europe, 1945–1967.* Palo Alto: Stanford University Press, 1968.

———. *The French in Germany, 1945–1949.* Palo Alto: Stanford University Press, 1962.

Wilmot, Chester. *The Struggle for Europe.* New York: Harper & Bros., 1952.

Winant, John G. *Letters from Grosvenor Square.* Boston: Houghton Mifflin, 1947.

Windsor, Philip. *City on Leave: A History of Berlin 1945–1962.* New York: Praeger, 1963.

Wolfe, Robert, ed. *Americans as Proconsuls: United States Military Government in Germany and Japan, 1944–1952.* Carbondale: Southern Illinois University Press, 1951.

Woodward, C. Vann. *Origins of the New South, 1877–1913.* Baton Rouge: Louisiana State University Press, 1951.

———. *Tom Watson: Agrarian Rebel.* New York: Macmillan, 1938.

Woodward, Sir Llewellyn. *British Foreign Policy in the Second World War.* London: H.M. Stationery Office, 1962.

Wright, C. Ben. *George F. Kennan: Scholar-Diplomat.* Ph.D. dissertation, University of Wisconsin, 1972.

Yarmolinsky, Adam. *The Military Establishment.* New York.: Harper & Row, 1971.

Yergin, Daniel. *Shattered Peace: The Origins of the Cold War and the National Security State.* Boston: Houghton Mifflin, 1977.

Zhukov, Georgii K. *Reminiscences and Reflections.* New York: Delacorte Press, 1971.

Ziemke, Earl. *The U.S. Army in the Occupation of Germany: 1944–1946.* Washington: Office of Military History, 1975.

Zink, Harold. *The United States in Germany 1944–1955.* Princeton: Van Nostrand Co., 1957.

ARTICLES

Acheson, Dean Gooderham. "On Dealing with Russia: An Inside View." *The New York Times Magazine*, 12 April 1959, pp. 27, 88–89.

Adler, Les K., and Paterson, Thomas G. "Red Fascism: The Merger of Nazi Germany and Soviet Russia in the American Image of Totalitarianism." *American Historical Review,* vol. 75 (April 1970).

Allemann, Fritz R., et al. "Berlin in Search of a Purpose." *Survey,* October 1966, pp. 129–138.

———. "East Germany: Ulbricht's Tottering State." *New Leader,* vol. 44 (14 August 1961), pp. 3–6.

Alsop, Joseph and Stewart. "Why We Changed Our Policy in Germany." *Saturday Evening Post,* 7 December 1946.

Anthony, Carl G. "The Berlin Crisis and Atlantic Unity." *Current History,* 1962, pp. 20–27.

Ausland, John C. "The Berlin Wall." *Foreign Service Journal,* July 1971, pp. 12–16.

Barker, Elizabeth. "Berlin Crisis: 1958–1962." *International Affairs,* vol. 39 (January 1963), pp. 59–73.

Barnes, Samuel H., et al. "The German Party System and the 1961 Federal Election." *American Political Science Review,* vol. 56 (1962), pp. 899–914.

Bennett, Jack. "The German Currency Reform." *Annals of the American Academy of Political and Social Science,* vol. 267 (January 1950).

Berkowitz, Morton, et al. "The Berlin Airlift: 1948." In their *The Politics of American Foreign Policy: The Social Context of Decisions.* Englewood Cliffs, N.J.: Prentice-Hall, 1977.

Berry, Lelah. "An Army Wife Lives Very Soft in Germany." *Saturday Evening Post,* 15 February 1947.

Bess, Demaree. "American Viceroy in Germany." *Saturday Evening Post,* 3 and 10 May 1947.

———. "Will We Be Pushed Out of Berlin?" *Saturday Evening Post,* 31 July 1948.

Bidault, Georges. "Agreement on Germany: Key to World Peace." *Foreign Affairs,* vol. 24, no. 4 (July 1946).

Bolton, Seymour. "Military Government and the German Political Parties." *Annals of the American Academy,* vol. 267 (January 1950), pp. 55–67.

Catudal, Honore M., Jr. "Steinstücken: The Politics of a Berlin Enclave." *World Affairs,* vol. 134 (Summer 1971), pp. 51–61.

Cecil, Robert. "Potsdam and Its Legends." *International Affairs,* July 1970.

Clay, Lucius D. "Berlin." *Foreign Affairs,* vol. 41, no. 1 (October 1962), pp. 47–58.

———. "The Engineer ROTC Camp of 1921, at Camp Humphries [sic], Va." *The Military Engineer,* vol. 12, no. 72 (1920), pp. 488–92.

———. "Popularizing ROTC Instruction." *The Military Engineer,* vol. 8, no. 69 (1921), pp. 230-32.

———. "Portable Footbridges of Kapok Pillows." *The Military Engineer,* vol. 15, no. 82 (1924), pp. 137–138.

———. "Some Observations as an Instructor." *The Military Engineer,* vol. 20, no. 3 (1928), pp. 216–18.

———. "With the Marines on Culebra Island." *The Military Engineer,* vol. 16, no. 86 (1924), pp. 147–48.

"Concan Finds a General." *Forbes,* 15 March 1959.

Detzer, Karl. "Clay of Berlin." *The Reader's Digest,* October 1948.

Deuer, Wallace R. "The Army in Power." *Survey,* February 1950.

Dorn, Walter L. "The Debate over American Occupation Policy in Germany in 1944–45." *Political Science Quarterly,* December 1957.

Dorst, Major James A. "Ft. Humphreys and Historic Belvoir." *The Military Engineer,* vol. 15, no. 82 (1923), pp. 332–34.

Drew, Elizabeth. "Dam Outrage: The Story of the Army Engineers." *The Atlantic,* July 1970.

Dulles, Eleanor Lansing. "The Soviet-Occupied Zone of Germany: A Case Study in Communist Control." *US Department of State Bulletin,* vol. 36 (15 April 1957), pp. 605–610; vol. 37 (17 June 1957), pp. 978–983; vol. 38 (14 April 1958), pp. 615–620.

Eisenhower, Dwight D. "My Views on Berlin." *Saturday Evening Post*, 9 December 1961.

Engler, Robert. "The Individual Soldier and the Occupation." *Annals of the American Academy*, vol. 267 (January 1950), pp. 77–86.

Fahy, Charles. "Legal Problems of German Occupation." *Michigan Law Review*, vol. 47 (November 1948), pp. 11–22.

Falk, Stanley C. "The National Security Council Under Truman, Eisenhower and Kennedy." *Political Science Quarterly*, vol. 79, no. 1 (1964).

Fischer, John. "The Army Takes Over." *Harpers*, vol. 190 (May 1945).

Franklin, William. "Zonal Boundaries and Access to Berlin." *World Politics*, vol. 16 (October 1963), pp. 1–31.

Friedrich, Carl J. "Rebuilding the German Constitution." *American Political Science Review*, vol. 43 (June 1949), pp. 461–482, vol. 44 (August 1949), pp. 704–720.

Gaddis, John Lewis. "Containment: A Reassessment." *Foreign Affairs*, vol. 55 (July 1977), pp. 873–887.

Galbraith, John Kenneth. "The Decline of American Power." *Esquire*, March 1972.

———. "Is There a German Policy?" *Fortune*, January 1947.

Gardner, Lloyd C. "America and the German 'Problem,' 1945–1949." In *The Politics and Policies of the Truman Administration.* Barton J. Bernstein, ed. Chicago: Quadrangle, 1970.

Gimbel, John. "American Military Government and the Education of a New German Leadership." *Political Science Quarterly*, vol. 73, no. 2 (June 1968).

———. "Cold War: The German Front." *Maryland Historian*, Spring 1971, pp. 41–45.

———. "James F. Byrnes and the Division of Germany." In Kendrick A. Clements, ed., *James F. Byrnes and the Origins of the Cold War.* Durham, N.C.: Carolina Academic Press, 1982.

———. "On the Implementation of the Potsdam Agreement: An Essay on U.S. Postwar German Policy." *Political Science Quarterly*, vol. 87, no. 2 (June 1972).

Gottlieb, Manuel. "The Reparations Problem Again." *Canadian Journal of Economic and Political Science*, vol. 16 (February 1950).

Green, L. C. "The Legal Status of Berlin." *Netherlands International Law Review*, vol. 10 (1963), pp. 113–138.

Griffith, William. "Denazification Program." *Annals of the American Academy*, vol. 267 (January 1950), pp. 68–76.

Guradze, Heinz. "The Landerrat: Landmark of German Reconstruction." *Western Political Quarterly*, vol. 3 (1950), pp. 190–213.

Hale, William H. "General Clay On His Own." *Harper's*, December 1948, pp. 86–94.

Hammond, Paul. "Directives for the Occupation of Germany." In Harold Stein, ed., *American Civil Military Decisions.* Birmingham: University of Alabama Press, 1963.

Harrington, Daniel F. "The Berlin Blockade Revisited." *International History Review*, February 1984, pp. 88–112.

———. "Kennan, Bohlen and the Riga Axioms." *Diplomatic History*, vol. 2 (Fall 1978).

Herbert, Major-General E. O. "The Cold War in Berlin." *Journal of the United Service Institute*, vol. 574 (May 1949).

Herring, Herbert. "The Department of State." *Harper's*, February 1937.

Herz, John. "The Fiasco of Denazification." *Political Science Quarterly*, vol. 63 (1948), pp. 569–94.

Hill, J. W. F. "Local Government in Western Germany." *Political Science Quarterly*, vol. 20 (1949), pp. 256–64.

Hoffmann, Stanley. "Do Nuclear Weapons Matter?" *New York Review of Books*, 2 February 1989, p. 29.

Howard, Michael. "Governor General of Germany." *Times Literary Supplement*, 19 August 1974.

Jessup, Philip C. "The Berlin Blockade and the Use of the United Nations." *Foreign Affairs*, vol. 50, no. 1 (October 1972).

———. "Park Avenue Diplomacy—Ending the Berlin Blockade." *Political Science Quarterly*, vol. 87, no. 3 (September 1972).

———. "The Rights of the United States in Berlin." *American Journal of International Law*, vol. 43 (1949), pp. 92–95.

Kahn, E. J., Jr. "Soldier in Mufti." *The New Yorker*, 13 January 1951.

Kelsen, Hans. "The Legal Status of Germany According to the Declaration of Berlin." *American Journal of International Law*, vol. 39 (July 1945), pp. 518–26.

Kennan, George F. "A Rebuttal and an Apology." In Thomas G. Paterson, ed., *Containment and the Cold War: American Foreign Policy Since 1945*. Reading, Mass.: Addison-Wesley, 1973.

——— ("X"). "The Sources of Soviet Conduct." *Foreign Affairs*, vol. 25, no. 4 (July 1947).

Koistinen, Paul A. C. "The 'Industrial Military Complex' in Historical Perspective." *Journal of American History*, vol. 56 (March 1970), pp. 819–39.

Krieger, Leonard. "The Inter-Regnum in Germany: March-August, 1945." *Political Science Quarterly*, vol. 64, no. 4 (December 1949).

Krieger, Wolfgang. "Was General Clay a Revisionist?" *Journal of Contemporary History*, vol. 18 (April 1983), pp. 165–84.

Kuklick, Bruce R. "The Division of Germany and American Policy of Reparations." *Western Political Quarterly*, vol. 23 (1970), pp. 276–93.

———. "The Genesis of European Advisory Commission." *Journal of Contemporary History*, vol. 4 (October 1969), pp. 189–209.

Lauterpacht, E. "The Position of the Western Powers in Berlin." *International and Comparative Law Quarterly*, vol. 8 (1959), pp. 207–12.

Loewenstein, Karl. "The Allied Presence in Berlin: Legal Basis." *Foreign Policy Bulletin*, vol. 38, no. 11 (1959), pp. 81–84.

Lubell, Samuel. "The Untold Tragedy of Potsdam." *Saturday Evening Post,* 8 December 1945.

Lutz, F. A. "The German Currency Reform and the Revival of the German Economy." *Economics,* vol. 16, no. 62 (May 1949).

Mason, E. S. "Reflections on the Moscow Conference." *International Organization,* vol. 1, no. 2 (May 1947).

Mason, John Brown. "Government, Administration and Politics in East Germany: A Selected Bibliography." *American Political Science Review,* vol. 53 (June 1959), pp. 507–23.

McClelland, Charles A. "Access to Berlin: The Quantity and Variety of Events, 1948–1963." In J. David Singer, ed., *Quantitative International Politics: Insights and Evidence.* New York: The Free Press, 1968.

Merritt, Richard L. "The Berlin Wall: What Was It All About?" *Journal of Political Science,* vol. 17 (February 1973), pp. 189–95.

———. "Politics, Theater, and the East-West Struggle: The Theater as a Cultural Bridge in West Berlin, 1948–1961." *Political Science Quarterly,* vol. 80 (June 1965), pp. 186–215.

———. "A Transformed Crisis: The Berlin Wall." In Roy C. Macridis, *Modern European Governments.* Englewood Cliffs, N.J.: Prentice-Hall, 1968.

Middleton, Drew. "Uncommon Clay." *New York Times,* 15 July 1945.

"Military Government." *Annals of the American Academy of Political and Social Science,* vol. 267, January 1950.

Morgenthau, Henry, Jr. "Our Policy Toward Germany." *New York Post,* 24 November 1947.

Mosely, Philip E. "Dismemberment of Germany." *Foreign Affairs*, vol. 28 (April 1950), pp. 487–98.

———. "The Occupation of Germany." *Foreign Affairs*, vol. 28 (July 1950), pp. 580–604.

———. "The Occupation of Germany: New Light on How the Zones Were Drawn." *Foreign Affairs*, vol. 28 (1950), pp. 580–604.

Mott, T. Bentley. "West Point: A Criticism." *Harper's*, March 1934, pp. 478–79.

Muhlen, Norbert. "The Wall: One Year Later." *National Review*, vol. 13 (28 August 1962), pp. 133–34.

Murphy, Charles J. V. "The Berlin Airlift." *Fortune* (November 1948).

———. "Somervell of SOS." *Life*, 8 March 1943.

Neumann, Franz. "Soviet Policy in Germany." *Annals of the American Academy of Political and Social Sciences*, May 1949, pp. 165–79.

Newmann, R. G. "New Constitutions in Germany." *American Political Science Review*, vol. 42 (June 1948), pp. 448–68.

———. "The New Political Parties of Germany." *American Political Science Review*, vol. 25 (August 1946), pp. 749–59.

Orion. "The Berlin Airlift." *Journal of the Royal United Service Institute*, vol. 94, no. 573 (February 1949).

Plischke, Elmer. "The 'Contractual Agreements' and Changing Allied–West German Relations." *Political Science Quarterly*, vol. 69 (June 1954), pp. 241–65.

———. "Denazifying the Reich." *Review of Politics* (April 1947).

———. "Denazification Law and Procedure." *The American Journal of International Law* (October 1947).

———. "Integrating Berlin and the Federal Republic of Germany." *The Journal of Politics*, February 1965, pp. 35–65.

Pollock, James K. "The Role of the Public in the New Germany." *American Political Science Review*, vol. 39 (1945), pp. 464–73.

———. "The West German Electoral Law of 1953." *American Political Science Review*, vol. 49 (March 1955), pp. 107–30.

Rigsby, L. W. "The Georgia Branch of the Virginia Clays and Their Celebrated Cousins." *Home and Family*, 4 July 1926.

Rostow, Eugene V. "The Partition of Germany and the Unity of Europe." *Virginia Quarterly Review*, vol. 23, no. 1 (Winter 1947).

Russell, William. "Re-education in Germany." *Foreign Affairs*, October 1948, pp. 68–77.

Schoenbrun, David. "The French and the Ruhr." *The New Republic*, 4 August 1947.

Sheehan, Robert. "Continental Can's Big Push." *Fortune*, April 1955.

Shuster, George. "American Occupation and German Education." *Proceedings of the American Philosophical Society*, vol. 97 (1953), pp. 159–62.

Simpson, J. L. "Berlin: Allied Rights and Responsibilities in the Divided City." *International and Comparative Law Quarterly*, vol. 6 (1957), pp. 83–102.

Smith, Jean Edward. "Berlin: The Erosion of a Principle." *The Reporter*, 21 November 1963, pp. 32–37.

———. "Berlin Confrontation." *Virginia Quarterly Review*, Summer 1966, pp. 181–202.

———. "The Berlin Wall in Retrospect." *Dalhousie Review*, Summer 1967, pp. 247–61.

———. "The German Democratic Republic and the West." *International Journal*, April 1967, pp. 231–52.

———. "The Red Prussianism of the German Democratic Republic." *Political Science Quarterly*, September 1967, pp. 368–85.

———. "Selection of a Proconsul for Germany: The Appointment of General Lucius D. Clay, 1945." *Military Affairs*, vol. 40 (October 1976).

———. "The United States, German Unity and the Deutsche Demokratische Republik," *Queen's Quarterly*, April 1967, pp. 51–66.

Tillman, Colonel S. E. "A Review of West Point's History." *Journal of the Military Service Institution of the United States*, January-June 1916, pp. 184–96.

Wagner, R. Harrison. "The Decision to Divide Germany and the Origins of the Cold War." *International Studies Quarterly,* vol. 24, no. 2 (June 1980).

Warner, Geoffrey. "The Division of Germany, 1946–1948." *International Affairs,* vol. 51, no. 1 (January 1975).
Wechsberg, Joseph. "Letter from Berlin." *The New Yorker,* May 26, 1962.
Whyte, Anne. "Quadripartite Rule in Berlin." *International Affairs,* vol. 23, no. 1 (January 1947).
Wright, C. Ben. "Mr. 'X' and Containment." *Slavic Review,* vol. 35, no. 1 (March 1976).
Wright, Quincy. "Some Legal Aspects of the Berlin Crisis." *American Journal of International Law,* vol. 55 (1961), pp. 959–65.
Zink, Harold. "The American Denazification Program." *Journal of Central European Affairs,* vol. 6 (October 1946), pp. 227–40.

ACKNOWLEDGMENTS

This book could not have been written without the assistance and cooperation of General Clay. Not only did he consent to several years of on-the-record interviews, but he freely made his files and papers available to me. When declassification problems arose, he intervened to resolve them. When the adjutant general once wanted to review what I had written, General Clay made a personal appeal in my behalf to the Secretary of Defense. The adjutant general was overruled. No request that I ever made to General Clay for information was refused. He insisted that I have full access, content to let the chips fall where they may.

In addition to my very obvious obligation to General Clay, my second debt is to Mrs. Marjorie Clay, who cheerfully endured my weekly forays into their family life both in New York and on Cape Cod. Like General Clay, she abhorred old papers and documents, but at my request carefully searched attics and basements for personal effects. And also like the general, she answered whatever questions I asked.

I also owe a special debt to members of the Clay family who have cooperated in tracing family history: Mrs. Zaida Clay Walsh, Douglas Davis, and Miss Louise Frix, of Atlanta; Eugene Herbert Clay, Jr., of Columbus, Ohio; and General Clay's sons, General Lucius D. Clay, Jr. (USAF), and Major General Frank Butner Clay (USA).

For information on Clay's Marietta boyhood, I am indebted to James Carmichael, Judge James J. Daniell, Professor James Quillian, Morgan McNeil, and Mrs. "Rip" Blair. Sidelights of his days at West Point were provided by his classmates Major General Hugh Casey and Colonel Charles "Chesty" Ward, as well as General Alfred Gruenther. Information concerning early duty at Camp Humphreys was provided by General Maxwell D. Taylor and Brigadier General Richard H. Groves, son of Lieutenant General Leslie R. Groves, who generously granted me access to his father's notes of that period. Clay's activities in the Philippines are partially recorded in the diary of Lieutenant (later Brigadier General) William L. Lee. Filemon Rodriguez, president of Filoil, Manila, graciously took time on a crowded visit to New York to see me and discuss his work with Clay in 1938. Claud Easterly of the *Denison Herald*, Denison, Texas, provided copious information about Clay's role in constructing the Red River Dam, as did Major General Richard Sverdrup of St. Louis.

For Clay's time in Washington, first in the office of the Chief of Engineers, later as Director of Materiel and deputy director of war mobilization, I am indebted to Robert A. Lovett, Goldwaithe Dorr, Charles Skinner, Lieutenant General Wilhelm D. Styer, Lieutenant General Glen Edgerton, Lieutenant General LeRoy Lutes, Lieutenant General Henry Aurand, and Brigadier General Max Tyler. Clay's wartime relations with Donald Nelson and the War Production Board were described by Harold Boeschenstein, Paul Cabot, Lincoln Gordon, Robert Nathan, and Joseph Weiner. His selection as Eisenhower's deputy for military government was explained by John J. McCloy.

Donald McLean, who was on Clay's personal staff in Germany, provided useful information about the period 1945–46 as did Major General William Whipple, James Boyd, Larry Wilkinson, John Kenneth Galbraith, William Draper, Edloe Donnan, Philip Jessup, Robert Murphy, Herman Wells, and W. Averell Harriman. Dean Acheson provided useful background material. Carl Joachim Friedrich, Clay's assistant on constitutional matters, supplied data on the drafting of West Germany's Basic Law. Brigadier General Telford Taylor and Judge Charles Fahy discussed working with Clay in the prosecution of war criminals and other legal matters. General Curtis LeMay: the Berlin airlift.

Clay's role in the Eisenhower campaign of 1952 was described by Herbert Brownell, Milton Eisenhower, Leonard Hall, Henry Cabot Lodge, Max Rabb, and Tom Stephens; his operations as chairman of the GOP Finance Committee (1965–68), by Assistant Secretary of Commerce Langhorn Washburn; his chairmanship of the Clay Committee on Highways, by Francis L. Turner, administrator of the Federal Highway Administration. For insight into Clay's eleemosynary activities, I am indebted to George M. Elsey, president of the American Red Cross; Dr. L. H. Foster, president of Tuskegee Institute; and Dr. Milton Porter and Richard Kerst of Columbia-Presbyterian Medical Center. His role as chairman of the board of the Federal National Mortgage Association (Fanny May) was described by President Alan Oakley Hunter; at Radio Free Europe, by Richard Durkee.

Material on Clay's return to Berlin in 1961 is drawn from interviews with General Lauris Norstad, General Bruce C. Clarke, and Lieutenant General Albert Watson. Details on Clay's business career were provided by Ellison Hazard, Paul Davies, Charles Stauffacher, and many others. Information concerning the release of the Bay of Pigs prisoners came from Robert Shea, Felix Larkin, Nicholas deB. Katzenbach, and Louis Oberdorfer.

General Clay's former secretaries, Captain Margaret Allen, Edna Shelley Gates, Marie Johnson, and Lisl Smejda, have been most helpful.

Among documentary sources, my especial thanks to Judith Schiff, curator of the Stimson Papers at Yale. Secretary Stimson did scholars an immense favor by passing a magic wand over his papers and saying "declassified." The Dulles Papers and the Forrestal Papers, both at Princeton, were useful yet more difficult to use. Dr. Rudolph Winnacher, historian of the U.S. Department of Defense, assisted magnificently in the declassification of Clay's records as Military Governor. The staff at the National Archives, once classification problems were resolved, could not have been more helpful. Specifically, William Cunliffe, Thomas Hohmann, John E. Taylor, and Gary D. Ryan in the Modern Military Records Division, and James J. Simpson at the records depository in Suitland, Maryland. Dr. Maurice Matloff of the office of the Chief of Military History made the facilities of his office freely available to me. The Manuscript Division of the Library of Congress, where I consulted the papers of Theodore Roosevelt, was also most cooperative, as was the Sam Rayburn Library in Bonham, Texas.

Because General Clay served every president from Woodrow Wilson to Richard Nixon, a trek through the presidential libraries was inevitable. Indeed, I know of few better ways to see the United States than to drive from Hyde Park (FDR) to Boston, Massachusetts (JFK); to West Branch, Iowa (HH); to Independence, Missouri (HST); to Abilene, Kansas (DDE); to Austin, Texas (LBJ) —and presumably, in the future, to California (RMN). One might quibble about the time and money required for such a trip, but certainly not about the cooperation forthcoming from the various library staffs. I am particularly grateful to Dr. James Mason of the Roosevelt Library; Dr. Thomas T. Thalken of the Hoover Library; Dr. Philip C. Brooks of the Truman Library; and Dr. John E. Wickman and Miss Jo Ann Wilkinson of the Eisenhower Library. I did not visit the MacArthur Memorial Archives in Norfolk, Virginia, but Dr. Philip P. Brower answered my various queries. At West Point, Mr. Thomas Tadulka of the Archives and History Section, USMA Library, was especially helpful, as were Colonels Thomas Griess, Roger Nye, and John Schilling of the permanent faculty.

For information concerning the political activities of General Clay's father, Senator Alexander Stephens Clay, I consulted the papers of Senator Clay, General John B. Gordon, and Governors Joseph E. Brown, W. J. Northen, and William Y. Atkinson at the Georgia Department of Archives and History. Unfortunately, Clay, Gordon, and Brown kept virtually nothing of importance—Gordon and Brown for good reason; Clay, I believe, simply because of family carelessness after his death. The papers of Hoke Smith at the University of Georgia proved interesting, but again the vast bulk had been destroyed. An exception to this apparent dearth was the voluminous papers of Tom Watson at the University of North Carolina. Unlike Gordon, Clay, Brown, and Smith, Tom Watson kept everything. The public records of Cobb County were useful in verifying vital property and probate statistics of the Clay family after the Civil War. Pre–Civil War public records in Cobb County were burned in anticipation of General Sherman.

To the Oral History Research Office of Columbia University and Mrs. Elizabeth B. Mason, I am eternally grateful for the typing of some twenty-five hundred pages of interview material with General Clay and others. The Clay interviews, plus those with Messrs. McCloy, Brownell, Lovett, Murphy, and Rabb, are open to scholars in accordance with the regulations established by Columbia University. To the late Professors Philip Mosely and William T. R. Fox of Columbia I am indebted for supplemental research funds and office space. To the University of Toronto I am indebted for sabbatical leaves that allowed me to complete the bulk of my research. The necessary funds were provided by the American Philosophical Society, the Canada Council, and the International Studies Program at Toronto. The University of Virginia invited me to spend the academic year 1987–88 in residence, which enabled me to complete the manuscript. My special thanks to Professors Robert Evans and Clifton McCleskey. The John F. Kennedy Institute of the Free University in Berlin appointed me a guest professor in 1989. The final revisions were completed at that time.

The manuscript was read at an early stage by Richard Arndt, Paul Ehrlich, and John Seaman. The entire manuscript was read by John Gimbel, Herbert Levine, and Katherine Koerner. It was typed, corrected, and nursed through many, many drafts by Brenda Samuels, Sandra McAuslan, and Elizabeth Jagdeo of the University of Toronto, and Gail Moore, Melody Roberts, and Betty Snead of the University of Virginia.

Finally, I am indebted beyond measure to my agent, Elizabeth Kaplan, of Sterling Lord Literistic, and to my editor at Henry Holt, Marian Wood. Without Elizabeth's encouragement, this manuscript would never have been completed. Without Marian's penetrating criticism and fine stylistic judgment, the manuscript would still be encumbered with the jargon of academe. If there are better editors, I am yet to meet them.

INDEX